The One Year® Book of Amazing Stories

THE ONE YEAR®

Book of Amazing Stories

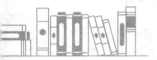

365 Days
of Seeing God's Hand
in Unlikely Places

Robert Petterson

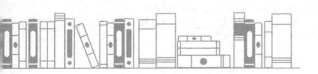

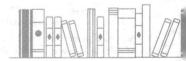

TYNDALE
MOMENTUM®

The nonfiction imprint of
Tyndale House Publishers, Inc.

Visit Tyndale online at www.tyndale.com.

Visit Tyndale Momentum online at www.tyndalemomentum.com.

Visit the author's website at www.robertapetterson.org.

TYNDALE, Tyndale Momentum, Tyndale's quill logo, *The One Year,* and *One Year* are registered trademarks of Tyndale House Publishers, Inc. The Tyndale Momentum logo and the One Year logo are trademarks of Tyndale House Publishers, Inc. Tyndale Momentum is the nonfiction imprint of Tyndale House Publishers, Inc., Carol Stream, Illinois.

The One Year Book of Amazing Stories: 365 Days of Seeing God's Hand in Unlikely Places

For information about special discounts for bulk purchases, please contact Tyndale House Publishers at csresponse@tyndale.com, or call 1-800-323-9400.

ISBN 978-1-4964-2401-3

Printed in the United States of America

24	23	22	21	20	19	18
7	6	5	4	3	2	1

*These 365 amazing stories are dedicated to three
generations of amazing females . . .*

JOYCE, *my wife,*
*a remarkable woman whose unfailing love and steadfast support
have given beauty, substance, and wonder to our story together.*

RACHAEL, *our attorney daughter,*
*a woman of force and unfailing compassion, champion of
the powerless, whose tireless work transforms the stories
of the sojourners among us from despair to hope.*

MAE *and* MIRA, *our granddaughters,*
*whose infectious joy, determination, and insatiable curiosity
will continue our amazing story for generations to come.*

Introduction

J. K. Rowling says, "There's always room for a story that can transport people to another place." Great stories take us to the hidden places of our unexplored imagination. They have the capacity to touch something deep within us—something that goes beyond mere facts and cold logic to empower us with transforming insights. Stories remind us that we are not alone and inspire us to believe that the impossible is actually possible. That's why God fills the Bible with epic tales of adventure, intrigue, and love—and why, when Jesus wanted to move people, he told stories.

The amazing stories tucked inside these pages are about real people like you and me. These folks have lived in every age and come from every walk of life. Yet the footprints they leave behind can embed themselves deeply in our own lives, often in ways that astound. In these stories, you will discover that there are no little people, small places, or unimportant encounters.

Some of these stories will ignite your imagination. Others will catch you by surprise as you discover amazing things about people you thought you knew. In each one, you will see God's truths illustrated in the most unexpected ways.

In the year ahead, you will unwrap a new story each day to recharge your spiritual batteries. Each will conclude with a thought-provoking life principle as well as an accompanying Bible verse to carry you through the day. In the back of this book, you will find sources allowing you to discover even more about each story. If you are a storyteller yourself, you may want to investigate the topical indexes, which will make it easy for you to access stories for your sermons, classes, public speeches, or after-dinner conversations.

It's my hope that these stories will inform, inspire, and transform you as much as they have me. Most of all, I hope they will inspire you to tell your own story. I believe this about you: the best lines and chapters of your amazing life story are still waiting to be written.

Dr. Robert Petterson

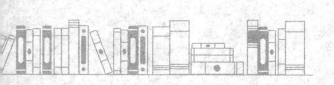

A Devastating Rescue

❧ ❧

Snow covered Bavaria like a fresh dusting of powdered sugar. On the banks of the icy Inn River, children were playing a game of "cowboys and Indians." The frosty air was filled with Sioux war cries and shouts of "Bang, bang! You're dead." Among the "cowboys and Indians" was a four-year-old boy. He was sickly and frail, small for his age, and wearing thick glasses. Yet he ran with determination, trying desperately to keep up with the galloping herd of children—until he tripped and fell over the embankment. His eyeglasses flew through the air as he broke through the thin sheet of ice. Unable to swim, the frantic boy was swept downriver toward certain death.

Johann Kuehberger was only five years old. But when he heard his playmate scream for help, he jumped into the icy waters and pulled him to safety. Little Johann was proclaimed a hero by the local newspaper in the town of Passau. No one was surprised when this courageous child grew up to be a priest. Johann Kuehberger would spend the rest of his life trying to save those in distress. But saving that childhood playmate from drowning would haunt him to his dying day. A fellow priest, Max Tremmel, revealed that Father Johann spent many sleepless nights obsessing over that rescue in the winter of 1894.

Little Johann might have grown up to serve God, but the child he saved went on to become one of history's most diabolical monsters. If only five-year-old Johann could have seen the future in that split second before he jumped into the river, he might have stopped dead in his tracks. Surely countless millions would have been spared terror and death—if only little Adolf Hitler had drowned that day.

Hitler often reminisced about his childhood games of "cowboys and

Indians" on the banks of the Inn River. But he never mentioned the near drowning. He wasn't about to spoil the Nazi myth of a superman Führer by admitting that he had been saved by a future priest of a religion he despised. Yet reporters have uncovered the story of his rescue from old files in Passau. A recent program on Bavarian radio got folks thinking: *What if Hitler had drowned?*

Every act has consequences. We can never know what the future will do with our decisions and actions. Sadly, Father Johann wasted far too many nights second-guessing himself. Ultimately, we cannot control the outcomes of our acts. But we can worry too much. Maybe you're filled with regrets or bitterness for the painful consequences of yesterday's choices. Or perhaps you hesitate to make decisions today for fear of how they will play out tomorrow. You might find some freedom from the paralysis of analysis if you remember this:

Do the best you can do, and leave the results to God.

———— ⚬౿ఌ⚬ ————

Commit your actions to the LORD,
and your plans will succeed.

PROVERBS 16:3

2

The Most Courageous Man in America

༄༅༅

In 1986 Italian runner Gianni Poli won the New York City Marathon in two hours and eleven minutes. In 2003, Mark Yatich of Kenya triumphed at the Los Angeles Marathon in a time of two hours and ten minutes.

But the greatest marathons of all time may have been run by the guy who finished dead last in both races, in the slowest times ever recorded. In 1986 he completed the New York City race in about ninety-eight hours. It took him a little more than 173 hours to cross the finish line at Los Angeles in 2003.

Before you write Bob Wieland off, you need to know that he completed both marathons using only his arms and torso. Bob has no legs. In 1969, while trying to rescue a fallen buddy in Vietnam, he stepped on a mortar round designed to destroy tanks. He sent this short note to his parents:

Dear Mom and Dad,
   I'm in the hospital. Everything is going to be okay. The people here are taking good care of me.
   Love,
   Bob
   P.S. I think I lost my legs.

Bob could have shriveled up in a wheelchair. Instead, he walked across America on his hands. That exploit took three years, eight months, and six days. He's the only double-amputee ever to complete the Iron Man and stumbled to shore. Yet when he was eased into the warm bath, the shock caused his body to go into death convulsions. There were only thirty-nine when a sentry, impressed by their bravery, stripped off his uniform and ran naked onto the ice. Again there were forty.

The next morning, the general ordered that their frozen bodies be burned and the ashes scattered on a nearby river. His legionnaires were shocked to find one still alive. His mother, who was among the camp followers, was summoned to convince this solitary survivor to recant. To everyone's surprise, she begged her son to stay true to the end—and he was burned alive with the corpses.

The forty martyrs of Sebaste tell an enduring story of the irresistible power of courage. A pagan legionnaire turned to Christ after one of those Christians came off the ice, then stripped naked to join them. A survivor was willing to be burned to death to keep that number intact. Four years later, Constantine I executed the caesar who had ordered those sacrifices. Sickened by pagan barbarity, and impressed by the faith of martyrs like those at Sebaste, Constantine made Christianity the favored religion of Rome.

Some 2,960 legionnaires followed orders that winter day. But forty did the right thing. Today, you may be tempted to cave in to pressure and violate your conscience. Don't you dare! The forty martyrs of Sebaste teach us that a single act of bravery can even change the course of history. *Courage inspires and ignites a spark of bravery in those watching.*

Fear not; you will no longer live in shame.
Don't be afraid; there is no more disgrace for you.
ISAIAH 54:4

Who Killed Superman?

୧୭୭୭୬

On June 16, 1959, police found George Keefer Brewer dead from a single gunshot wound to the head. Cursory evidence pointed to suicide. But the shell casings were in the wrong place, his body was covered with bruises, and witnesses waited for almost an hour to call the police. Many of these witnesses were unsavory characters, each with enough motive to kill him—especially those with Mob connections.

One thing is sure: George was unlucky in both life and death. His hulking good looks got him a part in *Gone with the Wind*, but after that it seemed that he could only get roles in forgettable B films. Then the Japanese bombed Pearl Harbor, and he was drafted. That seventeen-month stint in the army all but killed his career. So he took a starring role in a horrible little film, *Superman and the Mole Men*. He was almost laughed out of Hollywood. But the much-panned movie did get him a starring role in a new television series, *Adventures of Superman*. Just about every kid in 1950s America knew the opening line from the announcer: "Faster than a speeding bullet, more powerful than a locomotive, able to leap tall buildings in a single bound." George was now a superstar—to children. But he was still a B-list actor when it came to the big screen. Maybe that's why his life descended into a downward spiral of booze, bad luck, and unsavory friends. The world was shocked when the man with the stage name George Reeves was found shot to death. To this day, people ask, "Who shot the bullet that felled Superman?"

There is another mystery: Did George Reeve's mysterious death unleash a Superman curse? After Christopher Reeve played the superhero in four films, he was thrown from a horse and paralyzed for life. His costar Marlon Brando's career took a nosedive after *Superman*; his family disintegrated, and he ballooned into morbid obesity. Margot Kidder, who played Superman's girlfriend, was partially paralyzed in a car accident. Richard Pryor's life fell apart after he costarred in *Superman III*, and he ended up in a wheelchair. The child who played Superman as a baby ended his life by sniffing air freshener from a can. But none were more cursed by Superman than the original creators of the comic book superhero, Jerry Siegel and Joe Shuster. After being cheated out of the rights to their creation, they spent their lives fighting losing battles in court. They died without receiving any of the billions that their character generated.

Maybe kryptonite exists after all, fatal to anyone who touches this Superman first conceived by the German atheist philosopher, Friedrich Nietzsche, and later embraced by Adolf Hitler as the superior man who needs no God. But no one is faster than a speeding bullet, stronger than a locomotive, or able to leap tall buildings in a single bound. We need a much bigger power, from beyond outer space, to see us through life. You might want to remember these words when you think you are Superman or Superwoman:

Be careful who you trust. The devil was once a super angel.

––––– ⌘ –––––

Those who know your name trust in you, for you,
O LORD, do not abandon those who search for you.
PSALM 9:10

Tamerlane's Curse

ᥱᥕᦕᦎᥫ

Perhaps you think ancient curses unleashed on the modern world are only found in Hollywood movies such as *Raiders of the Lost Ark* or *The Curse of the Mummy's Tomb*. If you think they can't happen in real life, you might want to consider the amazing story of Tamerlane's curse. This fourteenth-century Mongol ruled a vast empire that covered most of modern-day Central Asia, Iraq, Iran, and Turkey. He was one of the worst butchers in history, often slaughtering whole people groups. When he was almost seventy years old, this genocidal maniac launched his final campaign, setting out with a massive army to conquer China. No enemy had ever prevailed against him, but a freak winter storm put an end to his unbroken string of victories. Trapped in impassable snowdrifts, Tamerlane died shivering in his blankets as winds and wolves howled around him.

The emperor's body was taken back to Samarkand, where it was embalmed and enclosed in an ornate tomb. These foreboding words were inscribed on the door to the crypt: "When I rise from the dead, the world shall tremble." That's why locals were frightened six hundred years later, when Joseph Stalin sent a team of archaeologists to bring Tamerlane's corpse back to Moscow. Muslim imams begged them not to unleash a curse by entering the tomb. But these were men of science, not superstition. Yet after breaking into the burial chamber, even they shivered at this inscription: "Whoever disturbs my tomb will unleash an invader more terrible than I." Maybe they should have run from that crypt, but they had their orders from the Communist boss of bosses.

Two days after the remains were shipped to Moscow, some 3.6 million German soldiers invaded Russia. Comrade Stalin, who had laughed at Tamerlane's curse, watched helplessly as the Nazi juggernaut rolled across the Soviet Union. Before the horror ended, twenty-six million Russians died. Surely the curse had come true: the world trembled as it watched Adolf Hitler, a butcher far more terrible than Tamerlane, unleash his invasion on those who opened the fourteenth-century tomb. It's no wonder Stalin sent Tamerlane's corpse back to its violated crypt, where it was reburied in an Islamic ceremony.

Even more amazing: within a month of the tomb being resealed, the tide of war turned at the Battle of Stalingrad. The surrender of the German army on the eastern front began the unraveling of the Third Reich. If he could, the six-hundred-year-old Mongol mummy would have been howling in wicked delight from his burial chamber.

What do you think? Coincidence or curse? At least this much is sure: no one has since dared to disturb Tamerlane's resealed tomb. You can be even more sure of this: God has warned us that curses will be unleashed on those who disobey commands inscribed in his Word. The evidence that they are being unleashed on our world today is too compelling to deny. So, just as we should seek God's blessings, we ought to fear his curses. Fearing God is out of fashion today, but there are some blessings for those who do so:

He who fears God fears nothing else; he who sees God sees nothing else.

It is a terrible thing to fall into the hands of the living God.

HEBREWS 10:31

The Biggest Nation of All

❧◦◦◦◦◦◦

Though his warrior father had carved out a kingdom for the crown prince, it was not big enough. This prince had a voracious appetite that could never be satisfied. That craving for more would send him to the ends of the earth in a never-ending quest that still astounds the world some 2,500 years later.

The crown prince was only twenty years old when his father was assassinated. After rounding up and ruthlessly executing all of his rivals, the boy conqueror began his long march across planet Earth. His army of some thirty thousand warriors blitzkrieged from the Balkans to India in less than thirteen years. They covered some ten thousand miles on sandaled feet, making the mechanized conquests of our high-tech military operations look almost slow by comparison.

The statistics of that amazing odyssey seem almost impossible. This ancient juggernaut conquered countless cities and nations that made up what are now Turkey, Iran, Iraq, Syria, Greece, Jordan, Israel, Pakistan, Afghanistan, Tajikistan, Arabia, Egypt, the Balkans, and part of India. Its empire stretched from the Aegean to the Himalayas, across three continents. The conqueror's rule spanned more than two million square miles of earth by the time he was thirty-two years of age.

When he reached the Indus River, his bone-weary army refused to take on the war elephants of India. After the better part of two decades, the troops wanted to go home. The ancient historian Plutarch writes that thirty-two-year-old Alexander the Great sat on the banks of the Indus and wept like a baby because there were no more worlds to conquer. Most historians figure that he would have marched his men all the way to China—if they would have followed him.

With an unsatisfied hunger that still gnawed at his restless soul, Alexander marched back to Babylon, where he drank himself into a stupor. In June of the year 323 BC, he died at age thirty-two. The cause of his death is still mysterious. Most likely it was typhoid fever, but some suspect that his generals, who carved up his empire after his death, might have poisoned him.

He was carried in an ornate casket back to Alexandria in Egypt, one of the more than seventy cities that he named after himself. That airtight burial box became the final resting place of a man for whom the world was never big enough. His tutor, Aristotle, often lamented that young Alexander could conquer the world, but he was never able to conquer his own passions or imaginations.

Perhaps the biggest nation of all is our imagination. Certainly, Pascal was right when he said that there is within us all a God-shaped vacuum as infinite as God himself. We can possess the whole universe and all that it contains and still not fill that vast emptiness within. If you have a soul hunger, you might want to remember this:

When too much is never enough, give yourself to the infinite one, who is more than enough.

⌘

You are a people holy to the LORD your God. Out
of all the peoples on the face of the earth, the LORD
has chosen you to be his treasured possession.

DEUTERONOMY 14:2, NIV

The Forgotten Explorer

❧

When his parents died, Matt dropped out of school and became a dishwasher. He was only twelve when a Baltimore ship captain took him on as a cabin boy. That skipper was the closest thing Matt ever had to a father. The captain showed the orphan how to read, write, and navigate a ship. Matt learned skills that would take him where no man had ever ventured.

When the ship's captain died, Matt was again on his own. He returned to Washington, DC, where he met the second man who would change his life. Captain Robert E. Peary was sailing south to survey the feasibility of a canal across Nicaragua. When he met Matt, he was surprised that an eighteen-year-old knew so much about navigation. So he hired the teen as his personal valet. During their two years in Central America, Peary's vision to explore the Arctic Circle ignited a passion in Matt. Their shared dream would yoke them together for twenty years of history-making exploration.

In 1895 they traveled to Greenland on a trip that turned to disaster. They barely survived the winter by eating their sled dogs. When they found refuge with an Inuit tribe, Matt became the first American to master their difficult language. He also learned how to build dogsleds, kayaks, and igloos, taking tips from the locals in surviving the harsh Arctic. Peary knew that his valet was the key to making it to the North Pole.

After several failed attempts, in 1908 they began their final shot at reaching the northernmost point on the planet. The two mushed north with forty-nine Inuits, more than two hundred dogs, seventy tons of whale blubber, and countless sleds full of supplies—slogging a trail through ice fields, across yawning crevices, and over towering glaciers. They did so in the face of howling winds, endless night, and temperatures that plunged to sixty-five degrees below zero. It was one of the most harrowing trips in history. As they finally came within sight of their goal, Captain Peary was exhausted, so Matt continued on, becoming the first man in history to stand at the North Pole. He then went back to get Peary. The captain was livid that his valet had planted the first flag, and forever after refused to speak to him. Matt later said that the North Pole was the place where his heart was broken.

The party arrived home to a hero's welcome. In 1909, their feat was like landing a man on the moon. Proud Americans feted Captain Peary with parades and receptions, applauding him as the first man to stand at the North Pole. Nobody took notice of Matt. Yet today the world knows it was really Matthew Henson who was the first to reach the North Pole. Maybe if he hadn't been African American or if he hadn't been Peary's valet, he'd have been recognized sooner. But some thirty-five years after the journey, Matt was finally awarded the Medal of Honor.

Perhaps you feel like Matthew Henson. You work hard, but others get the applause you deserve. Please don't let that make you discouraged or bitter. Remember this:

God sees everything, forgets nothing, and rewards what others miss.

———— ❧ ————

Look, I am coming soon, bringing my reward with
me to repay all people according to their deeds.

REVELATION 22:12

Saved by His Unborn Son

༄༅ༀༀༀ

Aron is addicted to living on the jagged edge. He has made more than forty solo winter climbs of Colorado's tallest mountains, equipped with nothing more than water, candy bars, and an ice ax. He never brings a cell phone, GPS, rope, or basic survival equipment. This daredevil was once buried up to his neck in an avalanche, nearly drowned in a river, and tussled with a bear. Yet what happened when he was solo climbing in Utah was beyond anything Aron could ever imagine.

As he was climbing up a crevice, Aron shook loose an eight-hundred-pound boulder, which crushed his arm against the canyon wall. He was now trapped by a hunk of rock bigger than the bed of a pickup truck. The pain was excruciating. He screamed, cursed, and prayed, but no one in heaven or on earth seemed to be listening. By day three, the last drop of water was gone. When day five dawned, he was facing hypothermia. He knew that he would die if he didn't extricate himself. So he came to an agonizing decision that still astounds us: he cracked the bones of his right arm against the rock, then used a multipurpose tool with a dull blade to saw off his lifeless limb below the elbow.

He managed to fashion a tourniquet to stem the blood flow, used his left arm to rappel seventy-five feet down to the canyon floor, and then walked seven miles before hikers saw him stumbling toward them, half-delirious and bleeding profusely. He was airlifted to the hospital in critical condition. Aron Ralston's amazing survival story astounded and inspired the world. But few people know the rest of the story.

During the last night of his 127-hour ordeal, it was freezing cold, and Aron was ready to give up, when a specter of a child showed up. The little boy was about three years old with blond hair. Aron says that the child threw his arms around his neck and held him tight. Six years later, in the final days of his wife's pregnancy, he told *Time* magazine he believed the child who visited him that night was his unborn baby, and he had waited seven years to see the boy again. Three years after Jessica gave birth to a baby boy in 2010, he claimed that his three-year-old blond toddler was the child who gave him hope nine years earlier.

A skeptic would say that Aron was hallucinating. A cynic might even accuse him of making up the story for personal gain. An orthodox Christian could dismiss any thought of the pre-conception appearance of a child as New Age hocus-pocus. Surely, there are mysteries beyond our understanding. Perhaps the best answer is the simplest: God hears our prayers, and he heard Aron's, too. Even when we cause our own messes, his grace and mercy is bigger than our stupidity and sins. What Aron saw that night is not nearly as important as the fact that God saw him through. And he will do whatever it takes to see you through too.

God adds extra to your ordinary and super to your natural.

———— ✤ ————

Jesus looked at them intently and said, "Humanly speaking, it is impossible. But not with God. Everything is possible with God."

MARK 10:27

16

History's Strangest Siege

～⌘～

Who knows what will change the course of history? King Richard the Lionhearted, the greatest knight in all of Christendom, had returned from a crusade in the Holy Land to wage war against the French House of Capet. Richard knew that his enemy, King Philip, was no pushover. So the Lionhearted quickly shored up a string of fortresses. His pièce de résistance was a marvel of medieval times: an impregnable fortress that he built on a steep limestone hill high above the River Seine north of Paris. When it was finished, even the Lionhearted was awed by this twelfth century engineering feat. He exclaimed, "Behold, how fair is this year-old daughter of mine." He called it Château Gaillard, or Strong Castle.

He was especially proud of the public latrines. Usually, the few toilets in a castle were reserved for the nobility. But King Richard was an enlightened world traveler who had learned that human waste causes disease. Besieged castles were more often doomed by the epidemics that raged inside than from the attacking armies outside. So he made sure that concealed chutes carried waste from the latrines to a distant place outside the castle walls.

Richard the Lionhearted was killed in battle before he saw the fate of his engineering masterpiece. But King Philip did come with his armies. The French bombarded the walls with everything they had and feverishly dug their tunnels to breach the fortifications. After six months, Château Gaillard stood unscathed. But the late King Richard's enlightened concern for the health of his defenders proved their undoing. At winter's end, a French soldier noticed steam coming from the base of an outer wall. The chutes to the public latrines were discovered. Frenchmen climbed up through human waste and into the toilets. Within hours, the most impregnable fortress in Europe fell.

Having seized Château Gaillard, King Philip was free to take Normandy from the English. For the first time in two hundred years the French controlled their whole country. The English loss of Normandy almost bankrupted Richard's brother, the new king of England. King John heaped ruinous taxes on England to recover his losses. Finally the barons revolted against the late Richard's brother, forcing the signing of the Magna Carta. That first taste of liberty would inexorably lead to a representative democracy over four hundred years later when the English Bill of Rights was signed. That leap forward in liberty led to America's Declaration of Independence a century afterward. But the chain of events that brought about the liberties we enjoy might never have happened had Frenchmen not climbed up through those public toilets that Richard built in 1198.

None of us know what will come of decisions we make. Our smallest acts are part of the countless threads woven together with innumerable others to form God's tapestry of history. Maybe that's why we should heed something that philosopher Immanuel Kant wrote:

Live your life as though your every act were to become a universal law.

Do not despise these small beginnings, for the LORD rejoices to see the work begin.

ZECHARIAH 4:10

The Ultimate Cold Case

✎⊙☙

Two children disappear in the dark of night, never to be seen again. These are not ordinary kids. One is Edward V, King of England. The other is his brother, Richard, the Duke of York. In the five hundred years since their disappearance in the summer of 1483, no bodies have been produced or examined. Accusations have been made, culprits identified, and motives suggested. But still, there is no conclusive proof as to who ordered the murder of the two princes or even if they were killed. It is the ultimate cold case.

The finger has long pointed to Richard III, the boys' uncle and regent to the throne. He had the most to gain from their deaths. He had long claimed that his nephews were illegitimate heirs. Around the time of the boys' disappearance he ascended to the throne of England. Sir Thomas More implicated him in his writings, and Shakespeare portrays him as a deformed monster in his play *Richard III*—the unspeakably cruel villain who sends killers to the Tower of London to smother the princes with their pillows. The bard paints a hauntingly tragic scene of two boys sobbing in fear, clutching on to each other as their killers approach their bed. Tradition holds that one of the king's noblemen confessed to carrying out the murder. But he confessed under torture ordered by the new king of England, Henry Tudor (Henry VII). He said that the boys were buried under a stairway in the Tower of London. Sure enough, the bones of two boys are said to have been found in that spot. Or was that a story cooked up by Henry's associates to discredit Richard and strengthen his claim to the throne?

Henry VII had a lot to gain from those boys' deaths, as they had a more legitimate claim to his throne. Did his men kidnap and kill them before or after Henry's army defeated Richard's in battle? In 1933 the bones again appeared. Doctors said that they seemed to be from a ten-year-old and a thirteen-year-old. But there was no DNA testing then. Recently, the remains of Richard III were discovered under a parking lot in England. The exhumed body bore no resemblance to the man described by Shakespeare. Nor does his psychological profile fit that of a man who would order the death of children. Scholars desperately want to test the bones of those boys, but both Queen Elizabeth and the Church of England refuse to allow this.

Forensic scientists are so much closer to solving this five-hundred-year-old case, but the more they learn, the more confusing and convoluted it gets. Maybe this amazing story of one of the world's oldest cold cases reminds us that not all mysteries are meant to be solved by us. Who killed those boys? God knows. He has already dealt with the matter. And he will deal equitably with every unsolved mystery in your life. So relax, and let him be God.

We need to do what we can do, and let God do what we cannot.

———— ∞ ————

Just as the heavens are higher than the earth,
so my ways are higher than your ways and my
thoughts higher than your thoughts.

ISAIAH 55:9

Antonina's Ark

ᏳᏯᏫᏔ

Antonina adored the wild outdoors. Mostly she loved nurturing the cuddly offspring of wild animals. She was grateful that her husband, Jan, was the keeper of the Warsaw Zoo. Every morning Antonina awakened to the sounds of one of the largest menageries of exotic animals in Europe. She turned the grounds of their villa into a Garden of Eden where she and her young son bottle-fed a variety of orphan cubs during birthing season. On any given day, visitors could see wild antelopes and zebras grazing on the Zabinskis' property. If asked to explain her love affair with wild animals, she would quickly say that, as a Christian, she was responsible to care for God's creation.

But the serpent stole into her Eden when the German blitzkrieg rolled across Poland and the Luftwaffe bombed Warsaw into rubble. The zoo was almost obliterated, along with many of the world's most exotic animals. Antonina was devastated when Nazi SS arrived to round up what was left. Most of the surviving animals were shipped to Germany. The SS turned the ruined grounds into their private game preserve, hunting down the few creatures that were left behind. After their killing spree ended, the renowned Warsaw Zoo was eerily empty.

When the Nazis unexpectedly made Jan the superintendent of parks, God opened doors that would turn a massacre into a miracle. Not far from their deserted zoo, one of the monstrous evils of the twentieth century was taking place in the Jewish ghetto. No lions or tigers could be more beastly than the SS predators who were systematically starving thousands even as trains were arriving to transport the rest to death camps.

So the Zabinskis hatched a plan to turn the rubble of dashed dreams into building blocks for something far better. Antonina later said that the destruction of their zoo was "not the dream of death . . . but merely 'winter sleep.'" Jan turned the empty zoo into a pig farm. The Nazis were amused. They could never imagine that the zookeeper was cleverly using his position as the director of Warsaw parks to smuggle pork into a starving ghetto to feed Orthodox Jews. Nor did they know that the empty cages in the zoo had been turned into a labyrinth of hiding places for more than three hundred Jews smuggled out of the ghetto.

You can read the amazing story of this heroic couple in Diane Ackerman's book *The Zookeeper's Wife*. If you find yourself at the Yad Vashem in Jerusalem, you can see their tree planted along the Avenue of the Righteous among the Nations, which honors Gentiles who risked their lives to save Jews during the Nazi Holocaust.

The story of the Zabinskis reminds us that God sometimes allows us to lose good things so that our hands are free to grab hold of better things. When Antonina's Garden of Eden was destroyed, she could have wallowed in the wreckage of her dreams. Instead, she and her husband replaced exotic animals with pigs to feed starving Jews and used the rubble of their zoo to build a Noah's ark to save endangered people. If your dream has died, this truth might help:

The rubble of broken dreams provides the building blocks of future hope.

———— ✑ ————

The LORD is close to the brokenhearted;
he rescues those whose spirits are crushed.

PSALM 34:18

The Evolutionary Man

✦

After their house was torched by white supremacists, his daddy's body was found on the railroad tracks. After his widowed mother had a mental breakdown, the eight children were parceled out to foster homes. When a family of do-gooders took him in, Malcolm Little was thrilled to be in a white home. But they saw him as more of a pet black puppy than a member of their family. They gave him a new name: Malcolm the Mascot. When he told a white teacher that he wanted to be a lawyer, the teacher sneered. "A lawyer?! That's not a realistic goal for a n—!"

Malcolm drifted to the East Coast, where he adopted street slang, became a hustler, peddled dope, and ran numbers, earning him a new name: Detroit Red. After he was arrested for armed robbery, Detroit Red was sentenced to ten years in prison. Fellow convicts called him Satan because of the way he cursed God, the Bible, and all things religious as a white man's tool to destroy blacks. That's when his sisters begged him to turn to the Nation of Islam. Malcolm was irresistibly drawn to its prophet, Elijah Muhammad, and his claim that whites were devils, and blacks needed to have their own nation. He came out of prison in 1952 as Malcolm X. His zeal caught the eye of Elijah Muhammad, and soon he was in the prophet's inner circle. By 1957 this Islamic sect was in the spotlight after a television exposé called *The Hate That Hate Produced* aired. When the charismatic Malcolm X became its most-sought-after spokesman, a jealous Elijah Muhammad ordered his assassination.

Malcolm X broke from the Nation of Islam. When he set out on a holy pilgrimage to Mecca, he told the world that he was now Malik El-Shabazz. Everything changed on that hajj. For the first time Malcolm saw Muslims of every nationality and color. He realized that black racism was as evil as white racism. He came home a changed man, preaching a message of reconciliation, not separation. He was rapidly becoming an agent for positive change when his house was firebombed on February 14, 1965. A week later, Nation of Islam assassins murdered him. El Hajj Malik El-Shabazz was only thirty-nine.

From Malcolm Little to Malcolm the Mascot to Detroit Red to Satan to Malcolm X to Malik El-Shabazz, his is an amazing story of personal evolution. We should weep for the white racism that turned him into a man called Satan. We ought to find his reverse racism abhorrent. But surely, we can find hope in his trajectory. Today he is celebrated as a martyr for his final fight for the dignity of African Americans and racial reconciliation. We can only guess what he might have become, if he only had a few more years to complete a transformation that was headed in the right direction. May all of us be continually transformed for the better, and may God give us the time to complete the transformation.

You are always one decision away from a totally different life.

―――――⚭⚬ℬ⚬⚭―――――

Don't copy the behavior and customs of this
world, but let God transform you into a new
person by changing the way you think.

ROMANS 12:2

The Singer Who Stopped World War III

࿇

Most of us have forgotten the civil war that plunged the Balkans into a genocidal nightmare during the 1990s. By 1999 the war was winding down. The Serbian militias had finally left Bosnia and Croatia. Hundreds of thousands of refugees were poised at the borders, waiting to return home. A column of thirty thousand NATO soldiers was advancing toward the strategic Pristina airfield.

That's when the precarious peace in the region was threatened. The Russians got there first, determined to fill the vacuum left by their fleeing Serbian allies. They pointed their artillery at the approaching NATO column and warned them to come no closer. It looked like a stand-off until a single word came by radio from US general Wesley Clark: "Destroy!" James Blunt was a captain in the British Life Guards and the lead officer at the head of the column. Again the order came from General Clark to attack the occupying force of two hundred Russians. Directly behind Captain Blunt was the elite Parachute Regiment, itching for a fight.

Blunt knew that obeying the general's command could lead to an international incident, maybe even World War III. Disobeying it would lead to court-martial. His cool judgment bought enough time for the commander of the British forces, General Sir Mike Jackson, to intervene with the words "I'm not going to have my soldiers start World War III." He gave orders to Captain Blunt to surround the airfield. Two days later, the Russians sent a message: "We have no food or water. Can we share the airfield with you?" After two weeks of negotiations, the Russians were enfolded into the peacekeeping force while staying outside the NATO command structure.

James Blunt always preferred crooning to commanding. He resigned his position to become a rock singer in England. His album had a hit song, "You're Beautiful." Another song, "No Bravery," became an anthem for the peace movement. He wrote that song outside the Pristina airfield during the 1999 standoff. He once said, "War is an absolutely ghastly thing. I wouldn't bother describing the things we saw." He also remains firm that if General Jackson hadn't intervened, he would have disobeyed General Clark's orders. The British general almost resigned in protest over Clark's insistence on destroying the Russians. Eventually Wesley Clark was relieved of his NATO command for "integrity and character issues."

The amazing story of rock singer James Blunt is another proof that history is God's story. He will write the last chapter and put the exclamation mark on the last line. General Wesley Clark could have started World War III. At least there might have been a war with Russia. It could have escalated to a nuclear holocaust. But God controls *his* story. He will even have an English rock-and-roll singer at the head of a NATO column to make sure that things are kept under his sovereign control. In an unstable world, that ought to make you sleep a bit sounder tonight.

Worry less and limit stress. God's got everything under control.

———— ∞ ————

The LORD is my light and my salvation—so why should I be afraid? The LORD is my fortress, protecting me from danger, so why should I tremble?

PSALM 27:1

26

The Real Lone Ranger

✧✦✧

Aficionados of cowboy films remember that thrilling score from the *William Tell* overture and a horseman on a distant hill yelling, "Hi-Yo Silver, awaaay!" After a pause, someone on screen would ask, "Who was that masked man?" Every kid in America knew the answer: He's the Lone Ranger!

But no one knew that the *real* Lone Ranger was Bass Reeves. During the Civil War, this aide to a Confederate officer finally had a gutful and rode west. After his escape, he had good reason to lose himself in the Oklahoma Territory. He learned enough Creek and Seminole language and customs to become a territorial scout, and he built a homestead with his bare hands. But things were about to change. The Indian Territory was a haunt of desperadoes, renegade Indians, horse thieves, rapists, and murderers. That's when "Hanging Judge" Isaac C. Parker was made the federal judge of the Indian Territory with dictatorial powers to clean up this cesspool. From his bench in Fort Smith, Arkansas, the hanging judge appointed James Fagan US marshal, authorizing him to hire two hundred deputy marshals. One of Fagan's first hires was Bass Reeves.

Reeves was thirty-eight years old when he began his legendary career. He was tall and imposing—a John Wayne figure of a man on a big white horse. He patrolled seventy-five thousand square miles of lawlessness, often traveling with a chuck wagon and cook. He also carried a large supply of chains and shackles, sometimes bringing in as many as twelve outlaws at a time to Fort Smith for a quick trial and hanging. When Bass Reeves went looking for the notorious Belle Starr, she turned herself in rather than face the most feared lawman in the Old West. He arrested more than three thousand felons in his illustrious career—more than any other lawman in US history. He killed fourteen desperadoes in the line of duty and was often the target of assassination attempts. Yet in spite of his many shoot-outs, he never took a bullet. When he died at age seventy-one, newspapers declared him to be the greatest lawman in the history of the Old West. Maybe that's why Bass Reeves became the inspiration for the Lone Ranger and the prototype of every Hollywood marshal from Matt Dillon to Rooster Cogburn.

So now you know the amazing story of the *real* Lone Ranger. But there is one more surprise: Bass Reeves was an African American, raised as a slave on an Arkansas plantation. He got to the Indian Territory by fleeing from his slave master, a Confederate officer. Yet hardly any of the newspapers that celebrated his exploits ever mentioned that he was a black man. But today we've taken the mask off the Lone Ranger and revealed that he was black Bass Reeves.

Maybe this is just a preview of a day when God will rip the masks off everyone, revealing and rewarding people who are the real deal, and exposing and punishing fakes, posers, and pretenders. Maybe we should take our masks off today and deal honestly with who we are while there's still time to get things right.

The problem with masks is that pretense finally lapses into character.

───── ✧ ─────

If anyone thinks they are something when
they are not, they deceive themselves.

GALATIANS 6:3, NIV

The Devil's Daughter

↬◦◉◦↫

Little Svetlana was only six when her mother died. It would be years before she discovered that thirty-one-year-old Nadya had not died of peritonitis but had shot herself. By the time she learned that her mother had committed suicide, Svetlana, like her mom, would do almost anything to escape her monstrous father. She later lamented that she was the devil's daughter.

It didn't start out that way. She remembered sitting on his lap, tickled by his thick moustache as he nuzzled her neck, being showered with kisses, and smelling his pipe-tobacco breath as he whispered how much he loved his "little hostess." But everything changed when she began to notice how many people in her papa's inner circle disappeared, never to be seen again. When she was seventeen, she fell in love with a Russian filmmaker. When her father disapproved, the arguments began. He had the final say when he shipped her lover off to the dreaded gulag. When Svetlana confronted her father, he beat her. Then she thought about all her aunts and uncles who had vanished for not keeping their mouths shut and began to experience the same terror everyone else felt in his presence. She never felt it more than when she sat near his deathbed. At the end, he sat up in bed, coughing, spitting up blood, and looking around with demonic fury while hissing like a serpent.

Only later did Svetlana Alliluyeva learn the full extent of her father's reign of terror that murdered twenty million people. In 1967 she fled to the West, leaving her two children behind. She left a note that said, "It is impossible to be always a slave." She thought she could find happiness, but she discovered that people were more interested in her infamous father than her. Disillusioned, Svetlana returned to Russia in 1984—only to discover that the children she had abandoned wanted nothing to do with her. So the devil's daughter fled back to the West, living a nomadic life between England and America. She plowed through failed marriages and disastrous romances. Olga, a third child born in America, was the only child who accepted Svetlana. She said her mother could only be satisfied by a man. Maybe she was still driven by a little girl's desire to be loved by her daddy. But that's impossible when your papa is a devil named Joseph Stalin. So she went looking for love in all the wrong places and died a lonely old woman in 2011.

The tragic story of Svetlana Stalin reminds every father that he needs to love his children. If a dad doesn't fill that father vacuum in a child's soul, no one else can ever fill it later on—unless, of course, it is our heavenly Father who ultimately satisfies every father longing. Tonight in America millions of children will go to bed in homes where there is no father. Even more are living with dysfunctional fathers. Don't let your children be counted among them.

Children don't look for love in all the wrong places when they start out life finding it in the right place.

<hr/>

The LORD is like a father to his children, tender
and compassionate to those who fear him.

PSALM 103:13

The Shaggy Hero

⌒◎⌒

Teens too often get a bad rap from the older generation. But every once in a while, a teenager rises up to make us all proud. James Persyn III has an impressive name, but he's a pretty ordinary fourteen-year-old from Shepherd, Michigan. He isn't very tall, and with his shaggy haircut, he could use a trip to the barber. He plays too many video games and watches too much television. But he astounded everyone on a January night in 2013. The teen was babysitting his brother and sister when he heard pounding on the front door. A college student outside was frantically screaming, "Let me in! Let me in!" It took courage for James to open that door.

The wild-eyed woman ran into the kitchen, shouting hysterically that a rapist had tried to kidnap her and had chased her to this house with murderous intent. She screamed that the children needed to hide quickly. James remembered his father's instructions that, in the case of danger, his kids should get into the bathroom that had no windows. James herded the woman and his two siblings into the empty tub and told them to keep quiet. He shut the door and ran into his bedroom to retrieve a hunting knife. He called Mr. Persyn on his cell phone and said, "Dad, you need to get home quick. There's a man outside, and he wants to kill us all."

James's dad sped off for his house. Meanwhile, the woman's enraged attacker poured gasoline all over the house and then set it on fire before he took off. James Persyn Jr. cut his lights as he neared his driveway. His heart sank as he saw the bottom part of his house on fire. He didn't know if the attacker was inside or if his family was safe. He smashed a window in an attempt to dive through. His kids were shaken, but the college girl had managed to calm down a bit. A police manhunt quickly found her attacker, Eric Ramsey. During the shoot-out, Ramsey was killed.

Later it was discovered that Ramsey was one bad dude. He had kidnapped the woman at gunpoint, tied her up, and taken her to his house, where he raped her. He was on his way to a deserted place where he planned to kill her when she jumped out of the moving car and ran up to the Persyn front door.

The teenager's calm handling of the situation and heroic stand against a crazed killer made national headlines. He was touted as a hero by the media. But his dad said, "I'm proud of my son. But he's not a hero. He just did the right thing." That may seem like a strange thing to say in an era of self-congratulation. But maybe Mr. Persyn is right. *Hero* is one of the most overused words in America today. By using the word indiscriminately, we have devalued and trivialized its once-sacred status. It's refreshing to hear someone say that doing the right thing is not necessarily heroic, it's just right.

Doing the right thing is always the right thing.

———— ❧ ————

Learn to do good. Seek justice.
Help the oppressed. Defend the cause of
orphans. Fight for the rights of widows.

ISAIAH 1:17

A Dog's Tale

⌒◌⌒

Stroll through Greyfriars on a rare sunny day, and it seems like an idyllic cemetery. But at night it becomes the rendezvous of ghost hunters. They claim it is the most-haunted graveyard in the world: a spooky place where body snatchers robbed graves; a makeshift prison where Presbyterian Covenanters were murdered; the place where the poltergeist of George MacKenzie, orchestrator of the unspeakable horrors endured by those Covenanters, is released each night to wander his killing fields. No wonder J. K. Rowling wrote her Harry Potter stories about wizards and witches in a coffee shop across from Greyfriars.

Yet at the entrance to the phantasmagoria of Greyfriars is the statue of a wee Skye terrier. Thousands of tourists come to this spot each year, proving that a dog's tale is better than any ghost story. This diminutive terrier was a familiar sight in the 1850s as he trotted beside his master on his nightly rounds. The policeman and his puppy were inseparable pals. But the man they dubbed Auld Jock was dying of tuberculosis. Scots openly wept when he was carried to Greyfriars on a February day in 1858. But most of their tears were for the forlorn little terrier leading the procession. After Auld Jock's burial, the dog he called Bobby refused to leave. Grave diggers shooed him away, but he clung to the freshly dug grave.

Stormy weather, freezing nights, and the ghost of George MacKenzie could not dislodge the grieving pet. The keeper of the churchyard, Auld Jock's family, and well-meaning locals couldn't entice him away. Month after month and year after year, he growled menacingly at anyone who came too close to his master's grave marker. Crowds came to Greyfriars just to see Bobby. The wee Skye terrier only left Auld Jock's gravesite at one o'clock each afternoon at the firing of the cannon in Edinburgh's old fortress. He would cross the cobblestone street to a pub where he was fed table scraps and then return to his faithful watch. The terrier lived well beyond his breed's normal life span, finally dying on Auld Jock's grave. He is buried next to his master, with these words on his granite marker: "Greyfriars Bobby—died 14th January 1872—aged 16 years. Let his loyalty and devotion be a lesson to us all."

Recently an English grinch tried to prove that this story was a Victorian hoax, using a series of dogs to impersonate Bobby. But even this spoilsport admits, "It won't ever be possible to debunk the story of Greyfriars Bobby—he's a living legend, the most faithful dog in the world, and bigger than all of us." Those of us who love our pets prefer to believe Bobby's amazing story. We are thankful to God for giving us our faithful companions. We even harbor a belief that they will be waiting for us in heaven. We might all agree with a pet owner's sentiments:

My goal in life is to become the person my dog already thinks I am.

-----⋐⋑-----

Just ask the animals, and they will teach you.
Ask the birds of the sky, and they will tell you.

JOB 12:7

The Chernobyl
Suicide Squad

೧᠗ல

It was the worst nuclear meltdown in history. Today the skeletal remains of the Chernobyl nuclear reactor stand like a gray and rusting ghost beside polluted waters—a grim sentinel reminding passersby of the failures of unbridled socialism. But in the early hours of April 26, 1986, it was the hottest place on earth. A failed test caused two explosions that took out Unit 4. Two workers were immediately killed by the blasts, twenty-nine more would die of radiation in the next four months, and the death toll continues to climb three decades later. Scientists say that those two explosions unleashed four hundred times the radiation of the bomb dropped on Hiroshima in 1945.

Within six hours the fires were extinguished, but a few days later the reactor core of Unit 4 was still melting down. A smoldering stream of reactive metal was flowing like molten lava toward a pool of cooling water beneath the destroyed reactor. Had that radioactive flow reached the water, it would have set off a massive explosion, leveling the whole power plant and unleashing a radioactive cloud that would have destroyed half of Europe, leaving it uninhabitable for the next five hundred thousand years.

It was imperative that someone go down below and drain the pool. But the basement was knee deep in radioactive water, it was pitch black, and the shut-off valves were most likely underwater. Three plant workers stepped forward as volunteers. They were warned that they would most likely experience radiation poisoning and die a slow and agonizing death in the months ahead, but that their families would be taken care of by a grateful government. So this suicide squad donned wet suits and gingerly stepped into water alive with radiation. They felt their way along pipes in utter darkness until they found the shut-off valves. When those above heard water flushing out of that pool, there was palpable relief followed by spontaneous joy. A world catastrophe had been avoided by this suicide squad. In the Soviet cover-up that followed, the names of these three heroes were lost. One died of a heart attack a few years later, and another disappeared. The remaining hero has asked to remain anonymous.

We should all be grateful for these three nameless and selfless heroes who stepped into a pool of death to save millions of people. No monuments have been erected to the Chernobyl suicide squad, but heaven knows their amazing story. And now you do too. It should give you a sense of inestimable value. God has always had the right people at the right time to make it possible for us to experience the life that he created us to enjoy. Each of us owes so much to people we will never know or long remember this side of heaven. So take time to thank God for the multitude of unknown and forgotten people. Rejoice in this:

We see farther because we stand on the shoulders of giants.

Since we are surrounded by such a huge crowd
of witnesses to the life of faith . . . let us run with
endurance the race God has set before us.

HEBREWS 12:1

Yanking on Superman's Cape

❦

The world watched in wonder as a kid from California's outback seized cycling's holy grail. No one rides the grueling 2,200-mile-long Tour de France alone. An unseen ogre climbs on every racer's back. Its name is pain. The farther the cyclist rides, the heavier it feels. The harder the cyclist pushes, the tighter it squeezes. The steeper the climb, the deeper it digs its sharp claws into muscles. But the kid carried the ogre all the way and stood wearing the yellow jersey in Paris, the first non-European to win cycling's most prestigious race.

The ogre climbed back on the kid's back later that year when he was hunting. He heard the explosion, felt the searing pain of the accidental discharge of shotgun pellets, and then went numb. There were sixty holes in his body, and blood was pouring from every one. He tried to stand, but his lung had collapsed, and he could barely breathe. During the surgery that followed, pellets were removed from his kidney, liver, and intestines. But thirty, including two in the lining of his heart, could not be retrieved. The accident would begin the process of lead poisoning that's rendered him increasingly nauseated and weak ever since.

But the French didn't call him Le Grand because he gives up easily. For the next two years, he worked until he was back in the race. Again the world watched in wonder as this comeback kid won the 1989 Tour de France. He became the first cyclist to make the cover of *Sports Illustrated* and was named its Sportsman of the Year in 1989. The next year, he won his third Tour de France. But lead poisoning was racking his body, so he retired. He was now the most famous and respected cyclist on the planet.

But superstars come and go. The new golden boy was Lance Armstrong. This American would eclipse all the others, winning a record seven Tour de France titles. But the man they used to call Le Grand knew the truth: Armstrong was a cheater—a cycling superman on steroids. The former star of cycling could have kept his mouth shut. No one likes it when someone yanks on Superman's cape. But Greg LeMond took a career-ending stand by accusing Armstrong of drug-enhanced performances. The outraged cycling world said that Le Grand LeMond wasn't so grand after all. He was labeled a jealous troublemaker, lost his endorsements, and was shunned by the cycling world. During that dark exile, his body was increasingly ravaged by lead poisoning. He calls that period "twelve years of hell."

The world now knows the facts: Greg LeMond was telling the truth, and Lance Armstrong was lying. Greg is now Le Grand again, the elder statesman of cycling, more respected than ever for his integrity. He would tell you that standing on the truth may come at a high price, but it is worth more than all the yellow jerseys and endorsements in the world. The amazing story of Greg LeMond reminds us of this:

People of integrity do what is right, not what is easy.

⌘

Remember, it is sin to know what you
ought to do and then not do it.

JAMES 4:17

The Aryan
Brotherhood of Africa

ↄⱺⱺ

The young lawyer fled the caste system of colonial India when he moved to South Africa. But, when he boarded a train to Pretoria with a first-class ticket, a white passenger complained. At the next stop, burly authorities tossed the Indian off the train. As he brushed the dust from his suit, he realized that he had encountered something more degrading than British snootiness: the rigid South African apartheid based on gradation of skin color. Blacks were called by the derogatory racial slur *Kaffir* and occupied the lowest rung of the caste system. On the middle rung were "colored people"—the lighter-skinned children of interracial marriages. Though they enjoyed more privileges, they were still segregated. The top rung of South Africa was reserved for whites alone. To his horror, the Indian lawyer discovered that he, like all other Asians, was lumped in with "colored" people.

So he started the Natal Indian Congress. For the next twenty years he honed the skills of nonviolent protest that would eventually drive the British out of India, dismantle segregation in America, and end apartheid in South Africa. Some 125 years later, he ranks among history's most revered heroes. And yet historians have uncovered a disquieting secret. To gain civil rights for fellow Indians, he tried to convince whites that Asians were superior to black Africans. In letters to the South African parliament, he referred to blacks as *Kaffirs*. In 1904 he wrote a letter to officials saying that unlike the African, the Indian had no "war-dances, nor does he drink Kaffir beer." When Durban was hit by a plague in 1905, he complained bitterly that Indians were being "herded together indiscriminately" with black Africans at the hospitals. In one of his letters he appealed to whites, saying "we are part of an Aryan brotherhood."

Who would have believed that Mahatma Gandhi would have used a term that is synonymous with white supremacy, from Adolf Hitler to the Ku Klux Klan! Yet it makes sense. Gandhi was enmeshed in an even worse system: the Hindu castes, established three thousand years earlier when Aryans invaded and conquered the darker-skinned indigenous peoples of India. They developed a religion that divided people into four castes, as well as a fifth group—the countless millions branded as outcasts or untouchables. In this religion, people are born into certain castes as punishment or reward for previous lifetimes. It is their *karma*, and it cannot be changed until their next life.

We are thankful that Gandhi fought against caste systems that exploited Indians. We celebrate the fact that Martin Luther King Jr. and Nelson Mandela used his methods to free people from oppression. We might wish that Gandhi would have fought as vigorously against the Aryan brotherhood that spawned racist social structures in India, Nazi Germany, South Africa, and America. We learn from Mahatma Gandhi's story that we all have our blind spots. That's why we have to keep reminding ourselves that any caste system that divides people into haves and have-nots is unbiblical and unhealthy.

Before we talk about how much we love God, we should show how much we love his children.

⋘⋙

If we don't love people we can see, how can we love God, whom we cannot see?

1 JOHN 4:20

A Letter from the Birmingham Jail

_✇

W ho would have believed that Michael would grow up to change the world? Surely the odds were stacked against a black baby born in the Old South. It helped that his preacher daddy saw him as a special gift from God. Maybe that's why this child prodigy entered college at the tender age of fifteen.

But his early success masked the deep scars of segregation. He first felt the sting of the Southern class system when a white friend invited him home. His playmate's mother chased Michael away while loudly berating her son for bringing a "colored boy" into the house. By the time he was a teenager, he no longer trusted a religion that looked the other way while folks practiced bigotry. The preacher's kid dismissed the Bible as myth and rebelled against church.

Everyone was shocked when he announced that he was off to seminary. But Michael didn't enter the ministry so much to preach the gospel as to use his pulpit to promote racial justice. He organized bus boycotts and peaceful protests. When redneck sheriffs unleashed their police dogs, he responded, "Throw us in jail, and we shall still love you. . . . Beat us and leave us half dead, and we shall still love you. But be ye assured that we will wear you down by our capacity to suffer."

Just when it seemed that Michael's nonviolent protests were finally paying off, the US attorney general ordered an investigation. Secret FBI wiretaps suggested his associations with Communist influences. Agents also uncovered evidence implicating him as a serial adulterer. When his wife found out, she threatened to leave him.

By 1963, many of his impatient followers were deserting to militant groups with slogans like "Burn, baby! Burn!" Michael hit rock bottom when he was thrown into Birmingham City Jail. With plenty of free time, he began to reread the Bible he had dismissed as myth. As he studied letters written by a jailed apostle some 1,900 years earlier, he realized that his hope wasn't in how much he loved others but in how much his Savior loved him.

Not only did Michael experience a conversion in Birmingham, so did the nation. Violent police reaction to his peaceful protests galvanized America. Not long after, he was awarded the Nobel Peace Prize. The name Michael appears on his birth certificate, but history remembers the moniker that his preacher daddy later gave him: Martin. By the time he was assassinated in 1968, Dr. Martin Luther King Jr. had unleashed a tidal wave that changed everything.

Every February the United States celebrates his birthday. But maybe you don't feel like throwing a party, because you still feel the sting of bigotry. Perhaps you are imprisoned in your own jailhouse, shackled to the ball and chain of some disability or disappointment. Could it be that, like Martin, you are deeply aware of your own hidden flaws and failures? Take heart. You just might find courage from a line that Dr. King penned in that Birmingham jail:

You must accept finite disappointment, but never lose infinite hope.

We know that in all things God works for
the good of those who love him, who have
been called according to his purpose.

ROMANS 8:28, NIV

The Perfect Boss

⁖⦵⦵⁖

Many decades after his death, ninety-one-year-old Rosa still remembers him as the sweetest boss anyone could ever have. She was only fifteen when she went to work at his mountain retreat. While her sister cooked for him, she served as a maid. She said that he was charming, always complimentary, and especially kind to his servants. In 1932, her boss was just getting over the suicide of the woman he loved. Because she and her sister shared a room above his bedroom, she remembers how her heart ached as she listened to him weep night after night.

Rosa remembers the first time she met him. She was scared until he smiled shyly and softly said, "Sorry to trouble you, but could you make me some coffee and bring some gingerbread biscuits to my study?" She was surprised at the Spartan nature of his room: an iron bed, one wardrobe, a small table, two chairs, a wooden box, and bare walls except for a picture of his mother.

Above all, she recalls how tenderly he loved his dogs: Wolf, Muck, and Blondi. He displayed an almost feminine gentleness with animals, cuddling kittens, picking up ducklings and kissing them tenderly. As his nation's leader, he passed the first laws in history to protect animals from abuse. She saw him walk around ants and other insects to keep from stepping on them. She often told friends that her boss couldn't possibly hurt a fly.

Though the household servants despised some of the thugs who came in and out of his mountain retreat, their boss never ceased to endear himself to the staff. Who could resist the way he held their children on his lap and sang lullabies to them in an almost childlike voice? At times, Rosa even saw a tear running down his face. She remembers how he took time to come to her sister's wedding and posed for a photograph with her family and how he used to insist that she take time off to go to church on Sunday mornings. The hardest part about getting married was leaving the kindest, most softhearted boss any working girl ever had.

Years later, Rosa Mitterer still finds it impossible to believe the bad things that they say about her big softie of a boss, Herr Adolf Hitler. She admits that the evidence of the Holocaust is undeniable, but she still finds it almost impossible to believe that he could have ordered it. This great-grandmother in Munich shrugs her frail shoulders and says, "I prefer to remember the charming facets of his personality." This amazing story is useful for reflection. We live in a telegenic age of celebrity, where style trumps substance and being cool gets more kudos than being correct. Like Rosa, we can be lulled into forgetting that even if bad ideas are wrapped in an alluring package, it doesn't make them any less destructive. Lest we be deceived by charm, we need to remember something Charles Spurgeon once said:

Discernment is not knowing the difference between right and wrong. It is knowing the difference between right and almost right.

———— ❧ ————

He will delight in obeying the LORD. He will not judge
by appearance nor make a decision based on hearsay.

ISAIAH 11:3

The Scotsman Who
Founded America

⤷⨀⥘

W as Johnny in the wrong place at the wrong time? Or was he right where he should be? Being caught by those French soldiers was the beginning of a nightmare. But it would also put Johnny on a path to change history.

No one would have guessed that this shy bookworm would be a world changer. But when the winds of the Reformation blew across Scotland in the 1500s, Johnny was caught up in a revolution. Even though he stayed in the background as a bodyguard to George Wishart, when the fiery Protestant preacher spoke out against the gross immorality of Cardinal Beaton, things got hot fast. The cardinal had Wishart arrested. Then the spiritual head of Scotland and his mistress watched from a bedroom window of his palace as the martyr burned. Not long after, angry Protestants stabbed the cardinal to death and hung him by his bloody bedsheets from the window where he had watched Wishart die. No one knows whether Johnny Knox was part of that mob, but we know that Wishart had ordered him to go home to his family. Instead, he was in that palace when French allies to the Scottish queen rounded up the cardinal's killers.

Young John was sentenced to slavery in the French galleys. Maybe he should have listened to Wishart and gone home. When he was miraculously released, he found his way through England to Geneva where he came under the tutelage of John Calvin. He returned to Scotland to stare down Mary, Queen of Scots, and to shape the emerging Protestant Church. He also brought to Scotland the Presbyterian form of church government he learned in Geneva, as well as Calvin's ideas of separation of church and state, checks and balances in government, capitalism, and the rights of the individual. In the stormy century that followed, hundreds of thousands of Scottish Presbyterians would flee to the colonies, bringing with them the radical ideas from Calvin's Geneva.

At the time of the American Revolution, the largest group of people in the colonies were Scots Presbyterians. Some twenty-three statements from their National Covenant in Scotland appear in the US Constitution. Thomas Jefferson, who was tutored by a Presbyterian professor, wrote the Declaration of Independence, a document that could have been penned by John Knox. John Witherspoon, a Scots Presbyterian who founded Princeton, helped shape that declaration. At Yorktown, all but one of Washington's colonels were Presbyterian elders. When it came time to establish a government, the founding fathers of America chose the republic envisioned by John Calvin. Can you imagine how many things might not have happened if John Knox had gone home the day Wishart was burned at the stake?

His amazing story is another proof that nothing is accidental. Every encounter today will be a divine appointment. So face your day with enthusiasm. You are essential to God's plan for the ages. Everything that happens today will be a small, but critical, part of shaping history.

Life is short, time goes fast, there are no rewinds or replays. So savor each moment as a precious part of a grand design.

We can make our plans, but the
LORD determines our steps.

PROVERBS 16:9

The Real Dr. Jekyll
and Mr. Hyde

❧

William Brodie was born with a silver spoon in his mouth and died with a rope around his neck. No one could have imagined this esteemed member of the city council hanging from the gallows. His grandfathers were prominent Edinburgh attorneys, and his father was a renowned businessman. William inherited a fortune of £10,000, along with four grand houses. He was already a successful cabinetmaker and locksmith. That's why he became the head of his guild and earned the title of the Deacon. When he walked down the Royal Mile in powdered wig and dark suit, Deacon Brodie was the picture of piety and prosperity.

But the Deacon was also spending nights at disreputable taverns where huge sums of money were lost at the gaming tables. And Deacon Brodie was one of the biggest losers. What money he didn't lose gambling went to support two mistresses and five illegitimate children. So the Deacon began to steal. His position as a locksmith allowed him to make wax impressions of keys and rob the houses of his clients. He moved from burglary to armed robbery when he fell in with a gang of cutthroats. Before long, he was as addicted to the thrill of thievery as he was to gambling.

No one would have guessed that the good Deacon was responsible for the rash of robberies in Edinburgh. One Sunday morning he used a key to enter a house, but the old lady who lived there was sitting in a chair, too sick to go to church. Deacon Brodie walked up to her, tipped his hat, and politely said, "Good morning, Madam." Then he calmly walked into the other room and pilfered her jewels. When later asked why she didn't tell the authorities, she replied, "I didn't believe that such a respectable gentleman could possibly do what I saw him do."

Deacon Brodie might have carried on his double life for years if he hadn't gotten greedy and attempted to rob the revenues of Scotland in the Excise Office. The robbery turned into a fiasco, and two thieves spilled the beans. The Deacon was now a fugitive with a price on his head. He got as far as Amsterdam, where he was captured and brought back to Edinburgh. The sensational trial lasted for twenty-one hours. Brodie was found guilty and sentenced to the gallows.

More than forty thousand people showed up on October 1, 1788, to watch him hang. Everyone admired the new scaffolds—the handiwork of Deacon Brodie, who had recently been commissioned to build a more effective gallows after a prior hanging had gone awry. He would be the first person to swing from his own handiwork. A century later, Robert Louis Stevenson used Deacon Brodie as the model for his infamous Dr. Jekyll and Mr. Hyde. The amazing story reminds us that none of us get away with our secret sins forever. Eventually, they catch up with us. Like Deacon Brodie, we often hang on the very gallows we construct ourselves. Maybe we should see what forty thousand people did on October 1, 1788:

Sins are like using a credit card. You enjoy now, but pay later.

———— ❧ ————

You may be sure that your sin will find you out.

NUMBERS 32:23

Ryan's Song

৵৩৬৩

R yan never wanted to be a social activist. Like most other boys in basketball-crazy Indiana, he just wanted to shoot some hoops. But Ryan wasn't like most other boys. He was born with hemophilia. A simple cut or bruise could cause hemorrhaging leading to death. As a result, the Indiana boy got more than his share of blood transfusions.

Yet in the early 1980s, no one was screening blood. Doctors had no way of knowing that the junior higher had received a transfusion of tainted blood until he came down with pneumonia and had to have part of a lung removed. When he tested positive for HIV, the doctors told his shocked parents that Ryan had AIDS and less than six months to live. If that wasn't traumatic enough, the junior high where Ryan was a seventh grader said that their son was no longer welcome.

As Ryan battled to regain his health and took classes by telephone, his mother fought school officials and parents to get her son readmitted to school. That eight-month battle would grip their community with hysteria and dominate national headlines. When this sweet kid was finally readmitted, he became the victim of bullying. Most students avoided him like he had leprosy. Someone spray-painted a slur on his locker, and he became the punch line for cruel Ryan White jokes. Most teens have enough trouble dealing with pimples and shouldering their backpacks. But Ryan had to carry the weight of his own terminal disease and the prejudice of an ignorant world. He never asked to be a spokesperson for those living with HIV and AIDS, but he took up the mantle at age fifteen, eloquently telling his personal story to the world.

It wasn't Ryan's fault that he was born with hemophilia or got a transfusion of tainted blood. He was just a Midwest teen who wanted to be accepted. Because he was willing to stand against ignorance, people living with HIV are no longer stigmatized, discriminated against, or defamed. Many A-list celebrities like Michael Jackson and Elizabeth Taylor became his friends. When he died too soon at age eighteen, Elton John said that he would give up fame and fortune to have one more conversation with his pal. Ronald Reagan admitted that he was too slow in responding to the AIDS crisis, but he credited the Indiana boy's heroism with waking him up. President George H. W. Bush signed into law the Ryan White CARE Act giving federal aid to those living with HIV.

It has been nearly thirty years since he died, and most folks have forgotten Ryan's amazing story. He was thrust into the public arena for only three years, but his life and death paved the way for untold thousands who live with HIV and AIDS. If every hero is a shadow of Jesus Christ, Ryan White surely reminds us of the one who took on our diseases, suffered abuse by a sin-sick world, and then gave us a blood transfusion so that we might have life. So let's remember Ryan White and give grateful thanks to Jesus today.

Christ came to comfort the afflicted and afflict the comfortable.

———— ✦ ————

God blesses those who mourn, for they will be comforted.

MATTHEW 5:4

The War Started by a Pig

࿐

The war is unknown to most Americans, and yet history hung on its outcome. Its origins were rooted in a border dispute between Great Britain and the United States. In the 1846 Treaty of Oregon, the Canadian border was set at the forty-ninth parallel. But had that line continued to the Pacific Ocean it would have given Victoria, British Columbia, to the Americans. So the line meandered south of Vancouver Island. And that's where the problems began.

South is an archipelago called the San Juan Islands, which straddled both sides of that meandering line. For years, the Hudson Bay Company had operated a large farm on San Juan Island. When American settlers came, they were despised as illegal squatters. Tempers were already frayed when a pig wandered off the Hudson Bay farm and began rooting out potatoes in Lyman Cutlar's field. When the American farmer shot and killed the pig, the British exploded. Charles Griffin stormed over to the American demanding satisfaction. "But your pig was eating my potatoes," protested Cutlar. "Rubbish!" snorted Griffin. "It's up to you to keep your potatoes out of my pig." Though Cutlar offered to pay ten dollars as restitution for the pig, Griffin reported him to the British authorities, who threatened to arrest him. His American neighbors fired off a petition for US protection to General William S. Harney, the commander of the Department of Oregon.

The virulently anti-British general sent a squadron of the Ninth Infantry, headed by future Confederate general George Pickett. When word reached Victoria, the governor of British Columbia sent three British warships to San Juan Island. By the time news of the escalation reached Washington, DC, and London, officials in both countries were shocked that the killing of a pig had caused a troop buildup of three warships, eighty-six artillery guns, and two thousand six hundred soldiers squared off against each other. A single spark might have ignited a third great war between the Americans and British since 1776. Fortunately, cooler heads prevailed. The kaiser of Germany was asked to mediate. When he decided in favor of the Americans a year later, troops from both sides left—and the San Juan Islands now belonged to the US. Thankfully, the only casualty of the Pig War was the pig.

This amazing story reminds us that the fate of history hangs on the thinnest of wires. Something as silly as shooting a pig can start a war between superpowers. Had the Pig War erupted into a full-scale conflict, the Civil War might have taken place shortly after instead of fourteen years later. If it had, England surely would have entered it on the side of the Confederates. It's doubtful that America and Canada would have the longest unprotected border in the world. We should never take peace for granted. In a world where the slightest provocation can ignite a nuclear holocaust, we can wring our hands in anxiety or get on our knees in prayer. What will you do?

Armed warriors wage wars, but prayer warriors avert them.

ᥱᥩᥰ

Don't worry about anything; instead, pray about
everything. Tell God what you need, and thank him for
all he has done. Then you will experience God's peace.

PHILIPPIANS 4:6-7

The Man behind
the Curtain

꿍

Lyman was a daydreamer. Born the seventh of nine children, he got little attention from his parents. A weak heart kept him inside. As a result, Lyman spent lonely days dreaming of fantasylands somewhere over the rainbow. He would expend his life searching for a pot of gold at the end of those rainbows. By his early thirties he had been a journalist, printer, postage-stamp dealer, and poultry breeder. Then he published a trade journal, only to fail at that too. He started his own theater, becoming its writer, director, and lead actor. Most of his plays were flops. When he fell in love with Maud, her mother warned her that Lyman was a flake. But mom's misgivings were no match for his ability to mesmerize Maud with his fantasies.

After they married, his theater went belly up. So he moved his family to the Dakota Territory, where he opened an emporium specializing in Chinese paper lanterns, Bohemian glass, and gourmet chocolates. But prairie farmers in the 1880s were not interested in novelties. This time the dreamer went bankrupt. When he moved to Chicago, his mother-in-law watched him captivate his children with magical stories and suggested that he write children's books. His first was called *Father Goose, His Book*, a collection of pictures and rhymes. He then wrote a novel for children. While searching for a title, he noticed the label on the bottom drawer of a file cabinet: O–Z.

Every publishing company turned down his manuscript until one offered to print it—if he paid the costs himself. He waited for what seemed an eternity before the first copies sold. It was Christmas of 1900, and he couldn't afford presents for his children. In desperation, he went to the publishing company in hopes of finding a royalty check. When it was handed to him, he didn't dare look at it. He arrived home with the check in his hand and gave it to his wife. When Maud peeked at the number she almost fainted. It was made out for $1,423.98—the equivalent of $40,000 today.

Everything changed for Lyman Frank Baum when the world fell in love with his book whose title was inspired by the file cabinet label, O–Z: *The Wonderful Wizard of Oz.* It became America's bestselling book. L. Frank Baum would write seventy books out of those fantasies that he dreamed up during his lonely childhood. In 1919, he died of the heart problems that kept him indoors as a child. He didn't live to see his book turned into a 1939 Hollywood movie or his beloved characters become indelibly etched in American culture. But his amazing story should encourage those who take longer to discover their true calling in life. It also proves that there are no wasted moments. Even a failure on the prairies of the Dakotas can teach something about tornadoes in Kansas and hope that comes after the storm, somewhere over the rainbow.

It takes the darkest storms to produce the brightest rainbows.

———— ❧ ————

All around him was a glowing halo, like a rainbow
shining in the clouds on a rainy day. This is what
the glory of the LORD looked like to me.

EZEKIEL 1:28

The Hit Man's Son

❦

Woody was only seven when his daddy took off. Like most fatherless boys, he was desperate to know about his missing dad. But whenever he asked his mom, she changed the subject. Years later, he heard about a sensational murder trial whose defendant had the same name as his missing father. When Woody asked his mother, she admitted that the accused murderer was indeed his absentee dad.

She also told him where his father, Charles, had been all those years: mostly in and out of jails and prisons. Woody's dad was a cold and calculating killer. He had just finished serving five years for the brutal murder of a Texas grain dealer. He had been sentenced to fifteen years but was let off for good behavior. When Charles wasn't killing someone, he could be quite charming, even fooling a parole board into thinking that he had found religion. But he wasn't out for very long before he was convicted of murdering a federal judge. When a drug cartel boss testified that he had paid Woody's dad $250,000 to do the job, the hit man got two life sentences.

So Woody developed a relationship with his long-lost dad in prison visiting rooms. Woody found him to be "one of the most articulate, well-read, charming people I've ever known." He also discovered that he was a con artist. During those years of trying to rebuild a father-and-son relationship, he struggled with whether Charles deserved his friendship or loyalty.

He finally decided that it was impossible to regain what had already been lost. But he could at least help his dad. Over the next several years Woody spent $2 million of his own money and countless hours with attorneys trying to get his father a new trial. He once said to reporters, "I don't know if he did deserve a new trial. [I was] . . . just being a son trying to help his dad." All his efforts came to naught when Charles had a heart attack and died in prison.

Perhaps this hit man's son channeled some of his father into those roles that terrify moviegoers: the psychopathic killer, mob boss, corrupt cop, or other chilling characters that won him Academy Award nominations. There is that flip side too: the son who forgave his father and worked to recover an unrecoverable relationship. You see that in the affable Woody Boyd, the bartender in the popular sitcom *Cheers*. But maybe Woody Harrelson's most demanding role was being a good son to the father who abandoned him for a life of crime. His is an amazing story of being faithful to the unfaithful, of forgiving the unforgivable, and of giving even when there is little or no return. In an age when people bail out of relationships if needs aren't being met, if you are one of that rare breed who is committed to going the distance in a stale marriage, conflicted family, soured friendship, or flawed church, take heart from the hit man's son. Woody might say amen to this:

The undecided look for escape; the committed search for solutions.

―⁂―

May the Lord make your love for one
another and for all people grow and overflow,
just as our love for you overflows.

1 THESSALONIANS 3:12

New York City's First Immigrant

⌒⌒⌒

Most folks mistakenly think that the first Africans arrived in North America as slaves in 1620. But a century earlier, a Moroccan-born slave called Esteban came with Spaniards to colonize Florida. Only four out of the original three hundred settlers survived. One of them was the African. The four lived among indigenous peoples on the Gulf Coast before miraculously finding their way to Mexico City. Their epic journey of survival caused a sensation in Europe. Later Esteban led a party of Spaniards north to what is now New Mexico and Arizona searching for lost cities of gold. For eight years, Esteban explored what is the American Southwest, taking notes on the flora, fauna, and landmarks used by later Spanish settlers and American frontiersmen. By the time Pueblo Indians killed this African trailblazer in 1539, he had opened up the Old West.

Almost twenty years before the Dutch brought those first slaves to Jamestown, the French hired a free African by the name of Mathieu da Costa to help explore what is now upstate New York and Canada. The ease with which he picked up indigenous languages made his services invaluable. Without this African, the French might not have opened up the northern areas of the Atlantic seaboard to European settlement.

And, six years prior to that slave sale in Jamestown, Juan Rodriguez arrived off Manhattan Island. The Dutch ship's logbook records him as "Spanish" and a "black rascal." Like Esteban and da Costa before him, this son of African slaves in Santo Domingo had a knack for picking up languages, making him essential to the Dutch enterprise. When the Dutch ship was ready to set sail, the "black rascal" from Santo Domingo insisted on staying behind. This entrepreneur was left with eighty hatchets, some knives, a sword, and a musket. He built a small trading post and parlayed those metal tools into a brisk trade with the indigenous peoples of Manhattan and Long Island.

Historians believe that this consummate survivor was there to greet and help the first Dutch settlers build New Amsterdam where the Hudson River flows into what is now New York Harbor. But this son of African slaves can lay claim to being the first immigrant on an island destined to become a megametropolis built on waves of immigrants. That's why, in the Washington Heights district of New York City, you will find a prominent street named Juan Rodriguez Way.

The amazing story of three intrepid black explorers should remind us of the rich contribution that Africa made to our earliest beginnings as a nation. It should also help us to see our rich tapestry of history, made up of so many colors, textures, and threads. Can you imagine the zillions of lines that have intersected down through the ages to make it possible for you to sit here, reading this amazing story? There are no random events in your life. Every encounter is a divine appointment. Each moment is another thread in God's astonishing tapestry.

Those who leave everything in God's hand will eventually see God's hand in everything.

―――― ⟡ ――――

All honor and glory to God forever and ever!
He is the eternal King, the unseen one who
never dies; he alone is God. Amen.
1 TIMOTHY 1:17

58

From Homeless to Harvard

ᘒᘒᘒ

By the time the sixties had turned to the eighties, her hippy parents were mainlining coke. While their kids starved, the couple spent welfare checks on cocaine and heroin. When cupboards were empty, the girls sucked on ice cubes. One night they divided a tube of toothpaste for dinner. Liz remembers her mother stealing money for her birthday gift and selling the television set and a Thanksgiving turkey to buy a hit of coke. She recalls going to school lice ridden, scruffy, and smelly. When the other kids began to bully her, she dropped out. While her parents slept away their days in a drug-induced stupor, she was a wild child on the mean streets of New York City.

Her mother often said, "One day life is going to be better." But Liz can't remember how many days she nursed her mother in that lice-filled, run-down flat. She does remember the day that her mom told her that she had tested HIV positive and had AIDS. Soon after, her mom died and was buried in a donated wooden box. When her dad couldn't pay the rent and moved into a homeless shelter, Liz was out on the streets. She fed herself by shoplifting food. She also stole self-help books that sparked dreams. She remembered how often her mother had said, "One day I'll fix my life." So she decided to fix hers. At age seventeen, this school dropout was hopelessly behind. But she came up with an audacious plan to finish high school in two years, completing a year each semester in an accelerated program. Not only did Liz accomplish that herculean task, she did it with straight A's. When a mentor took her to Harvard, she set her sights on being admitted to America's most prestigious college.

Her mother often said, "One day life is going to be better." That day came for Liz when she received a scholarship to pay for Harvard. It wasn't easy for this homeless girl from the streets of New York to fit in to an Ivy League school, but Liz Murray persisted to graduation. The scruffy, smelly shoplifter whom people avoided was now inspiring a nation. Oprah Winfrey gave her a Chutzpah Award. She shared her story on stages with world leaders like Bill Clinton, Tony Blair, Mikhail Gorbachev, and the Dalai Lama, and she wrote a *New York Times* bestseller, *Breaking Night*. Her life became the inspiration for a movie, *Homeless to Harvard*. Today Liz is married with two children, and she gives her time to helping homeless kids at New York's Covenant House. She still finds inspiration in a note that her dad gave her just before he died of AIDS: "Lizzy, I left my dreams behind a long time ago. Now they are safe with you."

The amazing story of Liz Murray proves that dreams can transform if we pay the price to make them come true. Lizzy's story is one of persevering effort that turns dreamers into achievers. Thomas Edison said it best: *Success is 10 percent inspiration and 90 percent perspiration.*

———— ✑ ————

Jesus told him, "Anyone who puts a hand to the plow
and then looks back is not fit for the Kingdom of God."

LUKE 9:62

When Patriotism
Isn't Enough

⌒⊙⊙⌒

The forty-nine-year-old spinster nurse in Brussels hardly fit the profile of a hero. Yet when hospitals filled to overflowing with the mangled casualties of the butchery, this English vicar's daughter mobilized her brigade of nurses to care for the disabled and dying of World War I. She put aside loyalty to country by making sure that soldiers from both sides got equal treatment.

There was a problem: anyone in Belgium who helped Allied soldiers escape through German lines would be shot as a traitor. But the English nurse continued to aid the British and French soldiers who found their way to her hospital. She and her nurses helped more than two hundred of them escape, many carrying vital intelligence back to Allied headquarters. When Germans found out about her clandestine operations, they sentenced her to die for treason. Clergy and diplomats pleaded for clemency, but Edith Cavell was executed by a firing squad on October 12, 1915.

In a world barely out of the Victorian era, the execution of an English vicar's daughter ignited a firestorm. Rudyard Kipling called it an attack on the flower of English womanhood. Such sentiment was a bonanza for British propagandists at a time when the war was going badly and military recruitment was down. Nurse Edith was the perfect martyr to ramp up the war effort. She was pictured as falsely accused, a fragile heroine fainting at the site of her execution. They described how she was executed in her nurse's uniform emblazoned with a red cross, without the courtesy of a blindfold, and how a coldhearted German officer shot her on the ground at point-blank range. Posters, fliers, and newspapers printed grotesque depictions of German brutes and slogans like "Murdered by the Huns."

Calls to avenge Nurse Edith doubled the number of recruits, did as much as anything to rally Americans to enter the war, and were critical to eventual Allied victory. The truth is: Edith admitted in court to aiding the Allied cause, refused to wear her nurse's uniform to her execution, and faced her death as bravely as any hero on the battlefield. This angel of mercy rose from her grave as an avenging angel. Propagandists may have appealed to Victorian ideals of fragile womanhood, but Edith was a brave woman who was willing to die in combat alongside men. It is a shame when women are forced to fill a vacuum left by cowardly men, but it is also shameful when we stereotype them as the weaker sex. If God used Deborah, Jael, and Judith as Israelite warriors, surely we should benefit from and celebrate women's bravery on every battlefield of life.

Courage knows no gender, and is the first quality of a warrior.

Barak told her, "I will go, but only if you go with me." "Very well," she replied, "I will go with you. But you will receive no honor in this venture, for the LORD's victory over Sisera will be at the hands of a woman."

JUDGES 4:8-9

The Slave Who
Civilized Europe

༄༅

Abu al-Hassan was the original Renaissance man, the Muslim Leonardo da Vinci. He was born in AD 789, when Europe was digging itself out of the Dark Ages. But in the Middle East, the caliphs of Baghdad were birthing a golden age. It was in that intoxicating world of Aladdin magic that Hassan began his life as the slave of Ibrahim al-Mawsili, the greatest musician of the East. When Mawsili saw a child prodigy in Hassan, he made the young slave his protégé. He also gave him the nickname Ziryab. But when the student outshone the master to become the darling of the royal court, the jealous Mawsili had him shipped off to Tunisia.

It wasn't long before Ziryab's fame as a poet and musician spread from North Africa to the Iberian Peninsula. When the sultan of Spain summoned him to his court, he introduced the West to the magic of Baghdad. Ziryab founded Europe's first music academy in Cordoba, introducing the lute that became the instrument of troubadours in the Middle Ages. He also reshaped European music. He was the consummate virtuoso, composer, poet, scholar, and fashionista. People wore the same drab clothing year-round until this trendsetter introduced the idea of fashions that changed with the seasons. He created colorful fabrics and designs that took Europe by storm. He opened a school of cosmetology and created facial creams, toothpaste, perfumes, and underarm deodorant. He taught women how to style their hair and men how to shave. He forever changed the hygiene of Europe when he popularized the idea of a bath a day instead of the old notion of once a week, month, or hardly ever.

Ziryab also changed the way we eat. We might not appreciate his introduction of asparagus and green veggies, but we are grateful that he popularized the idea of dessert with meals. This culinary master also introduced the three-course meal, crystal, floral arrangements, tablecloths, and napkins that make up our table art. He enhanced table conversation by importing scholars who enlightened Europeans on everything from astronomy to zoology. He changed the games people played after dinner by introducing chess. Ziryab was the trendsetter of the ages, a celebrity in the 800s who shaped our world today.

Ziryab's nickname literally means "black bird," reflecting the fact that he was descended from African slaves. This amazing story of a Muslim black man who helped civilize Christian Europe shows how so much of what has enriched our lives comes from every part of our diverse world. Though Jesus is the only one who can give us eternal life, he uses each and every one of us to redeem his fallen creation. Something John Stott wrote should broaden our horizons:

The overriding reason why we should take other people's cultural identities seriously is because God has taken ours seriously.

From one man [God] created all the nations throughout the whole earth. He decided beforehand when they should rise and fall, and he determined their boundaries.

ACTS 17:26

Generals and Slaves

✦⊙⊙⊙✦

Ghosts rise from old battlefields to fight for the heart and soul of a nation still divided. Instead of the blue and gray, the battle is now between red and blue states. Families, friends, churches, and races are still divided as they were in the 1800s. The ongoing civil war has never stopped being a culture war. It is now waged on news and social media: Twitter, Instagram, and Facebook. It has become a proxy war of metaphors wrapped in the symbols and images of Confederate flags and the statues of southern generals.

When it comes to statues, we might want to start with the general of the army. But remember, he is enshrined in military lore as one of our greatest tacticians. He graduated from West Point and at one time served in the US Army with distinction. We admire him for leading his armies to their first victory in the Civil War. His men would have marched to the ends of the earth for him, yet Union officers and Yankee politicians hated him for things that should offend our morals. Why has America had a love affair with him ever since Appomattox?

This legendary general once defended slavery. Maybe he didn't own any slaves of his own, but records show that he profited from his wife's slaves. Yes, they came with the estate that his wife inherited from her father. But he could have emancipated them earlier than he did. He admitted that slavery was evil, but his private letters show that he harbored deep racial prejudices. So maybe we should tear down the statues of this man, General Ulysses S. Grant. We should tear down those of Robert E. Lee while we are at it. He never wanted them anyway. He refused to wear his uniform after the war. He had little use for the Confederate flag. He wanted to see a divided nation healed. He would be the first to tear down his statues and lower the Confederate flag.

It is useful to keep images of an uncivil war in museums and history books to learn lessons that spare us the mistakes of the past. But we should reconsider erecting images of unresolved tragedies in the public square. Surely we don't need to defend or celebrate them. There are still issues to be settled, wrongs to be righted, and a nation in need of healing. Yet Christians must never put their hope in generals, politicians, demigods, messiahs, or the platforms of political parties. Our citizenship is in heaven, not in blue or red states. The civil war that still rages will not be solved until we look to the only Savior who can fix it. In the meantime, we should refrain from the sort of rhetoric and actions that unnecessarily divide. Abraham Lincoln gave some sage advice:

We should be too big to take offense, and too noble to give it.

Do all that you can to live in peace with everyone.

ROMANS 12:18

The Four Chaplains

◈

In an era of increasing polarization, it might do us all some good to remember an amazing act of heroism many decades ago. It took place during an era of nation against nation, race against race, and religion against religion, an era that began with ethnic cleansing and ended in the Holocaust.

On February 3, 1943, an army transport ship, the *Dorchester*, was ferrying nine hundred combat soldiers across the North Atlantic to join in the fight against Nazi Germany. It wasn't an easy passage. The winter crossing was stormy, making those aboard feel like they were riding a rodeo bull. Young boys in uniform were both homesick and seasick in hot, airtight compartments below deck. But their queasy claustrophobia would soon be forgotten when torpedoes from a German sub slammed into the *Dorchester*. The captain knew that his vessel was going down, and he sounded orders to abandon ship with all haste.

The pandemonium was heightened by the utter blackness of the stormy night. Young men were desperately searching for life jackets and trying to find lifeboats on a ship sinking in icy seas a hundred fifty miles from Greenland. In the midst of this chaos, four military chaplains became immortal heroes: Father John Washington, a New Jersey Roman Catholic; Reverend Clark Poling, a Reformed Church of America chaplain from Ohio; Reverend George Fox, a Pennsylvania Methodist; and Rabbi Alexander Goode, a Jewish leader from Brooklyn. Together, they did what chaplains are supposed to do as they guided soldiers to evacuation points, whispered courage in their ears, and helped them into lifeboats or over the side of the sinking ship. When life jackets ran out, the four chaplains peeled theirs off and gave them away.

Nearly seven hundred men died in the frigid waters that night, but more than two hundred survived—some wearing life jackets handed to them by the chaplains. One soldier said that he was going back to retrieve his gloves, but Rabbi Goode insisted that he take his. Witnesses remember seeing those chaplains for the last time, linking arms together and praying as the ship disappeared from sight—a Catholic priest, a Reformed pastor, a Methodist preacher, and a Jewish rabbi. They may have come from different regions of America, voted for different political candidates, believed disparate theologies, and worshiped with dissimilar liturgies, but they believed in the same God, fought under the same flag, and were willing to die for young men whose views and lifestyles they may not have embraced. It's no wonder that they were posthumously awarded one of the highest honors this nation can give to its military heroes.

In an age of intolerance, when almost anyone who doesn't agree with us is dismissed as an enemy to be ridiculed, we would do well to dust off the amazing story of four chaplains who linked arms together in unity to pay the ultimate sacrifice for others. If it causes any of us to become less divisive, the retelling of this story will be well worth it. We might even benefit from something Malcolm Forbes said:

Diversity is the art of thinking independently together.

———— ❧ ————

Are we not all children of the same Father?
Are we not all created by the same God?

MALACHI 2:10

The Woman Who
Never Backed Down

∾᷎⊙᷎∾

The McCauley girl never backed down to anyone. Maybe she got her grit from her grandfather. She remembers those days the KKK marched through their black neighborhood. Most folks hid behind locked doors. But her granddaddy stood ramrod tall in front of the farmhouse, his jaw set and shotgun cocked. No cowards hiding behind white sheets were going to intimidate him.

That willingness to stand up to bullies rubbed off on his granddaughter. When a young white man threatened her, the McCauley girl picked up a brick to hit him if he didn't back down. Her grandmother warned her that she would be lynched by age twenty. The girl retorted, "I would rather be lynched than live to be mistreated and not allowed to say 'I don't like it.'" Later she married Raymond, in part because he refused to be intimidated by white people. Together, they organized and agitated for civil rights.

She was smart enough to keep her resentment of racial injustice under wraps in an era of redneck sheriffs, lynching, and church firebombing. But when she got on the public transit and plopped down in the "colored" section, America was about to change.

On that chilly December evening in 1955 there were more whites than usual on the Cleveland Avenue bus route. The rules of segregation were brutally simple: blacks sat in the back of the bus. But they were expected to give up their seats if there were too many white riders. It was natural for the bus driver to charge down the aisle and demand that blacks in the first two rows of their designated section give up their seats to white passengers. It was natural for three of the African American passengers to get up meekly and move on back. It was also natural for Raymond's wife to set her jaw like her grandfather and refuse to get up.

At first, the white bus driver was flustered. He wasn't used to having his authority challenged. Then he got angry. Maybe she should have been scared. The driver could very well have thrown her off the bus. He was also carrying a pistol. Not long before, Claudette Colvin had been arrested when she didn't give up her seat. That summer, fourteen-year-old Emmett Till had been lynched for offending a white woman.

But Rosa's grandfather had raised her to not back down to bullies. She later said, "The time had just come when I had been pushed as far as I could stand to be pushed." Rosa's arrest by the police started a bus boycott that lasted 381 days. That Montgomery protest spread, Martin Luther King was thrust into prominence, and the dismantling of segregation began—all because a fed-up black woman refused to give up her seat. It's amazing what one act of courage can do to transform a nation.

Remember that Jesus went after the bullies in the Temple. A shepherd stood up to a bully named Goliath. Sometimes, like Rosa Parks, we shouldn't allow ourselves to be pushed anymore.

To sit passively in the face of evil is to be its silent accomplice.

———— ✑ ————

Jesus made a whip from some ropes and
chased them all out of the Temple.

JOHN 2:15

70

The Long Trek Home

✦

Made of the dust of the earth, we are prone to wallow in mud; infused with the breath of God, we sometimes soar. We are capable of acts of horror or feats of heroism. Case in point: those Uruguayan rugby players who survived a jetliner crash and the avalanche that followed. Twenty-seven passengers were left to face an uncertain future in an untenable place under unbearable conditions. They were trapped some twelve thousand feet high in the Andes Mountains on an ice plateau surrounded by drop-offs and jagged mountains. Their only shelter was a battered and perforated fuselage that gave little protection from icy winds and thin blankets that gave no warmth in temperatures below zero. They had no suitable clothing, no fuel for fire, no survival training, and no food.

When their dying radio brought news that the search for their missing jetliner had been called off, they could have given themselves up for dead. Yet these rugby players somehow endured seventy-two harrowing days on that windswept glacier. But the way they survived horrified the world. They dug up the frozen bodies of crash victims and ate their flesh. What those young men did has been the focus of ethical debates, articles, books, and films since 1972. Yet by focusing on the horror of their survival, we overlook the heroism of their escape.

Some two months into their ordeal, Nando Parrado and Roberto Canessa set out on an epic journey to find help. First they had to walk up a long ice slope at a forty-degree angle in street clothes and dress shoes through oxygen-poor air for three brutal days. When they arrived at the 14,774-foot vantage point, all they could see were jagged mountains in all directions. They wanted to cry. Instead, they whispered a prayer and headed for what looked like a distant valley. For the next seven days, they walked along sheer cliffs, across glaciers with crevices, down icy slopes, and over rugged peaks. They had no boots, ropes, crampons, ice axes, maps, or compasses. They slept out in the open, in winds twenty degrees below freezing, huddling in sleeping bags that had been stitched together from the insulation of the fuselage. They suffered hypothermia and frostbite. As they neared the base of the mountains, they had to cross flooded streams and fight through thick underbrush. Ten days after they set out, three horsemen spotted them. The next day helicopters flew to those who remained at the wreckage, their rescue made possible by the two who refused to remain.

Three decades later, *National Geographic* sponsored a team of elite mountain climbers, supplied with the best equipment available, to retrace the journey of Parrado and Canessa. Afterward, they concluded that the trek of those two was one of the greatest mountaineering and survival achievements of all time. The story of these rugby players proves that we are capable of anything, from the horrific to the heroic. Yet when we manage those infrequent moments of heroism we point to the only true and enduring Hero. John Piper put it well:

All heroes are shadows of Christ.

───── ✦ ─────

We have seen with our own eyes and now testify that the Father has sent his Son to be the Savior of the world.

1 JOHN 4:14

The Turkey That Soared

It's been decades since that day Michael electrified the world. Now folks show up at store openings to watch him perform silly antics in a chicken suit. Occasionally Michael gets a gig on a cruise ship selling inspiration mostly to old folks. He lives in a home filled with debris and memorabilia, still has his trademark laugh, snorts through his nose, and wears those pop-bottle glasses—the lovable nerd with a goofy smile, making a living off that one magical day in Calgary.

This son of a blue-collar family was a sickly, accident-prone child, the clumsiest kid on the playground. Yet, even if he was short on talent, Michael was long on dreams. He fantasized that he would someday stand on the podium as an Olympic medalist. Yet he failed at every sport he tried. His dad begged him to give up his impossible dream, but he refused.

Then Michael hit upon a novel idea. Great Britain didn't have a ski jumper on its winter Olympics team. It didn't matter that he had never ski jumped. There was an empty spot for the filling! The British Olympic Committee rejected him, but he wouldn't give up. He crisscrossed Europe, entering competitions, living in an old car, grubbing food out of garbage cans, shoveling snow, and scrubbing floors. He competed in thick, pink-and-white-rimmed glasses, wore six pairs of old socks in his hand-me-down boots, and used beat-up skis—the laughingstock of the circuit, he came in dead last in every competition. Yet, in a turn of events that could only have been dreamed up in Hollywood, Michael made the British Olympic team in 1988.

The world remembers Michael Edwards by his nickname, Eddie. His embarrassed teammates gave him other names: Fast Eddie. Slow Eddie. Crazy Eddie. Unsteady Eddie. Mr. Magoo on Skis. The Abominable

Snowman. But the one that stuck was Eddie the Eagle. In his qualifying jumps, he looked more like a turkey, falling flat on his face to the laughter of competitors, spectators, and commentators. But the lovable loser's determination inspired those at the ski jump venue, as well as a worldwide audience. Then came that magical jump. It didn't pull Eddie out of last place, but he did soar. When he stuck the landing, the announcer shouted, "The eagle has landed!" Eddie danced on his skis with the unbridled joy of a child, fist pumping the air in wild abandon. The crowd went crazy, caught up in Eddie's jubilation. The turkey who soared in Calgary became a worldwide sensation.

Today, Eddie dons a chicken suit and performs silly antics for the crowd at a supermarket opening, earning a few euros off that magical day when he became the stuff of Olympic legend. Eddie is the patron saint of every lovable loser who refuses to give up on dreams. He should encourage every person of mediocre talent who dares to believe that even turkeys can soar if they keep flapping away. Eddie the Eagle would probably agree with this:

Until you risk spreading your wings, you will never know how high you can fly.

⸎

Those who trust in the LORD will find new strength.
They will soar high on wings like eagles.

ISAIAH 40:31

The River of Doubt

&oe&

He had just suffered one of those rare defeats in his charmed life. At times like this, he had always turned to big adventure as his therapy. So he organized a trip down the Amazon River. Maybe an overweight man of fifty-four was foolish to challenge a monstrous river largely unexplored in 1913. But danger had always been Ted's drug of choice. So he used his fortune and charm to put together a first-class team of intrepid explorers and headed off to South America.

It didn't take long for Ted's party to realize that they were in over their heads. They had hoped to live off the land, but jungles know how to hide their bounty from intruders. Soon their food supplies were dangerously low. Then they lost a couple of canoes on a murderous stretch of rapids. As always, Ted played the hero. He pushed, paddled, pulled, and shoved as he rescued the canoes. When his leg was torn open, his exhausted party pulled him out of the rapids.

Ted was in excruciating pain, but he refused to show it. What was a nasty gash to a man who had chased outlaws in the American West, faced down elephants in Africa, charged into cannon fire, been hit by a streetcar, and been shot in the chest by a deranged man? Yet he was no match for deadly jungle microbes. By morning, he was burning up with fever and desperately needed to get to a doctor. But the rapids were impassable. If they were going to survive, they would have to hack their way through thick jungle. Yet the man who always led the charge said that he was too weak to go on. In a nearby bag was a vial of morphine. Ted would rather end things quickly than suffer an agonizing death. He was on the verge of breaking open that vial when his son Kermit figured out an ingenious way to get their canoes past the rapids.

Maybe he shouldn't have tackled the Amazon after he lost the presidential election of 1912, but Teddy Roosevelt thrived on big challenges. His courage and optimism in the face of extreme danger was the stuff of legend. The war hero who became America's youngest president and won the Nobel Peace Prize was bigger than life. When he passed away in his sleep five years after his trip down the Amazon, his former vice president quipped, "Death had to take him sleeping, for if Roosevelt had been awake, there would have been a fight." No one would have believed there was a day in the Amazon jungles when he was minutes away from giving up the fight. Maybe you are on your own river of doubt today. Before you give up, remember that Kermit figured out a way to get around those impassable rapids just before his dad broke open that vial of morphine. There's always a solution, if you hold on. Teddy Roosevelt would say "Bully!" to this:

A setback is often a setup for your comeback.

———— ✀ ————

Be strong and immovable. Always work
enthusiastically for the Lord, for you know that
nothing you do for the Lord is ever useless.

1 CORINTHIANS 15:58

Just Another
Night on the Job

୧ঌ৩৬৩

The cast of characters that toppled a US president is a who's who of saints and sinners. Some suffered shame, and others got fame. But no one can ever forget the Watergate scandal that transfixed the world and gave birth to a cynicism that has only intensified in the years since President Richard Nixon's resignation on August 9, 1974. Only time will tell how history will report Watergate in years to come. Who will be remembered and who will be forgotten? History is the most fickle and unpredictable writer. Too often she has amnesia, and then she remembers what we want to forget.

So far history has shown herself unpredictable when it comes to this scandal. Richard Nixon may have fled in disgrace, but he later wrote bestselling books on foreign policy and lived his final years as an elder statesman. *Washington Post* reporters Bob Woodward and Carl Bernstein were celebrated in the movie *All the President's Men*. Nixon's hatchet man, Charles Colson, came to Jesus in prison and later became one of evangelicalism's leading voices. White House counsel John Dean got out of prison and wrote a bestseller. G. Gordon Liddy, the mastermind of the Watergate burglary, had his own nationally syndicated radio program for twenty years. The media immortalized Judge John Sirica, Archibald Cox, and Sam Ervin for taking Nixon down.

But no one remembers the man who got the ball rolling. Without Frank Wills, the Watergate scandal would never have happened. Frank was an eighty-dollar-a-week security guard at the Watergate Hotel, working the graveyard shift on June 17, 1972, when he discovered tape across a door latch and removed it. When he discovered the latch taped again during a second inspection, he immediately called the police. When they arrived, they caught five burglars stealing Democratic National Committee files. Frank Wills was no hero. He was just a security guard doing his job. No one could have guessed that his quick action on a second-rate burglary would eventually implicate the Oval Office. Frank got little reward and no recognition. He did get a $2.50 raise from the security company and a bit part playing himself in *All the President's Men.* He bounced around after that and ended up in South Carolina taking care of his sick mother. He lived his last years in poverty and died of a brain tumor.

Frank didn't get any book deals. No one wanted to do a movie about a security guard doing his job. He barely even got fifteen minutes of fame for toppling a president. Reporter Bob Woodward did say that, of all the people involved with the Watergate scandal, Frank Wills was the only one who did his job exactly right. Woodward said of Frank, "Calling the police was one of the most important phone calls in history, and it was so simple and so basic." History may not write any lines about you, but God is writing a book on your life. So do the simple things and the basic things right. Let *His* story decide what to do with them.

Greatness is made up of a lot of small things done well every day.

Whatever you do, work at it with all your heart,
as working for the Lord, not for human masters.

COLOSSIANS 3:23, NIV

The Infinite Possibilities of Hope

❧

Sean knows what it's like to face the impossible. Twice he beat unbeatable odds. At age thirteen he came down with Hodgkin's disease. The doctors didn't think he would survive, but he did. When he was sixteen, he contracted Askin's sarcoma, a rare cancer that attaches itself to the walls of the chest. The prognosis is never optimistic, and its treatment has horrible side effects.

Sean may be the only person alive to have suffered both of these cancers. For sure, no one has gotten them both in such a short span of time. Doctors say that the odds of him overcoming both were the equivalent of winning four lottery tickets in a row using the same numbers. He survived his second cancer by being put in an induced coma for a year. At one point his parents were told that he had only two weeks to live, and a priest read his last rites. When he miraculously came out of that coma, he had only one functioning lung. Yet as he lay in his hospital bed watching the Ironman World Championship triathlon on television, he vowed that he would one day compete in it.

During the months of recovery that followed, an oft-quoted line inspired the teenager to go on: "The human body can live roughly thirty days without food. The human condition can sustain itself for roughly three days without water, but no human alive can live for more than thirty seconds without hope." He decided to test the infinite possibilities of hope. His first challenge was to crawl eight feet from his hospital bed to the bathroom. A few years later he climbed Mount Kilimanjaro. But he hadn't yet begun to test the infinite possibilities of hope. Over the next several years this cancer survivor with a single lung scaled the tallest mountain on each of the seven continents. He became the first cancer survivor to stand atop the granddaddy of them all: 29,229-foot-high Mount Everest. But he still hadn't tested the limits of hope. In his forties, he skied to the South Pole. Now he had completed the Explorers Grand Slam. But there was still that one remaining impossible goal. You guessed it: Sean Swarner traveled to Hawaii and competed in the Ironman World Championship.

This cancer survivor who was read his last rites has redefined the meaning of *impossible* by being the only person in history to climb the seven great summits of the world, ski to both the North and South Poles, and complete the Ironman in Hawaii—all on one lung. Now he is helping other people discover the infinite possibilities of hope as one of the world's top-ten motivational speakers.

Sean's amazing story is a reminder that God has given three precious gifts that will remain after everything else is stripped away: faith, hope, and love. Are you facing a mountain that seems too big to climb? Then test the possibilities of hope. They are too infinite to let you down.

When the world says give up, Hope whispers try it one more time.

———— ✎ ————

Three things will last forever—faith, hope, and love.

1 CORINTHIANS 13:13

The Night Witches

❧

Terrified Germans called these Russian bombers *Nachthexen*, "night witches." They came in so slow that radar couldn't spot them, their plywood bodies making a swooshing sound like the sweeping of a broom. When they dropped their incendiary bombs, the night skies were ablaze with a raging inferno.

Germans might have had more reason to call them the Night Witches had they known that these Soviet bomber groups were made up entirely of women. But the German army had only themselves to blame. Their killing spree had liquidated untold millions of men in Russia. That's when Colonel Marina Raskova lobbied Joseph Stalin to allow women to join combat units. Stalin agreed, ordering Colonel Raskova to organize three female bomber units. She recruited the fittest young women and then trained them to fly. One woman recalls that, after they put on flight clothes and cut their hair short, "We didn't recognize ourselves in the mirror— we saw boys there." Her most elite group was the 588th Night Bomber Regiment made up entirely of women, from the pilots to the mechanics.

It wasn't easy. They were subjected to sexual harassment, given cast-off uniforms that were several sizes too big, and forced to stuff sheets in their oversize men's boots. They had to fly antiquated Polikarpov Po-2 biplanes that were hopelessly slow, with canvas stretched over plywood frames and no armaments. It was a laughable idea that one of these flying fossils could ever tangle with a high-tech Luftwaffe Messerschmitt. The women who piloted these death traps were given no radar or parachutes. They operated with pencil, paper, triangle, and compass. They flew in open cockpits in freezing weather with frostbitten fingers. Yet they were tougher than any fighting men in the war, whether Axis or Allies.

In spite of all these obstacles, these daring aviators in plywood and canvas planes earned the dreaded title *Nachthexen*. The famed 588th Night Bomber Regiment flew more missions, dropped more bombs, destroyed more targets, and earned more medals than any other unit in the Soviet Air Force. After the surrender of Nazi Germany, their unit was disbanded, and they disappeared from memory—except among Germans who tossed in their beds for years afterward with nightmares of the *Nachthexen*. This amazing story of the Night Witches proves that victory doesn't come from the weapons in our hands as much as from the courage in our heart. Even a squadron made of canvas and plywood can win wars if its pilots are made of steel. Even a little boy can topple a giant with a stone and a sling, especially with God at his side. If you are facing some giant today, remember this:

God has put a stone in your hand for every giant you face.

———— ❧ ————

As Goliath moved closer to attack, David quickly
ran out to meet him. Reaching into his shepherd's
bag and taking out a stone, he hurled it with his
sling and hit the Philistine in the forehead.

1 SAMUEL 17:48-49

The Other Lafayette

✦

We might not know that this unsung hero existed if not for that engraving from the late 1700s. The etching captures the likeness of the Marquis de Lafayette, a French nobleman who became one of Washington's most trusted generals. But who is the black man holding the reins of the marquis's horse? The etching simply refers to him as Lafayette's *body servant, James.* James was the name given him by his master, William Armistead. When winds of freedom blew across the colonies, he begged his master to allow him to join the patriot army. Instead, Armistead loaned his slave to Lafayette as a body servant. But the marquis was an enlightened man who abhorred slavery. He could never understand why Southern colonials fought for freedom and yet subjected others to bondage. Lafayette was a rare man in the 1700s who could look beyond race or rank to see the person, and he saw something special in James.

When the British started offering emancipation to all runaways, he asked James to infiltrate the British ranks, posing as a fugitive slave. Lafayette's body servant pulled off the ruse, ingratiating himself with British commander General Cornwallis and his newest general, American traitor Benedict Arnold. When they asked James to spy for them, he became one of America's first double agents. The British never suspected that he was feeding their secrets to the Continental army. Lafayette boasted that James Armistead was his best spy. That African American's daring escapades rival those in any spy novel. His gathering of critical intelligence allowed Lafayette to defeat the British at Hampton and set up their army to be trapped at Yorktown. Without this black slave's dangerous and heroic work, the Continental army might not have won the last battle of the Revolutionary War.

A grateful Lafayette lobbied for James's freedom. But an ungrateful nation refused his request. James was returned to William Armistead as his slave. When the marquis visited Virginia in 1784, he was deeply distressed to discover that his best spy was still enslaved. He wrote to his friend, Washington, pleading for his freedom. It would take two years, but Lafayette's testimony moved the Virginia General Assembly to grant James Armistead his emancipation. James bought forty acres of farmland and raised a big family.

After he was emancipated, he changed his name to James Armistead Lafayette in honor of the French nobleman who saw beyond his station and the color of his skin to make him his most trusted spy. We should also be grateful to that Frenchman. Because he set a slave free to realize his fullest potential, we live in a free country where we can discover our fullest potential. The amazing story of the *other* Lafayette reminds us that we are also honored to take the name of the one who has set us free from sin to become all that we can be. But with honor comes responsibility: *If we bear Christ's name, we should reflect Christ's nature.*

<hr>

Follow my example, as I follow the example of Christ.

1 CORINTHIANS 11:1, NIV

Unbroken by Failure

He was seven years old when his family lost their Indiana farm. He had to drop out of school and go to work. Two years later his beloved mother died. When he was twenty-two years old he started a business. Within a year, it went belly up. He ran for the state legislature and lost. Someone hired him to run a store but fired him a few months later. So he applied to law school only to be rejected. A friend loaned him money to start another business. Within a year, he filed for bankruptcy. It took him seventeen years to pay off his debt.

Again he made a run at politics. He finally got a rare taste of success. The year he took office, he got engaged. It seemed that fortune was finally smiling on him. But on the eve of their wedding, his fiancée died of typhoid fever, and he plunged into suicidal despair. He spent the next six months in bed.

He recovered enough to get back into the political game but was defeated. His friends tried to cheer him up by pushing him into an arranged marriage. It would be the great disaster of his life, consigning him to twenty-three years with a difficult wife.

Again he ran for public office, suffering yet another defeat. Then his three-year-old son Edward died. After a season of grief, he finally won an election, only to lose his bid for reelection. When he limped home from Washington, DC, he ran for some minor office in his home state, only to be rejected again.

After licking his wounds for five years, he ran for the US Senate and lost. Sympathetic colleagues nominated him for vice president. He finished dead last among all the candidates. Two years later, he picked himself up off the floor and ran for the senate a second time. Again he was defeated, giving him the dubious distinction of being the biggest political loser in US history.

It's a miracle that two years later he somehow found the courage to run for America's highest office. In 1860, after decades of political failures and personal setbacks, Abraham Lincoln became the sixteenth president of the United States.

But his euphoria was short lived. As the country careened toward civil war, he was vilified across the South. Newspapers lampooned him, calling him the Gorilla from Illinois. When the Union dissolved, there were calls for the president's impeachment. His generals refused his orders, and cabinet members plotted against him. His eleven-year-old son died, and his wife descended into madness. In the end, he was denied the pleasure of savoring his greatest triumph when he was assassinated only six days after the Civil War ended.

As he stood by Lincoln's deathbed, the secretary of state whispered, "He now belongs to the ages." Two days later, on Good Friday, preachers across America eulogized Lincoln as the savior of our nation. If you have gone through a long stretch of defeats and are ready to throw in the towel, you might want to remember Abraham Lincoln's story in the light of something Leo Tolstoy wrote:

The two most powerful warriors are patience and time.

_____ ⟳ _____

Wait patiently for the LORD. Be brave and
courageous. Yes, wait patiently for the LORD.

PSALM 27:14

Denied in Life,
Together in Death

⊰♥⊱

This love story is tucked away in forgotten pages of America's colonial history. Few people know it. Those who discover it are surprised that such romance might have flowered in the cold soil of New England Puritanism.

He was a cantankerous sort whose public rebukes of his professors' lifeless faith got him expelled from Yale. So he became a missionary to the Delaware Indians. Though he was frail and sickly, as skinny as a beanpole and suffering from tuberculosis, he trekked deep into thick forests, sloughing through waist-deep snow to reach people dismissed by colonists as savages. In those gloomy woods, he plunged into extreme depression. Yet he somehow managed to pick himself up and preach the gospel to his beloved Delawares. He often coughed up so much blood that the snow around him was crimson after a sermon.

At age twenty-nine, his frail body gave out. He managed to ride half-dead to the home of Jonathan Edwards, the hellfire-and-brimstone preacher who loved him like a son. Edwards assigned the task of nursing the preacher to his seventeen-year-old daughter, Jerusha. This uncommonly beautiful teenager was the apple of her father's eye. Little did her preacher daddy know the price he would pay by putting the dying missionary in her care.

For several months, the girl gave herself wholeheartedly to nursing her patient. When doctors said that fresh air might help him, they went on long horseback rides together. We can only speculate about a budding romance between the two, but we do know that they took four days to ride to Boston on a trip that normally took two. Were they in love? Jerusha's daddy gives us reason to think so. He writes that, toward the end, the dying missionary smiled at his girl and said, "Dear Jerusha, are you willing to part with me? I am quite willing to part with you . . . if I thought I should not see you and be happy with you in another world, I could not bear to part with you." Two days later, David Brainerd died. Jerusha was at his bedside when he slipped into eternity.

Four months later, on Valentine's Day of 1748, Jerusha died of acute fever likely brought on by her care of David. A heartbroken Jonathan Edwards buried her next to Brainerd so that the two could rise together on Resurrection Day. He spoke of her as a flower cut down in the full bloom of beauty and took hope in the fact that David and Jerusha would indeed be together in another world.

If you go to Northampton, Massachusetts, you can see their names etched together on a weathered marker in the old cemetery. Listen to the wind, and you might hear the voices of two young lovers whispering, "We *are* happily together again in another world." That gives hope to all of us who believe that a father's gift of his most precious child to a dying man points to something more amazing:

You may not be perfect, but your Father thinks you're worth dying for.

This is how God loved the world: He gave his
one and only Son, so that everyone who believes
in him will not perish but have eternal life.

JOHN 3:16

Strong Heart

꿍

His mother gave him a Latin name that means "strong heart." She knew that her son needed to be strong in a world that was falling apart. Rome was in its death throes, and barbarian Goths were moving south to feed like vultures on its carcass. But Strong Heart grew up to justify the name his mother gave him. As a courageous pastor, this son of wealth brought hope to a terrified Rome. Christians and pagans alike celebrated his outrageous acts of charity. His joy was so contagious that even Rome's rulers turned a blind eye to his preaching.

Then a new emperor rose up to save Rome. Marcus Aurelius Claudius was determined to put an end to the Gothic menace. Every Italian man was conscripted into military service. Single men were forbidden to marry. Married men were prohibited from sleeping with their wives. Claudius wanted every ounce of energy focused on defeating the Goths.

But there were young lovers in Italy. When no one else dared to perform a wedding, lovesick couples found their way to the pastor who was famous for his compassion. Strong Heart defied an emperor and performed hundreds of illegal weddings. Almost all those nuptials ended with new believers' baptisms.

When word of the clandestine ceremonies reached the palace, Strong Heart was dragged before an irate emperor. But his contagious joy softened Claudius's hard heart. Palace observers wrote that the pastor could have walked away a free man had he not pressed Claudius to come to Jesus. Instead, the emperor angrily sentenced him to die.

Death row did nothing to blunt Strong Heart's joy. His jailer was so impressed that he brought his blind daughter to visit the prisoner, hoping that the man's exuberance would pull her out of a lifetime of self-pity.

Soon both were laughing, and within days they were in love. On the eve of his execution, the pastor wrote a final love letter to his sweetheart, signing it in a way that is still celebrated today.

At dawn, Strong Heart forgave each of his executioners and implored them to receive Jesus. They repaid his lavish love by beating him so brutally that his great heart exploded. Perhaps that's why a blood-red heart still symbolizes his life.

Scholars long speculated that Strong Heart's story was just another medieval myth. But archaeologists recently uncovered the remains of an ancient church in Rome. Chiseled in its doorway arch are the words of Pope Julius I honoring a man named Strong Heart who died on February 14. You may never have heard of Emperor Claudius, who died of disease around the same time, but today you remember Strong Heart, whose Latin name was Valentinus, and the way he ended that final letter to his sweetheart: "Your Valentine." Giving your heart away is risky. Too many folks try to protect their heart from hurt. If you are tempted to play it safe with love, remember Saint Valentine's story in light of something Mother Teresa once said:

If you give until it hurts, there is no more hurt, only love.

———— ⁂ ————

A new commandment I give to you, that you love
one another. . . . By this all people will know that you
are my disciples, if you have love for one another.

JOHN 13:34-35, ESV

Unleashing
the Power of Mom

❧

"Hell hath no fury like a woman scorned." So goes the oft-quoted line from an old English play. But it is only half-right. The truth is, hell has no fury like a mother scorned. Harm her child, and a mother's gentleness will turn to anger akin to heaven's wrath. Just ask Candy. On May 3, 1980, one of her thirteen-year-old twin daughters was on her way to a church carnival when a car careened out of control and onto the sidewalk and hit her.

It was bad enough that Candy Lightner had to identify Cari's mangled body while enduring a parent's worst nightmare. But what she heard from the police turned her grief into rage. Clarence Busch, the driver who hit Cari, was drunk at the time. Worse than that, he had a long rap sheet for drunk driving. The week before, he had been arrested for another hit-and-run accident while intoxicated. Just when Candy didn't think that she could get any angrier, the police officer informed her that drunk drivers were rarely prosecuted. Those convicted didn't get stiff sentences. He warned Candy that her daughter's killer wouldn't spend much time behind bars.

The grieving family had to endure a sham of a trial. Clarence Busch would only spend twenty-one months behind bars for killing a teenage girl on her way to church. Candy came to a conclusion that she would repeat often in the years to come: "Drunk driving is the only socially accepted homicide." This mom could have let her rage debilitate her. Instead, she harnessed it by uniting other moms and unleashing their power. When she started Mothers Against Drunk Drivers on a shoestring budget, she had no idea that MADD would change America. It got the attention of President Reagan, who asked Candy to become part of his National Commission on Drunk Driving. In five years she had mobilized six hundred thousand mothers in more than three hundred chapters across the country.

Because of MADD, laws were passed in all fifty states raising the drinking age to twenty-one. Licenses were revoked for those arrested for driving under the influence. The nation's legal blood alcohol content was lowered from 0.1% to 0.08%. The states with the toughest laws now treat alcohol-related deaths as murder that deserves a stiff sentence. We should be glad that Candy Lightner unleashed the power of mom. Since her daughter was killed, alcohol-related fatalities have dropped 40 percent. The story of a mother who wouldn't remain silent reminds us all to raise our voices for those who don't have a voice. God hasn't called us to be nice in the face of evil. Even Jesus got "mad" when bad people abused others. If you are a serious follower of Jesus, you need to remember this:

Those who speak for Jesus must be a voice for the voiceless.

❧

Speak up for those who cannot speak for themselves;
ensure justice for those being crushed.

PROVERBS 31:8

92

The House of Wisdom

༄༅

Tragedies visited on Iraq and Syria by a rampaging Islamic State were horrific enough. But the wanton destruction of priceless antiquities by ISIS thugs went beyond the pale. It is barbaric enough to rape the present, but it is monstrous to rob the future of its past. People can somehow move on from the wreckage of today, but they cannot go on to a more hopeful future without the wisdom of the past.

Yet the destruction of the world's heritage is nothing new. Hardly anyone remembers the House of Wisdom, but it was one of history's wonders. When Europeans were still digging out of the Dark Ages, scholars traveled across the globe to this magnificent center built by Caliph Harun al-Rashid. The House of Wisdom was the crown jewel of the golden age of Baghdad. In its size and scope, it rivaled the ancient library in Alexandria.

For five hundred years this House of Wisdom grew in grandeur as the agents of caliphs scoured the earth, using the immense wealth of Baghdad to buy up every manuscript, in every language, from every religion, on every imaginable subject, until they had cornered the market on the wisdom of the ages. The crème de la crème of intelligentsia came to this mecca of knowledge to study everything from astronomy to zoology. But its greatest contribution was the symposiums where scholars discussed, debated, and then distilled old truths into revolutionary ideas. Then they went home and disseminated what they learned to transform their societies. Without the House of Wisdom, Europe might not have climbed out from under the rubble of fallen Rome. The advances we enjoy would have come so much later.

But houses of wisdom must invariably crumble with age and neglect. Or fall prey to the barbarian. In the year 1258, Mongol hordes, led by the sadistic grandson of Genghis Khan, swept across Iraq. These mass murderers were the proto-ISIS of their day. They reduced Baghdad to rubble, slaughtered its people, and put an end to a golden age. That genocide was horrific enough if you were an Iraqi. What the Mongols did next was the crime of the ages. These mindless barbarians ransacked the House of Wisdom and threw the accumulated knowledge of ages past into the river. It was said that the Tigris was black with ink for days. Both heaven and history must have wept as the wisdom of the ages dissolved and dissipated into the murky waters. It would take the world centuries to recover from that monstrous tragedy—if, indeed, it ever has.

If we have been robbed of the House of Wisdom, we should at least salvage a lesson from its rubble: knowledge gained by the past can be so quickly stolen from the future. We ought to listen to the aged among us and soak up what they have to share. They, too, are houses of wisdom. We should insist that our children read the classics in an age when most are content with Google factoids. We ought to discuss ideas that matter instead of engaging in mindless chatter and social media trivialities.

Don't bypass houses of wisdom today. They may be gone tomorrow.

––––––– ✎ –––––––

Wisdom belongs to the aged, and understanding to the old.

JOB 12:12

From Libya with Love

❦

Mohamed Bzeek is one of many immigrants who make America better. This bearded gentle giant who hails from Libya is one amazing story. His wife, Dawn, was already taking in foster children when he met her, and they continued to care for foster kids when they married. But lots of folks in California open their homes to foster kids. Mohamed and Dawn were different. In the mid-1990s, they began taking in kids who were not only desperate for a home, but just desperate: terminally ill children who couldn't see, hear, or talk. This couple had a simple vision that they could fill the short lives of those dying kids with as much love as humanly possible. Since then, Mohamed has buried ten of his foster kids. But his heart never broke more than when he watched Dawn die from blood clots in her lungs in 2015.

Bzeek was determined to continue her vision to care for the most vulnerable. Nothing demonstrates that commitment more than watching him care for his most severely disabled foster child, a six-year-old girl who was born with microcephaly. She is unable to see, hear, or talk. She lies helpless for twenty-four hours a day, hooked to breathing tubes and wires. When no one else was willing to deal with her, this man from Libya took her in. He recently told a *People* magazine reporter, "The only way I can communicate with her is by touch. So I hold her. I want her to know that someone is here for her. Somebody loves her. She is not alone." Because Mohamed sleeps on a sofa next to her at night, she is never alone.

His story is even more amazing because he has his own special-needs son. Adam was born with osteogenesis imperfecta. His brittle bones make it difficult for the twenty-year-old computer science major to use his hands. So Mohamed helps his son complete his homework, take a bath, and tie his shoes. When asked about Adam, this proud father says, "He's the way God made him, but he's a fighter like all the other kids who have come to live with us."

Most folks can't figure out what has kept Mohamed Bzeek going for more than two decades of nonstop caring for those severely disabled kids. He could have given up when Dawn passed away. A lesser man might have said, "It was Dawn's vision anyway." When folks ask him why he still does it, Mohamed replies, "Even if these children cannot communicate, see, or hear, they still have a soul. They need somebody to love them. I tell them, 'It's okay, I'm here for you. We'll go through this together.'" What a beautiful world this would be if there were more amazing stories like this. The love of an immigrant from Libya challenges those of us who follow Jesus. We can all do much more than we've done for those who are neglected and abandoned. Mr. Bzeek would surely agree with something Mother Teresa said:

One of the greatest diseases is to be nobody to anybody.

―――――― ᘓᗝᘌ ――――――

Encourage those who are timid. Take tender care of
those who are weak. Be patient with everyone.

1 THESSALONIANS 5:14

Living for
Ninety-Nine Cents

⊷⊙☉⊶

Frank was in his early twenties, but he was already old and ravaged. He made his bed on a bench on the dark side of a park to avoid being spotted by a patrol car or hooligans. He gingerly arranged his blanket of newspapers. They didn't provide much warmth on a cold Toronto night, but they did shield him from pigeon droppings. Frank wondered for the umpteenth time how he had sunk so low.

He had been raised in a Montreal home with strong values, but he fell in with the wrong crowd. At age thirteen, he stole his first sip of alcohol. By the time he was eighteen, he was guzzling it. He loved how it made him feel invincible, but it also got him into a lot of trouble. When he was twenty-one, his dad kicked him out of the house.

Now he was on the mean streets of Toronto, homeless, jobless, and penniless. He had lost everything but his thirst for booze. A good night was surviving the violence. A good day was finding ninety-nine cents. For ninety-nine cents he could buy a bottle of cheap wine. If he got an extra fifty cents, he could rent a lice-infested mattress in some flophouse. But he lived for the first ninety-nine cents. Nothing mattered more than that bottle of wine. So he stood on street corners begging, "Buddy, can you spare a quarter, a dime, a nickel? Even a penny will do."

Things changed the day he heard a radio advertisement touting a program that helped alcoholics. Frank stood at a crossroads of crisis. If he used a dime to call the program, he would be ten cents short of that bottle of wine. Frank made the right choice. Since then, he hasn't had a drink of alcohol.

Frank O'Dea has gone on to be one of the most successful entrepreneurs in North America. When a businessman took a chance on a recovering alcoholic, Frank turned out to be a natural-born salesman. In 1975, he and a partner plunked down $1,000 in savings to buy a coffee kiosk in a shopping mall. That kiosk has grown to over three hundred cafés across Canada, and the company is now the country's largest specialty coffee retailer. Second Cup can now be found in many countries around the world. Watch out Starbucks! When Frank O'Dea was under newspapers on a park bench, he couldn't have imagined that one day he would walk a red carpet to receive his nation's second-highest honor, officer of the Order of Canada.

The amazing story of the man who lived for ninety-nine cents a day raises the question, "What am I living for today?" A bottle of cheap wine is a poor bargain in exchange for your life. So is a billion dollars, if it doesn't bring meaning now or eternity later. Sadly, a lot of folks sell their lives too cheaply. You might want to spend some time reflecting on what you are living for today.

Your life is too valuable to give it away too cheaply.

———— ✺ ————

What do you benefit if you gain the whole world but lose
your own soul? Is anything worth more than your soul?

MATTHEW 16:26

The Last Shot of
the Civil War

◈

If you think that the Civil War ended at the Appomattox courthouse, you might want to think again. There would be more gunfire before news of Lee's surrender reached combatants in the field. But the place where the last shot was fired makes for another amazing story.

The story began in Liverpool where Confederate agents purchased the merchant ship *Sea King*, the fastest and sleekest clipper ship ever built at the Glasgow, Scotland, shipyards. It was sheer beauty, with teak planks over steel frames. Displacing only 1,160 tons, it boasted three tall masts and a powerful auxiliary steam engine driving a propeller that could be lifted to reduce drag under full sail, allowing it to achieve speeds of up to sixteen knots an hour. The speedy cruiser was rechristened the CSS *Shenandoah*.

In October 1864 the ship slipped out of Liverpool under false papers. It sailed down the coast of Europe to Portugal where it was fitted with high-powered weaponry. The *Shenandoah* had sailed into the Madeira Islands as a beautiful clipper, but left as a high-speed death machine. Her orders from the Confederate secretary of the navy were ruthlessly simple: create havoc in the Yankee shipping lanes by capturing or destroying as many ships of commerce as possible. In the next thirteen months the *Shenandoah* would circumnavigate the globe, leaving a trail of destruction in her wake. In all of her travels, she captured thirty-eight ships, destroyed another thirty-two, and took a thousand prisoners. After creating havoc in the Atlantic shipping lanes, she went around Africa's Cape of Good Hope and across the Indian Ocean before pulling in to Melbourne, Australia, for repairs. Then the Confederate cruiser turned north, burning four Yankee whaling ships en route to the Bering Sea. Off the coast of Alaska, she ran into a whaling fleet out of New Bedford. Over the next several days, the cruiser captured twenty-four ships, burning most of them and sending the rest loaded with survivors to San Francisco. The master's mate's journal recorded the last shot in the *Shenandoah's* final rampage: "We brought her to with a shot from our 32-pounder Whitworth rifle, which whistled past her stern . . ." After claiming her final prize, the Confederate ship set sail for Liverpool where she surrendered to the Royal Navy.

That journal entry by the *Shenandoah's* master's mate proves that the Civil War's final shot was fired four thousand miles from Appomattox, somewhere in the Bering Sea between Alaska and Russia. It is another irony of history that this last battle of America's Civil War was fought by a ship that left England, and its final shot was fired by gunner John L. Guy, a seaman born in England. This amazing story reminds us that civil wars die hard—especially that civil war started by rebellious angels against God's Kingdom and his people. Like the CSS *Shenandoah*, Satan stalks life's stormy seas on a mission to search and destroy. We must be vigilant until Jesus returns to fire the last shot of this civil war—right between the devil's eyes. In the meantime, remember this:

The devil wins whenever we lose heart and leave the field to him.

———— ⌘ ————

Humble yourselves before God. Resist
the devil, and he will flee from you.

JAMES 4:7

The Unbreakable Porcelain Doll

Tis mother of thirteen lives in a farmhouse she calls Frog Hollow, enjoying the simple pleasures of rural Connecticut—gardening in a straw hat, feeding her menagerie of pets, or frolicking with her nine grandchildren. But it wasn't always that way. Maybe that's why she wears an opaque amulet to ward off evil spirits.

She grew up in Tinseltown, the daughter of silver screen royalty. In 1964 she became a star on television's first nighttime soap opera, *Peyton Place*. In steamy episodes full of sexpots and scoundrels, she oozed fragile innocence. America fell in love with this waiflike girl. She would parlay her porcelain doll image into movie fame. In *Rosemary's Baby*, she was bullied by Satanists and impregnated with the devil's baby. She went on to play the tragic Daisy Buchanan in *The Great Gatsby*. Her waiflike fragility screamed for a father-figure protector. She was only nineteen years old when Frank Sinatra flew her out to Palm Springs on his private jet. A year later, the forty-nine-year-old singer married the actress, who was his daughter's age. Their marriage became the butt of tabloid gossip and comedians' jokes. The porcelain doll was shattered two years later when Sinatra served her with divorce papers. Austrian composer André Previn, sixteen years her senior, came to her rescue. During their six-year marriage, they adopted three orphans and had three kids of their own. After their marriage collapsed, forty-four-year-old filmmaker Woody Allen rescued her. During their twelve-year, off-and-on-again relationship, three more kids were added to her growing family.

Woody Allen broke her heart when he engaged in a sexual relationship with one of her children and later married the girl. Frank Sinatra offered to send Mafia thugs to break Allen's legs. It seems that Ol' Blue Eyes was always there for her. Sinatra even fathered one of her sons when he was seventy-two years old. Maybe she was attracted to older men because she grew up with an absentee father. Perhaps she was a magnet to them because she seemed so fragile.

But Mia Farrow is anything but porcelain. She may have been born with a silver spoon in her mouth, but her life reads like a Shakespearean tragedy. She overcame childhood polio only to see her thirteen-year-old brother die, followed by the death of her father. She has survived marital breakups and raised thirteen children, some with severe disabilities. One committed suicide, another died of AIDS-related pneumonia, and still another passed away from heart failure. She is estranged from two of her kids. Yet this waiflike woman is made of pure steel. She was a goodwill ambassador to UNICEF, does refugee work in the Sudan, and is involved in several humanitarian causes. In 2008 *Time* magazine named her as one of the world's most influential women. Mia Farrow's amazing story proves the resiliency of the human spirit. Thankfully, we as believers also have the Holy Spirit to give us strength in difficult times. That's why Pierre Teilhard de Chardin wrote this:

We are not human beings having a spiritual experience. We are spiritual beings having a human experience.

⸺⸙⸺

The LORD God formed the man from the dust of the ground. He breathed the breath of life into the man's nostrils, and the man became a living person.

GENESIS 2:7

102

The Man Who
Saved the World

Tൟௐ

The world teetered on the edge of Armageddon in 1962 when John F. Kennedy and Nikita Khrushchev played their game of high-stakes poker. Only there would be no winner if either unleashed the dogs of war. A single launched nuclear warhead would start a chain reaction ending in total destruction.

It all started when Soviet Premier Nikita Khrushchev cut a deal with Fidel Castro. In return for Russian resources, the Cuban regime would allow the Soviets to install nukes ninety miles from the United States. When US spy planes photographed missiles pointed straight at the heart of America, President Kennedy called out Khrushchev. The Communist boss refused to back down. But the US was not going to allow a Soviet base in its backyard. American warships soon encircled Cuba with a naval blockade.

Kennedy had shoved a pile of nuclear poker chips across the table. It was now Khrushchev's play. The wily old fox gambled that the young US president was bluffing, and sent a fleet with contraband warheads toward Cuba. The world held its collective breath. Who would blink first? Or push the button? During those thirteen days of high anxiety, four Soviet submarines commanded by Captain Vasili Arkhipov shadowed American warships. Each sub carried nuclear warheads with the explosive power dropped on Nagasaki and Hiroshima.

The situation only got worse when US warships detected the subs. Next came the game of cat and mouse, search and destroy. The Soviets dove deep. For a week they sat in silence while conditions deteriorated.

As their batteries ran down, the air supply slowly played out. The heat in the subs was suffocating, and each submariner was rationed a single glass of water a day. Then the Americans began to drop explosives. Tempers finally snapped. Valentin Savitsky, captain of Sub B-59, was positive that war had started. He ordered his crew to launch their nuclear warheads. Had that happened, the other subs might have followed suit. But Vasili Arkhipov was in command of the squadron, and uncommonly cool under pressure. He vetoed Savitsky's order and commanded his subs to begin the long journey home.

They did not arrive to a hero's welcome. A Russian admiral said, "It would have been better if you'd gone down with your ship." Khrushchev's gamble had failed, and Brezhnev deposed him. Captain Vasili Arkhipov spent his final years in disgrace and obscurity. In 1989, he died of radiation poisoning. A decade after his death, the world finally learned about his heroism. He may have made a career-ending decision, but in that split second he saved the world from a nuclear holocaust. Thirty years after his death, his widow Olga says that she is proud of her hero husband. We should all be grateful for this Soviet naval captain. The amazing story of Vasili Arkhipov reminds us that God always has the right person at the right time in the right place to accomplish his sovereign purpose. No matter what our world is facing today, remember these words by Corrie ten Boom:

Never be afraid to entrust an unknown future to a known God.

———— ✑✐✑ ————

Our God is in the heavens, and he does as he wishes.

PSALM 115:3

The Siler City Cat House

❧

Siler City, North Carolina, was a nostalgic throwback to 1950s TV-sitcom America. Something straight out of *Mayberry R.F.D.* You'd half expect to see Sheriff Taylor, Barney, or Opie. Everyone in Siler City knew everyone else. Like most small southern towns, folks exchanged toothy smiles, polite pleasantries, and tidbits of juicy gossip softened with "bless her heart."

But the cat lady just didn't fit. When she drove in from California in her vintage Studebaker, everyone gave her a heaping helping of "Southern Friendly." After all, she was a big celebrity. But their syrup was laid on too thick, and she was by nature a stiff person. All that good-natured joking increasingly irritated her. When folks invited her to church suppers and services, she let them know that she wasn't a churchgoer. So they dismissed her as uppity and most likely one of those godless New Yorkers.

Those who remember her television persona would be shocked to know that she had become a recluse. By the 1980s, she lived mostly in the bedroom of her dilapidated house with scores of cats. She had turned her master bathroom into a 250-square-foot kitty box. Delivery boys from the Piggly Wiggly were overwhelmed by the peeling paint, moldy draperies, and stained carpets reeking of urine and covered with cat hair. The suffocating acid of the ammonia she used to mask the odors made them gag. Even her vintage Studebaker was covered in layers of feline hair, its once immaculate interior shredded. No one was surprised the day they discovered her decaying body in the back room.

Few of the townsfolk showed up at her funeral. None of the costars from her television series came either. You can't blame them. Andy Griffith and Ron Howard had knocked on her front door three years earlier, but she told them to go away. Today, you can find her tombstone etched with the name of her beloved television character, Aunt Bee. It's hard to believe that Frances Bavier was once a Hollywood pinup girl. It's even harder to believe that everyone's favorite Aunt Bee was a snob from the New York theater who disliked her costars on the cast of *The Andy Griffith Show.* In real life, she was the polar opposite of little Opie's beloved aunt. Why she opted to retire to her own "Mayberry" remains a mystery. When she discovered that people like Andy, Opie, Barney, Thelma Lou, Goober, Gomer, and Floyd lived there too, she locked herself up in her house of cats.

The amazing story of Frances Bavier may chip away at our nostalgia, but it can also help us be better. None of us can pretend forever to be somebody we aren't. The mask eventually cracks to expose a soul that has been rotted by years of deception. So, take off the mask while there's still time to let a healthy you shine through. When you think about Aunt Bee of Mayberry you might want to ask yourself this:

Do others love the real me, or the mask that I am wearing?

We don't try to trick anyone or distort the
word of God. We tell the truth before God,
and all who are honest know this.

2 CORINTHIANS 4:2

Tobacco Wives

✦

They were America's first mail-order brides. But they weren't looking for romance. These calculating spinsters boarded rickety ships to a faraway colony for cold, hard cash—and plenty of it. The Virginia Company was in big trouble when their first settlement started going under. Jamestown had enough men, land, and tobacco to make investors back in London very wealthy. But there was a scarcity of women. Genteel ladies in England were unwilling to immigrate to a place of death, disease, and deprivation. So discouraged men were hightailing it back to England. That's when the company's treasurer, Edwin Sandys, wrote to the directors about his goal to "make men more settled [and] less moveable . . ." and decrease the numbers ". . . who stay but to get something and then return for England." His answer was to make it attractive for women to come and domesticate the men.

Sandys came up with the novel idea of mail-order brides. It was the perfect idea at just the right time. Setting up housekeeping was prohibitively expensive, beyond most people's means in the 1600s. Unless they came from wealth, folks had to save for years to acquire a sufficient nest egg. Young women from the working class were forced to hire themselves out as domestics. The prospect of scrubbing other people's floors and emptying their chamber pots was not nearly as appealing as a home of their own in the New World. On top of that, Sandys opened the company's coffers to offer attractive incentives for working-class spinsters to immigrate to Jamestown: clothes, linens, free transportation, and a large piece of land. Once there, a mail-order bride was given room and board while she decided which of the eligible bachelors she wanted to marry. It was like *The Bachelorette*, seventeenth-century style.

Most of these spinsters were uneducated, unpolished, unattractive women with a few teeth missing. But they were gorgeous to men who had been isolated on a womanless frontier for years. Each woman was sure to snag a wealthy man because the lucky bachelor had to reimburse the Virginia Company with 150 pounds of tobacco—the equivalent of $5,000 today.

These mail-order brides may have been referred to as tobacco wives, but they became the backbone of Virginia and the ancestors of many of America's most famous founders. Edwin Sandys often said that his tobacco wives were the best investment ever made by the Virginia Company. Some four hundred years later every American should love these ladies who married for money. Without them, the Virginia colony would have withered on the vine. There would have been no Patrick Henry, George Washington, or Thomas Jefferson to give birth to the United States of America. God said from the beginning, "It is not good for the man to be alone" (Genesis 2:18). It always takes a woman before God can say, "It is very good." The amazing story of the tobacco wives proves this truth:

Often it's the princess who slays the dragon and saves the prince.

───── ✥ ─────

Reward her for all she has done.
Let her deeds publicly declare her praise.

PROVERBS 31:31

Can't Act. Slightly Bald.
Also Dances.

৻৩৩৶

It seemed that the boy from Nebraska was consigned to play second fiddle. He was a toddler when his mother dragged him with her to fetch his sister from ballet class. The four-year-old found a pair of discarded dance slippers in the corner of the classroom. After he discovered that he could stand on his toes too, he spent the rest of his childhood mimicking his big sister. He would dance in Adele's shadow for the next thirty years. When the talented eight-year-old girl and her little brother made a splash in Omaha, their stage mother took her little meal tickets to the Big Apple.

The young vaudeville hoofers debuted in an act with the clunky title "Juvenile Artists Presenting an Electric Musical Toe-Dancing Novelty." They appeared in second-tier vaudeville shows, forgettable Broadway musicals, and mediocre operettas for thirty years. What favorable press they got always focused on beautiful Adele. When she ran off to London to marry an English lord, her scrawny brother was left to dance alone. Going solo was a rude awakening. One critic wrote, "The two were better than the one." Fortunately, his old friends Ira and George Gershwin found a place for him in their Broadway shows. The middle-aged hoofer finally began to shine.

The Gershwins encouraged their friend that he was ready for the big time. So he boarded a train for Hollywood. Studio head David O. Selznick was on the road when Adele's brother took a screen test for RKO Pictures. An assistant was unimpressed. He scribbled a note that has become part of movie lore: "Can't act. Slightly bald. Also dances." Though distressed by his big ears and bad chin line, Selznick was so excited about his dancing that he offered Adele's little brother a contract. The rest is the stuff of Hollywood legend.

The hoofer from vaudeville would never again be a second fiddle to anyone. Moviegoers might have thought that Fred Astaire from Omaha was an overnight sensation, but he had paid his dues for thirty years in the shadows of his sister. He would go on to dance with legendary elegance across the silver screen with the greatest dancers in Hollywood. But they would always take second billing as *his* partners. His most famous partner was Ginger Rogers, who famously quipped, "I did everything Fred Astaire did, only backwards and in high heels." But she was never as famous as Mr. Astaire, who Russian ballet star Rudolf Nureyev called "America's greatest dancer." Mikhail Baryshnikov praised him as "perfection" and choreographer George Balanchine called him "the greatest dancer in the world."

Maybe you are lost in someone's shadow today. Make the most of it. It was in Adele's shadow that Fred Astaire learned how to dance solo. Perhaps you are destined always to play second fiddle. That's okay too. Remember, Fred Astaire could never dance backwards and in high heels like Ginger Rogers. When you recall the amazing story of Fred Astaire, remember that, until today, you probably never heard of his sister, Adele Astaire. So make this your credo:

If I'm called to play second fiddle, I'll play it like a Stradivarius.

———— ✦ ————

People should eat and drink and enjoy the fruits
of their labor, for these are gifts from God.

ECCLESIASTES 3:13

Never Too Old to Start

⌒◇◇◇⌒

When Anna Mary died in 1961, her doctor said, "She just wore out." Few folks logged more miles. Anna Mary was born before Abraham Lincoln took office. Times were tough for a farm family with twelve mouths to feed. She was twelve when she left home to work as a hired girl. At age twenty-seven she married Tom Moses, a hired hand where she worked as a housekeeper. The newlyweds moved to Virginia where they plunked down their $600 savings for a small farm. Anna Mary gave birth to ten children, but lost five in infancy. She worked her fingers to the bone, raised her kids, and made butter and potato chips to sell to neighbors.

After twenty years in Virginia, the couple moved to Eagle Bridge, New York, where Tom died in 1927. Anna Mary kept right on farming even though she was a sixty-seven-year-old widow. By the time she was seventy-six, her fingers were crippled by severe arthritis. She didn't mind quitting her farm chores, but she hated the fact that she could no longer stitch the embroidery that won blue ribbons at the county fair. A friend suggested that Anna Mary take up painting.

At an age when most folks are snoozing in a rocking chair, she became an artist. She decided to paint what she called "old timey pictures" of her life on the farm. Her paintings were primitive, one-dimensional, and out of perspective. She painted them on whatever surfaces she could salvage, painting with juices she squeezed from fruits. She did her work while sitting on a battered swivel chair at a cluttered kitchen table. Her first paintings were sent to the county fair along with jars of jams. Her jams won blue ribbons, but no one noticed her paintings.

Several years later, a New York art collector saw her primitive works hanging in a drugstore, selling for three to five dollars apiece. He bought them all, and then drove to her house to purchase what she had there. At eighty years of age, Tom Moses's widow had her first art exhibit in New York. She became an instant superstar. Her paintings were reproduced on Christmas cards, tiles, and fabrics. Over the next twenty years, this wisp of a woman with severe arthritis churned out more than a thousand paintings, twenty-five of them after she passed her hundredth birthday. In her nineties she was awarded two doctorates, feted by US presidents, became a member of the Daughters of the American Revolution and the Society of Mayflower Descendants, authored two books, was featured on the cover of *Life* magazine, and was celebrated as one of the world's greatest artists. When she finally wore out at 101 years of age, the world mourned the passing of the artist known as Grandma Moses.

The amazing story of Grandma Moses reminds us that it's always too soon to quit. When she could no longer hold a stitching needle, she picked up a paintbrush. While most folks give out, pull out, rust out, burn out, or flame out, Grandma Moses wore out by giving out to the very end. Hers is a story that says,

Work hard. Don't give up. Finish strong.

───── ⚘ ─────

Finishing is better than starting.
Patience is better than pride.

ECCLESIASTES 7:8

The Imperfect Story of Perfection

&⟨◉⟩&

Jimmy says that a third-grade teacher who taught him how to tie his shoes is his hero. Jimmy was born missing a hand. Classmates teased him unmercifully. Some cried because they were scared of his prosthesis. But Jimmy mostly hated the fact that other kids didn't want him on their team. Even if he managed to snag a ball, those shoelaces would come untied, and he'd get tangled in his feet.

But the one-handed kid loved baseball. He loved it so much that he threw away that clunky prosthesis and played catch with his dad for hours. He perfected the art of fielding the ball, shoving the glove between his arm and torso, grabbing the ball with his left hand and whipping it back to his father. Eventually the one-hander from Flint, Michigan, fielded as well as any other boy.

But it was impossible for Jimmy to tie his shoes. So his mom fixed them every morning. But she wasn't there during the day to retie them. That's when his third-grade teacher, Donn Clarkson, changed his life. The teacher put his hand on the boy's shoulder and said, "I've figured out how to do it." He took Jimmy out in the hallway and demonstrated how to tie his shoes with one hand. Jimmy later discovered that Mr. Clarkson had spent tedious hours figuring out the trick to tying shoelaces one handed.

Jimmy says that Mr. Clarkson's act of devotion was the most inspiring moment of his life. If someone would go to all that trouble for him, nothing was impossible for him to accomplish. He went on to the University of Michigan where he became a pitching phenom. After he won the Sullivan Award as America's best amateur athlete, he led the US team to a gold medal in the 1988 Summer Olympics. That year the California Angels drafted him in the first round. Fans who streamed into ballparks to watch him were amazed that he could field grounders and throw out runners as well as any two-handed pitcher in the majors. His best year was 1991 when he finished third in the Cy Young Award voting. But nothing compared to that magical game at Yankee Stadium in 1993 when he pitched a no-hitter. One-handed Jim Abbott from Flint, Michigan, had achieved baseball immortality in the house that Babe Ruth built.

Yet Jim often says that his many achievements and awards don't compare to Mr. Clarkson showing him how to tie his shoes. That third-grade teacher remains the greatest influence in his life. Having starred in America's pastime, Jim would tell you that his favorite pastime today is teaching kids how to tie their shoes. None of us can imagine the impact of a single act of kindness. As amazing as Jim Abbott's story is, Donn Clarkson's is even better. His kindness inspired an imperfect boy to go on to baseball perfection. Why don't you go out today and do an act of kindness? Only heaven will reveal its impact.

No act of kindness no matter how small is ever wasted.

—————— ⁕⊚⁕ ——————

Never let loyalty and kindness leave you!
Tie them around your neck as a reminder.
Write them deep within your heart.

PROVERBS 3:3

Seceding from the
Confederacy

≈◎◎◎≈

Most Americans have never heard of that little dustup in the heart of the Confederacy. Locals still want to keep it a secret. During the Civil War this land of swamps and thick forests was home to some of the most strident racists in the world. Later the Ku Klux Klan ruled the Piney Woods of Mississippi. Blacks who got out of line were lynched.

It's little wonder that the Confederacy saw this as prime recruiting grounds. Shortly after Mississippi seceded in 1861, Newt Knight was one of the first Jones County boys to sign up. Standing six feet four inches tall, he was as big as a house and quicker than a cat, the best marksman around, and as good a woodsman as Daniel Boone. Newt loved a good fight. But he soon tired of taking orders from Southern aristocrats in their spiffy parade uniforms. War was no game, and their harebrained tactics were getting good men slaughtered.

When Newt and his friends heard about a new law exempting slave-owning plantation gentry from the fighting, they had had enough. The Jones County boys deserted en masse. After the carnage at Vicksburg, there was an epidemic of desertions. In a frantic attempt to stop the hemorrhaging, Confederate major Amos McLemore was sent south to round up the deserters. By 1863, folks were already embittered that Confederate agents had been confiscating their animals and crops. McLemore's rampage through Jones County set off a firestorm.

That's when Newt Knight started a civil war within the Civil War by seceding from the South. He and his friends set up their own secessionist nation that was known as the Free State of Jones. The county seat of

Ellisville became ground zero in this battle against Confederate tyranny. The Union flag was soon flying over the courthouse, and an army of one thousand men and women, both black and white, was itching to fight. Two battle-hardened regiments were sent in to quell the uprising. Rebels were mowed down by superior firepower, mangled by hunting dogs, and hanged from trees. Yet even after Ellisville was seized by Confederate troops, Newt Knight continued to wage one of the most effective guerrilla wars in US history. By 1865, the weary Confederacy gave up the battle for Jones County. Three months later, it surrendered at Appomattox.

Newt might have remained a hero in Jones County if he hadn't violated the most sacred taboo of the Old South. He left his white wife and kids and ran off with a black woman with whom he had a slew of children. Today you will find a Confederate monument beside the courthouse in Ellisville. But there is no memorial to Newt Knight or the Free State of Jones. Racism dies hard in some parts of rural Mississippi. But things are changing at the local high school where Newt's black and white descendants mix freely together. Interracial dating is no big deal to them. But the freedom from tyranny that inspired the Free State of Jones is still dear to everyone. The amazing story of Newt Knight might recall what Ben Franklin said:

Make yourself sheep and the wolves will eat you.

———— ༺༻ ————

Beware of false prophets who come disguised as
harmless sheep but are really vicious wolves.

MATTHEW 7:15

The Founding Fathers
of Dirty Campaigns

క✫ⴄ◠

If you believe that political campaigns have never been dirtier, think again. Today's politicians are rank amateurs when compared to the founding fathers of dirty campaigns, John Adams and Thomas Jefferson. If the last campaign left you reeling, you should have been there for the presidential election of 1800. Surely it was the birth of the smear campaign in America.

Adams and Jefferson had been friends when they hammered out the Declaration of Independence and the US Constitution. But when Adams became the second president of the new nation, with Jefferson as his vice president, things soured. The tempestuous New Englander believed in a strong central government. The genteel Virginian was a proponent of states' rights. By the last year of their term, they were barely speaking to each other. On the eve of the 1800 presidential campaign, an embittered Jefferson was determined to keep Adams from winning a second term.

That campaign got ugly quickly. Jefferson's camp called the president a "hideous hermaphroditical character, which has neither the force and firmness of a man, nor the gentleness and sensibility of a woman." A campaign poster lampooned Adams as blind, bald, crippled, and toothless. The hot-tempered incumbent fired back that his opponent was "a mean-spirited, low-lived fellow, the son of a half-breed Indian squaw, sired by a Virginia mulatto father." Their campaigns dove deeper into the mud. Adams was branded a fool, a hypocrite, a criminal, and a tyrant. Jefferson was called an atheist, a libertine, and a coward.

With Election Day looming, the muck flew faster. As a Southern aristocrat, Jefferson was determined to appear above the fray while his hatchet man, James Callender, executed the most effective smear campaign in history. This master of dirty tricks convinced a majority of Americans that Adams was drawing up plans to attack France. Unlike Jefferson, the irascible Adams was willing to charge into the fray. He hysterically warned citizens that if his opponent won the election, men would have to hide their wives and daughters. America would be a wasteland of burning cities filled with rape and riot. Even Martha Washington bought his propaganda. The former First Lady told her clergyman that Jefferson was "one of the most detestable of mankind."

Yet Adams ended up covered in the most mud, and Jefferson easily won the presidency in 1800. The outgoing president was so bitter that he refused to attend his opponent's inauguration. The two didn't speak to each other for years. Through the intercession of friends, they finally buried the hatchet in the twilight of their lives. Ironically, they died within five hours of each other on July 4, 1826—exactly fifty years after they'd birthed a new nation.

We rejoice that these men were founding fathers of America. We are saddened that they also were the founders of dirty political campaigns. But their amazing story gives us some hope when we think our nation can't sink any lower. We've been dragged through the mud before and still managed to climb out of it. So let's slough on with hope.

We are never defeated in anything until we give up on God.

_____ ✑ _____

What we suffer now is nothing compared
to the glory he will reveal to us later.

ROMANS 8:18

The Persistent Fisherman

༄༅

Every morning before shuffling out the back door, the old man told the cook to keep the frying pan hot. Tonight he was going to bring that elusive fish home for supper. All day he would sit on the same battered lawn chair, under the same Florida sun, next to the same fishing hole, holding the same rod, while dangling the same hook. Day after day, month after month, and year after year, he waited for that fish to bite.

Occasionally, visitors came from Chicago or New York to pay homage to the old man at the fishing hole. They tried to mask their dismay upon seeing him. Though he was only in his late forties, he looked old beyond his years. His brain was eaten by syphilis, his face was scarred from earlier wars, and his body had been ravaged by prison. For a brief moment, his eyes would flicker in faint remembrance. He might respond with an incoherent grunt. But always his glassy gaze would quickly return to the hook in the water.

After awkward moments of silence, visitors would sadly slip away. There was a time when old Alphonse was Big Al. As America's most notorious and feared gangster, he ruled a crime syndicate as rich and powerful as the federal government. He was Public Enemy Number One. His detractors called him Scarface. His victims called him Sir. His stable of slick lawyers and bribed public officials kept him out of prison for years. No mobster had ever had a run like Scarface Al Capone.

But even the boss can't mess with the Internal Revenue Service. At thirty-three years of age, Big Al was sent up the river for tax evasion. When bribed officials allowed him to turn his cell into the Ritz-Carlton, he was carted off to the new maximum security prison at Alcatraz. There he experienced the true meaning of "hard time." After four years on the Rock, he was released for good behavior. The truth is, he was broken in spirit and addled by syphilis. He had spent most of his last year in the prison hospital, and the syndicate had moved on without him. The Feds figured that Alphonse Capone no longer posed a threat to anyone.

So old Scarface spent his final days near Miami, fishing for that elusive fish in a swimming pool that contained nothing but chlorinated water. You have to say this for addled Al: he was a persistent fisherman until the end. He died in 1947, at age forty-eight, still hoping to catch that fish.

Big Al's fishing story may sound crazy. But it's not as crazy as the everyday story of folks who keep fishing for what can never be caught. They actually believe they can find lasting satisfaction by hooking on to the things of this world. But the elusive fish never strikes. Maybe they're fishing in the wrong place, thinking they can fill that God-shaped hole inside with finite and temporary things.

Most folks go fishing all their lives without realizing that it's not fish they're after.

———— ❧ ————

The things we see now will soon be gone, but
the things we cannot see will last forever.

2 CORINTHIANS 4:18

The Healer's Song

‿⊙⊙⊙∽

The boy's name was derived from the diminutive form of the ancient Irish word *rón*, which means "seal." He must have felt like a baby seal at times, with his rubbery legs and flipper-like feet. Doctors told his parents that he would never walk. Kids at school teased him unmercifully. But his mother had him outfitted with clunky braces and then ordered him to wear shorts to show them off. She marched down the main street with her son shuffling awkwardly at her side. Both walked with their Irish heads held high.

He says that his folks instilled in him a faith in God and the gritty determination that no handicap could stop him. At age twenty, the Seal's legs were amputated below his knees. But that didn't stop him from winning four gold medals in the Paralympics or from becoming a world-class equestrian. Most people would have been satisfied to stop there, but the Seal was just beginning. The man without legs kept on climbing to the top of his class at a demanding medical school.

Maybe now he could relax and enjoy the view from the summit. But the Seal never stopped at the top. When his father reminded him that a song was the best medicine, he took up singing lessons at the age of thirty-three. After winning the BBC's version of *American Idol* and an international competition in France, he recorded his first album, *The Impossible Dream*. It sold a million copies, but he continued his practice in orthopedic sports medicine. Even then the Seal didn't stop climbing. He was awarded a position at England's prestigious Royal Opera School, and went on to star in *Madame Butterfly*. In 1998 he released another bestselling album, *My Life Belongs to You*. That year he founded the Irish Tenors. It wasn't long before the Seal ended up in the States, where he brought healing to the nation by singing moving hymns at funerals of firefighters and police officers killed at the World Trade Center. New Yorkers embraced him for his soaring rendition of "God Bless America" at Yankee baseball games. He was the soloist at Ronald Reagan's funeral and sang at President George H. W. Bush's eightieth birthday party, and he plays to sold-out arenas while selling millions of albums.

But he says that his greatest joy is in being the son of Mr. and Mrs. Tynan. They named their boy Ronan after the Irish word *rón*, or seal. But they gave him so much more by teaching their little seal that he could walk, run, and climb without legs. More than that, he could soar on a song. His mother never allowed him to feel sorry for himself. She pushed him to strive for more, and she taught him to hold his head high. His father inspired him to sing songs of healing. We are all the richer for Ronan's mom and dad. The amazing story of Ronan Tynan reminds us that real love is never wishy-washy. Maybe we ought to say something to our family and friends that Mrs. Tynan might have said to her little seal:

Life is tough, my darling, but then so are you.

———— ✿ ————

Rejoice in our confident hope.
Be patient in trouble, and keep on praying.

ROMANS 12:12

The School of Hard Knocks

〜◌◌◌〜

His stories are woven into the fabric of our lives. We are as familiar with their characters as we are with members of our own family. Our everyday language contains lines, phrases, and metaphors from his works. His fourteen novels have been adapted in more than three hundred films and television shows. He is far and away the bestselling author of all time. Indeed, the writer who called himself Boz remains a rock star almost 150 years after he died.

That's why you might be amazed to know where this literary giant was educated. Boz was only eleven when his debtor father was sent to Marshalsea prison. In Victorian times, the whole family often accompanied a man to debtors' prison. Boz would be scarred for life by his time in this horrific holding place for the derelict. He would later work as a child laborer in a warehouse to help pay off his father's debts. It's no wonder that his formal education was brief and in second-rate schools for poor children. He would forever after keep his early life a secret from friends, family, and readers. It was only after his death that his childhood shame was disclosed to a shocked world.

Boz could have allowed his early years to cripple his future, but he used them to his advantage. He honed his literary skills as a newspaper reporter, which is when he gave himself the pseudonym Boz. Even after he began to write his novels, his adoring public didn't know his real name. Maybe that was just as well. His books presented a scathing condemnation of poverty and injustice in the Victorian class system. He shocked readers with graphic images of poverty and crime, making it impossible for polite society to ignore the devastating consequences of social inequity. Yet he presented even his most down-and-out characters as sympathetic and heroic. He once said, "Virtue shows quite as well in rags and patches as she does in purple and fine linen." It's no wonder that his characters like Oliver Twist, Pip, Bob Cratchit, and David Copperfield became catalysts for social change. Without Boz, the world might have indeed remained a "Bah, humbug" of a place, ruled by the likes of Ebenezer Scrooge.

It's sad that Charles Dickens felt the need to create another name for himself. He wrote amazing stories but was ashamed of his own. Yet those childhood experiences created his stories. Without them, he wouldn't have known how Oliver Twist felt or what drove David Copperfield or what it was like to live in "the worst of times" or "the winter of despair." Without them, he could not have used his pen to bring about "the best of times" or "the season of light." This author seems to have never grasped that God writes our stories so that we might rewrite the stories of those we touch. Unless we experience our own bad times, we can never help others through theirs. From the amazing story of Boz we learn this truth:

We can only lead people out of places where we, too, have gone.

He comforts us in all our troubles so that we can
comfort others. When they are troubled, we will be
able to give them the same comfort God has given us.

2 CORINTHIANS 1:4

The Great
Candy Bar Debate

⁂

There were two big names in the United States in the early 1900s. One was Ruth Cleveland. Her father had been a bachelor in his late forties when he became the country's twenty-second president. A year later, Grover Cleveland shocked the nation by marrying twenty-one-year-old Frances Folsom, a woman less than half his age. She remains the youngest first lady in US history. When she gave birth to their first child in 1891, the nation went wild. Baby Ruth Cleveland was a media sensation. When she died of diphtheria at the age of twelve, Americans wept for "Baby Ruth" as if they had lost their own child.

In 1919, George Herman Ruth Jr. was a megastar. The Babe had pitched the Boston Red Sox to two championships, hurling a record twenty-nine consecutive scoreless World Series innings. He also set a record for home runs in 1919. Babe Ruth was traded to the New York Yankees that year and went on to become a baseball legend.

It was during that year that Chicago entrepreneur Otto Schnering and his Curtiss Candy Company made their own history with a log-shaped bar of caramel and peanuts that they called Baby Ruth. The price was only five cents, half the cost of a regular candy bar. Schnering unleashed an advertising tsunami when he hired airplanes to fly over cities, county fairs, and racetracks, dropping thousands of his new candy bars on paper parachutes. People devoured these delectable delights from the skies, and Baby Ruth became America's most popular candy bar.

While Otto Schnering claimed that folks loved his Baby Ruth bar because of its tastiness and low cost, the home run king knew better. As far as Babe Ruth was concerned, the Curtiss Candy Company was making a killing off his famous name. When he sued Schnering in court, the wily entrepreneur argued that he had named his candy bar after Baby Ruth Cleveland. The courts sided with Schnering. Yet Babe Ruth never gave up his battle to get his due from the Curtiss Candy Company, dragging out the litigation for the rest of his life. His daughter would carry on his futile fight for years afterward. It was the stuff of headlines and endless public debate.

Almost a century later, legal experts agree: Babe Ruth had a solid case. Baby Ruth Cleveland had been dead for fifteen years and was a fading memory for a fickle public. But the Babe was the biggest name in America—a megahero to every kid in the country. Why, then, did the Babe sue the Curtiss Candy Company? He surely didn't need the money. But maybe he did understand the worth of his name.

No one's name should be taken lightly. It shouldn't be stolen, exploited, or used in vain—and certainly not to market a candy bar. In one way at least, God is similar to Babe Ruth. His name is used to sell countless religious products. It has been bandied about to justify the most unimaginable acts of evil. God's name is misused by both the pious and profane. It is inexcusable to pirate someone's name the way Otto Schnering did Babe Ruth's—especially when it's God's name.

It's possible to take the Lord's name in vain, even if we never say a curse word.

————— ∞ —————

Our Father in heaven, may your name be kept holy.

MATTHEW 6:9

The Miracle That Won World War II

అదువు

The German blitzkrieg rolled across France and the Low Countries at lightning speed. Those who were left from the ravaged Allied armies retreated pell-mell toward the beaches of Dunkirk. Almost half a million troops were trapped with their backs to the sea. The German High Command boasted, "The British army is encircled, and our troops are proceeding to its annihilation." Desperate for a miracle, King George went on national radio to call the British to a day of prayer on May 26, 1940. On that Sunday, churches across the Isles overflowed with patriots praying for divine intervention. The string of miracles that followed make up one of history's most amazing stories.

On Monday, when panzer divisions were within ten miles of Dunkirk, Hitler inexplicably overruled his generals and called a halt to the German advance. The next day, a furious storm blew over Flanders, grounding the Luftwaffe. A few miles away, a mysterious calm settled over the English Channel, allowing a flotilla of boats—some as small as fourteen feet long—to set sail on glassy seas. It seemed that everything that could float left England, forming the largest armada the world had ever seen. British pilots flying above claimed that so many boats jammed the waterway that one could walk across the channel without getting wet feet.

For three days, the bulk of the Luftwaffe remained grounded. German generals watched helplessly while more than three hundred thousand Allied troops were ferried across the channel by fewer than a thousand naval and civilian craft. Seven hundred of these vessels were small boats manned by boys and old men. A paddle steamer called the *Medway Queen* made seven round trips, rescuing seven thousand soldiers. Some two hundred thousand men were taken off a long jetty called a mole. They stood massed and exposed while being strafed and bombed for three days. Witnesses said that they stood calmly, as if they were waiting for a morning bus to come by. Miraculously, relatively few were hit by the bombardment.

The British High Command had hoped to rescue thirty thousand soldiers during those forty-eight hours. Yet that strange flotilla, manned mostly by citizen sailors, accomplished the miraculous by evacuating ten times that many. Though World War II raged another five years, the "miracle at Dunkirk" proved to be a critical turning point. By allowing a trapped army to escape, Hitler sealed his own fate. Troops that escaped the beaches of Dunkirk would march victoriously through the streets of Berlin in 1945. It's no wonder that on Sunday, June 9, 1940, grateful congregations across England sang Psalm 124 in a national outpouring of thanksgiving: "The snare is broken and we are delivered."

Maybe you are trapped at your own Dunkirk today. Your back is against the sea, and the enemy is closing in for the kill. Yet the same God who visited Dunkirk in May of 1940 still does miracles today—especially for those who pray for them. So when all seems lost, stand firm with this credo:

Though hope is dim, I will not quit before my miracle arrives.

⸺❧⸺

Our help is from the LORD, who made heaven and earth.

PSALM 124:8

The Star of David Goes Jazz

❦

The old trumpet player had blown his heart out. He could no longer walk or fit into his shoes. His heart, kidneys, and liver were failing; his lungs were filled with fluid; his stomach was distended; and his memory was failing. As he languished in his hospital bed, the Star of David necklace that hung around his neck mystified doctors and nurses. Why was this African American man wearing a symbol of Judaism? Why did he insist on spending his last days in a Jewish hospital? Dr. Gary Zucker, his attending physician at New York City's Beth Israel Hospital, noticed an eerie transformation taking place. The jovial jester of jazz began to obsess about his own mortality and the deeper issues of life.

One day Dr. Zucker began to hum an old Yiddish lullaby brought over by his Jewish ancestors. To his shock, the old jazz musician began to sing along with him. Then he sat up and demanded pen and paper. From his deathbed in the Beth Israel Hospital, the patient furiously penned a memoir of his childhood in the Jim Crow South of the early 1900s. He wrote about wandering the streets of New Orleans, and how he was taken in by the Karnofskys.

At first he was a child laborer, working long hours for these Jewish junk dealers. He started at five o'clock in the morning, combing the streets with the Karnofsky brothers, collecting bottles, bones, scrap metal, and rags. Late at night, the boys delivered coal to houses of prostitution. Gradually, the little African American kid was enfolded into the Jewish family. He wolfed down their kosher food, learned Yiddish songs, and developed a love for music. He never got over the fact that white folks took him in despite being in the segregated South. Nor did he forget that these Lithuanian Jewish immigrants advanced him the money to buy his first musical instrument, a cheap horn from a pawnshop.

When the old man finally laid down his pen and fell back against his pillow in the hospital, he had filled seventy pages. Across the top of the first page he had scrawled, "Louis Armstrong + the Jewish family in New Orleans, LA, the year of 1907." Louis Armstrong wrote that it was Jewish music and language that had shaped much of New Orleans jazz and vernacular. Maybe it was because of the Karnofsky family that Armstrong transcended race and touched the whole world. One hears the joy of their Yiddish sing-alongs in his 1964 megahit that knocked the Beatles off the charts: "Hello, Dolly!" Their kindness is echoed in his memorable song "What a Wonderful World." The next time you see a photo of the late great Louis Armstrong, look for that Star of David. Remember the amazing story of a family who brought joy to countless millions by investing a few small kindnesses in a homeless boy from a very different background. The next time you hear that golden oldie "What a Wonderful World," think about this:

It doesn't take much to make a wonderful world. Just a small act of kindness each day will do.

――― ∞ ―――

Let's not get tired of doing what is good. At just the right time we will reap a harvest of blessing if we don't give up.

GALATIANS 6:9

The Swindle of the Century

⌒⊙⊙⌒

Bernie Madoff's Ponzi scheme stole billions from his gullible backers. But those who call Madoff history's greatest con artist never met the Prince of Poyais. This swindler not only scammed the equivalent of $5 billion in today's money, he actually managed to sell a country that didn't exist.

In the early 1800s, the British government was borrowing money on a massive scale, driving down the interest rates. English bond investors were forced to gamble on faraway places to find a better rate of return on their investments. It was the perfect setup for a swindler who introduced himself as the Prince of Poyais. Like charlatans everywhere, he oozed sincerity. His golden tongue painted the picture of a veritable Garden of Eden in Central America with rich resources waiting to be exploited. Before long, he had gullible investors salivating at the prospect of getting rich quick in the mystical land of Poyais. They couldn't believe their good fortune when the prince offered up a £200,000 bond from his realm with a return of 6 percent, among the highest offered anywhere in the world. Not only did he rake in a fortune from investors, he convinced hundreds of people to set sail for Poyais.

Shiploads of investors and settlers ventured out for his Central American country with promises of a tropical paradise rich with the world's most fertile soil and honeycombed with fresh streams of water filled with chunks of gold. What they found in Honduras was a tangled wilderness of impenetrable jungle filled with poisonous snakes and malaria. There were no ports, cities, or roads in this place of desolation, deprivation, and empty promises.

The Prince of Poyais was a scammer from Scotland by the name of Gregor MacGregor. He had spent his life selling false dreams to the gullible. His £200,000 bonds were as fake as the country he called Poyais. By the time he was exposed, he had already fled to France, where he played the same game with the same results. Mr. MacGregor could have written the words famously attributed to P. T. Barnum: "There's a sucker born every minute." When he was again discovered to be a fraud, he was forced to flee from those he had fleeced. He had to run to the ends of the earth to escape their vengeance. He died in 1845 in Caracas, Venezuela.

If you go to the MacGregor graveyard in Scotland today, you will not find his name on a grave marker or in the family's registry. His nefarious activities made him an embarrassment to his kin. But you can find the land that he called Poyais in the Black River region of Honduras. It's still a desolate and tangled wilderness, a perpetual warning to the gullible everywhere. If you don't want to be a victim of some Bernie Madoff or Prince of Poyais, hold fast to a tried-and-true rule:

If it seems too good to be true, it almost always is.

――――― ༺ঔ৩ঔ༻ ―――――

People who long to be rich fall into temptation and
are trapped by many foolish and harmful desires
that plunge them into ruin and destruction.

1 TIMOTHY 6:9

The Ultimate Closing Argument

☙◦◦❧

Clement Vallandigham of Ohio was never in doubt that he was right. This opinionated rabble-rouser would fight to the death to prove it. A descendant of Southern aristocracy, he was an implacable champion of the Confederate cause, even though he lived in the North. As the leader of the northern wing of the Democratic Party, known as the Copperheads, he campaigned long and hard against the policies of Abraham Lincoln and his Union armies.

This dogmatic Ohio lawyer would hold passionately to his Southern loyalties until the day of his bizarre death. After all, a person who is always right can never admit to being wrong—no matter how much it costs to defend his position. Maybe that's why Clement Vallandigham is remembered for one of the craziest stories in the history of American jurisprudence.

It all started with an 1870 barroom brawl in Hamilton, Ohio. Someone was shot to death in the melee. Although there was plenty of conflicting evidence, legal authorities arrested Thomas McGehan and charged him with murder. Clement Vallandigham was hired as his defense attorney. Though no one could say for certain what happened in the mayhem of that smoke-filled saloon, McGehan's doggedly opinionated lawyer had no doubt that his client was innocent. After all, the Ohio attorney had spent his whole life being right about everything and repeatedly fighting tooth and nail to prove it.

Vallandigham's defense was simple: the victim, Tom Myers, had accidentally shot himself with his own pistol. Clement was so sure that his strategy would win over the jury that he decided to demonstrate it to his team of defense lawyers. Using his Lebanon, Ohio, hotel suite as a mock courtroom, he pulled out a pistol that he believed to be unloaded. He cocked it and aimed the barrel at his stomach. To his shock, and to the horror of his fellow attorneys, when he pulled the trigger, the pistol discharged a forgotten bullet. Clement Vallandigham, the man who was always right—and willing to die proving it—fell fatally wounded onto the hotel floor. The dead attorney's defense team used his final argument to win the case for Thomas McGehan. It did little good. Four years later, an angry customer shot Mr. McGehan to death in his saloon.

It seems fitting that the lawyer who always believed that he was right and was willing to fight to the death proving his viewpoint would end his life by making his final point. Yet was it worth his life to get someone like Thomas McGehan off the hook? Maybe this is a more relevant question: Are you fighting battles that are worthwhile? Before you lose a marriage, a family, friends, a job, a reputation, and maybe even your life to prove a point, you should ask if the win is worth the cost. You might want to remember the amazing story of Clement Vallandigham's final defense and save your bullets for battles that really matter.

The aim of argument should not be victory, but progress.

Gently instruct those who oppose the truth.
Perhaps God will change those people's
hearts, and they will learn the truth.

2 TIMOTHY 2:25

134

The Day Jim Met Himself in *The Twilight Zone*

❧

Jim Lewis grew up feeling a gnawing emptiness. Something, or someone, was missing from his life. Like many adopted kids, he wondered about his biological roots. When his mother told him that he had a twin brother out there somewhere, he felt ambivalent. There are plenty of horror stories about reunions gone awry. But Jim Lewis was willing to take a risk. So he went looking for his lost brother.

What he discovered made him feel like he had descended into *The Twilight Zone*. When the identical twins were reunited on February 9, 1979, what they found out about each other is both amazing and eerie. Both were named Jim by their adoptive parents. Jim Lewis and Jim Springer grew up within forty-five minutes of each other. Both named their childhood dogs Toy. Both were married twice. Both chose to marry women named Linda. Both remarried women by the name of Betty. One named his son James Alan, and the other named his son James Allan. Both lived in the only house on their block. Both were chain-smokers, and both enjoyed drinking the same brand of beer. Jim and Jim were both passionate about woodworking. Both drove Chevrolets, and they ended up with similar jobs in law enforcement.

What Jim Lewis and Jim Springer discovered was beyond a case of shared genetics. Thirty-nine years after being separated at birth, they found the mirror image of themselves in one another. One could almost hear the iconic voice of Rod Serling giving an opening line in his golden oldie television show: "Jim meets himself . . . in *The Twilight Zone*."

The Jim twins proved to be a treasure trove for behavioral psychologists.

For years there has been a debate about whether we are shaped more by genetics or by our environment. Jim Lewis and Jim Springer presented the perfect case study: they shared the same heredity, yet they were raised in different environments. So the University of Minnesota put the reunited twins through a battery of tests. The results were groundbreaking. In a test measuring their personalities, the brothers scored so closely that it looked like one person had taken the test twice. The twins' brain waves were identical, and their medical histories mirrored each other.

The Jim twins have rewritten the way behaviorists look at personality development. Heredity may be more critical than environment. That makes sense if we believe that God wove us together in our mothers' wombs. Surely the experiences of our childhood determine the way we think, act, and react as adults. But we can take comfort in the fact that much of our hardwiring was set by our Designer before we were born. Our looks, personality, natural talents, emotional makeup, unique strengths, and weaknesses are set by his perfect design. Jim and Jim's amazing story may seem like an episode of *The Twilight Zone*, but it reminds us that we are perfectly made for our own zone. So don't try to make yourself into someone else.

You are a unique masterpiece, deliberately designed by God.

<hr>

Thank you for making me so wonderfully complex!
Your workmanship is marvelous—how well I know it.
PSALM 139:14

The Marathon Woman

cರಾಗಿ

When officials for the 1967 Boston Marathon saw K. V. Switzer on the registration form, no one thought it was anything other than a man's initials. Females were considered too delicate to run beyond 800 meters, so there was no reason for a place to mark gender on the entry form. No one could have figured that the K. V. stood for Kathrine Virginia.

Though there were no rules prohibiting women from running the Boston Marathon, it never occurred to officials that any woman would be crazy enough to attempt it. Coach Arnie Briggs of Syracuse University may have allowed her to train with the men's cross-country team, but he believed that a marathon was too tough for "fragile women." The coach said to her, "No dame ever ran the Boston Marathon!" But he made a deal with Kathrine: if she could run the twenty-six-mile distance in practice, he would take her to Boston himself. She met Coach Briggs's challenge, and he drove her to Beantown.

Kathrine showed up at the race wearing makeup and earrings. When a runner told her to wipe off her lipstick so that officials wouldn't notice her gender, she refused. As snow began to fall, she took off with the pack. A few miles into the race, a burly official in a heavy overcoat shook his finger at her. A few minutes later, the enraged man caught up with Kathrine, grabbed her by the shoulder, and cursed at her. Photographers captured race director Jock Semple trying to rip off her bib number. She stumbled forward in a state of bewilderment until a burst of anger energized her to finish the twenty-six-mile distance.

Sadly, Kathrine was disqualified from the marathon and kicked out of the Amateur Athletic Union. But her bib number, 261, became a symbol of fearlessness in the face of prejudice and rallied women in the fight for equality. Kathrine was among those pioneers who may never reap the fruits of their sacrifice but make it possible for later generations to experience what was denied them. That's why the world was excited on April 17, 2017, when Kathrine Virginia Switzer lined up with competitors for a second try at the Boston Marathon. She wore the same number, 261, that she had worn fifty years earlier. Though she was seventy years old, she finished the race in four hours, forty-four minutes, and thirty-one seconds, only twenty-five minutes more than it took her at age twenty in 1967.

Kathrine said, "We've come a light year, but we still have a long way to go." She may be right, but it is worth noting that Edna Kiplagat of Kenya won the women's division of the 2017 Boston Marathon in a time of two hours, twenty-one minutes, and fifty-two seconds, only six minutes slower than Dave McKenzie's winning time at Boston in 1967. Maybe all our daughters should be given the number 261 to show them that they can break through any ceiling. K. V. Switzer's amazing story reminds us that, though we've come a long way, we still have some work ahead of us. Let's allow this truth to energize us:

Gender equality is not a woman's issue. It is a human issue that affects us all.

―――――― ∾⊕∾ ――――――

When God created human beings, he made them to
be like himself. He created them male and female,
and he blessed them and called them "human."

GENESIS 5:1-2

Dynamite in
a Small Package

⌇⌇

You might not believe it looking at her today. This diminutive Jewish grandmother and guidance counselor to a generation of Baby Boomers was once a sniper in the Israeli army. Karola Siegel's childhood was shaped by the worst kind of trauma: her father was rounded up by the SS in Germany, and the rest of her family fled the country. She would never again see her parents, aunts and uncles, or cousins. They would all perish in the death camps.

Karola was the lucky one—if you could toss around the word *lucky* for a little girl who lost her whole family in the Holocaust. Her doomed parents had the foresight to send her to a boarding school in Switzerland, one step ahead of the Nazi roundups that consigned thousands of Jewish children to the gas chambers. In 1941, the letters from her parents ceased. Only after the war did she realize that they must have disappeared forever in the ghastly death camps. Like thousands of other displaced and disconnected Jews, this orphan found herself in an exodus to the promised land of Palestine. There she joined the *Haganah*, a fierce Zionist guerilla organization, and fought the occupying British army to establish the state of Israel. Later the Haganah fighters would go on to become the core of the Israeli defense force.

Karola's minute height at four feet seven inches made her a natural for slipping through barbed-wire fences. It also made her a perfect candidate to be a sniper, too small to be seen. Karola Siegel turned out to be a crack shot. She also excelled at throwing grenades with uncanny accuracy. Her commanders said that she was as tough as nails and as good a fighter as the Haganah ever produced. She proved that when she was severely wounded by an exploding shell during the Israeli War of Independence in 1948. Doctors said she might never walk again, but she fought her way back with gritty toughness. Within months, she was jogging. Some seventy years later, most folks would find it almost impossible to picture this grandmother as a commando.

Karola Siegel also excelled at throwing sexual barbs with hardened men on the front lines. Some thought that she had a potty mouth. Everyone agreed that no one was more eager than Karola to take on sexual taboos that almost no one else dared discuss in mixed company. That candor would one day turn her into a celebrity. Today, the world knows this Israeli sharpshooter and grenade thrower by the name she chose for herself, Ruth, and the last name that she got from her third husband, Manfred Westheimer. Dr. Ruth Westheimer went on to become America's irreverent sex therapist and a megapopular radio and television personality. You might not like Dr. Ruth's take on sexual morality or some of the controversial causes she has espoused during our culture wars, but this diminutive grandmother reminds all of those who struggle with their smallness:

Today's mighty oak is just yesterday's nut that held its ground.

———— ✦ ————

Do not despise these small beginnings,
for the LORD rejoices to see the work begin.

ZECHARIAH 4:10

The Fifty-Word Masterpiece

◈

American education was in a state of crisis in 1954. Reading levels among grade school children were declining. Primers left over from their parents' school days were out of date and boring. When *Life* magazine came out with a scathing exposé on the literacy of grade-schoolers, the public finally took notice. America was locked in a Cold War that would be won or lost in the dizzying new world of computers, space exploration, and high-tech weaponry. The future of the nation depended on American kids keeping up with Communist children.

So a worried nation turned to Theodor Geisel. This skinny egghead was an unlikely savior. He looked more nerd than Superman. He surely had the smarts, having gone to Dartmouth and Oxford. Yet by some standards, this brainiac had wasted his Ivy League education as a cartoonist for the advertising department of Standard Oil. His one dubious claim to fame was producing a creative ad on an insecticide.

In his spare time, Theodor created outlandish cartoon characters that were wedded to a mishmash of words and rhymes. He had written a quirky children's book that was rejected twenty-seven times before finally being published. Its sales were mediocre, causing Theodor to figure he would be consigned to the purgatory of corporate advertising for the rest of his dead-end career. But the world was about to discover the egghead in the back rooms of Standard Oil.

After that blistering exposé from *Life* came out, a concerned publishing house challenged Theodor to write a creative and fun book for six-year-olds using only 225 words out of the 348 in a standard first-grader's vocabulary list. He labored for nine months due to the word restriction, ending up eleven words over the publisher's request. Yet, in 1957, *The Cat in the Hat* came out to rave reviews and sales close to a million copies in its first three years.

Theodor would go on to make history with a series of books using his mother's maiden name, Seuss. The most amazing challenge in his Dr. Seuss series was the time Bennett Cerf, the founder of Random House, bet the author that he couldn't write a book using only fifty words. Theodor Seuss Geisel won that bet when he created his masterpiece *Green Eggs and Ham*. Bennett never paid up, but it didn't matter. Theodor would produce five of the top one hundred children's books of all time, selling more than six hundred million copies in twenty languages. He would give us the Grinch, Sam-I-Am, Horton the Elephant, and a plethora of other iconic characters that are now deeply embedded in our cultural consciousness.

But this genius of weirdness and wonder who never had any children of his own was proudest of the fact that he inspired generations of kids to enjoy reading. Some argue that Theodor Seuss Geisel just might have saved American education. When you consider your own legacy, you ought to remember something Calvin Coolidge said, "Nothing is more common than unsuccessful men with talent. . . . Persistence and determination alone are omnipotent." The amazing story of Dr. Seuss challenges us to never forget this truth:

Our greatest natural treasure is in the minds of our children.

———— ✿ ————

Children are a gift from the LORD; they are a
reward from him. Children born to a young
man are like arrows in a warrior's hands.

PSALM 127:3-4

The Curse of Camelot

❧☙

Joe and Rose had big plans. Both came from Irish immigrants who were treated like outcasts by Bostonian Brahmins. But Rose's daddy came up in the rough-and-tumble politics of Beantown to become its mayor. Some say Joe made his fortune supplying booze to mobsters. He bankrolled politicians who repaid him with deals that made him one of America's richest men. Joe allegedly used his ill-gotten gains to buy respectability with an ambassadorship to the royal court in England.

Yet scratch beneath the veneer of these nouveaux riches and you might discover the insecurities of an outcast past. Joe and Rose determined that their children would become American royalty. More drill sergeant than mother, Rose ran her home like a boot camp. Failure was never tolerated. Every week she weighed her kids to make sure no one was becoming overweight. A single gained pound earned a draconian diet. The smallest infraction of a rule produced a coat-hanger beating. No one was allowed to cry. Each child was expected to possess uncommonly good looks, graduate top of the class, excel in sports, display impeccable manners, and become a superstar.

But Rosemary, their oldest daughter, didn't fit the mold. She had been born with cognitive disabilities that kept her at the intellectual level of a fourth grader. When Rose and Joe sent her to boarding school, she repeatedly escaped. When Rosemary was twenty-three, Joe took her to get a lobotomy. The surgery left her in a severely debilitated state, and she was locked away in an institution. The lobotomy may have spared the family embarrassment, but many believe it unleashed the Kennedy curse.

Joe Jr., his parents' choice to become the US president, died when his World War II bomber blew up over England. Kathleen did her part to advance the family fame by marrying a British royal, only to die in a plane crash. Jack lost two children at birth, but he fulfilled his parents' dreams when he became America's thirty-fifth president—only to be assassinated. Ted was on the road to becoming president until his aspirations were derailed by scandal. Bobby was assassinated on the eve of capturing the 1968 presidential nomination.

Tragedy continued unabated into the next generation. One grandson recklessly totaled his car, paralyzing one of his passengers for life. Another grandson lost his leg to cancer. Four more grandchildren died tragically: one of a cocaine overdose, another in a skiing accident, still another in a plane crash, and yet another from a heart attack. These are only a smattering of the Kennedy heartaches. We may stand in awe of their political legacy. Yet we remember them more for that eerie curse. Was it unleashed when Rose and Joe decided to fix things by lobotomizing a special-needs child? Camelot might have been so much more beautiful had they seen Rosemary as a gift from God to be loved rather than a liability to be hidden. The Kennedy story surely proves this:

The greatest disability in life is the inability to see a person as more.

The LORD asked Moses, "Who makes a person's mouth?
Who decides whether people speak or do not speak, hear
or do not hear, see or do not see? Is it not I, the LORD?"

EXODUS 4:11

The Incredible Brain

❦

Your brain weighs about 3 pounds, making up less than 2 percent of your body weight. Yet it uses 20 percent of your total energy and oxygen intake—and for good reason! This cerebral sea contains 400 miles of blood vessels bringing nutrients to some 86 billion cells. A single piece of the brain, the size of a grain of sand, contains a whopping 100,000 neurons and 1 billion synapses in communication.

The amount of sights, sounds, smells, and other bits of sensory information that floods into the brain each millisecond is dizzying. In the average lifetime, the number of data bits stored in the brain adds up to the number 1 followed by a line of zeros 6.5 miles long. An ordinary person has about 50,000 conscious thoughts each day. All this information is processed at speeds up to 268 miles per hour, faster than Formula 1 race cars that top out at 240 miles an hour. Maybe that's why 100,000 chemical changes take place in your brain every second.

If you think that you control all your thoughts, think again. About 95 percent of your decisions are made in your subconscious mind, often processed by the incalculable bits of forgotten information stored away in your memory files. Then there's the "second brain" in your intestines, which contains 100,000 neurons producing 30 essential neurotransmitters, along with the "happy molecule" known as serotonin. That's why many of our decisions are gut reactions or feelings.

Here's the rub. According to Paul Reber, professor of psychology at Northwestern University, the brain can store 2.5 petabytes of data. That translates to 2.5 million gigabytes or 300 years' worth of television! It's impossible to bring to mind even the smallest fraction of those stored bits of information. But nothing taken into the brain can ever be erased.

Everything stored in our subconscious memory lasts a lifetime, even if we can't access it. Recollections pop up at the most inconvenient moments. Feelings caused by forgotten events can flood in when we least expect them, causing unexplainable anger, bitterness, sadness, and depression.

The brain that is so amazingly complex and powerful is also incredibly fragile. Even the most brilliant minds can snap. The most resilient people can plunge into the darkest despair. We are all a heartbeat removed from sudden head injuries, strokes, or aneurysms that can change everything. The older we get, the more likely we are to face memory loss or dementia. In many cases it's the stored memories, both conscious and unconscious, that plague and paralyze. We might wish that our memories could be erased like a virus in a computer. But those memories are hardwired forever. What we need is a new software program to help us to filter past experiences through new perspectives. God offers such a program in the Bible—a new way to look at old data. Energized by the Holy Spirit and equipped with the truths of Scripture, we can reinterpret everything for a healthier way of thinking. This much is true:

Unless we change our mind, nothing else changes.

⸺⁂⸻

Don't copy the behavior and customs of this world, but
let God transform you into a new person by changing
the way you think. Then you will learn to know God's
will for you, which is good and pleasing and perfect.

ROMANS 12:2

146

The Birdman of New York

❧

Nikola left his cheap hotel room each morning, repeating the same routine with clockwork predictability—shuffling to the same corner market, rummaging through the same threadbare pockets, and forking over the same amount of change to buy the same seeds. He would hobble to the same park, sit on the same bench, and feed his pigeons, often sitting among them until sundown. When he wasn't talking to his birds, the old man mumbled to himself in agitation.

Passersby dismissed Nikola as the strangest bird of all. If he saw a woman wearing pearls, the birdman would fly into a rage. He abhorred pearls and didn't mind ordering the offending person to go home and put on appropriate jewelry. If someone brushed up against him, he would react violently. He might have been covered with pigeon droppings, but he was deathly afraid of germs. No one would have guessed that ragged Nikola once occupied a lavish suite in the Waldorf Astoria. Back then, political leaders, titans of industry, and the crème de la crème of high society toasted his genius. Rudyard Kipling, John Muir, Mark Twain, and J. P. Morgan had been numbered among his closest friends. Now only pigeons came to pay homage to the crazy old man whose face had once emblazoned the cover of *Time* magazine.

People who watched the birdman argue with himself didn't know that he was working out his formula for a death ray that could knock ten thousand enemy airplanes out of the sky. Though British and American authorities had dismissed his idea as the ravings of a mad scientist, the Soviets had promised $25,000 for his plan. Onlookers would have been shocked to know that the birdman was the genius of the ages. Long before he spent his days feeding pigeons, he had created AC electricity and more than three hundred other inventions. As early as 1901 he had envisioned formulas for smartphone technology and the concepts that would lead to X-rays, particle beams, the Internet, and many other things we take for granted today.

Nikola had come to America in the late 1800s with four pennies and a dream. At times he dug ditches to make ends meet. Yet this towering intellect became the father of the electronic age. But Nikola's futuristic visions were so far ahead of his time that he bitterly gave up on a disbelieving world. He tore up his royalties in the Westinghouse company that would have made him a billionaire. In the end, Nikola Tesla, one of the greatest inventors of the twentieth century, preferred pigeons to people. Nikola Tesla died a recluse with large debts and a lifetime of unfulfilled dreams.

It has been said that there is a thin line between genius and craziness. Too often the greatest mind cannot comprehend what the simple faith of a child easily grasps. Even if you are a genius, you're crazy to ignore this wisdom:

If you gain everything but lose your soul, you have gained nothing.

———— ✍ ————

What do you benefit if you gain the whole
world but lose your own soul?

MARK 8:36

The Worst Singer in the World

܅܅܅

The New York City socialite actually thought that she could sing. Yet, more than seventy years after she died, her voice remains one of our nation's longest running jokes. Her recording of "The Queen of the Night" from Mozart's *The Magic Flute* continues to be played at dinner parties and watched by millions on YouTube for laughs. Her tone-deaf butchering of classical songs has been called a "story . . . of triumph over embarrassment" and she has been termed "the worst singer in the world."

As a child, Flo dreamed that she would grow up to be an opera star. For years she invested in voice lessons, and she practiced diligently. But money and hard work can't overcome zero talent. So Flo used her inheritance to create an alternate universe where she could live out her fantasies by becoming a generous patron of the arts. Her largesse gave her access to the greatest conductors, musicians, and soloists in the world. They were more than willing to stroke her ego in exchange for her contributions.

She founded the Verdi Club, which boasted four hundred members, including superstars of opera and symphony. Sometimes Flo wore flamboyant costumes and sang arias. Her horrific performances were greeted with wild applause. Great conductors such as Arturo Toscanini and Fausto Cleva gushed that her voice never sounded better. Maybe that's why she produced a record.

But no one fed Flo's delusions more than a mediocre Shakespearean actor by the name of St. Clair Bayfield. She kept him in high style, and he became her lover, manager, and chief cheerleader. Mostly, he shielded her from laughter and bad reviews. He even arranged for her to perform a concert at Carnegie Hall. The greatest musicians and singers in the world have graced this sacred stage. But on October 25, 1944, lines stretched around the block to hear America's worst voice. Most were US soldiers and sailors who had survived the fears and horrors of World War II by laughing at the 78 rpm recording of Flo's voice. The concert was a musical disaster, but the crowd cheered wildly as a blissfully oblivious Flo botched one song after another.

Flo went home thinking that her performance was a tour de force, but scathing reviews from newspaper critics were devastating. Five days later, Florence Foster Jenkins suffered a heart attack. Before dying a month later, she reportedly said, "People may say I can't sing, but no one can ever say I *didn't* sing." Who would have guessed that the recording of her concert would be one of the most frequently requested in the hallowed history of Carnegie Hall, or that her life would be celebrated in two movies, in a bestselling book, and on social media? We can either laugh at her delusions or admire her determination. She couldn't sing a lick, but she sang anyway. Indeed, she wrote a personal story of "triumph over embarrassment." Flo teaches us one of life's most important principles:

It is far better to try and fail than to fail to try.

───── ⁊⊚⊙⊱ ─────

As for you, be strong and courageous,
for your work will be rewarded.

2 CHRONICLES 15:7

The Real Hero in Those Swashbucklers

❧

Who would guess that the son of a black slave would become the inspiration for some of literature's most memorable heroes? He was the original swashbuckler: a dashing sword fighter who would become the prototype for the action heroes in his son's future novels.

When a French marquis left his plantation in Haiti to return home, he brought along his child, born of a black slave. Though his mixed-race son enjoyed the privileges of nobility, he also became the object of scorn in high society. One evening, an arrogant nobleman, pretending to mistake him for a lady's footman, abused him as he might a servant.

That public shaming drove the count to take fencing lessons. After several duels, he was feared as a great swordsman. He joined the queen's dragoons and overcame racial prejudice to rise in the ranks. When a new equality blew in on the winds of the French Revolution, he became a general in the Grand Army of Napoleon. His dark good looks, towering height, and swashbuckling bravery earned him the nickname Hercules. Soon he was one of France's most admired generals, leading an army of fifty thousand soldiers to smashing victories in Italy and Egypt. Along the way, he married a French girl with whom he had three children. Among them was his only son, whom he named after himself.

When his exploits upstaged Napoleon, the jealous conqueror sent him home from Egypt. His ship was captured by Corsican pirates, and he was held for ransom. Instead of paying the kidnappers, the French government left him to languish in an Italian prison. He never forgot that betrayal. Nor did his son, who idolized his swashbuckling hero of a father.

That boy would grow up to become one of France's most renowned novelists. His stories of heroism and cowardice, swashbuckling adventure and harrowing escape, betrayal and revenge, have thrilled countless millions of readers. You may have never heard of the count who was Napoleon's greatest general, but you probably remember his son, Alexandre Dumas.

You can see the swashbuckling count in Alexandre's most famous works: *The Three Musketeers,* "The Man in the Iron Mask," and *The Count of Monte Cristo.* He wanted the whole world to know the story of his father, who had been betrayed and forgotten by his country. The story of General Alexandre Dumas, the son of an African slave in colonial Haiti, is relived again and again by every swashbuckling hero who rides across the pages of literature or Hollywood's silver screen.

The count's novelist son reminds us of the power of a father or mother to shape a child and, through that child, the whole world. Every boy and girl needs a hero to emulate and an adventure to live. As parents and grandparents, we have the privilege of being the role models who inspire our children to reach for the stars.

Be the hero in the earliest stories of your children's memories.

❧

Every time I think of you, I give thanks to my God.

PHILIPPIANS 1:3

Cats and Rats

U golino may be the cat-hater of the ages. He grew up with all the superstitions of his dark age. Among them was the notion that black cats were harbingers of bad luck. If one of those dark felines crossed the path of medieval travelers, these unluckiest of people would quickly cross themselves and whisper prayers to their favorite saints.

But Ugolino's abhorrence of cats knew no bounds. Because he associated black cats with witches and demons, all cats should have run for cover when the College of Cardinals elected Ugolino de Conti to the papacy as Pope Gregory IX. With a zeal unrivaled by other pontiffs, he reorganized Catholic laws to whip a lax church into line and then created the papal Inquisition to root out heretics and witches.

Yet his lasting impact in history came from his little encyclical that is now filed away in the Vatican. Pope Gregory called it *Vox in Rama*. In it, he condemned black cats as tools of the devil and called on believers to rid Christendom of these demon carriers. Cats were killed by the hundreds of thousands.

That feline slaughter would come back to haunt Europe. In the Middle Ages, people barely fed themselves. Cats were forced to forage for their food. Their primary diet consisted of mice and rats. Few cat killers reasoned that murdering mousers would naturally bring about a dramatic increase in rodents.

Perhaps it's no coincidence that a hundred years after Gregory died, the Black Death (or bubonic plague) swept across the continent. Before this scourge ended, some twenty-five million people died. Whole villages and regions were depopulated. Civil order collapsed. History was dramatically changed, and not always for the better.

For years, there was great debate about the cause of this plague. Was the disease airborne or carried by fleas? One prevailing theory is that the pandemic was transmitted by fleas carried by rats. It's hard to pull the bad guy out of a lineup. But a good detective of history might well piece the evidence together this way: fewer cats, more rats, more fleas, more plagues, and more death. The evidence points an accusing finger at a superstitious old pope.

There is a sad irony in the Latin words of Gregory's *Vox in Rama* ("the Voice in Ramah"). Those are words from Matthew's Christmas story that speak of the wailing of mothers after King Herod's men had slaughtered their baby boys. How many mothers wept for lost children after that pandemic in medieval Europe? Pope Gregory IX fell victim to the law of unintended consequences. Black cats may be dreadful to some but not nearly as much as the Black Death. So, before you take action on anything, remember this cautionary tale about cats and rats. This warning might encourage you to spend some time seeking God's direction:

Sometimes your solution is worse than your problem.

"My thoughts are nothing like your thoughts," says
the LORD. "And my ways are far beyond anything
you could imagine. For just as the heavens are higher
than the earth, so my ways are higher than your ways
and my thoughts higher than your thoughts."

ISAIAH 55:8-9

Seeing the Extraordinary
in the Ordinary

એબ્ઓ

Moses was a bundle of contradictions. Though he was a supporter of the Union, he moved from Ohio to the mountains of southwest Missouri—a hotbed of Confederate sedition. Though he was opposed to slavery, he purchased a thirteen-year-old black girl named Mary. Moses hated doing it, but his wife, Sally, had just taken on a passel of orphaned relatives, and they were both overwhelmed carving a farm out of wilderness.

One dark night, Southern sympathizers kidnapped Mary and one of her children, George, and sold them to new slave masters in neighboring Kentucky. Moses paid a handsome reward to agents to find and rescue Mary and her boy. He didn't do it as much to get his property back as to console Sally. His wife had come to love Mary and her children as family.

Mary was never found. But Moses gave a prize horse to buy back her son. The boy became like a son to Sally. She saw genius in him that no one else would expect in a slave. While George's siblings worked on the farm with Moses, Sally taught George how to read and write. Moses' wife also had a knowledge of plants and herbs, which she shared with the inquisitive child. She gave him a love for botany that would one day astound and change the world.

When George was between ten and twelve, Sally insisted that he be sent off to school. Because of his brilliance, he was given opportunities that precious few African Americans were afforded in the 1800s. By the time he became the first black person to graduate from Iowa State University, he had established himself as one of the premier botanists in America. When he went on to head the agricultural department at the Tuskegee Institute, he was lauded as the most esteemed botanist in the world.

George's experiments on new ways of growing cotton saved the economy of the South. His innovations on the uses of crops such as peanuts, sweet potatoes, soybeans, and pecans have helped to alleviate world hunger. He invented hundreds of products, including plastics, paints, dyes, and varieties of gasoline. In an age when blacks were segregated, he became an agricultural adviser to the US president and a member of the prestigious British Royal Society of Arts. George's tombstone sums up his amazing life: "He could have added fortune to fame, but caring for neither, he found happiness and honor in being helpful to the world."

The next time you bite into a peanut butter and jelly sandwich or grab hold of something made of plastic, you might want to thank Sally and Moses Carver. When Sally sent George off to school, teachers asked the boy, "What is your name?" He replied, "I'm Carver's George." They said, "From now on you are George Carver." How much poorer the world would be today if Sally Carver hadn't seen something extraordinary in a slave child. Maybe that farm woman taught George Washington Carver something better than botany:

We rise highest by raising others up higher.

———— ⌘ ————

He lifts the poor from the dust and the needy
from the garbage dump. He sets them among
princes, placing them in seats of honor.

1 SAMUEL 2:8

Overcoming Prejudice

ꞔꙅꙮꙅꙷ

Bobby Shaw wasn't a bigot. Quite the opposite. He came from a leading abolitionist family in Boston. He attended church with the family of Harriet Beecher Stowe, the author of *Uncle Tom's Cabin*. Black parishioners shared the pews with him.

When the Civil War broke out, Bobby quickly signed up for action. But it wasn't for his parents' righteous cause of emancipation. He craved adventure. He got it at Antietam, the bloodiest battle of the war. His letters spoke in glowing terms about the camaraderie of soldiers, of guts and glory, flags waving, and bombs bursting in air. He came home to a hero's welcome.

The abolitionist governor asked if the hero would recruit and lead one of the first African American regiments in the Union army, the 54th Massachusetts Infantry. His abolitionist mother pled with her Bobby to take the assignment. But he wanted glory. He didn't feel that black soldiers could be disciplined or march bravely into battle without breaking in the face of cannon fire. Moreover, he was ashamed to lead a black regiment. He repeatedly refused until his mother's pleading pricked his conscience and he finally said yes.

It wasn't easy turning runaway slaves into a disciplined regiment. The reluctant colonel got little help from the war department to outfit his men. Yet by the time they marched south, Bobby was convinced that they were as fine a regiment as any in Lincoln's armies. The 54th proved him right by smashing the rebels on St. James Island in South Carolina. Two days later, this Massachusetts regiment marched into glory when Colonel Shaw volunteered to lead them in a suicide charge on the batteries of Charleston's Fort Wagner.

Shaw himself was killed. But the 54th did not buckle. By the time

Union bugles signaled retreat, Shaw's regiment had been decimated. But they proved themselves brave and faithful in a nation plagued by prejudice.

The Confederates refused the requests of the Union army to return Colonel Shaw's body. Instead, they contemptuously dumped it in the mass grave of his fallen soldiers, sure that there could be no greater shame for a white man than to be buried with Negroes. But Shaw's father wrote, "We can imagine no holier place than that in which he lies, among his brave and devoted followers, nor wish for him better company—what a body-guard he has!"

Subsequent generations have canonized Robert Gould Shaw as a champion of African Americans. The historical facts are not as kind. Colonel Shaw was not an outright bigot, but he had his prejudices and stereotypical thinking about race. It wasn't until he lived and worked with the 54th Infantry that Shaw's attitudes changed.

It is possible that many of us have "soft" prejudices toward others. Maybe our perspectives would change too if we got to know people who look, think, and act differently. Chew on this today:

There's no prejudice so strong as the conceit that one is not prejudiced.

They say to each other, "Don't come too close
or you will defile me! I am holier than you!"

ISAIAH 65:5

For Such a Time as This

❧❦❧

He was a megalomaniac. When his first queen refused to be paraded like a prize heifer before his drunken guests, he had her deposed. The maniacal ruler then held a beauty pageant to replace his first queen. The Jewish beauty was forced to become a contestant in this ancient version of *The Bachelor*.

When the Jewish beauty queen won, she became the king's plaything. She was packed off to the harem, put through extreme beauty treatments, and then sent to the royal bedchamber. It couldn't have been easy for her to walk into the lair of this beast and submit meekly to whatever brought him pleasure. He had already proven that he would banish a queen who failed to please him. What she endured that night was nothing less than rape. Such was the sad lot of this beautiful pawn of powerful men.

Meanwhile, her cousin earned the jealousy of a political rival—a virulent Jew hater. This anti-Semite manipulated the maniacal ruler into issuing an edict that all the Jews in his vast empire would be slaughtered on a set day. When her cousin got wind of the impending holocaust, he went to her and begged her to plead the Jewish cause to her husband. The beauty queen was terrified. If her husband banished his first queen for refusing to degrade herself at his stag party, what would he do to his second if she revealed that she was of the race that he had slated for genocide?

But her cousin responded, "Who knows if perhaps you were made queen for just such a time as this?" So this beautiful pawn of powerful men found her courage to face a maniacal husband and declare that she, too, was a Jew. Because no Persian shah could countermand even his own royal edict, she convinced him to allow the Jews to make a preemptive strike against those who were about to unleash the genocide. The queen used her feminine wiles to ensnare the evil rival of her cousin, making it look like he tried to seduce her. The enraged Persian shah, Xerxes, had evil Haman and his ten wicked sons impaled in the public square. To this day, Jews celebrate Queen Esther during their feast day of Purim.

A megalomaniac's trophy wife could have remained a beautiful pawn in the hands of men who played power politics. Instead, the pawn who became a queen risked everything. She made a perilous move that check-mated a kingmaker and saved the Jewish people. Esther's amazing story proves that none of us is a throwaway pawn in a board game of happen-stance. We have been put right where we are "for such a time as this." Each of us has a key role to play. So let's make the most of every moment to advance God's glory and others' welfare.

Even a pawn, in the hand of the Master, can take a king off the board.

———— ✐✐✐ ————

Who knows if perhaps you were made
queen for just such a time as this?

ESTHER 4:14

Fifteen Hundred Rejections

❦

He often hid traumatized in the bedroom while his folks threw invectives and punches like combatants in a heavyweight fight. When they finally called it quits on their marriage, he was shuffled between foster homes until he ended up in a high school for troubled youth. Nobody figured the kid from the broken home would go the distance.

But he had dreams of being an actor, writer, and director in Hollywood. His brooding good looks got him a few bit parts in minor movies. He cleaned lion cages at Central Park Zoo, ushered at a movie house, and even suffered the indignity of taking a part in a porn film to pay his rent. By 1975, this sometime actor and wannabe screenwriter had $106 in the bank, his wife was pregnant, and he couldn't pay the rent on his run-down apartment.

That's when he sat down and began to write a screenplay about a loser like himself. It was finished in less than four days. When he shopped his script around Hollywood, the wannabe screenwriter was rejected a total of fifteen hundred times. But he doggedly got up after each knockdown to go another round with the media moguls. Some were willing to buy the screenplay outright but wouldn't let him star in it.

But this determined screenwriter and actor wouldn't compromise. It was all or nothing. There would be no draw or split decision. Finally, United Artists took a low-risk chance. He could star in his own film. He was given a budget of $1 million and forced to finish it in twenty-eight days. It debuted to mixed reviews and small audiences. But word of mouth generated big buzz, and Sylvester Stallone's *Rocky* shot into the stratosphere in 1976. The Hollywood establishment was shocked when it became one of the biggest blockbusters of all time—grossing more than $100 million! Media elites were even more stunned when *Rocky* won the Academy Award for Best Picture in 1977.

The rest is cinema history. *Rocky* and its many sequels have grossed over $1 billion worldwide, making it one of the most successful movie franchises of all time. Sylvester Stallone has gone on to become one of the biggest action stars in movie history, with an estimated worth of $400 million.

Why have countless millions cheered for that washed-up Philly club fighter to go the distance with unbeatable Apollo Creed and then to go on to become the heavyweight champ of the world in *Rocky 2*? Why did we go back to some pretty awful sequels to watch him lose again and again, only to come back with the chant of "Rocky, Rocky, Rocky" reverberating through the arena? Sylvester Stallone's story is really his own, and it is ours. We know what it means to have our dreams shattered and to be repeatedly knocked down by life. But we also want to believe this:

As long as you can get up again, the fight is not yet lost.

―――――∞☙☞∞―――――

I have fought the good fight, I have finished the race, and
I have remained faithful. And now the prize awaits me.

2 TIMOTHY 4:7-8

The Strikeout King

❧

George struck out on the baseball field and in life. He grew up in a rough-and-tumble neighborhood called Pigtown. By age seven, he was already sneaking copious amounts of beer from the tap in his dad's saloon. Maybe that's why he got in so much trouble. He was sent to St. Mary's Industrial School for Boys, a combination orphanage and reformatory. After twelve years in that home for wayward boys, a defining word appears on his record: *incorrigible*.

But George could hit a ball farther than any other kid. After he broke almost every window in the neighborhood, a priest encouraged him to play baseball. If it hadn't been for Brother Matthias, George might have ended up in prison or the gutter. Instead, he became one of the most recognizable names in sports history.

To look at him, with his spindly legs and protruding beer belly, you would never guess that George was an athlete. You sure wouldn't know it from his lifestyle. Throughout his legendary career, he continually broke curfew—often showing up at game time hungover from drinking beer and downing a couple dozen hot dogs loaded with sauerkraut, mustard, and onions. If players today jack up their power with steroids, George diluted his with booze, women, and all-night poker games. Though he famously loved kids and performed outrageous acts of charity, his personal life was a mess of womanizing and debauchery.

Yet no one ever hit the ball like George Herman Ruth. He did his amazing feats before steroids or elongated seasons that pad statistics. He did it half-drunk, bloated by gluttony, and slowed by carousing. Who can forget that game against the Cubs in the 1932 World Series when the Babe was down in the count? The Chicago fans were screaming insults when he calmly pointed to the center field fence. He hit the next pitch more than five hundred feet over that fence.

His statistics are mind boggling. He held the record for home runs, with 60 in a single season, and 714 lifetime homers. In his amazing career he had 2,873 hits with 2,174 runs batted in.

But what most folks don't know is that the Sultan of Swat also held the major league record for striking out. After he retired, his strikeouts off the field caught up with him too. He desperately wanted to manage a team, but his lifestyle was too toxic. Baseball owners' repeated refusals to hire him as a manager broke his heart. In 1948, this bigger-than-life hero was reduced to a shadow of his former self by cancer. When he died at age fifty-three, he was celebrated as the greatest hitter of all time. Few remembered how often he struck out at the plate and in life.

What is true for the Babe goes for us, too. Either we will go for the fences or play it safe at the plate. Joe Sewell had the fewest strikeouts in a major league career, but who remembers Joe? You may strike out a lot if you go for the fences, but at least you'll hit a few home runs.

No one ever achieved greatness by playing it safe.

───── ⚬❦❧⚬ ─────

God has not given us a spirit of fear and timidity,
but of power, love, and self-discipline.

2 TIMOTHY 1:7

The City in the Clouds

⊶⊙⊙⊶

This true story is as exciting as an Indiana Jones movie. In 1911, Yale professor Hiram Bingham left Cuzco looking for Vilcabamba, the fabled lost city of the Inca. As the explorer traveled the dizzying heights of the Andes, he and his party were venturing into a ghostly realm that had been abandoned since sixteenth century Spanish conquistadors destroyed one of the world's great empires.

As they moved into the Urubamba Valley, a farmer told them about a city in the clouds atop a nearby mountain known as Old Peak. On a wet day in July, the explorer began the arduous climb up twisted and tangled trails. An eleven-year-old boy led him through mists into one of the wonders of the world—an ancient Inca city almost eight thousand feet high, hidden in the Andean clouds.

What Bingham discovered was breathtaking. It is rightly called one of the New Seven Wonders of the World—no city on earth has such spectacular vistas. The mysteries of that city in the clouds still confound historians and archaeologists.

Why was the city built? Was it a hideaway for royals or a holy city for temples and priests? Or was it designed as an impregnable fortress? The central temple is built in such a way that it serves as a perfect observatory to study the movement of stars and planets. How did Inca architects discover mathematical equations that confound engineers and astronomers today?

The labyrinth of stone terraces perched on the side of sheer drop-offs boggles the imagination. At one time the Inca grew crops with such a sophisticated irrigation system that they eclipse the fabled hanging gardens of Babylon. How did people without machinery drag those stone blocks up that eight-thousand-foot-high mountain? How did they cut and fit them so perfectly that they required no mortar to hold them together? How did they set them so tightly that the thinnest knife blade cannot be inserted between the blocks?

What about the biggest mystery of all: Why was this city in the clouds abandoned? The Spanish conquistadors never found the city. Only the ghosts who haunt these ancient ruins have the answers. Until the day he died, Bingham wrestled with the mysteries of the city on Old Peak, or—as it is called in the native Quechua language—Machu Picchu.

Surely this city was built as an extravagant act of worship to the Inca gods. The herculean effort that went into it beggars the imagination. The devotion of these ancient Incas should convict those of us who worship the one true God. Worship is more than a quick prayer at mealtime or a weekly one-hour service in air-conditioned comfort. This much is not a mystery: the God who created the glory of the Andes deserves more than halfhearted religion. Machu Picchu whispers this universal truth:

The worship of God is giving him the best of the best he has already given you.

History merely repeats itself. It has all been done
before. Nothing under the sun is truly new.

ECCLESIASTES 1:9

The Brain Is Faster Than the Tongue

❧

Jack's dad was a train conductor and a union organizer who worked fourteen hours a day. So Grace had to be both mother and father to her boy. Jack is quick to admit he became the man he is today because of her. He remembers those precious hours when they sat together at the train station waiting for his dad late at night. The life lessons he learned from his mom have transformed America.

Jack may be known for having an uncompromising toughness that reduces corporate heads to Jell-O, but he softens when he speaks about how his mom saved him from a childhood disability. Jack was a stutterer. That impediment rendered him insecure and shy. Yet his stuttering did not keep him from becoming a titan of corporate America.

Jack says that the secret to overcoming his disability was his mother assuring him that his stuttering was a sure sign of his superior intellect. He still smiles when he remembers her words: "No one's tongue could keep up with a brain like yours." His optimistic mom showed him that disabilities don't have to debilitate.

Jack also remembers another powerful lesson that he learned from Grace. As a five-foot-seven highschool athlete with limited abilities, he pushed himself with a relentless competitiveness that is still legendary today. Yet his obsession with winning made him a sore loser. When his team lost a hard-fought hockey game in overtime, he threw his stick across the rink and stormed off the ice. A few minutes later, Grace barged into the boy's locker room, angrily grabbed Jack by the scruff of the neck, and shouted, "You punk! If you don't know how to lose, you'll never know how to win!"

Jack was mortified, but he never forgot that lesson. Perhaps that's why Grace Welch gave America an exceptional son who became the CEO of General Electric. He would turn that staid old company into one of the great engines of our world economy. Along the way, Jack Welch mentored and launched some of the world's greatest CEOs. His books on management have become international bestsellers. In 1999, *Fortune* magazine named him the Manager of the Century. The *Financial Times* called him one of the three most respected leaders in the world. But maybe all those accolades should go to a woman named Grace from Peabody, Massachusetts.

We all need encouragers who will tell us our limitations don't have to limit us. It may be as simple as telling a stuttering child that his extraordinary brain is too fast for his tongue. Sometimes it's tough love that grabs a sore loser by the scruff of the neck and yells, "You will never be a winner if you don't learn how to lose well!" Children especially need to be affirmed. A word of encouragement may not produce the Manager of the Century, but it could make a bigger difference than you think. Jack Welch would probably agree with this:

Your greatest success is in making others successful.

Let us think of ways to motivate one another
to acts of love and good works.

HEBREWS 10:24

The Dumbhead

శాఖుల

To this day, some experts speculate that he was an idiot savant. He didn't speak a word until he was almost four years old. It took him several more years to figure out how to put together simple sentences. He didn't learn how to read until he was seven. His exasperated parents almost gave up on their slow-witted boy.

When he finally went to school, things got worse. His marks were the lowest in the class. He almost never turned in his homework. Teachers labeled him "a lazy dog." It was excruciating for the class to wait while he slowly mouthed the answers to the schoolmaster's questions. His class-mates called him a "retard" and his teachers ridiculed him as a *dummkopf,* or "dumbhead."

His academic failures continued unabated when he dropped out of high school. He managed to be accepted into a second-rate Swiss college after failing the entrance exam. Somehow he scraped by. But the faculty rejected his doctoral dissertation as "irrelevant and fanciful." He was still living up to his childhood nickname—"the dopey one."

He applied for jobs tailor made for his education as a physicist. Yet no one would hire him. He tutored young students, but their parents fired him. Finally he got a low-level job as a clerk in a patent office. He became a laughingstock when he couldn't figure out whether to put his socks or shoes on first or got lost on the way home or forgot that he had used his paycheck as a bookmark in some volume he had returned to the library. Most of the time he sat at his office desk, lost in realms of physics where no human mind had ever gone before.

Maybe he was an idiot savant after all. Who would have known that Albert Einstein's theory of relativity and its revolutionary formula $E = mc^2$

would change the world? Even after his theories were published, scientists mocked them as useless and irrelevant. They didn't call him dopey or dummkopf, but they did say that he had an irrational mind. But a few farsighted folk recognized his amazing genius, making him the professor of theoretical physics at the Universities of Zurich and Prague. He may have been the quintessential absentminded professor, but he proved that his critics were the dopes and dummkopfs when he went on to win the 1921 Nobel Prize for physics.

Imagine the surprise of the dumbhead's parents, classmates, professors, and critics if they could have looked at the cover of the December 31, 1999, issue of *Time* magazine and seen the banner headline above Einstein's photograph: "Person of the Century." *Time*'s feature article went on to say that his instincts embodied "the very best of this century as well as our highest hopes for the next." Be careful whom you write off as a dope or dummkopf. Some people are smarter than you think. Brilliance doesn't always come in conventional packages. Reserve your judgment and keep your opinions about others to yourself. Those people just might end up on the cover of *Time*.

Beware of outward appearances. They are usually deceiving.

———— ✎ ————

Look beneath the surface so you can judge correctly.

JOHN 7:24

The Peter Pan Syndrome

⌀⌀

What was done to little Mike was criminal. Had Joe forced his seven-year-old to work in coal mines eighteen hours a day, there would have been a public outcry. Instead, after Mike's abusive father drove him to megastardom, his fans thought he was the world's luckiest kid. Millions of tweens wanted to be just like him.

Years later, his bizarre behavior became tabloid fodder. The whispers of something sinister became public accusations. Mike was charged with a horrible crime: molesting children. When one of the accusers settled out of court for megabucks, public opinion declared the superstar guilty.

Many people have wondered what drove Mike to undergo painful surgeries that made him look perpetually young. Why did he build a fantasyland and invite young children to play there and at times sleep in his bed?

Maybe the answer is in the name that Michael Jackson gave his ranch—Neverland. Every child knows about that fantasyland where children never grow up and Peter Pan flies happily through a never-ending childhood. There is no compelling proof that Michael was a pedophile. He doesn't fit the profile. There is every reason to believe that he wanted to be Peter Pan.

We should weep for Michael. Even abused and disadvantaged children get to go to school and play with friends. Michael was denied all that by a father who drove his seven-year-old to work eighteen-hour days. He was turned into a sexual dancing machine with a soprano voice that made women swoon. At ten years of age, he was performing in strip clubs and hiding traumatized in his hotel bed while his older brothers engaged in debauchery with groupies. By age eleven, he was the biggest superstar on the planet, with a psyche frozen in time.

It's easy to see why Michael Jackson used his wealth to build Neverland with its fantastic toys, amusement rides, exotic animals, and a full-time magician. Those who want to think the best believe that he invited children to his sleepovers not to steal their childhoods through perverted acts but to recover what was stolen from him as a child, like an eleven-year-old boy frozen in time.

The nation feasted on his amazing talents without realizing that we were complicit in stealing his childhood. Then we turned on him when the joy that he gave us as a child superstar resulted in a dysfunctional adulthood. We should weep for the late Peter Pan. We might also wonder if things could have been different had Joe Jackson said to record moguls, "Not now. I want my boy to enjoy his childhood. Call back in ten years." Would things be better if we didn't push our own kids to grow up too fast by pressuring them to succeed too soon, or let them pressure us into allowing them to do adult things before they are ready? Perhaps Walt Disney said it best:

The trouble with the world is that too many people grow up.

———— ✺ ————

I tell you the truth, anyone who doesn't receive the
Kingdom of God like a child will never enter it.

LUKE 18:17

The Man Who Failed
Ten Thousand Times

❧

Al, as he was called as a child, first learned failure from his daddy, an excitable gadabout who seldom brought home a paycheck. He watched his mother slowly descend into madness as his family moved inexorably toward destitution. As if all that weren't bad enough, scarlet fever rendered little Al almost deaf. Maybe that's why he was a trouble-maker at school, labeled by his teacher as "unteachable." So his mother yanked him out of school. He would forever remain a fifth-grade dropout.

He hit the road at age twelve. He was quite the little entrepreneur, starting businesses only to have them fall apart. But his repeated failures were training grounds for a mind that would eventually change the world. When he was twenty years old, Al headed for Boston. In that citadel of academic powerhouses, the self-taught grade-school dropout began to invent new technologies. But highbrows saw his ideas as too futuristic. When he invented a machine that could tally votes at the ballot box, the Massachusetts legislature wasn't interested in something we now take for granted.

So Al headed for New York. There he invented two technologies that netted him $140,000 in 1870. Flush with success, he married sixteen-year-old Mary. Her death at age twenty-nine would be another tragedy in a long string of sorrows. But he did use his profits to start his laboratory in New Jersey. When it burned down, he stood on the ragged edge of bankruptcy. Yet, with his characteristic optimism, he rebuilt bigger, better, and more profitable facilities.

Over the next sixty years, the fifth-grade dropout led a technological revolution that would turn America into an economic juggernaut. He was in his eighties when he applied for the last of his 1,093 US patents. By now you may recognize Al as Thomas Alva Edison, the inventor of the lightbulb, phonograph, motion picture, and so many other modern marvels that changed our world. He was arguably history's most prodigious inventor.

Yet we would be wrong to celebrate his successes without remembering that he had far more failures. When someone asked about his many missteps, he famously replied, "I have not failed ten thousand times— I've successfully found ten thousand ways that will not work." Maybe he was nicknamed the Wizard of Menlo Park because people mistakenly believed that he magically snatched his ideas out of thin air. In fact, his creations came from exhausting hours of repeated experiments that produced repeated failures that spawned new observations that sometimes led to new inventions.

Maybe you feel like you are standing at the depressing end of a line of failures. Why don't you look at them the way Thomas Edison did: instead of failing, you've been successful in learning what won't work in the future. So keep plugging away with a credo that the Wizard of Menlo Park would embrace:

Failure is a detour on the road to success, not a dead-end street.

———— ✧ ————

Be strong and courageous! . . . For the LORD
your God will personally go ahead of you.
He will neither fail you nor abandon you.

DEUTERONOMY 31:6

Those Miracle Fruit Jars

Alexander was some kind of genius. In the age before supermarkets, when most Americans lived on farms or tended garden plots in town, preserving food for the winter ahead was a matter of life and death. That's why entrepreneurs like Mason and Ball became household names for mass-producing canning jars. But creating self-sealing lids for those jars became a vexing challenge. That's when Alexander Kerr's inventive mind discovered the secret worth its weight in gold.

The problem for Kerr was in finding the capital to mass-produce his product. In 1903 he partnered with John Giles to found the Hermetic Closure Company of Chicago. A year later, he changed the name to the Kerr Glass Manufacturing Company. He patented another of his inventions, the first threaded ring to hold the lid down—the same method used today.

Alexander had mortgaged his home, and he borrowed heavily to finance his new start-up. The competition was stiff and the American economy fragile. Those early days were tough sledding. Yet Alexander Kerr, who had been converted under the ministry of evangelist D. L. Moody, had committed to test God's promise to bless those who tithed—even when he had precious little to give.

That belief was severely tested four years after he started his company. It was 1906, and his fruit jars were being produced in San Francisco. On April 18 a massive earthquake hit. Some three thousand people were killed, and 80 percent of the city was destroyed. When Alexander received the news flash, his friends said, "You are a ruined man!" He responded, "I don't believe it. I know God can't go back on his promises!" He wired San Francisco. A devastating answer came back: "Factory in the heart of the fire. Undoubtedly destroyed. Heat so intense will be unable to find out anything for several days."

Those were faith-testing days for Kerr's family. About a week later, a second wire came from San Francisco: "Factory miraculously saved." Everything for a mile and a half on all sides of the factory burned, but the factory remained standing!

Kerr immediately left for the coast. It wasn't until he got to the site that he saw the amazing scope of God's miracle. His factory was made entirely of wood, containing huge tanks where the glass was melted at hot temperatures, fueled by oil. His building was the most flammable in the area. Yet the raging inferno came only to the edges of the Kerr factory, scorching its fences before jumping over his building to consume whole blocks around it. The fences were not burned, nor was the building singed. So complete was the miracle that not a single one of the thousands of jars was cracked by the massive earthquake or fires that followed.

Alexander later spoke in churches, reminding Christians of God's promise to bless those who tithe. If you are tempted to withhold that which belongs to God, you might want to ponder this:

The most impossible task in life is to outgive God.

Give, and you will receive. Your gift will return to you
in full—pressed down, shaken together to make room
for more, running over, and poured into your lap.

LUKE 6:38

Butterfly Miracles

ꜩꙄꙅ

Cancer had reduced six-year-old Christian to skin and bones. It was during his final days that nature bestowed its annual miracle. Millions of yellow butterflies invade northeast Oklahoma with a gentle firestorm of color and dance, covering the landscape and bringing unbridled joy after the bleakness of Oklahoma winter. But this gift seldom lasts more than a week before the yearly exodus of butterflies leaves on spring breezes.

Some friends went to the hospital to visit Christian. Though most of the butterflies had already flown away, one friend had managed to trap one for the dying boy. Christian peered at the imprisoned butterfly and then handed the jar to his mother, Marsha. "Mommy, please set him free. He's like me, in a place he doesn't like to be." Marsha opened the window, took the lid off the bottle, and let the butterfly soar away. A wistful smile crossed Christian's face. "I'm going to be like that butterfly when I fly away to Jesus in heaven."

Christian died a few days later. There are few events filled with more anguish than a child's funeral. Marsha and Gary dreaded going back to their country house filled with memories of their little boy. So their friends drove them back to the home they hadn't seen in weeks of hospital stay.

As the car turned in to the long driveway, an amazing sight awaited. The lawn was covered with a carpet of yellow butterflies. They rose by the thousands in a joyous aerial ballet. Marsha ran into their swirling midst. For several joyous moments, butterflies danced about her. She forgot her grief and began to laugh with childish delight. Then they rose en masse to catch winds to faraway places.

Grief returned as quickly as it had left, and Marsha stood alone in the yard where Christian had once played. Then a solitary butterfly returned and landed gently on her nose. It sat for several seconds, its wings gently caressing her tear-stained cheeks before flying away.

Nature has no explanation for butterflies awaiting a grieving mother two weeks after the annual migration had left. Marsha was convinced the butterfly that came back to caress her face was the one released from the hospital room. To this day, all of us are sure that we witnessed a miracle. God had orchestrated this dance of the butterflies to remind Marsha and Gary Dance of what their boy had uttered during his final days in the hospital: "I'm going to be like that butterfly and fly away to Jesus."

Did Christian know about one of nature's great miracles? When a caterpillar is ready to turn into a butterfly, it fixes itself to a branch and wriggles out of its outer skin. Underneath is the chrysalis, which hardens to protect the insect as it transforms. It literally creates its own coffin. Then it dies, only to break out of its coffin as a butterfly destined for the heavens. It's a story of resurrection. No wonder the day Jesus rose from the dead is symbolized by butterflies. Whenever you feel like hope is gone, remember Christian Dance's story and the truth it teaches:

If there were no death, there would be no butterflies.

It will happen in a moment, in the blink of an eye, when
the last trumpet is blown. For when the trumpet sounds,
those who have died will be raised to live forever.

1 CORINTHIANS 15:52

The Destructive Power of Bitterness

⁂

Life didn't welcome him with open arms. Born into a ragtag band of nomads on barren steppes, he was given the name Temujin. It most likely means "blacksmith." Maybe that was the best his parents could hope for their baby boy.

When a rival tribe poisoned his father, his widowed mother was left with a hungry brood, making them a drain on the meager resources of their ragged clan. So his family was banished. His mother and her seven children were forced to survive in a region of unspeakable harshness. Temujin never forgot that rejection. But he did learn how to live with an empty belly while facing the treeless brutality of the steppes with a survivalist's ruthlessness. It's said he even murdered his own halfbrother in a dispute over food.

When he was still a teenager, he and his wife were lured into a trap and captured by a band of nomads. He was tied to a pole at night and ridiculed and abused during the day. After enduring the endless indignities of slavery, Temujin made a daring escape. Determined to exact vengeance on all those who had betrayed his family, he became a feared warrior and cunning deal maker who united the clans and tribes of the steppes, forging the greatest confederation of horse warriors who ever galloped across the earth.

Once he had consolidated his power, Temujin's years of simmering bitterness exploded into a bloodlust that still astounds the world eight hundred years later. He hunted down those who had betrayed his family and punished them in the most horrific ways. Now he was ready to pour out his wrath on all the peoples of the earth.

The statistics are mind boggling. Riding fleet war ponies, Temujin's armies seized nearly twelve million square miles of territory—more than twice as much as any other world conqueror. His hordes slaughtered at least forty million people, putting him among the top three mass murderers in history. Tens of millions were killed in China. When the shah of Persia went back on a treaty, Temujin went berserk. His killing spree left three-fourths of the population of what is now Iran dead. It ranks as history's worst genocide. Temujin never left a score unsettled.

He also left no lasting legacy. Temujin was a destroyer, not a builder. History remembers him by the name that his Mongol chieftains gave him—Genghis Khan. But that memory comes with a shudder of horror and a thankfulness that he was long ago buried in an unmarked grave.

In contrast, billions of people worship a risen Savior who changed the world by teaching love and forgiveness. Love has the power to produce breathtaking oratorios, great art, and soaring architecture. It frees slaves, lifts the oppressed, and brings joy to the world. Yet we should never forget the story of Temujin and the destructive power of bitterness. It batters children, shatters marriages, gives birth to unimaginable horrors, and destroys whole civilizations. Whenever you are tempted to go over to the dark side, remember this:

A bitter heart eats its owner and spews poison on everyone it touches.

———— ☙❧ ————

Hatred stirs up quarrels, but love makes up for all offenses.

PROVERBS 10:12

A Bad Marriage That Saved America

⁓✺⁓

Few men were as unlucky in romance. Maybe women were put off by his rawboned ugliness. Certainly his hillbilly ways were not suitable for the high society to which he aspired. The woman he loved most died, and another broke off their engagement, declaring him to be beneath her.

When he spied Mary across the ballroom floor, he said that he wanted to dance with her in the worst way. She later quipped that he did exactly that—danced with her in the worst way! But she overlooked his two left feet. Her wealthy family disapproved of the country bumpkin, so the couple dated in secret. When he begged her to marry him, her kinfolk reluctantly gave in, and she left a fourteen-room mansion for his tiny apartment.

Never were two people more unsuited for each other. She was impulsive and demanding. He was quiet and stubborn. She couldn't stand his cracker-barrel ways. He hated the way she racked up debts. Her migraine headaches rendered her insufferable, and her bipolar outbursts made it hard to retain servants. So he carried dollar bills in his pocket to bribe the help not to quit. When a salesman barged into his office to complain about her bad behavior, he said, "Surely you can endure for fifteen minutes what I have endured for twenty years!"

Seldom has anyone been as miserable as Abraham Lincoln in his marriage to Mary Todd. The White House staff referred to her as "the hellcat." While the nation endured the deprivations of the Civil War, she went on bizarre spending sprees. Newspapers ridiculed her lavish spending. They also questioned her patriotism when the widow of one of her Confederate brothers moved into the White House. After her favorite son died of typhoid fever, she roamed the halls screaming hysterically. Finally, Abe led Mary to a window, pointed to a nearby insane asylum, and said, "Mother, control your grief, or I may have to send you there!"

No American president has ever had to overcome more odds than Abraham Lincoln. Generals refused to obey him, cabinet members plotted his demise, congressmen called for his impeachment, newspaper editorials vilified him, and his popularity with voters plummeted. Though only fifty-six years old when he was assassinated, he looked thirty years older. What kept him going?

Could it be that he was able to persevere through the Civil War by not bailing out on an uncivil war in his marriage? Did he win the nation's battle because he refused to be defeated by battles in his home? His wasn't a marriage made in heaven, but heaven used it to forge a man willing to stand on the front lines of battle. Did he learn that "a house divided against itself cannot stand" when it comes to a nation because he didn't allow Mary's mental illness to divide his own house? It's not by accident that polls ranking Abraham Lincoln as our greatest president also name his wife as our worst first lady. Today you may be aching to bail out of some unpleasant commitment. Could it be that God has put you in this bad situation to forge you for better things? Remember this truth from the story of the Lincoln marriage:

Effort will give its reward only after you refuse to give up.

———— ✦ ————

Keep on loving others as long as life lasts, in order to make certain that what you hope for will come true.

HEBREWS 6:11

The Bowl of Spaghetti

⌘

The simple fisherman was no theologian. He couldn't quote more than a handful of Scriptures. But that night at the dinner table he preached as eloquent a sermon as has ever been delivered on the meaning of the Cross. The son who watched his fisherman father would go on to earn a doctorate in theology and to preach the gospel worldwide, but this sermon would be the best he ever saw.

His sister was going to the prom. Kimberly and her date were having a pre-dance dinner at home. He was a farm boy on his first date, sitting uncomfortably in a starched shirt and J. C. Penney suit. To this day, no one can figure out what possessed Kimberly's mom to serve spaghetti and meatballs to kids dressed for a prom. Three bites into his meal, a meatball dripping with sauce fell off the farm boy's fork and rolled down the front of his tie, splattering all over his white shirt. Kimberly gasped. Her brother, the future preacher, stifled a giggle. But his sister's date looked like he wanted to crawl under the table in embarrassment.

The fisherman picked up the serving bowl of spaghetti and meatballs and dumped its contents down the front of his own shirt and into his lap. As he sat there drenched in pasta and tomato sauce, everyone at the table burst into laughter. His daughter and her date relaxed. Dad had saved prom night. With the help of a borrowed white shirt and tie, the prom kids climbed into the back of a '64 station wagon and were chauffeured by Kimberly's fisherman dad to the school gym.

The fisherman will never be mentioned in the roll call of great preachers. But his preacher son has taken that dinner table sermon by Arnold Petterson around the world. This storyteller is that son, Robert Petterson.

That night, when I watched my dad pour spaghetti all over himself, I saw the glory of the gospel.

All of us know what it's like for the meatball to fall off our fork, staining us with sin. Some folks laugh at us, while others shake their head in disgust. We want to crawl under the table in shame. But God the Son stepped out of heaven. He allowed God the Father to dump a supersize bowl full of our tangled mess of sins all over him. Do you see it dripping down his face, beard, and body? Now everyone is looking at him instead of us. Do you hear the laughter at the foot of the cross? Soldiers are mocking this strange Jewish Messiah hanging there like a bloodied rag doll. Religious leaders ridicule him too. "How dare this country bumpkin rabbi suggest that the Holy God of Israel would allow himself to be covered with shame? It would be laughable if it weren't so heretical!"

When my fisherman dad dumped that bowl of spaghetti and meatballs on himself that night, he showed me what my heavenly Father did at the Cross. Surely, Arnold Petterson's story illustrates this:

Because Jesus bore all our shame, there's none left for us to bear.

He personally carried our sins in his body on the
cross so that we can be dead to sin and live for
what is right. By his wounds you are healed.

1 PETER 2:24

The Man Who Loved Rachel

⚜

No one understood disappointment better than Andy. His capacity to withstand pain was legendary. At age thirteen, he ran off to fight in the Revolutionary War. When he and his brother Robert were captured, Andy refused to shine the boots of a British officer. He was slashed across the forehead with a sword. That blow gave him a lifetime of migraine headaches.

During their imprisonment, both brothers came down with small-pox. Their mother hiked forty-five miles and somehow got her two boys released. A few days later, Robert died from the pox. Not long after Andy recovered, his mother died of cholera. He barely had time to digest her death when news came that another brother, Hugh, died of heatstroke. During that season of grief, Andy formulated a credo that would serve him well in rough years ahead: "One man with courage makes a majority."

He arose to attack life with a vengeance. When Andy wasn't fighting with local Indian tribes, he was mixing it up in barroom brawls. The hurt within drove him to inflict pain on others. Then he fell in love with Rachel. But she was a divorcée, and he had big political dreams in an age when divorce was scandalous. After he married Rachel, they discovered a court's error that meant she was still legally married to her first husband. For years afterward, Rachel was the brunt of salacious gossip. Andy fought 103 duels defending her honor. People joked that his body carried so many bullets that it shook like a bag of marbles. A bullet lodged near his heart caused coughing spasms that left his handkerchiefs soaked with blood.

But he overcame his afflictions to become a military hero in the War of 1812. He parlayed his fame into a presidential run. The stakes were great in a nation on the edge of civil war. In one of the dirtiest political campaigns in US history, his opponents portrayed Rachel as a loose woman, unfit to be the first lady. During that brutal campaign, their sixteen-year-old adopted son died of tuberculosis. Yet with toughness that earned him the nickname Old Hickory, Andy won that election in 1828. But his joy was short lived when Rachel died of an illness of the heart and lungs. A grieving Andy was sworn in at an inauguration that turned into a riot when a mob of drunken supporters trashed the White House. Newspapers gave him a new nickname: King Mob.

Andy overcame the grief of those first days to serve two terms. He managed to steer America away from the brink of civil war and wipe out the federal deficit before retiring to Nashville to live out his final years. His bloated body was racked with a persistent cough, drenching his pillows in blood. During sleepless nights, he spoke incessantly of heaven and Rachel. On his deathbed, he gasped, "I go to meet Rachel. Follow Jesus and I will see you in heaven." If you are going through a tough spell, pull out an old twenty-dollar bill. As you look at the engraving of Andrew Jackson, recall the saying that saw him through his darkest days:

One person with courage makes a majority.

―――――⚬⚭⚬―――――

One of you routs a thousand, because the LORD
your God fights for you, just as he promised.

JOSHUA 23:10, NIV

The Shantung Compound

⌒◎⌒

Langdon was born in 1919, the son of a chaplain at the University of Chicago. After he graduated from Harvard University, he went to teach English in China, which was under Japanese rule at the time. When Japan bombed Pearl Harbor and the United States declared war, the Japanese began to round up citizens of Allied nations and cart them off to concentration camps. Langdon was sent to a former Presbyterian mission compound in the coastal province of Shantung. Some 1,500 prisoners were crammed into that pitifully small place. Most were pastors, priests, missionaries, and Christian educators.

As concentration camps go, the Shantung Compound was relatively civilized. No prisoners were beaten or tortured. But there was never enough food. Langdon lost fifty pounds, more than a third of his body weight. The biggest enemies were fear and boredom. Living space was at a premium. Privacy was almost nonexistent. Chalk lines were meticulously drawn to mark off personal space. For the next three years, inmates jealously guarded their few feet of real estate, ready to fight to the death if someone crossed the chalk line.

Years later, Langdon Gilkey wrote a disturbing bestseller entitled *Shantung Compound* about his dismay at the conditions in the camp. Even the most devout missionaries were not immune to gross selfishness. Clergymen squabbled with other prisoners over food even as they stole from communal supplies. Veteran missionaries refused to share any portion of their living space with new arrivals. One preacher argued that he needed all his space to write his sermons. Hypocrisy was rampant. Fundamentalists refused to share their meals with people who smoked cigarettes, treating them like the worst sort of sinners. Yet those same preachers grabbed all the Red Cross cigarettes they could to barter for extra tins of food.

In a camp full of missionaries, the only one who could be trusted to guard the communal food store was Dick Rogers, an alcoholic ex-soldier. But many a pious preacher, whose ration of food depended on Dick's strength of character, still considered him immoral because he drank.

Langdon was most disillusioned when the Red Cross delivered 2,100 food parcels to the compound. The Japanese decreed that, because the parcels came from the United States, each of the three hundred American prisoners would get first choice. The remaining 1,800 parcels were to be shared with the rest of the prisoners. But the American clergy caucused and formally protested that the Japanese were grossly unfair. They demanded that, because the parcels came from the *American* Red Cross, the three hundred US citizens should receive all of them!

Young Langdon Gilkey almost lost his faith as a result of the moral failures of Christians in that camp. Some sixty years later, he reminds us all that the best of saints have sinful hearts. Sadly, they will often sacrifice everything to meet their own needs. On the other hand, he saw heroic Christians who sacrificed everything to help fellow prisoners. Langdon Gilkey's story teaches us an important truth:

You do not own what you refuse to give away to others. It owns you. Only when you freely give it away are you free.

_____ ⸎ _____

Even though "I am allowed to do anything,"
I must not become a slave to anything.
1 CORINTHIANS 6:12

188

The Cover-Up
of the Century

ᘒᖆᘓ

The scandal rocked the nation and almost ended the career of a political superstar. It was 1931, and the candidate was about to run for the highest office in the land. But there was a dirty little secret that would have stopped his 1932 presidential campaign dead in its tracks. The candidate had entered into an illicit affair with a young woman half his age by the name of Angela. That would have been explosive enough. But even the most liberal voters would have been scandalized by a middle-aged bachelor's incestuous obsession with his niece.

Angela was ravishingly beautiful, a long-legged femme fatale who made heads turn when she walked down the street. Those who remember her say that she had a seductive, almost frightening, beauty that beguiled everyone she met.

Her uncle should have walked away from Angela when he set his sights on the nation's highest office. Instead he became more obsessed, moving her into a room in his apartment and forcing her to travel incognito in his black Mercedes as he barnstormed across the land. His bodyguards shadowed her every move. When she began a flirtatious affair with his driver, he fired the man. When she ran off to a faraway city, his agents dragged her back.

After she told her uncle that she had fallen in love with a Jewish musician, he exploded in his trademark fury. Neighbors complained to the police that a terrible fight had taken place. After he left in a rage for a campaign meeting, cops broke through the door to find Angela's corpse. She had died of a single gunshot wound. Her beautiful nose was shattered, bruises and cuts covered her body, and her uncle's 6.35mm Walther pistol lay beside her.

News outlets trumpeted the story across the world, and political opponents moved to exploit the situation. It was quickly becoming the scandal of the century, even fueling speculation that the uncle had killed his niece.

But the best cover-up team in history worked for this presidential candidate. His spin doctors went into damage control. Agents quickly removed Angela's body, a sham autopsy was performed, bribes and threats silenced officials, and the candidate's niece was hastily buried. To this day, calls to exhume the body have been met by silence from officials unwilling to dig up scandals of the past.

As far as cover-ups go, it was a political masterpiece. But it's too bad that the candidate's niece didn't live. She might have warned the world about the madman who would soon unleash an unimaginable reign of terror. Angela Raubal was perhaps the first person who was murdered by her uncle, Adolf Hitler. Millions more would be murdered after he became Germany's president.

Beware of damage control. Small indiscretions ignored can grow into monsters beyond our control—whether it's politicians getting away with murder, or you and I getting away with our sins. The skillful cover-up of a single murder can lead to the attempted cover-up of six million. Rejoice when your misdeeds are exposed while they are still manageable, changeable, and fixable.

The worst sins are the ones you get away with.

———— ❧ ————

You may be sure that your sin will find you out.

NUMBERS 32:23

Never Enough

⁓⊙⊙⊙⁓

Quince could never do enough. Though his parents lavished him with love, they also expected big things from their firstborn son. Maybe that's what fueled his insatiable desire to learn more, be more, and do more. This obsession would consume Quince's life, leaving him perpetually frustrated and unhappy.

By the time he entered Harvard as a teenager, he had mastered seven languages and translated Homer, Virgil, Plutarch, and Aristotle into English. He graduated with honors and quickly passed the bar exam. When a romance threatened his ambitions, he broke off the relationship and drove himself to build one of the most prodigious résumés in history.

He went to work for the government of his new nation, drafting several critical treaties and writing much of President Washington's farewell address. He became America's voice to the world when he served as US ambassador to several major European nations. If that wasn't enough, Quince was elected to Congress and the Senate before turning down a presidential appointment to the Supreme Court. This overachiever was also a member of the prestigious Academy of Sciences, a Harvard professor, and the US secretary of state. In spite of his dizzying success, his family pushed him to aim even higher.

In 1824, the man known to his friends as Quince became the sixth president of the United States. You remember him as John Quincy Adams. He was a man of uncommon courage who refused to compromise his abolitionist principles when America was careening toward a civil war. That courage cost him reelection.

Yet Adams was not finished. He became the only ex-president to serve again as a congressman. As a tireless crusader against slavery, he argued the landmark case of the *Amistad* slave ship before the US Supreme Court. His brilliant defense of human rights began the dismantling of the African slave trade. At age eighty, he was still fighting for the emancipation of slaves when he suffered two strokes on the floor of the House. He died within hours.

Seldom has a life achieved so much good for so many. Yet it was never enough. Look at the faded daguerreotype of Adams, the first US president to sit for a photograph. Study his many portraits. You will see a frowning and unhappy face. If you search the seventeen thousand pages of his personal diary, you will find precious few glimmers of personal satisfaction. One entry is especially haunting: "My life has been spent in vain and idle aspirations." To his dying day, this prodigious overachiever felt that he had accomplished little or nothing of value.

John Quincy Adams's story begs a question: When is enough, enough? It is one thing to be too easily contented with mediocrity. It is quite another to find little joy or contentment in a job well done. Overachievers everywhere need to stop occasionally and savor the little victories along the way. Maybe we should heed the epithet on the tomb of that overachiever Alexander the Great:

A tomb now suffices him for whom the world was not enough.

———— ✺ ————

True godliness with contentment is itself great
wealth. After all, we brought nothing with us
when we came into the world, and we can't
take anything with us when we leave it.

1 TIMOTHY 6:6-7

The Magnificent Seven

꿍

There were huge fortunes to be made in the Roaring Twenties. That's why the summit meeting at the Edgewater Beach Hotel in Chicago mesmerized the nation. Newspapers called the participants the Magnificent Seven. The collective power of these men was greater than that of the federal government.

Sitting at the great mahogany table was Charles Schwab, the president of the world's largest steel company. His lavish lifestyle was the stuff of tabloid legend. Less flamboyant, but equally powerful, was Arthur Cutten, the world's biggest wheat speculator. No one was more magnificent than Richard Whitney, who eventually became the president of the New York Stock Exchange. The stock market was a rampaging bull in the '20s, and Whitney rode it like a rodeo champion.

The man holding the most political clout was Albert Fall, one of the ten richest men in America, a US senator, and a key member of the president's cabinet. But he may not have controlled the future of America as much as Jesse Livermore, nicknamed "the Bear of Wall Street," or Ivar Kreuger, the Swedish industrialist who headed the world's largest monopoly. Surely attorney Leon Fraser was the least of the Magnificent Seven. But he would end up controlling the banking industry as president of the Bank of International Settlement.

Indeed, this was the greatest concentration of power and wealth ever assembled in one room. But that was 1923, only six years before the Great Depression. In 1950, a Chicago reporter decided to follow up on these power brokers to see what happened to them. The story he wrote is well worth recalling seventy years later.

Steel magnate Charles Schwab's fortune was wiped out in the crash of

1929, and he lived on borrowed money the last five years of his life. Wheat speculator Arthur Cutten died before he could be brought to trial. Richard Whitney, president of the New York Stock Exchange, was found guilty of embezzling millions. He had just been released from Sing Sing Prison in 1950. US senator Albert Fall was convicted of bribery in the biggest government scandal of all time. In 1944 he was paroled from prison to die at home. Jesse Livermore, Leon Fraser, and Ivar Kreuger all committed suicide when their financial empires were exposed as Ponzi schemes.

Ivar Kreuger was an avowed atheist. The rest of the Magnificent Seven may not have been atheists, but they lived as if God didn't exist. Take a deeper look at their individual stories, and you will discover that each had a soul hunger that could never be satisfied by all the profit, prestige, and power of this world. Their uncontrollable appetites led to their ruin. French philosopher Blaise Pascal said that there is a God-shaped vacuum within each of us. The finite stuff of this world cannot fill the black hole in us that could swallow whole universes and still be empty. That's why it's so important to ponder the tragic stories of the Magnificent Seven. Surely they prove Blaise Pascal's solution to our dilemma:

Only an infinite God can fill the infinite hole in each of us.

――――⊙⊙――――

Jesus replied, "I am the bread of life.
Whoever comes to me will never be hungry again.
Whoever believes in me will never be thirsty."

JOHN 6:35

Bringing Home the Gold

✧

Do you know who brought home the most gold medals from a single Olympic Games? If your answer is Usain Bolt, guess again. History's fastest sprinter won nine gold medals over three Olympics, but he doesn't come close. Mark Spitz amazed the world when he won seven gold medals in the 1972 Olympics. But Michael Phelps broke his record in the 2012 games. Phelps earned twenty-three gold medals over four Olympics, many more than the next closest Olympian!

But nobody did it better than Doug. Don't look for him among the roster of Olympians. As a middle-aged soldier, he was never going to compete. But he single-handedly made America a sports superpower in the 1928 Amsterdam games.

The games were only a year away when the president of the US Olympic Committee died, setting off a power struggle between America's amateur sports bodies. This rivalry almost derailed efforts to send a team to Amsterdam. But few Americans cared. The modern Olympic movement was still in its infancy, and the country was on the precipice of the Great Depression. Most folks figured that fielding a team was a waste of money.

At the eleventh hour, the Olympic Committee turned to Doug, hoping against hope that this tough-nosed superintendent of a military school could get the job done. Doug proved himself a dynamo. He barnstormed across America raising funds and hand-selecting his athletes, and then relentlessly pushed them to be the best in the world. He harangued coaches and made life miserable for slackers, arguing that this Olympic venture was war minus the weapons.

When Doug's hastily assembled team arrived in the Netherlands, he drove them harder. He personally attended every practice. After officials made an unfair decision and some of his Olympians threatened to quit in protest, Doug bellowed, "Americans never quit!" When he was criticized for being too tough on his team, he retorted, "We have not come three thousand miles to lose gracefully. We are here to win and win decisively!"

Americans certainly won decisively in 1928. No team ever took home a larger percentage of medals. Doug's Olympians won twenty-four gold medals, more than twice as many as the next two countries combined. The US powerhouse set seventeen Olympic and seven world records. Though their medal haul was a team effort, it's no stretch to credit Doug with single-handedly bringing home the gold.

The 1928 Amsterdam Olympics wouldn't be Doug's last epic campaign. You remember Doug as a great American hero in World War II: General Douglas MacArthur. With the same tough-nosed perseverance that produced one of history's greatest Olympic teams, he led American forces to victory in the Southwest Pacific. Maybe you are going for the gold in some area of your life today, but the odds are stacked against you. Perhaps, like some of Doug's Olympians, you are ready to quit in protest. You might want to remember the amazing story of the 1928 Olympics and something else Doug said:

On the fields of friendly strife are sown the seeds . . . of victory.

———— ঙ৩৩ ————

Be strong and courageous! Do not be afraid or discouraged. For the LORD your God is with you wherever you go.

JOSHUA 1:9

Unlucky in Love

❦

When it came to women, John couldn't win for losing. Every romantic relationship turned sour, and his one foray into marriage was a disaster. He died a childless old man with only one lifelong friend, his brother.

Maybe no woman could measure up to his indomitable mother. Perhaps he hadn't learned how to love as a child. His obstinate daddy and strong-willed mother constantly fought. John couldn't remember how many times his dad angrily stormed out of the house, abandoning his family for months at a time.

Yet, through his mother's mentoring, John became a towering intellect and spellbinding orator. People flocked to hear his sermons. Women were especially drawn to his charisma. His first romance was with Sally. But she was highborn, and the rigid class system of eighteenth-century England doomed their relationship.

So John fled to colonial America. There he set his sights on Sophy. She adored the charismatic clergyman, but he was slow to commit. Tired of waiting, she accepted a proposal from another suitor. When she asked John to perform the wedding, he angrily refused. His pettiness caused an uproar. So John went back to England, never to return to America.

When he got deathly ill, Grace nursed him back to health. John proposed marriage, but she called off the wedding and married someone else. John again felt the sting of rejection.

Three years later, he married the widow Molly. It was the biggest mistake of his life. John soon discovered that Molly was possessive, perpetually angry that she took second place to his ministry, and jealous when he spent too much time with wealthy women donors. It wasn't long before their arguments turned into screaming tirades.

Before he left on a preaching tour of Ireland, he cruelly said, "I hope I shall see your wicked face no more." When he returned, Molly came out of the house cursing and beating him with a broom. Preacher John quickly got back on his horse and galloped away. After she left him for good, he wrote in his journal, "I did not leave her. I did not send her away. I will not call her back."

Maybe no woman could ever measure up to John's mother, Susanna. It's one of the ironies of history that John Wesley preached towering sermons on Christ's love but was uncomfortable loving people. He healed so many broken hearts and yet managed to break his share of them. Wesley was a deeply flawed man. Yet God used him to spark the revivals that swept across colonial America, to found the Methodist Church, and to transform millions of lives.

Maybe you feel too flawed to be of use to God. You might take comfort from an old Puritan saying that applies to John Wesley and to all of us: *God can take a crooked stick and make a straight line.*

God chose things the world considers foolish in order to shame those who think they are wise. And he chose things that are powerless to shame those who are powerful.

1 CORINTHIANS 1:27

Too Big to Miss

◦◦◦

Judean winds whistle through the valley, calling the present to remember the past. As you pick up stones in a dried-up creek bed, through the ears of your imagination you hear the rattling of swords as ancient spirits rise to fight again. Then cars on a nearby freeway jolt you back to reality. You wonder if these passing motorists realize what took place in this Valley of Elah some three thousand years ago. Let your thoughts take you back to that magical day.

A giant lumbers out across that valley day after day. Goliath is the original Megatron, standing some nine feet tall. With his enormous bulk, armor, and weapons, he weighs in at some six hundred pounds—one gargantuan mass of bronze glistening in the Judean sun. The Philistines have found their weapon of mass destruction in this incredible hulk.

Half the valley shakes as he bellows his blasphemies across the creek in a voice that is Darth Vader on reverb. "Choose a man, and have him come out and fight me!" But the Israelites cower behind rocks, mesmerized, hypnotized, and paralyzed. For forty straight days they watch helplessly as the giant struts his awesome stuff.

Not much has changed in three thousand years. Every day, giants lumber forth to challenge us. We crawl out of bed and march out to battle, banging on shields and rattling sabers. We boast that *this* time we will beat our Goliath. Then the giant roars, and our courage melts.

According to tradition, Goliath had four brothers, all of them giants too. Giants come at us in packs. They appear in various shapes and sizes. Only you know the Goliaths you will face in your Valley of Elah. But God made you to be a giant slayer.

Look again. Do you see the herder of sheep from Bethlehem? He's just a pip-squeak boy. Get to know David, and you discover that he has feet of clay just like you. You may only have a few stones and a sling. Yet ablaze with God's Spirit, pip-squeaks with clay feet topple giants. And when they have the courage to walk out into the valley of giants, the people of God take heart. They rise up with a shout, inspired by a pip-squeak with a slingshot. Those who dare to be a David become the leaders who change the world.

Maybe it's all about perspective. King Saul was a mighty warrior, towering above everyone else in Israel. But Saul was a big man with a small heart. He took one look at Goliath and said, "That giant's too big to hit." David was the runt of the litter, but he had a heart bigger than all outdoors. He looked at Goliath and said, "He's too big to miss." David could have written the German proverb that says, "Fear makes the wolf bigger than he is." Perhaps David looked a thousand years into the future and saw his great descendant Jesus of Nazareth defeat Goliath when he crushed Satan at the Cross. If you are facing some giant today, remember this amazing fact:

When Jesus defeated Satan, he toppled all our giants too. We simply have to rise up and claim victories already won.

Thank God! He gives us victory over sin and
death through our Lord Jesus Christ. So, my dear
brothers and sisters, be strong and immovable.

1 CORINTHIANS 15:57-58

Stuttering to Stardom

❦

It was hard enough growing up black in rural Mississippi during the 1930s. But when the family moved to Michigan, the boy was traumatized. Shortly after the move, Todd began to stutter. Perhaps it was because of the move. Or maybe God was punishing him because he made fun of his stuttering Uncle Randy. When kids in school teased him, he was positive God had cursed him.

So Todd retreated into a world of self-imposed silence. He might stutter a few words in the safety of his home, but he was mute in public for eight long years. He says that he only felt safe talking to animals on the farm.

During those silent years, Todd learned to listen. He also developed a vivid imagination that found its expression in poetry. When he handed in a poem, his English teacher said that it was too good to have been written by a high school student. He challenged Todd to stand in front of the class and recite the poem. Only then would he prove that he had composed it. The truth is, this teacher had taken a keen interest in Todd, and was using this test to unleash his voice.

A trembling Todd began to stutter out his poem. Then it was as if a dam broke, and a torrent of words flooded out of his pent-up soul. He didn't lose his stutter, but he did go on to college and the army. When he was discharged, Todd headed for Broadway. He became a janitor, cleaning almost every toilet in every theater, until he got his first break in the play *Sunrise at Campobello*. He had a small moment on stage, delivering a single line: "Mrs. Roosevelt, supper is served." He got as far as "Mrs." and that dreaded letter: "M-M-M-M . . ." After stuttering through his one line, he almost ran off the stage.

Who would have guessed that mute Todd Jones would grow up to give the world its most recognizable voice: the deep, mellifluous, powerful, bass tones of a bigger-than-life man? Todd was a childhood nickname. But the world knows him as James Earl Jones, the iconic voice of Darth Vader in *Star Wars* and Mufasa in Walt Disney's *The Lion King*. He still stutters when stressed, but that hasn't kept him from carving out a towering acting career, or earning two Emmys, two Tonys, and an Academy Award for his performances in blockbuster films such as *The Great White Hope* and *Fences*.

Maybe you're insecure about your voice. God has given you something to say, but you don't know how to say it. So you remain silent when your world needs to hear you. Let the story of James Earl Jones inspire you to speak, even if your words come out stuttering. Yours may not become the world's most recognizable voice, but God wants to speak through you. Moses stuttered too. When he tried to talk God out of making him a prophet, the Lord said to him—and all of us:

Speak the truth, even if your voice shakes.

--- ❧ ---

Who makes a person's mouth? Who decides
whether people speak or do not speak . . . ? Is it not I,
the LORD? Now go! I will be with you as you speak.

EXODUS 4:11-12

Denied a Stage,
Given a Nation

✦

She was born with the voice of an angel. Her church choir called the six-year-old prodigy Baby Contralto. But her family lived on the poor side of town, and her hardworking daddy barely eked out a living. He did manage to scrape together enough to purchase a secondhand piano, but there was nothing left over for lessons. So his child prodigy trained herself.

When she was twelve, her daddy died, leaving her family penniless. By now Baby Contralto was able to sing soprano, alto, tenor, or bass. The world should be glad that her church choir, made up of poor folk, scraped together $500 to pay for the services of a well-known voice teacher.

Not long after, the New York Philharmonic Society discovered Baby Contralto. After performing at Carnegie Hall, she took Europe by storm. By the 1930s she was famous throughout Europe and the United States. Famed conductor Arturo Toscanini said that a voice like hers comes along once in a century. After she performed at the White House, her manager tried to book her at Constitution Hall in Washington, DC. But the owners of this iconic hall, the Daughters of the American Revolution (DAR), refused to allow the world's greatest contralto to sing there.

Their refusal makes no sense, unless you know Baby Contralto's given name, Marian Anderson. Although she sang before European royalty and US presidents, she was not even allowed to stay in most American hotels. The DAR also had a rule that only white artists could perform on their stage. People of color, like Marian Anderson, were restricted to the balcony.

So First Lady Eleanor Roosevelt arranged a concert at the Lincoln

Memorial. On a cold Easter day in 1939, the world's greatest contralto sang before seventy-five thousand people on the Mall and to a nationwide radio audience. The secretary of the interior introduced her with these words: "Genius, like justice, is blind. Genius draws no color lines."

One of the millions glued to their radios that day was a ten-year-old boy in Atlanta. Martin would later say that Ms. Anderson's heroic concert inspired his dream to change America. Twenty-four years later, Dr. Martin Luther King Jr. stood on the same steps at the Lincoln Memorial. In his famous "I Have a Dream" speech, he quoted lyrics from Baby Contralto's first song that day: "My country, 'tis of thee, sweet land of liberty . . . Let freedom ring!" Though Marian Anderson would become a legendary diva, win the Presidential Medal of Freedom and the Grammy Lifetime Achievement Award, she was most proud of that concert at the Lincoln Memorial and how it inspired a ten-year-old boy to change the world.

Sometimes the world tries to shut up the voice that God has given us. But there are truths that must be sung to the heavens. You may feel like a solitary little bird warbling your song into the face of a howling wind. But others are listening. So remember this:

The song of truth will find its echo in those who listen.

———— ⌒⌒⌒ ————

The LORD your God is living among you. He is
a mighty savior. He will take delight in you with
gladness. With his love, he will calm all your fears.
He will rejoice over you with joyful songs.

ZEPHANIAH 3:17

Singing to Johnny

❧

Christine was proclaimed one of the outstanding singers in America. She had big offers from record labels and was looking forward to a full schedule of concerts. Her agent predicted that she would be a recording star. Singing was her life and performing was her passion.

Everything changed that harrowing night Christine gave birth to baby Johnny. The doctor was inexcusably drunk. He broke several of the baby's bones as he pulled him from the birth canal. The violence of that delivery resulted in severe hemorrhaging of the newborn's brain. The inebriated obstetrician would lose his license to practice and later commit suicide. But that didn't help Christine's baby.

During the first year, eight doctors said that he could not possibly survive. For his first two years, she had to feed him every three hours with a special feeder. It took more than an hour to accomplish each feeding. During those two years Christine never left her home. She didn't get more than two hours of sleep at any one time. The voice that enraptured thousands now sang simple lullabies to a child with severe disabilities.

Johnny lived twenty-four years. He was totally paralyzed, only able to sit in a wheelchair with the assistance of a full-length body brace. Convinced that God had called her to care for her son, Christine never went back to the concert stage. She bathed, clothed, and lifted his limp body in and out of the wheelchair, spoon-fed him—and above all, sang to him.

Christine's husband, John Edmund Haggai, is a noted evangelist, author, and global missions leader. He wrote her story in his moving book *My Son Johnny*. What amazed him most was the way Christine showered their son with unconditional love for more than eight thousand straight days. She never once resented the fact that her music career died the day

Johnny was born. She felt that God had given her a voice to sing her boy into heaven. Even more amazing was the fact that she never complained that she was marooned in a small world with a helpless son who demanded every ounce of her energy and patience.

But the thing that most impressed John Haggai was that he never once heard Christine say an unkind word about the doctor who injured her son and destroyed her career. In fact, she wept when she heard that he had committed suicide. Her forgiveness of that obstetrician was as complete and unconditional as her love for Johnny.

Her husband proudly said that at age forty, after years of unending servitude, Christine possessed the youthful sparkle that would be the envy of any high school senior, and the charm and beauty for which any debutant would gladly give a fortune. Haggai believed that her ability to forgive made her more beautiful. Isn't that what makes Jesus so immeasurably beautiful? Nowhere do you see that more than when Jesus forgave those who crucified him. When we fail to forgive those who have hurt us deeply, or resent circumstances that derail our dreams, we need to remember something that Martin Luther King Jr. often said:

Forgiveness is not an occasional act but a permanent attitude.

He has removed our sins as far from
us as the east is from the west.

PSALM 103:12

The Secret Garden of Love

⌀

Jehan looked at life through a lawyer's eyes—he was cold, calculating, and rational. To this day he remains the poster child for rigid dogmatism. His theology has been vilified for producing an austere form of Puritan Protestantism.

Above all else, Jehan was a loner. He wanted nothing more in life than to escape to his library and churn out theological tomes. But he was a gifted preacher, and he seemed destined for the pulpit. Even so, he was determined to remain the lonely bachelor pastor. Yet his superiors begged their scholarly and unsentimental cleric to find a suitable wife.

So the reluctant Frenchman began his search, conducting it in the most unromantic way by interviewing candidates for the job. He even announced with his characteristic efficiency, "I plan to marry a little after Easter."

The first candidate was unsuitable because she did not speak French. The second was fifteen years older than Jehan. The third fell head over heels in love with the pastor, but after they started making plans for the wedding, he decided he didn't like her. He was so embarrassed by this debacle that he almost gave up.

It was now 1540, a year into his laborious search. Jehan was thirty-one when Idelette, a young woman in his church, lost her husband to the plague. She spoke French, held to his strict doctrinal views, and was pleasing to the eye. After Jehan cross-examined her like a prosecuting attorney, he pronounced her fit to marry.

Idelette was more than fit for Jehan. She would transform this cold lawyer-turned-preacher into a passionate lover. Both were frail and came down with illnesses shortly after their wedding, so the two were forced to spend quiet days at home together. They recovered to become a dynamic duo. Her love would empower him to change the course of history. He wrote that Idelette was "the faithful helper of my ministry" and "the best companion of my life."

Tragedy would draw them even closer. Their first child together died after two weeks, their second died at birth, and their third was born premature—only to die. Jehan's beloved Idelette was still in her thirties when she contracted tuberculosis and only forty when she lay on her deathbed. Every afternoon, the pastor would hurry home to his dying sweetheart and tenderly carry her into the warm sunshine of their garden for afternoons together. When she died, Jehan was inconsolable. He lamented, "My best life's companion has been taken from me." He would remain grief stricken to the end of his life.

History remembers Jehan Cauvin by his anglicized name, John Calvin. He is remembered as the crafter of Calvinism, the promoter of predestination, and the progenitor of Puritanism. His portraits show an austere and forbidding lawyer. Few people know the romantic side of this towering theologian—a secret passion born of a woman's love. Today, if you walk through a cemetery in Geneva, you will find his previously unmarked grave next to that of Idelette, their bodies waiting to rise together on Resurrection Day. On soft Geneva breezes you might hear a whisper that John Calvin would surely appreciate:

Unconditional love irresistibly opens closed hearts.

———— ✤ ————

Knowledge will become useless. But love will last forever!

1 CORINTHIANS 13:8

The Staying Power of a Momentary Lapse

⋅⊙⊙⋅

More than anything else, Wayne despised losing. He once said, "I've hated to lose ever since I was a kid and threw away the mallets when I lost at croquet." That determination to win drove Wayne to dizzying heights of success.

Long after his death, millions still revere him. And well they should. As a football coach, he stands among giants like Vince Lombardi, Knute Rockne, and Bear Bryant. This gruff, take-no-prisoners coach led his university's teams to two hundred and five victories during his twenty-eight-year tenure. He amassed thirteen conference titles and five national championships. His refusal to lose willed his players to win 80 percent of their games.

Yet there was a soft side to Wayne that few ever saw. He was one of the first coaches in his conference to recruit African Americans. Though he pushed his players to win on the gridiron, he was more concerned that they graduate. He was a molder of men and a comforter of the wounded. When a sportscaster asked Wayne to visit a young boy in a hospital burn unit, the coach said that he could stay only a few minutes. Instead of heading back to prepare for a big game, he stayed with the boy all evening. As he was leaving, the lad asked to see Wayne's Heisman Trophy winner. The next day, the All-American halfback visited the boy at coach's orders. His ex-players remember Wayne as the greatest influence in their lives. They recall him digging deep into his pockets to bail them out of financial problems and encouraging them in rough times.

Yet the world remembers Wayne for one momentary lapse of temper.

Folks should have seen it coming. There were earlier incidents, such as when a player sported a tie in the color of their biggest rival and Wayne angrily tore it off in front of a roomful of people. Meltdowns in front of reporters became frequent, and his tirades were embarrassing. Some said that the coach was losing it.

Then came the 1978 Gator Bowl. Wayne's Ohio State team was trailing by two points but had driven to the Clemson twenty-four-yard line as the clock was running out. They were in position to kick a game-winning field goal, when the coach inexplicably called for his quarterback to pass the ball. It was intercepted. As the Clemson player got up after being tackled, an enraged Wayne "Woody" Hayes slugged him in the face. The punch took less than three seconds. But a split-second decision ended a storied career.

More than a hundred years after his birth, Wayne "Woody" Hayes remains a legend in the Buckeye Nation. But try to talk about his achievements, and most folks will remind you of that one punch. A single rash act can destroy a reputation. Do you remember Pete Rose for holding multiple major-league records, or for being banned from baseball for betting on games? Do you recall Richard Nixon for opening the door to China, or for his Watergate debacle? That solitary punch teaches us all a powerful lesson:

A momentary lapse can ruin a lifetime of legacy.

Enthusiasm without knowledge is no good;
haste makes mistakes.

PROVERBS 19:2

The Lion Who Roamed Google Earth

෴

His mother named him Lion, but her little ragamuffin hardly looked like one. While she lugged stones at construction sites, Lion rode the back of his brother's bicycle to a nearby railway station to beg.

He idolized his nine-year-old brother, Guddu. Maybe that's why he insisted on going with him that night. Guddu left him asleep on a railway platform. When Lion woke up, his brother was gone. He was searching for Guddu inside a railroad car when the doors shut tight and the train began to speed down the tracks. Trapped and alone, he curled up in exhausted sleep. In the morning, lush forests rushed by in a blur of unfamiliar landscape.

When the train stopped in Calcutta, doors slid open and the lost boy was set free into the teeming masses. He wandered streets stalked by predators looking for children to sell to sex traffickers. Lion might as well have been on another planet—dark and sinister. At a police station, he didn't know the name of his village. When they showed him a map, he was unable to decipher names and places. So he was put in a home for street urchins and later transferred to an orphanage. But his good looks and personality made him perfect for adoption. Before long, Lion was off to Australia and the Brierleys.

Lavished with love by his adoptive parents, he grew into a proper Aussie. But he never forgot his village. Guddu appeared in his dreams, calling him home. Lion was now obsessed with finding his birth family. But when he looked at the map, he was overwhelmed by India's vastness.

He didn't know how far he had traveled from his home. He did know that there are almost a million villages in India. He calculated the speed of the train and how long he had been on it. He figured six hundred miles and drew a circle that big around Calcutta. But train routes radiate out from that city like a gigantic spiderweb. For five years Lion prowled Google Earth, zooming in on village after village as childhood memories flooded back. When he found the water tower at the station where his odyssey began, he hit pay dirt. He zoomed in to retrace the steps back to the village of his birth. Google Earth had taken him home!

A few months later, Lion experienced a joyful reunion with his mother. She never gave up hope that her Lion would return. He was shattered to discover that Guddu had been killed a month after they were separated, yet he found a passel of nephews and a niece. Today Saroo (the Hindi name for Lion) still lives in Australia, but he visits his Indian mother often. You can read his story, *A Long Journey Home*, or watch it in the movie *Lion*. It reminds us that we all long to go home. We should never take family for granted. Above all, we should long to go home to our heavenly Father. ***The best journeys in life always take us home.***

He returned home to his father. And while he was
still a long way off, his father saw him coming. Filled
with love and compassion, he ran to his son.

LUKE 15:20

Theo's Big Brother

ﻌﯣﺤﺤ

It was bad enough that Theo's older brother was ravaged in body and sick at heart. Now he was locked in an insane asylum because his neighbors said he was too crazy to be on the loose.

Maybe things would have been different if his preacher father hadn't been so austere or his mother so moody. Theo's older brother never felt loved as a child, nor could he shake the fact that his parents had given him the same name as their stillborn son, who had been delivered exactly one year before he was born. It's hard enough to see your name and birth date etched on a tombstone; it's devastating to feel that you're a replacement for the child your grieving parents really wanted.

He tried to curry favor with his father by studying for seminary and then volunteering to serve at a poor church other preachers avoided. He loved working among poor miners and potato eaters. They returned his love by nicknaming him Christ of the Coal Mines. It was the only time Theo's big brother ever felt loved. But before long, church leaders fired him for being too unconventional.

He tried his hand at art but insisted on painting subjects no one wanted to see on canvas. He sold only one out of more than two thousand paintings. He searched for romance, even resorting to bizarre acts in the name of love, but he was rejected by every woman except an alcoholic prostitute. It wasn't long before he, too, was drowning in booze.

Now he was in the asylum, looking through bars at a starry night. The world can thank Theo for believing that his older brother still had a spark of genius. If he hadn't brought art supplies to the asylum, perhaps his brother wouldn't have put on canvas what he saw through the bars. The lunatic laid his work aside with a shrug. No one would purchase this painting either.

When he was released, he took the painting to Theo's apartment along with the other unsold canvases full of sunflowers, reapers, and potato eaters. Theo promised to sell the works, but his older brother had already given up hope. Not long after, he shot himself. When Theo took his body to the church, the priest refused to hold a funeral for a man who had committed suicide. Instead, Theo took the coffin to a tavern, surrounded it with his brother's paintings, and celebrated his memory with drunks, starving artists, and prostitutes.

Theo died before he could sell his brother's paintings. But Theo's widow, Johanna van Gogh, made good on her husband's promise to Vincent. She might be shocked to know that one day Vincent van Gogh's *Starry Night*, seen through the bars of that asylum, would become his most famous work—or that one of his paintings would fetch as much as $82 million.

No life is ever wasted or without hope. Even in a hopeless asylum, we can still see a starry night through the bars. Theo's older brother gave up hope too soon. You won't, if you hold on to this truth:

It takes the darkest nights to produce the brightest stars.

———— ✧ ————

He counts the stars and calls them all by name.
How great is our Lord! His power is absolute!

PSALM 147:4-5

The Legend of the Lost Legion

❦

How did Rome lose an entire legion of some five thousand men—an elite army known as the Eagle? It is one of history's most enduring and unsolved mysteries, the subject of endless debate, speculation, novels, and movies.

The Ninth Legion was last seen in Britannia on the ragged edges of Rome's empire. When a coalition of Picts and other tribes invaded from the rugged highlands of Scotland, the legion moved into action. They were last seen marching into the swirling mists of northland forests where they vanished without a trace.

Or did they? Perhaps the answer to their disappearance is more mundane. Some scholars say that they were simply transferred. After all, this crack legion had fought in Hispania and Gaul before taking part in the Roman invasion of the British Isles in AD 43. Archeological digs in the Rhine Valley have uncovered evidence that legionnaires from Britannia were later barracked there. Yet it is inconclusive, hanging on fibers embedded in the rust of ancient sandal nails.

A dig near York, England, is more compelling. In AD 108 a gateway to a legionary fortress was built there. Its inscription credits the Ninth with its construction. This proves that the Eagle Legion was in the north of England just prior to the invasion of the Picts.

Maybe the most intriguing evidence is wrapped in the lore of Scotland. Local historian Andrew Hennessey tells about a labyrinth of underground caverns north of Hadrian's Wall. There have long been rumors of some ancient treasure in their unexplored depths. But because of the extreme danger from trapped gasses, they are off limits to hikers and spelunkers.

Hennessey relates an eyewitness account of explorers who defied warning signs and ventured deep into the caverns. There they discovered an underground lake on fire with methane gas. One of them climbed down into a deeper cavern. When he reached the bottom, he excitedly shouted that it was littered with the remains of dead horses and horse armor, skeletons clothed in Roman armor, weapons and shields, and a standard. (Was it the Eagle?) As the methane gasses began to render them all dizzy, the man's companions shouted to him to get out. But it was too late. They dragged his body up by a rope and hightailed it out of that chamber of horrors, leaving its mysteries locked deep within.

Could it be that the Scottish Picts lured the superior forces of the Ninth into this deadly labyrinth to gas them to death? We may never know. To check out the claims of those explorers, we would have to find our way into and out of one of nature's gas chambers. Some mysteries are best left to the realm of the imagination.

Perhaps we should rather focus on people who have lost their way *today*—those who have lost heart and hope, their moral bearings, sense of direction, or reason for living. We cannot rescue those long dead. But we can find the living dead and bring them home to our heavenly Father's house.

Get off the cruise ship and launch out in a lifeboat.

————— ∽◌◦◌∾ —————

Jesus told him, "Let the spiritually dead
bury their own dead! Your duty is to go and
preach about the Kingdom of God."

LUKE 9:60

216

The Prince of Preachers

At twenty-one years of age, he was his nation's biggest celebrity. His Sunday sermons were printed on the front page of newspapers and then reproduced and sold on London streets. The demand for these printed sermons was so great that more than a hundred million copies were sold worldwide. Explorer David Livingstone even carried them in his pockets as he hacked his way through African jungles.

So many people wanted to hear him preach that police had to be called in for crowd control. The biggest auditoriums in London weren't big enough. So he announced that he would preach in the music hall at the Royal Surrey Gardens. Polite society was scandalized. Vaudeville shows and circuses performed before raucous, beer-swilling crowds at the Surrey Music Hall.

British clergymen railed against him and newspaper articles condemned him as a publicity-seeking sensationalist. Yet on a Sunday evening in October of 1858, traffic jams stretched back seven miles as massive crowds shoved their way into the Surrey Gardens. As the young pastor stood up before the packed music hall, several people began to yell, "Fire!" Panicked people stampeded to the exits. Seven people were crushed to death and twenty-eight critically injured. The preacher boy was led out past twisted corpses laid out on the lawn. When he got home, he collapsed into his young wife's arms, sobbing uncontrollably. He was carried to his bed, where he lay in a fetal position for two weeks. In the days to follow, both preachers and newspaper editorials across Great Britain said that the tragedy was God's judgment on holding a church service on the devil's playground.

We can be glad that young Charles Spurgeon finally got up. He overcame suicidal despair to start a college, open a string of orphanages, and produce sixty-four volumes of the greatest sermons ever preached. At age twenty-three he ignored his critics and held services at the Crystal Palace, the largest auditorium in England. He spoke to the biggest crowds ever to hear a preacher. Four years later he opened the mammoth Metropolitan Tabernacle, the first megachurch in history.

Though he has been called the Prince of Preachers and countless millions have been transformed by his ministry, Spurgeon suffered severe depression for the rest of his life. Though his sermons were full of humor, he wrote, "Melancholy is my closest neighbor." There were times when flashbacks of that night in the Surrey Music Hall would come in the middle of a sermon, and he would have to be carried home in a stupor. He would experience seasons of enthusiasm, only to spend other months in bed. Before he died at age fifty-eight, he was revered as the greatest preacher of his age. But he was also morbidly obese and suffering from gout and rheumatism, all complicated by his bouts with depression.

Does it surprise you that such a great hero of the Christian faith should suffer chronic despair? It shouldn't. From the prophet Elijah to Mother Teresa, many of history's greatest saints have struggled with depression. But they have discovered that God's grace is often painted on the canvas of despair. In times of suffering, this truth deserves meditation:

The unwounded life bears no resemblance to Jesus.

───── ✦ ─────

I bear on my body the scars that show I belong to Jesus.

GALATIANS 6:17

Never Thin Enough

⊱⊰

From the first moments of her life, Frances Gumm experienced the sting of rejection. When her parents discovered that they were with child, her mother went looking for an abortionist. Ethel and Frank were vaudeville hoofers trying to break into the big time, and this pregnancy was most inconvenient.

Later they thanked their lucky stars that they kept this unborn child. Their little girl had more talent in her little finger than either of her mediocre parents. So Ethel became the ultimate stage mother, pushing her tiny tot toward stardom. When Frank's affairs became too unbearable, she dragged her little meal ticket to Hollywood, forcing her to perform in nightclubs and unsavory dives where no child should be. Frances later said that even when she was sick, her mother shoved her onto the stage with a warning: "You get out and sing or I'll wrap you around the bedpost and break you off short!"

When ten-year-old Frances was too tired to go on, some say her mother force-fed her pills that would lead to a lifetime of drug abuse. But Ethel's pushiness paid off. In 1935, Frances signed a contract with MGM and shot to stardom. She also fell into the hands of studio head Louis B. Mayer. He loved the teen's singing and dancing but hated her chubbiness. He publicly called her "my little hunchback" and privately dictated when and how much she could eat. From the time she was thirteen, her weight yo-yoed wildly, ranging from overweight to impossibly thin.

The studio fed Frances uppers and downers so she could work 24/7 churning out movies. She jokingly called these pills her "bolts and jolts." But her life was no joke. She never felt beautiful, thin, or loved enough. Maybe that's why she plowed through five marriages and numerous affairs.

Or why, at age forty-seven, she stumbled into a London bedroom and died from an overdose of barbiturates.

Her parents named her Frances, her friends called her Joots, and Hollywood remembers her as a legend. But we all remember her by her stage name: Judy Garland. She starred in a string of blockbuster movies such as *The Wizard of Oz*, *Meet Me in St. Louis*, *Easter Parade*, *A Star Is Born*, and *Judgment at Nuremberg*. Along the way, Judy recorded hit albums, sold out concerts, and starred in television and on Broadway. Judy Garland was talented, but tragically troubled. She once said, "If I am a legend, why am I so lonely?"

She never got over the way her mother and Louis B. Mayer berated and demeaned her for being too fat. Whenever she looked at a mirror or watched herself on the big screen, she seldom felt pretty enough. Is there anything sadder than to be created with so much talent yet never feel good enough? Maybe you are insecure about your looks. In a world obsessed with being thin and in, remember that it's not about the size you wear but how you wear your size. Stop trying to please others, and celebrate the person God made you to be.

Just be who you are. Everyone else is already taken.

———— ⌒✺⌒ ————

Thank you for making me so wonderfully complex!
Your workmanship is marvelous—how well I know it.

PSALM 139:14

History's Strangest Funeral

৬৩৬৩৩

S anta Anna lives on in infamy, at least in the heart of Texas where he gave no quarter to the Alamo. What many don't know is that he is also the founding father of Mexico who led colonials in a war of independence from Spain. For more than forty years, he was the towering figure south of the border. Historians call this period the Age of Santa Anna.

He is also remembered as the man who managed to lose half the country. When Texans declared independence, he marched north with a massive army. He had the Texans on the run when his army paused at San Jacinto. Late in the morning of April 21, 1836, he was preoccupied with a prostitute called the Yellow Rose when the ragtag army of Sam Houston showed up. It took less than eighteen minutes for the Texans to rout Santa Anna's grand army. The Mexican Napoleon limped home in disgrace, ridiculed as the man who lost the vast state of *Tejas* because he got caught in a moral compromise. He was forced to resign.

But Santa Anna didn't become Mexico's president eleven times by not being an opportunist. When Mexico refused to pay a debt to France, a French invasion force attacked Vera Cruz in 1838. The country again needed its Mexican Napoleon. In the battle for the city, a cannonball shattered Santa Anna's ankle. Doctors had to amputate his leg to save his life. While he was out of commission, the Mexicans paid their debt, and the French pulled out. Santa Anna may have lost a leg, but he gained a propaganda prop when he had it dug up. It was reburied with full military honors in a state funeral that included cannon salvos, speeches, prayers, and poems recited in honor of the general's lost leg. Before its burial, the grisly remains of the leg were placed in a crystal vase.

After that, Santa Anna won the presidency in a landslide. For years afterward, he had a habit of removing his prosthetic leg and waving it in the air for crowds to see how much he had sacrificed for his country. But he lost his prosthetic leg in the deciding battle of the Mexican-American War of 1847 when troops from Illinois seized it as a trophy of war. The Mexican Napoleon raced away from his final Waterloo, unwilling to sacrifice any more body parts for Mexico.

This amazing story of a cynical politician who used his leg as a propaganda prop is so different than the most amazing story of all: the selfless Savior who gave his whole body for the whole world on a Roman cross. No one had to dig that body up and put it on display. He rose on the third day in triumph, and unlike Santa Anna, he has never lost one square inch of territory or one person who belongs to him.

The tomb of Jesus is famous for what it does not contain.

———— ✦ ————

The Spirit of God, who raised Jesus from the dead, lives in you. And just as God raised Christ Jesus from the dead, he will give life to your mortal bodies by this same Spirit living within you.

ROMANS 8:11

Latrodectus Mactans

❧

Her name is *Latrodectus mactans*. The lady is black and beautiful, with an hourglass figure. It's her honeymoon night, and she dances before her husband to arouse his passions. More than anything *Latrodectus* wants babies. When the night of lovemaking is over and she is satisfied that she is pregnant, she gives him a fatal kiss—a dagger plunged into his body. On its point is poison fifteen times more toxic than the venom of a prairie rattlesnake. She then proceeds to eat her husband's body. It is a deliciously ingenious way to dispose of the evidence of her hideous crime.

It's not the first time that *Latrodectus* has committed such a ghastly deed, nor will it be the last. This serial killer waddles away, fat on the remains of her slain husband, to lay up to 750 eggs. She has earned her alias: the black widow. Anyone who has ever been bitten by the spider with the scientific name *Latrodectus mactans* can attest to the severity of her venom.

Forensic experts call women who kill their husbands black widows. Surprisingly, women are guilty of 41 percent of spousal homicides in America. Men most often kill outside their families. But women are far more likely to murder members of their own families—usually husbands. The number one reason is spousal abuse. The second is money.

The most infamous black widow was Belle Gunness. She stood at five-and-a-half feet tall and weighed a hefty 270 pounds. She was a rough farm woman who wore overalls, pitched hay, and butchered hogs. No one would have guessed that Belle was a femme fatale. But when she put on her corset and piled up her hair in the latest style, she became a lethal seductress. After she disappeared in 1908, investigators found more than forty poisoned victims buried on her farm. Before the books were closed, it was determined that Belle murdered forty people, including multiple husbands and all her children.

History crawls with black widows who devour men for their money. Lyda Trueblood poisoned four spouses, a brother-in-law, and her only child. Rhonda Bell Martin killed two husbands, her mother, and three of her children for their insurance. After autopsies revealed the grisly truth, this Alabama black widow was executed in 1957.

We are shocked and horrified at such stories. Yet they might hit close to home, especially if we are religious. Remember that God has always called Israel his bride. When Jesus came, he was the fulfillment of the prophecies that a Savior would come as a husband to rescue his bride. But the "black widow" religious leaders ensnared their husband in a web of deceit, pierced him with poison, and devoured his body. Yet he rose again. He loves us too much to leave us to our sin. So crush the spider and embrace the Savior.

It wasn't our nails but his love that kept Jesus on that cross.

God showed his great love for us by sending
Christ to die for us while we were still sinners.

ROMANS 5:8

The Deepest Pit of All

❧⊚⊚⊛❧

Betsie and her sister were two spinsters living out their middle years in the pleasant but predictable routine of a well-ordered life: working in the family clock shop; preparing meals for their aged father, Casper; and spending Sundays listening to long sermons in their Dutch Reformed Church.

The world might never have heard of these stay-at-home sisters had Hitler's blitzkrieg not rolled into Holland. At first, they continued on with their routine, determined to make the best of the German occupation. But everything changed the day a frantic woman showed up at their clock shop with suitcase in hand, fleeing an SS roundup of Jews. Casper quickly pulled her through the doorway. "In this household, God's people are always welcome."

At that moment, the clock makers became part of the Dutch Resistance. They turned their house into a clever labyrinth of hiding places for Jews, feeding and caring for them until they could be spirited away to freedom. But too many townspeople knew what they were doing. It was inevitable that the Gestapo would ferret out their clandestine operations. Eventually, the whole family was arrested. The two sisters descended into a kind of Dante's *Inferno*, transferred from one prison to another—each worse than the one before.

Finally, they ended up at the infamous Ravensbrück death camp. In that place where evil reigned, they were dehumanized and reduced to starving skeletons. Finally, at age fifty-nine, sweet Betsie gave out. Even as she lay dying, she showed Christlike love toward her guards. Her sister wasn't so forgiving. As she looked out the window of her barracks, she saw human ash rising from the crematorium. She bitterly complained that this nightmare was beyond God's grace. Betsie replied, "No pit is so deep that God is not deeper still."

Years later, Betsie ten Boom's sister would write a bestselling book called *The Hiding Place*. Corrie ten Boom traveled the world speaking about their experiences. After one lecture, an old German hesitantly approached her to confess that he had been a guard at Ravensbrück. For a moment, hatred rose up from deep within Corrie's soul. Then she remembered Betsie's words. The grace of God is deeper even than the deepest pit of our unforgiving bitterness. Corrie ten Boom had no choice but to forgive this former death camp guard.

If you visit the Yad Vashem World Holocaust Remembrance Center in Jerusalem, you will find the Ten Boom tree along the Avenue of the Righteous among the Nations, which honors Gentiles who risked their lives to save Jews during the Nazi Holocaust.

Is there a pit of bitterness deep in your soul where you harbor unforgiveness toward someone? Maybe you think the hatred is too deep to dig it up and drag it to the foot of another tree outside Jerusalem where God's Son died to atone for even death camp guards. But it is only there that every hurt can be buried and forgotten. If you doubt that those hurts and hatreds are too deep to be dug out, remember this:

God's grace is immeasurable, and his mercy is inexhaustible.

⌘

May you have the power to understand, as all
God's people should, how wide, how long,
how high, and how deep his love is.

EPHESIANS 3:18

226

Postcards from the Princess

❦

She was a little princess. The daughter of Hollywood royalty. The off-spring of two of the world's biggest stars. But along with her glitzy pedigree came the trappings of Tinseltown: addictions, broken marriages, and trips to the psychiatrist.

Most of all, the little princess was unspeakably lonely. Her mother was the songbird sweetheart of screen and stage, her father a teenage heart-throb whose records went solid gold. He was also the best friend of the husband of Hollywood's reigning movie queen. When his friend suddenly died, he felt it his duty to comfort the grieving widow. It wasn't long before the princess's daddy crossed the line between giving comfort and falling in love. When he abandoned the princess's mother to become one of the queen's trophy husbands, it made tabloid headlines.

The little princess was now like so many Tinseltown tots, shuffled between divorced celebrity parents on a merry-go-round of loneliness. There's a famous photo of her, sitting frail and tiny on a stool in the wings of a stage, watching wistfully as her famous mother performs for the audience. Her posture screams a silent message: "Mom, I'm so alone! I need you more than they do!"

But no one listened. Her dad, depressed after being jettisoned by the Hollywood queen, emotionally abandoned her. Successive husbands drove her mother into bankruptcy. So mom performed day and night to pay back the creditors. The princess became a dysfunctional loner. The fact that she was bipolar didn't help her in those years of estrangement.

She got her own starring role as Princess Leia in the Star Wars trilogy. Then she disappeared, descending into a season of mental illness. She wrote a book entitled *Postcards from the Edge*. In it Carrie Fisher described her schism with her mother, Debbie Reynolds. Miraculously, mother and daughter came together again to discover a closeness that had eluded them for years.

Carrie came back from the edge and blossomed under her mother's care. She told the *New York Times*, "My mother taught me how to sur-thrive." Yet, even the best friendships never last long enough. On December 27, 2016, the princess died after suffering a heart attack on a flight to London. Debbie was devastated. While preparing for her daughter's funeral the next day, she suffered a stroke and was rushed to the hospital, where she died less than twenty-four hours after her best friend's death. Her son, Todd, reported that earlier that day, his mother had said, "I miss her so much. I want to be with Carrie." Daughter and mother are indeed together, buried side by side in the eerie silence of a Hollywood cemetery.

Perhaps you are neglecting your family to pursue some dream. You may mistakenly think that you can repair the damage and restore the lost years later. Debbie and Carrie's story tells us to drop everything, rush home, and give ourselves to those God has given us. This much is surely true:

We will never have enough time to make up for lost time.

———— ∽◌◌◌∾ ————

Let us not neglect our meeting together, as some people do, but encourage one another, especially now that the day of his return is drawing near.

HEBREWS 10:25

The Forgotten Genius

⚬⊙⊙⚬

We recall JFK's bold prediction that the United States would beat the Russians to the moon. But we forget that the Russians were launching Sputnik satellites into space while NASA's rockets were blowing up off the launch pad. Cold War paranoia caused Americans to fear that Commie space stations would soon orbit the earth with nuclear missiles aimed at the US heartland. When the Soviets launched their first manned orbital flight, everyone conceded that they were lapping America in the race for space.

The finest engineering minds at NASA were stymied. How could they shoot a manned capsule into space and bring it back safely? More perplexing, even if they accomplished that, how could they put an astronaut into orbit around the earth and then bring him back? Traveling seventeen thousand miles an hour, a capsule missing its reentry point would be locked in orbit forever. But if it came in at the wrong point, it would fall so fast that it would explode into a fireball. The mathematical formula to calculate such a delicate operation had not been discovered. So America's elite engineers worked feverishly to solve the riddle.

In the west wing of NASA in Langley, Virginia, a group of human computers daily double-checked the figures produced by these engineers. These women—some of them with better minds than NASA's brightest men—were African American women. In the '50s and '60s they were still segregated in separate facilities, denied career advancement, and paid lower wages. If they took public transit to the Langley Research Center, they were relegated to the back of the bus.

But prejudice is not only evil, it's downright stupid. Among those black women was Katherine Johnson. A child prodigy, she had graduated from college at age eighteen. But as a computer for the all-male flight research team, her genius was discounted and ignored. In circumstances more amazing than if they'd been dreamed up by Hollywood, Katherine calculated the trajectory that would take Alan Shepard on the first US manned flight into space. She helped formulate the math that would get John Glenn safely out of orbit and back to earth. Glenn so trusted this woman that he refused to lift off until she double-checked the equations spit out by the new IBM computers. Later, Katherine Johnson contributed to the Apollo moon landing of 1969. Without her calculations, NASA might not have gotten its three astronauts back to earth.

For years, the world never heard of this unsung genius. Yet some fifty years later, at ninety-seven years of age, Katherine Johnson received the Presidential Medal of Freedom. You can read her story, and that of other African American women geniuses at NASA, in the bestselling book *Hidden Figures* or watch it in the 2016 movie by the same title.

Their recognition is long overdue. So is our realization that we should never judge people by color, gender, age, handicap, or religion. There are treasures hidden among those we stereotype as unworthy. Never forget this: ***When we are prejudiced, the people we hurt most are ourselves.***

❧

There is no longer Jew or Gentile, slave or free, male
and female. For you are all one in Christ Jesus.

GALATIANS 3:28

Diving into Stardom

✦

Charlie had big dreams. Maybe his Jewish parents fueled those hopes. Having escaped Europe on the eve of the Nazi Holocaust, they were grateful to the country that took them in, and they instilled a love for the American dream in their two sons.

Perhaps Charlie had such high hopes because he was so doggone smart. After earning top honors at McGill University, he was accepted for graduate work at Harvard and Oxford. But Charlie had lots of dreams. He wanted to be a great surgeon, and the prestigious Harvard Medical School seemed like a good choice. Yet his love of politics and debate could flower at Oxford. So it was off to the hallowed halls of England's greatest university. It was there that he met his future wife, Robyn. This scholar from Australia was every bit his intellectual equal and more. Together, they were the ultimate power couple.

When he switched to Harvard Medical School, he was set on his future as a great surgeon—until the day he skipped classes to play tennis. Afterward, he dove into a nearby pool to cool off. That dive took only two seconds, yet it would change his life forever. When he hit the bottom of the pool, his spinal cord was severed.

In an instant, he became a C5-6 quadriplegic. A two-second accident had shattered his dream of being a great surgeon. Most folks would have given up. But Charlie wasn't most folks. When the dean of Harvard Medical School visited him during his fourteen-month hospital stay and offered him a leave of absence, Charlie set his jaw and said he was coming back to classes. He didn't become a surgeon, but he did graduate from Harvard to become a psychiatrist. Even though he was confined to a wheelchair, he served with distinction as the chief resident at Massachusetts General Hospital.

But Charlie's dreams were too big for a psychiatrist's office. So he returned to his love for politics, becoming a speechwriter for Vice President Walter Mondale. Folks would be surprised to know that Charlie was a liberal Democrat back then. Today the world knows him as Dr. Charles Krauthammer, the conservative pundit on Fox News. He is a syndicated columnist for the *New York Times*, his opinions appearing in more than four hundred newspapers. When he was with the *Washington Post* he won the Pulitzer Prize. His books are bestsellers. He is also one of the top speed-chess players in the world. This media megastar exudes such brilliance, dignity, and strength that millions of viewers don't even know that he is a quadriplegic.

But don't ever ask him about his physical disabilities. Dr. Krauthammer gruffly deflects such negative talk. After all, Charlie is living his dreams. How about you? Do you have a dream that keeps you going? Maybe, like Charles, life has severed you from old dreams. But there are so many more out there, waiting to be grabbed. If you think dreams aren't important, you might want to ponder this:

People begin to die when they expect nothing from tomorrow.

─────── ✺ ───────

Why am I discouraged? Why is my heart so
sad? I will put my hope in God! I will praise
him again—my Savior and my God!

PSALM 42:11

232

The Newspaper Clipping

❧

They carried him from the Ford Theater to a boarding house across the street. The sixteenth president of the United States would not survive this assassination attempt.

When they emptied his pockets, they found two pairs of spectacles and a lens polisher, a pocketknife, a watch fob, a linen handkerchief, a wallet containing a five-dollar Confederate bill, and eight newspaper clippings—all singing his praises.

But there's one clipping that's most poignant: an editorial from a London newspaper, effusive in its praise of Lincoln. The clipping is neatly folded and now yellowed with age. It was unfolded so many times that it's falling apart at its creases. Fingers held it so often that letters at the edges of the columns are almost worn off.

That worn clipping is mute testimony to the deep wounds in Lincoln's psyche. No American president has ever been more vilified. Below the Mason-Dixon Line, he was alternately cursed as a tyrant or as a demon. Newspapers up North mocked him as the Gorilla from Illinois. His cabinet secretaries openly plotted against him. Senators threatened to impeach him. Generals refused to obey his orders, and his mentally disturbed wife wandered the hallways screaming at him.

How many times had this battered and berated president stolen away to read that London clipping, his eyes caressing each word of praise for affirmation denied to him by his own countrymen?

Now the national nightmare was over. The Union had been saved and the slaves emancipated. But Abraham Lincoln got no chance to savor victory. As he exhaled his last labored breath, a profound heaviness fell on those who surrounded his deathbed. Secretary of War

Edwin Stanton broke the silence when he whispered, "Now he belongs to the ages."

And now his deification began. The irony of his dying on Good Friday was not lost. On Easter Day, preachers mounted their pulpits to declare that Abraham Lincoln was the savior of America. When his funeral train moved slowly across the heartland, weeping citizens lined the tracks. In the next decade, almost every city, town, and hamlet in the north would erect memorials, monuments, and statues to Lincoln. His name would be affixed to street signs, buildings, and schools. America's most vilified president in life would become her most revered in death.

One thinks of an ancient proverb: "We build monuments to dead men out of stones we threw at them when they were alive." Why do we love people most *after* they have left us and sing their praises when they are no longer around to hear them?

We all need to be affirmed. More than that, we need to be affirmers. Don't wait until your family or friends are gone to tell them how much they mean to you. Take some time today to send a card, e-mail, or text with a word of praise to someone. Maybe that single yellowed clipping kept Lincoln going during the dark days of the Civil War. Perhaps your words of affirmation will sustain someone during their dark days ahead. Remember this:

There is no affirmation without the one who affirms.

———— ⌒∞⌒ ————

Encourage each other and build each other
up, just as you are already doing.

1 THESSALONIANS 5:11

The Long Prayer
That Changed America

࿐

Histotry vilifies him for his part in the infamous Salem Witch Trials. But he was also a towering intellect whose prodigious work in the sciences dragged colonial America into the Age of Enlightenment. His discoveries in plant hybridization changed the face of agriculture. His pioneering work in inoculation contributed to medical science that would save millions. If all that wasn't enough, this overachiever spoke seven languages and wrote 385 books and pamphlets, making him the most prolific author in American history. His epic seven-volume work, *Magnalia Christi Americana*, was the first written history of America.

It's no wonder that Benjamin Franklin sought out the old pastor as a mentor. They made for strange bedfellows, this conservative Puritan preacher and the skeptic of all things religious. But young Ben admired old Cotton for his scientific mind and humble heart. Though stereotypical opposites, they are equally woven into the fabric of our nation's DNA.

The Reverend Doctor Cotton Mather may be revered for his achievements or vilified for that nasty episode at Salem, but few historians recall his greatest contribution. For at least fifty years this intellectual got down on his knees at the break of dawn and prayed for a great spiritual awakening to sweep through the churches. That's 18,250 straight days of unceasing prayer!

Religion had grown cold in colonial America. The fiery faith of early Puritans had become dead orthodoxy. Harvard, the training school for preachers, was turning out intellectual snobs who put parishioners to sleep. Maybe that's why less than 10 percent regularly attended church or why America had become a tangle of drunkenness, incest, prejudice, and unspeakable cruelty.

When Cotton Mather challenged the church hierarchy, he made enemies in high places. When he promised to clean house at Harvard, they denied him its presidency. After he began to support the more evangelical Yale College, he became a pariah among the Puritan elite. But the church bigwigs couldn't stop him from crawling out of his bed every morning and praying for revival.

The end was drawing near for this preacher on a cold Sabbath morning in 1728. But those attending him on his deathbed said that he was still gasping out prayers for a great spiritual awakening. Little did he know that down the road in Northampton, a young preacher by the name of Jonathan Edwards was stepping into his grandfather's pulpit. Together with George Whitefield, John Wesley, and other firebrand preachers, Edwards would spark the Great Awakening revivals.

Cotton Mather's story is a reminder that our greatest act of patriotism is to pray. Maybe you have given up on seeing a spiritual revival sweep across our increasingly secular and immoral nation. Keep on praying. Cotton Mather would certainly agree with this statement by Billy Graham:

To get America back on its feet, we must get down on our knees.

———— ✄ ————

If my people who are called by my name will humble
themselves and pray and seek my face and turn
from their wicked ways, I will hear from heaven
and will forgive their sins and restore their land.

2 CHRONICLES 7:14

The Rain of Fire

❦

When Portuguese traders washed up on its shores after a storm in 1543, the West discovered Japan. Six years later, missionaries began to spread the gospel, helped in part by the fact that Japan was a collection of warring fiefdoms ruled by Samurai warlords. Some of these feudal lords saw these missionaries as useful tools to advance trade with the West and acquire modern European weapons. When they were baptized, their people followed suit.

But no one benefited from these missionaries more than the shrewd and venal lord of a little village situated on one of the world's great harbors. It wasn't long before ships from Portugal, Spain, and Holland were disgorging the riches of the West in his harbor. When he asked the Portuguese for warships and weaponry to help him subdue rival warlords, they insisted that he use this power to force conversions. In 1574, he demolished Buddhist temples and Shinto shrines while compelling sixty thousand of his subjects to convert to Christianity.

That little village grew into a prosperous city. In the late 1500s it was the center of Christianity in the Far East. It also got the attention of the regent Toyotomi Hideyoshi. He saw this growing foreign religion as a tool of Western imperialism. So he decided to rip Christianity out by its roots, beginning with the city by the harbor. Twenty-six priests and parishioners were crucified on a hill in its center. Over the next several years, thousands of Christians were martyred across Japan in the most barbaric ways.

But it was this city by the harbor that became the killing grounds of some thirty-five thousand martyrs. At scalding hot sulfur springs outside the city, executioners took boiling water and sprinkled it over those crucified, causing them to die an agonizing death. Many cried out to God for mercy but were answered with silence. It seemed that heaven had turned a blind eye to their suffering.

But maybe God did hear those cries in the killing center by the harbor. Some three hundred years later, a B-29 flying over that city dropped an atomic bomb called "Fat Man." The epicenter of that blast in Nagasaki was the spot where Christians had been martyred three centuries before. It is not without irony that thirty-five thousand people were incinerated in the immediate blast. Did the American War Department choose to bomb Nagasaki in retaliation for the martyrdom of Christians? Not likely! But it may not have been coincidence that sulfuric fire rained down from heaven on the spot where Christians had been scalded to death by boiling sulfur water.

One thing is sure. God loves his people with a holy jealousy. He does not turn a blind eye to their suffering. He will not remain silent forever. That's why we don't have to take matters into our own hands when we are abused. We can love our tormentors, knowing that God will judge evil in his time. If someone is wounding you today, take comfort from this truth: *God's justice is not blind. Nor does it sleep forever.*

Dear friends, never take revenge.
Leave that to the righteous anger of God.

ROMANS 12:19

238

Nowhere to Run,
Nowhere to Hide

‹ଈଓ›

Wilmer lived a gentleman farmer's pleasant life on his prosperous plantation near Manassas Junction in the rolling hills of Northern Virginia. Now that he had married a wealthy widow, life was good. Most of all, he enjoyed evening walks with his wife by the small stream that meandered through his plantation. Few people knew about this trickle of water called the Bull Run. But it wouldn't be long before the whole world knew about it.

Union forces were marching like toy soldiers from the north. They were followed, at a safe distance, by carriage loads of festive spectators from the nation's capital. They had come to watch their boys in blue rout a rebel army. They even brought blankets and picnic baskets. What would follow on that hot July day in 1861 was no picnic. An entertaining military spectacle turned into the bloody Battle of Bull Run on Wilmer's Manassas plantation. The carnage was so horrific that the good ladies and gentlemen watching from distant hills packed up their picnic baskets and hightailed it back to Washington, DC.

Wilmer McLean and his family had already fled the day before, after Confederate general P. G. T. Beauregard took possession of his house. When Wilmer returned to his plantation after the battle, his house had been ripped apart by cannon fire, his barns had been turned into hospitals, and his fields were a tangle of ruts and ditches. The horrors of war had hit too close to home for this man who loved the good life.

So Wilmer looked for a safe refuge—a place so far off the beaten path that this uncivil war could never find the McLean family. He discovered an out-of-the-way hamlet in the remote mountains of Virginia. He purchased a big home that used to be a tavern for mountain folk.

For four years his family enjoyed a respite from the nation's long nightmare, living in ignorant bliss—until an April day in 1865 shattered their solitude. A Confederate colonel rode out of the woods like a ghost and headed straight toward Wilmer. The Civil War had finally arrived at the McLean hideaway in the little hamlet of Appomattox Court House.

The colonel needed a suitable house for Generals Grant and Lee to work out the accords for ending the war. Wilmer had no choice but to offer his. Before the day was over, hundreds of troops overran his refuge. Within days, Union soldiers would loot his beautiful home, stealing almost everything as souvenirs of this momentous moment in American history.

Ken Burns said it best in his PBS Civil War documentary: "Wilmer McLean could rightly claim, 'The Civil War began in my front yard and ended in my front parlor.'" Wilmer also proved that you can only run for so long. There are no fail-safe hiding places. Trouble will find us. So we might as well break out of the cocoon of self-protection and live life to the full. There can be no adventure without taking risks. Here's a credo worth considering:

Playing it safe is the riskiest thing you will ever do.

———— ✺ ————

Farmers who wait for perfect weather never plant.
If they watch every cloud, they never harvest.

ECCLESIASTES 11:4

Composers
and Their Critics

❧❦❧

He came to England looking for greener pastures. He was good, but not in the same league with countrymen like Bach, Beethoven, or Mozart. Besides, the new king of England was from his homeland. Both were Germans, and both had the same first name: George.

The immigrant musician became a court favorite, and his star rose quickly. But he was his own worst enemy. His explosive temper made him enemies in high places. During one rehearsal, he dragged an actress to a second-story window and threatened to toss her out of it. It wasn't long before tabloids churned out stories about this bad-tempered German glutton with the crude accent, and he became persona non grata at the royal court.

After losing a fortune in the opera business, George was reduced to living in a small flat above a shop. Then he suffered a stroke, which blurred his vision and left him unable to play the keyboard or lead an orchestra.

About that time, the discouraged composer read a friend's libretto on the life of Christ. He was so moved and inspired that he locked himself away for twenty-three days. When George came out of his room, he had written a masterpiece for the ages. He exclaimed, "I did think I saw heaven open, and saw the very face of God."

With creditors in pursuit, he fled to Dublin with his magnum opus. He found backers to unveil it at a benefit concert. He chose, as a principal singer, an actress who had fled to Ireland after a scandalous divorce. Her performance would restore her reputation, and she would go on to become England's most famous star of the stage. The proceeds of that Dublin concert freed 143 debtors from prison.

Yet his oratorio was almost a flop. It debuted in London to mixed reviews. After John Wesley attended an early performance, he wrote, "There were some parts of it that were affecting, but I doubt that it has staying power." We might be glad that the esteemed reverend didn't leave his day job to become a music critic. King George himself had the good sense to stand in awe during its soaring climax. People still stand when the "Hallelujah" chorus by George Frideric Handel is performed. In spite of what early critics had to say, Handel's *Messiah* has endured as one of history's towering works.

You can divide the world into two classes: composers and critics. Critics are a dime a dozen. It takes no genius to criticize. It requires inspiration and perspiration to compose. So go out and compose something today. Leave criticizing and faultfinding to lesser folk. Never forget this enduring truth:

People who can, do. People who can't, criticize.

———— ✺ ————

Let everything you say be good and helpful, so that your
words will be an encouragement to those who hear them.

EPHESIANS 4:29

The Dance of Fools

S he stands aloof, like an eagle perched high above lesser creatures, look-ing down her haughty beak at the streets below. A celebration has broken out, and the riffraff celebrate with vulgar gusto. But her deepest disgust is in her husband, who has thrown off his royal robes and is danc-ing like a fool with the household maids.

It wasn't always like this. Once upon a time she was in love with the shepherd who had slain a giant. It was the stuff of fairy tales: the princess and the shepherd. When her daddy, the king, gave her to him in marriage it was headline news: "Royal Marries Commoner." But they did not live happily ever after. When her shepherd grew too popular, her father tried to kill him. She risked her life helping him escape. Lonely weeks turned to long months. When the king forced her to marry a mousy shadow of her shepherd, the princess prayed fervently that her hero would return to rescue her.

But disturbing news filtered back to the palace. Her fugitive first hus-band was now a Robin Hood, his band of outlaws living off the land while leading the king's men on a merry chase. He also took on new wives. When she heard the devastating news, her passions shriveled, and she walled off her heart until it became as cold as ice.

Then her father and brothers were killed in battle. A civil war erupted between her first husband and her father's royal house. When his rivals were eliminated, the shepherd demanded that she be sent back to him. Yet he reclaimed her not as a returning lover, but as a king taking back stolen property. Her second husband trailed behind, wailing hysterically and further humiliating her.

Weep for Michal, the proud daughter of King Saul. The shepherd once thought himself the luckiest man alive to marry her. Now she is his trophy wife, a political commodity to solidify his reign by connecting it to the old royal house. Weep for dreams dashed and for the bitterness that has robbed Michal of her joy in her king.

The Ark of the Covenant has been returned, bringing the very presence of God into Jerusalem. David has disrobed and is dancing like a mad fool in unbridled joy before his Lord. But when he returns exhausted from his worship, he is met by the ice queen who used to be a princess. She spits out pent-up anger: "How dare you disrobe and dance like a vulgar fellow?" She has forever shut the door to her king. He walks away, never to return to Michal's bedroom again.

A thousand years later, the great Son of David rides through the same gates of Jerusalem. As with the Ark of the Covenant, God's presence is in him. Indeed, Jesus is God in the flesh. The crowds dance like joyous fools before him. Soon this king, too, will disrobe to hang on a cross. High above in the Temple, the icy spirit of Michal lives again in religious leaders. They don't want their king either. So they shut the door to his love. How about you? Don't let Michal's sad story be yours.

The King has come! Open your heart and join the dance!

———— ༄༅ ————

You have turned my mourning into joyful dancing . . .
that I might sing praises to you and not be silent.

PSALM 30:11-12

Singing with Daddy

⌘

Her daddy was both a phenomenon and an anomaly. Though he was an African American, his silky smooth voice made him a pop icon when America was still segregated. No black singer had ever become such a crossover superstar, appealing to white and black audiences alike. His recordings became instant gold. The world was astounded when he got his own network television show in the fifties, when most blacks were still drinking from "colored only" fountains.

But racism still reared its ugly head. Her daddy's prime-time show was canceled when major sponsors were unwilling to take the risk of being associated with a black performer. Though his concerts to mostly white audiences were sold out, he was forced to stay in blacks-only hotels. After he purchased a luxury home in an all-white neighborhood, his neighbors signed a petition calling him "an undesirable." When they demanded that he sell, he refused.

America lost his silky baritone voice when he died of lung cancer at forty-five years of age. His little girl was shattered. Though she shared his musical DNA and had grown up around a veritable *Who's Who* of the greatest jazz and gospel singers in history, it was too painful to follow in her daddy's footsteps. Instead, she was determined to become a doctor— and maybe even cure the cancer that took her father's life.

But Natalie had inherited her daddy's golden voice, and it was crying out to be used. So she dropped out of pre-med. It wasn't long before her incomparable singing won her two Grammy Awards. She was ready for Las Vegas. But when she saw "The Daughter of Nat King Cole" on the marquee, she exploded. "I had to be myself, singing my songs in my own way."

More family tragedies followed. Natalie went through a dark season of drug addiction, during which she lost her career and came close to losing her life. The world can be thankful that she fought back with her father's courage. She regained the career that sold millions of albums and won nine Grammys.

But it was in 1991 that she finally embraced her daddy's legacy, recording her biggest hit album, *Unforgettable . . . with Love.* One song on that album became a blockbuster hit. A digitally restored recording of Nat King Cole's golden oldie *Unforgettable* was paired with Natalie's voice: a hauntingly beautiful duet spanning half a decade, with daughter and daddy harmonizing together. That duet propelled Nat King Cole's daughter to new heights of superstardom.

A few years later, on December 31, 2015, Natalie joined her daddy in death. But whenever you want to celebrate the power of legacy, you can put on a set of headphones and let that achingly beautiful and haunting duet fill your senses with joy. Embrace the legacy that your ancestors have woven into your DNA, for you can be sure of this:

You are made up of all those who have gone before you.

———— ✑✑✑ ————

The love of the LORD remains forever with those
who fear him. His salvation extends to the children's
children of those who are faithful to his covenant,
of those who obey his commandments!

PSALM 103:17-18

The Counterfeit Artist

His neighbors wondered how the recent immigrant always seemed to have so much cash. Some of it was in big bills. His small farm in New Jersey couldn't produce enough to give him that kind of spending money. When they asked the distinguished gentleman, he would demurely reply in a heavy German accent that he was receiving a pension from the Prussian army.

When he entered a small neighborhood grocery store to purchase some turnip greens, he handed the clerk a twenty-dollar bill. In 1887 not many people paid with bills that large. It wouldn't be easy to find change for twenty-five cents' worth of greens. Then as the clerk rummaged through her drawer looking for change, she noticed ink on her fingers. She was shocked. The German was a longtime friend. Surely he wouldn't give her a bill that wasn't genuine. The clerk shrugged off her suspicions and handed the man his change.

Later she had second thoughts. Twenty dollars was two weeks' salary in 1887. So she reluctantly summoned the local police. As it turned out, treasury officials had spent eleven years trying to track down the mysterious forger who had been circulating counterfeit bills in the Northeast. Having no clue as to his identity, agents nicknamed him Jim the Penman.

Nine years later, the German tried to pay a bartender with a fifty-dollar note. When the barkeep's wet hands smudged the ink, he called the authorities. Secret Service agents arrested Emanuel Ninger. When they searched his home, they found expensive paper and sophisticated paintbrushes. Ninger had taken weeks meticulously, painstakingly hand painting each bill. He may have created seven hundred counterfeit bills in eighteen years—many works of art, highly valued by collectors today.

Though the public admired him as a Robin Hood figure, the Feds weren't amused. Ninger spent six years in the penitentiary. When he got out, he took a stab at counterfeiting British pound notes. He just couldn't go straight. But his isn't the usual story of crime that doesn't pay. It's much more tragic than that. His is the story of a life and talent wasted.

When the Secret Service agents confiscated his counterfeiting paraphernalia, they also seized three portraits that he had painted. After his arrest, they were sold at public auction for $16,000. That averages out to more than $5,000 a portrait—a fabulous sum in 1896. Ninger later admitted that it took the same amount of time to paint a twenty-dollar bill as it did a $5,000 portrait. Yet when he got out of prison, he went back to counterfeiting! Emanuel Ninger's story of a wasted life begs a question of us all: Are we misusing our energy and talents in pursuit of lesser things when God has made us to create eternal things? Here's a contemporary take on something Sidney J. Harris once said:

People make counterfeit money; in many more cases, money makes counterfeit people.

⋯⋯

Don't store up treasures here on earth, where moths eat
them and rust destroys them, and where thieves break in
and steal. Store your treasures in heaven, where moths and
rust cannot destroy, and thieves do not break in and steal.

MATTHEW 6:19-20

The Price We Pay
for Greatness

そゆらか

The Simoni boy grew up in the golden age of art. Almost every Italian boy dreamed of growing up to be a painter, sculptor, or architect. The son of Lodovico Simoni harbored the conceit that he could be the greatest artist of all. Then his father's small bank in Florence went belly up, and his mother died.

The Simoni boy's prospects looked dim without a mother's care or a father's fortune. He was sent to a farm near a quarry where he lived with his nanny and her stonecutter husband. In addition to being cared for by his nurse, he learned how to handle a chisel and hammer.

He also learned to handle brush and canvas. Maybe that's why Lorenzo de' Medici, the Godfather of the Renaissance, took him under his wing. Simoni's boy was now enjoying the patronage of the richest man in Europe—until his benefactor died. Cast adrift, he realized that greatness would not be purchased on the cheap from someone else's purse. If he was going to paint and sculpt the human body, he would have to dissect and study its anatomy.

So he made his way to the church of Santa Maria del Santo Spirito on the outskirts of Florence. The poor, indigent, and diseased were dropped off at its charity hospital. Those who died were deposited in an airless, dark room full of rotting corpses in the hopes that their bodies might be claimed. Though this was the Renaissance Age, there was still plenty of superstition. Even priests and nuns refused to go into this haunt of departed spirits.

But young Simoni sneaked into that haunted room. Later, as a gift of gratitude, he carved a wooden crucifix for the church's high altar. Simoni spent weeks in that grotesque place, dissecting corpses and studying their anatomy. It beggars the imagination to think of the smells, gory sights, and diseases in that morgue during an era that knew nothing of embalming or antiseptic hygiene.

The Simoni boy later confessed that handling and dissecting those cadavers made him so sick to his stomach that he could keep nothing down. He went days without touching food or drink. Yet weeks later he walked out with a sketchbook that still astounds the medical and art world. No one ever knew more about the form and movement of the human body than the young Simoni.

The world has been immeasurably enriched by those horrifying days that Michelangelo di Lodovico Buonarroti Simoni spent alone in the morgue. Study his incomparable sculpture of David. Stand in awe before the Pietà. Or gaze in wonder at the ceiling of the Sistine Chapel. Who would have guessed that such breathtaking beauty was born in a house of corpses? People often say, "I would give anything to . . ." The truth is, we give almost nothing. Maybe that's why there is so much mediocrity in this world. When you think of something you would like to accomplish, recall the story of Michelangelo and his morgue. Know this too:

The cost of greatness is high, but the price for smallness is higher.

Work willingly at whatever you do, as though you
were working for the Lord rather than for people.

COLOSSIANS 3:23

A Message in a Bottle

❦

In 1972 *Voyager 2* was launched. Its projected journey was 1.4 billion miles. It passed Jupiter in 1979. Traveling at speeds of thirty-five thousand miles per hour, it hurtled past Saturn, Uranus, and Pluto before plunging into interstellar space in 1990.

Aboard the *Voyager 2* is a recording of the sounds of Earth. Babies crying and children laughing. Traffic jams and jackhammers. Singing of choirs, music of symphonies, and songs of romance. The pulsating beat of heavy metal rock music. The screams of airplanes and the fury of nature. A cacophony of sounds that capture the essence of life on this planet.

Those sounds serve as a time capsule, waiting for someone to make it play. Today, out in the distant vastness of the universe, a lonely spacecraft journeys toward an unknown destination, ready to break the silence of outer space with the sounds of humanity.

It has a surrealistic feel to it. Did the scientists at NASA put a message in a bottle and cast it into a cosmic ocean? Did they fear that we stand on the precipice of a nuclear, biological, or ecological holocaust? Were they afraid that our geopolitical house of cards might collapse into apocalyptic chaos?

Maybe *Voyager 2* is a cry for help from a distressed planet. A high-tech toss of the dice that some superior intelligence out there might hear the sounds of Earth. Like a bottle placed in the sea by a marooned sailor, *Voyager 2* bobs through the trackless reaches of the cosmic ocean with a recorded message: "If you are out there, this is Earth. If there is still time, help us. If our time has run out, remember us."

But there's good news for the programmers of *Voyager 2*, or for anyone else who has lost hope. There is someone out there, beyond the farthest expanse of our cosmic ocean. He knows that we exist. He never misses a single sound, especially our cries for help.

He didn't wait for us to perfect our technology so we could toss a bottle with a message into the interstellar seas. Two thousand years ago, he left heaven to come to a lost and dying planet. He humbled himself to enter the womb of an unwed teenage girl. From the moment of conception, this baby was fully God and fully human. His earthly name was Jesus. He was born to die so that he might redeem this Earth and all those who receive him as Savior and Lord. He rose from the dead and went back to heaven. But he's coming again to make everything right. Remember, history is his story. He writes it with a happy ending for those who belong to him.

As you consider your own salvation, think about the haunting story of *Voyager 2* and the happier story of heaven's great rescue operation that was launched just for you. Maybe this new take on something Saint Augustine said will resonate with your heart:

God has made us for himself, and his heart will be restless until we find our rest in his arms.

This is real love—not that we loved God, but that he loved us and sent his Son as a sacrifice to take away our sins.

1 JOHN 4:10

The Power of a Story

❧

It's not the warrior or kingmaker who changes the world, but the storyteller. Take Arthur. He is often dismissed as one of the many husbands of a Hollywood goddess. But he wrote a story that helped pull America back from the abyss of madness in the 1950s.

The world was locked in the Cold War, but a hot nuclear holocaust was a clear and present danger. America was ripe for Senator Joseph R. McCarthy and his Red Scare. The junior senator from Wisconsin boasted that he possessed a list of 205 high-ranking US officials who were closet Communists. His self-righteous patriotism and aggressive style made him the perfect candidate to become the grand inquisitor for an ideological housecleaning.

When he became the chairman of the Senate's committee on government operations, he launched investigations that soon turned into witch hunts, violating the constitutional rights of many in his crosshairs. More than two thousand government employees were forced to resign—many of them smeared on flimsy evidence, hearsay, and the secret testimony of others who were threatened that they would be next if they didn't cooperate.

Joe McCarthy was the undisputed champion of Americanism. Having cowed Washington, this bellicose bully went after Hollywood in a rerun of what happened in the nation's capital. Many actors and directors were branded as Communists and blacklisted on the flimsiest of evidence. Hysteria reigned as celebrities turned in their best friends as Commies. Not satisfied with the carnage he created in Hollywood, America's bullyboy went after the military. During the televised hearings, the army's chief counsel finally had a gutful. He thundered, "Have you no sense of decency, sir, at long last?" Like most bullies, McCarthy turned into a sniveling coward. The nation also had had a gutful. The Senate censured McCarthy, and he died ignominiously of hepatitis exacerbated by alcoholism.

America remembers that army lawyer slaying the giant McCarthy. But we often forget an equally powerful Broadway play. Arthur Miller wanted to speak out against McCarthy, but he would have surely been tagged as a Communist sympathizer and blacklisted. One day, as he read Charles W. Upham's 1867 study of the Salem Witch Trials in the 1600s, he saw a striking parallel to the witch hunts of Joe McCarthy: mob hysteria that corrupts a community, innocent people condemned on hearsay and flimsy evidence, civil rights violated, and coerced confessions. So the quiet playwright with the horn-rimmed glasses wrote one of the most powerful and enduring plays of all time: *The Crucible.*

The thousands who watched this historical drama knew that it was a thinly veiled exposé of the evils of McCarthyism. Many argue that Miller's powerful story did more to drive a stake through the Red Scare than anything else. Indeed, it is the storyteller who changes the world. Maybe that's why, whenever Jesus wanted to move people, he told a story. Each of us is a treasure trove of stories that have the power to transform others if only we will learn how to tell them well.

A story says something that cannot be said any other way.

⸎

One day Jesus told his disciples a story to show
that they should always pray and never give up.

LUKE 18:1

The Reluctant Spy

❧❧❧

Nate lived quietly in the shadows. As the sixth of ten brothers, he was mostly ignored. Frail and sickly, he stayed indoors by the fireplace. While other boys explored frontier forests, he burrowed into books. When his brothers plowed fields alongside their father, he talked poetry with his mother. By age eleven, this bookworm was fluent in Greek, Latin, and Hebrew. No one was surprised when he became Yale College's youngest student at age fourteen or when he graduated with top honors when he was only eighteen.

By now, colonial America was a hotbed of revolution. Down south, Patrick Henry electrified Virginia's House of Burgesses with his immortal words "Give me liberty or give me death!" But Nate was a gentle and meek scholar. Some even whispered that he was fainthearted or maybe cowardly. While other young men were taking up arms, this teacher retreated to the safety of his classroom.

Then came the British siege of Boston. Embarrassed to be thought a coward, he joined the local militia. Yet when his students marched off to war, Nate stayed behind. While they shed their blood on the battlefield, he hid in his classroom. But a sentence in a letter from a Yale classmate gnawed at him: "Our holy religion and the honor of God demand that we defend our country." That single line put steel in the frail bookworm's spine.

Soon after, he joined George Washington's army. When they made him a supply officer, he was relieved that his duties kept him far from battle. But a line in another letter jabbed at his conscience: "Now is the time for great men to immortalize their names in the defense of their country." When Washington needed a volunteer to spy out British troop strength on Long Island, Nate surprised everyone by impulsively stepping forward.

Never was a spy more fearful. Maybe that's why he was spotted within hours of landing in Manhattan. He was arrested and dragged before British general William Howe. He was summarily condemned as a spy, sentenced to death, and locked in a greenhouse for the night. We might wish that Nate faced his death with dignity. Instead, he shook with fear and vomited repeatedly. He asked for a Bible, but it was refused. At dawn he begged for a chaplain, but that, too, was denied. He was marched down the road to a tree by the local tavern. His knees buckled, but his resolve didn't. As the noose was placed around his neck, Nate quoted a line from Joseph Addison's play *Cato*, spoken by the Roman patriot Cato as he is being martyred: "I regret that I have but one life to give for my country."

When Nate's brothers came to reclaim his body, the British had already dumped it in an unmarked grave. Though the body was never recovered, a grateful nation hasn't forgotten Nate or his full name: Nathan Hale. Surely he immortalized his name with sacred honor in the defense of his country. If we wish to pass on to our children the liberties given to us at such great sacrifice, we ought to recall another line from *Cato*. Surely Nate had read these words too:

He who fears death has already lost the life he covets.

Greater love has no one than this: to lay
down one's life for one's friends.

JOHN 15:13, NIV

Mussolini's Last Bodyguard

∽⌒⊙⌒∾

Bruno's world had fallen apart, and the Grim Reaper was hot on his trail. How did his revolutionary idealism come to this? After he joined the elite Alpine regiments, he fell under the hypnotic spell of Italy's Fascist dictator, Benito Mussolini. He was proud when he became one of *Il Duce's* bodyguards. But by 1945 his dreams of a Fascist utopia had crumbled, and partisans were closing in on Mussolini.

Bruno was sent on a mission to clear a mountainside, but his troops were ambushed by guerillas. By playing dead, he was the only one to survive. Not long after, Mussolini and his mistress were executed, along with Bruno's colonel father. He and fourteen other officers were now in prison. One by one, the others were tortured and shot. Now it was Bruno's turn to face a firing squad. But a priest pled for his life, and he was set free. Once again, Bruno was the only one to escape death. But he had cheated death too many times to take any more chances. So he fled to South America, where some nine thousand SS officers and Fascist operatives had been welcomed by banana republic dictators.

In Argentina, Juan Perón made Bruno a construction manager. One day an angry worker hurled a shovel at his head, missing it by inches. It seemed that Bruno was always escaping death. So he and his new wife headed off to Bolivia to hunt for gold. There, a drunken miner began shooting a pistol, killing the man on Bruno's left and wounding another on his right. The Fascist was living a charmed life.

For the first time he looked at a Bible. Later, he was driving into the jungle when his shirt flew out of the car. All of his papers were in that shirt, but it was too late to go back over almost impassable roads. When a car with two missionaries came by going the other way, Bruno asked if they would look for his shirt. Later, he went to their church to pick it up. They never found the shirt, but Bruno discovered in Christ what his thirsty heart hadn't found before.

Then tragedy struck. As his wife was driving over the brow of a hill, they slammed into a car parked on the road. Tilly was killed instantly, and Bruno should have been. He was mostly paralyzed, but he slowly and painfully came back from the edge of death. By now he knew that God had repeatedly spared him for a bigger purpose. Mussolini's final bodyguard would go on to become Bolivia's greatest preacher. The young Fascist who had begun with revolutionary idealism ended by bringing the only revolution that can transform this world. Bruno Frigoli's amazing story should pose a question to each of us: Why has God spared me? Why am I still alive on this fragile planet? Could it be that he has a bigger plan for my life than I can ever imagine? This much is true:

The biggest tragedy isn't death, but a life devoid of great purpose.

Fight the good fight for the true faith. Hold tightly
to the eternal life to which God has called you.

1 TIMOTHY 6:12

Failing All the Way
to Greatness

❧

Larry's little brother had a lot to live up to. His brother was the star basketball player in the family. Though he was only five feet eight, Larry had a miraculous ability to do a double-pump reverse slam dunk. His ability to dribble like a Harlem Globetrotter, drain three-pointers from downtown, and go into the paint to outrebound six-foot-nine centers caused his coach to play him at all five positions on the court. College scouts drooled over his jaw-dropping play.

Larry's brother was a year younger, even shorter, and not nearly as good. Larry always won their endless games of horse and one-on-one, and that was okay for his hero-worshiping brother. But it also drove the kid to push himself harder to up his game.

Just before the scrawny boy's sophomore year, the coach invited him to join his older brother at a basketball camp. He figured that Larry's DNA must be in his little brother. The coach was disappointed. He admired the kid's raw speed and burgeoning skills but figured that he was destined to remain small of stature like the rest of his family. When the coach announced the varsity roster, all of the kid's friends who were six feet or taller were chosen. But Larry's brother was cut.

He was devastated, but this failure caused him to work harder until the next year, when he got the privilege of riding the bench while Larry starred on the court. Then Larry's kid brother miraculously grew five inches between his sophomore and junior year. To this day, no one can figure out how he eventually grew to six feet six in a family where no one has ever topped five feet ten. We do know that he went on to be a

McDonald's High School All-American, and he led his college team to the NCAA national championship, his Chicago Bulls to six NBA titles, and the US Olympic team to gold. He set more individual records than any other player. We also know that Larry's kid brother is now worth a cool $1.31 billion.

We sometimes forget that Larry Jordan's brother has also made his share of blunders on and off the court. Michael famously confessed in a CBS interview, "I've missed more than nine thousand shots in my career. I've lost almost three hundred games. Twenty-six times, I've been trusted to take the game-winning shot and missed." He will also tell you that, inch for inch, he is the second-best player in his family. He says, "When you say 'Air Jordan,' I'm number two, he's one."

Maybe you've been living in the shadow of those who are better than you. You could let their success fill you with discouragement, envy, or bitterness. Or you could be like Mike by plugging away until you get a five-inch growth spurt that takes you to the next level. Don't ever forget the essence of what Larry's brother said:

Failing over and over again is how you eventually succeed.

———— ✺ ————

The godly may trip seven times, but they will get up again.

PROVERBS 24:16

Let's Hear It for the Boll Weevil

❧❧❧

If you've ever been down to Coffee County in Southeastern Alabama, you know that there's not much to see. But it's worth the trip to stop off in the small town of Enterprise. There's not a whole lot to see there, either. But there is one attraction you won't see anywhere else in the world.

In the town square there is a thirteen-foot-high marble statue of a woman standing in splendor atop an ornate base in the middle of a fountain. Her arms stretch up in a pose of worship. This classic sculpture, looking like something you might see in Rome, seems strangely out of place in rural Alabama. But then you see what she holds in her hands as an offering to heaven: a giant, black boll weevil. More astounding are the words inscribed on her base: "In profound appreciation of the Boll Weevil and what it has done as the Herald of Prosperity."

Wait a minute! In profound appreciation of the boll weevil? The boll weevil is a herald of prosperity? Certainly not where there is cotton! And cotton was king for two hundred years in Coffee County. Boll weevils are especially fond of cotton. An infestation of these black devils can strip a cotton field bare in a few days. So why build a statue in "profound appreciation" of these voracious pests?

You have to go back to the late 1800s to answer that question. That's when a plague of boll weevils crossed over from Mexico, eating a destructive swath across the cotton patch of Southeastern America. By the time the insects reached Coffee County, panic was in the air. Cotton was the engine that drove the economy. There wasn't a living soul that didn't depend on cotton. By 1910 boll weevils covered Alabama like a swarming, crawling, devouring black flood. The annual yield of cotton was cut by 40 percent. Statewide revenue losses were more than 70 percent. Farmers lost whole crops. Many had to abandon farms that had been in their families for generations. Historians agree that, other than the Civil War, nothing devastated the South like the boll weevil.

To survive, cotton farmers had to turn to more diversified farming. Most of all they planted peanuts. By 1917, some twenty-four years after the first boll weevils arrived, Coffee County was producing more than one million bushels of peanuts annually. Enterprise had become known as the peanut capital of the world. Coffee County was more prosperous than it had ever been when cotton was king.

In that year of unprecedented prosperity, the grateful citizens of Enterprise erected their shrine to the boll weevil—the only memorial to an insect anywhere in the world. It was dedicated with a prayer of thanksgiving to God for allowing the greatest crisis in their history. Sometimes things have to fall apart before they can fall together. We may have to lose good things so that we can get better things. The folks in Enterprise would say amen to something Coach John Wooden often said:

Things turn out best for the people who make the best of the way things turn out.

———— ⚬⚬⚬ ————

Be truly glad. There is wonderful joy ahead, even
though you must endure many trials for a little while.

1 PETER 1:6

The Hand That Rocks
the Cradle

❦

Sukey was a feminist long before it was fashionable. In an age when girls were raised to please husbands and birth babies, she had bigger dreams. Her doting daddy treated her more like a son than a daughter. While other girls were learning how to cook and sew, he taught her Latin and Greek. When ladies retired to the parlor after dinner, she joined the men in the library.

Because she was allowed to soar intellectually, Sukey set her heart on publishing poetry a century before Jane Austen broke the gender barrier, and she fantasized about being the first woman admitted to Oxford. But her father clipped her wings by forcing her to marry Samuel, a mediocre preacher. She would spend her marriage in rural parishes with country bumpkins.

Their first parish was a dreary village with a mud cottage manse. She gave birth to seven children, only to watch three of them die. A careless midwife maimed the seventh for life. After six difficult pregnancies in eight years, Sukey almost died of exhaustion.

Things looked up when they were called to a richer parish. But Samuel managed money as badly as he preached. When their eighth child was born, he took to the road to earn extra income. He returned home enough times to sire five more children, who all died in infancy. After their manse burned down, Samuel abandoned his family. When he finally returned, Sukey birthed five more babies in rapid succession. He left it to her to educate their passel of kids. Both sons and daughters got as fine an education as the young scholars at Oxford.

When he was sixty-five, Samuel suffered a stroke. Sukey cared for him for seven years while they survived on charity. The feminist who dreamed of publishing poetry spent her life in obscurity. She gave birth to nineteen children, burying eight of them in infancy. Only seven were still alive when she died. You might be tempted to weep for her if you didn't know the rest of her story.

Her daddy nicknamed her Sukey. But history remembers her by her given name, Susanna, the wife of the Reverend Samuel Wesley. One of her sons, John, sparked a great revival in colonial America that birthed the Revolutionary War. Along the way, he founded the Methodist Church. Another son, Charles, penned more than nine thousand poems and hymns. Samuel Jr. became one of England's greatest scholars. Hetty became the poet her mother was never allowed to be. Two other daughters were prominent educators. All of Sukey's dreams, and so much more, were realized through the children she nurtured and inspired. One might argue that there would be no United States had there been no Susanna Wesley. Certainly, millions owe their spiritual lives to that woman.

Do you see your story in Sukey's disappointments? Have your dreams been dashed or your hopes postponed? Maybe life has deposited you at a wide spot on the road to nowhere. Is it possible that God has placed you here for bigger purposes than you can dare imagine? Take heart from Susanna Wesley's story:

God's gifts put our best dreams to shame.

⁓⊙⊙⊙⁓

"I know the plans I have for you," declares the
LORD, "plans to prosper you and not to harm
you, plans to give you hope and a future."

JEREMIAH 29:11, NIV

The Monkey That
Escaped the Nazis

⋄⊙⊙⊙⋄

Hans and his wife, Margarete, will never forget May 10, 1940. That day Hitler's blitzkrieg rolled across the French borders. As the Luftwaffe rained down fire from the skies, three million German soldiers followed in their wake.

Paris was in chaos as thousands fled. Hans and Margarete had more reason than most to flee. Both were German Jews with no illusions about what the Nazi SS would do to them. But they didn't act in time. Maybe they had lost their edge while enjoying the leisurely pace of Brazil when they lived there a few years earlier. By now, all the bicycles and vehicles were gone.

So Hans scoured the city for spare parts to build their bicycles. They stole out of town early one morning, leaving a lifetime of accumulated treasures behind. Yet hidden in their satchel was their most precious possession: the manuscript for a children's book.

Their journey was harrowing as they traveled by night and hid in barns by day. They faced their most dangerous moment at the border of Spain. Their Brazilian passports hid the fact that they were Jews. But their German accents caused Spanish border guards to suspect that they were spies. They held their breath as a guard scoured their satchel. When he was satisfied that the papers inside were only a manuscript for a children's story about a monkey, he let them go. From Spain, Hans and Margarete traveled to Portugal and on to Brazil.

When they got to South America, they had little money and few prospects for a job. So they took a steamer to New York, arriving with nothing but that manuscript. Through the intervention of a friend, Hans and Margarete were given an audience in the offices of Houghton Mifflin. At first, the publishers were skeptical. Why did they give the story of a mischievous male monkey the title of *Fifi*? Were children ready for a farcical story with colorful illustrations in a time of war?

We should be thankful that Houghton Mifflin took a chance on that story. We should be grateful because Hans and Margarete had the good sense to take their stories when they left everything else behind in Paris.

Several generations of children have been taught some of life's most valuable lessons by the adventures of a monkey that the publishers renamed Curious George. You may remember Hans and Margarete by their pseudonyms, H. A. and Margret Rey. Some seventy-five million copies of their Curious George books have been sold in more than twelve languages worldwide, and millions of children have watched that mischievous monkey escape thousands of slapstick dangers on television. But none was more hair-raising than the time he escaped the Nazis in 1940.

What if you had to run for your life like the Reys? If you could only take one or two things, what would they be? Very little of what you possess is all that precious. You might want to take an inventory of your belongings. It would surely tell you a lot about you and your life. No fact is more important than this:

When your life is summed up, your measure is more than your treasure.

———— ✶ ————

Wherever your treasure is, there the
desires of your heart will also be.

MATTHEW 6:21

Chariot Wheels in the Sea

The claim advanced by the Torah is the most controversial and endur- ing mystery of antiquity. How did 2.4 million escaping slaves walk through a divided Red Sea that later drowned the pursuing Egyptian army?

One explanation is that the Exodus took a route across a reed-filled shallow lake north of the Red Sea. Recent computer models touted by ABC News and Smithsonian.com suggest that a sustained wind shear could have blown the water back, allowing the Israelites to cross on mudflats. A shift of wind would have reversed the flow, drowning the Egyptians. That answer raises a bigger question: How did a whole army drown in six feet of water?

Another answer is that the crossing took place at the Gulf of Aqaba, much farther south than the traditional spot designated by Constantine's mother in the fourth century. The ancients called that place *Yam Suph*— their name for the Red Sea. But that site poses its own problems. The gulf is as deep and steep as the Grand Canyon. It would have taken days for 2.4 million people and all their livestock to descend down and up such a yawning canyon, even if they could do it.

But satellite photos astounded the world when they showed an under- water land bridge from Nuweiba (in Egypt) to Saudi Arabia. At both sides it slopes down at a gentle six-degree angle to a flat surface about nine hundred feet deep. More astounding are two ancient stone pillars, one in Egypt and the other in Saudi Arabia. The one in Arabia is etched with paleo-Hebrew words for Pharaoh, death, Egypt, King Solomon, and the Israelite word for God—YHWH. The best speculation is that Solomon erected these pillars to commemorate the Red Sea crossing some five hundred years before. He surely knew better than Constantine's mother or modern scientists where the crossing of the Yam Suph took place.

The amazing evidence doesn't stop there. In 2003, reporters interviewed a British diver who claimed to have sat in an Egyptian chariot cab among an underwater junkyard of chariot wells, ancient weapons, and other artifacts. More astounding is the footage taken by remote-controlled submarines that shows chariot parts encrusted with coral in the underwater land bridge. The most astounding image is that of a royal chariot wheel that remains untainted by time because coral cannot stick to gold or silver.

While the evidence is compelling, it does not answer every question. How did the waters part? A wind strong enough to do that would have buffeted the Israelites with the force of a hurricane. Could it have been a tsunami sucking the waters back before the sea came crashing back down on the Egyptians? That's highly unlikely. Ultimately, we are stuck with the necessity of a miracle.

Perhaps that leaves us right where God wants us: with enough evidence to bolster our wavering faith but enough questions to force us to depend on his Word with sustaining faith. Even chariot wheels on a video screen can't replace faith. We need to keep in mind something Blaise Pascal said:

Faith is different from proof; the one is human, the other is a gift of God.

The father instantly cried out, "I do believe, but help me overcome my unbelief!"

MARK 9:24

The Healing Town

෧ඁ෧෨

The amazing story of Geel, Belgium, is rooted in a tragedy. Some say that it is legend, but the townspeople swear it's gospel truth. In the seventh century, an Irish princess by the name of Dymphna fled from her incestuous, insane father. She found her way to the little village of Geel, where she was given refuge. There she lived as a virgin, helping the discouraged, suicidal, and mentally ill.

Dymphna's fame spread, and soon people were flocking to Geel. But the good news that attracted them found its way back to the Irish castle of the king. He traveled to Geel, where his men-at-arms seized his daughter. The king demanded she become his wife. When Dymphna refused his incestuous lusts, he had her beheaded. The villagers were distraught. What would they do with the mentally ill now that their caregiver was martyred?

At that critical moment, an amazing thing took place. The villagers of Geel made a vow to continue the princess's ministry to the mentally ill. In the fourteenth century, they built a church in honor of St. Dymphna. Soon medieval pilgrims were streaming to the shrine to find healing for their mentally ill kin. Sadly, most left in the dark of night, abandoning their relatives on the steps of the church and in its hospice. Soon the facilities built to care for the distraught, suicidal, and mentally ill were overtaxed.

Again, the amazing folk of Geel got together and agreed that they would open their homes to these needy visitors and enfold them into their families. By the 1930s, one-third of the residents of Geel—some four thousand people—were boarders suffering from some sort of mental illness. Their host families were mostly unschooled farmers and uneducated laborers. Yet by simply loving their guests as family, they provided them with arguably the best form of therapy they could receive. The

International Congress of Psychiatry declared last century that Geel was an example of best practices other places could duplicate.

How is it that simple farmers and laborers have been more effective than psychologists, social workers, and psychiatrists with advanced degrees? Studies have concluded that in most cases, families are better than facilities, and homes trump hospitals. There is no better cure for mental illness than acceptance and unconditional love.

Is it possible that there would be less mental illness if there were more hospitality? In an age of social media, where people are increasingly isolated, traditional families disintegrate, and homes become private retreats with locked doors, we might want to return to Geel to find an answer as old as the seventh century: before we can open our homes, we must open our hearts. Princess Dymphna just might agree with this provocative truth:

Entertainment is about impressing others. Hospitality is about serving them.

————— ❧ —————

I was hungry, and you fed me. I was thirsty, and you gave me a drink. I was a stranger, and you invited me into your home. I was naked, and you gave me clothing. I was sick, and you cared for me. I was in prison, and you visited me.

MATTHEW 25:35-36

Only the Lonely

꿈꿈꿈

As a child, Pyotr Ilyich dreaded rejection. His domineering mother repeatedly warned her insecure child that God would turn his back on Pyotr if he wasn't a good little boy! As hard as he tried, Pyotr was too much of a free spirit to please his stern parents. Despite the fact that he was a musical prodigy, his parents insisted that he train for a safe career in the civil service. When he decided to enroll in the music conservatory, his father refused to forgive him. His parents' rejection would twist his soul and unleash his manic genius.

Within a few years, Pyotr was composing music for the ages. Yet critics declared it too romantic, musicians deemed it shallow, and highbrows dismissed it as sentimental. That chorus of criticism plunged him into despair. But common folk flocked to his concerts, making him a superstar. His king proudly proclaimed him a national treasure. He should have been happy with those accolades, but Pyotr invariably allowed a single criticism to cancel out a thousand compliments. Years of rejection had so shattered his psyche that he was constantly suicidal.

A deep secret caused him his greatest anguish. Pyotr was a closet homosexual. If the truth ever got out, he would be ruined. So he tried to suppress his feelings by getting married. But his new wife was like his disapproving mother. His marriage ended disastrously. He longed to confess his homosexuality to a priest but feared being ostracized by the church. He surely wasn't going to tell his family.

When a homosexual lover exposed him to the world, he suffered a mental breakdown. A Russian court denounced him as a moral degenerate. Some historians speculate that, unhinged by this final condemnation, he ended his life, possibly by drinking arsenic-laced water.

The world knows Pyotr by his anglicized name, Peter—Peter Tchaikovsky. He is celebrated as the musical genius who wrote such masterpieces as the *Romeo and Juliet* overture, scores for ballets like *Swan Lake*, *The Sleeping Beauty*, and *The Nutcracker*, the stirring *1812 Overture*, soaring symphonies, and the opera *Eugene Onegin*. Who would have guessed that such breathtaking beauty was birthed by such a tortured soul?

Before he died, he penned these heartrending words: "None but the lonely feel my anguish." One of life's mysteries is how loveliness is born of ugliness or greatness is forged out of affliction. God always does his greatest work through the most flawed people. It might help us all to make this our faith credo when, like Peter Tchaikovsky, our story is filled with lonely anguish:

God can take my pain and use it to turn my life into a masterpiece.

Consider it pure joy . . . whenever you face
trials of many kinds, because you know that the
testing of your faith develops perseverance.

JAMES 1:2-3, NIV

The Man Who
Brought Bad Luck

꿍꿍

Some would say that Bobby was the luckiest kid in the world. Unlike his log cabin daddy, he went to the most elite schools in America. Not many kids get to be the son of a nation's leader or bear one of the most famous names in its history. Not only that, he was the only child in his family to survive to adulthood.

Because of family connections, he entered the army as a high-ranking officer. He was given a cushy job on the staff of the commanding general of the armies. Bobby not only came through that bloody war without a scratch, he had a front row seat at the signing of the treaty that ended it.

Bobby was the golden boy. But few people know about his luckiest moment. When the train he was traveling on stopped, he got out to stretch his legs. Just as he leaned up against a railroad car, it lurched forward, throwing him between the platform and the moving train. The kid would have died if a passerby hadn't pulled him to safety. The man who saved him was one of the greatest actors of his day. The president's boy surely recognized this superstar. But the celebrity didn't know who he had rescued until he received a letter of gratitude from the White House.

Later, Bobby's family name helped him become a successful corporate lawyer, the US secretary of war, and the foreign minister to Britain, and helped him make millions in lucrative business deals. Surely, Bobby—better known as Robert Todd Lincoln—was lucky in life.

But he wasn't so lucky for others. He had to sign the commitment papers to lock his mother away in an asylum. Mary Todd Lincoln never forgave Bobby for putting her away. He wasn't able to bring good luck to his father, either. As it turned out, the actor who saved his life that day at the train tracks was Edwin Booth, the brother of John Wilkes Booth—the assassin who later shot Bobby's father.

When Abraham Lincoln was carried from Ford's Theatre, Robert rushed to his bedside. He was in the room when his father died. Sixteen years later, he was serving as James Garfield's secretary of war when he witnessed an assassin fire two shots, one of which killed the president. On September 6, 1901, Robert was attending an event at the invitation of William McKinley when he heard that he had been shot. Twice he came to the bedside of a wounded president only to see him die too. Four US Presidents have been assassinated, and Robert Todd Lincoln was there for three of them. It's no wonder that he refused every president's invitation after that. He wryly observed that there was "a certain fatality about the presidential function when I am present."

Robert Todd Lincoln's amazing story raises a question: Are the circumstances of life a matter of blind luck? The Bible says no. History is really God's story. He uses even those events that are the results of our sins or foolish choices to write exactly what he wants into each chapter of our stories. He also reserves the Author's right to compose the final lines just the way he chooses. So take heart in this:

God is writing your life story, using both good and bad, to create an eternal bestseller.

The generous will prosper; those who refresh
others will themselves be refreshed.

PROVERBS 11:25

The Man Who Died
Three Times

⊷⊚⊶

Pastor Laszlo Tokes died three times. First he died to his dreams. He left a prestigious pulpit in his native Hungary when he felt God's call to a struggling church among despised minorities in Timisoara, Romania.

Then he died to his career. The Communist authorities put the squeeze on his bishop to muzzle his preaching. Pastor Tokes refused to compromise, so the bishop ordered him to vacate his tiny apartment in the church. After authorities canceled his ration card, his family survived on handouts from parishioners.

Finally he died to life itself. The secret police were coming to arrest him. Everyone knew that when the dreaded Securitate hauled anyone away, they were never seen again. His friends begged him to go into hiding. He responded with Martin Luther's words, "Here I stand. I can do nothing else. If I die, then I die."

A goon squad came in the dark of night on December 15, 1989. To their surprise, three hundred parishioners surrounded the church with arms locked together in solidarity. Inspired by their pastor's willingness to die, they were willing to give up their lives too. Word of their standoff with the secret police spread and thousands joined them. The bullies from the Securitate retreated, and a revolution that began with tearing down the Berlin Wall six weeks earlier came to Romania.

Two days later a hundred thousand people stormed Communist headquarters in Timisoara, shouting in unison, "God is alive! Jesus is alive!" Word of the uprising spread to the capital city of Bucharest, and almost a million people marched in the streets shouting, "God is alive! Jesus is alive!"

Dictator Nicolae Ceausescu was hiding in his mansion. This hard-line Communist had ruled the country with sadistic cruelty for twenty-four years. He created the Securitate with the largest network of spies and informants in Eastern Europe. Ceausescu declared Romania to be atheistic, but he demanded to be worshiped like a god. This hypocritical socialist and his scheming wife had systematically looted billions from the nation's treasury while living like capitalist royalty.

Yet a pastor's courage brought them down. As protesters surged through the streets, the army turned on their dictator. On Christmas Day, nine days after the Securitate had come to arrest Laszlo Tokes, a military court tried Nicolae and Elena Ceausescu on the charge of genocide. Within two hours they were convicted and executed. A pastor who died to self changed his country, but the dictator who lived for himself was swept into the dustbin of history.

The story of Laszlo Tokes reflects the sacrificial life of the Christ he served. Before there can be a resurrection, there must be death. This uncommonly brave pastor had to die three times before there was new life in Romania. What do you need to die to for things to change for the better? Laszlo Tokes's story proves that what happened in Jerusalem nearly two thousand years earlier can happen to us, if only we believe this truth: *Jesus cannot rise in you until you have died to yourself.*

***

My old self has been crucified with Christ. It is
no longer I who live, but Christ lives in me.

GALATIANS 2:20

Booed off the Stage

✑

From the time he was eight years old, Jerome knew that he wanted to be a comedian. Maybe it was because his sign-maker daddy was a closet comedian, or because he grew up in a wisecracking Brooklyn Jewish family.

While other kids were playing baseball, Jerome spent hours every day watching comedy on television to learn the art of delivering a joke. Over time, he honed his own brand of comedy that majored on wry observations about the mundane, everyday things of life.

He also grew up with every comedian's nightmare—bombing on the stage. He recalls the first time he performed stand-up comedy before an audience. Weeks before his debut, he meticulously wrote the script. Every morning he picked it up off his bed and rehearsed it over and over again. He stood before the mirror and practiced every facial expression, pause, and body movement. He knew what every storyteller or comedian knows—the lines don't matter as much as the timing, pacing, and delivery.

But when he stepped onto the stage, his mind went blank. He stood there for thirty seconds, searching his memory for the opening line. He may have looked like a stone statue on that stage, but inside he was going crazy.

The audience went from silent to fidgety to restless. Then the material came rushing into his mind like a tsunami. The humorous observations he had meticulously memorized came out in a rush of disconnected nonsensical words: "The beach . . . ah, driving . . . your parents . . ."

At first the audience nervously laughed, thinking that this was his shtick. Then it was evident that the kid on the stage was zoning out. After about three minutes, Jerome gave up and literally ran off the stage. Behind the curtains, he heard the booing and catcalls of people who had paid good money to laugh.

Jerome could have quit after that initial failure. A lot of folks would have. But the budding comedian came back to the same stage and performed flawlessly. We should be glad that he did. The world would be a lot poorer without the brilliant and humorous observations of Jerome Seinfeld, better known by his childhood nickname—Jerry.

He went on from that opening night debacle to become one of America's favorite comedians. His show, *Seinfeld*, was the highest-rated program on television during much of its nine-year run. His syndicated show, television specials, books, and live concerts have made him one of the top-ten comedians in the world, with an estimated worth of $820 million.

It's never easy getting up in front of people and talking. One of Seinfeld's funniest observations is that "according to most studies, people's number one fear is public speaking. Number two is death. Now, this means, to the average person, if you have to go to a funeral, you're better off in the casket than doing the eulogy."

Maybe you've been booed off the stage of life. Everyone has. The great ones have bombed more than anyone else. The issue is not whether you mess up but whether you get back up there.

Falling down is part of life. Getting up is living life.

Do not gloat over me, my enemies! For
though I fall, I will rise again.

MICAH 7:8

The Miracle at Naseby

ぐのⓈ◡

Nothing much ever happens in sleepy Naseby. Yet by happenstance of history, two armies collided there on the morning of June 14, 1645. The battle outside that little village would change the course of Western civilization.

Massed on the sheep pasture outside Naseby was the proud army of His Catholic Majesty King Charles I of England. His Royalist forces were shined and polished, their steel and muskets flashing in the cold sunlight under scarlet banners dancing in the breeze. Supporting the massed infantry were the Cavaliers, the finest swordsmen and cavalry in Europe, led by Prince Rupert, the swashbuckling nephew of King Charles. With swaggering bravado, he boasted that his Cavaliers would rout their ragtag enemy and be back in camp in time for lunch.

Across the field, the army of Parliament waited with fear rising in their throats. Mostly made up of drafted farmers and vastly outnumbered, they stood little chance at Naseby that day. While royal princes led the king's forces, Parliament's army was led by rugged Puritans more familiar with Bibles and plows than muskets and cannons. Among them was a farmer, Oliver Cromwell, leading the cavalry that would face Prince Rupert and his Cavaliers that morning.

Cromwell shouted out to his men, "Boys, keep your powder dry and your prayer books handy. Our battle is in the Lord's hands, and he alone gives the victory." As one man, his army fell to their knees. One by one, Puritan preachers among these farm boys began to cry out for supernatural strength.

At Naseby the prayers of country bumpkins overcame the polished steel of the royal army. Prince Rupert and his vaunted Cavaliers charged across the field, only to be outmaneuvered by Cromwell and put to flight. The army of Parliament surged forward and the rout was on. Prince Rupert was right: the battle was over before lunch. But it was the Royalists who were broken and in disarray.

The fate of a civil war that divided England was decided that day. It wasn't long before the rule of elected assembly replaced the absolute authority of the king. On the fields of Naseby, the blood of citizen farmers purchased a radical new government that would later flower in America.

Those of us who enjoy the freedoms of a government of the people, by the people, and for the people, should never forget the moment that turned the tide from king to Parliament that day. As Prince Rupert's Cavaliers charged across the field, Oliver Cromwell whispered a prayer to God before he pulled down the visor of his helmet: "If in the heat of battle this day, I should forget to remember thee, I pray that thou wouldst not forget me." Surely, the Lord did not forget him.

Cromwell's army was at its most lethal when it was on its knees in prayer. A battlefield may be looming before you today. Perhaps the odds are overwhelming. Before you pull down the visor to your helmet and march off to war, why don't you get down on your knees? The Battle of Naseby is another proof of this inviolate principle of warfare:

The greatest powers cannot overcome the humblest prayers.

―――――― ❧ ――――――

It is not by force nor by strength, but by my
Spirit, says the LORD of Heaven's Armies.

ZECHARIAH 4:6

The Longest-Standing Army

⁓⊙⊙⊛⌀

It is the longest-standing army in history. For more than two millennia, these eight thousand have stood their ground, rock solid and vigilant. They peer through stony eyes that have never flinched or closed. They are as ready for battle as they were the first day they stood on parade—fierce cavalrymen on warhorses, archers with bows cocked, artillery men pulling catapults, charioteers in speedy chariots, and auxiliary servants and civilian supporters.

There was a time when their uniforms were colorful and bright, each piece of their armor superbly crafted. Their faces were golden bronze back then. Time has aged their garb and grayed their faces, but they still stand guard against demons and other evil spirits. They have never taken a break, eaten a meal, or gone on furlough. No army has ever been more faithful to their mission.

Yet the world did not know about this amazing army until 1974, when Chinese farmers, digging a well, discovered their hiding place. More than two millennia have come and gone while the terra-cotta soldiers stand at attention. The reason for their existence, and the staggering conceit of a single warlord, is a tale worth telling and remembering.

Qin Shi Huang, founder of the Qin dynasty, had unified China after years of war to become its first emperor in 221 BC. He built cities and monuments to his glory, and then began the first version of China's Great Wall. But the mausoleum that he built near the city of Xi'an is the greatest monument to his towering ego.

Though it was never finished, it is the biggest burial complex in history.

Seven hundred thousand artisans and laborers worked for some thirty years to build and fill a twenty-square-mile compound with that massive army of life-size soldiers, each crafted in exact detail. Every aspect of a fully equipped army was duplicated in clay, down to the weapons and food storehouses for the lifeless soldiers.

Why this herculean labor and monumental expense? Emperor Qin Shi Huang wanted an army to accompany him into his afterlife. Though he could rule his own world, the underworld was beyond his control. He figured that a terra-cotta army, without human emotions or fears, could be trusted to guard him through eternity, no matter what spirits, demons, gods, or monsters might attack.

There is an irony to Qin's attempts to control his eternal destiny. Though his armies still stand at attention, his body remains in the ground.

All of us will enter the afterlife. Emperor and commoner alike will go naked to face God. But we don't need to go alone, or with fear. Nor do we need an army to protect us—not terra-cotta, human, or angelic. Jesus is enough.

As long as Jesus goes with us, we can go anywhere unafraid.

———— ༄ ————

Even when I walk through the darkest valley
I will not be afraid, for you are close beside me.
Your rod and your staff protect and comfort me.

PSALM 23:4

Saving Milly

❧◦ᏩᏭ◦☙

Most folks didn't think that Mort and Millicent's marriage would go the distance. Mort was a moderate Republican. Millicent was a fiery left-wing Democrat. Over the years, they began to drift in their marriage. It wasn't that they fell out of love. They were just too busy pursuing careers.

Millicent became a psychotherapist working with patients suffering from neurological disorders such as Parkinson's disease. That's how she knew something was wrong that day in 1987. She was signing a check and couldn't finish her name. She noticed a tremor in her little finger and a wobble in her left foot. Millicent was terrified. After tests were run, the news was devastating. Not only did she have Parkinson's disease, it was the most virulent strain.

She called Mort and told him to get home right away. He found her holding a bottle in her trembling hand. "This is Parkinson's medicine!" she screamed. "It's a horrible disease. I won't be able to walk. I won't be able to talk. I won't be able to eat. I'll be totally dependent on you." Her body racked with sobs. "You won't love me anymore. I know that you will leave me."

"I will never leave you," replied Mort. But Millicent wasn't convinced. She knew the statistics. More than 50 percent of husbands leave wives diagnosed with Parkinson's, and she was sure Mort would do the same. At that moment, he had to make a life-altering decision. He knew that Parkinson's victims became completely dependent on their families. If he became a caregiver to his wife, it would derail his career.

You may recall Morton Kondracke, who was the cohost of Fox News channel's *The Beltway Boys*. His rise in the media had been meteoric: ten years as a panelist on the PBS news program *The McLaughlin Group*, senior editor of the *New Republic*, Washington bureau chief of *Newsweek*, columnist for the *Wall Street Journal* and the *Washington Post*, and the most sought-after talking head on prime-time television.

In his book *Saving Milly*, Morton Kondracke wrote, "At that moment I made the decision to change from careerist to a caregiver." For seventeen years he devoted himself to caring for his wife. Eventually Milly was unable to walk or talk, and finally she was unable to swallow. Mort had to feed her, bathe her, and clean up her messes. Mort desperately prayed for Milly. As he spent less time in the newsroom and more in Milly's bedroom, he cried out to God, "What's my purpose here?" A simple answer came back: "Take care of Milly."

When Milly died on July 22, 2004, Mort's career was finished. He had been out of the game too long. But he would tell you that those years he gave to Milly were worth far more. Careers pale in significance to the care we give loved ones. If you put your life on hold to do what Mort did for Milly, let this encourage you during those often exasperating and thankless hours:

Careers will fade in importance and soon be forgotten, but heaven's applause for caregivers will last forever.

The Son of Man is going to come in his Father's
glory with his angels, and then he will reward each
person according to what they have done.

MATTHEW 16:27, NIV

The Exorcism of a Saint

❧

The old woman had lost her mind. At eighty-six years of age, she took a bad fall and broke her collarbone. Emaciated and frail, she also suffered from heart failure. So she was rushed to a hospital. During the day she curled up in a ball of silent despair. At night she screamed, ripped out her hair, and pulled wires from the monitoring equipment. Nothing could calm her high anxiety.

The archbishop was called to the old woman's room. He couldn't believe that this beloved and saintly woman was contorted in such convulsions of anger. He was sure that she must be demon possessed. So he called a priest to do an exorcism. When the priest saw who she was, he refused.

The archbishop insisted. "I command you to do it!" So he reluctantly obeyed his superior. The woman writhed and screamed while he performed his exorcism. When it was over, she fell into a deep sleep of utter peace.

Who would have guessed that an exorcism would need to be performed on a nun who had earned the Nobel Prize seventeen years earlier? For eighteen years she topped a Gallup Poll as the world's most admired woman. The people of India voted her the most beloved figure in their history. Years after her exorcism, she was canonized as a saint of the Roman Catholic Church.

Now you understand why someone as exalted as the archbishop was called to her room and why a priest hesitated to obey orders to perform an exorcism. Who would believe that Mother Teresa of Calcutta could be demonized? When reports of her exorcism were leaked to CNN, the world was shocked. How could a saint be under such attack by demons? Actually, it makes a lot of sense. Her closest friend, Sister Nirmala, told

CNN, "Mother Teresa often felt abandoned by God. But then, Jesus also felt abandoned on the cross."

Most of us have never come remotely close to exhausting ourselves in works of mercy the way Mother Teresa did for more than sixty years. If we did, we might find ourselves suffering with the kind of compassion fatigue that erodes the human soul. We might even find ourselves saying with Jesus, "My God, my God, why have you forsaken me?" (Matthew 27:46, ESV). If we really were a clear and present danger to the kingdom of darkness, we might find ourselves under the most severe kinds of demonic attack. Father Stroscio—who performed Mother Teresa's exorcism—said, "In the history of the church, hundreds of saints have gone through such things."

It is a risky thing to bring the love of Christ to places of suffering and despair. If you have committed to being light and salt where decay and darkness are at their worst, may your tribe increase! You might never be canonized like Mother Teresa, but you are one of those saints who puts a smile on God's face. When the enemy of your soul launches a frontal attack, don't let it fill you with doubt. It goes with the territory. Like Mother Teresa, you will overcome the darkness if you remember this:

The one who tries to bring you down is already below you.

———— ∞ ————

Humble yourselves before God. Resist
the devil, and he will flee from you.

JAMES 4:7

Freedom's Cry

✦✦✦

In an age when we demand our rights, the story of Johann and David is beyond amazing. These radical Moravians from Germany were the rarest of all Christians. They actually took Jesus at his word and were willing to live a gospel lifestyle—no matter the cost. When their leader, Count Zinzendorf, called them to go as missionaries to the Caribbean islands of St. Thomas and St. Croix, they didn't hesitate to do whatever necessary to get there.

The islands were covered with sugar plantations run by a handful of Danes. The vast majority of the population were African slaves who labored, languished, and died under the whip. Their slave masters ruled by intimidation and musket, living in constant fear of a slave uprising. The last thing they wanted was an influx of Moravian do-gooder missionaries teaching their slaves how to read and write, or that Jesus loved them. Such talk might lead their slave property to get big ideas about human dignity and freedom.

So the authorities refused to allow missionaries. Only slaves, slave masters, and traders were allowed to step foot on these Caribbean islands. That's when Johann and David came up with the bizarre idea to sell themselves as slaves. Who could be better to reach black slaves for Jesus than white men who willingly took on their slavery? The genius of their plan was that it was exactly what their Savior did some 1,700 years earlier.

When Johann and David arrived in Copenhagen, their fellow believers discouraged them from boarding a ship for the islands. They said that it was preposterous that white men could become slaves. These missionaries became the gossip of the Danish capital. The queen was so impressed that she took up their cause and made sure they found a way to the islands.

Johann and David were not allowed to become slaves, but they did find work as poor carpenters.

Johann Leonhard Dober and David Nitschmann's courageous faith opened the door for other Moravian missionaries to come to the Danish islands. Within a few decades they baptized some thirteen thousand converts. Later David Nitschmann accompanied John Wesley to America, where he helped spark the Great Awakening revivals that set the American colonies ablaze. He also helped start the Moravian work at Bethlehem, Pennsylvania.

These two men challenge our casual faith assumptions. Could it be that Johann and David had a better grasp of the gospel than we do? Jesus came as a slave, to do his heavenly Father's will. He willingly gave up his rights and freedoms to bring liberty to others. If we are to go into our world the same way he did, doesn't it make sense that Dober and Nitschmann had it right all along? Consider this in the light of their amazing story:

We are called to be like Christ, not other Christians.

———— ∞ ————

[Jesus] said, "Peace be with you. As the Father
has sent me, so I am sending you."

JOHN 20:21

The Red Priest

❧✺❧

Iosif Vissarionovich Dzhugashvili was born the son of a peasant cobbler. After his face was scarred by smallpox and his left arm deformed in an accident, he became the butt of other children's cruel jokes. It caused Iosif to grow up sullen and insecure, seething inside with a harsh and vindictive spirit.

It seemed that the passionate Orthodox faith of his washerwoman mother was Iosif's only saving grace. The little boy grew quite religious. Priests and parishioners alike said that he was pious and even saintly. Everyone agreed that Iosif had a bright future as a Russian Orthodox priest.

His mother managed to scrape together the tuition necessary to enroll him in the church school at Gori. Iosif flourished as a student, earning high praises from teachers and priests alike. Every night, his Orthodox mother prayed for her son to make a name for himself in the service of God.

After Iosif graduated with accolades, he was sent off to Tiflis Theological Seminary to begin his final studies. He might have gone on to a fine career as a priest if some fellow students hadn't introduced him to Messame Dassey, a secret and outlawed organization dedicated to liberating Georgia from Czarist Russia. Before long, he was reading the banned writings of Marx and Lenin.

When Iosif converted to the intoxicating religion of Communism, the seminary leadership was not amused. Iosif was unceremoniously expelled from the seminary. Maybe that's why he later became an implacable atheist and foe of religion. His dedication to Bolshevism took him into its inner circles and made the new name he gave himself one of the most feared in history.

You know Iosif as Joseph Stalin, the monster who later caused millions of his own subjects to toss fearfully in their beds at night and constantly look over their shoulders by day. Most historians agree that twenty million people were killed in Stalin's reign of terror. This avowed atheist once quipped, "One death is a tragedy; one million is a statistic." His belief that people were not created in the image of God but were soulless products of biological evolution allowed him to use them as cogs in the socialist state machinery and then toss them aside like scrap metal when they were no longer useful.

Who would have believed that Joseph Stalin once studied for the priesthood? Or that the cruel and vindictive streak behind a boy's mask of piety would lead to such terror? It has often been said that most wars have been caused by religion. The facts don't support that myth. While there have been too many religious wars, the greatest mass murderers—Genghis Khan, Adolf Hitler, Joseph Stalin, Mao Zedong, Napoleon Bonaparte, Pol Pot, and other perpetrators of history's bloodiest wars—have been atheists or irreligious men. Those who want to see peace in the world should hope and pray that George Washington's words are heeded:

Religion and morality are the essential pillars of civil society.

_____ ⌘ _____

Godliness makes a nation great, but
sin is a disgrace to any people.

PROVERBS 14:34

Decision at Twenty-Nine Thousand Feet

⌒⌒⌒

They spotted him just after sunrise, perched on a knife-edge ridge. He sat in the brutal cold without jacket, gloves, or hat. Australian climber Lincoln Hall had been left for dead. American guide Dan Mazur, two paying clients, and a Sherpa were just hours from the summit of Mount Everest on May 26, 2006, when they spied Hall.

The American had to react quickly. Would his team continue their assent to the top or help Hall? Mazur decided to help. Two other climbers passed them on their way to the summit. When asked to help, the two pretended not to understand. Mazur later discovered that they spoke impeccable English. Even more astounding was the fact that a week before Hall's rescue, British climber David Sharp died one thousand feet from the top while dozens passed by on their way to the summit. But Mazur's team lugged Lincoln Hall back down, forfeiting their prize.

Before we fault climbers who bypassed Hall and Sharp, we should consider what it costs to get to the summit. The weather on Mount Everest is so brutal that there are only two windows a year for climbing, each about ten days. Fewer than half the climbers succeed in their attempt. Close to three hundred have died trying.

Climbing Everest isn't cheap, starting at $45,000. It begins with an eight-day hike from Kathmandu to the seventeen-thousand-foot base camp. The entire expedition will take about two months. As they head out from base camp, climbers face soaring ice towers and crevasses so deep that one can only see darkness rather than bottom. It's beautiful, otherworldly, and dangerous. One misstep can lead to death.

Towering waves of ice—several stories high—crack and collapse to create avalanches that bury climbers alive or plunge them into crevasses. At twenty thousand feet the air contains half the oxygen that it does at sea level. The sun radiating off the snow can create temperatures of eighty to one hundred degrees Fahrenheit, leading to heat exhaustion, or plunge to fifty degrees below zero, bringing hypothermia. At twenty-two thousand feet, climbers must scale the Lhotse Face, a 3,600-foot wall of ice. At this point they are breathing bottled oxygen. Winds can blow 175 miles per hour, a category five hurricane. At twenty-three thousand feet, climbers are beyond rescue by helicopters.

Above twenty-five thousand feet, climbers enter the death zone. Many suffer swelling of the brain and fluid in the lungs. It's half a mile from high camp to the summit, but the final ascent will take eight to twelve hours. Oxygen is now one-third of what it is at sea level. If climbers make it up Hillary Step for a few moments on a summit about the size of a dining room table, they now face the most lethal part of the trip: descending the twenty-nine-thousand-foot monster. Slowed judgment and reflexes from exhaustion cause mistakes that lead to far more deaths than on the way up.

When Mazur and his team chose to rescue Lincoln Hall, forfeiting their dreams so tantalizingly close to the summit, it was an amazing act of mercy. Showing mercy is often messy, and it is seldom easy. It cost God's Son everything. It will cost us, too. But even if we are twenty-nine thousand feet up, we need to remember this:

Every breath in your life is a gift of God's mercy.

―――――⸺◌◌―――――

God blesses those who are merciful,
for they will be shown mercy.

MATTHEW 5:7

Lieutenant Butch and Easy Eddie

❦

The two men couldn't have been more different. Butch was a World War II fighter pilot who served aboard the USS *Lexington* in the South Pacific. His squadron was on a mission when he radioed that he was leaking fuel. He was ordered to return immediately to his aircraft carrier.

Reluctantly, Butch broke formation and headed back to the fleet. As he burst through the clouds, his blood ran cold. A squadron of Japanese bombers was headed straight for the *Lexington*. Lieutenant Butch O'Hare dove straight into the Japanese formation, his wing-mounted .50-caliber guns blazing. With single-minded focus, he fired until his ammo was spent. Butch then began to ram enemy planes, scattering the bewildered Japanese.

After Butch limped back to the carrier, the camera mounted on his plane showed that he had shot down five Japanese bombers. He was the first naval ace in World War II, and the first naval aviator to win the Congressional Medal of Honor. A year later, Butch O'Hare died in aerial combat at age twenty-nine.

There was another man about the same age as Butch. But Easy Eddie was no hero. This crooked lawyer represented Al Capone, manipulating the legal system to keep the mobster out of prison. Big Al made Eddie the highest-paid attorney in America. His estate was so big that it covered an entire Chicago city block. But Easy Eddie couldn't sleep at night, knowing that he had prostituted himself to the bloodiest mob in gangland history.

Most of all Eddie worried about the legacy he would leave his son. He loved that boy more than life itself, and he wanted him to grow up a better man than he was. But as long as he was associated with Scarface Al Capone, he could never pass on to his son the two most important legacies of all: a good name and a great example. To do that he would have to rectify the crimes he had committed. So he made a courageous decision to walk away from the rackets and testify against Big Al. A year later, Easy Eddie was brutally gunned down by gangsters in Chicago.

The disgraced attorney redeemed a tarnished family name with his final act of heroism. His son grew up proud of the example set by his father, Eddie O'Hare. Maybe it was Eddie's final act of courage that inspired his son Butch to charge that Japanese squadron on February 20, 1942, and later die a hero's death in aerial combat. The next time you fly into Chicago, you might land at O'Hare International Airport, named in honor of Easy Eddie's war-hero son, Lieutenant Commander Butch O'Hare.

Eddie was no saint. Few of us are. But like Easy Eddie, we can work to give our children a good name and a great example. Our sons or daughters may not get an international airport named after them, but we can make it our aim to help them be better than we are. The stories of Easy Eddie and his son, Butch, teach us a great truth:

Our story is the longest-lasting legacy we will leave to our heirs.

The love of the LORD remains forever with those who
fear him. His salvation extends to the children's children.

PSALM 103:17

The Warrior Saint

⁘

Henry V had invaded France in a dispute over who should rightfully wear its crown. The English won, and a treaty gave their monarch the French throne upon the death of its old king. When both kings died about the same time, the treaty was null and void. So the war was on again.

It was during this endless slaughter that a teenage girl began to hear voices and see visions. The pious revered her as a prophetess, cynics dismissed her as a lunatic, and priests whispered that she was a witch. But the maiden was sure that God had called her to go as a messenger to Charles, the French crown prince, with a simple prophecy: "God will give you the throne, and I am to lead your armies to victory."

In a scenario that seemed to have been scripted in heaven, the teen prophetess arrived at the royal city. But the prince was a cautious man, skeptical of audible voices from God. So he dressed as a commoner to test her. When she picked him out of the crowd and then recited the exact words of a prayer he had uttered in private, he was convinced that she was indeed heaven sent. He turned his armies over to this medieval maiden on a mission from God.

What happened next is the stuff of legend. A village maiden in men's armor led royal French knights and hardened foot soldiers to stunning victories. The English were sure that she was a sorceress! When she was left for dead outside an English fortress, the British held a trial to prove that she was a witch.

In one of the great scandals of church history, a jury of collaborating French clerics was assembled. Some seventy charges were brought, but the unschooled girl made such fools out of these churchmen that the trial was moved to private chambers. In spite of the worst kind of threats, she refused to repudiate her visions or voices. So on May 30, 1431, Joan of Arc was burned at the stake before ten thousand witnesses.

Most folks believe that she was officially condemned as a witch. The truth is more shocking. In desperation, that kangaroo court came up with the only charge that would stick: she had cut her hair and worn men's armor in violation of the Old Testament warning that a woman who dresses like a man is detestable to God.

In our age, executing a girl for cutting her hair short or wearing pants seems so medieval. Yet in some ways little has changed in six hundred years. When we can't defeat ideas, we figure out ways to attack people with charges that have nothing to do with the issues. But ridding ourselves of the purveyors of inconvenient truths won't make their notions go away. In 1920, the same church that earlier burned Joan of Arc at the stake made her a saint. Be careful whom you burn at the stake in your mind or with your tongue. They just might be seen as saints by future generations.

Before you write others off, wait a while. Time has a way of clarifying and humbling.

<hr>

Look! He comes with the clouds of heaven. And
everyone will see him—even those who pierced him.

REVELATION 1:7

296

The Recovering Skinhead

~⚬⚬~

Prison is the most segregated institution in America. Survival depends on hooking up quickly with a gang, almost always based on race: the Mexican Mafia, the Aryan Brotherhood, the Black Guerilla Family, or the Nazi Low Riders. But Frank spent his year in prison crossing racial boundaries, mostly hanging out with two black friends. The Aryan Brotherhood called him a traitor to the white race. But he ignored their threats, playing catch in the yard with his diverse group of friends while gang members gnashed their teeth.

When Frank got out of prison, he went to work for a Jewish antique dealer, shocked that a person who dealt in valuables would hire an ex-convict. He had never spent time with Jews before. Now he was eating kosher food, learning Yiddish idioms, and hanging out with the Jewish Anti-Defamation League. Later, he appeared with Bishop Desmond Tutu to speak out against racism in South Africa. He teamed with the Philadelphia Flyers to start Harmony Through Hockey, bringing kids from different racial backgrounds together on the sports field. He addresses high school assemblies across America, urging them to reject racism and bigotry. Frank is the poster child for racial harmony.

It's almost impossible to believe that he was once a neo-Nazi skinhead. Even when he was throwing a football with his black buddies in the prison yard, he had a swastika tattooed on his neck, and while working for the Jewish antique dealer, his shirt hid a tattoo of Nazi propaganda minister Joseph Goebbels. In fact, Frank was in prison because police confiscated a videotape of him kicking a kid from a rival skinhead group half to death. Frank Meeink was one sick-minded racist. He had organized a Philadelphia crew of neo-Nazi skinheads dubbed the Strike Force. He can't remember how many attacks he led against gays, college students, African Americans, and rival neo-Nazis. He now confesses, "I rarely went more than a week without beating on somebody." He was also a skinhead recruiter on his cable access show, *The Reich*. No one was more hard core in his white supremacy than Frank Meeink.

His story was anything but amazing, until he found himself in prison. To this day, Frank doesn't know how he got thrown in with those two African American convicts, but it changed his life. He found out that his racial stereotypes were based on lies. When he could no longer pigeonhole people of different races, it began to chip away at his white supremacy. When a Jewish antiquities dealer showed him kindness, it exposed the stupidity of his anti-Semitism. But a lifetime of stinking thinking doesn't go away overnight. That's why Frank Meeink called his memoir *Autobiography of a Recovering Skinhead*. Like all of us, just when he thinks that the wolves in his soul are sleeping, they rise up to howl again. But he is *recovering*—and dramatically so!

All of us need to be recovering from something unhealthy. What do you need to change? No matter how bad it is, it can't be any worse than Frank's sickness. The amazing second half of his story proves this:

A few bad chapters doesn't mean that your story is over.

I focus on this one thing: Forgetting the past and
looking forward to what lies ahead, I press on.

PHILIPPIANS 3:13-14

The Quadriplegic Ironman

෴

Ricky was born with the worst kind of cerebral palsy. Doctors said he would be a vegetable for life and recommended that his parents institutionalize him. But his brothers, Rob and Russell, were defiant: "We're going to bring our little brother home and treat him like a regular kid."

Ricky's mom, Judy, refused to surrender to her baby's disability. She spent endless hours doing physical therapy with Ricky, painstakingly taught him the alphabet, and then got state laws changed so that he could attend public school. A special computer allowed him to communicate using head motions to select letters and spell out words.

When he was fifteen years old, Ricky asked his dad if he could compete in a race. His dad agreed, and he pushed his son in a jerry-rigged chair that now resides in the Massachusetts Sports Hall of Fame. After the race, Ricky tapped out a message: "Today I felt like I wasn't handicapped." That started an odyssey that has taken him around the world, averaging fifty races a year, including thirty-four Boston Marathons and a nearly four-thousand-mile bike ride across America.

But it was at the Ironman triathlon in Kona, Hawaii, that a worldwide television audience witnessed Ricky's miracle. Only elite athletes are allowed to compete in this ultratriathlon of swimming, biking, and running. Ricky and his dad are the only tandem team ever allowed to compete. They came in close to last, but they were the big story in 1997.

The world watched fifty-nine-year-old retired air force colonel Dick Hoyt carry his mute, quadriplegic twenty-seven-year-old son into the Pacific. He swam 2.5 miles in open water, pulling Ricky in a rubber raft attached to his wet suit. After that, he completed the grueling 112-mile bicycle course with Ricky strapped to a seat on his handlebars. Finally, he ran the 26.2-mile marathon while pushing Ricky in a race chair. There have been few moments in sports as inspiring as when Team Hoyt crossed the finish line, Ricky's face grinning with unrestrained joy.

Today Rick Hoyt is a graduate of Boston University. With the help of his caregivers, he lives in an apartment where he develops computers to aid disabled people. Not long ago, he tapped out on his computer to a *Boston Globe* reporter, "When I am running, my disabilities disappear." The reporter said to his dad, "But don't you do the running for your son?" Dick replied, "No, Rick runs the races. I just loan him my arms and legs." He added, "There's nothing in the world that we can't do together."

The story of Team Hoyt should encourage us all. God has called us to run the race of life. Sometimes it seems beyond our abilities. But we have a heavenly Father who says, "If you do the running, I will give you my arms and legs. There's nothing that we can't do together." So keep on running, inspired by this truth:

Where our strength runs out, God's strength begins.

_____ ❧ _____

Those who trust in the LORD will find new strength.
They will soar high on wings like eagles. They will run
and not grow weary. They will walk and not faint.

ISAIAH 40:31

Feeding Cannibals

✦

Jonah Vatunigere was eight years old when he opened the door to his people's dark history by asking his grandfather, "What do humans taste like?" The old Fijian replied, "I've never tried it, but I still remember what grandpa said that humans taste like pork." Jonah shuddered, remembering the barbequed pork he ate the day before.

Today the subject of cannibalism is avoided in polite Fijian conversation. But there was a time when ships steered a wide berth around their islands. No one knows exactly how these gentle people developed an appetite for human flesh. Some speculate that, on the long sea voyages of the original settlers, food ran out and they resorted to cannibalism.

There was no human flesh more desirable than that of sailors or missionaries who dared set foot on the islands. For that reason alone we should stand in awe of those Christians who were willing to end up in cooking pots to spread the gospel. Among those brave people were James Calvert and his young bride, Mary. The Wesleyan Missionary Society of England sent this couple to the "cannibal islands" in 1838. Though the voyage was a terrible storm-tossed ride, their arrival was even more frightening. The ship's captain begged them not to go ashore, warning the couple that they would likely be eaten. But Mr. and Mrs. Calvert could not be dissuaded. Setting their jaws, they landed to the beating of drums.

Shortly after landing, they faced the traumatizing task of burying the remains of eighty victims of a cannibal feast. But they were not dissuaded from their calling. Both learned the Fijian language, and James traveled across the far-flung archipelago in a leaky canoe, preaching to folks who would rather devour him than listen to his words.

There was little response until an act of bravery that still amazes some almost two hundred years later. Among the other barbaric customs of the cannibal islands was that of strangling the women in the king's household when he died. James offered to have his fingers cut off in exchange for the life of a king's daughter. Though he was not taken up on his astounding offer, the monarch was so impressed that he became a Christian. The Calverts would see spectacular results in their seventeen-year ministry in Fiji: thirteen hundred churches, thirty thousand baptized converts, and more than one hundred thousand church attenders. They might be amazed to know that over one hundred years after they left the islands, the descendants of those Fijian cannibals have the highest percentage of church attendance in the world.

James Calvert is most remembered for his response to the ship's captain who warned that he and his wife would die if they set foot on the Fiji Islands. Calvert replied, "We died before we came here." This is the secret to standing strong for biblical convictions in the face of opposition. When you are tempted to cut and run, you might consider the Calverts' story in light of a line from Shakespeare's *Julius Caesar*:

Cowards die many times before their deaths. The valiant never taste of death but once.

Only in this way could he set free all who have
lived their lives as slaves to the fear of dying.

HEBREWS 2:15

The Day an Angel
Fed Angels

⌒◯⌒

Jaye was the child of a poor Southern family, growing up in a ramshackle house on a country dirt road. Times were tough, and food was in short supply.

She was playing in the yard on a hot summer day when she heard the clanging of chains. She looked up to see grizzled men dressed in black-and-white-striped uniforms shackled together and shuffling down the road. Two armed guards led the chain gang to a shade tree where they all sat down.

One of the guards knocked on the front door and asked Jaye's mother if his men could get a drink of water from the backyard pump. She agreed, but there was a look of concern as she pulled her girl into the house. Jaye watched from a window as prisoners were unchained one by one to hobble over and drink. After they quenched their thirst, guards and prisoners retreated to the shade.

Jaye's mother called her to the kitchen. In the blink of an eye, she had ferreted out the final tins of tuna in the cupboard. She used the last bread in the house to make a tray of tuna fish sandwiches. Alongside them stood two pitchers of ice-cold lemonade. She passed one pitcher to Jaye, and then, lifting the tray of sandwiches and the other pitcher, she led her out of the house and across the road.

Guards and prisoners began to stand up. But Jaye's mother said, "Oh no! Stay where you are! I'll serve you." With little Jaye at her side, she went down the line, filling each convict's tin cup with lemonade and giving each man a sandwich. A white woman serving lunch to black convicts on a chain gang was no small thing in the Deep South more than fifty years ago.

Each man silently ate his tuna fish sandwich and savored a tin cup of lemonade. Jaye remembers a quiet reverence like that in a cathedral. As the prisoners got up, one man said to Jaye's mother, "Ma'am, I've wondered all my life if I'd ever see an angel, and now I have. Thank you!" She softly replied, "You are all welcome. God bless you!" The prisoners moved on, their steps a bit quicker and their shoulders a little higher. Jaye never saw them again. But she remembers her mother mumbling a Bible verse about entertaining angels.

Jaye Lewis has grown up to be a wonderful writer of short stories. She still can't recall what her mother managed to scrape together from an almost empty cupboard to feed her own family that night. Some fifty years later, she knows one thing for sure: the same angel who served that chain gang served her family that night. Jaye's mother would disagree. She would quickly say that the real angel was more likely one of those prisoners. We never know when angels might drop by our house. They seldom look the way we picture them. Remember the story of Jaye Lewis's mother as you interact with others today. You might want to repeat this to yourself with each encounter:

I could be a person serving an angel, or like an angel serving people.

⎯⎯⎯ ❧ ⎯⎯⎯

Don't forget to show hospitality to strangers, for some who have done this have entertained angels without realizing it!

HEBREWS 13:2

When Faith Walked
across Niagara Falls

ക∕ഠ∕ൟ

N iagara Falls is some kind of monster. Less than a handful of dare-devils have challenged its fury and lived to tell about it. It's no won-der that more than one hundred thousand spectators gathered there and millions more tuned in to ABC to watch Nik Wallenda's death-defying aerial feat.

Nothing was left to chance in June of 2012. An eighteen-hundred-foot-long, two-inch-thick steel cable weighing seven tons was pulled across the falls by machines, stretched taut, and then secured by bolts driven deep into bedrock. Supporting cables were attached to the main wire to make sure it couldn't sway. The aerial artist wore the latest high-tech clothing and shoes. His sponsors required that he wear a harness that tethered him safely to the high wire. Protected by all these precautions, Wallenda com-pleted the walk to the delight of the crowd, ABC television, his corporate sponsors, and his nervous family.

If only you could have been there on June 30, 1859. This time the daredevil was the Great Blondin. His aerial acrobatics had thrilled audi-ences across the world. Yet Niagara Falls would be the Frenchman's greatest challenge. Blondin didn't take the same precautions that Nik Wallenda would take over a century later. Instead of a steel cable, he walked on a two-inch-thick Manila rope. No machines pulled it taut, and no cables held it steady. He refused to wear a safety harness. Instead of high-tech gear, he donned Turkish pantaloons and Persian slippers. He carried a wooden pole five times heavier than Wallenda's. Because his high wire was a thirteen-hundred-foot stretch of rope, Blondin walked downhill to the middle, some fifty feet below where he began, and back uphill to the end.

Wallenda performed his aerial extravaganza once. Blondin did his daredevil feats repeatedly over two summers, each time doing something more stupefying. He crossed that Manila rope on a bicycle, on stilts, and in the pitch black of night. Once he pushed a stove on a wheelbarrow and cooked an omelet high over the falls. On another occasion he climbed into a gunnysack blindfolded and then shuffled across that rope. As amazing as Wallenda's *one* feat might have seemed in 2012, Blondin's many stunts were far more electrifying in 1859.

But history mostly recalls that day when he asked ten thousand spectators if they believed that he could carry a man on his shoulders across Niagara Falls. The crowd responded with a roar of affirmation. He retorted, "Who then will get up on my back?" No one moved. So Blondin turned to his manager, Harry Colcord, and ordered him to climb up on his shoulders. Colcord was petrified, but he had promoted the Frenchman too long to back down. He later said that his half-hour ride on Blondin's shoulders was an eternity of terror.

Faith is not a spectator sport. It's one thing to experience adventure vicariously through someone else's high-risk faith. It's quite another to walk the high wire yourself. Today God may call you to climb on his shoulders and cross over some scary place. If so, something Corrie ten Boom wrote might help:

Never be afraid to trust an unknown future to a known God.

Faith is confidence in what we hope for and
assurance about what we do not see.

HEBREWS 11:1, NIV

When the Small Stand Tall

❧

From the time he was a royal baby, his tutors taught him that he was essentially a god. He married his sister so that the DNA of mere mortals wouldn't pollute his divine bloodline. When he ascended to the throne, he became the most powerful man on earth. But he couldn't sleep at night. A ragged band of immigrants had grown to two million people. No matter how hard this Egyptian pharaoh worked the Jewish slaves, they continued to multiply.

So the god-king called two Hebrew midwives into his throne room. Their blood must have run cold when he leaned forward and ominously whispered, "When you help the Hebrew women as they give birth, watch as they deliver. If the baby is a boy, kill him." This madman had worked out his "final solution" to the Jewish problem: work the men to death, kill their baby boys, and leave their girls to marry Egyptian men. Like Adolf Hitler, he might have boasted, "One day the Jews will be a distant memory."

But these midwives weren't snowflakes who melted when the heat was turned up. The book of Exodus says that they feared God and disobeyed a pharaoh. By standing tall, they gave life to millions of unborn babies yet to come.

Outwitted by two slave women, the god-king ordered the Egyptians to throw Jewish babies into the Nile River. But an ordinary slave couple refused to obey the world's most powerful man. After the midwives delivered their boy, they sent him in a basket down the Nile and into the bathing pool of the princess of Egypt. The baby's slave sister had the courage to bring his fearless slave mother to the palace to nurse him. During those formative years, this slave woman passed on her Jewish faith to her son Moses.

The world hardly remembers two midwives who defied a pyramid builder. The slave parents who showed such courage are practically lost to history. No memorials have been erected to the preteen slave girl who brought her mother to the palace of a genocidal maniac to nurse her rescued brother. But billions of Jews, Christians, and Muslims celebrate the life of the baby who grew up to liberate his people and forge the foundations of modern civilization.

We remember bigger-than-life players who dominate history's center stage while ignoring the small people on whose shoulders they stand. We forget two midwives whose courage gave birth to the unforgettable Moses. Most of us couldn't name the hardworking quarryman who taught the boy Michelangelo how to work with stone, the nanny who shaped the character of little Winston Churchill, or Billy Graham's mother. But God takes note of the small when they stand tall. Though he refuses to record the identity of a pharaoh, the names of two midwives, Shiphrah and Puah, are indelibly etched on the pages of Holy Scripture. You, too, may be small. But you, too, can stand tall when conviction demands courage. The story of Shiphrah and Puah recalls a Tanzanian proverb:

Little by little, a little becomes a lot.

———— ✦ ————

Do not despise these small beginnings,
for the LORD rejoices to see the work begin.
ZECHARIAH 4:10

The Factory
Worker's Daughter

୧ଚ୍ଚ

Melanija was desperate to get out of Sevnica. But Yugoslavia was a giant prison camp ruled over by a Cold War dictator, and the Iron Curtain kept the Knavs family locked in the grinding poverty of failed socialism. Melanija's father was an automobile salesman in a country where most folks couldn't afford a car. Her mother was a pattern-maker at a factory that produced children's dresses.

The factory worker's daughter could handle the modest lifestyle. But the grayness of her gray Communist-era home in the gray shadows of gray factories belching gray smoke into a world of gray dinginess strangled her soul. Then everything changed when Melanija moved to the capital. That's when she saw her first fashion magazine from the West. The moment she saw that wondrous kaleidoscope of color and design, she determined to escape the gray drabness of Eastern Europe. But the runways of Paris, Milan, and New York seemed as far away as distant planets.

Soon after, a photographer spied her walking among the street masses like a graceful swan in a puddle of shapeless gray goslings. When he invited her to come to his studio, the shy seventeen-year-old couldn't have guessed that she would one day captivate the fashion world. Her car-salesman dad and factory-worker mom would never have dreamed that their Melanija from little Sevnica would take them on a magic carpet ride to a world of penthouses and palaces.

After crisscrossing Europe, she moved in 1996 to New York City, where her breathtaking beauty graced the covers of America's leading magazines and captured the heart of a billionaire. Who would have guessed that twenty years later she would be standing beside the US president on Inauguration Day? As she stood elegantly statuesque in a blue cashmere dress, childhood friends watching by television in Slovenia must have giggled in delight at the stratospheric rise of Melanija Knavs. Those who once walked the runways with the Slovenian model who called herself Melania Knauss must have been amazed.

Every Cinderella has to believe that somewhere out there is a Prince Charming and that even a factory worker's daughter can become the First Lady of the land. You may say that such things only happen in fairy tales, Hollywood movies, or the crazy world of American politics. But for those who believe the gospel, there is a story infinitely better than Melania Trump's. Prince Charming came to rescue us from the gray shadow lands of unfulfilled dreams. He died slaying the dragon and rose again, and then hacked his way through the thistles and thorns of sin to find his Sleeping Beauty. He awakened her with a kiss and now calls her to come home as his bride to the golden tower emblazoned with his name. Maybe, like Melanija Knavs, you are living in a world of gray drabness. Dare to believe this hopeful statement by Hans Christian Andersen:

Every man's life is a fairy tale, written by God's fingers.

⎯⎯⎯⎯ ⁘ ⎯⎯⎯⎯

Humanly speaking, it is impossible. But not with God. Everything is possible with God.

MARK 10:27

"Viva Cristo Rey!"

୧ଡ଼ୠ

Hidden on a small island off the coast of Cuba is a prison so remote that the outside world didn't know it existed. After the Communist takeover of Cuba in 1959, thousands of Fidel Castro's enemies disappeared in the dark of night. Most were transported to this sinister place called Isla de Pinos—the Isle of the Pines. Among them was a twenty-three-year-old human rights activist, Armando Valladares. He had been sentenced to thirty years at hard labor. What was the crime that earned such a severe prison term? He refused to put a pro-Castro sign on his desk at work. He had been offered a lighter sentence if he would toe the Communist Party line, but he would not.

Valladares later wrote, "For me, it meant 8,000 days of hunger, of systematic beatings, of hard labor, of solitary confinement and solitude, 8,000 days of struggling to prove I was a human being . . . 8,000 days of testing my religious convictions, my faith, of fighting the hate my atheistic jailors were trying to instill in me with every bayonet thrust."

Daily, he watched prisoners being dragged before firing squads. Many were pastors and priests. Just before they were shot, they shouted, "Viva Cristo Rey!"—"Long live Christ the King!" An explosion of gunfire would be followed by deathly quiet. Inmates shouting back from their cells would break the silence: "Viva Cristo Rey!" Eventually the condemned were gagged prior to their execution lest their triumph in the face of death inspire the rest of the prisoners.

Though most of the Christians were Catholics like Valladares, he remembers a Protestant prisoner called the Brother of the Faith. Though repeatedly beaten, he sang hymns at the top of his lungs and shouted to fellow Christians to follow Christ to the end—especially as they were being led to the place of execution.

Valladares writes about the night that prisoners were hauled from their cells to a courtyard where guards began to beat them with rubber hoses and chains. A skeletal figure with long white hair and blazing eyes opened his arms and cried out, "Forgive them, Lord, for they know not what they do." Before he could finish, a lieutenant took quick aim and killed the Brother of the Faith.

Armando Valladares never forgot that martyr or other Christians who were light and salt in the human decay of that prison. After years of suffering the grossest of inhumanities, he was released from the Isla de Pinos. Somehow he made it to the United States and freedom. You can read his story in his book *Against All Hope*. There is a wonderful irony in the title of his book. Hope is the one thing we can never lose, no matter how much is against it.

People can live about thirty days without food, five days without water, and five minutes without air. But they can't live one second without hope. Valladares, the Brother of the Faith, and that company of Cuban martyrs never lost hope as long as they could shout, "Viva Cristo Rey!" Are you going through a tough spell right now? It might help to grab hold of Armando Valladares's story and this hope:

All the world is full of suffering. It is also full of overcoming.

———— ⌘ ————

Lord, where do I put my hope?
My only hope is in you.

PSALM 39:7

The Deadly Rehearsal

⤬

It was five weeks and counting until Operation Neptune. Nearly a quarter of a million men from twelve nations would take part in history's largest amphibious landing. Those who survived would face a monster: a vast network of tunnels, towers, pillboxes, artillery batteries, barbed wire, and land mines on towering cliffs. If any made it through that meat grinder, panzer divisions would be waiting on the other side.

Operation Neptune was one of history's great gambles. How do you keep such a colossal operation secret? One leaked word, and the Germans would turn D-day into an Allied debacle. The weather had to be just right. So did the tides. But the timing mattered most. So many moving parts. They all had to work in synchronized perfection, or the invasion would come apart at the seams. So the Allied brass came up with an idea: a dress rehearsal they called Operation Tiger.

On the Devon coast was a stretch of sand that was a mirror image of the beaches of Normandy. It was a perfect place to stage a mock invasion. Everything had been readied. On a moonlit night at the end of April, ships and landing craft hit Slapton Beach. The boys in London had set up the perfect dress rehearsal: dealing with seasickness, plunging into icy water, smelling the acrid explosives, and sucking sand on the beach while artillery shells whizz overhead. But the timing went terribly wrong. British artillery was supposed to bombard the beach *before* the American boys landed. Instead, they barraged their own allies at Slapton Beach.

This fiasco turned into pandemonium. U-boats were lurking nearby. When their radar picked up the massive flotilla, they moved in for the kill. An underwater hailstorm of torpedoes blew ships apart. Sailors were engulfed in flames. Landing crafts dumped soldiers into water over their heads. London radioed the ships to scatter. Hundreds of men were left behind in icy waters. As dawn broke over Slapton Beach, the sands were covered with mangled bodies and the seas were clogged with floating corpses.

The casualties were quickly removed, and the fiasco was covered up to keep the D-day invasion top secret. Yet the embarrassment at Slapton Beach was kept under wraps long after the war was over. But cover-ups never stay covered up. When old wreckage washed up on Slapton Beach in the 1980s, the story finally came out. Sadly, the men who gave their lives that night were never properly recognized. There is a small marker at Slapton Beach, but nothing like the grand memorials at Normandy. Yet the lessons learned in the Operation Tiger fiasco made the D-day victory possible. This amazing story reminds us that it is human nature to celebrate victory and cover up failures. Maybe we should erect memorials to the failures, too. After all, Slapton Beach fiascos prepare us for D-day victories. If you are in the aftermath of your own Slapton disaster, take heart from this:

Failure is not a loss. It's a gain, if you learn, change, and grow.

_____ ⌘ _____

When people fall down, don't they get up
again? When they discover they're on the
wrong road, don't they turn back?

JEREMIAH 8:4

The Amazing Visitations

⊷◉⊶

Tamrat watched in horror as a Socialist dictatorship brutalized his country. When people took to the streets to protest, they were slaughtered in the infamous Red Terror. Embittered, the doctor's son became an implacable atheist and radical Marxist. He fled to the mountains, where he spent fifteen years as a guerilla fighter, becoming a top-ranking military leader in the rebel army.

In the Ethiopian highlands, Tamrat met and married Mulu. They said their wedding vows while Russian aircraft bombarded their camp. When his socialist army seized control of Ethiopia, he became its prime minister. His boyhood friend took on the role of president. But when Tamrat began to doubt that rigid Marxism could solve the poverty of his ravaged country, his boyhood friend ordered him arrested on trumped-up charges. A kangaroo court found him guilty and sentenced him to eighteen years in prison. Mulu fled the country with their children, steps ahead of the police.

Although Tamrat was repeatedly tortured in prison, he was most haunted by the betrayal of his boyhood friend. After four years of solitary confinement, he sank into despair. His atheism brought no hope, so he studied Hinduism, Buddhism, and Islam. One night he suddenly became gravely ill. He was rushed to a medical clinic at the point of death. There, a Christian nurse risked everything to hand him a gospel tract.

A few nights later, Jesus appeared to him in his prison cell. The Savior said that he alone could change Tamrat's life and promised that he would never forsake him. Jesus appeared again the following two nights, and Tamrat surrendered his life to him. Later, a jailer smuggled a cell phone into his cell so he could call his wife. He wondered how she would react to his conversion. But she excitedly told him that Jesus had visited her on the same nights that he had come to Tamrat. With joy in his heart and a Bible in his hand, the political prisoner went through an amazing transformation.

Yet he couldn't overcome bitterness toward his betrayer. Then he saw a vision of Jesus on the cross forgiving his enemies. The dam of resentment broke. A weeping Tamrat prayed that God would forgive and bless his enemy. Maybe that's why, in a series of events that could only be scripted by heaven, he was released from prison after twelve years and led to an office where he forgave and embraced the startled president. A month later, he was reunited with Mulu and his children. Today the two carry on a dynamic ministry to world leaders. Not long ago, Mulu sat by the bedside of the man who betrayed her husband and held his hand while he was dying of cancer. Tamrat Layne would tell you that bitterness is the most miserable prison of all. Only by forgiving your enemy can you set yourself free.

Like Tamrat and Mulu, you just might unlock the floodgates of heaven's blessings too. Remember this:

Forgiving others is the best gift you will ever give yourself.

❦

Make allowance for each other's faults, and forgive
anyone who offends you. Remember, the Lord
forgave you, so you must forgive others.

COLOSSIANS 3:13

Candy Bombs

∽⊙⊙∽

In the Roaring Twenties, America went bonkers over aerial stunt shows by daredevils like Charles Lindbergh. The public couldn't get enough of those loops, rolls, and other high-flying tricks performed by madcap barnstormers. That's when the Curtiss Candy Company forever changed the world.

To promote a new candy bar called Baby Ruth, the company dispatched a Waco biplane to Pittsburg, Pennsylvania. On a sunny day in 1923, a fearless aviator flew low between buildings while performing death-defying tricks. As crowds gathered below, he dropped hundreds of Baby Ruths tied to rice-paper parachutes. Traffic was a mess, and mayhem erupted in the streets as people fought each other for this "manna" from heaven. Irate officials quickly passed a city ordinance against "candy bombs," but Baby Ruth eventually became the bestselling chocolate bar in America.

Down south in Florida, a local distributor for the Curtiss Candy Company decided to employ the same gimmick. After a biplane was loaded with Baby Ruths, his twelve-year-old son begged to go along for the ride, pleading that he could help by dropping the candy. After raining down Baby Ruths on the Hialeah racetrack, young Paul was head over heels in love with flying.

When the boy announced that he wanted to be a pilot, his father was not happy. He wanted his son to become a doctor. But Paul's mother, Enola Gay Tibbets, quickly supported her son's dreams. After college, Enola Gay's boy joined the army air corps. Paul would enjoy a distinguished career as a pilot, retiring as a brigadier general. But he is most remembered for the mission that he flew on August 6, 1945.

Colonel Paul Tibbets had proudly named his B-29 Superfortress the

Enola Gay after his mother, who encouraged his dreams to fly. When his B-29 flew from Tinian Island on that August day, it carried the product of a vast endeavor known as the Manhattan Project. At precisely 8:15 a.m. local time, the *Enola Gay* dropped "Little Boy" from thirty-one thousand feet. Forty-four seconds later, it exploded into a nuclear inferno, leaving tens of thousands of Japanese dead and dying. The first atomic bomb had turned Hiroshima into scorched ruin. The flight of the *Enola Gay* horrified the world, forever changing history. Yet General Tibbets went to his grave convinced that he had done the right thing, averting an invasion by Japan that might have cost a million lives.

Baby Ruths rain down from the skies on delighted folks at a racetrack. People tear open wrappers and bite into sweet, gooey pleasure. But a Hialeah afternoon can become a Hiroshima morning after. Many tools at our disposal are morally neutral—they can be used to bring joy or destruction, depending on whose hands they are in. The more powerful something is, the more potential it has to wreak havoc. In a world filled with eye candy, we should remember this:

Power is sweet, but its aftertaste can be most bitter.

———— ✦ ————

Better to be patient than powerful; better to
have self-control than to conquer a city.

PROVERBS 16:32

The Night of the Lepers

એઉનૂજી

The capital is under siege by the Arameans, and its citizens are dying of starvation. Profiteers are selling doves' dung for a year's wages and a donkey's head for a king's ransom. Just when the Israelite ruler thinks that things can't get worse, they do. Two women have agreed to kill and eat their own children. Having feasted on the first woman's baby, the second has reneged and hidden hers. The mother of the eaten child screams like a banshee.

This king is no saint, having shed his share of blood. Yet even he is appalled. He explodes in anger that God would allow these Jewish mothers to be reduced to such depravity. So he decides to kill God's representative—Elisha, the prophet. But the seer confronts the king with a prophecy: "By tomorrow, the Arameans will be gone and the city will have a glut of food." The ruler's right-hand man sarcastically replies, "Even if God opens the floodgates of heaven, this won't happen." Elisha snarls back, "Not only will it happen, but you will see it with your own eyes and not eat a bite of it."

Outside the gates, God orchestrates one of history's most amazing war stories. Four Jewish lepers sit in no-man's-land. Let's call them Harley, Charley, Farley, and Claude. The Israelites have locked them out of the city, and the Arameans keep their distance from them. Harley reasons, "If we stay here, we will starve to death. If we head for the Aramean camp, maybe they will throw some food to keep us at bay. Or they just might shoot us. But quick death by arrow or spear is better than slow starvation." So these four diseased outcasts tiptoe gingerly across no-man's-land. That's when a miracle for the ages takes place. God makes them sound like an attacking army. Hysteria sweeps through the Aramean ranks. Enemy soldiers flee pell-mell into the night, leaving everything behind.

It's the headline of the millennium: LEPERS ROUT ARMY. The four arrive at the tents, where they gorge themselves. Finding tents full of plunder, they begin to bury their fortune. Suddenly, Farley comes to his senses. "What we're doing isn't right. There's a city over there starving to death, and we must share the good news with them." So they hightail it back to Samaria. Never have four lepers been received with as much joy as Harley, Charley, Farley, and Claude!

A few hours later, food fills the city square. The king's cynical buddy is put in charge. The last thing he probably says in his life is "The line forms over here." A ravenous mob tramples him to death as they rush the stockpile. Elisha's words come true: "You will see it . . . and not eat a bite of it." Second Kings 7 doesn't tell us what happens to the lepers, but we shouldn't forget their amazing story—or the lesson they teach: if we have found spiritual food for the soul-famished cities of our day, we must not keep the Good News secret. This much is true:

When the truth is replaced by silence, the silence is a lie.

Publish his glorious deeds among the nations.
Tell everyone about the amazing things he does.

PSALM 96:3

A Sharecropper's Audacious Dream

❧❧❧

No one could have imagined that the sharecropper would change the face of sports. Growing up in a three-room shack, he lived at the dead end of poverty and racism. He suffered the horror of losing his best friend in a gruesome way: his hands were chopped off just before he was lynched by a redneck mob. He watched helplessly while his father was half beaten to death by three KKK bigots. The trauma of childhood formed a hard-shelled, take-no-prisoners exterior. It also turned him into a fast-talking huckster out to make a quick buck.

Fueled by anger, he traveled across America until he landed in California. There a guy by the name of Old Whiskey taught him to play tennis. One day he watched a tennis pro accept a winner's check for $100,000. He turned off his television set and decided that his future children would be his ticket to the big time. He scratched out a master plan that was seventy-eight-pages long. Later, when his two girls were young, he took them to public courts that were cracked and pockmarked. They hit balls over sagging nets while gang members sold drugs courtside.

But women's tennis was a white girls' game. Great players began as toddlers and were coached by pros in exclusive academies, learning the subtle intricacies of spin, lob, and drop shots for strategic tennis that mirrored chess games. The sharecropper had a radical idea: no girlie lobs, subtle slices, or long rallies. His girls would attack, overwhelming opponents with shock-and-awe power.

When he brought them to their first junior tournaments, they were dismissed as a freak show: ghetto girls in a country club setting. Tennis blue bloods rolled their eyes when their daddy boasted that his daughters would be the greatest tennis players in history. When he tried to cut an endorsement deal with Reebok before his girls turned pro, he pulled out charts from a grimy bag just as a cockroach ran across the table. He squashed it with his bare hand and then wiped its remains on his T-shirt. The huckster from Louisiana, with his toothy smile and braggadocio crassness, didn't belong in the rarified air of big-league tennis. Nor did his rough-cut girls.

They should have taken the audacious dream of Richard Williams seriously. His little girls, Venus and Serena, *did* go on to become the greatest tennis duo in history, winning thirty-three grand slam singles, seventeen grand slam doubles, and three Olympic gold medals. Serena holds the modern-era grand slam record with twenty-three singles titles, more than any man or woman. No athlete, male or female, has ever dominated their sport more than Serena Williams. On that day her dad saw a tennis pro collect a check for $100,000, he couldn't have imagined that his girls would now have a net worth of approximately $200 million.

Richard long ago dropped out of the limelight, his behavior an embarrassment to everyone. But there was that day when he had an audacious dream. People made a mistake to dismiss it as a sharecropper's fantasy. Richard proved the naysayers wrong. So will you, if you never forget this:

Don't allow small minds to tell you that your dreams are too big.

———— ✑ ————

Enlarge your house; build an addition. Spread out your home, and spare no expense!

ISAIAH 54:2

No Fairy Tale

∽◌◑◠◡

If the story wasn't true, you might think it to be a fairy tale. An ancient slave people were under a spell that caused them to forget they were once Children of the Light. When these slaves began to outnumber their masters, a wicked king feared that they might seize his dark realm. So he ordered the slaughter of their baby boys. As dragons of death stalked the dark land, a slave woman hid her newborn son in a basket on a river crawling with baby-eating monsters.

Fire angels watched over that baby, and a princess found him in the river. Though she was the daughter of the wicked king, she was kind and brave. She named him Delivered from Water and adopted him as her little prince. He grew up to be a mighty warrior, and he gained the admiration of the evil king. He led the armies of the dark realm to great victories. Delivered from Water had forgotten that he was a son of the enslaved Children of the Light.

Then one day this adopted prince of the dark realm saw an overseer beating a slave. The evil spell was broken, and he knew that he, too, was a Child of the Light. In anger, he slew the slave master. But darkness prevailed, and he had to flee to the desert.

For forty long years the prince wandered as a herder of sheep. He was eighty years old when the Light appeared as a mysterious fire in a twisted bush on a desert mountain. The Light told the shepherd that it was now time for him to free his people. "I can't do it!" protested the shepherd. "I'm not qualified—please send someone else."

The Light responded, "But I will be with you." He gave the old shepherd the supernatural power to turn a stick into a snake. "This is only the beginning of what I will do through you!" he promised. Then he sent him back to the dark realm to confront the evil king and set free the enslaved Children of the Light.

By now you are thinking that this is no fairy tale but a story from Sunday school. It appears in the Jewish Torah and the pages of the Christian Old Testament. It is the true story of Moses, whose name literally means "delivered from water." The delivered one went on to deliver God's people. All fairy tales—and every other story, including yours—are really reflections of a redemptive narrative that makes up the greatest story ever told. God has written your story too. Your personal history is really *his* story. Yours is very special and indispensable to *his* bigger story because *he* took the time to write it just for you. So go out and live another chapter, always remembering this:

No one loves a good story more than God. That's why he wrote yours.

——— ✧ ———

You saw me before I was born. Every day of my life
was recorded in your book. Every moment was laid out
before a single day had passed. How precious are your
thoughts about me, O God. They cannot be numbered!

PSALM 139:16-17

The Saint Who Took
Down the Mafia

∼⊙⊙⊙∼

When a cardinal refused to take a stand, the priest had to do some-thing. If the church remained silent in the face of evil, he would raise his voice—even if he was a solitary bird warbling in the face of a howling wind. So Father Pino went to war against a sinister force that had survived the turbulent history of his island and even profited from its misfortunes—the dreaded Sicilian Mafia.

As a boy, Pino had seen mobsters feast like parasites off the poor folk of his native Brancaccio, the most impoverished neighborhood in Palermo. In his first parish in the village of Godrano, the Mafia killed fifteen out of its hundred residents. Father Pino went door to door, begging villagers to forgive and be reconciled to the mobsters who bullied, extorted, and murdered their loved ones. But the priest also realized that we must not only forgive our enemies; sometimes we have to stand up to bullies the way David stood up to Goliath.

Pino appealed to the church hierarchy for help. But the cardinal of Palermo said that the Mafia was an overblown myth; a fantasy created by the media. The cardinal wasn't even sure it existed. He was more con-cerned about the threat of Communism than street hoodlums. But Pino refused to go along with the silent church. In 1990, when he returned to Brancaccio as the pastor of the Saint Gaetano parish, he declared war against the Mob. His Sunday morning homilies denounced Mafia vio-lence. When Mob bosses tried to bribe him, he refused their hush money. His church became the center of resistance to the *Cosa Nostra*. He warned his flock that true Christians could never engage in the age-old Sicilian practice of *omert*—turning a blind eye and taking a vow of silence in the face of Mafia violence. Slowly the Mob was losing its power in Palermo.

After the church hierarchy told him to tone down his rhetoric, his sermons got more aggressive. When the Mafia warned him to cool it, he turned up the heat. The more they threatened him, the more he spoke against them. By showing disrespect to the Mob dons, Father Pino signed his own death warrant. On September 15, 1993, while celebrating his fifty-sixth birthday, the courageous priest was gunned down in front of his church.

The Sicilian Mafia underestimated the power of martyrdom. Huge crowds marched in candlelight memorial parades carrying signs defying the Cosa Nostra. Father Pino's favorite saying was spray painted everywhere: "And what if somebody did something?" The church hierarchy finally rose up to challenge the godfathers of crime. Even the pope spoke out publicly against the Mafia. It's no wonder that the church beatified the Sicilian priest in 2013.

It has been said that the only thing necessary for evil to triumph is for good men to do nothing. Maybe there is an evil that you need to speak out against today. When you recall the story of Father Don Giuseppe "Pino" Puglisi, you might want to repeat this revision of his favorite question: *What if somebody did something, and what if that person was me?*

―――――∞⊙∾―――――

Who will protect me from the wicked? Who will stand up for me against evildoers?

PSALM 94:16

History on the Cutting Room Floor

❧❦❧

The local girls swooned over the handsome son of a sugar planter. This Cuban playboy was the area's most eligible bachelor. But he dreamed of being a movie star, so he found his way to the capital. In the 1940s this Caribbean city was the mistress of pleasure and the opulent garden of delights. Famous actors, directors, and talent agents flocked to Havana to sample her amusements.

It wasn't long before Mexican filmmakers noticed the Latin Adonis. He can still be seen dancing the rhumba as an extra in a forgettable 1946 film called *Holiday in Mexico*. He also had fleeting scenes as an extra in *Easy to Wed* and other movies. Then came his big break. Jerry Beeker, a talent scout for Paramount, spotted him in a Havana nightclub. Struck by his tall, athletic elegance and dark good looks, the agent invited the young Cuban to come to Hollywood for a screen test.

After a train ride across America, the aspiring actor met Beeker in his Hollywood office. The agent had already lined up a bit part for him in a movie called *Havana after Midnight*. It called for a Latin lover type who would deliver a single line: "Sí, Yanqui. Havana has the most beautiful and hot-blooded women in the world. You'll like it here." The sugar planter's son had hoped for more than a bit part as a Cuban heartthrob, but a small speaking part in an American movie was a big step up from being an extra in forgettable Mexican films.

With only a few days until the wrap, the young Cuban took a hotel room and waited for the movie to premier. Then the studio informed him that his one line had been cut. He barged into the office of the film editor,

Barney Pockler, and screamed that Pockler was ruining his chances at stardom. The film editor responded that the director had made the decision to cut his line because he lacked talent. The young man stormed off the movie lot and back to Cuba.

Barney Pockler's snipping of that single line would give him many sleepless nights a decade later. The United States and Russia were facing off in a nuclear showdown over Cuba, and the world teetered on the edge of Armageddon. Maybe if he hadn't shattered the dreams of an aspiring actor named Fidel Alejandro Castro Ruz, the young man might have stayed on in Hollywood instead of going home to start a revolution.

The great movements of history move on the smallest of gears. A single line is left on the cutting room floor, and Fidel Castro's life goes in a different direction. An art teacher tells Adolf Hitler that he has no talent, and the embittered young man becomes a monster. There are no throwaway moments, no unimportant actions, and no insignificant words. Before we speak, act, or react, we should take time to remember this:

Like a jigsaw puzzle, the big picture is made up of many small pieces.

———— ❧ ————

Whatever you have said in the dark will be heard in the
light, and what you have whispered behind closed doors
will be shouted from the housetops for all to hear!

LUKE 12:3

Unlocking the
Gift of Potential

৵ৄৢৢৄৢৄ৽

The imagination is a limitless universe existing somewhere in the human soul. It allows dreamers to go places and do things that are beyond their capacity. And every once in a while, dreams escape imagination and become reality—as they have for Patrick Henry Hughes.

Yet reality was something his parents didn't want to face. When their baby boy was born with severe birth defects, they focused on worst-case scenarios. The same imagination that is filled with dreams and visions has its bleak and dark places. And that's where Patrick John and Patricia lived. They knew that their son was born without eyes. They were told that he would be consigned to a wheelchair for life. But this information was given out in bits and pieces. They worried about what bad news would come next. Mostly they wondered about their baby's mental capacity. Their emotions went from denial to resignation to rage. They constantly asked God, "Why? Why this? Why us? Why him?"

Answers didn't come, but amazing things did. Six-week-old Patrick Hughes was screaming when his desperate daddy placed him atop the piano and began to play classical music. The baby stopped crying. In the months to come, the infant smiled and cooed whenever Patrick John put him in his lap and played that piano. One evening when his daddy played three notes on the keyboard, the nine-month-old reached out and played those notes back in rapid succession. When he was a toddler, he would listen to nursery rhyme songs and then plunk them out on the piano. America fell in love with this amazing kid when ABC's *Extreme Makeover* crew built for the Hughes a home that minimized Patrick

Henry's disabilities and maximized his abilities. When this blind kid in a wheelchair went to junior and senior high school, he was a fixture in the band and orchestra, inspiring his classmates that if he could unlock the gift of potential, so could they.

But the most amazing thing was yet to come. When Patrick Henry enrolled at the University of Louisville he figured he could play the trumpet in the prep band at his beloved Cardinals' basketball games. But he discovered that there was a requirement to participate in the marching band at football games. But how does a blind guy who can't walk do that? That's where imagination came to the rescue. Patrick Henry's dad took time off work every afternoon to attend the Louisville Marching Band practices. He learned the routines while his son mastered the music. You should have seen that dynamic duo work together during halftime shows. Patrick Henry played while Patrick John marched behind, wheeling him along. Together father and son make a single Hughes.

This amazing story teaches us that nothing is impossible if we allow dreams to escape imagination and become reality. Both father and son give all the credit to their Lord and Savior, Jesus, who empowers them to unlock the gift of potential. Patrick John and Patrick Henry might agree with something Albert Einstein said:

Logic will get you from A to B. Imagination will take you everywhere.

———— ✽ ————

Jesus told him, "You believe because you have seen me.
Blessed are those who believe without seeing me."

JOHN 20:29

Straw Dogs

⁓⊙⊙⊙⁓

An unpopular war in Vietnam polarized America in 1971. College campuses were rocked by demonstrations. Hippies and pacifists flashed peace signs, but there was no peace. During that turbulence, Hollywood legend Sam Peckinpah gave the nation a deeply disturbing movie. *Straw Dogs* was so brutal that forty years later it was still banned in the United Kingdom. It created a firestorm of controversy in America. That's exactly what Peckinpah wanted.

Straw Dogs is about an American college professor, Dr. David Sumner, who runs away from the violence in his land. He moves with his British wife, Amy, to an old farmhouse in the English countryside. Sumner is a pacifist who will go to any length to avoid confrontation. His unfulfilled wife abhors his weakness.

The professor hires several lads from the local pub to fix the roof on the farmhouse. Ignored by a husband hiding in his study, Amy prances around half naked, flirting shamelessly while the roofers drag out their repair job. David knows they are taking advantage of him but refuses to confront them. He sees the growing magnetism between his wife and one of the lads but retreats into the safe world of complex math equations. The bullyboys laugh behind his back, and Amy despises him all the more.

Emboldened by Amy's flirting and David's passivity, the lads slaughter a cat, hang it in her closet, and then giggle while Amy screams hysterically. They lure David away while one of them rapes his wife. Amy keeps her rape a secret, yet seethes in bitterness when her husband ignores her bruises and tears.

Events spin out of control. The village boys come in the dark of night to finish off the couple. The professor knows that his pacifism will not survive a night of terror. He somehow discovers his courage. While his wife cowers, he frantically runs from room to room trying to lock doors and board up windows. But there are too many openings. Someone breaks through the attic. Others come up through the cellar. David desperately fires a shotgun at one and swings an ax at another. Gore and carnage are everywhere, but he fights on in a frenzy until all the attackers have fled or been killed. Exhausted and covered with blood, the former pacifist whispers, "I will not allow violence against this house."

Sam Peckinpah posed hard questions to an America wrestling with Vietnam. Can pacifism stand in the face of evil? Will wickedness go away if ignored? If war isn't waged against evil when it is small, will we face an inescapable fight to the death when it grows into a monster? *Straw Dogs* is an allegory of spiritual warfare. We flirt with evil, thinking that we can charm the snake. Like Amy, we are caught by surprise when our pet becomes a predator. Or, like the professor, we passively sit by and allow evil to worm its way into our homes and seduce our loved ones. We shouldn't forget the story of a professor and his wife. They would probably agree with this truth:

The only way for evil to triumph is for good people to do nothing.

***

Look, I have given you authority over all the power
of the enemy, and you can walk among snakes and
scorpions and crush them. Nothing will injure you.

LUKE 10:19

The Only Place
without Prejudice

❧

Bessie was born to poverty and prejudice. She was both Native American and African American, which in her day meant she was starting life with two strikes against her. Her options were limited in the segregated South more than a hundred years ago, but her dreams were bigger than the skies above. Inspired by the exploits of the Wright brothers and World War I flying aces, she announced that she was going to become a pilot. Her wild dreams were met with laughter. Not only was she a person of color, she was a woman. So Bessie enrolled at the Oklahoma Colored Agricultural and Normal University, which today is called Langston University. She applied herself to an education that would afford her the few opportunities available to her in a segregated society—but her dream of flying wouldn't go away.

Bessie dropped out of school and followed her dreams north to Chicago in 1915. She applied to several American aviation schools, but she was repeatedly rejected. Her grit and determination set her on a five-year odyssey across America until the door of every aviation school was shut in her face. So she headed to France. When later asked why she kept on going, she replied, "I knew we had no aviators, neither men nor women, and I knew the race needed to be represented along this most important line, so I thought it my duty to risk my life to learn aviation and to encourage flying among men and women of our race, who are so far behind the white race in this modern study."

Bessie passed her training in Paris, and in 1921 she received her international pilot's license from the Federation Aeronautique Internationale.

She returned to America, where she barnstormed across the country, doing aerial stunts that men were afraid to attempt. Driven to prove the worth of her race and gender, Bessie upped the ante by attempting increasingly dangerous feats. No one was surprised when she fell to her death at thirty-four years of age.

Bessie Coleman's tragic demise made international headlines. More than ten thousand people attended her funeral. She never realized her greatest dreams, but she would be proud of Major Christina Hopper. Almost a century after Bessie's tragic end, this Ironman triathlete was the first African American female pilot to fly a fighter jet for America in combat when she flew an F-16 Fighting Falcon during the Iraq War. Google recently honored Bessie Coleman's life with their signature homage on her 125th birthday—a Doodle. Today, you might want to look up to the skies and remember the great aviator's saddest statement: "The air is the only place free from prejudices."

We can all honor Bessie Coleman with something better than a Doodle. We can work to make sure that there is no place, in the skies or on the earth, for prejudice against anyone. Voltaire was surely right when he wrote this timeless warning:

Prejudices are what fools use for reason.

My dear brothers and sisters, how can you claim
to have faith in our glorious Lord Jesus Christ
if you favor some people over others?

JAMES 2:1

The Boy They Called Scarface

ঽ৩৩৵

From the time he was a child, Francis Albert felt that the world was against him. When his mother went into sudden labor, he refused to be born. A doctor used forceps to yank him out, and that violent process tore open the left side of his face and ear. He was deposited in a kitchen sink while the doctor labored to save his mom's life. An aunt finally dunked the baby's lifeless body in cold water. Everyone was stunned when he screamed.

Years later, Francis bitterly confided to a lover, "They ripped me out and tossed me aside to die." Mostly he hated the scars left by the forceps. Later, he suffered more disfigurement from a botched mastoid operation. As a teen, his face was further scarred by cystic acne. He never got over the shame of his classmates calling him Scarface.

His stage mother forced him to enter talent shows, determined that his golden voice would lift his family out of poverty. Francis resented the fact that he could never do enough to please her. After kicking around as a small-time vocalist, he became the lead singer for the Tommy Dorsey Band. Years before the Beatles, his crooning caused teenage girls to scream and faint.

During World War II, Francis tried to join the army but was rejected as emotionally unfit. It was widely thought that he used his celebrity to shirk his duty.

Columnist Walter Winchell reported that Americans hated Francis more than Hitler. Yet he landed a starring role in an epic war movie and won an Oscar. It was rumored that Francis got his part because a

Mafia boss made the director an offer he couldn't refuse. Senator Joseph McCarthy called him a Communist. J. Edgar Hoover was convinced that he had ties to organized crime. Francis felt like the whole world was conspiring against him.

But his star rose in Las Vegas, and John F. Kennedy began to court him. Francis worked tirelessly to get the senator elected US president, only to feel the familiar sting of rejection when the Kennedy family decided Francis was politically toxic. He never recovered from the way he was tossed aside.

You remember Francis by his stage name, Frank. Ol' Blue Eyes made the whole world sing, but his personal life was tragic. He lived in fear of disappointing others and yet trusted no one. He was so embarrassed by his scars that he caked his face in Max Factor makeup. One of his wives said that he took twelve showers a day and constantly changed his clothes and makeup. He obsessed about people who had betrayed him. He alienated his kids and plowed through four marriages.

Daughter Nancy said, "Too bad my dad lived so much of his life before they came up with Zoloft." Francis was a control freak who carefully managed relationships to avoid being hurt again. His biggest hit summed up his life: "I Did It My Way." Those who knew Frank Sinatra best said that he died a lonely man, enslaved to a lifetime of resentments. His sad story sings a final warning:

When you try to control everything, you end up enjoying nothing.

———— ༄ ————

There is no fear in love, but perfect love casts
out fear. For fear has to do with punishment, and
whoever fears has not been perfected in love.

1 JOHN 4:18, ESV

When Death Births a Song

When the church boy performed in honky-tonks, his pastor warned that he couldn't play the "devil's music" on Saturday and direct the choir on Sunday. So the piano man surrendered his keyboard to Jesus. But if he couldn't bring church to the honky-tonk, that didn't mean that he couldn't take the blues to church. He became a trailblazer when he put religious lyrics to popular music. His synthesizing of the sacred and secular didn't always sit well with church folk, but a century later this African American is revered as the father of gospel music.

But Thomas is remembered most for a song birthed from unspeakable tragedy. He was thirty-two years old the day he left his wife alone in their Chicago apartment. Nettie was in her last days of pregnancy, and Thomas was scheduled to sing at a revival meeting in St. Louis. He was on the road when he remembered that he had forgotten his music case. He rushed home, where he found his wife sleeping. A voice whispered from within that he should stay with Nettie. But people were waiting for him to come and sing for the Lord.

When he finished singing, a messenger handed him a telegram with a single brutal line: YOUR WIFE IS DEAD. He rushed back to Chicago only to discover that Nettie had died giving birth to a baby boy. As he held his newborn son, he thanked God that at least some part of his wife had been left behind. But a few hours later, his baby boy died. He buried them together in a single casket.

Thomas wandered in a fog of unbearable grief. Then the fog turned to fury. What sort of God would take his wife and child? He was about to return to the honky-tonk life when he remembered that inner voice that had told him to stay home with Nettie. Grief was now replaced with guilt:

What if he had listened to the voice of Jesus instead of using his voice *for* Jesus? Maybe Nettie would still be alive.

A friend of his brought him to a nearby college, where he found a piano in the music room. He sat down at the keyboard and began to caress the ivories. A melody spontaneously flowed out of his soul along with a prayer in song: "Precious Lord, take my hand, lead me on, let me stand, I am tired, I am weak, I am worn; Through the storm, through the night, lead me on to the light: Take my hand, precious Lord, lead me home."

That gospel song, birthed out of Thomas Dorsey's heartbreak, has been translated into thirty-two languages and sung by millions of weary saints. It was Martin Luther King Jr.'s favorite song, the one sung at his funeral. Heartbreak is the greatest composer of songs. And nothing soothes the heartbroken more than a song.

Are you drowning in heartbreak? Maybe Thomas's story and song can become a lifeline of hope. You might even want to grab hold of this truth: ***God only allows his children to suffer if it gives birth to better things.***

―――――――◦§◦―――――――

What we suffer now is nothing compared
to the glory he will reveal to us later.

ROMANS 8:18

338

The Seamstress

෴

La Pola was opinionated and sassy, the poster child for political incorrect-ness. When officials of the Spanish king squashed liberties in her South American country, this fiery revolutionary became a rabble-rouser in the public square. La Pola's worried mother admonished her, "Your tongue is too sharp. Your words are as pointed as your sewing needles." She told her daughter that a woman's place was in the home and that she was putting her family in great danger. She breathed a sigh of relief when her outspoken daughter took up her needles again and went back to work as a seamstress.

Things were quieter in the streets of Bogotá when La Pola was sewing dresses for the rich wives of royal officials. No one suspected that she was silently listening to the wagging tongues of officials and their wives and then passing on their secrets to the rebels. Her ability to gather informa-tion made her an invaluable member of the resistance. This seamstress raised money, made uniforms for patriots, and used her seductive beauty to recruit new soldiers for the resistance. There might not be a Colombia today if La Pola hadn't learned to curb her fiery tongue while sewing qui-etly in the parlors of Spanish royalty.

But La Pola is celebrated in Colombia today for what happened after she was unmasked as a spy. At her trial, her old tongue came out razor sharp. She skewered the judges as traitors and electrified the spectators. Irate officials condemned her to be hanged. On the morning of November 14, 1817, on the way to the execution, priests begged her to pray for her soul. Instead, she defiantly spewed curses at the Spanish soldiers. She mocked the royal governor. When he ordered the drummers to play louder, she screeched above their din, "Assassins!" As she mounted the scaffold, she implored the soldiers to shoot the royal officials and beseeched the crowd to riot. It took a noose to finally silence La Pola's tongue. But her final words energized a faltering revolution. A young soldier by the name of José Hilario López was so inspired by her speech on the gallows that he would go on to lead the revolution to victory and become the first president of an independent Colombia.

Today this seamstress, Policarpa Salavarrieta, is commemorated every year in a national holiday in her honor. Her statue dominates the central square in Bogotá, and she is the only woman depicted on the country's paper money. For two hundred years she has been celebrated by poets and artists as La Pola, Colombia's first heroine.

This nineteenth-century seamstress teaches us the power of the human tongue. There are times when it is high treason to remain silent in the face of evil. There are other times when it is the height of patriotism and good sense to keep a rein on our tongues. May God give us the wisdom to know when to speak and when to shut up, never forgetting this truth:

In our tongues reside both the power to destroy and the power to give life.

The tongue is a small thing that makes grand speeches.
But a tiny spark can set a great forest on fire.

JAMES 3:5

Symphonies and Pyramids

He was a superstar long before the age of superstars. At age five, he wrote a concerto for the harpsichord. Before he was ten, he was composing and publishing violin sonatas. At twelve, he produced his first opera. When he was thirteen, he was the concertmaster of Europe's greatest symphony orchestra. By the time he died of exhaustion, this manic overachiever wrote numerous operettas, cantatas, hymns, oratorios, and arias. He composed forty-eight symphonies and a dozen operas. In his brief life, he gave birth to six hundred compositions!

His music was sheer perfection. His genius has never been matched. This whiz kid with the moniker Johannes Chrysostomus Wolfgangus Theophilus Mozart certainly had a lot of name to live up to.

But there was a dark side to the boy genius. In the 1700s he was living the destructive lifestyle of a modern rock superstar. He was only thirty-five when he collapsed from pneumonia. His drug-addicted wife was in such a stupor that she barely knew her husband had died. A handful of people went to his funeral, but a snowstorm prevented them from going to the grave site. By the time the weather cleared, the grave diggers could not remember where they had buried him. The grave of history's greatest musical genius has never been found.

Compare Mozart's unmarked grave to the most spectacular shrine ever built for a single person. Towering above desert sands outside Cairo, Egypt, it is the most visited grave site in the world. Over one hundred thousand slaves labored and died building the Great Pyramid. Its construction almost bankrupted a nation. After more than four thousand years this grave still stands in crumbling grandeur, although robbers long ago stole the body and plundered the buried wealth. Only a few history buffs remember the name of its original occupant: Pharaoh Khufu. Other than a grave that has become a popular tourist destination, Khufu has left no lasting legacy.

On the other hand, Mozart doesn't even have a weathered stone to mark the fact that he was here. Yet turn the lights in your den down low, slip a CD into the slot, close your eyes, and listen to the exquisite beauty of a Mozart sonata. Race along the highway with the convertible top down, and let the wind rush through your hair as a Mozart symphony blasts gloriously from the speakers. Attend his greatest opera and allow *The Marriage of Figaro* to inflame your senses with soaring passion. Although his body has long ago decomposed in that unmarked grave, his genius lives on forever. One thing is sure: if you look through your CD collection, you won't find anything by an Egyptian pharaoh named Khufu.

It matters little where any of us are buried. It does matter what we compose while still alive on this earth. Every time we love, touch, rescue, or encourage others, they become the living notes of a beautiful symphony that we are composing for the ages. Our life symphonies may not have the perfection of Mozart's musical genius, but they will bring joy and beauty long after we are gone. So live today with this in mind:

Everything will perish, and this world will pass, but the symphony you compose will last forever.

———— ✥ ————

Three things will last forever—faith, hope, and love—and the greatest of these is love.

1 CORINTHIANS 13:13

342

When Greatest
Isn't Good Enough

୧ᢙᢙᡆᢙᡃ

Mike was only twenty-nine years old when his life hit the wall. After he spent the weekend drinking, police clocked him at eighty-four miles an hour in a forty-five-miles-per-hour zone. He posted bail on a DUI charge, locked himself in his house, and refused to see anyone for seventy-two hours. Finally, he texted his agent, "I don't want to live anymore."

The world would have been shocked to know that this finely tuned machine was broken. His advisers begged him to get help. So he swallowed his pride and checked himself into an addiction treatment center, scared to death of opening up to others. This was the superstar who stood aloof, perpetually wearing headphones to block out the rest of the world and so absorbed in his personal goals that he didn't even learn the names of his Olympic teammates. Now he was going to have to bare his soul to other messed-up wrecks of humanity in this place of last resort for addicts.

As he stared at the peeling paint in the shower room, Mike couldn't believe how far he had fallen. History's most decorated Olympian must have seen himself as a train wreck, a time bomb ready to explode. Every minute of his life had been consumed with becoming the world's greatest swimmer. He had shut himself off from people and pleasure in his unswerving pursuit. In the process, he had become a swimming machine: an automaton who fueled himself on prodigious amounts of food, herculean amounts of weight lifting, and untold thousands of laps. Yet his life was as narrow as a single lane in a pool and as cold as the medals that adorned his neck. All the accolades and endorsements couldn't make up for his inability to find purpose beyond standing on the winner's podium.

When Mike was at his lowest, NFL superstar Ray Lewis gave him a copy of Rick Warren's bestseller *The Purpose Driven Life*. In that Arizona clinic, the broken swimming machine finally read the book. His mind was opened to a new way of thinking, and he began to believe there was a deeper meaning to his life. He later told *ESPN Magazine* that, after opening his life to God, he realized there was a bigger purpose for him on this planet. Mike would go on in his fifth Olympics to win more gold medals, bringing his record total to twenty-three. But this time there was a difference. Millions watching him at the Rio Games saw a playful Michael Phelps cheering on his teammates and then winning medals with the unrestrained joy of a kid winning his first medal at a YMCA swim meet.

The world is full of folks who have discovered that being the greatest isn't ever good enough. A question in a Peggy Lee hit song haunts all overachievers: "Is that all there is?" Saint Augustine answers Peggy, "God has made us for himself, and we will be restless until we find our rest in him." The amazing story of the swimming machine fixed by Jesus teaches us this:

The ultimate purpose in life is a life of ultimate purpose.

Whether you eat or drink, or whatever you do,
do it all for the glory of God.

1 CORINTHIANS 10:31

A Long Walk from
the Grave

⊸⊙⊙⊙⊸

Tragedy rocked America's heartland on April 26, 2006, when a tractor trailer swerved across the centerline into a head-on collision with a van full of people from Taylor University. Four students and a staff person were killed in the fiery crash. A surviving student was rushed to the hospital in critical condition. Her story still amazes the world a decade later.

The young woman, who was identified as Laura Van Ryn, age twenty-two, was so badly lacerated and battered that she lay for weeks swathed in bandages and unable to communicate. For thirty-five days, her worried parents sat by her bedside as she hovered between life and death. Don and Susie Van Ryn's only consolation was that they were spared the agony of Newell and Colleen Cerak, who had just walked away from the funeral of their daughter, Whitney, one of the women killed in the crash.

But the inscrutable God who gives also takes away. About five weeks into the Van Ryns' vigil, the woman in bandages stirred and yawned for the first time. They noticed that her teeth looked different from their daughter Laura's. As more bandages were removed, they were startled to see a navel piercing. So they whispered, "Can you tell us your name?" To their shock, the young woman they thought was Laura picked up a pen and wrote "Whitney." At that moment they came face-to-face with a jarring case of mistaken identity. Because Whitney Cerak and Laura Van Ryn looked eerily alike, the coroner at the scene of the accident put the wrong ID on Laura's body. So the Van Ryns lost a daughter they assumed was recovering in the hospital, and the Ceraks got back a child they thought they had buried a month earlier.

Whitney Cerak later spoke at a memorial service for her friend, Laura Van Ryn, whose body had been mistakenly buried in a grave marked for her. More than a decade later, she is happily married and the mother of three children. She doesn't remember those weeks in the hospital, but will always treasure the way the Van Ryns kept a prayerful vigil at her bedside. Though they still grieve for Laura, Don and Susie Van Ryn take great joy in Whitney's happy life. They could be bitter at the tractor trailer driver who only served two years in prison after pleading guilty to five counts of reckless homicide. They could be angry at God for allowing them to have false hope for five weeks, only to have it snatched away—along with their beloved daughter. Instead, theirs is a story of amazing faith. Don Van Ryn told Matt Lauer on the *Today* show, "There are just some things that can't be explained, but the faith that we have in God has gone so deep."

Maybe you are facing a heartache that makes no sense. You've asked life's most difficult questions: "Why? Why me? Why this? Why now?" Sometimes there are no answers. But Don and Susie Van Ryn would surely agree with this:

When we put our troubles in God's hands, he puts his peace in our hearts.

Tell God what you need, and thank him for all he
has done. Then you will experience God's peace,
which exceeds anything we can understand.

PHILIPPIANS 4:6-7

Failing Forward

The only thing that Harland had ever succeeded at was failure. He was just five when his daddy died, leaving his family penniless. At age fourteen, he dropped out of school and hit the road. He worked as a farmhand but soon quit. He became a streetcar conductor but was fired. At age sixteen he lied about his age and joined the army. It wasn't long before he was drummed out of the service. He headed to Alabama, where he tried his hand as a blacksmith. He failed at that, too.

After an unbroken string of failures, Harland found his calling as a locomotive fireman. He figured that he had finally found himself. He was on top of the world when he fell in love and got married. She announced that she was pregnant the day he came home to tell her he had been fired again. A few weeks later, his young wife gave away all their possessions and moved back in with her parents.

Then came the Great Depression. Harland couldn't win for losing. After studying law by correspondence, he was licensed to practice. But he lost his career when he got in a fistfight with one of his clients in a courtroom. He got a gig as a ferryboat captain but was fired after several accidents. He managed a gas station but lost that job when he shot a competitor in an argument over signs.

Later in life he became the chief cook and bottle washer in a little restaurant in Corbin, Kentucky. His establishment became so popular that it put the town on the map, earning him a prestigious award from the governor. Harland was finally a winner. But the new highway bypassed the town, and Harland had to sell his eatery for a fraction of its value. At age sixty-five he was back to square one.

Not long afterward, the mail carrier delivered his first Social Security payment. When he looked at that $105 check, something inside him exploded. He had struggled all his life and had nothing to show for it. So he took that check to the bank and began a fund to start a new venture. That franchise would become one of the most successful in US history.

The man who didn't succeed until he had logged a lifetime of failures, who didn't get started until it was time to stop, was Harland Sanders. You remember him by the title the Kentucky governor gave him: colonel—Colonel Harland Sanders. The business he started with a $105 Social Security check and a "finger lickin' good" recipe was Kentucky Fried Chicken. That little venture that Harland started late in life has become a global empire of twenty thousand stores in 125 countries, generating an annual revenue of $23 billion.

Colonel Sanders's story teaches us that it's never too late to succeed. On the other hand, it's always too soon to give up. No situation is beyond hope. No sin is beyond redemption. No failure is final. Maybe you are on the verge of giving in or giving up. If so, look again at seventy-year-old Harland. He would agree with this:

Failure is never final or fatal, as long as you fail forward.

The godly may trip seven times, but they will get up again.
But one disaster is enough to overthrow the wicked.

PROVERBS 24:16

The Magnificent Fraud

❧

After an epic battle, Shah Jahan was the undisputed master of a vast subcontinent. Yet it was a hollow victory. His wife had just died in childbirth. For nineteen years the princess of Persia had been his soul mate. Their love was the stuff of storybook legend. In an age when Asian kings kept their wives in harems, she was his chief adviser. She even rode by his side into battle.

His grief was monumental. Those who heard his anguished howling were sure that he had gone mad. When he emerged from his chambers, his courtiers and servants gasped in horror. In only eight days his black hair had turned white. He demanded that his subjects join him in mourning. Those caught smiling in public were executed. The shah's sorrow reduced his vast kingdom to a place of utter desolation.

Then he turned his grief into a frenzy of activity. He imported the finest architects and craftsmen to build the world's greatest monument to love—a magnificent mausoleum that would house the treasured remains of his wife. More than twenty thousand workers took twenty-two years to build it at a cost of billions in today's dollars. Centuries later, it remains one of the architectural marvels of history. It has been dubbed the eighth wonder of the world. When the building was finished, the shah ordered the architectural plans destroyed, the architects murdered, and the hands of the master craftsmen cut off so that their genius could never create anything to rival his magnificent memorial to his wife.

Perhaps you have seen the monument that Shah Jahan erected to his wife, Mumtaz Mahal: the breathtakingly beautiful Taj Mahal. The wife of a British officer was heard to say, "I would gladly die tomorrow if some man loved me enough to put such a building over my grave." An Indian poet wrote of the Taj Mahal, "Only let this one tear-drop, this Tajmahal, glisten spotlessly bright on the cheek of time, forever and ever."

But do you know the little secret that will never appear in a tourist guidebook? Indian researchers have discovered that the ornate burial box does not contain the ashes of Mumtaz Mahal. She is thought to be buried somewhere else, in an unmarked grave. How did this happen? Did Shah Jahan know the awful truth? There are plenty of theories. One is that when Shah Jahan visited the work site, he tripped over a box that had been carelessly left among the rubble. He angrily ordered it to be thrown away. Terrified workers tossed it into a nearby garbage pile where it disappeared forever. But that story is impossible to confirm.

But this much is true: the eighth wonder of the world perpetrates one of history's greatest frauds. It stands as mute testimony to the tragedy of wasted endeavors. It also raises a question: Are we building magnificent facades that hide empty boxes? One day we will stand before God and give an account for how we have invested his resources. It's good to reflect on an old Italian proverb:

When the game is over, both king and pawns go back into the same box.

———— ✥ ————

We must all appear before the judgment seat of Christ,
so that each of us may receive what is due us for the
things done while in the body, whether good or bad.

2 CORINTHIANS 5:10

The Forgotten Fallen

❧

They rise from the hills of Boston, the fields of Saratoga, and the swamps of South Carolina. Their faded red uniforms hang tattered on bodies mangled by weapons of terror. You will not hear or see them except through the ears and eyes of imagination. Yet if you listen where redcoat and rebel once clashed in freedom's battles, you might hear the moaning of the nameless forgotten.

They were shipped far from home: British conscripts and German Hessians press-ganged into service. They flooded in by the thousands, in scarlet-red uniforms, high-stepping to fife and drum on a mission from king and parliament. They little understood the fiery speeches from colonial rabble-rousers about "taxation without representation" or "the rights of free men." These boys in red coats only knew that they, too, were fighting for God and country. So they marched ramrod straight like toy soldiers into the yawning jaws of death. European battle tactics had come face-to-face with a new kind of guerilla warfare where farmer soldiers and frontier sharpshooters fired with deadly accuracy from behind trees and rocks before disappearing into forest mists. Some twenty-five thousand British boys and ten thousand Hessian boys fell on colonial fields, their bodies mangled by cannon fire, shattered by musket ball, or ravaged by disease and gangrene.

No one much cared. They were expendable to rich old men in the royal courts and parliaments who profited from this war. The colonials despised them as dirty redcoats, murderers of patriots, the illegal army of foreign tyrants. So they were buried in mass graves and trenches far from family, without monuments or grave markers. No one in England or Germany wanted to take on the expense of bringing their remains home for proper burial. None in America thought of these fallen redcoats as patriots who bravely sacrificed life and limb for their country.

In all of the United States, there is only one marker specifying the names of British soldiers: Lieutenant William Calderwood and Ensign John Finley, whose names are etched on a single gravestone in Beaumont, South Carolina. Shouldn't we remember the rest—the thirty-five thousand who never returned home to be celebrated for their heroism or remembered by a gravestone? Shouldn't the country where they fell see them as more than redcoats trying to snatch our liberties? Many of them likely knelt before the same God that George Washington prayed to before battle. They, too, left behind grieving parents, widows, and orphans.

War may mark men and women as enemies, but they are really brothers and sisters who both fight and die for their countries. They face the same loneliness, shed the same blood, and die with the same horror and pain. Maybe before we are caught up in self-righteous jingoism, we who are God worshipers should consider this enduring truth:

Those who worship their nation often say that God is on their side. Those who worship God first ask if their nation is on his side.

———— ⁊⊙⊙⊙ ————

He stood at the entrance to the camp and shouted, "All of you who are on the LORD's side, come here and join me."

EXODUS 32:26

Sermons from the Crypt

◈

His German name was Karl der Grosse. At age twenty-nine, he was crowned the ruler of a tiny kingdom in what is now modern-day France. Few people at his coronation thought that King Karl would one day reshape the map of Europe.

At the time of Karl's ascension in 771, Europe was a collection of petty fiefdoms, plagued by superstition and ignorance, poverty and pestilence. In the south, Islamic armies had conquered Spain. Vikings were raiding from the north. Ruthless hordes were riding in on the winds of the east.

In this apocalyptic age, Karl rose up to rescue Christendom. Standing six feet four inches tall in a day when the average European stood five feet three, this giant of a man declared war on all those who opposed Christendom. By sheer brutality, he dragged Europe out of the Dark Ages. Over the next forty-two years he fought fifty-three wars. When he defeated an army or captured a city, he insisted that everyone convert to Christianity. Those who refused were slaughtered. After one battle 4,500 Saxons were beheaded when they refused baptism. Their wives and children were driven into a river and drowned. After that, no one dared to oppose Karl's evangelism by intimidation.

By the cross and sword, he carved out an empire that went from the Atlantic to Russia, earning the nickname the Scourge of Christ. Then he spent his final years building monasteries and universities, trying to atone for his reign of terror. He died as one of the most powerful men in the world, outliving four wives and leaving behind five mistresses, eighteen children, and a united Europe.

Two centuries later, workmen accidentally broke into Karl's burial crypt under the cathedral in Aachen, Germany. As they peered into the musty darkness, they saw a two-hundred-year-old skeleton encased in cobwebs and tied with rotting ropes to a throne. Bones were covered with the tatters of what was once a rich robe, now eaten away by time. A crown was perched sideways on a grinning skull.

As the workers inched closer to the macabre remains of the man who once ruled Europe, they saw a table holding a large Bible. The right index finger of the skeleton was resting on a verse in the open book. The workmen called for a priest. Holding a candle close to the Bible, he read the Latin verse of Jesus' words: "What do you benefit if you gain the whole world but lose your own soul?" (Mark 8:36).

Historians recall that on Christmas Day in the year 800, a grateful Pope Leo III gave Karl der Grosse a new name: Carolus Magnus or Charles the Great. History remembers him by a single name, Charlemagne. Each of us has been shaped by the way he transformed history. Yet as he coughed out his last words from a blood-drenched silk pillow, he ordered his body to be buried in a way that would give a message: both the great and small will appear equally naked before God to give an account for their lives down here. We might all want to remember the last sermon preached by an emperor's skeletal remains:

The only judgment that ultimately matters is the Final Judgment.

～∽⬯∾～

He is coming to judge the earth. He will judge the
world with justice and the nations with fairness.

PSALM 98:9

354

The Most Expensive Book in the World

⁓⊙⊙⊙~

It is the bestselling book of all time, but few folks are aware that it's also the most expensive—not the Gutenberg Bible, but that paperback copy you can purchase on the cheap at Walmart. This bestseller is so accessible that the average American evangelical owns about four copies. Yet these Bibles remain mostly unread. Maybe we wouldn't let them gather dust if we knew their amazing and costly history.

Thousands of years before a single line was penned on an ancient scroll, an unbroken chain of storytellers retold the world's greatest story. A man who was once a fugitive inscribed its first lines 3,400 years ago. Over the next thousand years, prophets, poets, and kings wrote the rest of the Old Testament. Most of them were scorned, exiled, or killed. When Jesus came as the living Word, he was abandoned, abused, and crucified. The apostles who authored the New Testament all died as martyrs except John, who was exiled. The Bible was surely inked in the blood of martyrs.

It's no wonder this book was priceless to generations of saints who paid whatever cost necessary to preserve and pass it down from age to age. Even so, by the fourteenth century only a few hand-copied Bibles existed. The cost of producing them was so prohibitive that only kings, bishops, and wealthy merchants could afford to own one. Many priests never read a Bible, and because it was written in Latin, it was unintelligible to unschooled laity. Maybe that's why Europe descended into a dark age of spiritual ignorance and superstition.

Reformers paid a horrific price when they dared to translate the Bible into the languages of the common people. After John Wycliffe and his associates translated the Bible into English, he and his followers were severely persecuted. In 1415, the Council of Constance declared Wycliffe a heretic. His corpse was dug up and burned, and his ashes were scattered in a nearby river. That same council condemned the Bohemian priest John Huss as an archenemy of the faith for translating the Bible into the Czech language. He was burned alive at the stake. Englishman William Tyndale became a fugitive with a price on his head. Yet he sent copies of his Bible translation back to England in bales of hay, even though it exposed him to grave danger. He was finally caught and strangled at the stake before his body was consumed by fire. But his translation became the basis for the King James Version of the Bible.

The number of people who suffered martyrdom to produce, preserve, and preach the Bible is legion. This book is a bestseller because it is God's revealed truth, empowered by his Holy Spirit to transform lives. But it is rendered even greater by the storms it has weathered and the price that has been paid to pass down the most enduring and amazing story in history. Surely such a treasure shouldn't be left unread. Maybe Charles Spurgeon said it best:

Visit many good books, but live in the Bible.

When I discovered your words, I devoured them.
They are my joy and my heart's delight.

JEREMIAH 15:16

The Other Fire That Night

❧❧❧

You might think that this megadisaster on October 8, 1871, would have captivated America. Yet the rest of the country hardly noticed. More than a century later, only a handful of historians recall the Great Peshtigo Fire of 1871.

It started as a stationary low-pressure system that sucked freakishly hot weather into the upper Midwest. It ended with the largest forest fire in the recorded history of North America. Upper Wisconsin and Michigan were ripe for disaster. Loggers had cut down huge swaths of forest, leaving behind massive piles of brush. Thanks to a building boom, thousands of new wooden houses had been hastily put up. The railroad had laid miles of new track, hacking away trees while leaving behind huge mounds of sawdust, bark, and branches. A man-made tinderbox was waiting for a spark to ignite a firestorm.

Several smaller fires had been kindled that day, but night winds shifted and the flames were fanned into a raging inferno that raced toward the little town of Peshtigo, Wisconsin. The firestorm engulfed the 1,600 residents before they knew what hit them. Shifting winds created a tornado of fire that obliterated the village, leaving behind only blackened bricks, twisted metal, and charred bones. The fire was so hot that it turned sand into glass. More than 800 people died from fire and smoke or drowned in the river trying to escape. Half the population of Peshtigo perished in less than an hour.

But the worst was yet to come. Flying embers from the Peshtigo conflagration ignited nearby forests. By now the tornado had turned into a hurricane of fire, devouring logging camps, farms, and villages in its path. No one knows exactly how many people died, but the official numbers are staggering: up to 2,400 known dead and 1,500 left homeless. But there were hundreds of others unaccounted for. Some 2,400 square miles, or 1.5 million acres, of northern Wisconsin and Michigan were destroyed before heavy rains finally came.

It was the largest forest fire in American history, but few outside Wisconsin or Michigan knew about it. The attention of the world was focused on a fire that struck Chicago the same day. Though the Chicago fire of October 8, 1871, was much smaller, with 250 fatalities, it was given the grandiose title the Great Chicago Fire. It garnered all the headlines. The Peshtigo Fire might have been big news in Wisconsin and Michigan where 2,400 people died and 1.5 million acres of forests and farms were destroyed, but editors across America did not consider that "other fire" newsworthy.

Nothing much has changed. The media still confounds us with what it considers newsworthy, often dismissing as unimportant what we think is most critical. In an age of celebrity and tabloid news, that which the wise consider trivial and trashy is the pabulum of the masses. We shouldn't be surprised that the Chicago Fire is remembered while the Peshtigo Fire is forgotten. Maybe that's why we should consider what's important in an age of trivial pursuits:

Great minds discuss ideas. Average minds discuss events. Small minds discuss people.

God blesses those who hunger and thirst
for justice, for they will be satisfied.

MATTHEW 5:6

A Frog Who
Married a Queen

એૹૹ

I t wasn't easy finding Larry. The reporter had to comb through county records and then drive down a dusty road through rusty gates to a ramshackle house. Who would have figured that Larry would fall so far so fast?

Some twenty years earlier, he had been the toast of Hollywood celebrities at Michael Jackson's Neverland Ranch. He might have been a blue-collar builder whose total assets amounted to a few tools and a pickup truck, but on that magical day he was ruggedly handsome—Joe Six-Pack in a J. C. Penney suit, living a fairy tale; the frog who marries a silver-screen queen.

There would be no fairy-tale ending for Larry. Twenty years later he was bloated, bleary eyed, and out of money. Alcohol had reduced him to a shadow of the man who once traveled the world in private jets and on luxury yachts with Hollywood royalty. His memory was fading and his words were slurred.

He showed off a few trinkets from his marriage to the Hollywood queen. He was especially proud of the wedding photo. She looked stunning in her $25,000 dress, and he was handsome in his off-the-rack suit. He looked like the cat that swallowed the canary. In reality, he was the canary who was about to be eaten by the cat and spat out five years later.

This was not a marriage made in heaven. The carpenter totaled his truck while driving drunk. A judge committed him to the Betty Ford Clinic. There he met the movie queen who was there to get clean. After a quick romance, the two got hitched. This was his third marriage and her eighth. She often boasted, "I've only slept with men I'm married to." But she quickly tired of each husband. She once said, "The excitement is in the getting, not the keeping."

The Neverland Ranch marriage was the first time that Elizabeth Taylor married a frog like Larry Fortensky. She said to her wedding guests, "I've finally found a man who can keep me happy." Larry grinned like a Cheshire cat, kidding himself that he could accomplish what a hotel mogul, movie stars, and a US senator had failed to do. It wouldn't be long before she would give him the boot too.

When the reporter finished the interview, Larry sat hunched over in a daze. Maybe he was lost in a dream of what could have been. Or he was thinking about his only daughter who hadn't spoken to him for years because of a fight over money from his divorce settlement. Or perhaps he was looking at his reflection in the mirror behind that wedding photo, seeing how much he had deteriorated since that day at the Neverland Ranch. As the reporter got up to leave, Larry whispered, "Divorce makes you a lot less than you used to be." Divorce seldom makes anyone bigger. If you are ready to bail out of a tough marriage, you might want to remember Larry's story. It screams a warning to couples everywhere:

Divorce is like an amputation. You may survive, but there's less of you.

[Jesus] said, "'This explains why a man leaves his father
and mother and is joined to his wife, and the two are
united into one.' Since they are no longer two but one,
let no one split apart what God has joined together."

MATTHEW 19:5-6

Life Without Limbs

❧

When they brought her baby, she cried, "Take him away—I don't want to see him." Her husband tried to calm her. "He's beautiful." But she saw this misshapen newborn as a terrible mistake. Before they arrived at the hospital, she had a premonition that something was dreadfully wrong. Her husband was at her bedside when he saw little Nick emerge without arms. He almost vomited. He would have fainted if the nurses hadn't pushed him out of the delivery room. Had he stayed, he would have seen that his son also had no legs.

It was an act of bravery for that couple to bring home a baby who was little more than a head and torso. It was months before Nick's mother came to terms with a boy without limbs. The road ahead was even more difficult for Nick. When he was six, doctors tried to fit him with artificial limbs that were more of a nuisance than a help. When he went to public school, classmates teased and bullied him. At age ten, he felt worthless and wanted to commit suicide at the prospect of being a lifetime burden to his parents.

His dad and mom pulled him out of the crisis by telling him that, if he set his mind to it, he could do anything other kids did. His disabilities didn't have to define or disable him. So the boy without arms and legs learned how to swim and fish, snowboard and surf, play pool and putt a golf ball, brush his teeth and wash his hair. Millions who have watched Nick Vujicic on YouTube videos go away amazed at what a person without limbs is capable of doing.

When he was nineteen, Nick became a motivational speaker. This Australian overcomer has become a globe-trotter, traveling more than three million miles to fifty-eight countries, carrying a message of hope to world leaders as well as the discouraged, disadvantaged, and disabled. He now lives in the United States, where he heads his own nonprofit called Life Without Limbs. He not only shares his personal faith in Jesus Christ but also delivers this inspiring message: no matter what our disability, no dream is beyond our reach.

Nick is now happily married to a Japanese American beauty named Kanae. A few years ago they welcomed their first child into the world, a little boy they call Kiyoshi. You should see the man without arms giving high fives and hugs to his son, or wrestling with him on the floor. Everything Nick thought to be impossible as a suicidal boy has come true. Anyone who follows Nick Vujicic's amazing story surely agrees with his father's assessment: he *is* a beautiful person. Each of us is a special needs child. We all have some kind of disability. But we don't have to let those challenges define or disable us if we will believe what Nick's dad told him one day:

You are a gift, just differently packaged.

———— ✺ ————

"Rabbi," his disciples asked him, "why was this man born blind?" . . . [Jesus answered,] "This happened so the power of God could be seen in him."

JOHN 9:2-3

The Unlikely Leader

❧

If Jimmy could make it, anyone could. Rejected by his parents and shunned by his schoolmates, he retreated into a lonely world of self-loathing. His only comfort was stuffing himself with food until he became grotesquely obese. His flabby white face was covered with pimples and scarred with acne. He reeked of body odor and stuttered whenever he opened his mouth.

One day everything changed for this social outcast. As he walked down a London side street, he looked into a doorway and saw a ragtag collection of fellow losers seated on folding chairs. A sign told him that this was the meeting hall of the Communist Party. A well-dressed man greeted him warmly with this line: "No matter who you are, we can turn you into a leader of men."

Jimmy took the seat closest to the door. The speaker was Douglas Hyde, the editor of the Communist newspaper the *Daily Worker*. Hyde concluded his mesmerizing speech with a bold claim: "I don't care who you are, if you give yourself to the Communist Party, we will turn you into a leader." A tiny seed of hope was planted in Jimmy's heart. He waddled to the podium and stuttered, "C-c-c-comrade, I w-w-w-want you to t-t-turn me into a l-l-leader of m-m-men."

Hyde later wrote in his book, *Dedication and Leadership*, that he groaned within. He had never seen sorrier human material. But he had made a promise. So he gulped and welcomed Jimmy into the brotherhood. The new convert was sent out to the mean streets of London to hand out the *Daily Worker*. He was ridiculed, spit upon, and assaulted. When he returned with his soul battered and bruised, he whimpered, "I c-c-can't d-d-do it!" But his comrades wouldn't let him give up. Slowly but inexorably, Jimmy was transformed from a loser into a leader. The despairing stutterer became a dynamic speaker. The former recluse became the greatest union organizer the Communist Party of Great Britain had ever seen. Years later, his death was front-page news. Factories shut down as thousands attended his funeral.

There is a postscript to Jimmy's story. It has to do with Douglas Hyde, the man who first gave him hope. Hyde left the Communist Party and embraced Christianity. He believed that Christ offered more hope than did Lenin. But when Hyde wrote *Dedication and Leadership* in 1956, disillusionment with the church was setting in—in particular, the Pope's harsh treatment of those on the political left. Hyde said that although Communists believe humans are soulless products of evolution, they often have more faith in their message to transform people than do most Christians. By the time he died in 1966, he had moved away from organized religion. On his deathbed he declared himself to be an "agnostic Christian."

How tragic! Douglas Hyde looked at the church of Jesus rather than the Jesus of the church. Jesus took twelve losers who were misfits like Jimmy Reid and transformed them to change the world. He still does that two thousand years later. If we remember this truth, we will never lose heart in what he can do for us and others:

God formed us. Sin deformed us. Jesus will transform us.

Anyone who belongs to Christ has become a new person.
The old life is gone; a new life has begun!

2 CORINTHIANS 5:17

The Beauty and the Brains

❧

The Austrian bombshell possessed a beauty that drove men wild. In 1933 she shocked the world by appearing nude in a low-budget film with the provocative title *Ecstasy*. It got her in hot water with the pope, who publicly condemned her. It also got her noticed by media moguls in Tinseltown. Before long she was an MGM megastar—the glamor queen of the silver screen, starring with such leading men as Clark Gable, Spencer Tracy, and Jimmy Stewart. During World War II, American servicemen voted her their favorite pinup girl. She was arguably the most beautiful star in the golden age of Hollywood.

But the glamor queen saw her beauty as a curse. She wrote in her autobiography, "[My face] attracted six unsuccessful marriage partners. It has attracted all the wrong people into my boudoir and brought me tragedy and heartache for five decades. My face is a mask I cannot remove: I must always live with it. I curse it." Mostly, she lamented the prejudice that haunts so many beautiful people: the assumption that they are shallow, that beauty and brains can't coexist in the same person.

Few people would have guessed that this Hollywood starlet was a closet scientist who worked late into the night on inventions and designs. As a Jew, she felt compelled to help defeat Adolf Hitler. So she began to formulate an invention that would change the future of warfare and modern technology. Her brilliant ideas were born of the same principles that operate a player piano.

To the untrained eye, her sketches are tangled mazes of wires and switches. Yet scientists today are amazed at the brilliance that unlocked the secrets of sonar technology. When she took her drawings to the navy, they wondered what piano notes had to do with submarines. They couldn't believe that a Hollywood beauty's idea of "frequency hopping" would amount to anything. But by the Cold War era, her ideas became an integral part of the American defense system. Without the discoveries of this film star, missiles may not have flown undetected. A torpedo might not have been guided by radio waves. Khrushchev might not have backed down during the Cuban Missile Crisis. Who knows—maybe drones wouldn't even be flying over Afghanistan today. And the Wi-Fi that drives social media might not exist.

Yet when a silver-screen megastar known as Hedy Lamarr presented her ideas to the US Department of the Navy, the brass told her that she should use her looks and celebrity to sell war bonds instead of wasting time with "this silly inventing." Even then, they couldn't see the brilliance behind the beauty. The Hollywood glamor queen would carry the sadness of that prejudice to her grave. We might wonder if much has changed in the seventy-five years since. In an age of celebrity that worships at the altar of beauty, we need to reevaluate how we look at others. The story of Hedy Lamarr teaches us a powerful fact:

If you judge a book by its cover, you might miss an amazing story.

———— ∽◎∾ ————

People judge by outward appearance,
but the LORD looks at the heart.

1 SAMUEL 16:7

Feathers in the Wind

⸎◌⸎

He was on a business trip when his heart was broken. As he looked across the dining room, he saw his pastor. Why was the good reverend in this restaurant so far from home? As he hurried across the room to greet the pastor, he froze in his tracks. His pastor was with a woman who wasn't his wife, and they were holding hands by candlelight.

The businessman felt like a bomb had gone off in his face. Then he remembered that he was an elder with an obligation to protect the flock from a wolf in sheep's clothing. His first reaction was to confront his philandering pastor. But he didn't want to create a scene. So he fled to his hotel room and called his wife. She was quick with advice. He needed to call an emergency meeting of the elders. He hung up his phone and began to pack. She picked up hers and began to call her friends. The news spread like wildfire. By the next day, the two-timing pastor was the talk of the town. By evening, clergy several states away had heard about the affair. A "concerned" friend informed the pastor's wife. Her husband returned home to a full-blown scandal. He protested his innocence, but the genie was out of the bottle.

By week's end the church auditorium was packed for a congregational meeting that was more like a public hanging. Hardly anyone noticed the pretty blonde. They were more captivated by the reverend and his tight-lipped family as they walked down the aisle. A hush fell over the crowd as he stepped into his pulpit. The assembled vultures expected a public confession. Instead, he said, "I have come to tender my resignation. My family is deeply wounded, and my reputation soiled. In choosing to believe the worst, you have done things that cannot be undone." He then stepped down to the front row and took the hand of the pretty blonde.

"I'd like to introduce you to my baby sister. She is the woman who was in the restaurant with me. Her husband had just left her, and I drove three hundred miles to bring comfort." With that, he and his family walked out past a stunned congregation.

In the days that followed, frantic knocking on his front door went unanswered. Phone calls were not returned. As the movers went about their work, parishioners stood in the driveway and pled with the pastor to stay. He finally picked up a pillow, tore it open, and shook the feathers into the wind. "If you can find and return all these feathers, and if every word of gossip can be returned to your mouths unsaid, then things can be made right again."

This true account is told with the names of pastor and church kept secret to protect hearts still fragile and broken years later. This story of a rush to judgment should remind all of us to be careful about what we assume to be true. We will be even more careful not to spread gossip or slander if we remember this:

We reveal the most about ourselves when we speak about others.

Do not judge others, and you will not be judged. For you will be treated as you treat others. The standard you use in judging is the standard by which you will be judged.

MATTHEW 7:1-2

Two Days Late and a Month Short

❧❧❧

It's the Fourth of July! Not even the Grinch can steal the patriotism that swells up in American hearts on this day. So break out the sparklers, throw a few dogs on the grill, and enjoy fireworks at sunset. After all, today is America's birthday. Or is it?

Not according to John Adams. On July 3, 1776, he wrote to his wife, Abigail, that the Second Continental Congress had voted to declare independence from England the day before. Mr. Adams gushed, "The Second Day of July, 1776, will be the most memorable epoch in American history. . . . It ought to be solemnized with Pomp and Parade, with Shows, Games, Sports, Guns, Bells, Bonfires and Illuminations, from one End of this Continent to the other from this Time forward forever more."

Why, then, don't we celebrate our nation's birthday on the second day of July? Maybe it's because it took another day to edit the Declaration of Independence. The final copy wasn't approved until July 4. Philadelphia waited until July 8 to celebrate with parades. General George Washington didn't hear about its ratification until July 9. It wouldn't be until August 30 that London got the word.

The revised version was approved by voice vote on July 4, 1776, but not signed. The actual signing didn't begin until John Hancock scrawled his signature across the middle of the page on August 2, 1776, a full month after the voice vote. The others affixed their signatures over the next several months. The last person to sign was Thomas McKean of Delaware, who signed the Declaration of Independence more than a year later. Only in 1777 was the document fully ratified. Now you know the truth: our July 4, 1776, celebration is two days late—or a month to a year too early.

All this begs a question: When is our nation's true birthday? Maybe its origins can be traced to Mount Sinai and the Law received by Moses more than three thousand years ago. Or to the democracy of ancient Greece. Or to the birth of Christianity some two thousand years ago. We can see parts of its blueprint in Plato's *Republic* and Augustine's *City of God*. It is foreshadowed in the Magna Carta and written in blood on the fields of Naseby, where Oliver Cromwell's Parliament army triumphed over King Charles of England, giving birth to representative democracy. Without the Great Awakening revivals fifty years earlier in colonial America, there might have been no revolution in 1776.

The dream that is America has been reborn on the fields of Gettysburg, on the beaches of Normandy, in the Mekong Delta, in the deserts of Iraq and Afghanistan, and in thousands of other places where the blood of patriots has been shed. Our freedoms are purchased on the installment plan—not just by patriots who signed their own death sentences in 1776 but every day of every year by those who pay the ultimate price to keep liberty alive for each new generation. People are willing to do so because they understand what W. E. B. DuBois said:

The cost of liberty is less than the price of repression.

Christ has truly set us free. Now make sure that you
stay free, and don't get tied up again in slavery to the law.

GALATIANS 5:1

The Silent Hero

❧

Her story has moved millions. This dynamic speaker is also a disability rights activist, a renowned painter, and a bestselling author. Her first book has sold more than three million copies and has been translated into about forty languages. Through her Internet ministry, she gives hope to disabled and discouraged people around the world. Yet few people notice the man who stands in the shadows offstage. Unlike his wife, Ken is no celebrity. He would remind you that he is just a retired high school history teacher. So he silently waits while she signs autographs. After the lights dim, he gets her back to the hotel or airport. This quiet man is, after all, her arms and legs.

Ken's celebrity wife is a quadriplegic who has been consigned to a wheelchair for the past four decades. When she was seventeen, a diving accident crushed her spine. Since then she has had no feeling from the neck down. She could have given in to despair, but instead this gutsy woman taught herself how to paint, holding the brush in her teeth. When she won awards for her paintings, she was interviewed by Barbara Walters on prime-time television. Then she taught herself how to type without fingers. She wrote a bestseller that inspired millions of readers. That catapulted her into a speaking ministry that would exhaust most folks—even those who don't live in constant pain.

Her first date with Ken was a little unorthodox. While at the movies, he had to empty her leg bag and dump the urine outside behind a tree. From that moment on, he knew that life with her would be a tough road. Friends warned them not to get married. Ken would be signing up for a lifetime of 24/7 caregiving. What if he folded under the load? And what about her? How would she feel if he became resentful?

Thirty-some years after Ken pushed her down the aisle, he would tell you that marriage to a quadriplegic is no picnic. Every day he has to put on and take off her makeup, help her onto and off of the toilet, charge the wheelchair batteries, lift her in and out of bed, turn her over during the night, and do all the shopping and housekeeping. He had to be her rock when she got stage 3 breast cancer and underwent a mastectomy.

There were times Ken did get resentful. When he fell into a deep depression, he and his wife had to get brutally honest with each other to save their relationship. But Ken Tada would tell you that his marriage to Joni Eareckson is the best thing that happened to both of them. True love really does hold on, especially when it's grounded in Christ. Both Ken and Joni say that persevering through pain together produces indescribable intimacy.

Maybe you want to bail out of a tough marriage, a dysfunctional family, or a disappointing friendship. You will never grow by taking the easy way out. Ken and Joni's amazing love story teaches us this:

Relationships enjoy compatibility but endure by commitment.

Love never gives up, never loses faith, is always hopeful, and endures through every circumstance.

1 CORINTHIANS 13:7

A Tale of Two Families

❧

This amazing story of two families spans several generations. Both trace their lineage back to two men who lived in colonial America. One called himself Jukes. But his name isn't so important. He was constantly coming up with a new alias to stay a step ahead of the law. Jukes was, according to his neighbors, "a shiftless, lazy no-account." The little that he managed to scrape together was mostly gained by his marginal skills as a petty thief. But Mr. Jukes was never clever enough to outwit the local sheriff. He was constantly in and out of jail. His wife was a woman of low morals who spent too much time in a drunken stupor.

At the turn of the twentieth century, a series of sociologists managed to uncover twelve hundred descendants in the Jukes family tree. Some three hundred were professional beggars. More than a hundred were convicted criminals. Sixty were thieves and pickpockets. At least four hundred of them were drunkards or drug addicts. Another seven were convicted murderers, although several more were suspects. More than fifty of them spent time in mental institutions. Of the twelve hundred descendants discovered by the educators, only twenty ever learned a trade. Half who did learned their trade in prison. Less than two hundred of Jukes's descendants finished high school, and none attended college. The Jukeses' family record was one of pauperism and prison, imbecility and insanity, prostitution and panhandling, drunkenness and drug abuse.

One sociologist also studied the family tree of a colonial contemporary of Jukes. He was a preacher, as were his father and grandfather. Scholars say that he was the greatest theologian and philosopher ever produced by America. His dynamic preaching sparked a great spiritual awakening that birthed the American Revolution. Maybe you remember this third president of Princeton, the Reverend Jonathan Edwards, and his famous sermon "Sinners in the Hands of an Angry God." But you may not have ever shaken his family tree to see what fell out.

A total of four hundred descendants have been traced to Jonathan Edwards and his wife, Sarah. Among them was a US vice president, three US senators, three governors, three mayors, thirteen college and university presidents, and thirty judges. Around sixty-five of Edwards's progeny were college professors. Another hundred were ministers, missionaries, or seminary professors. Eighty were public office holders. In his family tree were one hundred lawyers and sixty medical doctors. Several descendants had written books, published newspapers, or been editors of journals. Until the beginning of the twentieth century, every major industry in America had as its founder or promoter an offspring of Jonathan and Sarah Edwards.

Most families are mixed bags of success and failures. Few are as dismal as Jukes's descendants, or as stellar as Edwards's progeny. But the contrast cannot be missed, nor the lesson dismissed. Parents have a profound impact on their world for generations to come. Nothing is more important than the responsibilities and possibilities of parenthood. The story of two families shouts a message:

Your children will become who you are, so be who you want them to be.

———— ∾ ————

Direct your children onto the right path, and
when they are older, they will not leave it.

PROVERBS 22:6

Be Careful Little Eyes
What You See

⋘⊙⋙

Little Theodore never felt like he belonged. It would be years before he figured out why. By then his rage was off the charts.

His teen mother named him Theodore Robert Cowell, giving him her maiden name. She took her baby to Philadelphia to live with his grandparents. Ashamed of being an unwed mother, she told her son that she was his sister. He would be an adult before he discovered that his "big sister" was really his mother, and that his grandparents weren't Mom and Dad. He never forgave that deception.

When he was four, his mom took him from the only home he had ever known and moved across the country. Theodore never recovered from the trauma of that move or the fact that his mother was incapable of showing affection. To make matters worse, she married an abusive alcoholic. The boy withdrew into a shell of bitter loneliness. Though he grew up to be quite handsome, Theodore had few friends or dates. He could never shake his paranoid fear of intimacy.

At age twelve, he found some porn magazines in a garbage dump. Through soft porn he tried to connect with women without risking intimacy. But the flesh is never satisfied. So Theodore graduated to the hard stuff. He tried to break his addiction by incessantly repeating a mantra he learned in Sunday school: "Be careful little eyes what you see." But he couldn't overcome the weaknesses of his flesh.

After the only girl he ever loved broke up with him, Theodore snapped. Somewhere outside Seattle, he killed his first victim. Before he was finished, he became the most prolific murderer in US history. Some experts say that he may have tortured and murdered as many as one hundred women in a cross-country killing spree. On the night before he was strapped into the electric chair at the Florida State Prison, Theodore "Ted" Bundy confessed to Dr. James Dobson,

> There was an unfulfilled longing in my heart. I thought that pornography could fill the emptiness. My mind was always focused on the wrong things. They became the doorways that allowed sinister spirits to come inside me. Violence became part of my fantasies. I drank lots of alcohol to reduce my religious inhibitions. When I committed my first murder it seemed like I was possessed by something awful and alien.

Ted Bundy spent the last night of his life praying with a minister. He wept over the horror and pain he had inflicted on his victims. In the early morning hours, Theodore finally smiled and said, "My eyes will soon see something beautiful for the first time." What will you look at today? Herman Melville wrote, "Eyes are windows to the soul." If you recall Ted's story, you might take this truth seriously:

Eyes are glass doors through which the visible world enters to take control of the invisible soul.

―――― ∽◌∾ ――――

Your eye is like a lamp that provides light for your
body. When your eye is healthy, your whole body
is filled with light. But when your eye is unhealthy,
your whole body is filled with darkness.

MATTHEW 6:22-23

Boomerang Justice

❧

Many are convinced that the territorial governor committed suicide. Anyone who knows his story might see how he'd be tempted to do so. After all, the murder of an innocent man was committed on his watch. He had sworn to uphold the law. But one morning a lynch mob dragged a battered man into his courtroom, demanding that he be hanged. The governor knew the man was not guilty, but he caved to the mob. That act of judicial cowardice will live forever in infamy.

He had left the capital with high hopes as the new territorial governor of a high desert country crawling with outlaw gangs. If he managed to clean up the territory, he would return home to a hero's welcome. When he galloped into the territorial capital at the head of his federal troops, everyone knew there was a new sheriff in town—a tough law-and-order man. He might as well have been called "the hanging judge." He made the streets safe for decent folk and ruthlessly hunted down outlaw gangs. With grit and determination, he lasted a decade in a place that had chewed up and spit out governors every two years.

Yet history remembers this territorial governor for hanging that innocent man. He tried to reason with the lynch mob, but they wouldn't listen. He tried to get the bloodied man to admit to some crime, but he refused. He had some of his marshals beat him savagely, hoping that this bludgeoning would satisfy the mob. Instead, they screamed even louder for a lynching. Finally, he brought out the meanest desperado who had ever appeared on a wanted poster—a gunslinger and a bank robber. He offered to hang him in place of the innocent man, but the mob refused. So he caved in to keep peace in the territory.

His attempt at compromise didn't work. The territory erupted into a violent range war. The judge was called home in disgrace, his political career in shambles. A few years later, according to people who claimed to know, he went to a bluff above a river and jumped to his death. People said he committed suicide because he couldn't get that innocent man out of his mind. You remember that governor by his infamous name: Pontius Pilate. The wild territory was Judea.

The innocent man he "hanged" was Jesus.

Did Pilate finally commit suicide? That is debatable. But one thing is certain: Jesus stands before us today, just as he stood before Pilate. He asks us to choose what we will do with him. He will not go away, so we must decide. The choice we make has eternal consequences. There is irony in Governor Pilate's story: this judge will stand in heaven's courtroom before the one he hanged on a tree outside Jerusalem. Their roles will be reversed. Now Jesus will be the judge.

He will be your judge too. Are you ready for that day? You will be if you receive him as your Savior and King. You will avoid the fate of this governor if you learn from the tragic story of Pilate's encounter with Jesus:

Either crown him or crucify him, but never compromise him.

———— ∞ ————

Together they will go to war against the Lamb,
but the Lamb will defeat them because he is
Lord of all lords and King of all kings.

REVELATION 17:14

378

The Real Wonder Woman

⌒⊙⊙⌒

Meet Wonder Woman. Don't let her looks deceive you. This twenty-seven-year-old Nigerian woman doesn't appear indestructible. Her face, neck, and arms are disfigured, her huge nose is a hodgepodge of plastic surgeries, and her lower lip is enlarged. When she walks down the street, people stare. What they see is a difficult enough sight. If they could look beneath her clothes, they would see a mass of hideous scars.

On December 10, 2005, Kechi took a short ride on Sosoliso Airlines Flight 1145. Those fifteen minutes changed her life. As the plane neared its destination, it flew into turbulent winds; it was a roller-coaster ride followed by a sudden drop. Someone yelled, "Are we landing already?" No one had time to answer. The airliner slammed into the ground, bursting into flames and killing 107 people. It is a miracle that Kechi survived the impact and the fireball that roared through the shattered airliner. Only she and one other passenger made it out alive.

Kechi awakened in the hospital to see her mother through a haze of morphine. As it wore off, she felt searing pain. Her whole body was on fire. Her nose was almost gone, as were her lips. She later said she was glad she didn't see herself in a mirror. Instead, her mom tenderly said, "Kechi, you are still beautiful." Her family flew her to a burn hospital in Galveston, Texas. Recovery took seven years. Each little step forward, including the slightest movement of her arms and facial muscles, came with excruciating pain. There were one hundred plastic surgeries over the next thirteen years.

Yet this Nigerian woman walks down the streets of Houston with her reconstructed head held high. People stop and gawk at her, but she returns their stares with a smile as big as Texas. She walks with the confidence of one who knows that Jesus sees her as beautiful. Instead of feeling resentment, she confesses that all things work together for the good of those who love God (see Romans 8:28). How did she make it through the years of pain and reconstructive surgeries? She says that she sang away the sorrows, scars, and stares.

The world finally saw her in season 12 of NBC's *America's Got Talent* when she walked onto center stage. The audience gasped when they first laid eyes on this severely disfigured woman. Then she began to sing her mesmerizing song. As Kechi Okwuchi's angelic voice soared to its dramatic conclusion, the audience stood as one person, along with notoriously critical judge Simon Cowell. The applause was deafening. Judge Howie Mandel told Kechi, "You're one of the most beautiful women I have ever met." This Wonder Woman could not have known when she awakened in the hospital that she would one day stand on one of America's biggest stages as one of our most beautiful women.

Maybe you are sitting on an ash heap today. You look at your scars and wonder if beauty will ever come again. Dear friend, take heart from Kechi's amazing story. This much is true:

We can overcome the tragedy we never thought we could live through.

———— ❧ ————

He will give a crown of beauty for ashes,
a joyous blessing instead of mourning.

ISAIAH 61:3

Christianity in Shoe Leather

❦

Not much ever happened in little Northfield, Massachusetts. Who would have guessed that one of its ragged orphans would change the world? Lyman was only four when his daddy worked himself into an early grave. By the time he was seventeen, he could barely read or write. With two dollars in his pocket, he headed for Boston to work in his uncle's boot shop.

His pious uncle asked him to promise to go to church on Sundays. But the unschooled teen struggled with the big words in the sermons. He invariably fell asleep. Fortunately, a Sunday school teacher took an interest in the slow learner and led him to Jesus. When church elders heard the news, they shook their heads and declared that Lyman would be of little use to God's Kingdom.

Soon afterward, he moved to Chicago to sell shoes. What he lacked in book learning and social graces he made up for in dogged determination, becoming the Windy City's best shoe salesman. He also joined a church where he irritated everyone with his unpolished zeal. His butchered grammar and fractured theology became wildly unpopular. Finally, a delegation of elders advised the shoe salesman, "Leave praying and speaking to those who can do it better."

So Lyman went to the slums of Chicago to set up a Sunday school. People joked that he was too ignorant to teach even unschooled street kids. Yet by sheer tenacity, he dragged thousands of ragged children to his Sunday school. His venture was so successful that it attracted a lawyer from nearby Springfield. Abraham Lincoln often spoke about the Sunday when he watched "legions of ragamuffin kids study the Bible."

Then the shoe salesman started his own church. Mostly, he attracted unschooled hicks. When his church was destroyed in the Great Fire of 1871, he teamed up with a gospel singer and became a traveling evangelist. His poor preaching made him the nation's laughingstock. He spoke so fast that folks couldn't follow. A reporter held a stopwatch and counted his words. Lyman topped out at 230 words a minute. He also topped the scales at four hundred pounds of weight!

But this obese shoe salesman was determined to get the gospel out by any means. Who would have figured that he would personally lead more than a million people to Christ? Or that he would earn the title Prince of Evangelists? No one expected someone with his lackluster background to establish the largest Bible college in America, one of the world's biggest publishing houses, and a string of schools that sent five thousand missionaries overseas during his lifetime, making America the largest missionary-sending nation in history!

The world remembers him by his full name, Dwight Lyman Moody. There's not a Christian in the world that hasn't been affected by that shoe salesman. D. L. Moody proves that none of us are so devoid of talent that we can't do so much more, if only we would take up the challenge that spurred him to greatness:

The world has yet to see what God can do with a person fully consecrated to him.

———— ✆ ————

[Jesus said,] "Very truly I tell you, whoever believes
in me will do the works I have been doing, and
they will do even greater things than these."

JOHN 14:12, NIV

The Dangling Telephone

They found her cold body tangled in sheets. A telephone receiver dangled from a cord by the bed. Detectives concluded that she had tried to make one last call. Folks in her hometown always said that the Mortenson girl would end up dead before her time.

Actually, she really wasn't the Mortenson girl. No one knew the identity of her real daddy. She was only six when her mother, Gladys, was carted off to the insane asylum, leaving her to be shuffled through too many foster homes, where she was abused and mistreated. In one of these homes, a renter molested her and then purred, "Here, honey, take this nickel and don't tell anyone what I did to you." She later complained, "I found out early on that I was only worth five cents." Even after she grew up to be a Hollywood goddess, she saw herself as little more than a sex object.

She often said, "I want to be loved for myself." Yet Norma Jeane Mortenson constantly reinvented herself. As a child she adopted her mother's maiden name and became Norma Jean Baker. When she married at age sixteen, she was Norma Jean Dougherty. Later she wed a baseball legend and turned into Norma Jean DiMaggio. During her short marriage to a renowned playwright she was Norma Jean Miller. But it was as a twenty-year-old model that a Hollywood publicist gave Norma Jean her most famous name, Marilyn Monroe.

Though she parlayed her sexy blonde persona into megastardom, she always felt used and dirty, like a molested little girl. Maybe that's why she plowed through three failed marriages and unhappy romances with the most powerful men in the world. She lamented, "I'm just a small-town girl in a big world trying to find someone to love." Toward the end of her short life, she observed, "A wise girl kisses but doesn't love, listens but doesn't believe, and leaves before she is left."

At age thirty-six, her life was out of control. In desperation, she called an actor friend. After listening to her talk incessantly about how unloved she felt, he impatiently hung up. Popping lethal barbiturates, she frantically tried to call someone who would listen. The next morning, the phone was found dangling by her deathbed.

The editor of *Vogue*, Clare Boothe Luce, later wrote a poignant piece on Norma Jean's death. She asked, "What really killed this love goddess who never found love?" Ms. Luce believed the answer was in that dangling phone. "Marilyn Monroe died because she never got through to someone who would love her."

In his haunting tribute to Norma Jean, "Candle in the Wind," Elton John sang, "Loneliness was tough, the toughest role you ever played." It's the hardest role that any of us ever play. Clare Boothe Luce concluded, "Millions of people are trying to get through to someone who will love them." There is someone who loved us enough to step out of heaven and die on a cross to open the lines of communication. This ought to give you the confidence to pick up the receiver.

He's been there all the time, waiting patiently on the line.

――――――ﾟﾟ――――――

Call to me and I will answer you, and will tell you
great and hidden things that you have not known.

JEREMIAH 33:3, ESV

Off Screen

cᴏᴏᴏ

Lucille LeSueur brought a new style to Hollywood: not classic beauty, but strong features; not delicate femininity, but animal magnetism; strength softened by glitzy jewelry, designer clothes, and extravagant hairstyles. She was the ultimate fabrication of Hollywood mythmakers.

Lucille was a chorus girl in a second-rate Broadway review when she was discovered and signed by Metro-Goldwyn-Mayer in 1925. But the movie studio had to do something about her name. Lucille was too ordinary, and LeSueur sounded like "the sewer." So the company's public relations team ran a magazine competition to choose a new name. It would become one of the most famous in Hollywood history. With her new brand, the former Lucille LeSueur clawed her way to the top, cutting off all ties to her dirt-poor Texas roots and reinventing herself as a film legend without a past.

But nothing made her a bigger hit with her fans than when she adopted the daughter of an unwed mother. Then she adopted twins. The Hollywood queen lavished those kids with storybook nurseries, doting nannies, toys galore, and parties with pony rides, clowns, magicians, and balloons. All this was staged and filmed to project an image: the Hollywood goddess as an adoring mother of adorable orphans—a fairy tale straight out of central casting.

Yet little Christina, her oldest daughter, knew the truth, and so did the studio heads. Behind the scenes, Lucille LeSueur plowed through four marriages and a string of affairs. By age thirty-seven, her drinking binges and wild mood swings had made her box-office poison. So she continued to play the adoring mother in an attempt to recover her image and career. But when the camera crews left, all semblance of peace shattered.

Christina was thirteen when her Hollywood mom almost choked her to death, punched her in the face, and slammed her head against the floor. She still recalls the night her mother dragged her out of bed and beat her over the head with a can of scouring powder because she'd left soap streaks on the bathroom floor. She still has nightmares about being beaten with wire hangers for the way she hung up her clothes.

Lucille LeSueur, better known as Joan Crawford, was no glamor queen at home. A year after the actress died, Christina wrote a sizzling exposé called *Mommie Dearest*. Her bestseller spawned a movie that forever destroyed her mother's legend. Though Joan Crawford's defenders have panned *Mommie Dearest* as the lies of an ungrateful child, Christina asserts that her book is gospel truth.

Her story teaches us that no matter how careful we are to project a certain image of ourselves to the watching world, those who really know us will tell the rest of the story. So will God. He knows the truth—the whole truth. One day he will open the book on your life and expose your secrets to everyone. It might help to remember this:

The truth may hurt today, but your lies will haunt you forever.

Whatever you have said in the dark will be heard in the light, and what you have whispered behind closed doors will be shouted from the housetops for all to hear!

LUKE 12:3

The Secret No One Knew

⌘

He was a national treasure—the kind of comedic genius who comes along once in a generation. He first entered people's living rooms as an alien from a distant planet, a jabbering motormouth whose nonstop craziness made viewers laugh until they ached. Over the years he morphed into characters that are indelibly etched in our cultural consciousness: a crazy disc jockey in Vietnam, a grandmotherly nanny, a doctor named Patch Adams, a teacher, a psychologist, a president, and a psychotic killer. Peter Pan flying through Neverland. Teddy Roosevelt running amok in a night at the museum. And a creepy voyeur at the photo shop. No one has ever run the gamut of emotions the way Robin did. He made us laugh. And he made us cry.

It's no wonder Robin was nominated four times for an Oscar, winning an Academy Award. He amassed two Screen Actors Guild Awards, three Emmys, four Grammys, and six Golden Globes, plus numerous other honors. Yet he had so much left to give his fans who were craving more. That's why the world was devastated when he was found dead in his California home on August 11, 2014. Even more distressing was the report that he had hanged himself. It was common knowledge that he had struggled with drugs and alcohol. Though he made millions laugh, he suffered with severe bouts of chronic depression. After he married Susan, his last three years seemed to be the happiest of his tortured life.

But those who were closest to Robin Williams knew that things weren't right. He had been diagnosed with Parkinson's three months earlier, and there was something even deeper going on. It was as if an emotional dam had broken, and the old depression swept over him like a flood, along with confusion and paranoia. Only after the autopsy did Susan discover the awful truth. Her kind and generous husband had a debilitating brain disease called Lewy body dementia. This frequently misdiagnosed disease is no garden-variety depression. It is the second most common neuro-degenerative dementia after Alzheimer's, causing fluctuations in mental status, hallucinations, paranoia, and the impairment of motor function. Doctors say that, at best, Robin Williams had only three painful years left to live. What a tragedy for Susan and his children. We are all the poorer for his passing. Surely, the great ones *do* die too young.

The story of Robin Williams reminds us that life is unpredictable. We should live each moment to the full, giving as much joy as possible to the watching world. When we are gone, like Robin Williams, we should be both missed for what we have taken away and celebrated for what we have left behind. His story gives us a powerful credo for life:

Live the way you want to be remembered after you're gone.

Blessed are those who die in the Lord from now on. Yes, says the Spirit, they are blessed indeed, for they will rest from their hard work; for their good deeds follow them!

REVELATION 14:13

The Folly of
Unnecessary Battles

❦

The largest battle ever fought on American soil began with a search for shoes. Before the butchery ended, it had exacted fifty-one thousand casualties. It was the worst slaughter in our history.

Historians now agree that the battle should not have been fought. If only the commanding general of the Army of Northern Virginia had read *The Art of War* by Sun Tzu, a single principle espoused by that Chinese warlord might have stopped him dead in his tracks: "There are roads which must not be followed, armies which must not be attacked."

But General Robert E. Lee had set out on a desperate gamble to turn the tide of a war that was going from bad to worse. If the Confederacy could win a major victory, England and France might be willing to throw their much-needed support behind the Southern cause.

Lee's troops broke out of the Shenandoah Valley and marched north toward Philadelphia. But an army marches on shoes, and many of General Lee's ragged Confederates were marching barefoot. In late June, scouts reported that there was a supply of boots at Gettysburg. Lee moved quickly toward the Pennsylvania town. But Gettysburg stood at a junction of ten roads. It's not surprising that Lee's army ran smack-dab into General George Meade's Army of the Potomac.

As the sun dawned on July 3, 1863, Lee held all the cards. He had caught Meade's Union army out of position. His army could either take the open road to an undefended Philadelphia or move south unchallenged to attack Washington, DC. Either way, he could strike a blow that would change the tide of war.

Yet Robert E. Lee inexplicably attacked Meade's army at Gettysburg, even though the Union forces were larger and better armed, and controlled the high ground. At first, Lee's old magic worked. Then his cavalry under Jeb Stuart went on a wild-goose chase. When he lost Stuart, General Lee lost his eyes. Unable to follow Meade's troop movements, he was outmaneuvered.

His generals begged him to retreat, but pride got the best of Lee. He ordered fifteen thousand men to march across a mile of open field against Federals dug in on Cemetery Ridge. Leading the Southern charge was General Pickett's infantry. Two-thirds of Pickett's men were mowed down in a senseless slaughter. Among them were three generals, eight of ten officers above the rank of captain, and three thousand soldiers. The rebels suffered six thousand casualties in a single hour. Pickett later complained, "That old man killed my boys." The shattered Army of Northern Virginia retreated in disgrace, and the sun began to set on the Confederate cause.

Sun Tzu was right: there are some armies that should never be fought. Wasted battles dissipate our strength on lesser things. Robert E. Lee's folly at Gettysburg reminds us to think well before we waste precious resources on labors and battles that give little in return. Maybe our story will turn out better if we remember something Coach John Wooden once said:

Don't mistake activity with achievement.

<hr />

Always give yourselves fully to the work
of the Lord, because you know that your
labor in the Lord is not in vain.

1 CORINTHIANS 15:58, NIV

The Son for a Son

⌒⊙⌒

We remember him by a single name: Barabbas. We know precious little about him except that he was a terrorist. But his name unlocks an amazing story. It's a combination of two Hebrew words that mean "the son of a father." In his day, rabbis were given the honorary title of Father—much like priests in Christendom centuries later.

Barabbas was a common nickname for a rabbi's son. The boy likely attended Hebrew school and synagogue, observed the traditions and rituals of Judaism, and memorized Torah law. Ancient manuscripts also give him a first name: Yeshua, or Jesus. It is shocking that history's most infamous terrorist was the son of a rabbi and named Jesus.

This preacher's kid grew up longing for the Messiah promised by the prophets. But his land was under Roman tyranny, and his fingers itched to tear down their banners. So he joined a group of terrorists called the *Zelotes*. Some were known by a more sinister name: *Sicarii*, or "dagger men." Like suicide bombers today, they slipped into crowded marketplaces to create mayhem and terror with their deadly weapons. They also used their daggers in robberies to finance their revolution.

Jesus the preacher's kid may have started out like Robin Hood. But soon terror became his only game. He struck that Passover when the streets of Jerusalem were packed with pilgrims. His fellow *Zelotes* whipped the crowds into a frenzy of protest. But legionnaires from the Fortress of Antonia charged the street demonstration. The gutters soon ran with the blood of slaughter, and Barabbas was captured, along with two of his lieutenants. Roman justice was swift and brutal. Later in the week, on Friday morning, Jesus the rabbi's son was about to be crucified.

But you know the rest of the story. He was dragged from his dungeon into the governor's court. Before him was that screaming lynch mob. Next to Pilate was a beaten and bloodied man—a rabbi like his father. He was facing death too, just like the rabbi's son. To his amazement, the Roman shouted, "Which one do you want me to release to you: Jesus Barabbas, or Jesus who is called the Messiah?" (Matthew 27:17, NIV). They were the most ironic words in history. The rabbi's son or the rabbi? Jesus the pretend messiah or Jesus the true Messiah? Jesus the son of a father or Jesus the Son of the Father? Jesus the terrorist or Jesus the peacemaker? Jesus the destroyer or Jesus the giver of life? To humanity's shame, the mob chose the lesser Jesus.

But this is the real scandal of the ages: Jesus hung on our cross too. All of us are children of some father. We might be religious, like the preacher's son. But we are just as rebellious. Our crimes are not hidden from the Lord. But the Son of our Father in heaven took our place and our punishment. We don't know what Barabbas did with his reprieve, but his story reminds us of this fact:

Jesus gave his life for you so that you might give your life to him.

God made Christ, who never sinned,
to be the offering for our sin, so that we could
be made right with God through Christ.

2 CORINTHIANS 5:21

The Lost City of El Dorado

❧❦❧

Beginning as a stream in Peru, the Amazon increases in volume to become the mightiest river in the world. Its basin is nearly the size of the continental United States. Forty percent of all rivers in South America drain into its inland sea of jungles and swamps. By the time this monster reaches the coast, it is about two hundred miles wide at its mouth, vomiting fifty-seven million gallons of water into the Atlantic every second. Miles out at sea, sailors can dip into salty ocean and drink its fresh water.

The Amazon's vast reservoir of untapped riches is also a monstrous Venus flytrap, consuming those foolhardy enough to enter. Its dangers are legion: armies of fire ants and pools of piranhas that strip prey to the bone within seconds, flesh-eating worms and insects, poisonous plants, giant snakes, meat-eating predators, mazes of quicksand, and villages inhabited by Stone Age headhunters. Yet like the Sirens of ancient mythology, the Amazon lured its hapless victims with tales of the lost city of El Dorado, or "the Golden One."

In 1542, Francisco de Orellana led the first ill-fated expedition into the Amazon to find El Dorado. Along the way, almost four thousand men perished from disease, starvation, and the poisoned arrows of headhunters. Later expeditions resorted to cannibalism to survive. In 1561, conquistador Lope de Aguirre went crazy in his search for El Dorado, slaughtering his own children and men. In the centuries that followed, the death toll mounted as thousands more searched in vain for the mysterious city. By the late 1800s, archaeologists concluded that the lost city was a cruel hoax.

Then came the most famous explorer of all: legendary Percy Fawcett, the original Indiana Jones. In 1925, he confidently ventured into the heart of the Amazon to find what he called "the lost city of Z." He never returned. To this day, his fate remains a mystery. Those who failed to find him or his remains decided that the lost city of El Dorado was indeed a myth.

Today we know the truth. Thanks to satellite imagery, scientists have uncovered an ancient city in the Amazon basin, complete with the remains of bridges, moats, roads, and city squares dating from AD 200 to 1283. Covering many square miles, the city supported more than sixty thousand people. This discovery proves that the Amazon once supported a rich civilization that predated the Inca Empire. What happened to it is as big a mystery as the fate of Percy Fawcett.

This much we do know: a lot of misery and death might have been spared if early explorers had possessed Google Earth. The story of El Dorado, and those who vanished looking for it, reminds us that we have a sure source that gives true directions in an age when people are lured by deadly myths—something better than Google. It's called the Bible. Unlike El Dorado, which hides its wealth, God's Word promises this:

The Bible is a gold mine, waiting for someone to seize its riches.

―――― ∞ ――――

Reverence for the LORD is pure, lasting forever.
The laws of the LORD are true; each one is fair.
They are more desirable than gold, even the finest gold.

PSALM 19:9-10

From Africa with Love

⌒⊙⊙⌒

There was once an African queen who heard about a powerful king in faraway Asia. She was told so many tall tales about this king that she found it impossible to restrain her curiosity. So she left her Ethiopian palace and embarked on a long journey. When she arrived in the fabled Asian kingdom, the queen came face-to-face with the world's richest man.

His lifestyle still boggles our imagination three thousand years later. He sat on a throne of pure ivory overlaid with gold. The plates and goblets at his lavish banquets were made of pure gold. Every morning he dressed in snow-white robes to ride out in a chariot made of the finest cedar, inlaid with gold and ivory, carpeted in tapestries woven with gold thread, and pulled by the finest horses on earth. A bodyguard of sixty warriors accompanied him: the tallest and handsomest men in his kingdom, arrayed in Tyrian purple, each with long black hair sprinkled daily with fresh gold dust.

His vast estates included parks, zoos, temples, libraries, universities, and lavish resorts. A thousand delights awaited him in his palace of pleasures: the world's most beautiful women, orchestras, choirs, singers, dancers, magicians, and circus acts to rival the Cirque du Soleil.

This hedonist was also the greatest thinker in antiquity. His court was filled with the brightest of scholars who traveled across the globe to learn from his renowned wisdom. He wrote four books that are among the towering classics in history, and he composed wise sayings that are still repeated today, as well as three thousand poems and more than one thousand songs. As a military strategist, he had no peer. His unparalleled skills at diplomacy achieved peace in the Middle East.

After spending months with the Asian king, the African queen gushed,

"All that I heard is not even half of what I have seen." You remember this Ethiopian queen by her kingdom's ancient name, Sheba. The Asian king was Solomon. The Ethiopian left with memories to last several lifetimes. Some believe she also carried Solomon's baby in her womb, which would mean all of her descendants, including the last emperor of Ethiopia, Haile Selassie, carried Solomon's DNA. The Queen of Sheba also brought Judaism to Ethiopia. A thousand years later, an official of the Ethiopian royal court traveled to Jerusalem to worship at the Temple. On the way home, a church deacon told him about Jesus and baptized him. The court official brought Christianity back to Africa, making the Ethiopian Orthodox Church the oldest continuing Christian body in the world—all this because a curious African queen decided to visit an Asian king!

The king wrote a biblical love story called the Song of Solomon. Many scholars believe that he was writing about his love affair with the African queen. But it is also an allegorical story of God's love for his people. Having read the story of an African queen and her Israelite lover, you might want to read the Song of Solomon to see how passionately the king of heaven loves you. Those who have already embraced this king will agree with this: *What you have heard about Jesus is not half of what there is to see.*

———— ✧ ————

I didn't believe what was said until I arrived here and saw it with my own eyes. In fact, I had not heard the half of it!

1 KINGS 10:7

The Power of
a Single Supper

<svg>cⁱⓄⓖ◡</svg>

He had been promised clemency by Mr. Lincoln but was now imprisoned on suspicion of engineering the president's assassination. He was innocent, but an angry nation was in no mood to go easy on the former president of the Confederacy. Jefferson Davis was a traitor to his country, and he needed to suffer the consequences of rebellion. The government had three options: charge him with murder for plotting Lincoln's assassination, charge him with treason for engineering rebellion, or charge him with war crimes for the Confederate treatment of Union prisoners. Angry citizens wanted him hanged. Some offered to build the gallows.

But the nation was embroiled in the impeachment trial of a US president, so Jefferson Davis was held without trial for two years. He was shackled in a small room in Fort Monroe, and kept under suicide watch, without a moment's privacy. A guard stood over him at meals, with orders to force-feed him if he refused to eat. But the worst part was being treated not as a former head of state but as a despised traitor. His warden, General Nelson Miles, was especially disdainful.

After he had been caged for months like an animal in a zoo—poked at and stared at, without even being able to use the toilet in privacy, his despair turned to seething bitterness. As a Southern aristocrat, he resented the rudeness of his captors. As a Confederate, he begrudged the way the North was punishing the South. As a Christian, he was appalled by the malice of fellow believers. As a West Point graduate, he was infuriated by the disrespect shown to him by the officers at Fort Monroe. As a former US senator, he was appalled that the government was denying his Constitutional rights.

Things improved for Davis a year later, when he was moved into larger quarters and his wife, Varina Howell Davis, took up residence at Fort Monroe. From her personal memoirs, we discover an amazing story. Though her husband was a churchgoer who prayed daily and read the Scriptures, he refused to let go of the raging resentments shredding his soul—until the day a chaplain set Communion before him. Bitterness toward his jailers, the federal government, and his current circumstances gushed up like bile. How could he have a mystical union with Christ if he was divided from others by hatred and prejudice? As he reached for the elements, he asked God to forgive him for his bitterness and to bless his enemies. According to Varina, everything changed after that. A year later, charges were dropped and the Jeffersons left Fort Monroe for their home in Mississippi.

Perhaps you are bitter toward people or circumstances. Try taking your resentments to the Lord's Table. Some say that you have to rid yourself of them *before* you take Communion. The amazing story of Jefferson Davis teaches us that God can cleanse our souls as we eat the Supper. So hurry to the Table and discover the power in a single meal.

Feed on Christ, and your resentments will starve to death.

Jesus said again, "I tell you the truth, unless you
eat the flesh of the Son of Man and drink his blood,
you cannot have eternal life within you."

JOHN 6:53

A Victory in Defeat

❧❧❧

The east was on a collision course with the west in 480 BC. The world watched in awe as the largest army in history poured into Europe. Heading this colossal war machine was Xerxes, the king of Persia. His army numbered almost two million foot soldiers, eighty thousand horsemen, twenty thousand chariots, camel-riding Arabs, and war elephants from India. Xerxes had crafted the most lethal weapon of mass destruction that humankind had ever seen. The Greek historian Herodotus wrote that when this beast from the east marched, the ground shook. When it stopped to drink, pools were dried up and rivers reduced to a trickle.

You may remember Xerxes as the husband of the biblical heroine Esther. This self-proclaimed "king of kings" spent four years amassing his titanic force to crush tiny Greece. It was the mismatch of the ages. Greece was a collection of city-states warring against each other. Athens was mired in social stagnation, and Sparta was in economic shambles. Never was a nation so vulnerable. Yet five Greek cities managed to scrape together about five thousand soldiers. They were outnumbered 430 to 1. But at their core were three hundred Spartans. These three hundred had been trained since childhood to stand or die in battle. Every Spartan mother sent her sons off to war with this warning: "Come home with your shield, or on it."

The Greeks took their stand in a narrow pass, fifty feet wide, with the sea on one side and towering cliffs on the other, at a place called Thermopylae. This battleground has become hallowed in military history. It is to the Greeks what the Alamo is to Texans. In that narrow pass a heroic handful held back the Persian hordes for two days. When Xerxes finally unleashed his crack storm troopers, the Greeks annihilated them.

But on the third night, a traitor showed the Persians a secret trail through the cliffs into Thermopylae. Sure death was coming with the breaking dawn. Dismissing the rest of the Greeks, General Leonidas led his three hundred Spartans, along with some loyal Thespians, to a mound where they made their final stand. When their weapons were gone, they fought with hands and teeth until the last man died. As the end neared, a runner was sent home with the message that still echoes down the corridors of time: "Stranger, tell the Spartans that we behaved as they would wish us to, and are buried here."

This small band of Spartans died without knowing they were changing history. They bought enough time for the Greek cities to raise a great army. Their heroism triggered a surge of national pride that led to decisive victories at Salamis and Plataea. The power of Persia was broken. The future of civilization shifted from Asia to Europe. Athens became the world's most influential city. Greek culture and democracy would give birth to the modern world. Maybe you are facing overwhelming odds. Perhaps you have suffered a crushing defeat. Take heart from the story of three hundred Spartans. Surely it teaches us a valuable lesson:

There are some defeats whose triumphs rival victories.

———— ✺ ————

Some nations boast of their chariots and horses, but we boast in the name of the LORD our God. Those nations will fall down and collapse, but we will rise up and stand firm.

PSALM 20:7-8

Skiing to the North Pole

✧✧✧

Maybe you think you are too old or too tired, or you've done it all. So you kick back in your La-Z-Boy recliner to binge on television. After scarfing down some empty calories, you doze off while your muscles grow softer and your willpower dissipates. Don't try to sell your worn-out excuses to Barbara Hillary. This eighty-something-year-old African American dynamo will tell you to get up and get going.

Whether she's in her hometown of Queens or trekking to the North Pole, Barbara is always on the lookout for new challenges and adventures. Maybe her career in nursing, in which she specialized in gerontology, allowed her to witness firsthand the dangers of growing old without purpose. So after she retired as a nurse, she took up a second career as an explorer. When she announced that she wanted to trek to the North Pole, people said she was crazy. But this senior citizen was undeterred. She learned to cross-country ski and logged countless hours of cardio and strength workouts. Beachgoers did a double take when they saw her pulling a sled loaded with bags of sand down a Long Island beach.

Before Barbara could head out for the North Pole, she had to fight a bigger battle with cancer. Then this retiree on a limited income had to find a way to come up with thousands of dollars to finance her trip. Yet she refused to give up her dream. She kept thinking about another African American, Matthew Henson, who became the first man to reach the North Pole a century earlier. She was determined to be the first African American woman to accomplish the same feat. At seventy-five years young, Barbara Hillary flew by helicopter to the farthest reaches of Norway. From there she pushed and clawed her way on skis into unimaginably cold winds, her fingers stinging with frostbite and her body aching beyond belief.

On April 23, 2007, she realized her goal when she finally stood at the North Pole.

But Barbara still wasn't ready for the La-Z-Boy. Next she set her sights on the South Pole. It proved almost impossible to find sponsors who believed that someone pushing eighty could accomplish such a feat. But at age seventy-nine, she flew to Union Glacier below South America. Braving temperatures of forty degrees below zero, Barbara trekked to the South Pole. But don't tell Barbara that it's good enough to be the first African American to make it to both poles. At eighty-five years of age, she is still going strong as she crisscrosses the country in her third career as an inspirational speaker.

This amazing story of an octogenarian Energizer Bunny proves that age, health, gender, race, finances, or past achievements should never keep us from dreaming up new challenges or setting out on bigger adventures. No one should end up merely speculating, contemplating, ruminating, meditating, or cogitating. So turn in that La-Z-Boy for a new adventure. If you're afraid to take a risk, you might want to remember something Mark Twain wrote:

Why not go out on a limb? That's where the fruit is.

─────── ⧯ ───────

If you cling to your life, you will lose it, and
if you let your life go, you will save it.

LUKE 17:33

The Leper Who Became a Saint

⌒⌒⌒

Who could have imagined that Jozef would one day be canonized as a saint? As the seventh child of a poor coin collector, he got the family leftovers. He didn't have access to much education, and he did poorly in school. But he had a heart for the underdog. No one was surprised when Jozef applied to be a priest. Nor were they shocked that he was initially rejected as uneducated and unintelligent. When he applied to be a missionary, he was turned down as unsuitable. Only after they couldn't find anyone else to go did they finally send him.

Jozef arrived in Hawaii in 1864, during a year of great panic. Leprosy had found its way to paradise, and it was spreading like wildfire among native Polynesians. Protestant missionaries said that this was God's judgment on the licentious lifestyle of the islanders. American planters threatened to seize the islands by armed force if something wasn't done.

Lepers were rounded up and shipped to a deserted peninsula on Molokai Island. It was isolated and windswept, accessible only by a mule trail over steep mountains. The lepers might as well have been dumped on the moon. In this place of sorrow, they waited to die in ramshackle huts amid filthy squalor. A few Protestant missionaries and Catholic priests visited, but most quickly left.

About that time, Jozef remembered his ordination as a priest. His superiors had covered him with a funeral pall to symbolize his death to the world. When he begged his bishop to go to the leper colony as its resident priest, he was signing his death warrant. When he left for Molokai, he knew he was never coming back. Outside of Jesus, no one ever loved lepers more than Jozef. He built a church with his own hands, dug a reservoir, founded a school, and brought stability. He made coffins and dug the graves for six hundred lepers. Maybe he loved them too much when he kissed them on their lips, shared his tobacco pipe with them, and dipped his fingers in their poi—a traditional dish made of mashed taro root. But he cared more about the outcasts than he did about hygiene. It wasn't long before he turned a place of sorrow into a sanctuary of hope.

A decade after he arrived, he accidently put his foot in scalding water. When he saw the blisters but felt no pain, he immediately sent word to his superiors, "I have leprosy. Please send a confessor." He ministered four more years while his body was eaten away. In his last weeks he wrote a letter to his brother: "I thank God very much for letting me die of the same disease and in the same way as my lepers." The world remembers Jozef by the name he took when he became a priest, Father Damien. When he died, church bells rang in mourning across the islands. Every year, Hawaiians celebrate the memory of this Belgian priest. In 2009, he was canonized as Saint Damien. He is called the patron saint of those with leprosy, HIV, and AIDS. His service to the sick and outcast continues to be a source of inspiration to people worldwide. When we are reluctant to identify with those Jesus called "the least of these," we might want to remember this:

Each sick and outcast person is really Jesus in disguise.

———— ⁊⳯⳨ ————

The King will say, "I tell you the truth, when you did it to one of the least of these my brothers and sisters, you were doing it to me!"

MATTHEW 25:40

Too Smart to Be President

✦

He skipped down the street of a small college town, following a butterfly with childlike wonder. Bystanders chuckled at this elderly sage with clownish face, droopy mustache, and goofy smile. His baggy tweed coat was rumpled and his long hair unkempt. His wife had laid out his socks, but he once again forgot to put them on. If it weren't 1952, you would think that this old man was a hippy from the '70s.

The butterfly disappeared, and he mumbled to himself in a soft German accent. He remembered that his wife earlier shoved him out the door and pointed to the classroom down the street. So he retraced his steps. If you looked closely, you would see a wrinkled letter sticking out of the back pocket of his trousers—a communication from his Israeli friend, Chaim Weizmann. The world would have been shocked to know that Weizmann was begging this absentminded Jewish professor to take his place as the next president of Israel.

But the professor had more pressing business today. He was being paid to drum physics equations into the heads of *dummkopf* students. There was a time when teachers had called him a dumbhead too. His life had been an unbroken string of failures until he stumbled upon an equation that won him a Nobel Prize. He might have been the world's foremost physicist in 1952, but he was hardly the right stuff for the presidency of a fledgling nation fighting for survival.

Leadership requires an organized lifestyle, and his was a hopeless clutter of chaos. His long-suffering wife was beyond frustrated with his inability to accomplish the simplest tasks. Speaking of wives, he was a disaster as a husband. He plowed through marriages, had several extramarital affairs, and fathered at least one illegitimate child. Women found him irresistible, and he couldn't resist them. He hardly possessed the moral character to lead a nation. Then there was that question of security clearance. When he offered his genius to help America create its first atomic bomb, he was turned down by a government that suspected he was a spy. Even now, the CIA believed that he spied for the Soviets. How did Weizmann come up with this harebrained idea that Albert Einstein could be the next president of Israel?

Dr. Einstein didn't conceive the Theory of Relativity or win the Nobel Prize because he was a *dummkopf*. We will never know what motivated Chaim Weizmann's offer, but we do know that the Princeton professor turned it down in 1952. A man who couldn't remember to put his socks on in the morning, or how to come home to his wife at night, has no business as a head of state. You may never discover something like $E = mc^2$, but you can be as much of a genius as Einstein if you stick to what you do best. God made each of us to shine in some area of life. This amazing story about Albert Einstein confirms this genius bit of advice from Lana Del Rey:

Doing what you love is freedom. Loving what you do is happiness.

God has given each of you a gift from his great variety
of spiritual gifts. Use them well to serve one another.

1 PETER 4:10

The Godfather
and the Priest

She was the crown jewel of Europe and the birthplace of the Renaissance. In this magical city, banking families controlled the wealth of the world, Michelangelo created his art, Galileo pondered the movements of the solar system, Dante studied poetry, and Machiavelli tutored princes on how to wield power. Surely, Florence stood at the crossroads of history.

Yet behind the scenes, a puppet master pulled the strings. He was the boss of bosses, the godfather of Florence—Lorenzo the Magnificent, patriarch of the Medici banking cartel and the richest man in Europe. In public, he was a great patron of the arts and church. Because of his largesse, artists like Michelangelo, Botticelli, and Leonardo da Vinci were able to make the world more beautiful. He also bankrolled the soaring cathedrals that made Florence the envy of Christendom.

But anyone who scratched beneath the thin veneer of Renaissance beauty would find Lorenzo's Florence to be a Hollywood spectacular of decadence and drag, prostitutes and political graft, where nothing and nobody could be trusted. Lorenzo supported an unspeakably corrupt pope in order to elevate his own nephew, Giulio, to the papacy. At Lorenzo's insistence, the pope made fourteen-year-old Giulio a cardinal. When Giulio later became pope, he would fill offices of the church with hoodlums from the Medici family and would make the Vatican treasury his personal piggy bank.

Yet during Lorenzo's age of gilded decadence, a reformer rose in Florence—the Dominican friar Girolamo Savonarola. This firebrand thundered against the worldliness of Florentine Christians and exposed church corruption. Some fifteen thousand people regularly packed the great cathedral in Florence to hear him preach. Repentant people brought their opulence to the city square to be burned in what Savonarola called "the bonfires of the vanities." This Renaissance "John the Baptist" called for Lorenzo to repent and the Borgia pope, Alexander, to step down.

The Borgias reacted with fury. Pope Alexander excommunicated Savonarola. The pope's son, Cesare, rushed to Florence to orchestrate the friar's burning at the stake. Shortly before his martyrdom, Savonarola gave an amazing prophecy: "It matters little what you do to me today. Within forty years a man will rise up in the north to bring a reformation that can't be stopped." Some twenty years later, during the papacy of Lorenzo's son, Martin Luther rose in the north country of Germany to spark a reformation that couldn't be stopped. Today Lorenzo the Magnificent lies forgotten in an ornate tomb while simple friars and monks like Savonarola and Luther are celebrated. Not far from Lorenzo's mausoleum, a vendor sells a T-shirt that the godfather of Florence, the Borgia gang, and the corrupt popes would despise. But Savonarola and Luther would probably buy and wear the shirt with this slogan:

Your ego is not your amigo.

When they saw the courage of Peter and John
and realized that they were unschooled, ordinary
men, they were astonished and they took note
that these men had been with Jesus.

ACTS 4:13, NIV

The Widow Who Laundered a Fortune

❦

Ray was a milk-shake-machine salesman who knew a good thing when he saw it. When he walked into that hamburger joint on the edge of the California desert he knew he had discovered a gold mine. The fifty-two-year-old Oak Park, Illinois, salesman convinced the McDonald brothers that he could sell their franchise to the whole world. No one imagined that he would turn their fast-food operation into an international juggernaut that would sell more than a hundred billion burgers.

Ray saw himself as the Walt Disney of fast-food America, creating a wholesome family image with his golden arches, Ronald McDonald, Happy Meals, and playgrounds. But his private life was anything but wholesome. Most folks don't know that the salesman from Oak Park cheated the McDonald brothers out of their franchise, forcing them to accept an offer they couldn't refuse—a paltry $2.7 million for an empire now worth $106.4 billion. Ray always knew a good thing when he saw it. And he would stoop to any dirty tricks to get it. The same went for women. Ray Kroc was a serial home wrecker.

At age fifty-two, he met Joan, a twenty-eight-year-old beautiful blonde piano bar singer. He set her husband up in a string of McDonald's franchises while he pursued her. After twelve years, he finally busted up Joan's marriage to Rollie and took her on as his third wife. It would not be a marriage made in heaven. He had a violent, ungovernable temper and a taste for Early Times whiskey. Joan took Ray to divorce court, but opted to stay married to his money. She figured that she could put up with the unhappiness of living with Ray as long as she could use his fortune to do good in the world. Philanthropy became Joan's magnificent obsession.

When Ray died in 1984, she inherited the controlling stake in the company. After she gave away countless millions, folks called her Saint Joan of the Golden Arches. For the rest of her life, she practiced radical charity—some of it planned, a lot of it spontaneous. She was a pioneer in the hospice movement and funded early AIDS research. In 2003 she was told that she had terminal cancer. So she threw herself a birthday party and invited people who had no idea that they were getting, as their presents, the bulk of her estate. Her $235 million gift to NPR saved that network. The $2 billion that she gave to the Salvation Army was used to build recreational centers in poor neighborhoods across America. Almost all of her vast estate went to charities.

The story of Ray Kroc is not so amazing as the one about his Robin Hood wife who took his wealth and gave it away to those who needed it so much more. The next time you drive by a McDonald's, or stop in to buy a Happy Meal, remember Joan Kroc's story. Better yet, skip that burger and fries, and contribute the money to make someone else a happier person.

Rather than counting your blessings, be the blessing other people count on.

———— ✦ ————

When someone has been given much,
much will be required in return.

LUKE 12:48

The Unwanted Boy

❧❦❧

Benny was born out of wedlock to an immigrant mother who was abandoned by her lover, a country doctor. It wasn't easy being the love child of an unwed mother, especially during the late 1800s in rural Tennessee. Teased unmercifully, he learned to fight back with fists and bulldog tenacity. But his hard-shell exterior masked the shame he felt as the town ragamuffin. Mostly, Benny hated the town gossip about the things his mother did at night to make ends meet.

Sometimes the boy would slip into the church house by himself. His shabby clothes and outcast status caused him to hide in the back pew. Most of the time, he would slip out before the benediction. But that day he waited too long, and the aisle was clogged with people. Benny was unable to avoid the preacher.

He grabbed the boy by the shoulder and said, "You must be the child of . . ." Looking perplexed, he repeated, "You must be the child of . . ." Benny shrank back in embarrassment, figuring that it wouldn't be long before someone chimed in that he was the son of a tramp. But the pastor slapped him on the back and exclaimed, "Now I recognize you. You're a child of God. You go out there and claim your rightful inheritance!"

A few months later, Benny's mother put him in an orphanage, and he was later reunited with his father. With the new opportunities afforded by his doctor daddy and a dogged determination forged in early childhood, Benny did go out and make something of himself. But he would tell everyone that when a Baptist preacher told him to go out and claim his rightful inheritance, it was the turning point in his life.

Years later, Benny was living out his last years in the Tennessee mountains of his childhood. One evening, as he left a restaurant, he passed by a vacationing seminary professor, Dr. Fred Craddock, the professor of preaching at Candler School of Theology in Atlanta. Benny engaged him in some easy mountain banter. When Dr. Craddock told him that he taught young men how to preach, the old man broke into a wide smile. He told the professor about the preacher who inspired him one Sunday morning when he was an unwanted boy. Then he whispered, "You tell your preacher boys that they can change lives by helping folks believe the best things about their future."

As Benny shuffled out of the restaurant, Dr. Craddock asked his waitress, "Do you know who that old man is?" "Everyone knows him," she said. "He's a legend hereabouts. His name is Ben Hooper, the most famous lawyer in this state, and a two-time governor of Tennessee."

You can read Ben Hooper's story in his autobiography, *The Unwanted Boy*. It proves that there is a transforming power in believing the best things. Please don't allow the traumas of childhood, disabilities of adulthood, opinions of others, sins of the past, or your own negative self-talk determine who you are. You are a child of God. Go out and claim your inheritance today! Ben Hooper's triumphant story celebrates this unalterable transforming truth:

The future you see is most often the future you get.

————— ❧ —————

[Jesus said,] "Everything is possible for one who believes."

MARK 9:23, NIV

Paco's Papa

⌒⌒⊙⌒⌒

Ernie felt like God had played a cruel joke on him. Born a free spirit, he was raised in a staid Victorian house on Main Street in a Midwestern town. His mother crammed her religion down his throat, and a perfectionistic father demanded that Ernie excel in everything he did. Ernie felt smothered. He later wrote that he grew up in a town of wide lawns and narrow minds.

His folks wanted him to become a doctor, but he loved to write. After high school he escaped to Kansas City to work for a newspaper. His parents were scandalized, but his editors said that he was a boy genius. His wanderlust led him to join the Red Cross ambulance corps on the Italian front in World War I. It was exhilarating until he was severely wounded. In the hospital he fell in love with a volunteer nurse named Agnes. Ernie returned home to Illinois confident that she would soon join him as his wife.

A few months later, he received a devastating letter. Agnes had fallen in love with someone else. Ernie never got over that rejection. He began to drink heavily. Though a rising star in the literary world, he was gaining a reputation as a barroom brawler. Rage and alcoholism would torment Ernie to the end.

One day Agnes showed up at his father's lake home. When he opened the door, she pleaded, "Ernie, please forgive me and take me back!" Without a word, he slammed the door in her face. A few years later, when his father took his own life, Ernie snarled, "Everyone who commits suicide rots in hell." When his mother died, he refused to attend her funeral. Over the years, booze and bitterness dismantled Ernie. He plowed through four marriages. Even though his friends called him Papa, his children lived in fear of his rage. At age sixty-one, he put a shotgun to his head and pulled the trigger.

His family called him Ernie, but the world remembers him as Ernest Hemingway. He wrote novels like *For Whom the Bell Tolls* and *A Farewell to Arms*. He was awarded both the Pulitzer and Nobel Prizes. As a writer, Hemingway was a giant. As a celebrity adventurer, he was bigger than life. But the real Ernie never ceased being the bitter little boy who couldn't do enough to please his parents.

None of Hemingway's stories capture his deep wounds more than the one about Paco. After he wrongs his father, the boy runs away to Madrid. Paco's father follows him to the city. Unable to find Paco, his father takes out a newspaper ad: "Paco, meet me at the Hotel Montana, twelve noon, Tuesday. All is forgiven. Papa." When the father arrives at the hotel, he finds a lobby filled with eight hundred young men, all named Paco.

Ernie captures his and our hearts' longing. Whether we are the Prodigal Son in the far country or the older brother keeping all the rules at home, we want to know that our father loves us unconditionally. What a difference it would have made for Ernest Hemingway—and would make for all of us—to grasp this:

God loves each of us as if there were only one of us.

———— ✿ ————

When God our Savior revealed his kindness and
love, he saved us, not because of the righteous
things we had done, but because of his mercy.

TITUS 3:4-5

The Film No One Wanted to Make

⁓◌◌⁓

The walnut rancher's kid was always dreaming. He dreamed of becoming a star athlete, but was too small. He aspired to be a race-car driver until he was in a bad accident. He dreamed of being a writer of fantasies, but didn't get far with that. His biggest dream was more far fetched. He wanted to take those Flash Gordon B movies from the thirties and forties, with their cheesy special effects, and turn them into dazzling epics for future moviegoers.

He did go on to film school and direct small indie films. He made a few waves with his experimental picture, *THX 1138*, but moviegoers weren't ready for his vision of a cold dystopian future. So he tried to buy the rights to the Flash Gordon series, but couldn't swing the deal. Then he wrote his own script—a sci-fi spectacular with the cheesiness of a Flash Gordon romp coupled with new special effects. But when he shopped the idea, studios turned him down. United Artists said no, as did Universal and Disney.

In the meantime, he did hit pay dirt with a little movie that became a big hit. His *American Graffiti* even earned an Oscar nomination in 1974. Fox was finally willing to take a chance on his goofy space saga, but only if he agreed to direct the sequel to *American Graffiti*. They were so sure that his sci-fi film would go belly up that they invested a paltry amount in his movie. He agreed to take no salary as long as he got the lion's share of the profits and the exclusive rights to any sequels and toys that his sci-fi movie might spawn. When he went to North Africa to film his project, the Fox heads figured that the money they made on the sequel to *American Graffiti* would more than make up for the few million they lost on a movie about a civil war in a faraway galaxy.

We will never know what happened to the studio heads that took a pass on *Star Wars*, but George Lucas got the best deal in Hollywood history. Fox's shortsightedness allowed Lucas to independently make *The Empire Strikes Back* and *Return of the Jedi*, the biggest movies ever self-financed outside the studio system. Even Lucas couldn't have guessed how many millions he would make just off toys from his Star Wars sagas. He parlayed his profits into his own major studio, Lucasfilm. Ironically, Disney, which said no to that first Star Wars film, bought Lucasfilm in 2012 for $4.6 billion. What about that sequel to *American Graffiti*—the one that Fox said couldn't miss? It hit the theaters in 1979, making a tepid $15 million. *The Empire Strikes Back* made nearly $600 million worldwide when it came out the next year.

The amazing story of George Lucas inspires us not to give up, even in the face of naysayers. It also warns us to beware of being afraid to take a chance on someone else's dreams. Sticking with a safe thing is not always the smart move.

Playing it safe in a changing world is the riskiest thing you can do.

––––––––– ༄༅ –––––––––

Farmers who wait for perfect weather never plant.
If they watch every cloud, they never harvest.
ECCLESIASTES 11:4

The King of the Mountain

⋘◉⋙

The descent from the mountaintop can be so painful. Just ask the old boxer. Sportswriter Gary Smith interviewed him on one of the saddest sports specials ever aired. Too many blows to the head in too many fights over too many years had slurred the ex-champ's words. Those closest to him had begged him to get out of the ring, but he refused to stop until his crown was taken from him.

Shuffling and shaking with tremors, the old boxer led the sportswriter to a weathered barn behind his farmhouse. Photos, posters, and portraits showed the ex-champ in his prime, his sculpted arms raised, fists pumping the air, and face glowing with unbridled exuberance. But the pictures were faded and covered with bird droppings. Pigeons now made their home where he had once trained.

Shaking his head in embarrassment, the old champ shuffled slowly to the photos and turned them over one by one. He then limped to the door and stared off into the distance. The silence was eloquently painful in that barn. He turned to Smith and quietly slurred, "I had the world, and it wasn't nothin'. Look now."

Long ago, the champ *did* have the world. Most experts agree that Muhammad Ali was the greatest fighter ever to dance across the ring. He won the world heavyweight championship three times and was the most recognized athlete on the planet. His face appeared on the cover of *Sports Illustrated* more times than any other person. As long as he was floating like a butterfly and stinging like a bee, he commanded the limelight and mesmerized his adoring public with nonstop chatter. An entourage followed in his wake, constantly stroking his king-size ego. Muhammad Ali was "King of the Mountain."

As the interview ended, the champ was clearly worn out. Parkinson's was reducing him to uncontrollable tremors. His daughter said that it was time to take him back to the house. He shuffled out past pictures of "The Thrilla in Manila" and "The Rope-A-Dope in Zaire," now faded and covered with pigeon droppings. It was too painful to watch. Mercifully, the cameras faded to a commercial featuring a new sports superstar plugging a product. But those haunting words still hung in the air: "I had the world, and it wasn't nothin'. Look now."

Most of us know the king of the mountain game. It's as primitive as it is brutal. The object is to get to the top of the pile. So we push, claw, and crawl to stand higher than anyone else. But getting to the top is a dubious victory. Already, those below are trying to topple the king. Be careful when you hang those victory posters. Pigeons are making their nests in the rafters. You can learn a lot from the story of Muhammad Ali. You can learn even more from the king who came down from heaven's mountain as a suffering servant. He became a lamb and ended up the Lion of Judah. The greatest story ever told teaches us this:

The best way to find yourself is to lose yourself in the service of others.

—————— ✑✑✑ ——————

The Son of Man came not to be served but to serve
others and to give his life as a ransom for many.

MATTHEW 20:28

When Wickedness Prospers

⟡

They died four thousand years ago, but their story still haunts. The saga began when Abram and Sarai left the Persian Gulf and followed God to what is now Israel. God had promised the old man that he and his wife would have a child who would inherit the land forever and bless the whole world. Old Abram believed God's promises by sheer faith. But this was where the story went south. A famine struck. Like so many in our world today, the couple was forced to flee poverty and steal across borders into a land of plenty. They were constantly on the move as aliens without status. The pharaoh of that land was a collector of women. When his agents spied Sarai, the king summoned Abram. This vulnerable immigrant was a pawn in the familiar story of the powerful exploiting the weak. To save his skin, Abram passed Sarai off as his sister and allowed Pharaoh to take her into his bedroom. In a world that took advantage of women, she had no choice but to put her trust in God.

The God who loves the exploited struck Pharaoh's palace with a plague before he could take her to his bed. When the Egyptian discovered the truth, he rebuked Abram. It's a sad day when a pagan has to remind a believer to do the right thing. To appease Abram's God, Pharaoh loaded the deceiver down with gifts and deported him back to Canaan as a wealthy man. Maybe sin does pay. Or does it? Among their ill-gotten gains was a beautiful young slave by the name of Hagar. Weary of waiting for God to bless her barren womb, Sarai decided to use the slave girl as a surrogate mother. Old Abram agreed, conspiring in a terrible sin. The woman who was almost violated in Egypt when her husband betrayed her now pushed him to betray God by doing the same to an Egyptian woman. This power couple became as exploitive as a pharaoh, and Hagar gave them baby Ishmael.

Yet God showed himself faithful by giving them a son named Isaac. Hagar's son and the supernaturally born son became bitter rivals. So the couple banished Hagar and her son. Again, it seemed that the couple dodged the bullet of sin. Or did they? From Ishmael came the Arab people, and from them came Muhamed, the father of Islam. Islam claims God's promise of the Holy Land and the world because Ishmael was Abram's first son. The family feud between Ishmael and Isaac has turned the Middle East into a war zone and filled the earth with terror. This feud born of an ancient couple's faithlessness will not stop until Isaac's great Son, Jesus, ends it at Armageddon. The amazing story of Abram, Sarai, Hagar, and their sons teaches us that God is faithful in spite of our faithlessness. Yet he loves us too much to let us sin and get away with it. This much hasn't changed in four thousand years:

You can choose your sins, but you cannot choose their consequences.

———— ✤ ————

An evil man is held captive by his own sins;
they are ropes that catch and hold him.

PROVERBS 5:22

The Man Who Was Bigger Than God

⌒⌒⌒

After his classmates made fun of him, Howie threw away his hearing aids. He lived the rest of his life with an incessant ringing in his ears. It nearly drove him insane. When his prayers for relief went unanswered, he set his credo for life: if you can't depend on God, you have to be your own god.

Fearing the bacteria that bred in the dampness of Houston, his hypochondriac mother sent her son to live in dry Southern California. There, he discovered the two loves of his life: Hollywood and aviation. Lost in the magic of a movie, he forgot the ringing in his ears. Soaring high in an airplane, it stopped altogether.

Then his parents died, making him the world's wealthiest orphan. Howie boasted, "I'm richer than God!" He became the king of Hollywood, producing a string of films. Along the way, he engaged in sexual affairs that led to incurable syphilis. But that didn't stop him from becoming king of the skies or from building history's largest airplane. The world was stunned when he flew to Paris in half the time it took Charles Lindbergh—and then flew around the world in three days. He made a fortune in World War II as the biggest supplier of airplane parts. After he purchased shares in Trans World Airlines, he became the first multibillionaire in history. Howard Hughes now bragged that he was more powerful than God.

Yet his bravado masked his spreading syphilis. His old fear of germs returned with a vengeance. He moved to Las Vegas for the clean air, purchased a hotel and casino, and lived like a hermit in a sanitary bubble on the top floor. His agents bought up the surrounding casinos to extend his safe zone. He spent millions bribing the president to stop nuclear testing in Nevada, lest he be exposed to radiation. He funneled a fortune to the CIA to stop Russia from unleashing biological warfare. Howard Hughes was now the ultimate control freak.

Toward the end, he was downing hundreds of pills every day. He would eat little besides green peas, and he had each one measured so he wouldn't choke to death. He kept a team of doctors on full-time alert, wore surgical gowns, used Kleenex boxes for shoes, and wouldn't allow anything to touch his exposed skin. If a flu or cold epidemic hit the area, a private jet would quickly whisk him away.

In spite of all his precautions, he fell into a coma when he was seventy and died in transit to the hospital on April 5, 1976. He was the richest man in the world, but his six-foot-four-inch frame had been starved down to ninety pounds, his body covered by filth and his arms riddled with holes. X-rays showed broken needles lodged under his skin. The autopsy revealed a brain eaten by syphilis. He was so unrecognizable that the FBI took fingerprints to confirm his identity. The story of a man who thought he was bigger than God screams a warning to all of us who try to control our world. We might relax more if we remember this:

Worries don't come from thinking about the future but from wanting to control it.

―――――⚬⚭⚬―――――

Cast your burden upon the LORD and He will sustain you;
He will never allow the righteous to be shaken.

PSALM 55:22, NASB

Unit 731

❧❧❧

Some seventy-five years later it still remains one of the dirtiest secrets of World War II. Most folks have never heard of the "Asian Auschwitz" or the notorious Unit 731. While the world was focused on the Nazi Holocaust and the sensational Nuremberg trials, these monsters were packing up their tools of torture and heading back to respectability in Japan. And the US government conspired with them to perpetrate one of the most shameful cover-ups in history.

Today only the ghosts of nearly a quarter million dead are left of what was a four-mile square of barbed-wire horror in Northeast China. At its epicenter was the headquarters of Unit 731. Its name was innocuous enough: The Epidemic and Water Purification Unit. But its real mission was to do medical tests on mostly Chinese and Korean prisoners. At first, the medical doctors and scientists were trying to learn how to save the lives of Japanese soldiers. Prisoners were tied to stakes, just close enough to live bombs so that the detonation would mangle their bodies without killing them. To simulate battlefield conditions, the horrifically wounded would be operated on without morphine or anesthesia.

Later, as the war began to go badly for Japan, Unit 731 worked frantically to develop chemical and biological warfare. Thousands of prisoners were infected with germs, had their limbs amputated or frozen, underwent vivisection, were used as targets to test the effectiveness of new explosive devices, were burned alive with flamethrowers, or were killed en masse by chemical weapons. All the while, emotionally detached scientists recorded the data in clinical detail. How did they do it? They referred to their victims as *matures* which means "logs." It was easier to think of the prisoners as pieces of wood rather than screaming human beings.

The ultimate tests came when chemical and biological weapons were field-tested on Chinese towns and villages. After air strikes, Japanese scientists would come in wearing hazmat suits to test the bodies of the mass murdered so they could improve the effectiveness of their weapons. And yet the Allies brought none of these mad scientists to justice after the war. The sadistic head of Unit 731 was even celebrated for his service. Why this monumental miscarriage of justice? The US government, eager to get a jump on the Soviets, offered the Japanese scientists immunity in exchange for their data. Most of the doctors in Unit 731 became respected leaders in the postwar Japanese medical community. To this day, Japan has never admitted to or apologized for what happened in China.

The story of Unit 731 is another reminder of the human capacity for inhumanity. What is amazing is that the United States not only conspired in the cover-up, but also used data gained by war crimes to prepare for its own wars. We can only hope that justice delayed is not justice denied. Those who wait upon the Lord remain confident of this:

Nothing can remain secret forever, nor will any crime go unpunished.

⚬⚬⚬

All that is secret will eventually be brought into
the open, and everything that is concealed will
be brought to light and made known to all.

LUKE 8:17

The Cinderella Man

❦

Jimmy had been a contender. Now he was a club fighter, slugging it out for a few bucks and beers. When he broke his right hand, he was forced to quit the ring. After he lost his job as a day laborer, he had to take handouts to feed his family. The former heavyweight contender was now a welfare recipient.

Yet through a series of events that could only have been dreamed up by a Hollywood scriptwriter, Jimmy found himself in a Long Island stadium fighting Max Baer, the undisputed heavyweight champion of the world. Baer took sadistic delight in knocking his opponents senseless. Two fights earlier, he had beaten a challenger to death in the ring. In his last fight, he had battered another into permanent brain damage. Baer's managers had booked the fight with Jimmy thinking that the washed-up bum from Hoboken would be an easy walkover.

Jimmy desperately needed the money. He went into that fight as a staggering twenty-to-one underdog. Yet on June 13, 1935, Jim Braddock scored the greatest upset in sports history by beating Max Baer. He has been dubbed the Cinderella Man for his magical feat. When asked how he overcame such overwhelming odds, Braddock replied, "No matter how many times I'm knocked down, I always get up and fight one more round."

His upset victory gave hope to a nation mired in the Great Depression. In 1935, one out of every three men in America was standing in a soup line. Less than 25 percent of those who did have a job were earning an adequate wage. The suicide rate was at an all-time high. But when Jimmy Braddock got up off the canvas to fight one more round all the way to the world championship, he gave down-and-outers everywhere a shot in the arm.

If you are down on the canvas today, it might help you to discover the story behind Jimmy's miracle win. Most folks forget that early on Braddock was a perennial contender. But he always lost to the best boxers. He had a powerful right hand, but his left was weak. Top fighters exploited that weakness to beat him. When he broke his right hand, his career was as good as over. He gamely took on lesser fighters, but he repeatedly broke his right hand because it was his only weapon. Finally, severe arthritis set in to that hand, forcing him to use his left when he went to work as a longshoreman. Day by day, that left hand became increasingly stronger.

Max Baer came into that fight without fear of Braddock's left hand. It turned out to be the cocky champ's fatal mistake on that magical June night in 1935. Sometimes God takes away good things to give us better things. You may be trying to slug it out with your version of a weak left hand. Like Jimmy you've even given up hope that you can ever be a contender again. Don't give up dreams that once gave you hope. Make Jimmy Braddock's credo your own:

No matter how many times you're knocked down, always get up off the canvas and fight one more round.

⸎

I have fought the good fight, I have finished
the race, I have kept the faith. Now there is in
store for me the crown of righteousness.

2 TIMOTHY 4:7-8, NIV

The Last Lecture

༺ဖ༼ၜ༽ဖ༻

Doctors told Randy that he had advanced pancreatic cancer. When he was advised that he had only a few months, this forty-seven-year-old professor at Carnegie Mellon University wrestled with the inevitable question faced by the terminally ill: how would he spend his last days? Randy wasn't the sort of man to waste precious time on self-pity or in a frantic race to complete some bucket list.

Instead, he remembered a parlor game sometimes played when professors get together: *The Last Lecture*. What if you only had forty-five minutes to give your final lecture to students? Teachers have been known to while away hours debating about which knowledge is most critical to pass on to their pupils.

Randy Pausch wasn't playing a parlor game on September 18, 2007, nor did he have to imagine what he would say at his last lecture. Standing before a packed hall at Carnegie Mellon University, Professor Pausch chose as the title of his last lecture, "Really Achieving Your Childhood Dreams." The man about to die chose to tell his students how to live. There was nothing maudlin or cheesy about his last lecture. Instead, he gave an optimistic talk, filling the auditorium with laughter and tears. Students said that it was reminiscent of Robin Williams's final speech in the movie *Dead Poets Society.*

Little did the professor know that his last lecture would go viral. When advance word of it appeared in the *Wall Street Journal*, columnist Jeff Zaslow drove three hundred miles from Detroit to hear it. He said that it was the most electrifying moment of his life. He likened it to watching Babe Ruth hit his last home run or Michael Jordan make the final jump shot to win the NBA finals. Zaslow posted a five-minute highlight video of the lecture on the *Journal*'s website. He's still amazed at what happened next. People forwarded the clip at viral speed. Within hours, hundreds of thousands had seen it on YouTube and other social media. ABC's *Good Morning America* interviewed the professor the next day. Millions logged on to ABC's website to learn more. Within months, there were six million hits on the YouTube site that carried the full video of that final lecture. Pausch reprised his talk on an *Oprah Winfrey Show* episode that reached ten million people. With Zaslow's help, he authored a book entitled *The Last Lecture*. It remained on the *New York Times* Best Sellers List for more than a hundred weeks, selling five million copies. It's since been translated into forty-eight languages to become an international bestseller.

Randy Pausch passed away quietly at his Chesapeake family home on July 25, 2008. Millions mourned the passing of a college professor who only wanted to give a last lecture to his students. Maybe the cards are stacked against you. You couldn't have been dealt a worse hand than this Carnegie Mellon computer professor. But his amazing story should give you hope that it's never over until it's over. We should all take time to reflect on something he said to his students:

We cannot change the cards we are dealt, just how we play the hand.

Be strong and courageous! Do not be afraid or discouraged.
For the LORD your God is with you wherever you go.

JOSHUA 1:9

Little Herbie Steals a Quarter

స్త్రిఖ్యం

Herbie was the sweetest little boy in the Maywood neighborhood of Indianapolis. He might have grown up to be an angel if his doting mother hadn't died when he was four years old. Instead, his harsh father bullied him at home, turning him into a playground bully at school.

By the time he was a sixth grader, he was a back-alley brawler and petty thief. He dropped out after middle school and became a drifter. At age twenty he was arrested for stealing a car and joined the navy to avoid prosecution. But he soon deserted and was dishonorably discharged. He got married, but his violent temper killed the romance, and the marriage ended in a bitter divorce. After he and a buddy held up a grocery store, he was sentenced to twenty years for armed robbery. When he entered the Indiana State Prison, he snarled, "I will be the meanest SOB you ever saw when I get out of here!"

When he was paroled eight years later, his gang became the most prolific bank robbers in US history. His daring jailbreaks became the stuff of tabloid legend. He bragged to a reporter, "All my life I wanted to be a bank robber, carry a gun, and wear a mask. Now that it's happened, I guess I'm about the best bank robber they ever had. And I sure am happy."

The public adored him as something of a modern-day Robin Hood, but Herbie was a vicious psychopath who hobnobbed with notorious gangsters like "Pretty Boy" Floyd and "Baby Face" Nelson. J. Edgar Hoover declared him Public Enemy Number One and launched the biggest manhunt in US history to bring him to justice.

Maybe you remember Herbie by his full name: John Herbert Dillinger.

Mary Dillinger's little angel had grown up to be the meanest man you ever saw. Not long before he was shot down in an FBI ambush, John Dillinger confided to a friend, "I can trace my life of crime back to when I was nine years old. I stole a quarter from my old man's wallet. I was scared that he would find out and give me a beating, but I got away with it. After that, stealing became easy."

Little Herbie stole a quarter. It didn't seem like a big deal at the time. But it led to a lifetime of choices that created John Dillinger, Public Enemy Number One. No choice is insignificant. Your decisions are the hinges on which your destiny hangs. French philosopher Albert Camus wrote, "Life is the sum of all your choices." John Dillinger was no philosopher, but he would probably agree with Camus.

You will make thousands of choices today. A few may be carefully weighed, but most will be impulsive or unconscious. The vast majority probably won't warrant a second thought. But none will be unimportant. So do yourself a favor. Reflect long and hard on the story of a little boy who stole a quarter. Your decisions today may not lead to such high drama, but this much is true for each of us:

Monumental consequences are shaped by momentary choices.

⚬⚬⚬

Trust in the LORD with all your heart and do not lean on your own understanding. In all your ways acknowledge Him, and He will make your paths straight.

PROVERBS 3:5-6, NASB

The Disability That Set
a World Record

Im Dong-Hyun of South Korea is some kind of magician with a bow and arrow. He wasted little time in breaking the first world record of the 2012 Summer Olympics. His score of 699 out of a possible 720 in the opening round of the archery competition may have been the most astounding world record in the London Olympics. But it was no fluke. Dong-Hyun broke the world record *he* set four years before in the Beijing Olympics. Winning gold is old hat for this world-record holder. He was only eighteen years old when he led his South Korean archery team to gold in the 2004 Athens Olympics.

In an age of Olympic superstars like Michael Phelps and Usain Bolt, you might not think that Im Dong-Hyun's prowess is such a big deal—until you discover that this eagle-eyed archer is legally blind. He has 20/200 vision in his left eye, the one he looks through to see a target. His right eye isn't much better. That means he has to be ten times closer to the target than someone with 20/20 vision. But his blindness gets him no breaks. He still has to stand the same seventy meters from the target as competitors with perfect vision.

On top of that, Dong-Hyun achieves near perfection without wearing corrective lenses. He says that eyeglasses get in the way. So, how does he see his target? He has to somehow distinguish between the bright colors of the various rings. Yet that makes his world records even more amazing. His myopia renders colors fuzzy and blended together, like different-colored paints dropped into a glass of water. After he set his Olympic and world record, this legally blind South Korean joked with reporters, "If I couldn't see the colors at all, now that would be a problem."

A person with 20/20 vision would be hard pressed to read a newspaper at arm's length, but this Olympic archer with 20/200 vision has to distinguish between blurred rings of color on a target the size of a grapefruit three-quarters of the length of a football field away. Yet when awed reporters tried to make a big deal out of his myopia, he brushed aside their questions with this response: "I don't have a stick, I don't have a blind dog. It's unpleasant when people say I'm disabled. All this interest in my sight is not welcome."

This multiple gold medalist in a sport that requires a steady hand and eagle eye refuses to allow his disability to disable him. He is adamant that no one has to be handicapped by a handicap. If you've been deprived of an eye that can see, you can still develop an inner eye that seldom misses the bull's-eye. This amazing story of Im Dong-Hyun reminds us of one of life's miracles: an uncommon weakness in one area always develops an uncommon strength in another. All of us who have some handicap can adopt this credo:

My abilities are stronger than my disabilities.

———— ✍ ————

I am glad to boast about my weaknesses, so that
the power of Christ can work through me.

2 CORINTHIANS 12:9

The Monster in the Monk

❧

Little Grozny was a bundle of contradictions—one part piety, and the other psychopath. It's no wonder! At age three, he was declared the crown prince of a medieval kingdom in its death spasms. After his daddy died, his family turned the palace into a nonstop soap opera. When they weren't stabbing or poisoning each other, they were plotting how to rid themselves of the little crown prince.

The cruelest blow of all came when his conniving mother locked him in a dungeon. This Jezebel ruled the nation while her lonely child feared for his life. He often wished that he could escape to a monastery. The priests who tutored him may have smiled at his angelic prayers, but they should have seen telltale signs of the sinister. When he wasn't voraciously reading, he loved to torture little animals. His rage became unpredictable and uncontrollable. He would spend hours in prayer, only to get up off his knees to berate and beat servants. He was barely a teen when he raped his first victim.

But this walking time bomb also became a cunning expert at his own *Game of Thrones*. He played the dim-witted prince after nobles poisoned his mother. But when he was thirteen, he orchestrated the execution of the ringleader. Three years later, he was crowned king. He changed the title of his office to czar, or caesar, and set about building a new Rome on the Volga. In the following years, Grozny expanded his small kingdom of Muscovy by conquering more than a billion square acres. He championed the poor, stopped the Mongol hordes, and Christianized Russia. Then he announced that he was going to retire to a monastery. But peasants and priests begged him to remain on his throne.

This Russian caesar might have wished for his grandfather's name, Ivan the Great. Instead, history has called him Grozny—the Russian name for *terrible*. Indeed, this Ivan was cruel, paranoid, maniacal, and schizophrenic. He beat one of his sons to death with an iron bar. He probably murdered a baby son. He terrorized his remaining son until the boy went insane. While he worked tirelessly to establish the Orthodox faith, he also martyred priests who opposed him. His paranoia caused him to murder sixty thousand of his citizens. But his lasting legacy of terror was his *oprichniki*, a network of six thousand secret police. His diabolical creation was the forerunner to the KGB and the prototype for police states ever since. When he finally died of a stroke in 1584 while playing chess, people everywhere breathed a collective sigh of relief.

The amazing story of Czar Ivan is as perplexing as it is terrible. How can a person be both pious and a predator? It is a mystery as old as humankind. Yet this story of Ivan the Terrible offers equal warning and hope. It warns that within every monk lurks a monster. Yet it gives hope that there is a monk longing to escape from every monster. The ancient North African theologian, Origen, reminds us of this fact:

The power of choosing good or evil is within the reach of all.

———— ✦ ————

Don't let evil conquer you, but conquer evil by doing good.

ROMANS 12:21

A Lifeline from the Asylum

❦

He was one of those wretched souls locked away in an insane asylum in the 1800s. He insisted that he wasn't crazy. But the science of psychology was still in its infancy. In those days, asylums were more like prisons. The misdiagnosed, the mildly eccentric, and the "raving lunatics" were all thrown in together. Methods for treating the mentally ill were cruel and primitive. If you weren't mentally unstable when they committed you, you were certain to lose your sanity afterward.

When he finally died, the workers who came to clean up his cell discovered a poem scribbled on the wall next to his bed. The doctors were perplexed. How could a lunatic articulate such beauty? Actually, they weren't his words. Before they locked him away in the asylum, he had memorized lines written by a Jewish rabbi some nine hundred years earlier. He must have scratched them on the wall as a lifeline of hope when he was drowning in a rising sea of insanity. Years later, a discouraged evangelist turned these lines into the last stanza of a famous hymn:

Could we with ink the ocean fill
And were the skies of parchment made,
Were every stalk on earth a quill
And every man a scribe by trade,
To write the love of God above
Would drain the ocean dry.
Nor could the scroll contain the whole
Though stretched from sky to sky.

435

O love of God, how rich and pure!
   How measureless and strong!
It shall forevermore endure
   The saints' and angels' song.

Maybe you have joined the countless millions who have sung the hymn "The Love of God." You probably didn't know that it was based on the words of a medieval rabbi who was defending a group of Jews from anti-Semitic attacks or that it was later scribbled on the wall of an insane asylum. There's something poignant about this poor soul clinging to those words as the light of his soul slowly dimmed and then went out. Were these words his last touch with sanity?

How that story was passed on is a story in itself. A worker who cleaned the room wrote them in pencil on a scrap of paper. That paper passed through many hands over several years. A discouraged evangelist found it lying on an apple crate in the corner of a room and turned its words into the third verse of his hymn.

These words run like a thread of hope through so many stories: a rabbi running for his life; an inmate fighting to keep his sanity; an evangelist trying to find hope; and countless millions who have been inspired by a hymn. Isn't the sustaining power of a story amazing? Now the words have found their way to you. Maybe you should scribble them on your wall too.

Hope is the raw material from which faith builds the house.

Hope does not put us to shame, because God's
love has been poured out into our hearts through
the Holy Spirit, who has been given to us.

ROMANS 5:5, NIV

The Man
Who Knew Infinity

ॐ

The college dropout spontaneously scribbled equations with a grand elegance that soared like Beethoven's symphonies. It's no wonder that this twenty-five-year-old Hindu from India attracted the attention of Cambridge professor and world-renowned mathematician G. H. Hardy, who famously wrote, "Beauty is my first test; there is no permanent place in the world for ugly mathematics."

Back in India, the karma of that young mathematician, Srinivasa Ramanujan, was set in a rigid Hindu caste system. To make matters worse, the prejudice of Victorian England, still ruling in India at the time, would never allow an Indian to soar. His intuitive genius was also a curse. After he discovered an out-of-date math book, he spent almost every waking hour at a deserted temple courtyard writing out equations in the sand. Although he had no idea where they came from, his calculations were complex beyond the grasp of scholars at Oxford or Cambridge. He spent so much time in his magical world of equations that his other studies fell by the wayside. When he lost his scholarships, he was forced to apply for government assistance. After he published a paper in the *Journal of the Indian Mathematical Society*, he managed to land a job as a clerk. It was during his time as a low-level numbers cruncher that he sent his work to G. H. Hardy. At first, the Cambridge professor thought it was a hoax. When he realized that the Indian genius was for real, he paid Ramanujan's way to Cambridge.

There never was a more unsuited pair. One was a devout Hindu and the other an implacable atheist. Ramanujan was warmly sentimental.

Hardy was cold and detached. The Hindu's genius was intuitive, flowing out of a romance with mathematics. The atheist was wired like an engineer, building his equations on classical methodology. But during their five years together, Hardy taught Ramanujan how to master the science of mathematics, and the Indian took the atheist to unexplored realms that were almost spiritual.

When a mystified Hardy demanded that his Indian student explain how he came up with his equations, he replied, "They flow out of my worship of God." Such esoteric thinking confounded the professor who had long ago abandoned his belief in God. But together, this unlikely pair discovered the circle theory that led to advances in modular forms that are unraveling the mysteries of black holes. Great minds have proven that Ramanujan unlocked the secrets to infinity, but they are no closer to figuring out how. Before he died in 1920, this Indian had intuitively gone to places that today's math geniuses are still unable to find.

After his Indian friend died of tuberculosis at age thirty-two, a grieving G. H. Hardy confessed, "The fact that I again believe in God, I owe to Ramanujan." We don't have to be geniuses to figure out a profound equation in Ramanujan's amazing story. When finite beings worship the infinite God, we get a glimpse of infinity. Those of us who worship Jesus Christ can learn this from that Hindu genius:

When our finite best flows out of worship, the possibilities are infinite.

———— ✸ ————

Whether you eat or drink, or whatever you do,
do it all for the glory of God.

1 CORINTHIANS 10:31

Kissing the Beggar's Lips

e was christened Giovanni, the Italian name for John. His mother named him after John the Baptist in hopes that he would be devoted to Jesus. But Giovanni was hardly devout. As the son of a wealthy cloth merchant, the boy was a spoiled rich kid. Though his father hoped he would take over the family business, Giovanni frittered away his days listening to troubadours in the marketplace. At night he played the fop, prancing from one debauchery to another. He wasted his father's money on prostitutes and his energy in street brawls. Yet he existed in disillusionment and despair.

One day a beggar in the marketplace asked Giovanni for a handout. His rich young friends shoved the panhandler aside. But Giovanni remembered a line he heard at Sunday Mass: "When you feed the hungry, you minister to Christ." He grabbed hold of the beggar, gave him everything in his pockets, and kissed him full on his lips.

That evening he informed his family that he wanted to give everything away to the poor. His enraged father forced Giovanni to enlist in the army, and he was sent off to war. After he was captured, he said that Christ visited him in his prison. When he returned home, he no longer wanted to party with his friends. They jokingly asked if he was planning to marry and settle down. He replied, "Yes, I shall soon wed Lady Poverty." He moved into a charity hospital where he fed and bathed the most repulsive of the sick. On winter nights he climbed into bed with lepers, wrapping them in his arms to keep them warm.

By day, this son of wealth sat on the steps of the cathedral begging for money to feed the poor. When his father's cardinal friend, the confessor to Pope Innocent, came up the steps, he begged for permission to start a new order to minister to the poor. With the pope's blessing, he gathered disciples who gave away all their possessions to follow Jesus. They crisscrossed Europe, ministering to the poor, comforting the sick, and evangelizing the forgotten. Giovanni was the only missionary that the caliph ever allowed to preach in North Africa. This supreme leader of Islam said, "He is the rarest of all Christians who truly lives out his faith."

While still in his early forties, Giovanni caught a fatal disease from a sick wretch that he had held in his arms. In October of 1226 he fell prostrate on the cold ground and whispered, "Welcome, Sister Death." Then he gasped his final words to his brothers: "I have done my part. May Jesus teach you to do yours." You remember Giovanni di Bernardone by the name his father later gave him: Francesco. History memorializes him as Saint Francis of Assisi. His last words challenge each of us. Have we done our part? If you don't know what your part is, ask Jesus. If you already know but find it impossible to accomplish, Jesus stands ready to give you what Saint Francis said makes it possible:

To give largely, liberally, and cheerfully requires a new heart.

I will give you a new heart and put a new spirit
in you; I will remove from you your heart
of stone and give you a heart of flesh.

EZEKIEL 36:26, NIV

Wright-Mare in Wisconsin

❧

Lloyd was proud of his architectural marvel. He called it Taliesin in honor of a Welsh bard and his romantic poems. The Chicago architect planned to enjoy plenty of romance in his Wisconsin getaway. And that's exactly why the locals were scandalized. Whenever they spoke about Lloyd's house, they put the emphasis on the last syllable: Talie-*sin*. Some tried to get up a petition to bulldoze it. Others threatened to burn it down. The school superintendent warned that the goings-on there would corrupt the morals of area children.

What caused this firestorm? After Lloyd had finished the house of a wealthy client, he stole the man's wife. When he ran off to Europe with Mamah Borthwick, he abandoned his wife and six children. That was scandalous enough in the big city of Chicago. But there was outrage in Spring Green when he built a love cottage for his mistress. Lloyd couldn't care less. He was the world's greatest architect. Laws and rules applied to lesser people. He once said to a reporter, "Two women were necessary for a man of artistic mind—one to be mother of his children and the other to be his mental companion, his inspiration and soul mate." But Lloyd's plans would be turned upside down on August 15, 1914.

Lloyd was away when his mistress and two of her children sat down to lunch on the porch at Taliesin. Workers were eating in the dining room. Barbados native Julian Carlton was serving lunch. After Julian served the soup, he took an ax outside, where he hacked Lloyd's mistress and her children to death. Meanwhile, the workers in the dining room saw fluid spreading across the floor. Suddenly, the liquid erupted into a blazing inferno, and the door to the dining room was shut and locked. Some of the workers managed to bust through the door, only to be met by Julian with his bloodied ax. By the time townspeople arrived at the burning love cottage, seven people, including three children, had been brutally murdered. Julian had swallowed muriatic acid. It would take him seven agonizing weeks to die.

The conventional wisdom in 1914 was that Mamah got what she deserved for breaking up Lloyd's happy family. But what about the man who was above convention? He immediately set about to rebuild his love cottage. A year later he moved in with another lover. The world remembers Frank Lloyd Wright for his wondrous architecture. But few folks remember the getaway that he built in Spring Green or what happened there. Maybe the Taliesin tragedy is a morality tale. Certainly, we ought to grieve for the innocent victims. But we should also question Lloyd's assumption that we can ignore the laws indelibly written into creation by its Creator. When we are tempted to think that we are the exception to the rule, we ought to recall something Robert Louis Stevenson wrote:

Sooner or later, everyone sits down to a banquet of consequences.

———— ✿ ————

My experience shows that those who plant trouble
and cultivate evil will harvest the same.

JOB 4:8

The Price We Pay for Love

⌒⌒⌒

Clive wrote about faraway places he never visited. He created magical worlds seen through children's eyes though he was a middle-aged college professor. He wrote a bestselling book on love even though he had never experienced romance. Later he authored a book on the problem of pain in spite of the fact that he was living a comfortable life. When his nation's capital was being bombed into rubble, he lifted the spirits of his countrymen with rousing radio talks. Yet he lived far from the bombs in a peaceful university town.

In short, Clive was the world's foremost expert on things he had never experienced. The biggest excitement in his life was sitting at the same table in the same pub on the same evening every week with the same cronies, creating adventures that they would never experience in places they would never visit. Beyond that, he was a slightly dumpy professor who shared a cluttered cottage with his bachelor brother.

Then Clive's life was turned upside down by a visiting author from America. Joy would give him the greatest happiness in his life, only to leave him to cope with unbearable grief.

The two were polar opposites. She was a recent divorcée while he was a confirmed bachelor. Where he was stodgy, she was flamboyant. He was boringly conventional. She loved to flout tradition. He was a staunch Anglican. She jumped impulsively from Judaism to communism to evangelicalism. Yet in spite of their stark differences, Joy and Clive formed a deep friendship that eventually blossomed into love.

Just when the fifty-eight-year-old bachelor ratcheted up his courage to propose, she discovered that she had terminal bone cancer. He wanted to call off the wedding, insisting that losing a wife would be too painful. Joy responded, "The extent to which we love each other now is the extent to which you will feel pain after I'm gone. That's the deal."

It took Clive several days to realize that having Joy now was worth the pain later. On March 21, 1957, they were married in her hospital room. The next few years were deliriously happy. Then she died of cancer, plunging him into suicidal despair that almost destroyed his faith. He recovered enough to write *A Grief Observed*. A haunting line leaps off one of its pages: "I not only live each endless day in grief, but live each day thinking about living each day in grief."

Three years after cancer stole his beloved Joy, he collapsed in his bedroom and died. The world hardly noticed the passing of this author of the beloved Chronicles of Narnia because a young American president was assassinated in Dallas on the same day. But fifty-four years later, C. S. Lewis is remembered as a towering giant who changed the landscape of literature. Maybe you're facing the loss of someone or something very special. Perhaps you are grieving for a loss already suffered. You might take some solace in "the deal" offered by Joy Davidman to her fearful English bachelor:

The pain of your loss is living proof of the joy you possessed.

―――――― ❦ ――――――

May the God of hope fill you with all joy and peace
as you trust in him, so that you may overflow
with hope by the power of the Holy Spirit.

ROMANS 15:13, NIV

Victoria's Secret

❧

If her English subjects had known that their Christian queen was intimately involved with an Indian servant by the name of Abdul Karim, they might have rioted. So Victoria's secret was kept under wraps. After her death, the Muslim servant she affectionately called *Munshi* was deported to India where he died in obscurity. Their letters and notes were destroyed. Any mention of Abdul in Queen Victoria's journals was blotted out by her daughter, Beatrice. The book on their story was closed. But history is a book that refuses to stay shut.

A few years ago, Indian journalist Shrabani Basu stumbled onto the cover-up quite by accident. But the evidence was sketchy. So Ms. Basu played the detective, following clues that eventually led her to the smoking gun in India: Abdul's missing diaries and personal letters from Victoria. They were a treasure trove of startling evidence that proved deep intimacy between an old English queen and her young Indian footman. Ms. Basu was astounded by the way Victoria ended her letters to Abdul: "your closest friend" or "your true friend" and even "your loving mother." But the journalist's biggest breakthrough was her discovery that Abdul had taught Victoria how to write in Hindustani. She returned to England where she was allowed to research journals that survived only because Victoria's jealous children did not understand the Hindustani their mother had used to write to her Indian servant.

In those journals, Shrabani discovered Victoria's heart. She also found a love story that was not sexual, but made of that rarest of intimacies birthed by soul mates—a transcendent friendship. This servant dared look deep into the eyes of a distant and haughty queen. He was warmly personal while others treated her with stiff deference. He gently pointed out her faults while others pandered to her whims. He listened to her heart while others heard only her voice. He intrigued and excited a dowager queen who was weary and wounded by life. So she opened her heart to someone from an alien world. He taught her to love curry, shared the mysteries of India, and recited verses from the Koran. He became her teacher, adviser, and confidant.

Palace snobs spoke of him with racial slurs and said he "forgot his proper place." The Prince of Wales told her that she was insane. Officials worried that Abdul would convert their queen to Islam. That never happened, but Victoria was immeasurably enriched because she was willing to step outside her royal bubble. Abdul received the friendship of a lifetime because he risked stepping outside "the proper place" society had defined for him. The amazing story of friendship between a Christian queen and her Muslim servant should inspire us all to step out of our own bubbles. We don't have to abandon our values or beliefs to get to know people who are different or who think differently. But like Victoria and Abdul, we might just grow from gaining new perspectives. This much is surely true: *No one ever grows inside their comfort zone.*

Notorious sinners often came to listen to Jesus teach. This made the Pharisees and teachers of religious law complain that he was associating with sinful people—even eating with them.

LUKE 15:1-2

446

Wandering to Glory

❧

John was a vagabond, trying to find himself. A long-haired, bearded hippy before there were hippies. A free spirit who climbed trees, and then sat there for days playing his recorder and meditating. A new Saint Francis of Assisi, traveling the road to wherever the unwanted, unwashed, and unloved needed Jesus.

He had fought for the British against the Japanese in Burma. He came home to a war hero's welcome. He left home and took to the road to shake off horrors he had witnessed in Burma. He tried to join a Benedictine monastery, but found it too restricting. He hooked up with Carthusian monks, but their lifestyle was too demanding. Along the way he lived in attics, huts, and even a hen run. He spent some time as the caretaker of an estate owned by the church, but had a falling-out with its administrators. So he moved on again. Family and friends couldn't figure out whether he was following God or running from himself. They wondered, "When is John finally going to find himself and make something of his life?"

The road took John to the African country of Rhodesia. Somewhere outside the capital, he stumbled onto a leper colony. John was appalled that eighty lepers had been abandoned in this place of filth, hunger, and thirst. For the first time in twenty-five years, he decided to stay put. He lived in their huts, drove out the rats that gnawed on them at night, cleaned their sores, cut their nails if they still had fingers or toes, sang them to sleep at night, and buried them when they died. He helped his lepers build a church and led them in their worship.

But the Rhodesian Leprosy Association was threatened by this bearded Jesus freak who saw their lepers as people to be loved rather than statistics to be reported. Officials ordered John to leave the colony. So he lived in a tent on a hill nearby. Then a farmer gave him a tin hut just outside the wire fence surrounding the colony. For the next six years he lived outside that fence in order to help the lepers inside. It all ended on a September evening in 1979, when a squadron of Robert Mugabe's guerrillas showed up. Because he was a white Englishman, they saw him as a tool of colonialists. After publicly degrading and then interrogating him, the Marxists took him down the road and shot him. The vagabond had finally found himself. He had found himself as a lover of lepers. When he embraced them, he found himself in the arms of Jesus. When he was tortured and shot, he found himself as a martyr. When he died, he found himself in glory. The amazing story of John Bradburne gives hope to all of us who are still trying to find ourselves. It reminds us to be patient with others who are still searching for their purpose. It takes some folks longer to find themselves. So take heart in this:

God orders our steps, our stops, and our detours along the way.

———— ❧ ————

The LORD directs the steps of the godly.
He delights in every detail of their lives.

PSALM 37:23

The Broken Harpsichord

ଏଡ୍ରେଉ

The old composer was in the twilight of life. He was only fifty-seven years of age, but he seemed so much older. Always misshapen in appearance, he now looked like a hunchbacked gnome. A tempestuous past had finally worn his soul down to a nub. He had overcome so much. His mother tried to abort him, his grandfather rejected him, and his father almost destroyed him. Though he was a musical prodigy, his dyslexia made it difficult for him to read or write. He was ugly in appearance, melancholy in temperament, and painfully shy. Rejected by every woman he ever loved, he would live out his life in loneliness.

Almost all of his fees went to support a family left destitute by his drunken father. Yet poverty didn't impede productivity. He drove himself with perfectionistic frenzy to earn the approval he craved. Some two hundred years later, his soaring symphonies still leave us breathless. They also reveal the inner rage that drove him to write such gloriously tempestuous scores.

Just as he experienced success, he contracted an incurable disability. He drove himself to compose as many works as possible in the short time left. As his disability increased, so did his miraculous output. Yet his obsessive-compulsive personality, fueled by emotional turmoil, ruined almost all his friendships. Critics complained that his symphonies were strange, overtly extravagant, and even risqué. He would utter these cynical words on his deathbed: "*Plaudite, amici, comoedia finite est.*" (Applaud friends, the comedy is over.)

In his final days, he spent long evenings playing a broken-down harpsichord that had been sold cheaply at auction. Its finish was faded; keys were missing. And it was hopelessly out of tune. Yet tears of joy flowed down the composer's face when he played that wreck of a harpsichord. Those watching said that the malformed body became serenely beautiful. Maybe he had finally begun to relax after fifty-seven years of frantic turbulence.

His servants would look at each other with sly grins. You would think that old Ludwig van Beethoven was hearing a symphony from heaven instead of the sour notes on a broken instrument. And maybe he was! As you may know, the disability that should have ruined his career was the loss of his hearing. It was a miracle that he could have written symphonies for the ages when he was going deaf. Now he existed in a world of total silence. But he was hearing the music that the harpsichord *should* make, not the sour notes it *did* make.

Do you ever feel like Beethoven's wreck of a harpsichord—faded and peeling, with your best days behind you? Are you a few ivories short of a full keyboard? Remember this, dear friend: God has purchased you with the priceless sacrifice of his only begotten Son. He's not deaf like Beethoven. He hears all your sour notes. But he chooses to enjoy your best ones and loves you all the more for those that aren't so good. The story of Beethoven's harpsichord gives this hope:

God plays his most beautiful symphonies on broken instruments.

_____ ⌘ _____

Don't be afraid, for I am with you. Don't be discouraged,
for I am your God. I will strengthen you and help you.
I will hold you up with my victorious right hand.

ISAIAH 41:10

History's Forgotten Half

❧◈❧

Colonial America was mostly little towns, villages, and hamlets. The majority of people lived on rural farms or in frontier cabins, isolated from each other and the ideas that were reshaping the rest of the world. Dr. Giles Goddard believed that a new nation was ready to be birthed, if only its people could get a vision. He drummed into his children, M. K. and William, that the news and the mail would be the catalysts. Newspapers would publish the ideas and events that shaped public opinion. A great postal system would circulate those ideas.

After the good doctor died, his children put feet to their father's vision. They started the first newspaper in Rhode Island, opened another in Philadelphia, and then landed in Baltimore, where they founded its first newspaper. While M. K. printed the paper, William went on the road to open new mail routes. Working in tandem, they expanded their circulation until the Baltimore newspaper became one of the most powerful voices in the colonies. When bullies tried to silence the paper's call for revolution, M. K. refused to back down. Maybe that's why this courageous journalist was chosen to print and circulate the Declaration of Independence. When war came, M. K. was an equal opportunity offender, criticizing the British army for its cruelties and General Washington for his ineffectiveness. Both Tories and patriots were angry. Hotheads tried to destroy the printing presses. M. K. even faced mob violence. But the publisher and editor believed that muzzling a free press would destroy freedom. M. K.'s refusal to back down is one of the reasons we enjoy freedom of the press in America today.

After the Revolutionary War ended, William came back to Baltimore. A bitter sibling rivalry resulted in M. K. being forced out, so she focused on her job at the post office in Baltimore. Yes, *she*! M. K. stood for Mary Katherine. Had a male-dominated world known that M. K. Goddard was a woman, her newspaper might never have gotten off the ground. It was because she was a woman that William was able to seize the newspaper. It was because of her gender that the postmaster general replaced her as Baltimore's postmaster. He said that the job required travel that was "beyond the capacity of a woman." Her appeal to the US Senate and President Washington fell on deaf ears. So the woman who was worthy to be the postmaster general of America, and even its next president, ran a little bookstore in Baltimore for the rest of her life.

History has largely forgotten her. But if you look again at the Declaration of Independence, you will see the signatures of fifty-six men and the name of its printer, Mary Katherine Goddard. Her amazing story reminds us of the tragic history of gender inequality. We talk about the founding fathers and ignore our founding mothers. They are history's forgotten half. Nobel Prize winner Malala Yousafzai reminds us of a critical truth:

We cannot all succeed when half of us are held back.

———— ✍ ————

My dear brothers and sisters, how can you claim
to have faith in our glorious Lord Jesus Christ
if you favor some people over others?

JAMES 2:1

The Monster from Milwaukee

෴

The most horrifying thing about Jeffrey wasn't what came out in his sensational trial. For most folks, it's what happened to him later on in prison. Jeffrey was a serial killer before mass murders became commonplace news in America. Today we hardly get time to digest one act of terror before we are confronted with another. But in the early 1990s, Jeffrey's horror story captivated the nation. Eleven corpses had been found in his apartment. Before the investigation ended, it was discovered that he had murdered and dismembered at least seventeen young men. But the grisly discovery that horrified America was the fact that this sadistic killer also cannibalized his victims.

Search the Internet, and you will find pictures of the monster from Milwaukee sitting in the courtroom during his trial. He sits serenely with steely eyes and an impassive face. There are no signs of remorse or hints of regret. It's no wonder that the world cheered when he was sentenced to life without parole. Even that seemed like too little justice. How could the state ever exact enough retribution for those that this monster had lured into his chamber of horrors?

But this is what folks still find most disturbing: Jeffrey Dahmer became a born-again Christian in prison. He publicly repented for his despicable deeds. After he was baptized, he sent letters of apology to his victims' families. Most people were skeptical, dismissing his newfound faith as a jailhouse conversion. Others were outraged, arguing that God would never forgive such a monster.

Then Jeffrey did the craziest thing in his crazy life. He asked to be released from solitary confinement. Prison officials told him that he was signing his own death warrant. But the born-again serial killer wanted to share his faith. So he was transferred to the general prison population. The chaplain was so impressed by Jeffrey's spiritual growth that he made him his assistant. The monster from Milwaukee was now reading the Scriptures and serving Communion.

At the same time, fellow prisoners were plotting to kill him. When an inmate slashed his throat, he miraculously survived. His parents begged him to return to solitary confinement. Jeffrey responded that prison was his mission field. A few days later, he was beaten to death in a prison restroom. When the news of his death was broadcast on November 28, 1994, the nation cheered. It was Thanksgiving Day all over again.

Yet there was one fly in the ointment of justice. The prison chaplain told skeptical reporters that Jeffrey Dahmer was truly saved and in heaven. That claim sparked a national debate: Aren't there some sins and sinners so heinous that they are beyond God's grace? Maybe these questions are more relevant: Are some sins in your life beyond God's grace? Can others hurt you so badly that they are beyond your forgiveness? Jeffrey's story is disturbing, but it drives us to consider something Corrie ten Boom said when she was faced with forgiving those who abused and killed her sister in a Nazi concentration camp:

No pit is so deep that God is not deeper still.

I could ask the darkness to hide me and the
light around me to become night—but even
in darkness I cannot hide from you.

PSALM 139:11-12

Truth and
Its Consequences

༄༅༄

The lush rain forests of Guatemala are a garden of sensual delights. Yet they blush with shame as the mute witnesses to unspeakable horror. Trees recall the screams of the dying and the rapid fire of automatic weapons. Volcanic soil covers mass graves. Villages are deserted and decaying, their men and boys shot and their women and orphans hiding among the undocumented up north.

If those mute forests could at least point accusing fingers, our eyes would turn toward Guatemala City. On its outskirts stands a two-story concrete building guarded by high walls, barbed wire, and soldiers with Israeli rifles. It is the military intelligence school built and operated by the CIA. The ties between American intelligence officers and the Guatemalan army go back to the CIA's Operation Success, which helped army generals stage a coup against President Jacobo Arbenz in 1954. For four decades the CIA aided the generals as they sent their armies into the countryside to root out guerrillas. In the chaos, military death squads depopulated whole villages. Only the forests will ever know how many victims of mass murder lie buried and forgotten beneath their soil.

But the forests don't have to testify. God was watching too. He raised up a hero in Juan Gerardi Conedera. As the auxiliary bishop of Guatemala, Gerardi could have played it safe by cozying up to the oligarchy of power just as the church hierarchy had always done. But this bishop was a man of monumental integrity. Because he adored Jesus, he loved the indigenous Mayan people who had suffered the most. So he set out to expose a nearly four-decade cover-up. His truth commission uncovered chilling firsthand accounts of torture, massacre, and the erasing of whole villages. The evidence of genocide that he gathered was as exhaustive as it was horrifying.

Bishop Gerardi knew bringing this evidence to light would mean putting his own life on the line. He was proven right when military agents tried to assassinate him. He fled to El Salvador, but was refused entry. For three years he hid out in Costa Rica. After the election of a new government, he thought it was safe to return. But Guatemala is never safe for those who uncover its dirty secrets. On April 26, 1998, two days after the bishop released his four-volume report, he was bludgeoned to death. In the sensational trial that followed, a few scapegoats were convicted: the sergeant who assassinated Gerardi and a colonel who orchestrated his actions. But those who ordered the hit were never brought to justice.

The amazing story of Bishop Gerardi reminds us that truth has consequences. Uncovering it may lead to martyrdom. Facing it can bring shock and shame. But no one can run from it forever. Those who sow the wind, reap the whirlwind. Guatemala has descended into chaos. The brutal reign of generals has been replaced by the sadistic rule of drug gangs. And Guatemala sits in the Central American triangle known as "the homicide capital of the world." Indeed, truth has consequences. So does the big lie. The forests know what we forget:

Truth hurts for a moment, but lies will destroy forever.

A false witness will not go unpunished,
and a liar will be destroyed.

PROVERBS 19:9

456

The Midnight Ride

⌒⌒⊙⌒⌒

There was a time when every grade-school kid in America knew that opening line from Henry Wadsworth Longfellow's most famous poem: "Listen, my children, and you shall hear of the midnight ride of Paul Revere." Few events are etched more indelibly in Americana than that ride. Yet there were three riders on April 18, 1775. William Dawes rode in another direction to warn citizens that redcoats were on the march. Samuel Prescott raced down another road to call patriots to arms. But only one reached his appointed destination. Paul Revere was captured by British sentries. William Dawes fell off his horse and had to limp back to Boston. Only Prescott managed to reach Concord in time to warn the village.

Longfellow should have written "The Midnight Ride of Samuel Prescott." Or he could have penned a poem about an epic ride two years later by sixteen-year-old Sybil Ludington. This girl was the eldest of Colonel Henry Ludington's twelve children. Her father commanded the militia of Dutchess County in New York. That's why he was the first to get the news that the British were burning nearby Danbury. The colonel needed to assemble his militia quickly. But it was near the end of April, and his citizen soldiers had returned to their farms for spring planting.

So Colonel Ludington chose the best rider in Dutchess County. Sybil bolted out of their farmyard that evening, riding like the wind to the villages south, and then turned west past farms and hamlets, then north through forests and farmlands to the farthest reaches of the county. When she finally turned south again, dawn was breaking. Patriot farmers were already assembling in the Ludington farmyard. The colonel led his militia seventeen miles down the road to Ridgefield to join the battle against the British. The tide of the Revolutionary War was turned when citizen soldiers stopped the redcoat advance at Ridgefield.

Few people remember the teenage girl who made that victory possible. Her life afterward was rather ordinary. Years later, few folks showed up at a funeral for an old woman who had been widowed for forty years. She is buried under a decaying gravestone that misspells her name Sibbell. Yet on one glorious night, she galloped into history. Her ride was twice as far as Paul Revere's. Three men rode out of Boston on a moonlit night, but Sybil's ride was through the driving rain. The roads from Boston to Concord were smooth, but those in Dutchess County were narrow and winding, full of ruts and potholes, and crawling with outlaws. All she had for protection was a stick. Maybe every schoolchild should remember the midnight ride of Sybil Ludington. Her amazing story shows that sometimes it takes a girl to do a man's work. Ability alone should determine who gets the job, or the reward for doing it well—not age, or gender, or race, or religion, or pedigree. If you are in charge of any enterprise, your success hangs on doing this one thing right:

Get the right person at the right time in the right job.

———— ⁊✺⁊ ————

I remember your genuine faith, for you share
the faith that first filled your grandmother Lois
and your mother, Eunice.

2 TIMOTHY 1:5

George Washington's Liar

୧୭୧

No one imagined that Ben would become the stuff of legend. But when this shopkeeper heard that British troops had massacred citizens in Boston, something inside him exploded. He cried out in a town meeting, "Good God, are the Americans all asleep and tamely giving up their glorious liberties?" When revolution broke out, he organized a militia and led it down the road to join the fight in Boston.

Then he came up with an audacious idea. If he took Fort Ticonderoga in nearby New York, he could capture enough cannons to blast the British out of Boston. After a forced march, Ben's little militia caught the redcoats napping and took the fort. His feat galvanized a revolution badly in need of a victory. After he was promoted to colonel, he marched his men across Maine's rugged wilderness in freezing November and attacked Quebec with only about a thousand men. A musket ball tore through his leg, leaving him lame. But he limped home a hero. After that, he led his men to a string of stunning victories.

Jealous superiors grudgingly promoted him to brigadier general. He had hoped for more. Maybe that's when bitterness took root. Finally, George Washington made him a major general. He alone understood what military experts now affirm: Ben was the greatest general on either side in this war. Ben's star reached its zenith at the Battle of Saratoga. The colonials were in retreat when Ben wheeled his horse around and charged into British cannon fire. His horse was shot out from under him, and he was badly wounded. But his courage rallied the Americans, and victory was snatched from defeat.

Yet there was a dark side to Washington's favorite general. The public hero was a private thief who regularly diverted war funds into his personal accounts. As military governor of Philadelphia, his embezzlement became so egregious that he was court-martialed. Ben appealed to Washington, "Having become a cripple in service to my country, I little expected such ungrateful returns." In a move that still confounds historians, Washington countermanded the court-martial and gave Ben command of the most critical fortress in America's defense system.

Within days, an embittered Ben cut a secret deal to turn the fort over to the enemy in exchange for £20,000 and a commission as a general in the British army. You remember Ben by his birth name, Benedict. The fort he betrayed was West Point. Had the war ended at Saratoga, Benedict Arnold would be celebrated as a hero. Instead, his very name is synonymous with treachery.

It is a baffling mystery: How could George Washington, a man famous for never telling a lie, be so completely conned by one of history's greatest liars? Today, you will be assaulted by a blitzkrieg of lies, cleverly disguised by the enemy of our souls. Maybe the answer to why George Washington and all of us are so easily conned is found in a statement by the Dutch humanist Erasmus:

Our minds are so formed that we are far more susceptible to falsehood than truth.

Dear friends, do not believe every spirit, but test the
spirits to see whether they are from God, because
many false prophets have gone out into the world.

1 JOHN 4:1, NIV

Flying without Wings

❧

An oft-quoted proverb says, "Idle hands are the devil's tools." But Jessica Cox doesn't have any hands. Or arms, for that matter. So she uses her leftover body parts to live an action-packed life. From the time she was a toddler, she had to use her feet to do what other tiny tots did with their hands. She was fitted with prosthetic limbs, but they were too clunky. So she shelved those artificial arms. Jessica says that nothing can substitute for the tactile ability of flesh and bones.

From the time she was a baby, she was determined to do everything that everyone else did. At age three she was the only armless kid in her gymnastics class. At age five, she was outswimming the other kids by kicking her legs faster than they could spin their arms. She was the only armless kid in dance class, and the first one without arms to sign up for tae kwon do. As a teenager, Jessica walked down the runway as an armless model.

In 2008, she became the first woman without arms to get a pilot's license. Other pilots are amazed that everything they do in the cockpit, she can do even better with her feet. This armless wonder woman not only flies high, but has learned to kick high too. She is the first person without arms to get a black belt in tae kwon do. People are amazed when they see her pick up nunchucks with her toes and then use them with deadly accuracy. Just in case idle feet can also be the devil's tools, Jessica has learned to surf. Athletes with two hands and arms find it hard enough to wrestle with a surfboard in surging sea. But she pops right up and then defies the laws of gravity when she cuts back and forth across the waves without arms and hands to give her balance.

Jessica Cox still hasn't put a pencil between her toes and checked off all the boxes on her list of unfinished amazing feats. But she has taken up playing the piano. She and her husband, Patrick, have been working together on the theme song from the Disney movie *Frozen*. He plays with his fingers while she uses her toes. A line from "Let It Go" could have been written about Jessica Cox: "It's time to see what I can do to test the limits and break through . . ." This armless overcomer has never let any moss grow under her feet. Now she is traveling the world speaking to disabled people. She wants them to hear her amazing story so that they will be inspired to soar without wings—or legs, or sight, or any other missing part of what people call normal. Surely the last lines of the song that Jessica and Patrick are learning to play on the piano sums up her life: "Let the storms rage on. The cold never bothered me anyway!" All of us could sing those words about ourselves if we would adopt this credo:

Being challenged is inevitable. Being defeated is optional.

The LORD will withhold no good thing
from those who do what is right.

PSALM 84:11

The Ship That God
Couldn't Sink

⤸⊙⊙⤵

In the spring of 1912 the world stood in awe. A colossus was setting out on her maiden voyage. The pride of the White Star Line was a marvel of modern engineering. At 882 feet long, she was the largest ocean liner ever built. The docks were packed with Brits who came to watch this floating palace steam out to sea.

With Victorian smugness, the press proclaimed that the impossible had been done with the building of this unsinkable ship. It was the apex of Darwinian evolution. The captain boasted, "Even God himself cannot sink the *Titanic*." Man was not only master of the seas; he was greater than God himself!

Some forty-eight hours later, on a clear April night, the ship *Titanic* grazed the side of an iceberg. It was so slight that most passengers hardly felt it. Yet it tore a three-hundred-foot-long gash in the hull. Within three hours the "unsinkable" *Titanic* sank four hundred miles south of Newfoundland, taking fifteen hundred people down to a watery grave.

It was a voyage doomed by pride. The *Titanic* exuded the class system of the late nineteenth century. On its luxurious top deck were opulent staterooms reserved for society's elite like Vanderbilt, Astor, and Gould. Below them were the second-class decks for the more moderately well-off bourgeois. In the *Titanic*'s bowels were third-class decks crammed with poor immigrants and ship's workers.

The White Star Line was so paranoid about keeping the social classes separate that the doors between the decks were locked and chained. As a result, hundreds of passengers were trapped below. Hundreds more died needlessly because arrogant shipbuilders were cocksure that they had built a megaship that even God couldn't sink. As a result, they didn't think it necessary to provide enough lifeboats.

When news of the tragedy reached England, frantic relatives rushed to the Liverpool offices of the White Star Line to discover if their loved ones had survived. Outside the office was a single wooden board. On it were listed two columns of names. At the top of one was the word "SAVED." Topping the other was the word "LOST." No one was listed according to status or wealth. Astor, Vanderbilt, and Gould were listed among immigrants, waiters, and maids.

Only one thing mattered to those who rushed to the White Star offices to learn their loved ones' fates: were they lost or saved? It would do us all good to stand there at the offices of the White Star Line with those folks on a cool April morning in 1912. We should realize that the SS *Earth* is like an ocean liner plowing through cosmic seas. She is divided into social classes: winners and losers, haves and have-nots, celebrities and nobodies. So many of us are striving to move up to a higher deck. But there's an iceberg out there. Sooner than we think, a sinkable SS *Earth* will collide with the end of time. Only one thing will matter on that day: Are you saved or lost? Before we hit that iceberg, we need to grab hold of this:

Jesus Christ is not one of many ways to heaven. He is the only way.

There is salvation in no one else! God has given no
other name under heaven by which we must be saved.

ACTS 4:12

Letters from Lizzie

❧❦❧

Lizzie allowed herself to be defined by everyone else. Her readers declared her a prodigy when she published four books of poetry before she was twelve years old. By the time she was seventeen, she was the toast of the literary world. Yet her adoring public never saw her. Doctors had declared her an invalid for life after a spinal injury. Years later, her readers would have been shocked to know that England's greatest female poet was a thirty-nine-year-old recluse who seldom left her bedroom. But a struggling poet had fallen in love with her poetry. The two carried on a romance through some of the most passionate love letters ever written.

When he showed up to visit Lizzie, her Victorian parents were outraged. Her father informed the young man that he wasn't good enough and showed him the door. But Lizzie escaped her father's cold house and ran off to Italy with her young poet. In that sunny climate she regained her health and wrote her best poetry. But her angry parents gave her a new definition: ungrateful daughter.

Lizzie wrote them every week for the next decade, begging their forgiveness. After sending more than five hundred unanswered letters, she received a package from her father. She excitedly ripped it open and then burst into tears. In that parcel were all the letters that Lizzie had sent every week for ten years. None had been opened. Her poet husband tried to console his brokenhearted wife, but she never recovered from her parents' final rejection.

What parent wouldn't be thrilled to receive from their children the sort of letters written by Elizabeth Barrett with the encouragement of her poet husband, Robert Browning? We can't help but feel outrage at her parents and sorrow for Lizzie's heartbreak. But the real tragedy for Elizabeth

Barrett was in how she allowed others to define her. Doctors declared her an invalid, so she stayed in bed. Her family decided what was best for her health, so she became a recluse. It was only when her authoritarian father declared that her poet lover wasn't good enough that Lizzie finally found the courage to escape a world defined by others. Yet having once escaped their narrow boundaries, Lizzie would spend the rest of her days in a world of sadness that she allowed her unforgiving parents to create for her.

Lizzie's story whispers a warning to all of us: we cannot allow others to define who we are. We live in a fallen world of flawed sinners. By definition the assessment of others, whether positive or negative, is faulty at best and downright wrong at worst. Only the God who created and is recreating us in his image has the right to define who we are. So start living by this credo:

Strong people let God define them. Weak people let others define them.

See what great love the Father has lavished on us, that
we should be called children of God! And that is what
we are! The reason the world does not know us is that it
did not know him. . . . What we will be has not yet been
made known. But we know that when Christ appears,
we shall be like him, for we shall see him as he is.

1 JOHN 3:1-2, NIV

The Kingdom
Built on Failure

⌀☙

He was a dreamer in a world of broken dreams. When his daddy's farm went belly up, he and his brothers delivered newspapers to keep the family afloat. In high school, he was an incorrigible daydreamer. While other kids took notes, he doodled. At age sixteen, he dreamed about going off to fight with the doughboys in World War I. So he quit school, but army recruiters told him he was too young. He went off to Europe anyway, dreaming about big adventure. He ended up as a Red Cross driver, chauffeuring bigwigs to meetings far from the battlefront. He returned home to a job at a Kansas City company making commercials. He drew cartoons he had created when he was doodling away his school years. But the editor claimed he lacked imagination and good ideas. It was another failure.

So the dreamer headed out to Hollywood. He tried acting, but got nowhere. He took a job at the bank, but he hated that. In 1921, he launched Laugh-O-Grams. It flopped. When he couldn't pay the rent, he ate dog food. He created Oswald the Lucky Rabbit, but Universal Studios stole his idea. He tried to sell a cartoon about a talking mouse, but MGM rejected it. They said that a giant mouse on a big screen would terrify women. They advised the dreamer that no one would buy the idea of talking animals. Maybe that's why he couldn't get his *Three Little Pigs* distributed. When he gave a sneak preview of *Snow White and the Seven Dwarfs*, college students walked out halfway through the film. *Pinocchio* was a box-office flop, as were many of his films that would later go on to be childhood classics.

Those of us who grew up on his magic would be shocked to know that more of this dreamer's ideas failed than succeeded. Yet we are eternally grateful that Walt Disney was one of those rare dreamers who didn't let broken dreams stop the dreaming. His unending parade of memorable characters, classic films that set the record for Oscars, unforgettable songs, and Magic Kingdoms have brought joy to billions of people. His indomitable optimism might be best captured in the words of one of his classic Disney songs, *When You Wish upon a Star*. Close your eyes and you can almost hear Jiminy Cricket singing those magical lyrics. It truly doesn't make a difference who you are. This amazing story of the dreamer who overcame his broken dreams reminds us that dreams can come true if we have the courage to pursue them. As the Fairy Godmother said in Disney's *Cinderella*, "Even miracles take a little time." So don't allow delays or disappointment to kill your dreams.

If you still have a heartbeat, there's still time for your dreams.

———— ᶜᵒᑲᵒ˒ ————

"In the last days," God says, "I will pour out my
Spirit upon all people. Your sons and daughters
will prophesy. Your young men will see visions,
and your old men will dream dreams."

ACTS 2:17

The Goose
from Goose Town

తుంఁ⌒ం

He was nicknamed the Goose. Maybe it was because he hailed from Goose Town. Perhaps it was his fiery temper. When he flew into a rage, he looked like an attacking goose. Yet this peasant dreamed of becoming a gentleman. A single question haunted him: How does a goose become a swan? When he decided that religion was the answer, he became a priest. His sermons packed the Bethlehem Church of Prague, and his bishop bragged that he was the best preacher in Europe. Still Goose felt like he couldn't do enough to be God's swan.

Everything changed when he read a book by the English Reformer John Wycliffe, who claimed that regular folk could get to heaven through faith in Christ's work alone. In Wycliffe's radical theology, Goose found his answer to being transformed into heaven's swan: if his goodness wasn't enough, there was more than enough goodness from heaven!

When he began to preach Wycliffe's message, the Goose ignited a firestorm that got him labeled an archenemy of the faith. He was arrested and imprisoned in the archbishop's palace. In November of 1414 the Vatican convened a council at Constance to deal with him. There, he was jailed in a Dominican monastery, where raw human sewage from the latrines rained down on him. Though he was suffering from pneumonia, he was dragged day after day to face the full fury of a church gone mad. During a break in his trial, he was moved to a castle dungeon where he was shackled for several more months. When the council reconvened, he was carted off to a Franciscan priory, where inquisitors tortured him in a last-ditch effort to break his resolve. Goose still refused to recant.

Finally, he was excommunicated and condemned to the stake. As he neared the place of execution, someone used his nickname as a taunt: "Your goose is cooked!" Wood and straw were piled up to his neck, and a fire was set ablaze with Wycliffe's books as kindling. The Goose died singing an old, traditional hymn. Later, his tormentors scattered his ashes in the Rhine River. But that didn't stop Czech patriots from rising up with the shout, "Remember the Goose!" With that cry of freedom, they threw off the shackles of the medieval church to establish a free nation.

There is an inspiring epilogue to Goose's story. As he was chained to his stake, he uttered a prophecy: "You may cook a goose today, but a hundred years from now a man will rise up whose call for reform cannot be suppressed." Exactly 103 years to the month after Goose was arrested, Martin Luther nailed his ninety-five theses to a door in Wittenberg, igniting a reformation that could not be suppressed. On that day a cooked goose rose from his ashes and soared like a swan. Some six hundred years later the world remembers Goose by his given name, John Huss. If you long to see changes in your life, start with a secret that John Wycliffe gave to the Goose:

When your goodness isn't good enough, there is a goodness from heaven more than good enough.

———— ✦ ————

[The Lord] said to me, "My grace is sufficient for
you, for my power is made perfect in weakness."
Therefore I will boast all the more gladly about my
weaknesses, so that Christ's power may rest on me.

2 CORINTHIANS 12:9, NIV

The Parting Shot

ം🙰🙰

S ome folks are just sore losers. Long after they've lost the battle, they still insist on the final word. The British surely did on November 25, 1783. Two years earlier General Cornwallis had surrendered at Yorktown. For all practical purposes, the Revolutionary War ended that day. Yet it took two more years for the peace accords to be hammered out in Paris. During that time, twenty-seven thousand British troops remained in control of New York City. Another thirty-five thousand loyalists remained hunkered down on the Hudson.

The newly elected president of a new nation could not enter the city where he was to be inaugurated. So he waited impatiently outside Princeton, New Jersey, while negotiations moved at a snail's pace across the Atlantic. The Treaty of Paris was finally signed on September 3, 1783. Word didn't reach the president-elect until the first of November. But even then Washington couldn't march triumphantly into New York City. English troops still had to be transported home. British General Carleton was still dismantling seven years of bureaucratic apparatus. Thousands of loyalists had to hightail it out of town while British regulars were still there to protect them from mob violence. It was a logistical nightmare that had taken eight months. It would be twenty-five more days before the last longboat ferried the final redcoats to their waiting ship in the harbor.

That final day of evacuation came on November 25, 1783. General Clinton entered the city at the head of a column of smartly uniformed American dragoons. Thousands of patriots waved banners and cheered until they were hoarse. The crowning moment was to be the lowering of the Union Jack. Upon the president-elect's arrival, cannons were to fire rounds as the nation's new flag rose. But the British were still smarting over their defeat. Earlier that morning, redcoats had nailed their Union Jack to the flagpole. Then they had greased the pole so no one could shinny up to rip it down. As they watched in glee from their ships, several Americans tried to climb up the pole, only to slide back down. Officials began to panic, and the crowd grew restless. But Sergeant John Van Arsdale ran two blocks to a hardware store and made a purchase that saved the day. Pounding nails into the pole as cleats, Van Arsdale climbed to the top, tore down the Union Jack and replaced it with Old Glory.

The last laugh was on the sore losers. American ingenuity had bested British spite. On their way out of the harbor, angry British fired at Staten Island, but their shells fell harmlessly short. The British should have seen that as a harbinger of things yet to come. Eventually the sun would set on the British empire as surely as it was rising with the American flag. Sometimes it is better to take your lumps. It's hard to figure out why you lost as long as you are lashing out at others. When former General Electric CEO Jack Welch threw a temper tantrum after losing a high school hockey game, his mother said something that changed his life:

You will never be a winner until you learn to be a loser.

It's not good to eat too much honey, and
it's not good to seek honors for yourself.

PROVERBS 25:27

Seeing with Ears

❧

When Aquanetta studied her toddler's face, she discovered that he couldn't see out of his left eye. A trip to the doctor was devastating. He said that little Ben had retinoblastoma. Not only had the cancer blinded his left eye, but it was in his right one too. The toddler's only hope was chemotherapy and radiation. The treatments failed. The doctor told his mom that the only way he could save her son was to surgically remove both his eyes. After the surgery, the toddler's eye sockets were fitted with prosthetics, but he was totally blind.

Yet little Ben somehow figured out how to click his tongue the way dolphins do to find their way around. The echo that returned from his clicking was like sonar, telling him how far away an object was, and even what it was. Ben Underwood amazed everyone with his ability to use his ears to see. He learned how to shoot hoops, Rollerblade, engage in karate, play video games, and even run up and down stairs. The world was mesmerized by this blind wonder kid performing amazing feats on his YouTube videos. He became an inspiration to disabled kids everywhere.

Mostly, Ben transformed Aquanetta's life. She had lived on the ragged edge as a single mom with five kids. She was addicted to crack cocaine and homeless. After authorities took her children away, she finally went straight. When she got her kids back, she worked two jobs to hold her family together. But it was Ben's blindness that healed her, his faith in Jesus that drew her back to God. Though he was without eyes, he had an uncanny way of seeing a person's heart. He often told his mom that being sightless was an advantage because he couldn't see people based on outward appearances. As she grew spiritually, she got another pair of eyes too.

When he was fifteen, Ben's cancer returned with a vengeance. He never complained after he was told that he was terminal. As death closed in on him, he faced it as another assignment in his life. He knew he was going to see again, and the first person he would see was Jesus. Ben was buried on what would have been his seventeenth birthday. Two thousand people attended his funeral. His friend Stevie Wonder sang, and his mom shared how Ben had given her the gift of faith. In an interview she said, "He didn't just die. He put [death] on and wore it and taught me how to do it."

The amazing story of Ben Underwood is a reminder that God has given us other eyes that see so much better. There are the eyes of faith, the eyes of the heart, and the eyes of the spirit. We are all nearsighted and sometimes even blind when it comes to our normal way of seeing. We need to pray that God will let us see beneath outward appearances and beyond what appears to be reality.

A blind man who sees is better than a seeing man who is blind.

❧

Jesus placed his hands on the man's eyes again, and
his eyes were opened. His sight was completely
restored, and he could see everything clearly.

MARK 8:25

474

The Man Who
Changed Washington

೮ഗ൫ഗ৩

The Reverend Peter Miller made plenty of enemies taking on unpopular causes. But none upset the townsfolk of Ephrata in Lancaster
County more than when he left the pulpit of the Reformed church to join
a commune of mystics. Michael Widman, who took over Miller's pulpit,
especially hated the former pastor. In every sermon, the new preacher
castigated Miller as a heretic. Whenever Miller came into town, Widman
would scream insults at him. But Peter always responded to his tormentor
with a smile, saying, "God loves you, as do I."

Later, Widman quit his pulpit and purchased the town's tavern. When
the American Revolution began, he formed a militia. But pacifist Peter
Miller refused to take up arms against the British. Widman mocked him
as a coward. But the fact that Miller declined to join the militia didn't
mean that he wasn't a patriot. In fact, he was one of George Washington's
most trusted spies.

One night, when British officers visited his tavern, Widman cursed
them and their General Howe. When the redcoats drew swords and pistols, he jumped out the window. He spent days in hiding while they
combed the countryside looking for him. Fearing for his life, he turned
himself in to the British and offered to spy for them. The loudmouth who
bullied Peter Miller for not bearing arms against the English was now
spilling his guts to them. General Howe was so disgusted by Widman's
cowardice that he had him thrown out onto the streets.

The disgraced tavern owner returned to Ephrata under the cover of
dark. When his wife found out what he had done, she told everyone.

You might think that Peter Miller rejoiced that his tormentor had been exposed as a fraud. Instead, when word came that his old enemy had been sentenced to hang for treason, Miller walked seventy miles to Valley Forge to plead for Widman's life. General Washington responded, "I'm sorry, Peter, but I cannot release your friend Michael." The reverend replied, "My friend? Sir, he is my worst enemy!" Washington responded, "If you would walk all this way to beg a pardon for your worst enemy, that makes a difference. I will release him to you."

The pacifist took the coward by the arm and led him home. Widman would pay a terrible price for his treason. He lost his tavern, was despised by his wife, and became an outcast. Peter Miller was the only one who refused to abandon him. Maybe that's why a postscript to this story is so touching. Not long after Widman's escape from the gallows, the notorious traitor Joseph Bettys had a rope around his neck when his family arrived to plead for his life. Washington was so touched that he personally removed the noose from Bettys. He then issued a directive to his army to show compassion toward captured enemies. Later, he issued more pardons than any president in US history. Is it possible that the father of our country was changed the day Peter Miller pleaded for the life of his worst enemy? Maybe we can change our world by remembering this:

We will defeat our enemies when we make them our friends.

You have heard that it was said, "Love your neighbor and hate your enemy." But I tell you, love your enemies and pray for those who persecute you.

MATTHEW 5:43-44, NIV

Carpenter to the Stars

His boyish good looks got him a gig with Columbia Pictures as a contract player, earning $150 a week. Nothing came of that. So he tried his luck at Universal Studios. In 1966 he got a bit part in a forgettable film: *Dead Heat on a Merry-Go-Round*. Moviegoers weren't impressed with the movie and studio execs were even less enamored with him. One of the suits told him, "You'll never make it in this business." After that, he was poison at the studios.

What does a man with Midwest values do when his dreams of acting go up in smoke? He gets a job. So the Hollywood hopeful became a fixer-upper. In the evenings he went to a library to read books on carpentry. He progressed from handyman to carpenter to craftsman. Word got around that this magician with a hammer and saw could do high-end jobs worthy of a celebrity's mansion. That's when he met a young director named George Lucas. The director was doing a low-budget film for Fox and needed to fill a small role with a blue-collar type. Lucas was glad that he could get the carpenter for cheap. No one figured that his little movie would become box-office gold.

That surprise blockbuster may have generated Oscar buzz, but the carpenter wasn't stupid enough to quit his day job. Even big stars can wait a long time between movie roles. And this carpenter was no star. For the next four years, he plugged away at his carpentry. He got a couple of small roles from one of his customers, Francis Ford Coppola. But the man who wanted to be a star continued to be a carpenter for the stars. One day his old friend George Lucas asked if he would read a few lines with some aspiring actors who were auditioning for another low-budget movie he was directing. Lucas had no intention of casting the carpenter. He had already decided to use actor Christopher Walken in that role. He just needed the carpenter to read the lines as a stand-in. The more Lucas listened to him read, the more his gut told him that the carpenter was the perfect choice to play Han Solo in his new film, *Star Wars*. The rest, as they say, is history. The carpenter to the stars would go on to be a star. His iconic characters, Han Solo and Indiana Jones, are the stuff of movie legend.

The carpenter, who didn't get off the launching pad until he was in his midthirties, has become Hollywood royalty. No one was ever bigger than Harrison Ford. He still picks up his carpenter's tools but only as a hobby to relieve the stresses of stardom. His amazing story reminds us that most dreams in life are delayed. How we wait for success to come may define us more than any success that comes to us. Going to work as a carpenter might be even more heroic than Han Solo blasting a stormtrooper or Indiana Jones finding the Holy Grail. So remember this in your waiting times:

Doing small things well is a great thing.

———— ✿ ————

If you are faithful in little things,
you will be faithful in large ones.

LUKE 16:10

The Miracle on Flight 255

❦

The pilots were in a hurry to take off that Sunday evening. If they didn't clear the runway quickly, they wouldn't beat the noise curfew at their destination in Phoenix. So the McDonnell Douglas rumbled down the runway despite the fact that the pilots hadn't gone through their taxi checklist. Had they done so, they might have discovered that they didn't have electrical power to the aircraft takeoff system. They also would have known that the slats and flaps of their airliner were not extended enough.

As Flight 255 lifted off the Detroit runway, the jet began to rock laterally. It struck a light pole, severing eighteen feet off its left wing and igniting stored fuel. The right wing was seared off as it ripped through a car rental building. Rolling crazily out of control, the jetliner careened through traffic and slammed into an overpass on Interstate 94. It then exploded into a fireball, scattering its charred remains across several miles.

It was one of the worst tragedies in airline history. One hundred fifty-four passengers and crew members perished, as well as two motorists on the highway. Only a handful of airline crashes have killed more children and wiped out more entire families than Flight 255.

The Detroit medical examiner was one of the first people on the scene. He shook his head and declared that it was impossible that anyone could have survived. As rescuers combed through the burned corpses in the eerie darkness, it seemed that his initial assessment was correct.

Then someone heard a child's faint whimper. Miraculously, four-year-old Cecelia Cichan was huddled under the charred body of her mother, next to the remains of her father and brother. The little girl was critically injured and bearing scars that she will carry for the rest of her life, but she was alive!

After the rescuers pulled the child from the wreckage, the medical examiner closely studied the position of the bodies. He concluded that in the terrifying seconds prior to impact, somehow Cecelia's mother managed to wrap herself around her little girl. Her body not only cushioned the impact but also took the full fury of the fireball that roared through the disintegrating cabin.

Cecelia's mother's act of love gives us a glimpse of what Jesus did on the cross. Our world careens out of control like Northwest Flight 255. Like those reckless pilots, humankind has repeatedly violated the safety rules laid out by our loving Creator. As a result, the flames of destruction race toward us. But Jesus wraps himself around God's children. On the cross, he takes the full fireball of hell. Like little Cecelia, we emerge from life's wreckage wounded and scarred. But we have a second chance at eternal life because Jesus shielded us from destruction.

Thirty years later, Cecelia is a wife and mom herself. Every day she thanks God for a mother who was willing to wrap herself around her daughter. Have you allowed Jesus to wrap himself around you? If he has, are you content to remain in the only shelter that will stand up to the firestorms of life?

If Jesus is your refuge, you no longer have to search for other shelter.

[Jesus said,] "How often I have longed to
gather your children together, as a hen
gathers her chicks under her wings."

MATTHEW 23:37, NIV

When Whales Fight Back

❧

Their oils lit up the world and lubricated the machines of the Industrial Revolution. Ambergris from their bowels gave perfume its staying power. Baleen from the jaws of some whales made skirt hoops and corsets, and ivory from the teeth of others was etched with art. The whale was worth its weight in gold. So iron men set out in their wooden ships to seek slaughter and fortune. Why did these mighty leviathans allow puny humans to harvest them without a fight? They had size, speed, and the biggest brains on the planet. Bull whales were as big as whaling ships. Their raw power could crush a whaleboat and send its harpooners to a watery grave. The story of the whaling ship *Essex* proves that.

The *Essex* had journeyed from Nantucket to slaughter sperm whales two thousand miles west of South America. Its whaleboats were launched to reap the bounty. But this time a whale turned on its killers. The boat of first mate Owen Chase was splintered to pieces. The remaining whaleboats hightailed it back to the ship. The horrified crew watched helplessly as the eighty-five-foot whale charged into the *Essex* with leviathan fury and circled back to ram it again. Twenty whalers abandoned the mangled ship to embark on a three-month ordeal of survival that was both heroic and horrific. Only five men survived the voyage. And they survived only because they resorted to cannibalism.

Captain Pollard never lived down the fact that he ate his cousin. After trying whaling one more time, he ended his days as a night watchman. Owen Chase wrote a sensational book about the final voyage of the *Essex*. Chase became a captain of whaling ships and made his own fortune. But he had recurring nightmares about the fury of that one whale. He plowed through four marriages and was finally committed to an asylum for the insane. Yet there was that one line in Chase's book: "I could distinctly see him smite his jaws together, as if distracted with rage and fury." It would inspire young Herman Melville of New York City to write one of literature's towering masterpieces: *Moby Dick*.

The amazing story of a whale that fought back raises the question: Why do the powerful so often allow the few to prey on them? A few lions ravage massive herds of wildebeests that could stomp their predators to death. A handful of Bolsheviks seized Russia. A small party of fanatics liquidated six million Jews. Why do the masses of humanity allow an elite few to control and even destroy them with sharpened harpoons? Maybe we are like whales. These most powerful of God's creatures are the least aggressive. The attack on the *Essex* is the rarest of instances where one ever fought back. Self-defense is a God-given right. We should use it when evil threatens our families, churches, or country. Dietrich Bonhoeffer left us this warning:

Silence in the face of evil is itself evil. God will not hold us guiltless.

Look, I have given you authority over all the power
of the enemy, and you can walk among snakes and
scorpions and crush them. Nothing will injure you.

LUKE 10:19

Searching for Heaven

৵৹৵

John couldn't remember how often he had gone to bed with an empty belly. His single mom barely eked out a living in a tollbooth. When she dragged herself home at night, she had little energy left for her son. Maybe that's why he grew up with a legendary appetite for food, booze, women, and applause.

When his mom died, John dropped out of school and headed for Broadway. When he failed to make it on the stage, he was on to Hollywood. There he landed bit parts in forgettable movies. Along the way, he discovered a knack for slapstick comedy, a flair for music, and the ability to dance with uncommon grace. He channeled those talents into a nightclub act. But he was better known for the orgies in his hotel suite. John was drowning in a sea of booze. His Tinseltown buddies whispered, "Our funny fat friend will never make it."

But John did make it when he landed the lead role in one of television's first sitcoms: *The Life of Riley*. By 1950 he was hosting a variety show that became the highest-rated program on television. Every week, millions tuned in to watch him glide across the stage with America's most beautiful dancers. He created comic characters that are etched in television legend. None is more beloved than bumbling bus driver Ralph Kramden. He parlayed that role into his biggest sitcom, *The Honeymooners*. By now you remember John by his stage name, Jackie. Jackie Gleason starred in twenty-seven movies, recorded sixty-five albums of music, and won almost every award in stage and film before being inducted into television's Hall of Fame.

He made the whole world laugh, but his private life was no laughing matter. He made millions of dollars, only to waste his fortune trying to satisfy his insatiable appetites. Little Johnny grew into fat Jackie, but he could never fill his emptiness. He confessed to friends that there must be something better out there beyond this world. So he became obsessed with parapsychology, UFOs, and extraterrestrials, accumulating the world's largest private library on the paranormal. Jackie even built one of his luxury homes in the shape of a UFO.

Before Gleason died, Mort Sahl of WRC radio asked him, "Jackie, as a man who has seen and done it all, is there anything left that you still want to do?"

The entertainer replied, "I want to see the face of God."

Sahl chuckled uneasily. "Do you mean that you want to go to heaven?"

"I suppose so," replied Gleason. "But mostly, I want to see God." Then he quietly said, "But I don't know how to get to heaven."

Down deep, everyone wants to see God. Saint Augustine said, "God has created us for himself, and we will be restless until we find our rest in him." Are you hungry today for more? French philosopher Blaise Pascal declared, "Nothing less than heaven will ever satisfy earthlings." Gleason would agree, but he didn't know how to get to heaven. God's Son has an answer for Jackie, and for all of us:

In Jesus you see the face of God. Through him you get to heaven.

Jesus answered, "I am the way and the truth and the life. No one comes to the Father except through me."

JOHN 14:6, NIV

The Sweet Potato That Destroyed China

୧ᢙᢙᢙ

Did you know that the sweet potato destroyed China? If you find this to be an outrageous claim, just ask Charles Mann, the author of the bestselling book *1493*. Better yet, take a trip back to 1492 when Columbus landed in the Bahamas. His great contribution wasn't in discovering America. Voyagers from North Africa may have done that before Christ.

Columbus *did* speed up globalization. Horses, pigs, and smallpox were imported to the New World from Europe. Lemons, oranges, and slaves came from Africa. Spices found their way from Asia. Before Columbus sailed, the French never smoked a cigarette, the Irish hadn't tasted a potato, and the Italians had no tomato sauce. Those commodities existed only in the New World. Columbus didn't discover America, but he opened its treasure trove to the world.

That brings us to the sweet potato, a tasty tuberous root indigenous to South America, and silver, another prevalent natural resource. When a Spanish galleon stumbled upon a Chinese fleet in Manila, traders from China finally saw something they wanted from the West: the New World silver on that Spanish ship. Soon huge fleets of Spanish galleons were transporting tons of Peruvian silver to Manila in exchange for Chinese silk, porcelain, and spices. It was a trade deal made in heaven, until a Chinese merchant saw sweet potatoes on a Spanish ship.

When that trader tasted a baked sweet potato, it was love at first bite. He bought up all the potatoes in the Spanish fleet. Sure enough, the sweet potato became wildly popular in China. Soon the Spanish were bringing bags of these delectable delights along with their silver. The best part of this sweet deal was that the potatoes could be planted in the rocky soil of mountains above fertile rice valleys. But the sweet potato craze led to greedy farmers clearing forests to plant more. Eventually, tropical rains eroded the deforested mountains.

Floods came to the valleys below, wiping out the rice. Famine led to food riots. As emperors of China retreated inside the Forbidden City, warlords rose up to quell the anarchy. Millions were slaughtered. As China's infrastructure collapsed, pestilence stalked the land. A weakened China was taken over by European powers, and it did not recover until fifty years ago—all because of the sweet potato!

Here's a compelling question: What's the "sweet potato" that could destroy America—that thing we crave today that might be remembered as a tragedy four hundred years from now? Could it be our iPhones? We are as crazy about our handheld devices as the Chinese were about their sweet potatoes. Everywhere we go, people ignore each other while staring at a screen, communicating with folks who aren't in the room. Social media multitasking is producing an attention-deficit generation. Never has friendship been so cheaply gained or so easily disposed of as on Facebook. Will future generations talk about the "Apple" that hastened the end of deeply genuine relationships? Today, why don't you put your handheld devices aside and engage in some meaningful face-to-face conversation? Remember this before you pick up today's version of the sweet potato:

Posting on social media while socializing is unsocial.

———— ∞∞ ————

Let us not neglect our meeting together,
as some people do, but encourage one another.

HEBREWS 10:25

The Hero of Nanking

⋘⊚⊚⋙

They found her lifeless body in the kitchen. The fifty-four-year-old missionary had committed suicide. Earlier that year, she had swallowed a bottleful of sleeping pills. This time she succeeded at killing herself by inhaling gas from her oven. Why did Minnie end her life this way? Nobody can know for sure. But maybe an answer is tucked away in her diary: "Had I ten perfect lives, I would give them all for China."

Minnie Vautrin had worked tirelessly as a missionary educator building the Ginling Women's College in Nanking. Her school had produced the first female college graduate in Chinese history. But her tireless work was taking a toll. She wrote in her diary, "I don't know if I can go on much longer." Her friends begged her to take a furlough. And she might have, had the Japanese not invaded China. She was taking a break up north, when word came that Nanking was under siege. Close to a million Chinese refugees had poured into the city. Most foreigners had fled. But Minnie returned to Nanking. Though Ginling College was in the safe zone, she took no chances. She ordered that trenches be built, walls shored up, supplies stockpiled, and the dormitories made ready for refugees from the holocaust to come.

The siege turned into an orgy of mass murder and rape. The Japanese beheaded thousands of Chinese soldiers who had surrendered. Then they turned on the citizens of Nanking. Some three hundred thousand bodies were soon rotting in the streets. Blood flowed down gutters and into rivers. But the Chinese girls and women suffered most. As many as eighty thousand were raped in the most unspeakable ways. Refugees from the terror fled to Ginling College. Many were rape victims. Others were a step ahead of their rapists. Minnie hung out a huge American flag and stood at the gate when Japanese soldiers arrived. They waved blood-stained bayonets in her face, but she refused to budge. She stayed awake day and night, personally guarding the front gate. Once, she nodded off to sleep, only to awaken to the screams of one of her girls being raped. She never forgave herself for that. But she did save ten thousand female Chinese refugees that hid behind her walls. Later, she exhausted herself helping rape victims find their families or learn to survive on their own. But friends saw that she was slowly unraveling.

In 1940, colleagues brought the shell of a woman home. Minnie tried to recover. But on May 14, 1941, she finally gave up. There are no easy answers to why a warrior like Minnie committed suicide. She wished for ten perfect lives to give to China. Maybe she just wore herself out stuffing ten lifetimes into a single life of service. Or perhaps the answer is simpler than that: Minnie was the last victim of the Rape of Nanking. The amazing story of this Christian missionary who is still celebrated as a national hero in Communist China proves this truth:

Greatness is not in what you accumulate, but in what you give away.

Even the Son of Man came not to be served but
to serve others and to give his life as a ransom for many.

MARK 10:45

Hugs for the President

⌒⌒⌒⌒

Michael felt like an outsider. Maybe it was because he was an adopted kid, or because his Hollywood parents never had time for him. When his folks divorced, he was devastated. After his actor dad married Nancy, things got worse. His new stepmom tolerated no competition for her husband's heart. Eventually, Nancy froze Michael out of the family circle. The lonely boy longed for two things from his father: a hug and the three words "I love you." He got neither.

Michael watched from a distance as his dad went from being president of the Screen Actors Guild, to governor of California, and finally to president of the United States. The only time he was useful to his father was when he was trotted out at some political event to bolster the family image. Michael would stand there with a plastic smile hiding the pain of never cracking the circle of love shared only by Ronnie and Nancy.

Then he turned to Jesus. By grasping how much his heavenly father loved him, he got over his bitterness toward a distant earthly dad. But he still ached for his father to embrace him and say, "I love you." He was devastated when he heard that his dad was in the first stages of Alzheimer's. The clock was ticking. Would Michael ever hear those three words?

One day he saw his dad in a crowded room. His old wounds throbbed again. What would Jesus do? Michael knew the answer. He walked across the room and embraced his startled father. "Dad, I love you." For a moment, the old man was confused. Then he replied softly, "I love you, too." Michael says that every time he saw his father after that, he would hug him and say, "Dad, I love you." After a while, the old president no longer recognized who he was. But he still knew that Michael was the one who always hugged him. Whenever his son came into the room, President Reagan's face would light up as he opened his arms wide for his hug.

Michael saw his dad for the last time a few days before he slipped into a coma. As Michael pulled out of the driveway, his wife tugged at his arm and pointed to the house. His father was standing on the porch, a frail ninety-three-year-old, arms spread wide, waiting for the hug that his son forgot to give him.

At the funeral service for President Reagan, Michael was still shuffled to the outer edges. Nancy never acknowledged his presence. But he had the look of a man at peace. A few days later, he wrote in a news column, "The best gift that my father left me was the knowledge that he had a personal relationship with Jesus, and is waiting for me in heaven." Maybe you're waiting for a certain someone to show you love. Why don't you take the initiative? Reach out and give a hug. Michael would say amen to this truth:

Hugs are like boomerangs. Eventually they come back to you.

He returned home to his father. And while he was
still a long way off, his father saw him coming.
Filled with love and compassion, he ran to
his son, embraced him, and kissed him.

LUKE 15:20

Shot for Going to School

❧

She just wanted to go to school. It was a simple desire, granted to most girls in the rest of the world. But this wasn't the rest of the world. Taliban thugs controlled the Swat Valley in Pakistan. These Islamic terrorists decided that women were getting too uppity, and their daughters were going to be more so if they went to school. So they cracked down on schools that admitted girls. But the pint-size teenager spoke out against these bullies. When her blogs went viral, they decided that she was a threat to their regime.

On an October day in 2012, she was riding a school bus when a Taliban assassin jumped on board waving his gun. "Which of you girls is Malala Yousafzai?" When her friends looked at Malala, he shot her in the head. She should have died on that bus. Instead, the bullet traveled the length of her head and down into her shoulder. Pakistani doctors stopped the hemorrhaging, and she was flown to England for further surgery. As news of this cowardly shooting went global, countless millions prayed for her recovery.

When fifteen-year-old Malala woke up in the hospital, she was an international celebrity. But she wanted more than fifteen minutes of fame. Her life had been spared for a purpose. She would spend her second life as a spokesperson for the education of girls and women. She wasted little time taking advantage of her celebrity, embarking on a dizzying whirlwind of interviews, talk shows, and social media chats. She met with world leaders, spoke to opinion makers and took part in symposiums. Along the way, she managed to raise more than $8 million for girls' education, including opening a school for Syrian refugees. At only fifteen, this Pakistani teenager had become the world's most powerful advocate for women's rights.

The Taliban thugs who sent that assassin to shut her up had unleashed their worst nightmare. They must have yanked at their beards the next year when she addressed the United Nations General Assembly or the year after when she became history's youngest Nobel Peace Prize laureate. The girl that the Taliban shot now has them in her crosshairs. When she finishes her education at Oxford, she plans to go into politics. She has aspirations to follow in the footsteps of her childhood hero, the first woman prime minister of Pakistan. If Malala Yousafzai becomes Pakistan's prime minister, the Taliban may try to assassinate her the same way they did Benazir Bhutto. But don't count on it. They already tried, and it backfired. Besides that, when they killed Benazir Bhutto with a car bomb, they only succeeded in lighting a fire under Malala, who has gone on to have a far greater voice on the world stage. The Taliban just can't win for losing.

The amazing story of the girl who was shot for going to school proves once again that God is always in control. The bad guys may seem to be winning, but they are only tools in God's hands. If someone is doing you harm, take heart in something that Max Lucado said:

In God's hands intended evil becomes eventual good.

———— ✠ ————

The LORD turns my darkness into light.

2 SAMUEL 22:29, NIV

The Possibilities and Limits of Forgiveness

❦

Eighty-nine of Simon's relatives were murdered in the Nazi Holocaust. As far as he knew, his wife was one of them. He barely escaped death several times while funneled through five SS killing centers. One day while he was still imprisoned, a nurse came looking for a Jew. Any Jew would do. An SS officer had made a deathbed request to talk to one. She led Simon to a man swathed in bandages. He had been burned over most of his body; only his eyes were visible, and he couldn't talk above a whisper.

The Nazi officer ordered Simon to sit on the edge of his bed. He introduced himself as Karl Seidl and said that he was raised a Catholic and had joined the SS against his father's wishes. He then gasped out his final confession as if this Jew were his priest. Seidl spared none of the horrifying details of his years as a Jew killer. He told Simon about the day he found a house where two hundred Jews were hiding and ordered his men to set the building afire. He described the screams of people burning alive. He added that he had personally shot every man, woman, and child who had tried to escape that inferno.

When Seidl finally finished his confession, the room was deathly still. Simon shook with hatred. But SS Officer Seidl desperately wanted absolution. In the mind of this dying Nazi, Simon sat in the place of every Jew he had dehumanized or murdered. Seidl whispered with urgency, "Jew, will you forgive me?" Simon sat for several seconds looking down at the SS officer and then got up and walked away, leaving Karl Seidl to die without absolution.

Two years later, Simon's camp was liberated. He had survived the last year on two hundred calories a day. Miraculously, he was reunited with his wife. He went on to become the world's most celebrated Nazi hunter. Until he died at age ninety-six, he fought anti-Semitism and kept the memory of the Holocaust alive.

Yet Karl Seidl haunted Simon until the day he died. Simon constantly tortured himself with questions about whether he was right in refusing to forgive the SS officer. He remembered a day when his work detail passed a German military cemetery. He saw a sunflower on each grave and wondered if there was one on Seidl's. In 1976, Simon Wiesenthal tried to bury the ghost of Karl Seidl by writing a bestseller entitled *The Sunflower*. In it he discussed the possibilities and limits of forgiveness, asking the questions that haunted him since he walked away from Seidl. In his book, fifty-three distinguished theologians, jurists, human rights activists, Holocaust survivors, and victims of other genocides respond to his questions. They prove one thing: there are no easy answers to forgiveness. Apart from Jesus there are no ultimate answers.

Some two thousand years ago, hardened religious leaders nailed a rabbi from Nazareth to a cross. This Jew responded to those who dehumanized and murdered him, "Father, forgive them." Simon Wiesenthal thought that forgiveness was a gift you give someone else and Karl Seidl wasn't worthy. If you think someone hasn't earned your forgiveness, you might want to remember this:

Forgiveness is the gift that you give yourself.

----- ⚘ -----

If you forgive those who sin against you,
your heavenly Father will forgive you.

MATTHEW 6:14

494

A Resurrection in
the Valley of Death

୬ୄ୵ଡ଼ଡ଼ୄ

W hen Phil and Stan kissed their wives good-bye, it was for the last
time. On September 19, 1968, the Iowa farm boy and his buddy
from Australia climbed into the highlands of New Guinea, going where no
Westerner had ventured before. But Stan and Phil wanted to bring Jesus
to the Yali people. Their vision was audacious. The Yali were headhunters
and cannibals, living in the Stone Age. These most-feared of the mountain
tribes were called lords of the earth.

Officials warned Phil and Stan that it was sheer suicide to enter the
Yali heartland. But the Iowa farm boy and the Australian outbacker were
not easily cowed. They had already hacked their way through impassable
forests, carved an airfield out of tangled jungle, and built a mission station
with their own hands. Stan had fought the Japanese in World War II, survived a ruptured appendix in the jungle, and pulled five Yali arrows from
his body in an earlier attack. Phil said, "They can't kill me. I died the day
that I gave myself to Jesus."

As the missionaries went over the mountains into the Seng Valley,
they were entering misty shadowlands of witchcraft, revenge killings,
and human sacrifices. Distant drums warned that shamans were stirring
up their people to destroy these white devils. On September 25, 1968,
Stan Dale and Phil Masters went down under a hail of arrows as the
Yali swarmed over them. Remembering that these missionaries had talked
about a resurrection and fearing that they might come back to haunt
them, the Yali hacked their bodies to pieces, ate them, burned their bones,
and scattered their ashes into the wind.

When Yali drums carried the news of their death down the valleys of the Snow Mountains, it seemed like a monumental tragedy. They left behind two grieving widows and ten orphaned children. No one was available to finish the translation of the Bible into Yali. Persecution broke out against the handful of Yali believers. Stan Dale's widow went back to Australia, never to return. Phil Masters's widow cried out in despair, "Why, God? What did we do wrong?" For all practical purposes, the vision to reach the Yali was over.

But God had other plans. Three months later, a plane crashed in Yali territory. Everyone on board died except for a nine-year-old boy. A Yali believer found and hid him. When a party of missionaries came to retrieve the boy, Yali leaders were sure that the spirits of Stan and Phil had returned. In fear, they invited the missionaries to share their gospel. Today there are one hundred churches among the Yali. The lords of the earth have come to Christ and are sending their own missionaries to neighboring tribes. Who would have guessed that fierce cannibals would become gospel preachers? When your dreams have been shattered, remember the story of two martyred missionaries and a tribe of headhunters. What's true for them is also true for you:

It's not over until it's over, and then it's still not over.

⁓⊙⊙⊙⁓

As for me, I know that my Redeemer lives, and he
will stand upon the earth at last. And after my body
has decayed, yet in my body I will see God!

JOB 19:25-26

The Flood That Changed America

⌒⊙⌒

I n our conceit, we often think we can defy natural law and get away with it. Nothing proves that more than the Great Mississippi Flood of 1927. For millennia the mighty Mississippi rolled southward like a mile-wide tide. When heavy rains fell and fed it on its way down, this sluggish river became a flood, overflowing its banks and turning plains on either side into river bottom. For thousands of years, these floods gifted the earth, providing a rich ecological soup for a food chain that filled the prairies and skies with abundant wildlife. As the floods receded, they left behind the most fertile lands in the world.

But America went west, and the Mississippi became a great highway, moving people and commerce. Cities and towns were built along its banks to profit from the wealth that traveled its rolling tide. Farms were built on its rich bottomlands, and towns grew up to market their produce. Floods that once gifted the land were now viewed as monsters that destroyed property and lives. So the mighty Mississippi had to be corralled and controlled. In the 1870s, levies were built along the river. America's best engineers protested that they would only compress the river and increase its destructive power, but their warnings were ignored.

For more than fifty years, those levies held. But successive floods created cracks and crevices. In 1927, disaster struck. The flood of the century roared down from the north, blowing out levy after levy, flooding twenty-seven thousand square miles, leaving a million people homeless, and killing hundreds. The damages were close to eight billion in today's dollars. This natural disaster would change America. Greedy and racist officials opened the levies to flood the farms and neighborhoods of African Americans. The Republican administration rushed to help whites but ignored blacks. Thousands of people of color were pressed into labor gangs to clean up the mess. Their misery birthed the blues, sparked an exodus of southern blacks to northern cities, and turned them away from the party of Abraham Lincoln to the Democratic Party.

The Great Mississippi Flood of 1927 allowed the federal government to take over the corralling of the Mississippi with stronger levies. Old Man River now rolls subdued and docile down to the Gulf. Once rich bottom-lands are ingested with fertilizers. Wildlife has disappeared. The silt that once built marshlands no longer flows as thick. As wetlands disappear, the seas move closer to New Orleans. So do hurricanes like Katrina. But instead of the abundance left behind by Mississippi floods, hurricanes leave only death and destruction.

The amazing story of this 1927 flood reminds us God is the creator and architect of natural laws. We cannot build cities in floodplains or in the path of hurricanes without consequences. Nor can we rearrange nature without affecting its ecological balance. We can't defy the laws of gravity by jumping off high cliffs or sow our wild oats without expecting a harvest. The sooner we learn to respect and obey God's laws, the healthier and happier we will all be.

God has built inevitable consequences into his unalterable laws.

They have planted the wind and
will harvest the whirlwind.

HOSEA 8:7

Old Woom's Winnie

∽◕◔◔∾

Great things were expected of this firstborn son of a British lord. But the person who was perhaps the greatest influence on his life was not someone with prestige and power; it was his nanny. That woman became the love of this lonely boy's life. As an adult, he often shed tears when he remembered the substitute mother he affectionately called Old Woom. She gave him the nickname Winnie.

When little Winnie wasn't frolicking in the park with Old Woom, he sat alone at his bedroom window watching soldiers drill across the boulevard. He imagined that if he could come back from war as a hero, he might earn his parents' love.

At age seven he began his odyssey through prep schools. He hardly ever saw his folks, except for fleeting moments during holidays. But that didn't keep him from driving himself to make them proud. Not even a speech impediment could stop him once he set his mind on something. This earned him another nickname: pigheaded. He wore that unkind epithet as a badge of honor.

He applied to his nation's leading military college, only to fail the entrance exam three times. Once he got in, he barely made the grades to stay in. As a young officer his career was undistinguished. He came home to run for parliament and was defeated. He headed off to South Africa to fight in the Boer War, but was captured.

When Winnie got back home again, he rose in the ranks of government with the help of family connections. He was finally elected to parliament, but was condemned when he ordered troops to fire on striking miners. During World War I, as first lord of the Admiralty, he committed the greatest blunder of his career when he insisted that British troops seize Gallipoli in Turkey. Over a million soldiers were drawn into that unnecessary battle. Military brass warned Winnie that an advance into the teeth of Turkish artillery was suicidal. But he wouldn't back down. One admiral resigned, calling Winnie pigheaded. Before this debacle ended in defeat, there were a quarter of a million casualties on both sides. Winnie was sacked.

But with his trademark pigheadedness, he bounced back to become chancellor of the exchequer. Against all advice, he pigheadedly made monetary changes that plunged England into a depression. Again he was fired. When he stood pigheaded against his party's unwillingness to take a stand against Communism and Nazism, Winnie spent his next decade in political isolation. No one would have guessed then that his nation would soon need his pigheadedness. The world remembers Winnie as Prime Minister Winston Churchill, whose refusal to back down saved the world from totalitarianism.

Later, he went on to win the Nobel Prize. In 2002, a BBC poll named him the greatest Briton of all time. When asked the secret to his success, Churchill replied, "Success is the ability to go from failure to failure with no loss of enthusiasm." If you are discouraged today, you might want to recall a line in a speech that pigheaded Winnie gave at Harrow during the worst days of World War II:

Never give in, never give in, never, never, never, never give in!

As for you, be strong and courageous,
for your work will be rewarded.

2 CHRONICLES 15:7

Premature Burials

❧

Most folks have never heard of *taphophobia*—the fear of being buried alive. It may sound like the stuff of Gothic horror, but for some, there has been good reason for taphophobia. During the Middle Ages, plague victims often dug their way back out after being too hastily buried by frightened grave diggers. John Duns Scotus was one of the most venerated scholars in the 1300s. He was buried with the full honors befitting a man of his esteem. The next day they discovered his bloody-handed corpse beside his gravesite. He didn't die before he was laid in the coffin, but he did kill himself clawing his way out.

Lest you think that bungled burials are a thing of the past, you might google what happened in Peraia, Greece, during 2014. A woman was pronounced dead from cancer. But after she was buried, her children heard her screaming. When the body was exhumed, the autopsy showed that she had died of a cardiac arrest in her coffin. Could there be anything more terrifying than being buried alive?

The thought of a premature burial caused women in the Victorian era to go into hysterics. One time an attending physician and medical inspector had certified that a man was dead. He was dressed in his funeral suit and laid in the coffin. A splendid service was conducted, and the mourners processed to the graveyard. Just as the coffin was about to be lowered into the hole, the supposed dead man awoke from his trance. When the vicar and undertaker sent a bill for their services, he refused to pay on the grounds that he hadn't ordered them. The vicar and undertaker sued him in court. There was a wave of taphophobia when news of this sensational lawsuit was published in 1842.

This hysteria was heightened by one of Edgar Allan Poe's later horror stories, "The Premature Burial," which was published complete with graphic illustrations. No one profited more from this panic than the makers of coffins. Newspapers and periodicals carried etchings of caskets with air tubes attached. Others came with megaphones and bugles to alert those above ground that all was not well below. Some had ingenious contraptions with strings to be attached to the limbs of the buried and connected to flags that could be raised. The manufacturers of these fail-safe coffins made a killing off of Victorian taphophobics. We may be undecided about whether a story of premature burials is creepy or comedic, but it reminds us that there is one thing worse than being buried alive—and that's coming back to life after you are dead and not being prepared to meet your Maker. Maybe you've wagered your eternity on an assumption that death is the end. But it is the riskiest wager you will ever make. Those of us who've put our trust in Jesus for our eternal life are not worried about what takes place after the funeral. We have already made our arrangements for a certain journey beyond the grave.

What we do in life will echo in eternity.

———— ✺ ————

Each person is destined to die once and
after that comes judgment.

HEBREWS 9:27

The Compassionate Puritan

❧⊙❧

Few people have lived or died as well as Jon. He graduated from Yale at the top of his class at age seventeen. While still a teenager, he wrote a paper on metaphysical theology. He then penned a treatise on atomic theory two hundred years before Albert Einstein's work on the topic. Many scholars rate Jon as America's greatest philosopher. His books on metaphysics are masterpieces. No other American has produced more national leaders among his descendants.

Shortly before Jon became the president of Princeton, his scientific curiosity focused on advances in medicine. The science of inoculation was primitive, but when smallpox ravaged colonial America, Jon volunteered to be a human guinea pig. On March 22, 1758, several days after he was inoculated with an experimental vaccination, he died from the disease.

Jon possessed one of the most brilliant minds in American history. His quest for knowledge was insatiable. But if you assume that he took that inoculation for the advancement of medical science, you would be wrong. Most folks would find it hard to believe that he did it because of compassion. History remembers him for his famous sermon "Sinners in the Hands of an Angry God." His portraits reveal a stern Puritan. His call for repentance sparked the revivals that shook colonial America. When he rebuked church leaders for their hypocrisy, he made enemies in high places. After he called out his parishioners for their lukewarm faith, they fired him. History recalls Jonathan Edwards either as a brilliant-but-coldly-rational philosopher or a hellfire-and-brimstone preacher.

Most folks don't know that he spent a year's salary to purchase a black slave and then set her free. He begged Christians everywhere to do the same. Later, he worked among the Mohicans and took up their cause when most colonists despised them. His home was often filled with individuals from various Native tribes, much to the distress of his neighbors. After he was thrown out of his church, he was offered pulpits in prestigious parishes but became a missionary to the impoverished Housatonic tribe of New Jersey. He made even more enemies by going after crooked politicians who tried to steal their land.

When his Native neighbors began dying by the thousands from smallpox, he took that high-risk inoculation in hopes that a cure would be found. He refused to heed friends who argued that his life was too important to risk. The love that compelled him to plead with colonists to flee from hell also drove him to die for those they despised as savages. In his final hours, Edwards's throat was so constricted that he could hardly eat, drink, or breathe. With his final gasping words, he instructed his daughter Lucy to give a portion of his estate to the poor. His physician said that he had never seen a man die with as much calmness and grace as Edwards. Jonathan Edwards not only died well but also lived better by lifting others' burdens. This story of the third president of Princeton University should inspire us with this truth:

A life well lived is not measured in how many positions we've held, but in how many people we've helped.

✧

Pure and genuine religion in the sight of God the Father means caring for orphans and widows in their distress.

JAMES 1:27

Loving Daddy's Killer

⟨◦⟨∅⟩◦⟩

Steve was only five years old when his pilot daddy flew that Piper cruiser into Ecuador's jungles. Five missionaries were determined to make contact with the Waodani. The neighboring Quechuas called them the Auca, a term that means "naked savages." What else would you call people who spear their incapacitated elderly to death and bury their unwanted babies alive? Both Quechua and Spaniard saw the Waodani as wild dogs to be hunted down and destroyed. But no one dared to venture into the heart of Waodani country where savages of the spear and blowgun showed no mercy to intruders.

Those five missionaries were signing their own death warrants. But one of them, Jim Elliot, lived by a credo that they all shared: "He is no fool who gives what he cannot keep to gain what he cannot lose." The place where they landed became the river of no return when Waodanis attacked the five intruders, spearing them repeatedly and hacking them to death with machetes. The savagery of their martyrdom shocked the world. The response of their families was even more shocking. Jim's widow, Elisabeth, wrote a book called *Through Gates of Splendor*, which tells the story of the five martyrs. The murdered pilot's sister Rachel Saint went with Elisabeth to live among the Waodani killers, who didn't perceive women as a threat. Rachel lived there for almost four decades before dying of cancer. All of the killers came to Christ, and Rachel became a sister to Mincaye, the man who had speared her brother to death.

When Steve began to spend the summers with his Aunt Rachel, Mincaye complained that the boy was useless in the jungle. Rachel replied, "You killed his father, now you teach him how to live." Mincaye became a surrogate father to Steve, training him in the ways of the jungle. When

Steve was fourteen, he asked Mincaye to baptize him in the river near the spot where Mincaye had killed Steve's father, Nate Saint. When Rachel died, the Waodoni asked Steve Saint to live with them. He and his family spent a year and a half in their village. His children came to revere Mincaye as their grandfather.

A reporter for *USA Today* probably spoke for lots of folks when he said that he could "forgive Mincaye, maybe. But love him, that's morbid." Steve admits that it would be, if God wasn't in the equation. He confesses that it was painful losing his dad, but God turned evil around for good. He got a great father in Mincaye, amazing adventures as a jungle boy, and life with Stone Age tribesmen, and his kids got an awesome Waodani grandfather. Steve is most grateful that the martyrdom of those five missionaries in 1956 motivated thousands of people to take the message of Jesus Christ to tribes like the Waodani. This amazing story of Mincaye and the Saint family is another reminder that life is not a series of random, freak events. God knows exactly what he is doing.

God specializes in turning crucifixions into resurrections.

You intended to harm me, but God intended
it all for good. He brought me to this position
so I could save the lives of many people.

GENESIS 50:20

506

Let's Roll

⋘⊙⊙⋙

Forty passengers and crew members who boarded the United flight in Newark thought they were headed west. Four others were intent on another destination. About the same time, fifteen other al-Qaeda members were boarding three other flights—one in Washington, DC, and two in Boston. Their objective was to turn these airliners into guided missiles. Their targets couldn't be more strategic: the World Trade Towers, the symbol of America's financial might; the Pentagon, the brain center of her military power; and likely the Capitol, the emblem of her democratic ideals. These nineteen terrorists were not so intent on killing thousands of people as they were on murdering the concept of America.

As the thirty-three unsuspecting passengers settled back for a five-hour flight to the West Coast, they couldn't have imagined that the other four were ready to storm the cockpit and wrest control of Flight 93 from its seven crew members. But the unimaginable happened. Now the jetliner was turning toward Washington, DC, as a terrorist missile in the hands of kamikaze pilots. To this day, no one knows whether their target was the Capitol dome or the White House—but the worst-case scenario would have been the Capitol building with its congress members, senators, and other government officials. A hit there would have plunged the US into chaos.

The terrorists warned passengers that they had a bomb and would detonate it if anyone got out of line. But news of the other attacks had reached Flight 93. They knew that they were part of a bigger plot, that their jetliner was now a guided missile. They didn't know the target, but they knew that the results would be catastrophic. So they agreed to take back Flight 93, or die trying. Loved ones on the ground begged them by cell phone to play it safe. But the stakes were too high. Tom Burnett made a last call to his wife: "I know that we are all going to die. There's three of us who are going to do something about it. I love you, honey." Todd Beamer was heard on an open line: "Are you guys ready? Let's roll!" Flight attendant Sandy Bradshaw made her final call: "Everyone's running to first class. I've got to go. Bye."

The cockpit recorder captured the final minutes. As passengers tried to break through the cockpit door, the hijackers took the jet into a roll. But these determined heroes kept battering the door. So the terrorists made a desperate decision to take the jetliner into a nosedive. It slammed into a Pennsylvania field at 580 miles per hour, instantly killing everyone on board, scorching hundreds of acres, and scattering debris in an eight-mile radius. The impact buried the black box twenty-five feet down. One can only imagine the damage that jetliner could have done to the Capitol. This amazing story encourages us not to play it safe while the bad guys hijack our families, churches, institutions, culture, and country. Todd Beamer's final words call us all to action: "Are you guys ready? Let's roll!"

It's better to die for a cause than to live a life that is worthless.

───── ∾⊙∾ ─────

If our hope in Christ is only for this life, we are
more to be pitied than anyone in the world.

1 CORINTHIANS 15:19

The Army
That Attacked Itself

࿐

The cartoon character Pogo famously said, "We have met the enemy and he is us." He could have been talking about the fiasco that took place in 1788. The armies of Austria were all that stood between Europe and the military might of the Ottoman Empire. They had beaten the Turks to Karansebes in present-day Romania. Whoever held Karansebes would control the Danube River. The Austrians knew that the Turkish armies of the Ottoman sultan were also racing toward this strategic city. Mounted scouts were sent out to reconnoiter the surrounding area. They didn't spot any Turks, but they did come upon a band of gypsies. While inspecting their wagons, the scouts found a large store of schnapps, which the enterprising gypsies offered at cut-rate prices. It wasn't long before the Austrians were getting rip-roaring drunk.

The carousing of the scouts attracted a column of infantrymen who asked their compatriots to share their schnapps. The soused scouts refused, and the thirsty infantrymen threatened to seize their liquor by force, which led to fisticuffs. In the melee, someone fired off a shot. That's when chaos ensued. Half-drunk scouts and fully spooked infantrymen began shooting at each other. Then someone yelled, "The Turks are attacking!" Panic over Turks replaced animosity over schnapps, and they all hightailed it back to Karansebes.

Just when things couldn't get any crazier, they did. The Austrian army was made up of mercenaries from several nations. When the sentries yelled, "Halt! Halt!" in German, those rushing back took it to be "Allah! Allah!" Pandemonium broke out in Karansebes, as soldiers began screaming that the Turks were upon them. An officer ordered the artillery to fire away. Cannonballs hit no imaginary Turks that night, but did wreak havoc among real Austrians. Panicked soldiers shot at shadows and anything else that moved in the night. It would be as laughable as a scene out of the movie *Blazing Saddles* if ten thousand Austrians hadn't been injured or killed that night.

Two days later the Ottomans arrived, expecting a battle. What they found was the carnage of an army that had destroyed itself. The Turks easily seized the city of Karansebes. So who won the Battle of Karansebes and who lost? The answer is the same. The Austrian army was the only one in history to win and lose the same battle. Some skeptics think that such a battle could not have happened, but the evidence is quite compelling. Those of us who have watched spouses quarrel or families feud or churches split or nations dissolve into civil wars know that armies often turn in on each other instead of fighting the enemy out there. These battles can start over things as silly as sharing the schnapps. Are you at war with loved ones right now? There are too many *real* foes out there to be wasting our energy fighting our natural allies. Here's a play on the words Sun Tzu wrote:

He will win who knows when to fight and when not to fight.

———— ⚬⊙⚭ ————

We are not fighting against flesh-and-blood enemies,
but against evil rulers and authorities of the unseen
world, against mighty powers in this dark world,
and against evil spirits in the heavenly places.

EPHESIANS 6:12

The Curse of
the Control Freak

e⊙⊙౿

He was as famous for his craziness as for his paintings that sold for as much as $10,000 in the 1940s. He saw himself as the last of the bohemians: an avant-garde artist in a world of bongos, beards, and beatniks. Hollywood celebrities were drawn to his hillside ranch for wild parties that he hosted in a toga worn over red long underwear. As they wandered his forty-eight-acre junkyard, they marveled at a mishmash of sculptures created out of salvaged wood, rusted bedsprings, and other recycled junk. When the artist stripped naked to show off his body covered with tattoo art, it was the signal for a night of free love, drugs, and alcohol to begin. J. H. Zorthian was a hippie years before the Age of Aquarius.

Most of his Hollywood celebrity guests could not have guessed that there was a time when this crazy Armenian was a conventional mural artist. Back then he lived in a Pasadena neighborhood with an heiress wife and three children. One morning he read a newspaper account about a child who had been run over by a car. Fearing that his own children might suffer a similar fate, he began plotting how he could guarantee his kids' safety in an accident-prone world.

Zorthian's paranoia drove him to sell his home on the streets of Pasadena and purchase a twelve-acre plot in the Altadena Hills at the end of a winding, deserted road. At each turn, the artist posted a sign: "Children at Play." He constructed a fenced-in play area that no automobile could approach. Then he built a house with every safety design possible. Finally, he added a garage. Only one car was allowed to drive up to it, and that was Zorthian's.

After the ranch house was finished, he walked the property in deep thought, considering what other dangers might threaten his children. His last project to tackle was the garage. What if he backed out and accidentally ran over one of the children? Zorthian quickly sketched plans for a protected turnaround, but before the concrete could be poured, heavy rains came. It would have been finished by that weekend if it hadn't rained. Instead, when Zorthian had to back out of the garage on Sunday, his toddler son, Tiran, ran into the path of the car and was killed.

Friends said that J. H. Zorthian never recovered from that tragedy. It caused him to plunge into a free-flowing bohemian lifestyle. Could it be that there's a happy medium between the two extremes of control freak and irresponsible? The more you reflect on Zorthian's story, the more this makes sense:

Do the best you can. Then relax and leave the results to God.

∞

We can make our own plans, but the LORD gives the
right answer. People may be pure in their own eyes,
but the LORD examines their motives. Commit your
actions to the LORD, and your plans will succeed.

PROVERBS 16:1-3

The Scandalous Missionary

↻↺

A clipper ship sailed from Liverpool on the winds of prayer. On board was a wild-eyed, twenty-one-year-old visionary on his way to China as a missionary. In 1853 Hudson Taylor might as well have been going to the moon. Only a handful of Western missionaries had ever ventured to this land teeming with millions.

After landing in Shanghai, he was appalled to discover that locals dismissed missionaries as agents of colonial powers promoting Western religion and culture to destroy the Chinese way of life. Most missionaries hid behind the walls of their compounds, spoke through interpreters, and were waited on by Chinese servants. When they left their compounds, they were often carried on litters by porters. Their sense of superiority was palpable.

So Hudson traded in his European fashions for Chinese clothes. He shaved his head and grew pigtails. Instead of spending time with English businessmen and diplomats, he lived among Chinese peasants, eating their food, observing their customs, and mastering their language. Older missionaries were scandalized by the behavior of this upstart. Fellow Europeans called him a traitor to his own kind. Hudson stubbornly replied, "China is not to be won for Christ by ease-loving men and women. . . . In everything and at every time—even life itself must be secondary." He set out to the interior where no white man had gone before. After four years he had a handful of converts and a bad case of hepatitis.

So he returned to England, crisscrossing the country looking for helpers. His Chinese garb and pigtails may have caused a sensation, but there was almost no interest for China in the churches. Hudson fell into one of his frequent bouts of depression. He lamented, "Can all the Christians in England sit still with folded arms while these multitudes [in China] are perishing?" At the end of his rope, he got a vision: he would call men and women to radical mission. They would go to China without raising support, trust in the Lord to supply their needs, be required to adopt a Chinese lifestyle, and go inland to the most difficult places. He called his audacious idea China Inland Missions. A year later, Hudson Taylor left England with his family and sixteen raw recruits.

For the next thirty years, he wore himself out. He saw as many as two hundred patients a day as a midwife, and directed more than half of all the missionaries in China. Along the way, his wife passed away at age thirty-three, and four of his eight children died before the age of ten. He battled bouts of depression and finally collapsed with a complete physical and emotional breakdown. But his scandalous vision of a radical Christian life brought thousands of missionaries to the Far East. Were he to come back today he would be shocked to see that by 2030 China will have more churchgoers than America. Hudson Taylor's amazing story reminds us of something we often forget in an age of ease-loving faith: true Christianity is countercultural. It is radical. It is even scandalous. To paraphrase David Platt:

Christianity isn't about catering to, but abandoning ourselves.

───── ∽◌∾ ─────

I want to know Christ and experience the mighty power
that raised him from the dead. I want to suffer with
him, sharing in his death, so that one way or another
I will experience the resurrection from the dead!

PHILIPPIANS 3:10-11

When Dogs Routed
a Tank Division

⁂

Some of the most colossal blunders have taken place in military history. Many have been devastatingly tragic. Others have been downright silly, like the one that happened in Russia during World War II.

The Soviet Union was reeling under the withering assault of the German blitzkrieg. Within weeks, the Nazi advance had killed four million Russian soldiers. It seemed that Moscow would soon fall. At the cutting edge of Hitler's war machine were the panzer divisions. These sleek tanks raced forward like chariots of fire, leaving a wake of devastation and death. The clumsy and antiquated Russian tanks were no match for the German juggernaut.

These were frantic days in the Kremlin war room. Joseph Stalin demanded quick answers. When the generals and commissars didn't have any, they were sacked or shot. Panic and despair set in. No one knew how to stop the dreaded panzers, until a hotshot young commissar came up with an ingenious idea: dog bombs. His plan was to train dogs to run up under the advancing German tanks with bombs strapped to their backs. The commissar convinced his skeptical superiors that his plan was foolproof.

Hundreds of dogs went through a quick but intensive training program. The day came to put Operation Dog Bomb into action. Russian and German tanks were massing across from each other when a small convoy of Russian trucks pulled up on the field between the two armies. Canines jumped out of the trucks, bombs strapped to their backs. Russian trainers pointed them toward the panzers and blew their whistles.

The Germans looked on in astonishment as packs of dogs came running at them. Suddenly, the dogs stopped and looked both ways in confusion. Then, they turned tail and ran back toward the Soviet battle group and up under *their* tanks. Russian tanks were blowing up right and left. The Russian battle line collapsed in chaos as drivers tried desperately to get away from the pursuing dog bombs.

Surely this was one of the most bizarre battles in the annals of military warfare. Never before or since has a pack of dogs routed a division of tanks! How did this fiasco happen? It seems that the boys in the Kremlin made a slight miscalculation in their preparation. They trained their dogs using *Russian* tanks. The commissar who conceived the idea of dog bombs disappeared from sight after this fiasco.

So many battles have been lost because of bad planning and preparation. The best dog bombs in the world won't work if the dogs are trained on the wrong tanks. Wars are won and lost in the training that takes place before battles begin. The small battles that you face every day are the basic training for bigger wars ahead. Learn your lessons well today so that you will be prepared for what comes tomorrow. Take time to train your children and prepare your family for inevitable battles ahead. You might want to remember this key to success:

The will to prepare is more important than the will to succeed.

———— ✦ ————

Physical training is good, but training for
godliness is much better, promising benefits
in this life and in the life to come.

1 TIMOTHY 4:8

From Rags to Riches

❧

She has written make-believe stories filled with magic, but her personal story may be the most magical one of all. Joanne was raised in grinding poverty. On top of that, she cared for her mom who battled debilitating multiple sclerosis. During that difficult time, she began to write notes for a book on paper napkins she found on tabletops. She was twenty-five when her mother passed away and she was finally able to devote more time to her book. To make ends meet, she taught English in Portugal where she met Jorge. After a miscarriage, they got married, and she later gave birth to Jessica. But her rocky marriage imploded. So she headed home to the UK with little Jessica and only three completed chapters in her briefcase.

It was hard to concentrate living in a cramped apartment as the single parent of a baby, while jobless and flat broke. She worked on her book in cafés while Jessica slept in a nearby baby carriage, but she was getting nowhere. Joanne's world was unraveling. She had lost her mother, suffered a miscarriage, and seen her marriage collapse in only thirteen months, and she was now living on welfare. The book she had sketched on paper napkins was going nowhere. As far as she was concerned, she was the biggest failure on earth. She fell into a suicidal depression. Yet somehow she found the resiliency to finish those last chapters.

Joanne's struggles continued when several publishing houses rejected her manuscript. Finally, Bloomsbury of London decided to take a chance on a story about Harry, Hogwarts, and wizardry. Even then they asked her to change her name, Joanne Katherine Rowling, to J. K. Rowling because they were afraid that boys wouldn't read a book authored by a woman.

The world should be glad that Bloomsbury took a chance on Harry Potter. Since that first book, Joanne K. Rowling has sold almost five hundred million copies in her series, won scores of literary awards, and had her novels turned into blockbuster movies. She now has a net worth of $1 billion. Some fifteen years after she was penniless and suicidal, J. K. Rowling was listed in *Forbes* as one of the richest and most powerful women in the world. Yet she never forgets her roots. Maybe that's why she has given a large portion of her earnings to charities.

This amazing rags-to-riches story reminds us that it's always too soon to give up. Night is always darkest just before dawn. The psalmist says that weeping may last for a night, but joy comes in the morning. The key is to keep on plugging away until the dawn breaks. If you are going through a dark time, you might want to take heart from a mantra that J. K. Rowling repeated during her blackest nights:

Happiness can be found even in the darkest of times, if only one remembers to turn on the light.

⸙

Night is the time when people sleep and drinkers get drunk. But let us who live in the light be clearheaded, protected by the armor of faith and love, and wearing as our helmet the confidence of our salvation.

1 THESSALONIANS 5:7-8

Conceived in Shame,
Born for Greatness

୧୦୬୭୭

The boy was an outcast, rejected by his father and scorned by his brothers. History remembers his exploits, but the shame of his youth is hidden away in ancient Torah commentaries. It is well known by Jewish rabbis but seldom talked about among Christian scholars.

The boy's father, Yishai, was a member of Judaism's high court, revered as one of the four guardians of the Torah, a man of considerable wealth, and a descendant of Israel's most famous family. He lived on a ranch outside the village of Beit Lechem, south of Jerusalem. His beautiful wife, Nitzevet, gave him seven handsome sons who all grew up to be mighty warriors.

Yishai's life should have been idyllic, except for a single blot on his family name. His grandfather had married a widow from a nearby pagan nation. Any descendants born of that forbidden union were unclean to the tenth generation. Torah law, which Yishai so zealously guarded, said that he and his boys were impure because of his grandfather's illicit marriage.

Over the years, Yishai became obsessed about this stain on his family name. But he did rejoice in the fact that God had given him seven sons. And he wanted to keep it at seven because that was the Hebrew number for blessing. So he shut his bedroom door to his wife. But Nitzevet was determined to bear another child. After tricking and seducing Yishai, she conceived an eighth son.

Yishai never forgave her. Nor did he accept the child of that deception. He encouraged his other sons to reject their kid brother. The little boy ate at a separate table with his disgraced mother, and his brothers publicly mocked him. Eventually, the despised son was exiled to distant fields to care for the flocks. Shepherds were the outcasts of Jewish society. When Yishai sent his son into the wilderness, it was tantamount to saying that his son was dead to him.

At this point the Bible picks up the boy's story. A disillusioned prophet left a disobedient king to anoint a new man for Israel's throne. God led him to Yishai's farm outside Beit Lechem. A proud dad paraded his seven strapping sons before an impressed prophet. But God whispered, "Beware, Sammy! You're looking at the outward appearances, but I look at the heart." The prophet asked Yishai if he had another son. "Yes," replied the rancher. "But why would you be interested in a shepherd boy?"

Yet the boy had become an eagle eye with a slingshot, killing lions and bears while growing close to God in the lonely wilderness. By now you may have guessed that the boy Samuel wanted to see was David. We call Yishai "Jesse" and Beit Lechem "Bethlehem." Jesse's grandfather was Boaz, who broke Torah law by marrying a Moabite woman named Ruth. The story of an outcast boy who grew up to be a giant slayer is just one of many that prove this undeniable principle:

God forges greatness in the furnace of loneliness and affliction.

―――――⌘―――――

When you pass through the waters, I will be with
you; and through the rivers, they shall not overwhelm
you; when you walk through fire you shall not be
burned, and the flame shall not consume you.

ISAIAH 43:2, ESV

The Night Mars
Invaded New Jersey

∽◌∾

There was a time when radio was king. But no one knew just how powerful electronic media was until that October evening in 1938. Some six million listeners were tuned in to the CBS program *The Mercury Theatre on the Air* when the show was preempted by a frantic news bulletin: "Toronto, Canada. Professor Morse of McGill University has observed a total of three explosions on the planet Mars." Another urgent bulletin followed: "It is reported that at 8:50 p.m. a huge, flaming object, believed to be a meteorite, fell in the neighborhood of Grover's Mill, New Jersey."

The announcer said that CBS had dispatched reporter Carl Phillips to the scene. Twenty seconds later, Phillips was on the air. He described the mass chaos of crowds stampeding over police barricades to see the meteorite. A nationwide radio audience could hear the sounds of sirens, horns, and people shoving and shouting. Soon this bedlam in New Jersey would grip the nation.

Phillips interviewed Princeton scientist Professor Pierson, who declared excitedly that this was not a meteorite but something encased in a metal not found on Earth: a cylindrical shape, something extraterrestrial! The reporter interrupted the professor: "Just a minute! Something's happening! Ladies and gentlemen, this is terrific! This end of the thing is beginning to flake off! The top is beginning to rotate like a screw! The thing must be hollow!"

The radio audience could hear the shouts of panicked bystanders. "Look, the darn thing's unscrewing!" "Keep back, there! Keep back, I tell you!" "Maybe there's men in it trying to escape!" Phillips was now screaming about something like a gigantic gray snake coming out of the top. It had tentacles, was as huge as a bear, and glistened like wet leather, with huge black eyes like a serpent. Its mouth was V-shaped, with saliva dripping from rimless lips that seemed to quiver and pulsate.

Reports were coming in rapid fire: spaceships were hovering over the Hudson River; the monster from the space cylinder was incinerating people with heat rays; Martian tripods were obliterating undermanned state police; a report from the governor of New Jersey had declared martial law; and highways were clogged as people fled the aliens.

By now millions of listeners across America were panic stricken. Hysterical people ran into the streets. Phone lines were jammed. Most listeners didn't wait around to hear the final words from *The Mercury Theatre*: "You've been listening to the CBS presentation of Orson Welles and *The Mercury Theatre* in an original dramatization of *The War of the Worlds* by H. G. Wells."

This innovative use of dramatized fiction became national head-lines: RADIO LISTENERS IN PANIC—*New York Times*. RADIO FAKE SCARES NATION—*Chicago Herald*. US TERRORIZED—*San Francisco Chronicle*. The legendary career of Orson Welles was launched, and so was the mega power of mass media. Decades later we are still blitzed by entertainment sold as news, much of it biased or false. That is good enough reason to look for the straight scoop in the Bible. The best thing about the true news is that it is also good news.

Truth is powerful, and it will still prevail after every lie has been exposed.

———— ✺ ————

All Scripture is inspired by God and is useful to
teach us what is true and to make us realize what
is wrong in our lives. It corrects us when we are
wrong and teaches us to do what is right.

2 TIMOTHY 3:16

Men against the Sea

๛

W hy does it still fascinate more than two hundred years later? The mutiny took place on the smallest of British naval ships, with a crew that numbered only forty-six, on an ignoble mission of carrying breadfruit plants from Tahiti to the West Indies as cheap food for slaves. Yet the mutiny on the *Bounty* has generated endless studies, novels, and major movies.

Could it be that the conflict on that speck of a ship is a metaphor for the battles of our own age? Two days after the mutiny, George Washington became president of a new democracy. Three months later, French citizens toppled their king. The old order was under siege and so was Captain William Bligh. He represented God and king, law and order, discipline by the book, and duty before pleasure. He was willing to sacrifice himself and every member of his crew for the good of ship and country. Opposing him was master's mate Fletcher Christian, the man who put individual rights above the common good, romanticism over reason, happiness before patriotism, and unfettered freedom ahead of the rule of law. Bligh was old school, while Christian was the champion of a new morality. In every movie about the mutiny, Bligh is the bully and villain, while Christian comes off the hero. It makes sense because Fletcher Christian personifies the values of Hollywood way back in 1789. But Hollywood movies seldom tell the rest of the story.

When the mutineers put Bligh and seventeen of his loyalists in a tiny twenty-three-foot open boat and set them adrift out in the middle of a vast ocean, they might as well have been sentencing them to death. Yet somehow this law-and-order villain of Hollywood movies managed to pull off history's greatest feat of seamanship. In an epic forty-seven-day test of endurance, he willed his men through cannibal islands and across stormy seas 3,618 miles to safety. And old-school Bligh lost only one man in the process.

On the other hand, the rebel without a cause took his mutineers back to the sexual pleasures and unfettered freedoms of Tahiti. Then fearing the hangman's noose, they took their women to a desolate rock called Pitcairn. There the fugitives from British justice scuttled the ship and turned their island into a Hobbesian den of mayhem and murder. A few years later, an American whaling ship would discover a single fugitive mutineer and a few women and kids in a pigsty of filth and ignorance. All the others had been murdered, and Fletcher Christian was long dead.

Hollywood doesn't tell you the end of this story, but we ought to recall the fate of the HMS *Bounty* when we put Captain Bligh and traditional values adrift and turn the USS *America* over to those who promote unfettered freedoms over moral absolutes and compassion over law and order. Bligh might not be as likable as Fletcher Christian, but he will take us to safety. That surely beats the depravity of Pitcairn's Island. Aristotle put it well:

At his best, man is the noblest of all creatures. Separated from law and justice, he is the worst.

<hr>

How I delight in your commands! How I love them!
I honor and love your commands.
I meditate on your decrees.

PSALM 119:47-48

The Fifteen-Minute Superstar

⤜⊙⊙⊙⤛

Hardly anyone remembers Jamie Foss, or the television show that gave her fifteen minutes of dubious fame. The program aired in 2004 with auditions held across the nation. Contestants were chosen by three celebrity judges and then flown to Hollywood to take part in a nationally televised competition. Each contestant was given vocal coaching, makeovers, and critiques of their performances. The grand prize was a recording contract, along with the promise of becoming America's next superstar. Week after week, singers were eliminated until a winner was crowned on the final episode.

If you are thinking *American Idol* or *The Voice*, you are wrong. Its name was much more grandiose: *Superstar USA*. But its premise was the polar opposite of those other televised competitions. Three celebrity judges intentionally eliminated anyone who had any talent, while praising outrageously bad performances and advancing the worst singers to the next round.

The judges and those who tuned in to *Superstar USA* were laughing at these wannabes with inflated egos. The premise of the show was that you could never go wrong banking on people's capacity for self-delusion. The Danish philosopher Søren Kierkegaard was right when he wrote, "There are two ways to be fooled: one is to believe what isn't so; the other is to refuse to believe what is so."

The final contestants performed in front of a live audience. By now the judges had winnowed the group down to the worst singers. The producers deceived the studio audience by saying that the performers were terminally ill teens whose last wish was to perform in front of a live television audience. Compassionate spectators gave standing ovations to some of the ghastliest performances in the history of American television.

At the end of the final show, judges chose the worst performer and crowned her the winner. Jamie was overwhelmed with joy at being crowned *Superstar USA*. But her exuberance was short lived. The host let her in on the dreadful secret: she was the worst of a season full of America's worst singers. That moment was so crushing to Jamie, and so embarrassing to almost everyone watching, that *Superstar USA* was canceled after one season. There is no nudity so offensive to people as the naked truth.

Jamie did get a check for $50,000 and a recording contract. As you might imagine, thirteen years later the record company still hasn't produced her CD. The joke was on Jamie. It's so easy to believe what isn't so and yet so hard to believe what is. *Superstar USA* only ran for one season, but the ultimate reality show, *Spirituality USA*, runs every day of every year. The judges told Jamie what she wanted to hear. Lots of folks will do the same for us. But the embarrassment and pain that Jamie Foss endured will one day pale in comparison to ours if we allow false flattery to delude us about ourselves. Today, someone or something might smack you in the face with harsh reality. You'll be better for it, if you remember this lesson from Jamie's story:

Reality denied will always come back to hurt you more than the truth.

—————— ⚬⊙⚬ ——————

Faithful are the wounds of a friend;
profuse are the kisses of an enemy.

PROVERBS 27:6, ESV

America's Fairy Godmother

⋖◌◌◌⋗

"Jesus loves the little children, all the children of the world. Red and yellow, black and white, they are precious in his sight." So go the words of a Sunday school song. Danielle would probably add a verse about how Jesus loves all the *neglected* children of the world. Outside of Jesus, few people love the discarded kids of America more than Danielle Gletow of Trenton, New Jersey.

Danielle and Joe were excited about starting a family of their own. But they knew that the country was filled with the cast-off children of broken homes. So they decided to adopt. As the process dragged on, they elected to become foster parents. "These kids are here already," Danielle reasoned. "They don't ask to be born into their circumstances." The couple took in several foster children before they adopted their daughter, Mia. It wasn't long after the adoption that Danielle gave birth to Lilian. But a houseful of kids still wasn't enough. The couple couldn't shake the fact that there were still thousands of kids being shuffled from home to home. How could a couple with limited resources help these castaways feel loved?

Danielle knew that most foster kids live in a world of shattered hopes and dashed dreams. So she stepped out in faith and started a nonprofit called One Simple Wish. Foster kids across America can go to a website and submit a single simple wish to be met by donors. Danielle quit her high-paying marketing job and personally donated the first $10,000 to get One Simple Wish going. What started out on a prayer and a shoestring budget has grown to a million-dollar nonprofit that operates in nearly every state, with more than eight hundred partners. From a football to a doll to a trip to the Denver Zoo, some forty thousand children have had their simple wishes granted. The gifts may seem small, but to these children each gift is tangible evidence that someone out there cares for them. One Simple Wish has blessed the lives of hundreds of kids who had given up hope that any dream could ever come true.

Danielle Gletow has won awards and been feted on major television shows. CNN has labeled her a hero, and *Family Circle* has listed her as one of the "Most Influential Moms in America." But all those kudos don't impress Danielle as much as the thousands of thank-you notes she has received from foster kids. They think of her as the "fairy godmother to America's foster children." Mostly Danielle is glad that, after she gives 110 percent to neglected children during the day, she can lay her head on her pillow at night and know that something like One Simple Wish can change the world, one child at a time. Can you imagine what a nicer world this might be if each of us performed a single simple act of kindness for someone each day? We never change the world all at once, but just a wee bit at a time. Remember this old African proverb:

How do you eat an elephant? You do it one bite at a time.

There was a believer in Joppa named Tabitha
(which in Greek is Dorcas). She was always doing
kind things for others and helping the poor.

ACTS 9:36

The Chambermaid's Choice

eᔑᓍᓂᓂᔐ

Maria had hoped that her second marriage would make for a better future. Though born the daughter of a cook, she had dreams of being in high society. But at sixteen, she fell madly in love with a nobleman's valet. When they married, she consigned herself to be dismissed as one of the serving class. After Maria gave birth to a son, her valet husband died. At age eighteen she was a grieving widow and a single mother. Not long after, her little boy died too.

Then she got a second chance at love. But when her young musician took her home to meet his prominent family, they looked down their haughty noses at this girl from the serving class. His father would ever after refer to her as "the chambermaid." Her husband's family would always view her as an inferior interloper. It was no wonder that Maria's second marriage soon soured.

She later referred to her life as "a chain of sorrows." The couple's first child died six days after he was born. The "chambermaid" would bury five of her eight children. But her worst heartache was watching the decline of a husband who enjoyed the tavern more than practicing his music. If he wasn't in a drunken stupor, he was with other women. Then the beatings began. After he took advantage of her in one of his brutal rages, Maria discovered she was pregnant. She determined that she wasn't about to bring a child conceived by rape into her miserable world.

She found her way to a woman who traded in concoctions that induced miscarriage. Three drops of that deadly liquid would kill her baby. Any more might end her life too. She dumped it all into a cup of tea. But before she was able to drink it, the cup was accidentally knocked off the table.

At first she was hysterical. Then she resigned herself to the fact that God must have a purpose for her unwanted child.

He turned out to be a strange little boy, often reclusive and unresponsive. But he did have his family's love for music. When a local teacher took him on as a piano student, no one imagined that she was gaining a prodigy. Maria was forty years old when Wolfgang Mozart allegedly declared that her son was destined for greatness. Two months later, the teenage prodigy rushed home to be at her deathbed. She told her son that giving birth to him was the best thing she ever did in her unhappy life.

We should all be grateful that Maria van Beethoven did not abort little Ludwig, a child of rape who would grow up to write the world's greatest symphonies. Maybe you, too, were unplanned or unwanted. But God conceived you as his masterpiece. Perhaps you are facing a tough choice or difficult circumstances. Answers never come easily in times like these. Hopefully Maria's story and that of her unwanted child, Ludwig van Beethoven, might give you courage to do this:

Trust God. He knows who belongs in your life and who doesn't.

———— ❧ ————

I was thrust into your arms at my birth. You have
been my God from the moment I was born.

PSALM 22:10

A Magnificent Case
of Malpractice

ভ৶৻৩৶৶

Frances Jane was six weeks old when she became violently ill. Because the family doctor was away, another was called to the home. When he put hot mustard poultices on Frances's eyes, her mother protested. But the doctor insisted that hot mustard would draw out the infection. Instead, his quackery burned the screaming baby's corneas. Even as little Frances whimpered in pain, scars were beginning to form over her eyes. In the weeks after, her mother realized that her baby was not responding to visual stimuli. Her worst fears were realized when *real* doctors confirmed that the quack had blinded little Frances for life.

A year later, the blind baby's father died of pneumonia. Her mother was forced to take a job as a maid. So little Frances was put in the care of her grandmother. That lady would become the greatest influence in the little girl's life by teaching her "to see the world around her." Daily, she took Frances on nature walks, vividly describing sights that her granddaughter could only see in her imagination. She also read the Scriptures to the blind girl, whose memory was so extraordinary that eventually she could quote the first five books of the Bible, all four Gospels, the Proverbs, Song of Solomon, and most of the Psalms. Frances also became a poet. This girl accomplished more without eyes than do most sighted people.

Just before she turned fifteen, she enrolled as a student at the New York Institute for the Blind. When she graduated with honors, she became a teacher there. She published her poetry and was invited to perform it before the joint session of the US Congress. The applause was deafening. But it was as a composer that Frances excelled. She wrote more songs than any person in history—some nine thousand hymns. Her most famous was "Blessed Assurance." She has been dubbed America's Hymn Queen. Frances and her blind husband could have grown wealthy off her royalties, but they chose to live in a cramped apartment, spending their time and money ministering to drunken bums in the Bowery.

The world remembers Frances by the nickname that her grandmother gave her: Fanny. Fanny Crosby always thanked God for that quack whose malpractice made her blind. Without it, her grandmother wouldn't have taught her to see with her heart rather than her eyes. She wouldn't have developed the eyes of her heart to write all those wondrous hymns that have blessed millions. She said that she was the most fortunate of all people for when she crossed over to heaven and regained her sight, "the first face that shall ever gladden my sight will be that of my Savior." Her amazing story reminds us to remember this great truth:

Sight is useless when the heart is blind. Sight is unnecessary when the heart sees.

The god of this age has blinded the minds of unbelievers,
so that they cannot see the light of the gospel that
displays the glory of Christ, who is the image of God.

2 CORINTHIANS 4:4, NIV

The Song of a Human Trafficker

༄༅༙

Johnny was a latchkey kid. His mother had died, and his father was a ship's captain off at sea. Abandoned and adrift, he roamed the streets as a pickpocket and troublemaker. When Johnny's sea captain father returned, he took eleven-year-old Johnny aboard his ship, figuring that the rough life of a sailor might knock some sense into his prodigal son. Instead, his boy became even more unruly, creating mayhem in almost every port of call.

His disgusted father finally gave him his walking papers. Johnny signed on to another vessel where he attempted desertion by jumping ship. He was captured by the shore patrol and publicly flogged. When the word got around that the ship captain's son was incorrigible, no respectable vessel would sign him on. So Johnny became a deckhand aboard a slave ship, hauling human cargo to the Americas.

Just when it seemed that he couldn't sink any lower, Johnny was enslaved by a man named Amos Clow, whose African mistress took special delight in having a white slave as her personal plaything. After he escaped, he was possessed with an implacable hatred for Africans. When he became the captain of his own slave ship, his brutality knew no bounds.

It took a violent storm to mark the beginning of change in his life. On a return trip to England, when it seemed that his ship was about to sink, Johnny cried out to Jesus for salvation. It took a few more years for this new convert to quit the slave business, yet God was slowly transforming his racist heart.

Eventually, Johnny felt called to the pulpit. The archbishop of York rejected him because his past was too scandalous. Finally, he was given a small parish. But curious crowds came to hear this notorious slave trader turned preacher. He wrote almost three hundred hymns to accompany his sermons. Eight years after he became a pastor, Johnny penned history's most famous hymn, "Amazing Grace."

A single line in the first stanza jumps off the page: "Amazing grace, how sweet the sound, that saved a wretch like me." Surely, the Reverend John Newton knew firsthand the power of sin to reduce humans to utter wretchedness. When he later wrote a pamphlet on the slave trade, his exposé on the wretchedness of human trafficking helped bring about the abolition of slavery in the British Empire three decades before America's Civil War.

Over the past several years many hymnals have replaced the term "wretch" in "Amazing Grace" with words that are less offensive to a culture obsessed with positive self-image. But maybe we lose something of the grandeur of God's grace when we minimize our own sinful condition. To take the "wretch" out of "Amazing Grace" is to cut the very heart out of a hymn celebrating the immensity of God's love for us. Old Johnny Newton might even say this:

Take the wretch out of "Amazing Grace," and you take the amazing out of grace.

God is so rich in mercy, and he loved us so much,
that even though we were dead because of our sins,
he gave us life when he raised Christ from the dead.
(It is only by God's grace that you have been saved!)

EPHESIANS 2:4-5

Moral Pap for the Young

⌀⌀⌀

The girl grew up hobnobbing with America's greatest minds. She borrowed books from Ralph Waldo Emerson's library, walked with Henry David Thoreau at Walden Pond, discussed literature with Nathaniel Hawthorne, and became friends with abolitionist Frederick Douglass. Among her acquaintances was one of America's earliest suffragettes, Julia Ward Howe.

Louisa grew up to be a towering intellectual, social activist, and hardcore feminist. Her activism left her no time for the silliness of romance or foolishness of marriage. Although she fulfilled her duties as a maiden aunt, she really didn't like kids. She wanted to be a poet like Emerson, write philosophy like Thoreau, or help Frederick Douglass emancipate slaves. If she did stoop to penning a novel, it had to speak to society's ills the way Nathaniel Hawthorne did. So Louisa fought against slavery and registered women to vote. When the Civil War broke out, she served as a nurse in military hospitals. Occasionally, she played the part of the aunt, but found little girls to be utterly boring.

When publishers asked her to write a novel about girls coming of age, the spinster suffragette protested that that sort of book was "moral pap for the young." But when they promised to publish her father's book of philosophy if she wrote the novel, she grudgingly agreed. Who would have believed that the maiden aunt who had no time for girlish romance would write a classic book that has enchanted millions of romantic girls? No one was more surprised about the success of *Little Women* than its reluctant author, Louisa May Alcott.

Her friends would have been even more surprised to know that this perpetual tomboy used the pen name A. M. Bernard to write pulp fiction about the perils and passions of Pauline, cross-dressers, spies, revenge, weak heroines being rescued by strong men, and smoking hashish. Later she wrote Gothic romances for the *Atlantic*. These melodramas include racy exchanges we might not expect from Louisa May Alcott. Those who knew the New England spinster would have been shocked to discover that mercury poisoning had weakened her immune system, causing her to suffer from severe vertigo and hallucinations. Few people know that the author of *Little Women* died at age fifty-five, addicted to opium and fantasizing about romances she never experienced.

The amazing story of Louisa May Alcott reminds us that things are seldom as they seem. Most of us are a bundle of contradictions. Made of the earth's dust, we wallow in mud. Filled with the breath of God, we aspire to fly in the heavens. This is why we desperately need the filling of the Holy Spirit. Without God's indwelling power, we too easily go the way of the sinner rather than the saint.

A saint is a sinner who gets up and tries one more time.

Protect me, for I am devoted to you. Save me,
for I serve you and trust you. You are my God.

PSALM 86:2

536

The Asterisk in an Obituary

❧❧❧

S he was as cute as a button, the first crush for a generation of boys. But the final three years of her twenty-seven-year battle with multiple sclerosis were a waking nightmare. Once the most recognizable teen on the planet, she was now unable to recognize anyone. She existed in a coma-like state, propped up in an electrically controlled chair, nearly blind, unable to speak or go to the bathroom on her own. In those last three years she was fed through a tube. Her throat had to be cleared several times an hour to prevent her from choking to death.

There was a time when she was a pop culture icon. No one received more fan mail than America's favorite Mouseketeer. In 1960, a nationwide poll voted her teenager of the year. Dubbed America's sweetheart, she went on to drive young men crazy in movies like *Beach Blanket Bingo* and *How to Stuff a Wild Bikini*.

She broke hearts across the land when she married her agent in 1965. Even Linus deadpanned in a *Peanuts* cartoon strip, "How depressing . . . Annette Funicello has grown up!" After the wedding, she stepped out of the limelight. But no baby boomer could ever forget the darling of *The Mickey Mouse Club* who became a beach blanket beauty.

Annette began to lose control in her legs when she came out of retirement to do a movie in 1991. A deeply religious woman, she was afraid that people would think she was drunk. So she went public about her MS. America applauded her gutsy battle with this degenerative disease. When she dropped out of sight again, no one knew how much MS was ravaging her. Nor would anyone have recognized her in the end. But her family had a front-row seat to her nightmare. In announcing her death in April of 2013, her children said, "Our mother is now dancing in heaven."

Within a week of Annette's passing, Google recorded millions of hits on her life and death. Almost every article contained a single throwaway line: "In 1986, she married her second husband, horse trainer Glen Holt." Glen was only an asterisk in Annette's obituary.

Few folks know that Annette Funicello's first husband was abusive or that this horse trainer gave her refuge when she had nowhere to go. Within a year of their wedding, she was diagnosed with multiple sclerosis. Yet during those last years, he bathed her, lifted her on and off the toilet, changed her diapers, and attended to her every need. In the end, America's sweetheart was ravaged, bloated, and comatose. It's easy to love the girl of our fantasies, but Glen loved her in dirty diapers and with bloated flesh—not for a while, but for nine thousand straight days.

When asked if it was a burden, he replied, "How can it be when you love somebody?" Maybe you are one of those unsung heroes who is caring for someone. If you're tired and wondering how long you can hang on, know this:

Anyone can carry a burden to nightfall. Heroes get up and do it again tomorrow.

———— ✍︎ ————

Let us not become weary in doing good, for at the proper time we will reap a harvest if we do not give up.

GALATIANS 6:9, NIV

Touching All Bases

⋘⟐⋙

Bruce Beyer was happy with his adoptive parents. How could he not be? In 1967, he joined nearly one thousand war protesters who turned in their draft cards in the largest act of civil disobedience in US history. When agents came to arrest him, he punched one of them, earning a prison sentence. While out on appeal, he fled to Canada. His jumping bail cost his adoptive father a year's salary. Yet ten years later, his dad walked with him across a bridge back into America.

When Bruce suffered heart problems, he needed to discover his family history. So he sent in one of those DNA kits to Ancestry.com. Then he did some sleuthing. When he found out that he was related to Benedict Arnold, he recalled how often he was called a traitor when he fled to Canada. He discovered that his birth father was journeyman baseball player Joe Tipton, who played for seven major league teams, including the world champion Cleveland Indians in 1948. Bruce was excited until he realized that Joe Tipton is famous for "the most lopsided trade in baseball" when the Chicago White Sox traded him for Nellie Fox. Fox would go on to be a Hall of Famer while Tipton is a baseball footnote. But his adoptive dad, Bob, is in the University of Buffalo's Hall of Fame for football. Folks think that Joe Tipton would have been ashamed that his son was a draft dodger. But Bruce knows that his adoptive dad was willing to walk with his "Benedict Arnold" across that bridge.

Most of all, he learned how much he was loved by his birth mother, Pamela. She was eighteen when she fell for a married baseball player. Pamela was sent away to Buffalo to have Joe's baby. After his adoptive mother died, Bruce found an old letter from Pamela in his adoptive mother's papers. In it, she said, "I'm thinking about how happy you must be because now you have a little baby boy, a boy I love more than life itself." She wanted her son to know she desperately wanted him, but he "needed the love of two parents." She speaks of a pink flower that she holds in her hand to remember her little boy. The letter is both fragrant and heartrending. She ends it by saying, "God knows it hurts to let him go, though. My thoughts and love will be with you three forever." Later Pamela's sister sent Bruce a Christmas ornament on which his birth mother had stitched the word *passion*. Next to it was a pink flower, a reminder of her great passion: a son she had given away at birth.

This amazing story is one of selfless love: a mom who was willing to live with a broken heart for the good of her child, an adoptive mother who opened her heart to a baby boy, and an adoptive father who loved his boy unconditionally. May we all love and be loved like that.

Love is not if or because, but anyway and even though and in spite of.

We know what real love is because Jesus gave
up his life for us. So we also ought to give up
our lives for our brothers and sisters.

1 JOHN 3:16

The Treasure of the Salinas de San Andreas

❧❧❧

When Billy Ford headed across the Guadalupe River, he couldn't have known that he was about to push America to the brink of war. Had the sheriff understood the high stakes that night in 1854, he might have formed a bigger posse than seventeen Americans, ten Mexicans, and an Englishman. He surely needed more firepower than his sixty-four-pound howitzer, especially if he was going to seize the Salinas de San Andreas.

Acre for acre, this was the richest land in Texas, worth its weight in gold. As far back as prehistoric times it had been a bonanza. Aztecs and Mayans traveled great distances to extract its riches. In 1647, a Spanish king granted Don Diego de Vivar exclusive rights to mine its wealth, making his family fabulously wealthy.

By 1854, powerful men were willing to sell their souls to possess the Salinas de San Andreas. But Sheriff Ford should have known better. For more than two hundred years, Comanches, Apaches, Spaniards, Frenchmen, Mexicans, Americans, and Tejanos had fought to the death over this treasure trove of the Trans-Pecos. Somewhere in the badlands of Texas, Ford's outgunned posse ran into an army of Tejanos. After a deadly shoot-out, he hightailed it back to New Mexico.

Some twenty-three years later, this simmering conflict erupted again. Like a scene out of the cowboy comedy *Blazing Saddles*, several small armies converged west of El Paso. Mexican federales crossed the Rio Grande, Apaches rode in from the west, Comanches swooped down from the north, vigilantes stormed out of El Paso, and five hundred Mexican

American locals rushed to protect their claim to the Salinas de San Andreas. Just when things couldn't get crazier, hired gunslingers came in by railroad just as Texas rangers arrived from Austin. In the confusion that followed, Tejanos captured Texas rangers, Apaches scalped vigilantes, Comanches shot it out with gunslingers, and federales fled back across the Rio Grande. The Ninth Cavalry, made up of African American buffalo soldiers, finally galloped in to restore order. This fiasco looked like an eye-poking contest between the Three Stooges, but it garnered world headlines and almost caused a war between the United States and Mexico.

What was this treasure that made men crazy with greed? It wasn't gold, oil, or cattle. But it was the richest salt preserve in North America. Unless you hail from West Texas, you have probably never heard about these shoot-outs. After the San Elizario Salt War, America turned to cheaper salt from Kansas. Today Salinas de San Andreas is a deserted stretch of badlands.

In a day of cheap table salt, it's hard to believe that more wars in history have been fought over salt than have been waged over gold or religion. People can live without gold or oil but not salt. Jesus said, "You are the salt of the earth" (Matthew 5:13). We are to do what salt does: heal, preserve, and bring flavor to life. So get out of the shaker and spread yourself around.

Salty Christians make others thirst for Jesus, the Water of Life.

∽⊙∾

You are the salt of the earth. But if the salt loses
its saltiness, how can it be made salty again?
It is no longer good for anything, except to
be thrown out and trampled underfoot.

MATTHEW 5:13, NIV

The Man of a Thousand Faces

∽⊙⊙⊙∾

No one could play someone else better than Richard. Born into a vaudeville family, he began performing onstage while still a toddler. By the time he was a teenager, he was a master impressionist who could transform himself into a variety of characters. But it was at home that Richard honed the fine art of the masquerade. Dominated by an overprotective mother, he learned to play whatever role made her happy. By the time he was an adult, Richard didn't know who he was anymore. Maybe that's why he plowed through four marriages and his children complained that they never really knew their father.

Who would have guessed that this master impressionist and comic genius was lost and miserable? Toward the end of a brilliant career spanning sixty films, Richard was interviewed by Kermit the Frog on *The Muppet Show*. The puppet said, "Just relax and be yourself."

Richard responded, "I can't be myself, because I don't know who I really am anymore."

After years of cardiac trouble brought on by anxiety, alcohol, and drugs, Richard was told that his heart was dying. Racing against the clock, he tried to mend fences. He confessed to a son that he shouldn't have abandoned his first wife. He deeply regretted alienating his kids. Mostly, he wished he hadn't wasted his life trying to be what others wanted him to be.

Not long after that, Richard collapsed of a heart attack. He was rushed to a London hospital, where he died on July 24, 1980. He was only fifty-four years old. His son Michael tearfully spoke to reporters about the last days that he shared with his dad: "It marked the beginning of an all-too-brief closeness between us."

Michael's dad was born Richard Henry Sellers. But the world remembers him by his screen name, Peter Sellers. He portrayed such memorable characters as Dr. Strangelove and Inspector Clouseau, the bumbling master of disguise in the Pink Panther movies. Before Sellers died, an article in *Time* magazine quoted one of his friends as saying, "Poor Peter! The real Peter disappeared a long time ago. What remains is an amalgamation of all the characters he has played, and he is frantically trying to unsnarl the mess to find out who he really is."

Film critics agree that Peter Sellers was the greatest comedic genius since Charlie Chaplin. No one was funnier than Inspector Clouseau. Nothing is sadder than the story of the actor who played him. His life is summed up in a Smokey Robinson song: "Ain't too much sadder than the tears of a clown when there's no one around. . . . I'm hurt and I want you to know, but for others I put on a show." Hopefully those words aren't your story too. Don't settle for brief moments of closeness such as those Michael shared with his dad at the end. You can experience authentic relationships with those who matter, if you remember this:

To try to be someone else is to waste the person you were created to be.

·ᨀᨀ·

You made all the delicate, inner parts of my body
and knit me together in my mother's womb. Thank
you for making me so wonderfully complex! Your
workmanship is marvelous—how well I know it.

PSALM 139:13-14

The Flying Parson

❧

No one would have guessed that Gil was a world-class runner. He was more stocky than sinewy, and his thick glasses made him look like a bookworm. While other runners were stretching, he was in the locker room reading his Bible. When they were psyching themselves up, he was praying. Before each race, he told his competitors that Jesus loved them, and so did he. So rivals and reporters dubbed Gil the Flying Parson, the Pacing Parson, or the Iron Deacon.

But when the starter gun fired, everyone discovered why Gil had earned that other nickname: the Killer. Gil was not blessed with blazing speed or a great finishing kick. So he would get out in front early and set a punishing tempo. One by one, the other runners would fall back, unable to keep up with his grueling pace. Through the 1940s Gilbert dominated the mile. Yet no one would have given Gilbert a plug nickel after he flopped on the world's biggest stage. In 1941 the world's greatest milers had been assembled at Madison Square Garden. The stands were packed with spectators puffing away on cigarettes and chomping on cigars. Tobacco smoke hung over the track like a suffocating fog. Gilbert's eyes were stinging, and he was overwhelmed with nausea. When the starter's gun went off, he almost vomited. He suffered a miler's worst nightmare when the entire field lapped him. He almost gave up after that disaster.

But Gilbert kept on running with dogged determination. In 1943 he received the Sullivan Award as the outstanding amateur athlete in the United States. On March 11, 1944, he returned to the place of humiliation. The stands were packed, and the same pall of stale tobacco smoke hung over Madison Square Garden. But this time Gilbert ran like the wind, breaking the world indoor-mile record by a tenth of a second!

A week later, he beat his world record time at Chicago Stadium. He then stunned the track world by hanging up his shoes and becoming a pastor.

Pastor Gilbert's retirement lasted until 1947 when the old itch returned. Like his hero, Eric Liddell, he felt God's pleasure when he ran. On the eve of his comeback, he said, "I believe that I can do God's work better this way than not running." He had his best season in 1948 when he won a string of victories and again broke the indoor world record for the mile. He was America's best hope for the 1,500-meter run in the 1948 Olympics. But a week before the trials, Gilbert came down with the mumps and then tore his Achilles tendon. It was the end of the storied running career of the Flying Parson, Gil Dodds. But this champion for Christ went on to preach the gospel across the world. When he died of a brain tumor at age fifty-eight, he could say with Paul, "I have fought the good fight, I have finished the race, I have kept the faith" (1 Timothy 4:7, NIV). Whatever you face today, remember this:

When your legs can't run anymore, run with your heart.

———— ✤ ————

I press on to reach the end of the race and
receive the heavenly prize for which God,
through Christ Jesus, is calling us.

PHILIPPIANS 3:14

546

Thomas Clarkson's Box

⌘

Thomas carried his wooden box everywhere. Inside was a miniature chamber of horrors. Whenever he opened the lid and allowed people to peek in or showed its gruesome contents to an audience, their revulsion was palpable. And that's exactly the reaction that Thomas intended to create with his box.

As a student at Cambridge, Thomas entered an essay contest that posed this question: "Is it lawful to make slaves of others against their will?" His research exposed him to one of history's most monstrous crimes: the mass enslavement and murder of at least twenty million Africans who were transported as human cargo to the Americas. Thomas also discovered that British slave ships had carried nearly four million Africans to English sugar plantations.

His passionate essay won him first prize and created a great sensation in 1785. Thomas then gathered like-minded Christians to form the Society for Effecting the Abolition of the Slave Trade. The passion of this fiery red-haired giant convinced William Wilberforce, a member of Parliament, to join a crusade that would take four decades to win. Most Englishmen loved their sugar, molasses, and rum too much. To make matters worse, wealthy sugar planters bankrolled members of Parliament. Despite the untiring efforts of Wilberforce, lobbyists for big sugar got the votes needed to keep slavery legal.

But Thomas Clarkson kept fighting year after year, crisscrossing the British Isles to speak against slavery. He visited slave ships and interviewed slavers. Along the way, he collected evidence for his box. A gang of sailors tried to assassinate him on the Liverpool docks. But those toughs hadn't counted on the fists of that red-haired giant. Paid assassins shadowed him, but he kept filling that box. He became the best-known man in England while traveling more than a hundred thousand miles on horseback and speaking to more than a million people. Wherever he went, he opened that box to reveal his evidence: ship's diagrams of slaves stuffed like sardines in their holds, the records of slaves thrown into the sea to collect insurance on "lost cargo," and the diabolical instruments used by slavers. But even more effective were the beautiful works of art created by Africans, as well as a chart proving the intellectual contribution of Africa to the world—showing that these slaves were not subhuman, to be bought and sold like cattle.

Slaves were finally given their freedom in the British Empire in 1833. Most folks give the credit to Wilberforce's work in Parliament. But historians know that the lion's share of credit goes to Thomas Clarkson and his box. When he died at age eighty-six in 1846, he was still working to see slavery abolished in the United States. The amazing story of this towering giant and his wooden box reminds us that the world is full of evidence of the human condition, but there is a Savior who came to emancipate those enslaved to so many dehumanizing masters. Those of us who have been set free by Jesus have the evidence. We just have to open the box.

If you have something worth fighting for, go out and fight for it.

———— ✌❀❀ ————

Fight the good fight for the true faith.

1 TIMOTHY 6:12

The Preacher and the Gunslinger

⚜

His preacher daddy christened him John Wesley, hoping that his baby would grow up as godly as his namesake. His daddy's hopes were dashed when his little angel stabbed a classmate during a school-yard squabble. Maybe if he hadn't excused John Wesley's violence with pious platitudes, he might have saved a lot of lives.

John Wesley was only fifteen when he figured it was his right to kill an "uppity" black man. But Federal troops thought otherwise. The teen killed four soldiers in shoot-outs. After hiding out, he decided to go straight by joining a cattle drive on the Chisholm Trail. But the trail boss needed John's six-shooter more than his cowboy skills. Along the way, he killed seven more men. When he got to Abilene, Kansas, he shot three more. He gained instant fame when he made the legendary Wild Bill Hickok back down.

Tired of the killing, John Wesley decided to hang up his guns. He married Jane, who gave him three children. He hoped to make it as a rancher, but ran afoul of the law. John Wesley Hardin just couldn't go straight. He killed four more men before surrendering to the sheriff of Cherokee County. He got his religion back in that jailhouse and then escaped to return to ranching. But his reputation always caught up with him. He got in big trouble when he killed a state police captain. He escaped by taking two cattle herds up the Chisholm Trail. He might have gone straight this time if he hadn't shot a deputy. After that, he couldn't run far enough. But he did gun down five more men before Texas rangers finally captured him.

John Wesley Hardin was sentenced to twenty-five years in prison.

There, he studied theology, taught Sunday school, and read law books. After sixteen years, he was pardoned for good behavior. He passed the bar exam and then headed for El Paso, where his fame got him plenty of clients. He might have made it this time, if he hadn't committed adultery. When the angry husband threatened to expose his affair, John Wesley hired corrupt lawmen to assassinate him. But John didn't pay his hired killers for their work, so one of them caught John by surprise in a saloon and shot him. The fastest gun in the West died instantly. He was only forty-two years old.

John Wesley's amazing story is also one of the saddest: a preacher's kid who wanted to live up to his first two names, but ended up being remembered by his last. He was another in a long line of gunslingers who finally ran into someone quicker. He should have believed the Good Book his daddy preached: "Those who use the sword will die by the sword" (Matthew 26:52). Every day we face the same choice: Will we live by the Word of God or trust in our quick draw? The key is to hang up our guns before it's too late. John Wesley Hardin didn't figure this out, but you can:

It's never too late to be who you might have been.

———— ⌘ ————

He will take our weak mortal bodies and change them
into glorious bodies like his own, using the same power
with which he will bring everything under his control.

PHILIPPIANS 3:21

The Man in the Iron Lung

❧

Robin Cavendish was one of those lucky people who was born on third and thought he hit a triple. A dapper gentleman, he zoomed around in a sports car, played a wicked game of cricket, and danced the tango like Fred Astaire. No one was surprised when he married beautiful Diana, the belle of the ball. After all, Robin lived the ultimate charmed life. He and his wife headed off to Africa, where they enjoyed the privileged life of English colonials in 1950s Kenya.

But one day Robin suddenly felt faint and collapsed. When he was paralyzed from the neck down, the doctors delivered a devastating diagnosis of polio. He was flown back to England and stuffed in an iron lung in a metallic row of other warehoused polio victims. The doctors informed Diana that her husband would die within three months. But she refused to believe their prognosis. Even when Robin wanted to die, she wouldn't let him give up. She insisted on taking him home to be surrounded by loved ones instead of existing in a living morgue, entombed in a state-of-the-art medical sarcophagus while technicians robotically checked dials and air hoses.

When doctors tried to block their path, Robin said, "Why do you keep disabled people in prison?" In 1962, his friend Teddy Hall, an Oxford math professor, designed a wheelchair with a respirator. Now that he was no longer confined to a bed, Robin tracked down the records of every polio victim in England to see how many had survived more than a year in an iron lung. His findings were bleak. So he launched a campaign petitioning the health department to provide wheelchairs like his to free polio victims from iron lungs. Over the years, he allowed himself to be used as a guinea pig for the development of voice- and breath-activated equipment.

His vision gave birth to a plush hotel complex with facilities for the severely disabled, where their families could go on holiday. He traveled in his specially equipped van across Great Britain as a tireless advocate for disability rights. He never regretted his polio but in fact saw it as the blessing that opened the door to his life's calling. When he died on August 8, 1994, he had outlived the doctor's prognosis by thirty-six years. He set thousands free from iron lungs and gave new mobility and dignity to people with disabilities around the world.

There are people who live with extraordinary courage, but few do it day in and day out for thirty-six years as did Robin and Diana Cavendish. Their amazing story teaches us that we should never allow others to define our future. Nor should we allow our weaknesses to limit it. When we break through barriers, we inspire others. An obituary in the British newspaper the *Independent* said of Robin Cavendish, "Though professing to be an unbeliever himself, he had a capacity for making other people feel closer to God." Those of us who are believers never have an excuse to let anyone but God define us and our possibilities!

Other people's opinions don't define your reality.

―――――⋇―――――

You are a chosen people. You are royal priests,
a holy nation, God's very own possession.

1 PETER 2:9

The World's Most-Admired Woman

❧

No one would have ever guessed that scrawny little Agnes would one day light up the world. Like most folks in her poverty-stricken eastern European country, she seemed doomed to a dead-end life. After her widowed mother had exhausted herself trying to find an eligible bachelor for the mousy girl, Agnes announced that God had called her to be a missionary. Everyone said she was crazy. But eighteen-year-old Agnes headed for the faraway city of Dublin, Ireland. After learning a smattering of English, she moved to Asia where she kicked around from school to school, seemingly consigned to teach schoolchildren forever.

Everything changed when Agnes went on a spiritual retreat to a nearby city. There she stumbled upon the worst slums on earth. She was overwhelmed by the poverty and disease. At thirty-six years of age, the diminutive spinster heard Jesus tell her to bring his light to this place of darkness. She called other women to join her in ministering to the poorest outcasts in India.

The world doesn't know her as Agnes: after she committed herself to ministry, she changed her name to the patron saint of missionaries, Teresa. Who would have figured that the Gallup Poll would one day declare this pint-size Albanian woman the most admired woman of the twentieth century? Or that she would win the Nobel Prize? Or that her order would grow to 4,500 sisters in 153 countries giving themselves to the poorest of the poor? Who would believe that from her one-room cell in a Calcutta convent, she would oversee a worldwide string of hospitals, hospices, AIDS centers, orphanages, and schools?

When Mother Teresa won the Nobel Prize, reporters asked her how we should promote world peace. She shocked everyone with her simple answer: "Go home and love your family." When they asked her to describe herself, she replied, "By blood, I am an Albanian; by citizenship, an Indian; by faith, a Catholic nun. As to my calling, I belong to the world. As to my heart, I belong entirely to Jesus."

When a delegation of nuns came to Calcutta to discover the secret to Mother Teresa's success, the head of one order asked, "Why are you growing while so many other orders are dying?"

Mother Teresa quietly replied, "I give them Jesus."

"I know that," replied the woman impatiently. "But can you be more specific? Do your sisters object to wearing habits? What about the rules of your order? How do you enforce them?"

"Only one thing matters. I give them Jesus," she replied again.

"Yes, yes, I know that!" persisted the woman. "But there's got to be more than that!"

The little nun walked up to the woman and said in the sternest voice possible, "I give them Jesus! There's nothing more!"

Jesus alone can change the world. By giving Jesus only, even a humble nun from a hardscrabble upbringing can change the world. So can we, if we remember this from Agnes's story:

Religion does not save or transform people. Only Jesus does.

We all, with unveiled face, beholding as in a mirror
the glory of the Lord, are being transformed
into the same image from glory to glory.

2 CORINTHIANS 3:18, NKJV

The Race of the Century

ꙮꙮꙮ

In the 1930s the sport of kings was still the king of sports. And War Admiral was the undisputed king of race horses. In 1937 this son of the legendary Man o' War won the Triple Crown. War Admiral was sleek, powerful, and unbeatable. He was the toast of Kentucky bluegrass aristocracy and the darling of the East Coast horse-racing establishment.

Out on the West Coast, Seabiscuit was tearing up the tracks. He had won eleven of fifteen races in 1937 and was the leading money winner in America. But the West Coast racing circuit was considered second tier. Meanwhile, War Admiral was winning the Triple Crown by beating the crème de la crème of East Coast thoroughbreds. War Admiral was king, while Seabiscuit was Cinderella. War Admiral was Nob Hill, and Seabiscuit was from the wrong side of the tracks—the blue-collar horse who had overcome tough breaks and defeats. The two horses were a perfect metaphor for depression-era class divisions in America: working class versus country club, have-nots versus haves, union workers versus bosses, shantytown versus high society.

When reporters clamored for a race between the two, the nation went wild with enthusiasm. The race was scheduled for the Pimlico racetrack on November 1, 1938. But Pimlico only held fifteen thousand spectators. So it was scheduled on a Tuesday workday to keep hordes of Seabiscuit fans from attending. Even so, forty thousand fans poured onto the grounds—a sweating, shoving, seething sea of blue-collar stiffs packing the stands, hanging from the rafters, and crowding the track. Newsreels rolled and flashbulbs popped. President Roosevelt left a cabinet meeting to listen to the race, and forty million people crowded around radios across America.

Seldom does a sporting event transcend the arena to become a social phenomenon. But 1938 was a tough year in America. The country was trying to climb out of the Great Depression. Soup lines were still long. Nazi Germany was unleashing the dogs of war. The empire of Japan had ignited a holocaust of mass murder. Seabiscuit was a big underdog facing impossible odds against a powerful and unbeatable foe—just like millions of Americans.

When the Cinderella horse upset War Admiral that magical day, famed reporter Grantland Rice proclaimed, "A little horse with the heart of a lion and the flying feet of a gazelle yesterday proved his place as the gamest thoroughbred that ever raced over an American track." Seabiscuit would bring new hope that folks from the wrong side of the track could still win, the jobless could climb out of a depression, and citizen soldiers could defeat monstrous enemies overseas. The amazing story of Seabiscuit reminds us that the battle is not always won by the strongest. The fastest racer does not always cross the finish line first. The underdog with heart can win the race. So take heart from this today:

Passion and courage always beat talent and speed.

I have observed something under the sun.
The fastest runner doesn't always win the race, and
the strongest warrior doesn't always win the battle.

ECCLESIASTES 9:11

Scrubbing the Tombstone

୧◦⊙◦ଠ

It happened in a split second. A single explosive moment. But that tackle at the Ole Miss football game would intertwine their lives forever. When the defensive back hit the Vanderbilt fullback, a sickening pop could be heard throughout the stadium. But it was the tackler who lay motionless. The impact had broken four vertebrae in his spine, paralyzing him for life. Chucky Mullins's courage would captivate America. President George H. W. Bush visited him in the hospital, encouraging the quadriplegic to fight on. Through herculean effort, Chucky got back to classes in a wheelchair. Tragically, he died from a blood clot a year later. But his legend has only grown in the three decades since. Every year, the Ole Miss player who earns the Chucky Mullins Courage Award gets to wear his hallowed number 38, and when the Rebels charge onto their field, the players touch the bronze head of Chucky's statue.

Amazingly, Brad Gaines got up from that tackle and went back to the Vanderbilt huddle. Until that moment, the fullback had led the Southeastern Conference in pass receptions and had pro scouts salivating. After that, he fell apart emotionally. Against his coach's advice, he went to see Chucky in the hospital. He wanted to flee when he saw all the tubes and monitors. Mullins was down to 120 pounds, unable to move or feed himself. But he smiled at Brad and whispered to him to come closer. When the fullback bent down, Chucky said, "It's not your fault." Brad appreciated Chucky's absolution, but he never played another down after that season. Nor did he watch another football game for eight years. Yet the two men became inseparable friends. When Chucky died, Brad was invited to ride the Ole Miss team bus and sit with Chucky's teammates at his funeral.

It's been almost three decades since that tackle, and the memory still reduces Brad to tears. Though he is back coaching kids on the football field, he says that part of him died that day. Three times a year, he drives more than three hours each way to Russellville, Alabama: on the anniversaries of that tackle, Chucky's death, and Christmas. He scrubs the gravestone, cleans the plot, and sits in silence to remember a day in October of 1989 when everything changed. He still sobs as if that tackle happened yesterday. Why does he make those pilgrimages? Is it to remember a friendship born of tragedy, or are they acts of penance because he can never quite accept those words whispered in a Memphis hospital: "It's not your fault"? This amazing story is a bittersweet reminder of that moment when our sins inexorably intertwined our lives with Jesus Christ. He never whispers from the cross, "It's not your fault." But he does say, "I have paid the price for your misdeeds and mistakes." There's no need to rehearse our faults, to blame ourselves, or to do acts of penance. The Gospels assure us of this:

God's part is to forgive. Your part is to leave the guilt behind.

Now there is no condemnation for those
who belong to Christ Jesus.

ROMANS 8:1

The Forgotten Father

ᴖᴑᴖ

We celebrate the hallowed names of patriots who founded America, but hardly anyone remembers Joseph Warren. Yet he was perhaps the most influential of the Sons of Liberty. This child prodigy enrolled in Harvard at age fourteen and became Boston's youngest doctor at twenty-two. He counted among his patients Samuel Adams, John Hancock, and two future presidents: John Adams and John Quincy Adams. His skill as a physician gave him access to the royal governor, British generals, and the leading loyalists of Boston. But he raised a strong voice for independence. In 1775, on the five-year anniversary of the Boston Massacre, he donned a toga and gave a rousing speech for liberty to a massive crowd at the Old South Meeting House. British officers stood in the back, making menacing signs, but the firebrand was not intimidated.

When the English Parliament suspended civil rights after the Boston Tea Party, Dr. Warren penned the Suffolk Resolves that called for a boycott of British goods and for colonial militias to prepare for a fight. When the doctor learned from loyalist friends that the British were ready to march on Lexington and Concord, he sent Paul Revere on his midnight ride. He then ordered Benedict Arnold to march to Fort Ticonderoga to capture the cannons needed to blast the British out of Boston.

While other Sons of Liberty headed to the Continental Congress in Philadelphia, the doctor decided to stay in Boston and fight. He took up a musket and joined the defenders at Bunker Hill. Though the Massachusetts provincial government had appointed him a major general, Joseph knew that he was more orator than general. So he joined volunteers at the fiercest point of the fighting. A year before the Declaration of Independence was signed, Dr. Joseph Warren became the first casualty of the Revolutionary

War when a British musket ball shattered his head. After the battle, the thirty-four-year-old doctor was buried in a shallow grave at Bunker Hill. Ten months later, Paul Revere helped identify his remains from a false tooth that he had crafted for the good doctor.

Historians are agreed that, had Joseph Warren lived, he would have been our nation's most charismatic leader. The royal governor of Boston, Thomas Hutchinson, wrote that he would have become "the Cromwell of North America." Loyalist Peter Oliver said in 1782 that "George Washington would have been an obscurity." Yet few remember that Dr. Joseph Warren, the orator whose fiery speech sparked the revolution, was the first American to die on a battlefield for our country.

Dr. Joseph Warren's amazing story reminds us that we stand on the shoulders of forgotten heroes as much as the shoulders of those whose names we celebrate. This patriot didn't live to see the Declaration of Independence. Perhaps the greatest heroes are those who give their lives so that others who come behind them will experience what the heroes themselves never will. In this age in which we live for the here and now, we would do well to remember this:

We haven't come this far only to come this far.

All these people earned a good reputation
because of their faith, yet none of them
received all that God had promised.

HEBREWS 11:39

The Other Rosa Parks

❧❦❧

Every schoolkid in America celebrates Rosa Parks, but probably no one remembers Elizabeth Jennings and her act of courage a century earlier. This African American woman was running late for church services, where she was the organist. When the horse-drawn streetcar stopped, there was no placard that said Colored Riders Only. But she was in a hurry, so she boarded in violation of New York City's segregation laws. When the burly conductor ordered her to get off, she stubbornly replied, "I don't know where you were born, but you are a good-for-nothing impudent fellow for insulting a decent person on her way to church!" Replying that he was from Ireland, the conductor began shoving Elizabeth as she tenaciously clung to the window frame. The driver began to tear at her dress and smash her bonnet. It took two brawny men to throw that diminutive church organist onto the sidewalk.

Slavery may have been outlawed in the North, but New York City still had some harsh segregation laws. On the eve of the Civil War, Elizabeth Jennings finally had a gutful. She wrote a letter of protest to the *New York Tribune*, where abolitionist Horace Greeley was the editor. Then she sued the trolley car company. Her white lawyer had just passed the bar. But young Chester Arthur, who would become the president of the United States some thirty years later, won that case against the Third Avenue Railroad Company. The judge's ruling seems antiquated today: "Colored persons if sober, well behaved, and free from disease," could not be excluded from public conveyances. But it was a landmark decision. It would take several more years for New York's segregation laws to be dismantled, one courageous battle at a time. In 1863, the Irish would run amok in the city, turning their rage on blacks. Eleven African Americans were lynched, burned alive, or beaten to death by white mobs. Another two thousand would be made homeless before federal troops moved in to restore order.

It was during that terrifying time that Elizabeth Jennings Graham buried her only child. She later started the first kindergarten for black children in New York City, and then she faded into obscurity. Hardly a word about this courageous woman appears in the public record. Today you will find her decaying grave marker in the Cypress Hills Cemetery of New York City. She is buried next to her baby boy and a few thousand mostly Irish Union soldiers. Elizabeth Jennings's story is no less amazing than that of Rosa Parks and Martin Luther King Jr. It reminds us that great changes are seldom the result of monumental events. Rather, they are the sum of countless forgotten acts of heroism by ordinary people in insignificant places over decades and centuries. Your good deeds may not be remembered or celebrated, but each has a part in creating the world your children and grandchildren will inherit. So keep on doing the small things well.

Small acts, when multiplied by millions of people, transform the world.

The very hairs on your head are all numbered.
So don't be afraid; you are more valuable to
God than a whole flock of sparrows.

LUKE 12:7

The Day the Music Died

❧

*R*olling Stone magazine called his suicide "the day the music died." He might not have become a hostile loner who hated authority if his parents hadn't turned his childhood home into a war zone. Yet this alienated teen found his escape in a cast-off guitar that unlocked his genius. His blistering music, raw lyrics, and angry performances introduced a new word to the pop lexicon: *grunge*. By 1993 his band had recorded two megahit albums. The band's signature song, "Smells Like Teen Spirit," became the anthem of Generation X.

Kurt was now the biggest rock star on the planet. Yet he couldn't shake the angst of a tortured childhood. While he screamed at the world, painful stomach spasms shrieked back at him. When prescription drugs didn't work, he shot up heroin to kill the pain. In an attempt to create the family he never knew as a child, he got married. But his rocker wife was also hooked on heroin, and they fought as viciously as his parents had—until the baby came.

Kurt said that his daughter was the only pure thing in his life. Then his wife confessed in a *Vanity Fair* interview that she used heroin during her pregnancy. Kurt just about lost his mind fighting legal battles to keep authorities from taking his child. His screaming fits with his band, Nirvana, became tabloid fodder. After he almost died of an overdose in Italy, he returned to Seattle and locked himself in a room with loaded guns. His wife called 911, and police raided his estate.

By now his wife was running scared. She flew to Los Angeles to kick her drug habit, and begged Kurt to do the same for their baby's sake. He checked himself into a clinic where a psychiatrist said that he was a seething volcano, reliving his childhood traumas as if they had just happened.

When he got out, he promised to let go of the past. He flew home to Seattle, locked himself in his guesthouse, and took his own life.

When the news hit the media, teens across America locked themselves in their bedrooms. MTV said that Nirvana was to the '90s what the Beatles had been to the '60s, and Kurt Cobain's suicide was as catastrophic as John Lennon's murder. *Rolling Stone* magazine declared him the voice of a lost generation.

Kurt had so much to live for. Within ten years he sold fifty million albums. Nirvana was the flagship of Generation X. Fans worldwide were ready to make its next album another megahit. *Rolling Stone* ranked him the twelfth best guitarist of all time, and MTV listed him as the seventh greatest singer in pop history. In 2006 he surpassed Elvis as the top-selling deceased celebrity, and in 2014 he was elected to the Rock and Roll Hall of Fame. Weep for the troubled superstar who couldn't let go of past resentments. As you look to the future, allow this lesson from Kurt's story to be a springboard for success:

No one ever moved forward while chained to the past.

———— ◦ა◎ঌ◦ ————

One thing I do: forgetting what lies behind and straining
forward to what lies ahead, I press on toward the goal
for the prize of the upward call of God in Christ Jesus.

PHILIPPIANS 3:13-14, ESV

The Imaginary Home

❦

I t's not the state song of West Virginia. But don't tell that to the almost seventy thousand raucous fans who fill Milan Puskar Stadium in Morgantown to watch their beloved Mountaineers play football. Fans are whipped into something like a religious fervor as they belt out those words of a John Denver megahit:

Country roads, take me home to the place I belong.
West Virginia, mountain mama, take me home, country roads.

Bill and Taffy Danoff of the Starland Vocal Band had just performed in a Washington, DC, concert with folk-rock and country singer John Denver. After the show, they asked Denver to come over to their place to look at a song they had just written, although they originally had Johnny Cash in mind for it. John almost didn't make it because he got in an accident.

When Denver finally arrived, it was past midnight. He had thought about going back to the hotel, but after he saw the song, he was forever grateful that he hadn't let it slip away to Johnny Cash. He made some changes to the song and asked if they could sing it in their concert the next evening. The crowd went crazy, and John Denver knew that he had a hit song. They flew to New York where he recorded "Take Me Home, Country Roads" with Bill and Taffy singing backup. It became a megahit, has been enshrined in the Grammy Hall of Fame, and is surely the late, great John Denver's signature song.

But the folks of West Virginia, who have made this their favorite song, would be shocked to know that John Denver had never been to West

Virginia. Neither had the song's writers, Bill and Taffy Danoff. Bill got his inspiration from postcards sent by a West Virginia friend and from his time as a kid in Massachusetts listening to a powerful station out of Wheeling. He told NPR in 2011 that hearing that station was like hearing from somewhere far away. As far as he was concerned, West Virginia could have been in Europe.

The amazing story of a song that so wonderfully captured West Virginia but was written and recorded by three people who had never been there, speaks to the heart of every Christian. We have never seen Christ, but we know him. We have never been to heaven, but we sing songs about it. There is someplace over the rainbow that we know, even though we've never been there. The world we know lasts for a moment, but our home is heaven, and we eagerly await our Savior who will come from that place that is more real than any place we have been before.

Heaven will only be inherited by those who already have heaven in their soul.

———— ✿✿✿ ————

Since you have been raised to new life with Christ,
set your sights on the realities of heaven.

COLOSSIANS 3:1

The Shortest War
in History

ભ&©ન્

O ut of all the years in recorded human history, only 268 of them have been without a war. The longest war was waged between Christian and Muslim kingdoms on the Iberian Peninsula for 781 years! The shortest took place on an East African island. When Europe's powers sat down to carve up Africa, Germany turned Zanzibar over to Great Britain. The British were glad to stay out of local affairs, as long as the strategic island remained a safe haven for their warships. But when Khalid bin Barghash seized the throne of Zanzibar after allegedly poisoning his cousin, the British braced for trouble. In a Machiavellian move, London demanded that the new sultan abdicate in favor of their man, Hamoud bin Muhammed. When Bin Barghash stalled, the British ambassador delivered an ultimatum: abdicate by 9:00 a.m. local time on August 27, or face the full fury of the greatest empire on earth.

The sultan had no idea of what he was up against. He not only refused to cede his throne, he barricaded himself in his fortress with three thousand loyalists. The Royal Navy moved five heavily armed warships into the harbor and took dead aim at his fortifications. British diplomats begged the sultan to give up his throne or their warships would unleash their fury. But Bin Barghash was positive that civilized Europeans wouldn't do such a barbaric thing. It's too bad that the sultan of Zanzibar didn't have a crystal ball, or he might have looked two decades into the future to see Europeans unleash a world war that left forty million casualties. The sultan surely miscalculated when he figured that Europeans were civilized or chivalrous on the eve of the twentieth century.

At nine o'clock the British proved they could kill with the same promptness with which they served their afternoon tea. Just as they promised, their warships unleashed a barrage of firepower. The sultan's fortress disintegrated under the onslaught of modern artillery. In less than an hour, five hundred of his followers were dead. He hightailed it over to the German consulate. At exactly 9:40 a.m. the British guns were silent, and the fortress was in ruins. The shortest war in history had taken exactly thirty-eight minutes. But its terrible carnage was a horrific preview, in 1896, of a coming century in which wars would slaughter 160 million people.

The story of the world's shortest war is amazing because it is also a preview of a much shorter war yet to come. The ultimatum was delivered by Jesus two thousand years ago. Pretenders have stolen his throne. There is still time for them to abdicate. But like Khalid bin Barghash, these false kings will miscalculate the resolve of their Foe. They will bring armies to a place called Armageddon. The King of kings will unleash something far more terrible than English artillery; he will let loose the full fury of heaven. You want to be on the right side on that day. If you haven't bowed your knee to the King of kings, do it now—while there's still time.

If history is His Story, God gets to end it the way he chooses.

I saw heaven opened, and a white horse was standing
there. Its rider was named Faithful and True,
for he judges fairly and wages a righteous war.

REVELATION 19:11

A Shoemaker
Who Changed the World

❧

Willie was a stuttering plodder. The only job he could get was as a shoemaker's apprentice. The only girl who would marry him was Dorothy, who suffered from mental illness. But everything changed for Willie when he read a runaway bestseller. Most who read Captain Cook's journal were captivated by the exploits of a daring explorer. But Willie saw vast human needs in faraway places. He fashioned a world globe from leather scraps. After staring at it, he sobbed, "Here am I, Lord. Send me!"

Protestants were not sending foreign missionaries in the 1700s. When Willie stammered out his vision at a meeting of Calvinistic Baptists, an old pastor angrily shouted, "Young man, sit down! When God pleases to convert the heathen, he will do it without you or me!" Others tried to dissuade Willie by reminding him that he was a shoemaker saddled with a crazy wife. Someone said, "Face it, William: you're unfit." He stuttered, "B-b-but I c-c-can p-p-plod!"

For the next eleven years, Willie plodded until he could read the Bible in Latin, Greek, Dutch, and French. He was finally licensed to preach. When he wasn't in the pulpit of his tiny church, he rode across England, stuttering a message: "Expect great things from God. Attempt great things for God." Fortified by that credo, he gathered like-minded pastors to establish the Baptist Mission Society. He was so poor that he couldn't contribute a single penny to his new venture.

Yet he managed to collect a handful of missionaries and some pitiful resources to go to India. In 1793 they might as well have been going to the moon. His wife sat on the dock, refusing to leave. Twice Willie had to get on his knees and beg her to board the ship. When the missionaries arrived in India, Hindu radicals tried to kill them. The British East India Company refused to let them travel inland. Willie's five-year-old son died, and Dorothy lost her mind completely.

Willie labored seven years before he saw his first conversion. After twenty years, he had only a handful of converts. His first wife died, and then his second. But he continued to plod. When he died in 1834 at age seventy-three, he had translated the Bible into thirty-four languages, founded India's first college, established forty-five teaching centers, alleviated famine by teaching new agricultural methods, and worked to free Indian women from the cruelest sorts of bondage.

If you visit India today, you can find Willie's statue close to the parliament building. Even Hindus celebrate him as one of their nation's greatest heroes. History recalls Willie by his full name, William Carey. He has been dubbed the Father of Modern Missions. But he would be more impressed to know that some twenty-five million people in India have called Jesus Christ their Savior, and today there are five times more Christians in India than in England. Maybe you're just a plodder like Willie, in a place as small as a village cobbler's shop. Yet as long as you can plod, you can do so much more, if only you do what he did:

Expect great things from God. Attempt great things for God.

I am the LORD, the God of all the peoples of
the world. Is anything too hard for me?

JEREMIAH 32:27

The Mysterious Monk

✧

Joseph Matthäus Aigner had a death wish. But when he tried to end his unhappy life, a mysterious monk showed up at the most inopportune time to stop him. The skeptic might attribute this to sheer coincidence. A Buddhist could call it *karma*. A Christian would call it God's intervention. At the very least, it makes for another amazing story.

Aigner was blessed with decent talent. He would never become a great artist, but this Austrian journeyman made a good living as a portrait painter in the 1800s. Yet young Aigner was tormented by visions of grandeur. He could not rest until he produced a masterpiece. Alas, his mediocre talent reduced his aspirations to pipe dreams. At age eighteen he gave in to one of his frequent bouts of despair and tried to hang himself. Just as he was about to step off into midair, a monk of the Capuchin order mysteriously appeared. The good brother stopped Aigner from committing suicide.

At age twenty-two the artist again attempted suicide. As he was slipping the noose over his head, the same Capuchin monk appeared to stop Aigner from hanging himself. Again, he disappeared as quickly as he came. The Austrian artist never did learn the mysterious monk's name. Eight years later, the portrait painter joined a rebellion against Austrian authorities. He was captured and sentenced to hang as a traitor. Once again, on the eve of his execution, the same Capuchin monk showed up to plead with the authorities to spare him. When he was pardoned, did Aigner figure that heaven had orchestrated the appearances of this holy man? We will never know. But for the next thirty years, the artist lived the safe bourgeois existence of a successful portrait painter without further attempts at cutting life short.

But deep despair always lurked in the shadows. At age sixty-eight,

Joseph Aigner finally succeeded in committing suicide—this time with a pistol. No one showed up to stop him. But when they couldn't find a priest who was willing to officiate the service for someone who committed the cardinal sin of suicide, the same Capuchin monk showed up from seemingly nowhere to conduct the funeral. Afterward, he slipped away without giving his name. Was he perhaps an angel? No one can be sure.

The amazing encounters of an artist and a mysterious monk form a story of statistical impossibilities. No rational person could assign these four encounters to sheer coincidence. For those of us who believe that heaven is intimately involved in what happens on earth, there are no chance encounters. The God who created us for his own glory and loved us enough to send his Son to redeem his children never takes his eyes off us. He is closer to us than our own breath. Such a thought is both frightening and comforting. This much is surely true:

No one is sent by accident to anyone.

Our Father in heaven, may your name be kept
holy. May your Kingdom come soon. May your
will be done on earth, as it is in heaven.

MATTHEW 6:9-10

Vengeance and Survival

⊱⊶⊷⊰

The Siberian tiger is a monster—the largest cat in the world. The biggest ever measured was just short of thirteen feet in length; the heaviest weighed 1,025 pounds. Not only does the king of Russian forests have the bulk of an industrial freezer, it can leap twenty-five feet through the air and can vertically jump over a basketball hoop. No one ever wants to face this fearsome predator in the territory it has marked as its killing field.

Vladimir Markov should have known better when he went tiger hunting. But the Chinese were paying big money for the pelts and parts of these magnificent beasts, and the poverty of Russia made the payoff worth the danger. Besides, in the battle of man against beast, humans usually win. Isn't the cunning and firepower of a rational man superior to the savage instincts of a beast? Why else had poachers exterminated one-third of Siberian tigers in a decade?

Markov came upon a monster tiger feasting on his kill. His bullet hit the beast, but it ran off in wounded rage. It angrily watched from the brush as Markov dragged its half-finished meal away. It then staked out Markov's cabin, where it went on a rampage, systematically destroying everything that had the poacher's scent. Afterward, the Siberian tiger waited for forty-eight hours until Markov returned home. It pounced on the poacher, dragged him kicking and screaming into the nearby forest, and proceeded to eat him—not so much for food, but because it had a score to settle. This wasn't a spontaneous or instinctual response of animal savagery, but revenge that the beast had held in its mind for two days.

What happened next was something that had never been recorded in Russian history. The tiger began to stalk other humans in a manner that was chillingly premeditated, like the vigilante Charles Bronson in his Death Wish movies, as if it was methodically exacting revenge for every tiger shot by poachers. The man-eater seemed to be equal parts beast, human, and demon. Though the monster tiger was shot several times, bullets had little more effect on it than harpoons on Moby Dick. Finally, the authorities turned to an almost superhuman Russian woodsman, Yuri Trush. Trush and the tiger stalked each other in an epic duel between superman and supertiger. The fight ended with an earsplitting roar, a majestic leap by the beast, and a split-second reaction and deadly shot by Trush. The tiger lay dead at his feet, and locals breathed a sigh of relief.

This amazingly true story of man against beast reminds us of the enemy of our soul, the raging lion, who stalks us. His memory is long, and his revenge knows no bounds. But the Son of God became a man, stalked him, and defeated him at the Cross. There is nothing more dangerous than a wounded beast, but we have no need to fear this raging cat. Take heart from this truth:

The enemy may roar, but he has been declawed, defanged, and put on God's leash.

———— ✣ ————

Only by your power can we push back our enemies;
only in your name can we trample our foes.

PSALM 44:5

The Man Who Volunteered for Auschwitz

࿐

Inmate 4859 was one of those cursed souls doomed to Auschwitz. But unlike the others consigned to this camp of horrors, Witold Pilecki volunteered for the assignment. As a cavalryman, he earned the Polish Cross of Valor twice. After the German conquest of Poland, this hero continued to lead partisan guerrillas in an underground fight against the Nazi occupation.

In 1940 the Gestapo rounded up several of his resistance fighters and sent them to Auschwitz. At the time, little was known about the Nazi concentration camps. So Pilecki volunteered to get sent to Auschwitz to gather intelligence. After he allowed himself to be arrested, he was brutally beaten, tortured, and then hauled off to the camp. As Inmate 4859, he suffered stomach ailments, typhus, pneumonia, infestations of lice, backbreaking labor in extreme weather, soup crawling with worms, and unspeakable cruelty at the hands of sadistic guards. Yet he managed to put together a resistance organization in the camp and gather incriminating evidence of mass genocide while avoiding detection by seven thousand SS personnel. His reports of atrocities in Auschwitz were smuggled out to Warsaw and then on to London. Sadly, the Allies did not believe that the gassing of more than a million Jews could be taking place. When he broadcast on a jury-rigged radio from inside the camp, the world heard of the Holocaust for the first time. Until the day he died, Pilecki could never get over the fact that the Allies failed to bomb the railroad tracks on which death trains traveled or destroyed the gas chambers and crematoriums at Auschwitz.

When the Gestapo closed in, Inmate 4859 became one of the few prisoners to escape from the death camp. His detailed reports estimated that 1.5 million Jews would be gassed by March of 1943. He begged both the English and Russians to help his partisans liberate the camp, but they showed no interest. After the war, he continued his armed resistance against the Soviet occupation of Poland, smuggling out reports of their atrocities. On May 8, 1947, he was captured. Before his trial, KGB operatives subjected him to severe torture. He said to his wife, "Compared to them, Auschwitz was just a trifle." He refused to reveal the identity of his comrades or confess to crimes at his show trial. On May 25, 1948, Witold Pilecki was taken from his cell and shot in the back of the head.

It would be fifty years later, after the fall of Communism, before the amazing story of Inmate 4859 would be told. His one-hundred-page report on what took place in Auschwitz forever shuts the mouths of Holocaust deniers. If all heroes are shadows of Jesus Christ, then Pilecki's willingness to go into that Nazi death camp to rescue the doomed surely recalls Christ volunteering to come to earth and descending into hell to save a world of cursed people. May we, like Witold Pilecki, be willing to enter into the suffering of others to bring about their redemption. Inmate 4859 might agree with Saint Augustine:

It was pride that changed angels into devils; it is humility that makes men as angels.

_____ ⳩ _____

He humbled himself in obedience to God
and died a criminal's death on a cross.

PHILIPPIANS 2:8

The Man of a Million Lies

⸻

His Italian mother named him after the apostle Mark in the hopes that he would always tell the gospel truth. Yet when he later wrote a bestseller about his travels, cynics called it a book of a million lies. He was nicknamed Mark of a Million Lies.

In the 1200s, Europeans found it impossible to believe Mark's tales of a twenty-four-year odyssey that took him across the steppes of Russia, over mountains in Afghanistan, through deserts in Persia, and around the Himalayas into the far reaches of Asia.

Mark was one of the first Europeans to enter China. Through amazing circumstances, he became a favorite of the most powerful man on earth. Kublai Khan ruled over a domain that eclipsed the ancient Roman Empire. Mark saw cities that made Western capitals look like roadside villages. The khan's palace dwarfed the largest cathedrals and castles in Europe. It was so massive that its banquet hall could seat six thousand guests, all dining on plates of pure gold. He saw the world's first paper money and marveled at the explosive power of gunpowder. It would be five hundred years before Europe would produce as much steel as China manufactured in 1267, and six hundred years before the Pony Express would equal the speed of Kublai Khan's postal service.

Mark began his journey home to Venice loaded down with gold, silk, and spices. According to some accounts, tucked away in his pocket was a recipe for that Chinese culinary delight, pasta. The khan had sent him on his way with a royal guard of one thousand men. By the time they reached the Indian Ocean, six hundred had drowned or died of disease. A ragged Mark barely limped home, most of his riches lost along the way.

Folks dismissed his stories, and it wasn't long before he landed in jail. In that lonely dungeon, he dictated his fantastic yarns to a writer of romance novels. Those stories were marketed as *The Travels of Marco Polo*. But a skeptical public dismissed it as a book of a million lies.

Mark got out of that prison and went on to make another fortune. Yet he never shook that moniker, Marco the Liar. As he lay on his deathbed, his family, friends, and parish priest implored him to recant his fabrications lest they land him in hell. Mark spit out his final words: "I have not even told you half of what I saw."

Medieval cynics dismissed his stories as the tall tales of a lunatic or a liar. Yet history has established the credibility of *The Travels of Marco Polo*. A century later, another Italian read Mark's stories. By the time Christopher Columbus finished them, a dream was sparked that he, too, could discover new worlds.

Is there anything sadder than folks who are afraid to dream big or explore new worlds? Don't you dare be one of them! Allow Mark's story to send you out today with a sense of excitement, keeping this in mind:

You haven't seen the half of all the wonders that are still out there.

Eye has not seen, nor ear heard, nor have entered
into the heart of man the things which God
has prepared for those who love Him.

1 CORINTHIANS 2:9, NKJV

The Triumph of Bubbles

When Belle Silverman was born with bubbles in her mouth, her immigrant mother gave her a nickname that lasted a lifetime. Yet life was anything but bubbly for the girl called Bubbles. Brooklyn neighbors exclaimed that her golden curls and precocious talent made her a Jewish Shirley Temple. Those compliments became a curse when her obsessive stage mom stole Bubbles's childhood by dragging her to endless auditions for roles in radio, movies, and vaudeville. Mrs. Silverman was sure that her Shirley Temple look-alike was their ticket out of poverty. Repeated rejections at those auditions traumatized little Bubbles. So did the look of disappointment in her mother's eyes.

When she was sixteen, her voice teacher said that she was tailor made for the opera. But nothing ever came easy for Bubbles. She spent ten frustrating years on the road trying to make it in second-tier operas. The New York City Opera turned her down seven times before they accepted her. When Bubbles finally snagged a starring role, critics panned her performances as uneven. Leading opera houses refused to let her appear on their stages. It was only after she went to Europe and won over the toughest opera fans in the world that critics begrudgingly recognized her magnificent voice.

Even when she became a star at the Met and *Time* magazine dubbed her America's Queen of the Opera, her adoring public never knew that Bubbles was raising two children with disabilities. One of them was severely cognitively disabled. She spent a fortune building a sanctuary for her kids in Martha's Vineyard. After they moved in, it burned to the ground. Then her husband collapsed with a stroke. She cared for him for eight years while raising two children with special needs and juggling a demanding career.

You might think that a lifetime of setbacks would make Belle Silverman from Crown Heights a sour woman. But the lady nicknamed Bubbles plowed through her troubles with infectious joy. Barbara Walters called her the happiest person on earth. After a *Sixty Minutes* interview, Mike Wallace said that she was the most impressive person he had ever met. When he asked her how she had overcome bitterness to be so bubbly, she replied, "I can't control the circumstances of my life, but I can choose to be joyful."

You may remember Belle Silverman by her stage name, Beverly Sills. When Belle died in 2007, a *New York Times* obituary proclaimed the Brooklyn-born coloratura soprano to be America's most popular opera star since Enrico Caruso. But to family and friends, she will always remain Bubbles. Two years before her death, she summed up her challenges and triumphs to a *Times* reporter: "Man plans, and God laughs. I've never considered myself a happy woman. How could I be with all that's happened to me? But I choose to be a cheerful woman." When you face speed bumps on life's road, it might help to recall this line from Bubbles:

Circumstances are often beyond your choice, but you can choose to be cheerful.

———— ✤ ————

Worry weighs a person down;
an encouraging word cheers a person up.

PROVERBS 12:25

Looking for That Home

❦

S he hated the gritty, grimy oil-patch town on the bayou. Port Arthur was oil tanks and refineries, sulfur and salt water, rednecks, wildcatters, and a wild child who was stuck there by an accident of birth. Her friends called the wild child Pearl. But she felt more like a grain of sand stuck in the soft muck of the oyster's slimy flesh.

It didn't help that she was overweight and that her face was scarred with acne. When the mean girls ridiculed her, Pearl became a rebel. She traded in the bobby socks and pleated skirts of the 1950s for oversize men's shirts and baggy jeans. Pearl became the first girl in her school to wear a miniskirt. But she was no Twiggy, and when she squeezed her plus-sized body into that little skirt, she was called a promiscuous pig. But Pearl couldn't care less about what they thought. As far as she was concerned, she never did belong in Port Arthur.

Pearl's ticket out of town was her voice. It was raw and real, made for the folk-rock sound that was sweeping America. Pearl's tough-talking, hard-drinking, outrageous persona didn't fit the oil patch, but it was perfect for the Woodstock age. After kicking around coffeehouses across Texas, Pearl headed out to San Francisco. Her career didn't gain much traction, but she became hopelessly addicted to amphetamines and other drugs. So she headed back to Port Arthur.

Then she got her big break as lead singer in the San Francisco rock group Big Brother and the Holding Company. Jazzed by heroin, amphetamines, and bourbon that she guzzled during her performances, Pearl enflamed audiences with her unrestrained sexuality and gutsy sound. Her success also created jealousy with the band. So Pearl went solo. She wowed audiences from Woodstock to the Monterey Pop Festival, recording some hit singles and a successful album. But she moved from place to place like a gypsy, looking for that elusive paradise she dreamed about in Port Arthur. She also plowed through lots of lovers. Yet she lamented, "On stage I make love to twenty-five thousand people, and then I go home alone."

The first lady of rock 'n' roll was found dead from an overdose of drugs in a Hollywood hotel on October 4, 1970. She was only twenty-seven years old. Shortly after her death, her second album, *Pearl*, was produced. You remember Pearl by her birth name, Janis Joplin. Her most famous hit, "Me and Bobby McGee," was on that album. A haunting line captures her unfulfilled longing: "One day up near Salinas, Lord, I let him slip away. He's lookin' for that home, and I hope he finds it." Not only are Bobby McGee and Janis Joplin looking for a home, so are all of us. Whether we live in oil-patch Port Arthur or posh Beverly Hills, God has made us for himself. Until we find our refuge in him, we will have restless soul syndrome.

If we desire that which the world cannot satisfy, it is because we have been made for another world.

———— ✦ ————

Surely your goodness and unfailing love will
pursue me all the days of my life, and I will
live in the house of the LORD forever.

PSALM 23:6

The Reluctant Hero

❧

Alvin was a rabble-rouser. One of eleven children born to a poor mountain family, he grew up fighting for every last scrap. Along the way, he became a master woodsman and champion marksman. All those skills were necessary to put food on the table when his daddy died. Alvin spent only a few months in school, rendering him almost illiterate. He also fell in with a gang of ruffians who drank too much moonshine and got into too many hillbilly brawls.

But when his best friend was killed in a bar fight, Alvin found Jesus and joined a local church. With all the fanaticism of a reformed rogue, he gave up drinking, smoking, gambling, cussing, dancing, and violence of any kind. Yet about the time Alvin got religion, America was dragged into World War I. In 1917 the Tennessee mountain man got drafted by the army. He applied for conscientious objector status but was denied. After two days in prayer, he reluctantly reported for duty. No one was a better marksman, but Alvin made it plain that he wouldn't carry a weapon or shoot another human being. Some of his fellow soldiers accused him of cowardice. But an officer used a well-worn Bible to show him that just wars can accomplish God's greater good. Once Alvin came to the same conclusion, he became a dedicated soldier.

No one would have ever guessed that this conscientious objector would be dubbed "the greatest soldier in history." What happened on October 8, 1918, is the stuff of legend. Alvin was part of a company of eighteen Americans caught behind German lines in France. Their sergeant was killed along with half the company. Alvin took charge. He began to pick off the Germans one by one. As each enemy soldier fell dead, Alvin yelled that if they surrendered, the shooting would stop. Within minutes, the American corporal had killed more than twenty-five Germans. The remaining ninety came out of their trenches with hands held high. They were in for the surprise of their lives when they realized a lone Tennessee mountain man had done all the shooting. As Alvin and his handful of American boys made their way back to the Allied lines, more Germans surrendered. Alvin York had single-handedly killed twenty-five enemy soldiers and captured over a hundred others.

No soldier in American history has ever done more in a single military encounter. Nor has any been honored more than Sergeant Alvin York, who was awarded the Congressional Medal of Honor, the Distinguished Service Cross, the Badge of Nobility, and the French Croix de Guerre. The reluctant hero went back to Tennessee, where he married his sweetheart, had eight children, and established the York Institute to give kids the education he never had. He was prouder of that institute than his exploits in France or those medals. His amazing story reminds us that Christians can still be warriors. The godly should never look for a fight. But even Jesus made a whip and drove money changers out of the Temple. We should never back down from fighting the good fight for that which is right.

What is important is not to fight, but to fight the right enemy.

Thank God! He gives us victory over sin and
death through our Lord Jesus Christ.

1 CORINTHIANS 15:57

A Teacher's Final Lesson

ictoria had a single passion. From the time she was a little girl, she dreamed of being a teacher. When other girls were riding horses or dressing up like Cinderella, little Victoria was lining up her dolls like students and teaching them the three Rs. More than anything else, she wanted to mold young minds—the younger the better. That's why she studied to be an elementary school teacher and was working on a master's degree to become even more proficient.

Victoria's aunt Debbie says that she was ecstatic when she called to say that she had obtained her first job at an elementary school in Newtown, Connecticut. Five years later this bubbly goofball, with her infectious laugh and warm hugs, was everyone's favorite teacher. No one worked harder to prepare innovative lesson plans. At the beginning of her fifth year at the school, she posted a line on social media: "This is going to be the best year ever." What happened on December 14, 2012, would turn that happy prediction on its head.

Shortly after the opening bell, twenty-year-old Adam Lanza shot his way through the front door. He had already gunned down his mother, Nancy. This crazed young man came dressed to kill, wearing military fatigues and carrying an arsenal: a semi-automatic AR-15 assault rifle, Glock and Sig Sauer pistols, and plenty of ammo. Before the massacre at Sandy Hook Elementary School was over, he slaughtered twenty six- and seven-year-old children as well as six adults. Victoria knew that he was systematically moving from room to room, executing teachers and kids. She quickly got some children out of the room, and shoved others into the classroom closet. When Lanza came into the room, she stood defiantly in front of a huddle of six-year-olds and took a burst of gunfire. The police later found her lying on the bodies of the children she tried to save, like a mother hen covering her chicks.

At Victoria Soto's funeral, an overflowing crowd sang "Amazing Grace," one of her favorite hymns. Singer Paul Simon, a friend of her family, sang as a tribute one of his most famous songs: "The Sound of Silence." Its lines hauntingly capture Victoria's passion: "Hear my words that I might teach you. Take my arms that I might reach you. But my words like silent raindrops fell and echoed in the wells of silence." Victoria's voice may have been silenced, but the minister reminded everyone, "Her last act was selfless, Christlike in laying down her life for her children." Surely, the last lesson she ever taught her kids was her best.

The amazing story of Victoria Soto reminds us of the old adage that actions speak louder than words. The greatest lessons in life are caught, not taught. Our children watch what we do more than they listen to what we say. Jesus said that people would know that we are his disciples by the way we love one another, not by the way we preach the gospel.

A mouth will say anything, but actions will tell everything.

Just as you can identify a tree by its fruit, so
you can identify people by their actions.

MATTHEW 7:20

The Man Who
Fell to Earth

༄❦༄

Whated Russians couldn't do with their missiles, they tried to accomplish with rockets. The Cold War was heating up, and the Soviets were looking to score a propaganda coup. So they rushed Sputnik 1 to the launching pad in 1957. Shortly after, Laika became the world's most famous dog when she was put in orbit. Russia got out of the starting blocks first, and the space race was on.

Yuri Gagarin was sent to Star City outside Moscow as one of twenty cosmonauts. He underwent rigorous training, including brutal sessions in centrifuges to prepare for the g-forces of a rocket launch. Gagarin was chosen for the first manned spaceflight because Soviet premier Nikita Khrushchev wanted a broad-faced Slavic peasant, born of the soil, to show the power of Mother Russia. The cosmonaut arrived at the launchpad feeling a mixture of excitement and fear on April 12, 1961. The Soviets had rushed their schedule to stay ahead of the Americans, and their space capsule was little more than a metal cone perched precariously atop the third stage of an R-7 rocket. Soviet scientists knew that it had serious design flaws. But Kremlin bosses were willing to sacrifice cosmonauts for the glory of Communism.

Gagarin may have been only five feet two inches tall, but he was twisted like a pretzel inside that bucket of bolts grandiosely named the *Vostok* spaceship. He radioed, saying, *Poyekhali!*—"Let's go!" The rocket shook, rattled, and roared as it slowly lifted off the pad. The cosmonaut felt like he was being crushed by the g-forces. Then came that rush of relief as the capsule was catapulted into space. Gagarin was floating on celestial seas, the first man in history to see Earth shimmering like a blue pearl from space. But reentry was a terrifying free fall. The spaceship disintegrated as cables failed, insulating panels flew off, and bolts shook loose. Gagarin had been ordered to stay with the craft so the Soviets could claim the altitude record. Yet he knew the record would be forfeit if the pilot wasn't alive. At 4.3 miles above Earth, he parachuted out of *Vostok*'s death spiral. There were no television cameras to capture his landing. He walked to a farmhouse where an old peasant woman made the sign of the cross when she saw the man in a space suit. After he said, "Hello, comrades," a girl asked, "Are you from outer space, or have you fallen from the skies?"

The Soviets lied to the world when they announced that Yuri Gagarin had landed his spacecraft. But he knew the truth: he had barely made it back alive. The amazing story of the man who fell from the sky reminds us that, without Yuri Gagarin's first manned spaceflight, a lagging United States might not have been motivated to work harder and put American astronauts on the moon. We can become better when others defeat us— even if they cheat like the Soviets did. In victory, we celebrate. But in defeat, we evaluate.

Winners are not people who never fail, but those who never quit.

⎯⎯⎯ ⁂ ⎯⎯⎯

As for you, be strong and do not give up,
for your work will be rewarded.

2 CHRONICLES 15:7, NIV

A Mouse That Roared

୦ଡ଼ିତ୍ରୁ

He hated the name that his missionary mother gave him at birth. As a runt fighting for a spot on the rugby fields, he figured that *Henry* was a sissy's name. But it wasn't as bad as the nickname his classmates gave him: the Mouse.

After college, the Mouse returned to China to teach chemistry at a boys' school. When bloody civil war broke out, he went where the fighting was fiercest. His wife begged him not to go, but he was determined to go to those in greatest need. When the Japanese later invaded China, the Mouse sent his family to Canada but refused to leave his mission. It wasn't long before he landed in a concentration camp. He was a quiet hero in that barbed-wire mission field before a brain tumor threatened his life. Winston Churchill pleaded with the Japanese to release him. But when the prisoner exchange took place, the Mouse gave up his spot to a pregnant woman. Not long after, he died in that Japanese camp.

Why was this prisoner so important that the British prime minister personally intervened for his release? Perhaps Churchill recalled a day twenty years earlier when the Mouse roared on the center stage of Olympic history. In 1924 Henry was known by his middle name, Eric. Sportswriters called him the Flying Scotsman. You might have watched his inspiring story in the Oscar-winning film *Chariots of Fire*. At the Paris Olympics he won a gold medal. But a number of Olympians did that in 1924.

The Mouse made headlines for another reason: he refused to run when he discovered that the qualifying heats for his races were set for Sunday. Raised a strict Presbyterian, he believed that it was a sin to compete in athletics on the Sabbath. So the Mouse decided that standing on principle trumped running for gold. When the British Olympic committee pleaded with him to run for king and country, he refused to budge. His stand seems quaintly old-fashioned in an age where sports dominate our Sundays.

The Mouse went to church while others competed. He lost two gold medals but gained the respect of the world for his unwavering integrity. Later that week, he did win a gold medal, setting a world record that stood for a decade. Could it be that this principled stand in Paris produced a hero in China twenty years later? Maybe it was his character as much as his athletic prowess that led to a 2002 poll naming him Scotland's most popular sports figure of all time.

Mice can roar like lions when there's conviction in their bellies. A single mouse standing its ground has been known to stampede bull elephants. You might not agree with Henry Eric Liddell's views on the Sabbath, but in an age of compromise his story is worth remembering. There are some principles that far outweigh gold medals. Certainly this much is true:

If you don't stand for something, you will fall for anything.

———— ⌘ ————

Wide is the gate and broad is the road that
leads to destruction, and many enter through
it. But small is the gate and narrow the road
that leads to life, and only a few find it.

MATTHEW 7:13-14, NIV

The Woman Who
Tore Down the Wall

⟲◈⟳

The history books will never tell you that Nellie Clyde Wilson ended the Cold War. But too often history overlooks its most important people.

Nellie was a little wisp of a woman, born the youngest of seven kids in a small town on the road to nowhere. Despite her strict Presbyterian upbringing, she fell head over heels in love with a dashing Irish Catholic named Jack.

It wasn't long after the wedding that Jack began to show his true colors. Brought up in a family of hard drinkers, Jack had a taste for whiskey. Jobs were hard to come by, and it didn't help that Jack's drunkenness got him repeatedly fired. Their family was forced to move at least ten times in fourteen years. Nellie eked out a meager living by taking in sewing and laundry, and somehow managed to make the meals stretch for Jack and their two boys. Most months she barely scraped together the rent money. Yet she never lost her sense of humor or optimism. Her youngest boy often recalled that she was the most positive woman in his life.

Mostly, her boys observed the way she loved Jesus. They went with her to the jailhouse, bringing hot food to prisoners. They watched her subsist on crackers because she had taken her meal next door to a sick neighbor. When Jack complained about her tithing to the church, Nellie good-naturedly replied that God would make their 90 percent twice as big if he got his tenth.

Nellie was a bit player in small-town America. You might never have known who she was if it hadn't been for her sons. They flourished under her unbounded optimism and grew strong observing her heroic faith. She steeled them with discipline and lavished them with love. Every night she read her boys stories about good and evil. Her youngest son's favorite was about a knight in shining armor who conquered an evil empire. From Nellie, this little boy learned how to dream big and overcome impossible odds. She nurtured his love for acting and told him that he could change the world. Most of all, she taught him to love God.

The world remembers this wisp of a woman by her married name: Nellie (Nelle) Clyde Wilson Reagan. The son she nicknamed Dutch grew up to live out his mother's bedtime story, becoming the knight in shining armor who triumphed over an evil empire. President Ronald Reagan often said that his mother was the most influential person in his life.

Could it be that this diminutive washerwoman from a small town in Illinois was the one who tore down the Berlin Wall and set millions free from Communist tyranny because of a dream that she instilled in her son?

As you ponder your own life story, you might take heart from something that Nellie wrote in her well-worn Bible:

You can be too big for God to use, but you can never be too small.

———— ∽⚬ঔ∾ ————

He gives grace generously. As the Scriptures say,
"God opposes the proud but gives grace to the humble."

JAMES 4:6

Collapsing to Victory

❧

K ayla is some kind of warrior. This collegiate track star enters her events knowing that she will have to deal with postrace trauma. She never forgets that she's running on borrowed time. Every race may be her last because on any given morning Kayla may wake up unable to walk or move again. Yet she keeps on running with courage that astounds the track world.

This amazing young woman may be one of America's top runners, but she also battles multiple sclerosis, a disease that attacks her central nervous system—inducing chronic fatigue, blurred vision, loss of balance, numbness, tingling, and weakness of limbs. These symptoms would be a death knell for most competitors, but they spur Kayla to make the most of her borrowed time.

She was a fourteen-year-old soccer player when the symptoms of MS first appeared. The initial attacks caused lesions and scarring on her brain and spine that affected her ability to control her legs, making it impossible to play soccer. But she could still run. Although she started out as one of the slowest runners on her high school cross-country team, she gamely fought through a rigorous training schedule. Through gut-wrenching determination, this overcomer became the captain of her Mount Tabor team. She won the North Carolina state championship, set the twenty-first best time in the United States, and went undefeated in meets during her senior year. She is now a scholarship runner for Lipscomb University in Nashville, majoring in molecular biology with an eye to becoming a forensic scientist. Though she battles constant fatigue, she is as successful in the classroom as she is running track or cross-country.

Kayla lines up for every race knowing that the body heat from running will cause her to lose all feeling in her legs. So she uses the swinging gait of her arms to control her pace. She knows that if she falls, she'll struggle to get up to complete the race. As she crosses the finish line, she collapses helplessly into the arms of her coaches and is carried away like a limp doll. Only after she lies on the ground for ten minutes or more does the feeling return—like hot needles of burning pain. When this award-winning bundle of courage is asked why she continues to put herself through the pain and anguish, she says that she does so to prove to every MS sufferer and every other disabled person that they don't have to be sidelined by their afflictions.

This amazing story of Kayla Montgomery is a reminder to all of us that we never know when we will run our last race. Even those of us without a disability like MS have no guarantee that we will even get out of bed tomorrow morning. Like Kayla, we need to squeeze the most out of every precious second today, because the present is all we have for sure. This is an incontrovertible truth:

The past is a memory, the future is a maybe, and now is the moment.

———— ✧ ————

Do not boast about tomorrow,
for you do not know what a day may bring.

PROVERBS 27:1, NIV

Sixty-Six Shining Lights

❧❧❧

Nineteen-year-old Britney excitedly called her mother from the Hotel Montana in Port-au-Prince. Cherylann still remembers some of the last words she ever heard from her daughter: "They love us so much and are so happy." A few days later she texted, "I want to move here and start an orphanage myself."

A few hours later, a 7.1 earthquake struck Haiti, killing more than two hundred thousand people, and leaving millions homeless. Britney was among fourteen students and faculty from Florida's Lynn University who were there to work with handicapped orphans. When her parents heard that the Hotel Montana had collapsed in the quake, they were frantic with worry. For two days they sat by the phone and television. They even appealed to President Obama to send people to find their daughter.

Then on Thursday morning, Len and Cherylann were sure that they spotted Britney's photo among eleven Lynn students who had been found alive. They happily sped off to the airport to fly down to Florida, telling Boston reporters that they wanted to be there to welcome their daughter when she stepped off the helicopter from Haiti. Hours after they arrived in Florida, the president of Lynn College informed them of the devastating news that the rescue teams had been wrong. Their daughter was still missing. On a single Thursday they had run the gamut of emotions from worry to exhilaration to despair. They waited for thirty-three days before they got the devastating news that Britney's body had been found in the rubble of the Montana Hotel. The pain they felt was unimaginable. There can be no sorrow greater than burying a child before their time.

How does a family recover from unspeakable heartache? The Gengels decided to fulfill Britney's dream. They made sixty-seven pilgrimages to

Grand Goave, a small fishing town two hours' drive from Port-au-Prince, to work on the Be Like Brit orphanage. They chose this site because it would have been the next site on Britney's itinerary before she died. Today, a beautiful $1.8 million campus employs seventy-eight Haitians, and is home to sixty-six orphans. Len and Cherylann Gengel chose the number as a living symbol of the thirty-three days they waited before Britney's body was found: thirty-three boys and thirty-three girls.

"When you lose a child it's the most unnatural act of mankind," says Len Gengel. "But at the same time, out of the darkness and out of our grief and pain we have these beautiful sixty-six shining lights." Britney Gengel's amazing story proves the enduring power of a dream. An earthquake cannot crush it, nor can the grave. Her family's amazing story reminds us that the darkness of grief can give birth to sixty-six shining lights. There can be no resurrection without a death. The dark night of the soul cannot last forever. Neither will yours, if you rise up to turn the hurt into something that gives hope. Surely Britney and her parents would agree with Victor Hugo:

Even the darkest night will end, and the sun will rise.

⚜

Weeping may last through the night,
but joy comes with the morning.

PSALM 30:5

The Teenage Cardinal

❦

No one was ever born with a bigger silver spoon in his mouth than the son of Lorenzo the Magnificent, godfather of Florence and head of the most powerful banking cartel in Europe. Not only was Lorenzo the patron of such artists as Botticelli and Michelangelo, he also built cathedrals and funded the Vatican. But Lorenzo's largesse was not without strings. He cut a deal with a corrupt pope, Innocent VIII, to make his son Giovanni a cardinal at age thirteen. The skids were now greased for the Medici cartel's eventual control of the Vatican. After Pope Alexander VI took the Holy See into the sewer and Pope Julius II waged his unholy wars, huge bribes got Lorenzo's pampered rich kid elected Pope Leo X in 1513.

Leo's election was tantamount to a Mafia takeover. Immediately, the young pope stacked the college of cardinals with his cousins. He then proceeded to go on a spending spree. When he raided the Vatican treasury to finance a war, securing his nephew as the Duke of Urbino, he narrowly escaped being poisoned by angry cardinals. But his brush with death didn't stop Leo. He spent huge sums of money to make Saint Peter's Basilica the showplace of Christendom. When challenged, the spendthrift responded, "Since God has given us the papacy, let us enjoy it." He joked, "What good is it to have Saint Peter's keys if we don't use them to unlock heaven's bank?" His efforts to make Rome the cultural center of the world drained the papal treasury within two years. Leo was reduced to selling off his Vatican palace, piece by piece. He sold papal indulgences—the ecclesiastical version of "get out of jail free" cards in the game of Monopoly. Folks bankrupted themselves to buy their way out of hell or purgatory.

When Martin Luther took his stand against Leo, the pope shrugged, saying, "Nothing will come of that dustup in Northern Germany." By the time the genie was out of the bottle, never to be put back again, Leo was in over his head. His papal bull of 1520, *Exsurge Domine*, condemned Luther's Reformation. But the German laughed and invited his friends to a barbeque, saying, "I plan to roast a papal bull." To the delight of his dinner guests, he threw Leo's *Exsurge Domine* into a roaring fire. The rich kid who became a cardinal at age thirteen died between his silk sheets at the age of forty-five. During his disastrous papacy, he had bankrupted the Vatican, brought about a schism in the church, and dissipated his own personal fortune. He did leave behind the magnificent Saint Peter's Basilica, but it came at a terrible price.

This amazing story shouts a warning. The Peter Principle was alive and well in Saint Peter's. We can all rise to a place that we are incompetent to handle. If we get there too soon, it can be disastrous. Giftedness is something we get from God. Competency is earned through experience. Character can only be gained by persevering through life's tribulations. All three take time to develop.

The greater the achievement, the greater will be its danger.

<hr />

It's better to wait for an invitation to the head
table than to be sent away in public disgrace.

PROVERBS 25:7

The Angel in the Red Bandana

❦

Was Welles Crowther an angel? His mother said that he was just her little boy who grew up to be a hero. But there are plenty of folks who will tell you that he was the angel in a red bandana on that September day in 2001. His father's voice still shakes with both grief and wonder when he talks about what happened after that second airliner hit the south tower of the World Trade Center: Welles "ran toward the danger, not away from it."

Welles was a rookie equities trader working in the Wall Street district when the terrorist attack took place. But the twenty-four-year-old also had training as a volunteer fireman in Upper Nyack, New York. So he took off at a run to the buildings that others were fleeing. He pulled out a red bandana and wrapped it around his face as a mask of protection against dust and smoke. Then he ran up the stairs, getting as high as the seventy-eighth floor of the south tower. Nobody knows how many times he went up and down those stairs in the choking dust and searing heat, but he managed to get at least eighteen people out of the building to safety. No one knew his name, but afterward stories began to circulate about a mysterious man referred to as "the angel in the red bandana" who rescued folks until the tower collapsed in on him.

Welles Crowther was just one of several heroes who gave their lives to save others at the World Trade Center. Disasters bring out the best and worst in people. They will invariably expose the weaknesses of some and reveal the strength of others. There will always be criminals, looters, profiteers, cowards, victims, survivors, and heroes in every catastrophe.

By definition, the heroes are always in the minority—but these brave few inspire us all to be better long after they have sacrificed themselves for others.

Six years later, nearly a thousand people gathered at the Lafayette Theater not far from New York City for the premier of a documentary movie, *Man in Red Bandana*. The ornate old theater from the 1920s displayed the world's largest red bandana, some twenty by twenty feet in size. Many of those in attendance wore red bandanas in honor of an "angel" who gave his or her life to save others. Almost two decades later, Welles's mother, Alison, says, "Young people come up to me over and over and over again and say, 'We want to try to be like Welles.'"

The amazing story of the angel in the red bandana is a testimony to the staying power of heroism. In an age that is all too self-seeking, people still admire self-sacrifice. It never goes out of fashion. That's why, two thousand years after he died, people may reject the Christian religion, but they still admire the Jesus who gave his life for others on an old rugged cross. When you live with the same sacrificial love as Jesus, you have preached the only gospel that still attracts people.

Love is not possible without sacrifice, and sacrifice is not possible without love.

There is no greater love than to lay
down one's life for one's friends.

JOHN 15:13

The Fixer

❦

Marty was a fixer. Although his mother loved him, she was a harsh disciplinarian. His coal-miner daddy constantly berated and bullied him, and as hard as he tried, Marty could never quite please his earthly father. So he figured that maybe he could please his Father in heaven. This obsession would almost destroy his life.

To fix things with his coal-miner father, he went off to college and law school where he drove himself to earn top honors. But his dormitory was a medieval version of the movie *Animal House*. Marty took a vow of chastity, but he couldn't control his sexual fantasies. He whipped himself with thornbushes and plunged into icy ponds, but couldn't rein in his youthful lusts. While traveling through the thick forests one day, he was caught in a violent storm. As lightning danced about him, he was sure that a vengeful God was about to exact retribution. He screamed, "Help me, Saint Anna! I will become a monk." Having survived the tempest, he entered a monastery. His coal-miner daddy never forgave Marty for that.

He threw himself into the cloistered life with a frenzy, fastidiously keeping all the rules. He said, "If ever a monk got to heaven by his monkery it was I." Marty earned a doctorate, taught at the nation's premier university, and became a prolific writer. He also excelled at doing good deeds. But none of that calmed his angst. He confessed, "I lost touch with Christ the Savior and Comforter, and made him the jailor and hangman of my poor soul."

A frantic Marty went on a pilgrimage to Rome, where he hoped to find salvation. Instead he saw debauchery. Princes of the church lived in luxury, priests kept mistresses, holy offices were bought and sold, and sinners tried to bribe their way out of hell. Disillusioned, Marty found his way to marble stairs in the Vatican. He climbed up those steps on his hands and knees, kissing each one and repeating the *Pater Noster* (Our Father). After this self-imposed torture, his elbows and knees were reduced to a bloody pulp. He fell into a heap of exhaustion and cried out words written by Paul: "The righteous shall live by faith!" That moment, the boy who never satisfied his earthly father died. The man who worked to please his heavenly Father was born again. A revival began in Marty's soul that would spark a great reformation years later.

Martin Luther was the consummate fixer. He tried to fix things with both his earthly daddy and heavenly Father. He was constantly trying to fix others. Maybe you have his fixation. Are you worn out yet? Why don't you relax and let God do the fixing? Now is the time to remember that there is a God, and none of us are him. In fact, this is why Jesus came:

None of us has enough to do enough to fix enough. Only God's grace has enough to fix all that is broken.

⋯⊙⋯

It is by grace you have been saved, through faith—
and this is not from yourselves, it is a gift of God—
not by works, so that no one can boast.

EPHESIANS 2:8-9, NIV

The Curse of Macbeth

⟡⊙⟡

It is one of the bard's most celebrated plays, but it is considered bad luck in the theater world to utter the word Macbeth. That's why actors traditionally refer to it as "The Scottish Play." William Shakespeare may have telegraphed the curse when he penned one of its most famous lines: "something wicked this way comes." Then there are the black magic spells in the incantations of the three witches in his opening scene.

At its first performance in the early 1600s, the boy who played Lady Macbeth became violently ill and died before going onstage. Shakespeare himself had to play the Scottish queen. King James I was so disgusted by the play's bloody violence and occult themes that he banned it for several years.

No one takes more risks than actresses playing Lady Macbeth. On several occasions, those playing the wicked queen were chased out of the theater by an angry mob. One actress almost died when she fell off the stage during the sleepwalking scene. In 1926 an actor got so caught up in his part that he actually tried to strangle Lady Macbeth onstage. Luckily, other players pried his hands loose from the hysterical actress.

In 1849 the play so riled up an audience in New York City that the theatergoers started a riot that spilled out into the streets. Before order was restored, about thirty people were killed. In 1937 a piece of heavy staging mysteriously fell, barely missing Laurence Olivier. Had it fallen a few inches closer, the venerable Olivier would have been crushed to death. In the same presentation, the tip of a sword flew from the stage, hitting a theatergoer and causing him to have a heart attack. But no production of Macbeth was more disastrous than the one in 1942 starring John Gielgud. Three actors died during its tragic run, and the costume designer committed suicide.

In 1953 when Charlton Heston played the lead in the cursed play, he suffered a bad motorcycle crash during rehearsals. His legs were also burned badly in a performance. Later it was discovered that his tights were mysteriously soaked in kerosene. The list of mysterious deaths, violent illnesses, unexplainable accidents, and other weird happenings goes on and on.

The amazing story of the curse of Macbeth could be dismissed as co-incidence. We might chuckle at the superstitions of actors who refuse to utter the word *Macbeth*, or directors who ban it on movie sets. Or we could see the danger of the occult. The real incantations of witches, even written in script, or acted out on stage, have power. Playing with a Ouija board; allowing palm readers, dealers of tarot cards, or horoscopes to tell your future; or dabbling in the magic arts come with risks. Beware of video games, books, or movies that open the door to a real and frightening world of evil spirits and their dark lord.

We shouldn't play games with someone who plays for keeps.

———— ⚮ ————

You, Timothy, are a man of God; so run from all these
evil things. Pursue righteousness and a godly life,
along with faith, love, perseverance, and gentleness.

1 TIMOTHY 6:11

Helper of the Helpless

❦

When her Irish father died after losing his business, Amy had to drop out of school to help her mother. One day, as her family was leaving church, a beggar woman came out of the shadows to ask for help. As other parishioners hurried by, Amy was embarrassed to be seen with the vagabond and hid her face in shame. When she and her mother stopped at a restaurant to have tea and biscuits, Amy looked up to see a beggar girl with a dirty nose pressed against the window, looking at her food. At that moment, the Irish girl quietly promised God that when she grew up, she would help the helpless.

Amy didn't have to wait long to fulfill her promise. On Saturdays she went with her pastor to hand out tracts and food in the slums of Belfast. The women were too poor to buy hats, so they covered their heads with cast-off shawls. People of means ridiculed them as the "shawlies." But Amy loved these ragamuffins. She got together a group of ladies to knit fine woolen shawls that these ragpickers and factory girls could wear with pride. When their "betters" in churches refused to accept Amy's shawlies, she gathered the money to purchase a building so they could have their own services.

Amy did all this while suffering neuralgia that kept her chronically fatigued and bedridden for days. When she announced that God had called her to the Far East to work with even poorer women, people said she was crazy. But Amy headed for Japan in 1893. She learned the language and tried to wear a kimono, but it was too thin, and the cold caused her neuralgia to flare up. She spent weeks in bed, unable to move. She also managed to go out to peasants in rural villages. But the freezing weather was making her useless. So Amy headed for the warmer climate and even poorer women in India.

There, Amy learned about girls sold into temple prostitution. The woman who had helped ragamuffins in shawls gave herself to outcasts in saris. She dyed her skin dark and donned a sari so that she could steal into temples and free the prostitutes. She was chased by irate Hindu priests, arrested by authorities, and warned by other missionaries that she made Christians look foolish. But opposition didn't stop the woman who promised God that she would help the helpless. In fifty years Amy freed hundreds of girls from sex trafficking—in spite of the fact that she was often too helpless to get out of bed. But during her bouts with neuralgia, Amy Carmichael wrote books that have inspired the faith of millions.

This amazing story inspires us to ask if there are people who need our help. They may be as close as a girl pressing a dirty nose against the restaurant window, looking longingly at our food. They might be as far away as the victims of sex trafficking in India. But we just might become helpers of the helpless if we take to heart something Amy often said:

You can give without loving. But you can't love without giving.

———— ❧ ————

The generous will prosper; those who refresh
others will themselves be refreshed.

PROVERBS 11:25

Sarah's House of Spirits

こめのかめめ

When Sarah wed William Winchester, she married into a vast fortune from the famous repeating rifle that won the West. But when her only child, Annie, died in July of 1866, she became mentally unstable. Fifteen years later, her husband died of tuberculosis. Though she was now one of the richest women on earth, she had no peace. Then a spiritualist medium told her that her tragedies were divine retribution for the death wrought by Winchester rifles. She was instructed to move west and use her ill-gotten fortune to build a house for the spirits of those killed by Winchesters. As long as she kept building those abodes for spirits, she would stay alive. So Sarah moved to San Jose, California, purchased a six-room house, and began to add rooms for Winchester spirits.

What this paranoid woman built over the next four decades is one of history's most amazing architectural monstrosities. Twenty carpenters worked in shifts twenty-four hours a day, seven days a week. Sarah designed each room after consulting the dead in nightly séances. By the time she died in 1922, her Winchester Mystery House had one hundred sixty rooms in twenty-four thousand square feet over six acres. It contained two thousand doors, ten thousand windows, forty-seven fireplaces, forty stairways, thirteen bathrooms, six kitchens, an elevator, two basements, and a hidden attic.

But it's not its size that makes Sarah's masterpiece so amazing as much as its maze-like corridors, doors, and stairways that lead to nowhere, or its sheer drop-offs, rooms within rooms, and shortcuts that lead in endless circles. It's a Gothic puzzle designed to confuse vindictive spirits. Sarah's fixation with the number thirteen runs throughout the house: chandeliers with thirteen lights, thirteen sink drains, sets of thirteen clothes hooks, and thirteen bathrooms. To cancel out the evil vibrations of the number thirteen there are many features with the lucky number seven. The heiress had several master bedrooms built so that she could sleep in a different room every night to confuse vengeful spirits that were searching for her.

When Sarah Winchester died of a heart attack at age eighty-three, her will was written in thirteen sections and signed thirteen times. It came as no surprise that none of her heirs wanted her house. Today, passersby stop to gawk and wonder what would possess someone to build such a monstrosity. The amazing story of Sarah's spirit house is a testimony to the power of paranoia and the dangers of the occult. Answers to life are not found in Ouija boards, tarot cards, horoscopes, or séances. In an age obsessed with the occult, we need to remember that the Holy Spirit alone speaks through the only Book that reveals the only way to the peace and security poor Sarah never found in her spirit house.

You can't walk with God while holding hands with the devil.

⸙

When you look up into the sky and see the sun,
moon, and stars—all the forces of heaven—
don't be seduced into worshiping them.

DEUTERONOMY 4:19

The Chief Inspirator

❧

Toan has an amazing story to share. He was born into a war-ravaged world on the verge of collapse. By the time he was taking his first toddler steps, he was trying to keep up with his family as they fled the advancing Communists. Somehow, his family managed to get to the United States with a total of four dollars between them. Ten people were crammed into a tiny trailer house in Sacramento. They hardly spoke English, and jobs were hard to come by, but the same determination that got them to America lifted them out of poverty.

Toan worked hard at his studies. After college, he parlayed his good looks and smarts into a career as a television reporter in San Francisco, and cohosted the PBS show *California Heartland*. The immigrant kid from Vietnam was living the American dream. But few folks knew that he had just gone through a family tragedy. Toan was in Wisconsin working in his first job as a television reporter when he got the phone call that his dad was dying of stomach cancer. Toan immediately quit his job and moved back to Sacramento to care for his father. He bathed him, fed him, cleaned up his messes, and watched the cancer consume his body. He was with his dad 24/7 until he died several months later.

Shortly afterward Toan watched his aunt and both grandmothers pass away. Seeing four family members die within a year changed the direction of Toan's life. He saw the spirituality that sustained his loved ones in their darkest moments and was nourished by the personal stories that gave their lives meaning. It was during that season of reflection that the TruthDare podcast was birthed in Toan's mind. In his innovative podcasts he interviews people from all walks of life, challenging them to share the spiritual motives that drive their lives and to tell stories of how they overcame challenges. He believes that there are heroes among us, and their stories can inspire the rest of us to be heroes. In one podcast he interviewed a fifty-one-year-old UCLA lecturer who gave up his home to a homeless woman and her four children for a year. Toan has also started an organization called Community Heroes, which encourages schoolchildren to become agents of change.

Toan Lam could have been satisfied to live the American dream as a television personality. Instead he is helping others fulfill their dreams. He calls himself the chief inspirator—instigating and motivating others to be all they can be. Toan has an amazing story, but he's more interested in you sharing yours. He says that our story connects with others to show them that no matter what they are going through, they are not alone and there is hope. We should all take Toan Lam's credo to heart:

There is only one you. Treasure your gift. Hone it. Use it to help others. Service is the key to joy.

───── ✦ ─────

We are God's masterpiece. He has created us
anew in Christ Jesus, so we can do the good
things he planned for us long ago.

EPHESIANS 2:10

Barbarians at the Gates

༄ཻ

The city of Carthage was a marvel of the ancient world. Founded by the seafaring Phoenicians, it stood majestically on the Gulf of Tunis in North Africa with two artificial harbors—one built for commercial shipping and the other boasting more than two hundred battleships. Twenty-three miles of massive walls surrounded the city, making it impregnable. With half a million inhabitants, it was one of the largest cities in the world. Its armies were led by generals like Hannibal the Great. Its navies sailed the world, even to the Americas some five hundred years before Christ. Carthage ruled the seas and became fabulously wealthy and powerful as a result.

But kings invariably come and go, and empires rise and fall. A city-state on the Tiber River now challenged the city-state on the Gulf of Tunis. In 264 BC the first of three successive wars was fought between Rome and Carthage. Historians call them the Punic Wars. The savagery and destruction was horrific. In the Second Punic War, Hannibal brought his war elephants across the Alps and almost destroyed Rome. But the city on the Tiber got its revenge in 146 BC, during the Third Punic War. The three-year Roman destruction of Carthage was the ancient version of the Siege of Stalingrad in World War II. The Romans tore down the walls and slaughtered seven hundred thousand people. The fifty thousand who survived this genocidal holocaust were sold into slavery.

As a handful of Carthaginians made their final suicidal stand in the temple of their god Eshmun, the Roman general Scipio Africanus stood in the nearby Tunisian hills watching the burning city. We might expect the conqueror to be smiling in triumph. But the Greek historian Polybius wrote that the Roman "burst into tears, and stood long reflecting on the inevitable change which awaits cities, nations, and dynasties, one and all, as it does every one of us men." At that moment, Scipio Africanus had a frightening premonition: just as the sun was setting on Carthage after seven hundred years, so it would one day set on his city. Rome might be called the Eternal City, but no city, nation, or civilization is eternal. In August of AD 410, the barbarian Visigoths sacked Rome, and the city that had stood proudly on the Tiber for eight hundred years suffered the same fate as Carthage.

Some would say that the barbarians are again at the gates. The amazing stories of the fall of Carthage and Rome remind us that none of us can put our hope in cities, nations, civilizations, armies, navies, generals, or our own manufactured gods. There is only one eternal city whose builder and architect is God, only one Savior, and only one inevitable ending: Jesus will return, the kingdoms of this earth will all fall, and the King of kings alone will rule forever. The Carthaginians in 146 BC and the Romans in AD 410 would say amen to this:

When the final line is written, it will be too late to change your story.

‒‒‒‒‒‒ ৎ৯৩৩ ‒‒‒‒‒‒

This is all the more urgent, for you know how late
it is; time is running out. Wake up, for our salvation
is nearer now than when we first believed.

ROMANS 13:11

History's Greatest Athlete

❧

When Bright Path left Oklahoma for the Carlisle Indian Industrial School, he was just another kid off the reservation. But everything changed when he walked by the high-jump pit on the athletic field. When curiosity got the best of him, he casually ran toward the high bar in street clothes and effortlessly cleared it, surpassing the school record. His feat got the attention of the school's athletic director, the legendary Pop Warner. The Native American phenom soon became a star on the track team. But it was on the football field that he took America by storm as a halfback, placekicker, and defensive back, leading little Carlisle to an upset victory over number one Harvard and then blowing out top-ranked West Point the next year. He earned all-American honors both years. No one was surprised when he was named to the US Olympic team in 1912. But everyone was astounded when he won both the pentathlon and decathlon at the Stockholm Olympics, causing Sweden's king to declare him the greatest athlete in the world.

Bright Path returned home to a hero's welcome. But when it was discovered that he had received meal money while playing in minor league baseball games, the Olympic committee revoked his amateur status, stripped him of his gold medals, and expunged his name from the records. Bright Path spent the next several years in a dizzying effort to prove that he was still the greatest athlete in the world. He starred in major league baseball, batting .327 in his last season. At the same time, he played pro football. He even spent a year as the president of the new NFL while scoring touchdowns on the playing field. When his body finally gave out at age forty-one, he got roles in sixty Hollywood films.

But Bright Path couldn't shake his resentment over losing those gold medals. He plowed through three marriages and all his money. He lived his last years in a trailer in small-town California, digging ditches to make a buck, his once magnificent body broken by alcohol abuse. By now, the world had forgotten about the Hercules named Wa-Tho-Huk, or Bright Path. But things turned around in 1950, when the Associated Press named him the greatest athlete in the first half of the twentieth century. A year later Burt Lancaster played him in the Hollywood movie *Jim Thorpe—All-American.* In 1953, at age sixty-four, Bright Path died of a heart attack in his trailer. In 1983, some thirty years after his death, the Olympic committee finally righted a wrong by restoring his medals and records.

The amazing story of Jim Thorpe reminds us that it matters little what others say about us. They may take away our medals, expunge our exploits from the record, and even forget what we once did—but God keeps a record, and eternity will shout out our deeds for all to know. So don't allow shortsighted people to rob you of the personal satisfaction and joy of a job well done.

The best reward of a thing well done is having done it.

—

The Son of Man will come with his angels
in the glory of his Father and will judge
all people according to their deeds.
MATTHEW 16:27

The Cop Who Couldn't Be Bought

⌒⌒⌒

Paco may have been a heroic New York cop, but fifty years later he is still hated by police in Gotham. Maybe the fact that he was a whistle-blower is the reason he gets hate mail from officers across America. But law-abiding citizens everywhere still applaud Paco for exposing the rotten core of the Big Apple.

His proud immigrant family christened him Francisco, but Brooklyn buddies nicknamed him Paco. Though his daddy barely eked out a living in his tiny shoe-repair shop, he told his son that he could achieve his wildest dreams. He also instilled in him a commitment to uncompromising honesty. With those old-world values, Paco worked hard to realize his dream to be a New York cop. When he graduated from the police academy, he gave his all to be the best officer on the force. He was rewarded by being made a detective, and he worked tirelessly as an undercover cop to clean up the sixties and seventies drug epidemic.

But it wasn't long before Paco became disillusioned with a police department riddled with corruption. Cops were taking bribes from crime bosses, stealing confiscated drugs to resell on the streets, and even murdering those who didn't play by the rules. Clean cops refused to snitch on rogue officers, sticking to a code of silence that allowed corruption to flourish. When the Knapp Commission began its hearings, Paco was one of the few policemen willing to step forward and testify. His integrity made him the most-hated man in every police precinct. During a drug raid ten months later, Paco was shot in the face by a dealer and left to die by his fellow cops. Paco would have died if a tenant hadn't called 911.

During his months of recovery, he received nonstop harassing phone calls and hate mail.

When Paco realized that he was as good as a dead man, he went into a kind of witness protection program—hiding out from the police. But a grateful nation still remembers him as the incorruptible cop made famous by the Hollywood film *Serpico*. In his eighties, Frank Serpico remains deaf in one ear from that bullet. A statement by the police officer who took the 911 call still haunts him: "If I knew it was Serpico, I would have left him there to bleed to death." He still fights bitterness toward a corrupt police department that stole his childhood dream. Yet his willingness to sacrifice that dream to clean up police corruption put officers across America on notice that citizens depend on these guardians of public safety to operate with integrity.

The amazing story of Frank Serpico reminds us that there are things bigger than our personal dreams. Success at any price is failure. Maybe a clean cop by the name of Paco understood a question that Jesus asked: "What should it profit a man to gain the whole world and lose his soul?" We should never forget that a single soul is infinitely more valuable than anything this world can offer.

A lie may take care of the present, but it has no future.

Honesty guides good people; dishonesty
destroys treacherous people.

PROVERBS 11:3

Three Minutes and Seventeen Seconds That Changed Football

❦

Nate never wanted to be a trailblazer. As an all-state, star football player, he just wanted to play college ball. But it was the 1960s, and the powerhouse Southeastern Conference didn't have a single African American playing football on any of its rosters. So the SEC presidents decided it was high time to integrate sports in the South. The University of Kentucky took the lead.

Nate remembers being invited to the Kentucky governor's mansion in the winter of 1965. It may have been the first time an African American teen had eaten in its dining room. Sitting next to Nate was Greg Page, a huge defensive end. Governor Ned Breathitt made an impassioned recruiting speech, pleading with the two to blaze a trail for integration. He admitted that it wouldn't be easy, but that the governor's office, the university, and the athletic department would give the two their full support.

It wasn't easy. Greg and Nate became roommates, shuffled off to the edges of the dormitory in a kind of soft segregation. Greg should have been the first African American to play a game in the SEC, but he severed his spinal cord on the practice field several weeks before the first game. Nate grieved for his best friend. He was lonely as the only African American on the team. He wanted to quit, but he had promised to be a trailblazer. When he went into that opening game against Mississippi, he made history. He only played three minutes and seventeen seconds, due to his injured shoulder. He didn't really care that he was the first African American to play in an SEC game. Greg had died the night before.

After Greg Page's heart-wrenching funeral, the team traveled to Nate's first game in the Deep South. The atmosphere at the Auburn University stadium was hostile. State troopers behind the Kentucky bench waved Confederate flags. Fans were shouting racial obscenities at Nate and chanting, "Put LeRoy in!" "Give LeRoy the ball!" "Kill LeRoy, shoot LeRoy!" Five games into the season, he received the cruelest blow of all: because he had missed so many classes while keeping vigil at Greg's bedside, the coach pulled his meal ticket. He was forced to fend for himself while his white teammates ate sumptuously at the athletic table. He was now totally ostracized and alone. After five games, he transferred to Western Kentucky.

Nate Northington bears no regrets and resentments for how he was treated in 1967. He went on to lead Western Kentucky to a 1970 Ohio Valley Championship. But he is proud of that three minutes and seventeen seconds against the University of Mississippi that changed football. Today there is a new statue outside the Kentucky stadium. It features the first four African American players at the University of Kentucky. Among those figures in bronze are Nate Northington and his friend Greg Page. Their story reminds us that we've come a long way. We still have further yet to go in so many areas of life, but those three minutes and seventeen seconds prove one thing to us all:

How much time we have isn't as important as how much we do with the time we have.

―――――⟡⟡⟡―――――

Make the most of every opportunity in these evil days.

EPHESIANS 5:16

The Jewel Thief Who Became a Cop

ᴄᴏᴏⓌᴏ

Like a lot of career criminals, Larry started out as a small-time hood. He got hooked watching his dad make easy money betting on sports. By the time he was in his early twenties, he was a small-time bookie on the mean streets of New York City. The excitement of living in the fast lane drove him to graduate to the major leagues of gambling. It wasn't long before mobsters noticed his potential. When he became a consistent earner, he moved up the ranks of organized crime.

Then Larry discovered easier money than gambling: robbing jewelry stores. In seven years, his heists from twenty stores got him $15 million in diamonds alone. But it wasn't the money that mattered most. Larry loved the excitement of getting away with robbery. He got his biggest rush by taking over a whole store, tying up folks, and watching them squirm in fear. Before long, he made the FBI's Most Wanted list. Though the rush was greater, so was the risk. One night, Larry slipped up. That stupid mistake got him twelve years in a federal penitentiary.

When he walked into that lair of hardened criminals, he was scared to death. He thought, *It can't get any worse than this.* But it got a whole lot worse when he was put in solitary confinement for a year. Larry thought he would lose his mind until the guy in the next hole spoke to him through an air vent. That friendship was his only touch of sanity. Then, one night, his unseen friend said, "I love you, brother, but I'm checking out." The next morning Larry saw his friend being wheeled away on a gurney. He had committed suicide. Larry felt like he had been kicked in the stomach. Then he heard a silent voice whisper, "I have plans for you." Larry knew instantly that Jesus was speaking. He also knew that he was supposed to make sure that other kids didn't end up in prison like his dead friend.

Larry Lawton dedicated his life to Christ. When he got out of prison, he started Reality Check, a program for at-risk teens, giving tough talks about the consequences of crime. His Reality Check has become one of the most successful teen programs in America. Larry is proudest of the fact that he is the only ex-con in American history to be made an honorary policeman after the Lake St. Louis Police Department swore him in on August 16, 2013. The amazing story of Larry Lawton proves that no one is beyond redemption. Check the Bible. Some of God's choicest heroes did stints in prison. If you are living through the consequences of sin or foolishness, don't let tough times steal your hope. God is preparing you to help others to go through the same struggles. Your ability to overcome will give you the credibility to help others facing the same difficulties.

Bad times are redeemed when they are used to make others better.

We can rejoice, too, when we run into problems and
trials, for we know that they help us develop endurance.
And endurance develops strength of character, and
character strengthens our confident hope of salvation.

ROMANS 5:3-4

The Secret Mission
That Changed America

જીબ્ડ

History always walks the high wire. A slight misstep and the future instantly changes. Take Joe, a Boston gangster who made his millions running illegal booze. Joe hobnobbed with mobsters like Lucky Luciano and Al Capone. But he had grandiose plans that required respectability. So he married into political royalty, used his ill-gotten gains to bankroll big-name politicians, and bought himself an ambassadorship to England. The rumrunner was now listed among the crème de la crème of society's elite. He and his ambitious wife, Rose, ruthlessly drove their children to be the next generation of America's leaders. But his biggest plan was to put his namesake oldest son in the Oval Office.

Joe Jr. was his father's golden boy. Old Joe sent him to the most prestigious schools, made sure that sportswriters covered his exploits on the athletic field, and got him into the best clubs. But Joe Jr. threw the old man a curveball when he quit Harvard to join the navy in World War II. When he became a decorated fighter pilot, old Joe was thrilled. Nothing would get his son more votes than coming home a war hero. When it was finally time for Joe Jr. to come home, his father was relieved. He had Joe Jr.'s political future mapped out: congressman, senator, and then the first Irish Catholic president in US history. But the high wire of history is tricky. A single misstep, and the future is forever altered.

It was one thing for the former gangster to sell his son as a war hero, it was quite another for Joe Jr. to actually want to be one. When the Allies needed someone to take out a German site ready to launch deadly V-2 rockets at London, navy lieutenant Joe volunteered. Operation Aphrodite was nothing less than a suicide mission. Joe Jr. took off loaded down with twelve tons of explosive torpedoes. Some fifteen minutes into his flight, his plane exploded over England. If Joseph Kennedy Jr. hadn't volunteered for that fatal mission, he well might have become the president of the United States. But history walks the high wire. Instead, his younger brother John became president, accomplishing old Joe Kennedy's vision. But those plans fell off the high wire when a sniper's bullet took John's life in Dallas. Bobby Kennedy seemed poised to take up the mantle until that postelection night when he too was felled by an assassin's bullet. Ted Kennedy might have become president, if he hadn't wrecked his car and walked away, leaving a girlfriend to die in the waters of Chappaquiddick.

The amazing story of Joseph Kennedy and his boys teaches us that we may propose, but God will always dispose. None of us can change the past, control the present, or determine the future. There are too many moving parts to manage or manipulate. You might want to pray Francis Chan's prayer:

God, interrupt whatever we are doing so that we can join You in what You're doing.

———— ✺ ————

You will keep in perfect peace all who trust in
you, all whose thoughts are fixed on you!

ISAIAH 26:3

When Saints Doubt

⁓⊙⊙⊙⁓

The corruption of organized religion had so sickened him that he fled into the wilderness to find God. He subsisted on locusts and wild honey and exchanged his city clothes for rough-cut camel hides. His beard and hair grew unruly, his brown body hard and wiry. In the loneliness of the desert, God gave a harsh message to penetrate hard hearts. In the hot furnace of Dead Sea badlands, heaven forged steel that would have to stand against the onslaughts of the forces of darkness.

When the time was right, the firebrand came out of the desert with the sting of a scorpion, preaching hellfire and brimstone. People who were disillusioned by the shallowness of the Temple and synagogues streamed out into the desert to get that old-time religion. The prophet's message was simple: "Repent, for the kingdom of God is near." Untold thousands wept over their lackluster faith and went into the Jordan to undergo ritualistic Jewish cleansing.

The desert firebrand had another message: he was preparing the way for the Messiah. One day, Yeshua bar Yosef from Nazareth stood at the edge of the crowd. The prophet knew instantly that he was the one. He pointed a bony finger at his carpenter cousin and said, "This is the Lamb that takes away the sins of the world." Yeshua replied, "Baptize me, Ioánnes, to fulfill all righteousness." After the baptism, the prophet saw the Holy Spirit fill his cousin and heard God's voice say, "This is my Son, in whom I am well pleased."

After that day, the desert prophet's ministry decreased as Yeshua's increased. But God had one last job for the one we call John the Baptist. Scandal had rocked Judea when Herod Antipas, the puppet king of the Romans, stole his weaker brother's wife. So the prophet hurried to Herod's winter palace to deliver the last sting of a desert scorpion. The king was not amused, and John found himself locked in a dungeon. He was ready for martyrdom, but he wasn't prepared for the doubts. Maybe he had baptized the wrong messiah. Perhaps Yeshua was just a carpenter. Sometimes the mind can play tricks. So John sent a desperate message to Yeshua: "Are you the one, or is there another yet to come?" Yeshua didn't rebuke his cousin's doubts. Instead, he sent back a gentle but assuring answer: "The blind see, the deaf hear, the lame walk, lepers are cleansed, and the good news is preached to the poor."

The amazing story of a doubting saint should encourage us all. There's not a hero in the Bible who didn't doubt. Perhaps there can be no *real* faith until we have nothing else to hold on to. If you are suffering doubts, Jesus would say what he said to John, "See what I am doing all around you. Let the evidence chase your doubts away."

When your doubts create mountains, allow your faith to remove them.

———— ☙ ————

LORD, sustain me as you promised, that I may live!
Do not let my hope be crushed.

PSALM 119:116

The Comeback King

✑✑✑

It was hyped as the Rumble in the Jungle. Las Vegas bookies said it was the mismatch of the century. But the dictator of Zaire had shelled out millions to secure the first heavyweight championship ever staged in Africa. The champ was twenty-five years old. An Olympic gold medalist. An undefeated six feet four inches of sculpted muscle and lethal power. His record was 40–0 with thirty-seven knockouts. He had demolished Joltin' Joe Frazier and Kenny Norton. His opponent was seven years older, past his prime, and desperately trying to become a serious contender again. Some sixty thousand spectators in the stadium in Kinshasa, and a worldwide TV audience, wondered if the fight would go beyond two rounds.

The challenger laughed and played the clown. For seven rounds, he did his rope-a-dope maneuver, covering up while the champ wore himself out punching. In the eighth round, lightning struck—a withering punch coming out of nowhere. Ka-pow! The stunned champ fell like a mighty oak tree. He somehow got up off the canvas, but it was too late. The referee stopped the fight. Muhammad Ali had won back his title, and George Foreman tasted defeat for the first time in his meteoric career.

Foreman had fought his way out of poverty to become king of the mountain. Now he was dethroned and determined to get his crown back. He demolished five opponents. One more win, and Ali would have to give him a rematch. But that fifth fight went the distance, and George lost on points. He collapsed in his dressing room, convinced he was going to die. Overwhelmed by the smell of death, he cried out to God. He says Jesus reached down and saved him. He also called him to preach the gospel. So the former champ became the new reverend. He opened a youth center for at-risk kids and began to enjoy the simple pleasures he had denied himself for so long. He told National Public Radio, "You get a second chance to live and it makes a better person out of you. You realize that wasn't really a loss for me in Africa—it was a gain I didn't appreciate."

In his midforties, out of shape and overweight, the Reverend needed money for his youth center. So he got back in the ring. The sports world laughed, but fans were pulling for him. In 1994, the sentimental favorite squared off against the champ. This time George was smiling, not scowling. To the delight of the watching world, the forty-five-year-old reverend became the oldest boxer in history to win the heavyweight championship. Most folks know him as the smiling bald guy who sells George Foreman grills on television, the guy whose net worth is $300 million. But he would tell you that his real worth is found in Jesus Christ and in the work he does to get kids on the right track. He says that he owes it all to that loss in Zaire. He might flash a smile and suggest this:

Take a closer look at your loss, and you just might find a gain.

The LORD says, "I will give you back what you
lost to the swarming locusts, the hopping locusts,
the stripping locusts, and the cutting locusts."

JOEL 2:25

The Decision

⌒⊚⌒

No one had ever climbed the west face of Siula Grande, a towering twenty-one-thousand-foot high peak in the Andes Mountains. But on June 8, 1985, Joe Simpson and Simon Yates accomplished that amazing feat. A blizzard was barreling toward them, and they had to get down fast. Their epic descent would create controversy and fuel ethical debates thirty years later.

The two had climbed three thousand feet down when Simpson's ice ax failed to take hold, and he fell fifteen feet, shattering his right leg. Yates could have abandoned his crippled partner. Instead they crawled down the face of Siula Grande, tied together Alpine-style, three hundred feet at a time. After nine exhausting hours, Simpson slid down the ice and over a cliff. He was dangling from a rope one hundred feet below. Yates yelled over the side, but he couldn't hear anything in the howling wind. For more than an hour, he held on until totally exhausted. He faced an agonizing choice: either he would go over the cliff to his death with Simpson, or he would have to save himself. Simon Yates cut the rope.

Joe Simpson fell more than a hundred feet into a yawning crevasse below, landing on a narrow ice bridge. He was now utterly alone in pitch black, sobbing like a baby. Somehow, he managed to crawl deeper into the darkness. Then he saw light streaming through a hole. He was now out in the open again, crawling across a vast glacier on his elbows. With each move of his body, the fractured leg bones shifted. He was delirious with pain. Stuffing snow in his mouth, he continued an epic crawl to the end of the ice field. He faced six more miles of jagged rocks to the base camp. More than once he lost his bearings, but he kept going by singing songs and quoting Shakespeare. After four days, he smelled the most beautiful fragrance of his life: the odor of human excrement coming from the camp latrines. When guilt-ridden Yates found him, Simpson wept uncontrollably.

People still debate the ethics of Yates cutting his partner loose to die so that he might live. Simpson is quick to say that, if the roles were reversed, he would have done the same. He bears no grudge against Yates. But their relationship has been strained ever since. Simpson actually feels sorry for his former climbing partner. He told *People* magazine, "[Yates] made the incredibly brave decision to save me. But he's known as the guy who cut the rope, and I'm the guy who crawled out and wrote the book." This amazing story reminds us that life hands us difficult decisions. So often they have to be made too quickly. There will always be plenty of second-guessers. It's easy to be an armchair ethicist when you aren't on the ice cliff in a blinding blizzard. But the one who has to make the decision and live with the consequences is the only one who has the right to second-guess. This much is true:

Most often, the hardest thing and the right thing are the same.

***

Who are those who fear the LORD? He will
show them the path they should choose.

PSALM 25:12

The Unexpected Hero

⌒⊙⌒

Danny was small for his age. But what he lacked in size, he made up for in smarts. Among the brightest kids in school, he set his sights on becoming a surgeon. Yet everything changed for this second-generation Japanese American teen when he walked to church that December morning.

He saw the Zeros flying overhead, heard the roar of bombs, and looked at plumes of smoke rising from sinking battleships in Pearl Harbor. This aspiring surgeon ran to the Red Cross station to assist with the wounded. For five sleepless days and nights, he helped patch up mutilated military personnel while growing increasingly angry.

So he headed for the recruiting office to sign up for the war against Japan. On the way, he heard racist catcalls. "Hey, Jap, get out of here!" "He might be a spy!" He was told that, though he was a US citizen, he was now classified as a 4-C or enemy alien. He was undraftable, not fit to serve, a danger to America, and a potential spy. Like 120,000 other Japanese Americans, Danny was faced with sitting out the war in an internment camp.

He could have been bitter. Instead, when the war department came up with the idea of an elite division of Japanese Americans fighting Germans in Europe, Danny was quick to sign up. No Americans ever served with more distinction than the 442nd Regimental Combat Team, earning more than nine thousand Purple Hearts, fifty-two Distinguished Service Crosses, twenty-one Congressional Medals of Honor, and seven Presidential Unit Citations.

And no one was ever more willing to give everything for his country, as Danny proved one bloody day in Italy. When ordered to take a German fortification, he led his men into the fray, his Thompson submachine gun blazing. He was almost there when a bullet ripped through his abdomen, barely missing his spine. He continued charging until a rifle grenade shattered his arm, leaving it barely hanging from his shoulder.

Lieutenant Dan looked down at his useless right arm and saw his own grenade gripped in its hand. He ripped it out with his left, lobbed it at the enemy, and continued on until he was shot in the leg. He then passed out and rolled downhill, where his men found him. Danny's heroism inspired his men to victory that day. He lost his arm, but a grateful country awarded him the Medal of Honor.

With only one arm, Dan had to give up his dream of being a surgeon. But after spending twenty months in hospitals recovering from his wounds, he did go on to study law and become a prosecuting attorney. In 1962, he was elected to the US Senate in a political landslide. You may recall this Japanese American as nine-term senator Daniel Inouye of Hawaii, the second-longest-serving senator in US history. With the same courage that seized a German fortification, the late Senator Inouye fought against corruption and injustice on the floor of the US Senate.

What have you lost? Has that loss shattered your dreams? Then remember Danny's story, and take heart from this:

You might lose something good, but you could gain something better.

———— ❧ ————

For his sake I have discarded everything else, counting
it all as garbage, so that I could gain Christ.

PHILIPPIANS 3:8

630

From Trailer Park
to Tinseltown

 birth

In the urban slang of our day, she was a courtyard kid—a social outcast who didn't fit in with the preppies, jocks, nerds, hoods, goths, or any other teen tribe. Other kids called her the trailer girl. But a trailer was the best her mom could afford on a secretary's paycheck. So the scrawny trailer girl went to school in cast-off clothes that were two sizes too big. Because she was ostracized or bullied by the snobby kids at school, she learned to scrap and fight for everything she ever got. She found her groove at the aquatic center, where her determined grit made her a top-ranked swimmer. She also discovered that she had an uncommon talent for acting. The secretary had instilled in her trailer kid the attitude that she could achieve any dream, if she was willing to pay the price. But she also warned her that she had to make a choice: the Olympics or Hollywood. Each demanded too high a price to do both. The girl chose Hollywood.

When the secretary lost her job, mom and daughter headed to Los Angeles in an old Oldsmobile, with only seventy-five dollars to their name. They lived in that wreck of a car while the trailer girl went looking for roles. Meanwhile, her mom headed to a pay phone with a roll of quarters. She spent whole days pestering studios to give her daughter an audition. The hard work paid off with bit parts in television series, minor roles in forgettable movies, and a starring role in a box office disaster. The trailer girl got her big break when she landed the lead role in a 1999 indie movie—the true story of a transgender boy who was murdered by bigots. She received a paltry $3,000, but that role in *Boys Don't Cry* won her several critics' awards, a Golden Globe, and an Oscar for best actress. Her career was off and running. After several starring roles, she signed on with Clint Eastwood to do *Million Dollar Baby*. That role earned her a second Oscar. Hilary Swank often says that it was her childhood as an outsider, ostracized and bullied, that helped her make those two Oscar-winning roles come alive with such gut-wrenching realism.

Most folks would never guess that this Tinseltown superstar comes from Trailertown. The scrawny girl in thrift shop baggy clothes now has her own high-end line of sportswear that those snobby girls from her high school probably couldn't afford. Nor would any of them begin to look as good as she does when modeling them. The Cinderella girl has this mission statement on her fashion line's website: "I want to make a choice every single day to step into my fullest potential, to not leave any stone unturned on my journey of discovery." Her amazing story helps us remember that we are all a work in progress. Her journey reminds us that, as long as we have a breath, none of our stories are finished. Hilary Swank might even say amen to this challenge:

Go after your dream, no matter how unattainable others say it is.

_____ ༄ _____

As for you, be strong and courageous,
for your work will be rewarded.

2 CHRONICLES 15:7

Blinking a Bestseller

❦

Could there be anything more horrifying than locked-in syndrome? The afflicted are sentenced to a *living* death—an Edgar Allan Poe horror story of someone buried alive in his own coffin. It is usually caused by a brain stem hemorrhage. The victim is left quadriplegic, with no way to produce speech or facial movements. But the real horror is that the victim is aware of everything—they are able to think, see, and hear, but unable to communicate except by blinking their eyes.

Jean-Dominique, the editor in chief of the French fashion magazine *Elle* never imagined that he would live such a nightmare. But, after a devastating stroke left him a quadriplegic, he was shipped off to a hospital on the coast of Normandy. He seemed to be in a state of vegetation until a nurse took him outside in a wheelchair. But that nurse did him no favors. The bracing wind awakened his senses, but he was still unable to do more than blink his left eye. He might as well have been a swimmer locked in a diving bell or a caterpillar entombed in his own cocoon.

But Jean-Dominique's girlfriend, Florence Ben Sadoun, became the unseen hero of his amazing story. Two or three times a week she would make the long drive from Paris to hold his hand for hours at a time, read to him, and joke with him. She was part of a small posse of true friends that he called his "personal bodyguard." Over that year, Florence aided her Jean-Do to write a book. He used a method called the Silent Alphabet— a blinking of the eye like Morse code to spell out letters. It took Jean-Dominique Bauby more than two hundred thousand blinks of his left eye to write what would become a runaway international bestseller: *The Diving Bell and the Butterfly*. Later, millions of moviegoers pulled out their hankies when they watched his story in a film by the same title.

Sadly, the movie misrepresented Florence in the story. Screenwriters made Bauby's previous partner, Sylvie, the faithful heroine who stayed by his side. The real backstory is that Sylvie hardly ever visited her former lover in the hospital and was in New York City with her new boyfriend when Jean-Dominique Bauby died in 1997. Yet Florence was sitting by his deathbed holding his hand as she had for the past year. She was there to caress his lifeless face as he passed away. She still smiles when she thinks about that day Jean-Do's soul escaped the diving bell and broke loose from the cocoon to soar like a butterfly into eternity.

There are few things more amazing than someone with locked-in syndrome blinking his left eye a quarter of a million times to dictate a best-selling book that has inspired millions—unless it is a woman who inspired him with her unselfish love. Florence may have been removed from the movie, but heaven knows the truth. And now, so do you. This amazing story should encourage all of us to never give up. It is a reminder of a quote inspired by C. S. Lewis's work:

Hardships often prepare ordinary people for an extraordinary destiny.

Here on earth you will have many trials and sorrows.
But take heart, because I have overcome the world.

JOHN 16:33

Left Behind in Africa

❦

No one could imagine that Davie would end up buried with the mighty in Westminster Abbey. He was one among several dirty little urchins living with impoverished Scottish parents in a single tenement room. The boy was only ten years old when he began working twelve hours a day in a factory. The fact that he managed to eke out a formal education and become a medical doctor is a testament to his towering intellect and spirit.

He left England in 1840 and headed out to Africa as a medical missionary. Yet he is remembered as one of history's greatest explorers. He crossed deserts, scaled mountains, and hacked his way through jungles that no European had ever seen. Along the way, he found one of God's signature creations. Africans called it Smoke That Thunders, but he named it Victoria Falls. By 1859, he had traversed the continent, returned home a national hero, and received the accolades of the prestigious Royal Geographical Society. The British government commissioned him to lead an expedition down the Zambezi River. He came across bodies of water unknown to Europeans, but he also witnessed Arab slave traders massacre whole villages of black Africans. The explorer would spend the rest of his life crusading against slavery. He was the first doctor to find a connection between malaria and mosquitoes, and he was years ahead of his time when he saw quinine as the remedy for the tropical disease.

In 1866 the doctor headed into the unexplored interior of East Africa looking for the source of the Nile River. When he vanished from sight, the *London Daily Telegraph* and the *New York Herald* sent journalist Henry Stanley into the heart of Africa to find him. When Stanley finally stumbled onto Davie, he uttered one of history's monumentally obvious questions:

"Dr. Livingstone, I presume?" One can imagine the only other white man within hundreds of miles responding, "Do you think I could be anyone else?" Stanley tried to convince David Livingstone to come home with him. But the medical missionary refused to leave his beloved Africans. A year later, he was felled by dysentery and malaria. He had given away all his quinine and had nothing left to save himself.

The villagers found Dr. Livingstone on his knees in front of his cot. He had died praying. They cut open his body, took out his heart, and buried it in their soil. Then they carried his corpse hundreds of miles to a British outpost. The whole of Great Britain mourned when he was buried in Westminster Abbey. Today, you can find his grave marker in London and his statue in Edinburgh. But you will have to go to Africa to find his heart. Little Davie from the one-room tenement couldn't have imagined that more than 380 million of his beloved Africans would today claim his Savior as theirs. His amazing story reminds us that God can make good use of our intellect, gifts, and determination. But he makes the best use of a heart sold out to him. If that's all you have, it's more than enough.

Having a soft heart in a cruel world is courage, not weakness.

People judge by outward appearance,
but the LORD looks at the heart.

1 SAMUEL 16:7

Crawling a Picket Fence to the Olympics

❧

Six-year-old Glenn hated that potbellied stove in the one-room school-house. Every morning, he and his brother had to walk two miles into freezing prairie winds to light the fire that kept students warm. But one day someone made the terrible mistake of putting gasoline in the kerosene jug. When Floyd tossed the lit match into the stove, there was an explosive flash, engulfing both boys in flames.

Floyd died within minutes after help came. Glenn nearly died too. The pain Glenn experienced was excruciating, followed by no feeling in his legs. The doctors said that they needed to be amputated. But after losing one son, his mother was not about to let her other son lose his legs. After several weeks, they sent little Glenn home in a wheelchair along with a pair of crutches. A century ago there were no skin grafts or transplants. The doctors said that he would never walk again. But if the boy was to keep his legs, the family would have to massage them every night. Glenn later said that those nightly massages were more painful than the fire that left the horrific scars.

On a summer's day in 1919, Glenn's mom took him outside. A few minutes later, he was pulling himself by his elbows toward the picket fence. When he reached it, he pulled himself up until he was standing on legs that felt like they were being stabbed with red-hot needles. Day after day, the boy pulled himself along that picket fence until he wore a path at its base. Then he made a discovery that changed his life: his legs didn't hurt when he ran. The boy was soon running six miles a day across Kansas prairies. Like the movie character Forrest Gump, he was fond of saying,

"I ran and ran." By the time he was in high school, Glenn was running faster than any boy in Kansas. In his last schoolboy race he set a national high school record for the mile. He went on to the University of Kansas where he set the collegiate record.

After winning the Sullivan Award as America's outstanding amateur athlete, he won twenty races during a whirlwind tour of Europe. In 1934 he shattered the world record for the mile. He broke the world record again at the 1936 Berlin Olympics, but got a silver medal when a New Zealander ran it in six-tenths of a second faster. Few athletes have dominated the mile more than the Kansas Ironman. Almost a century later many experts say that, given what he had to overcome, Glenn Cunningham may have been the greatest miler in history. He often said that he owed it all to two things: that gasoline fire and the picket fence. His amazing story proves that adversity and perseverance add up to success. Without adversity there is no need for perseverance. Without perseverance there is no value in adversity. Glenn's picket fence reminds us of this fact:

Perseverance is not a single long race, but many short races one after another.

<hr/>

Blessed is the one who perseveres under trial because,
having stood the test, that person will receive the
crown of life that the Lord has promised.

JAMES 1:12, NIV

The Deli Sandwich

೧ംᠥᡐᠥ

Archduke Franz Ferdinand, heir to the throne of the Austro-Hungarian Empire, arrived in Sarajevo on Sunday morning with all the pomp and ceremony accorded a future emperor. It was a beautiful day for a parade, but the archduke's security had no idea that six assassins were in place along the route. Yet because the Black Hand terrorist organization had chosen rank amateurs, the operation soon turned into a comedy of errors. The first assassin got cold feet and ran. The second threw a grenade at the car, but it bounced off before detonating. The others were so distracted by the festivities that the royal limousine sped by before they had a chance to squeeze off a shot. By now, Gavrilo Princip was the only assassin who hadn't run away. But he knew that the plan to blow up the archduke had blown up.

By now it was almost lunchtime, and even anarchists have to eat. So he walked away from the crowd to a nearby deli. Perhaps he didn't want to take his cyanide on an empty stomach. According to some sources, he went inside and ate a sandwich. When he came back outside, he couldn't believe his luck. The royal limousine had rolled up to the intersection outside the deli. The driver had made a wrong turn and was trying to back up when the engine stalled. Gavrilo Princip ran up to the car and began firing. His bullets hit Ferdinand in the neck and his wife Sophie in the stomach. Princip then turned his pistol on himself, but bystanders tackled him to the ground. The royal limousine sped off, and soon after the archduke and the duchess died from their wounds. Eight co-conspirators were convicted of treason and murder.

People have been fascinated by the "coincidences" of June 28, 1914. What if Gavrilo Princip had not stopped at that deli for a sandwich?

What if the limo driver had not taken a wrong turn? Or if the car had not stalled when backing up? Ferdinand and Sophie would have gone home to Vienna after that parade. But all those things *did* happen, putting an anarchist and an archduke on a collision course. That assassination started the dominoes falling that led to World War I, resulting in the death of thirty-seven million people, rearranging the landscape of Europe, and setting in motion future events that led to World War II and the bloodiest century in history.

Random events lined up perfectly that day to change history. Or *was* history changed? Is it possible that the individual decisions made by an archduke, assassin, and driver, along with the responses of world leaders that led to a world war were all part of the inexorable march of history to its preordained conclusion? Some argue that the sandwich that led to World War I only proves that wars are caused by the stupidest things. If that's the case, nothing makes sense, and we ought to all be very afraid. But if we believe that even stopping for a sandwich is part of a divine plan that never changes, we can relax in what C. S. Lewis wrote:

History is a story written by the finger of God.

Whatever the LORD pleases, he does, in heaven
and on earth, in the seas and all deeps.

PSALM 135:6, ESV

The Paralyzed Action Star

⁓⊙⊙⊙⁓

He has single-handedly vanquished Nazis, Commies, mobsters, bruisers, and drug cartels. That's why you might be shocked to discover that this mega action hero has suffered partial paralysis since birth. When his birth was taking too long, an overeager medical intern grabbed a pair of forceps, clamped them on to the baby's tiny head and began to yank—severing the nerves to the newborn's eyelids and lips and partially paralyzing his face. He would grow up with a droopy eyelid, a hanging lower lip, and slurred speech. Those impediments would subject him to endless ridicule as a child and would add to his tough-guy persona as an adult. They would also help create memorable movie roles.

Childhood was never easy for the boy with paralyzed facial muscles. He often hid in terror, watching his parents' violent arguments turn to fisticuffs. When they finally divorced, he was shuffled between mom, dad, and foster homes. It seemed like those forceps were a metaphor for his crazy childhood—being yanked from place to place while the nerves of his emotions were being severed. His heart became as paralyzed as his face. When bullies in Queens and Philly pushed him around, the scrawny kid began to build that famous muscular body by lifting concrete blocks. The teenager was fast becoming a juvenile delinquent, with an interior as hard as his exterior. After he was expelled from fourteen schools, his mom figured out a way to ship her hoodlum son to a school in Switzerland. There the kid from the rough neighborhoods of Queens found his groove acting in student plays.

He came back to America ready for the movies. But Hollywood wasn't ready for him. Agents said that his drooping eyelid and lower lip made him look lazy and unintelligent. His slurred speech made him sound like a blue-collar working stiff or an East Coast Mafia capo. He might make it as a character actor, but never as a leading man. So the aspiring actor took small parts as hoodlums, worked as a movie usher, cleaned cages at the Bronx Zoo, and degraded himself in an adult film to pay the rent. But those facial and speech liabilities would become the stuff of stardom when Sylvester Stallone wrote, directed, and starred in his Oscar-winning film about a washed-up, punch-drunk boxer from the mean streets of Philly: Rocky Balboa. They were perfect for his Rambo character and for other action-hero roles that have brought $2.5 billion into the coffers of Hollywood.

The deeply spiritual Sylvester Stallone would agree that those forceps that paralyzed his face were God's instruments to shape his future for good. That medical intern was put there for a purpose in his life. Maybe you are trying to make sense of why God has allowed particular people or certain circumstances to bring adversity to your life. Could it be that God has given you an opportunity in that thing you see as a problem? The Bible is clear about this:

We serve a turnaround God who specializes in turning evil into good.

———— ∽∾∽ ————

O Sovereign LORD! You made the heavens
and earth by your strong hand and powerful
arm. Nothing is too hard for you!

JEREMIAH 32:17

Starving for a Stranger

❧❦❧

Franciszek waited for fifty-three years to join his long-lost friend. Yet they were total strangers. They met briefly but never spoke to each other. Franciszek was a sergeant in the Polish army when the Germans seized Poland. After months in a Gestapo prison, he was sent to Auschwitz. What he saw in that pit of depravity gnawed at his Catholic faith. He didn't know if his wife and sons were alive, but he was sure he had been cast into Dante's *Inferno*. One thing kept Franciszek going: a shred of hope that he would survive and find his missing family.

Hope vanished when a roll call revealed that a prisoner had escaped. The deputy commandant ordered a reprisal: ten inmates would be chosen at random, locked in the hunger bunker, and starved to death. As the identifying numbers were rattled off, his heart stopped: "Prisoner 5659." That's when Franciszek broke down. Sobbing hysterically, he screamed, "I'm only forty-one, too young to die! I have a wife and children!" At that moment, a frail and balding man stepped forward. "I'm a Catholic priest from Poland. I would like to take his place because he has a wife and children." So the SS seized the Franciscan father Maximilian Kolbe, Prisoner 16670, and locked him in the bunker with the other nine.

When Franciszek went back to his cell block, the other prisoners were angry. Father Kolbe had been their priest and confessor. It wasn't fair that a holy man should die in the place of a coward; that a saint should be sacrificed for a sinner. Meanwhile Kolbe was ministering to the starving while he starved. After ten days, he was one of just three still alive. An SS doctor came into the bunker and killed Father Kolbe with an injection of carbolic acid. Franciszek survived the death camp. After the war, he found his wife. Tragically, his two sons had been killed. But the Franciscan priest's willingness to die for him had restored his faith in God.

He often felt unworthy of Kolbe's sacrifice. Yet he made it his goal to spend the rest of his days telling others the story. He also felt like the spirit of the priest was walking with him. They became best friends. Franciszek Gajowniczek was at the Vatican when Kolbe was beatified as a saint. When he finally died at age ninety-three, his widow told reporters that, in his last days, the old man felt that his friend was calling him to join him in heaven. She smiled and said that the two best friends were now reunited for eternity. Their amazing story is a lovely metaphor for those of us who are Christians. Jesus stepped forward and took our place, and ever since, we have fallen more and more in love with him as our friendship deepens. One day, he will call us home to be with him forever. But until that day, we have a story of his love to tell everyone who will listen.

If Jesus died for us in public, we can't live for him in private.

———— ✿ ————

Thank the LORD! Praise his name! Tell the nations
what he has done. Let them know how mighty he is.

ISAIAH 12:4

Two Minutes
That Changed History

୧୭୧ଡ଼ୢ

He slumped over his desk in weariness. His face looked like the cracked leather of his old chair. Some fifty-one thousand boys had been slaughtered on a Pennsylvania battlefield, and he was expected to say a few words in memorial to the fallen. So he labored deep into the night for something better than pious platitudes from a worn-out politician.

But inspiration didn't come easily. His screaming wife was suffering one of those migraine headaches that had turned their loveless marriage into a nightmare. He laid his pen aside and escaped next door with his half-written speech. His neighbor agreed that it was a poor start. Overwhelmed with melancholy, he fell into his lonely bed for another sleepless night.

Early the next morning, he caught his train for a grueling journey to the battlefield. He again tried to finish his speech, but it hardly mattered anyway. The main eulogy was to be delivered by Edward Everett, the golden-tongued orator from Massachusetts. The lonely man on the train was invited as an afterthought to give a few closing remarks. The invitation bluntly stated that he should speak a couple of minutes at most. No one ever wanted to follow an Edward Everett speech. And he felt that the words he had scratched out were unworthy of this hallowed occasion.

At ten o'clock in the morning on November 19, the tired man rode across the battlefield being dedicated to the fifty-one thousand slaughtered boys. Most of their corpses still lay in hastily dug graves. More than ten thousand spectators had jam-packed the fields around the grandstand, waiting for Everett's speech. America's greatest orator didn't disappoint.

His address lasted more than two hours, making it the longest speech in US history. When he finished, the applause was thunderous.

Then the next speaker, who was an afterthought, got up to deliver his closing remarks. They lasted two minutes, containing only 272 words. When he finished, he was greeted with deathly silence. His heart sank. Slumping next to his friend Ward Lamon, he whispered, "My talk went sour." To the day he died, the man would rank this as his worst speech. To his surprise, applause began to ripple across the fields, growing into a deafening ovation. *Harper's Weekly* later reported, "It was the perfect piece of American eloquence." Newspapers hailed it as the greatest speech in history. Edward Everett said that in just two minutes Abraham Lincoln had captured the heart of Gettysburg better than his two-and-a-half-hour speech.

There was a time when every schoolchild memorized these remarks by a speaker who was invited as an afterthought only because he was the president. That Gettysburg Address gives a simple message: we cannot allow the dead to have died in vain. It is always up to the living to continue the work of those who died to give us a heritage. You might want to find a copy of those two minutes delivered by Abraham Lincoln at Gettysburg. Reading it may inspire you to remember this:

It is for the living to complete the unfinished work of the dead.

———— ⁂ ————

All these people earned a good reputation because of
their faith, yet none of them received all that God had
promised. For God had something better in mind for us,
so that they would not reach perfection without us.

HEBREWS 11:39-40

A Righteous Evil

⟨⟨◌⟩⟩

The old daguerreotypes portray a bony scarecrow of a man, with bushy hair, flint-hard face, and blazing eyes—a desert prophet ready to wield the terrible swift sword of the Lord. Yet he was a rare white man, in a culture marinated in racism, who not only fought slavery with a holy zeal but also socialized more with blacks than whites. He not only preached the gospel of racial reconciliation, he was a leader in the Underground Railroad that helped thousands of slaves escape to Canada.

But the prophet got increasingly impatient with do-nothing politicians who worked harder at compromise than emancipation. When yet another concession to national unity allowed the Nebraska and Kansas territories to decide whether or not to permit slavery, he and his five sons galloped out of Ohio, armed for war. After Missouri raiders massacred the antislavery citizens of Lawrence, his abolitionist warriors rampaged across Kansas exacting retribution. They dragged pro-slavery men out of their homes and butchered them in front of their families. A horrified nation dubbed this guerilla war Bleeding Kansas. Little did they know they were watching the preview of a coming civil war. The Ohio abolitionist John Brown was now a household name—lionized in the North and loathed in the South.

In 1859 he tried to seize the Federal armory at Harper's Ferry. It was an audacious but disastrous gamble. Maybe he wanted to foment an uprising of slaves, or set up a free state in the mountains of western Virginia, or just shake things up. Within hours John Brown's band of fanatics was surrounded by a thousand militiamen. Two days later he surrendered to US Lieutenant Colonel Robert E. Lee. He was found guilty of murder, conspiracy to incite a slave uprising, and treason against Virginia.

On December 2, 1859, he was hanged in front of a crowd of jeering Southerners, among them actor John Wilkes Booth.

The raid on Harper's Ferry further polarized the nation. Panic gripped the South, increasing calls for secession. Up North, radical abolitionists were fired up by John Brown's "martyrdom," declaring that war was the only solution. Before his raid, the pro-slavery Democrats were heavily favored to win the presidential election. Afterward, Abraham Lincoln and his antislavery Republicans won. Civil war was now inevitable. Union soldiers later marched into battle singing, "John Brown's body lies a-mouldering in the grave, but his soul goes marching on." Surely the terrible swift sword was now the Grim Reaper's bloody scythe.

Today John Brown remains as controversial as he was 150 years ago. In an age of polarization, much like the 1850s, perhaps it is enough to say that he represents the best and worst angels in us all. Most of us want to see the right things happen (or at least our idea of what's right). But like John Brown, we too often work for what's right in the worst ways. History bears sad witness to unimaginable evil done in the name of God, country, and the public good. The amazing story of John Brown serves as a warning to us all:

The wrong means will never get us to the right ends.

———— ✧ ————

There is a path before each person that
seems right, but it ends in death.

PROVERBS 14:12

The Candy Man Can

❦

Milton grew up in the age of Vanderbilt, Carnegie, and Rockefeller. These titans of industry built empires of steel, oil, and railroads. Their massive plants belched out smoke, turning factory towns into grimy gray nightmares where overworked and underpaid workers were as replaceable as parts on their assembly lines. But Milton had a vision of a workers' paradise, where employees would be treated with dignity and prosperity.

He was only fifteen when he went to work sixty to eighty hours a week for a Pennsylvania confectioner to learn candy making. Then he borrowed a hundred dollars from his aunt to open a candy shop in Philadelphia. For six years, he spent his nights making caramels and taffies and his days selling them from a pushcart. Finally, his health gave out, and his business collapsed. In 1882 he headed out to Denver to make it rich in the Colorado silver rush. Milton didn't strike silver, but he did discover that adding fresh milk to caramel made it richer and extended its shelf life. So he traveled to Chicago with his new secret and opened another candy store. Again he went belly up. The same thing happened when he moved to New Orleans. He headed up to New York City to start over yet again but went bankrupt. So he went home to Lancaster only to discover that his family had given up on him. They refused to loan him any more money, but he also refused to give up on his dream. When a former employee invested his life savings in Milton's fifth start-up, the candy man finally had his first success, which allowed him to secure a loan of $250,000. With that cash infusion, he became America's caramel king.

But Milton isn't remembered for caramels. When he went to the 1893 World's Fair in Chicago, he learned a new method for mass-producing milk chocolate. Now he was ready to realize his life dream: a utopian city of the future. He not only wanted to build a state-of-the-art chocolate factory but also a beautiful city for his employees. It featured affordable housing with sanitation systems and electricity, paved streets with names like Chocolate Avenue and Cocoa Avenue, schools, department stores, trolleys, churches, a library, a hospital, a zoo, an open-air theater, and an amusement park. When the depression came and other industries were firing employees, Milton kept his workers busy with projects to beautify and enlarge their utopian city and to start one of the best orphanages in America.

His mass-produced chocolates turned these candies from a luxury for the rich to an affordable treat for the masses. You know Milton's city as Hershey, Pennsylvania. He proved that giving dignity and prosperity to employees is also profitable. His company sales skyrocketed from $600,000 to $20 million by 1921. That golden oldie hit song could have been written about the amazing story of Milton Hershey: "The Candy Man . . . makes the world taste good." So the next time you take a bite out of a Hershey bar, think about people in your life in the light of something the original candy man knew:

People who feel appreciated will always do more than what is expected of them.

―――― ☙ ――――

This is what the LORD Almighty said: "Administer true justice; show mercy and compassion to one another."

ZECHARIAH 7:9, NIV

Only One Came Forward

◌◞◍◟◌

Mordecai was seven years old when he decided that God had called him to be an evangelist. He started by preaching to barnyard animals. He even tried to immerse a cat in a water trough. When the feline began to scratch and claw, the budding evangelist threw him down and screamed, "Go on . . . go to hell!" It's no wonder Mordecai grew up to be a "hog-jowl and turnip-green preacher"—country slang for a parson who gets in people's faces. Whenever he brought his gospel tent to town, he would ask the locals to identify their most notorious sinner. He would then make a beeline for that person. Atheists, agnostics, and backsliders went into hiding when Mordecai Ham came to town. Once he found his prey quivering behind a haystack. "What are you going to do to me?" whimpered the farmer. Ham responded, "I'm going to ask God to kill you! You're an atheist. If there is no God, my prayers won't hurt you. If there is a God, you deserve to die because you are making atheists out of your children." A few days later, the evangelist baptized the unbelieving farmer and forty-one of his relatives.

Mordecai Ham regularly railed against the evils of alcohol. When angry moonshiners threw rocks at the church where he was preaching, he stormed outside to confront the hillbilly ruffians. Their ringleader threatened him with a knife. "You are a coward, pulling a knife on an unarmed man!" snorted Ham. "So I'm going to ask the Lord either to convert you or kill you." The man walked away cursing the preacher. The next day, the bully was found dead in his bed. The other three moonshiners died in a sawmill explosion. Mordecai has been dubbed the Chuck Norris of the revival circuit. He railed against every sin listed in the Bible—and some that weren't. In the twilight of his "hog-jowl and turnip-green" ministry, handsome

Hollywood preachers came selling a softer gospel using Madison Avenue techniques. Folks stopped listening to the hellfire and brimstone of old Mordecai Ham. It seemed that he was washed up.

One night a pitiful handful in a half-filled service came forward. Mordecai Ham went back to his hotel room and wept in despair. Maybe he should have paid attention to one of those converts that night: a gangly North Carolina boy by the name of Billy Graham. In an age that measures success by the numbers, we need to step back and reevaluate what really matters. The impact we can have through a single prayer, a single conversation, a single act of kindness, or a single [you fill in the blank]—on a single child, man, or woman—is both incalculable and underrated. A child learns to walk one step at a time, and a race is finished by putting one foot in front of the other. Mordecai Ham died years ago, but what happened that one amazing night should encourage us with this truth:

A single person doing the right thing, for the right reason, at the right time has the power to change the whole world.

Each one of you will put to flight a thousand
of the enemy, for the LORD your God fights
for you, just as he has promised.

JOSHUA 23:10

Lessons from
the Concentration Camp

⋙⊙⊙⋘

Some were Orthodox, others Hasidic, and still others secular. Among them were the fashionable and the threadbare, the scholar and the blue-collar worker, the socialite and the pauper, the beautiful and the plain. The showers were the great equalizer. Treasures were confiscated, heads shaved, and clothes exchanged for striped pajamas. They were marched lockstep to identical lice-infested bunks in identical barracks. The labor, hunger, and disease would eventually strip them of their last distinguishing features: whether thin or fat, old or young, healthy or sickly—they'd all be reduced to the same skeletal grotesqueness.

No one would have known that Viktor Frankl was a prominent psychologist and neurologist in Vienna. During his journey through the horrors of the Auschwitz and Kaufering concentration camps, he lost everything. When he was liberated, he discovered that his pregnant wife and most of his relatives had perished. Many Holocaust survivors became disillusioned with God or even gave up on the idea that there was any ultimate meaning. Dr. Viktor Frankl was not one of them. In 1959 he channeled his experiences in the death camps into an international bestseller, *Man's Search for Meaning.* He wrote the book in nine days, but it had been percolating in his mind for decades.

Frankl said that the difference between those who survived the camps and those who didn't usually came down to one thing: *meaning.* He remembered a science teacher who said, "Life is nothing more than a combustion process, a process of oxidation." Frankl responded, "Sir, if this is so, what is the meaning of life?" He later noticed that those who saw transcendent meaning, even in the most horrific of circumstances, were the ones who triumphed over the horror. He said that the Nazis could take away all their freedoms but one: the freedom we all have to choose how we will respond to life.

Viktor Frankl became the most renowned psychologist in the postwar world. We must surely grieve for all the Holocaust took from him, but we can be equally grateful to Dr. Frankl for showing us that we can find sense even in the senseless. He was a prophetic voice when humanism and hedonism slowly stripped spiritual meaning from Western life. Before his death in 1997, he became increasingly concerned about the American search for happiness rather than meaning. He was certain that our narcissistic pursuit of pleasure was producing an epidemic of soul emptiness. Maybe we should dust off *Man's Search for Meaning* and read it again. The Library of Congress labeled it one of the ten most influential books in the United States. The amazing thing Frankl learned in the Nazi death camps applies to our postmodern "affluenza": those who put their hope in pleasure, power, peace, and prosperity soon died when they lost it. Those who found a transcendent meaning—even seeing God at work in terrible circumstances—found the will to survive and even triumph. Today you might want to think about something Frankl wrote:

Our main motivation for living is our will to find meaning in life.

<hr>

You guide me with your counsel, leading me to a
glorious destiny. Whom have I in heaven but you?
I desire you more than anything on earth.

PSALM 73:24-25

The Man Time Forgot

✺

Some people are just lucky. Or maybe they deserve a second chance at life. Or better yet: God is the God of second chances. Just ask Cornealious "Mike" Anderson. He was unemployed and looking for an easy score when he and a buddy held up a Burger King manager making a night deposit. Mike was hiding out at his girlfriend's apartment when the police caught up with him. He was arrested and convicted of armed robbery. The judge gave him thirteen years in prison. But his attorney appealed the verdict, arguing that the evidence had been illegally seized. So Cornealious was out on a twenty-five-thousand-dollar bond. It took two years for the case to get to the Missouri Supreme Court, where judges unanimously agreed that his rights were not violated, and he had to serve his sentence.

But because of a clerk's error at the Department of Corrections, Cornealious was never served with papers. He asked his attorney what he should do, and the lawyer told him that it was the responsibility of the state to arrest him. So he went on with his life. Only this time, he did it the right way: got married, started a family, built a successful business, became a model citizen and churchgoing man. He renewed his driver's license, registered his business, voted in elections, and listed his residence on documents. But it wasn't until thirteen years later, on the day he was scheduled to be released from prison, that a Department of Corrections computer revealed he had never been incarcerated.

Cornealious was arrested by marshals at his home on July 23, 2013. The legal sparring went on for months. His lawyer argued that he should be released for time served. The attorney general responded, "The law is very clear: you don't get credit for time served when you are out on bail."

When the national media picked up the story, people bombarded the attorney general's office with pleas for clemency. So the state bowed to public pressure and let Cornealious Anderson go free.

The feel-good story of 2014 didn't last long. Six months later, he was arrested for second-degree robbery when a woman accused him of snatching her purse. Those who had championed his cause were heartbroken. But a thorough investigation discovered that he had an airtight alibi. It also found that police had used questionable procedures. The St. Louis circuit attorney's office publicly apologized for their shoddy handling of the case. For the third time in fourteen years, Cornealious "Mike" Anderson walked away from jail a free man. One might argue that his first time was luck. His second was because of a life well lived. His third was a case of mistaken identity. Or we could say that this is another story of amazing grace. Folks often complain that life isn't fair. The truth is that if God gave us what we really deserved, we would all be in big trouble. But God is the God of second, third, and a gazillion more chances. Cornealious might say amen to this truth:

God is never fair. Instead, he goes beyond fair to mercy.

―⚬⚭⚬―

He does not punish us for all our sins;
he does not deal harshly with us, as we deserve.

PSALM 103:10

Pitching Your Tent toward Sodom

∽◦⑥◦∾

He left his city along the Euphrates River and headed north with his uncle. They crossed Iraq into Syria, and then Uncle Abe's new God called them to move on to the land of promise. But high desert country could not sustain both the uncle's and the nephew's herds in the same place. After their herdsmen fought over grazing rights, they decided to split.

When his nephew chose the lush plains east of the Jordan River, Uncle Abe gasped. The cities of that region were cesspools of depravity: demonic gods, infant sacrifice, unthinkable perversions, and horrific cruelty. But Lot could only see grazing lands that would fatten his herds and markets that would fatten his wallet. The Genesis account says that he "pitched his tent toward Sodom" (Genesis 13:12, KJV). In short, Lot kept his family outside that wicked city, but placed his tent in such a way that his wife and daughters were able to see its bright lights. Over time they were seduced from a distance. They pestered Lot to move them into Sodom until he finally acquiesced to their pressure. Eventually, Abraham's nephew became a member of the city council. But his business interests caused him to keep his mouth shut in the face of evil, even as his wife and daughters abandoned Uncle Abraham's God for the pleasures of Sodom.

Then angels appeared with a warning: judgment was coming, and Lot's family must flee immediately. The angels literally dragged the reluctant family away from Sodom and Gomorrah. No one knows whether the region was hit by a meteorite or an earthquake, but huge fissures opened, and methane gasses spewed out in geysers of hot fire and liquefied salt, raining down a holocaust that turned sand into glass balls and stones into charred lumps. Lot and his daughters ran into the mountains to the east, but his wife couldn't tear herself away from the cities she loved. Liquefied salt washed over her, instantly encasing her so that she became a pillar of salt.

The worst was yet to come for Lot. As his two daughters cowered in the mountains above, they must have thought the whole world had been destroyed. They figured that their daddy was the only man left on the planet. So they got him drunk and took turns seducing him. Could the righteous man, who pitched his tents toward Sodom, have sunk any lower than incest? His sons became the progenitors of the Ammonite and Moabite nations, taking on the immoralities that Lot's daughters had picked up in Sodom. Lot's tale is the sad story of a man who lost his place in the family of Abraham, then his own family, and finally his legacy. His amazingly sad story warns us that a life of small compromises eventually leads to a tipping point and a plunge into catastrophe. We would do well to remember Lot and something Ralph Waldo Emerson wrote:

Sow a thought, you will reap an action; sow an act, you will reap a habit; sow a habit, you will reap a character; sow a character, you will reap a destiny.

———— ∽◌∾ ————

Sin is crouching at the door, eager to control you.
But you must subdue it and be its master.

GENESIS 4:7

Surrendering to Lord Nelson

⌒⊙⊙⌒

More than two centuries after his heroic death in 1805, his legend remains bigger than ever. His majestic statue towers 169 feet high, surrounded by massive brass lions, on the square named after his greatest naval battle. It is such a symbol of Great Britain's power that Adolf Hitler planned to take it back to Berlin after he conquered England. This one-armed admiral of the British Royal Navy was so legendary in his day that he couldn't walk down the streets without creating Nelson mania. He often disobeyed the cautious orders of the Admiralty, but his reckless abandon won naval victories, and his daring exploits made him the darling of an awestruck nation. His scandalous affair with a diplomat's wife was tabloid gold, adding to his dashing mystique.

But it was his final battle that placed him forever at the apex of England's pantheon of legendary heroes. Napoleon's armada had been targeting England for invasion. All that stood between France and the terrified island nation was Admiral Horatio Lord Nelson's undermanned fleet. But at the Battle of Trafalgar off the coast of Spain, Nelson led his navy to a smashing victory. It was one of history's signature sea battles. But Lord Nelson was mortally wounded by a sniper's bullet. His body was put in a barrel of brandy and brought back to a hero's welcome. He was buried in St. Paul's Cathedral as the whole of Great Britain wept in grief.

Lord Nelson was especially celebrated for the chivalry and kindness he showed his vanquished foes. After one of his victories, the defeated commander was escorted aboard Lord Nelson's flagship to surrender his sword. Having heard of the British admiral's graciousness, the defeated commander walked boldly across the deck and extended a hand as if the two were equals. Nelson stood stiffly with his right hand at his side and then sternly said, "Hand over your sword, and I will then shake your hand." The legendary admiral understood a principle of war: first there must be a surrender, and then there can be friendship. A war can never end until one of the parties submits to the other. Some of our country's greatest allies were once our fiercest enemies: England, Germany, and Japan. But there had to be a surrender, followed by the cessation of hostilities, before friendship could be forged.

This amazing story of Lord Horatio Nelson is a reminder of the war of the ages between God and his rebellious creation. Jesus can never be our Savior until he is first our King. We have to hand over our sword and throne before we can take his nail-scarred hand in friendship. The same principle is true in the wars that wreck our marriages, homes, friendships, and churches. Paul said that husbands and wives, parents and children, and even bosses and workers must lay down the sword and submit first to King Jesus and then to one another's needs before we can really have relationships that are truly loving and satisfying.

You cannot extend the hand of friendship until you first lay down the weapons of war.

Submit to God, and you will have peace;
then things will go well for you.

JOB 22:21

Barefoot in the Snow

❦

Titus proved that heroes come in all sizes. He was no bigger than a peanut, a seven-year-old second grader riding in a truck seat on a bitterly cold Colorado night. Tammy Hall and her three kids had just left a Thanksgiving dinner gathering when her pickup hit a slick spot on the road. She lost control of her truck, and it rolled five times before it landed in a crumpled heap. Tammy was thrown from the cab and lay unconscious in the snow. The air was well below freezing at twenty-three degrees Fahrenheit, with the windchill much colder. Titus miraculously survived the crash unscathed, as did his sisters, Tiffany, age four, and Tierra, age one, who were still strapped in their child safety seats.

After calming his frightened sisters, seven-year-old Titus shoved the door open and crawled out of the pickup truck. He was clad only in a thin pair of pajamas and no shoes. He had to walk through mud and ice in socks that were soon soaking wet. Then he climbed under an electric fence and managed to push open a heavy gate. In the pitch black of a freezing night, he began to run across deep snow in his wet socks and pajamas. After a quarter mile, he was heaving in exhaustion, but he trudged on until he reached the lights of the Galeton Dairy. When he saw a dairy employee, he began to holler, "Help, there's been an accident." But the Spanish-speaking worker only understood when the panting and shivering boy kept repeating, "My mom! My mom! My mom!"

The dairy worker immediately called 911, and emergency vehicles rushed to the scene of the accident. They found Titus's mother still unconscious in the snow and close to hypothermia. She had a broken neck, broken back, and ten broken ribs. She was rushed to the emergency room where doctors said that she was in critical condition. The medical personnel are sure of one thing: if seven-year-old Titus hadn't run in soaking wet socks through the snow and freezing cold to find help, his mother probably would have died that night. Paramedics and police are also sure of one thing: that second-grade boy was some kind of hero.

Tammy learned some valuable lessons that night. She shouldn't have been talking on the cell phone or driving without a seat belt. She also discovered that Titus was her little man when it counted most. When the seven-year-old was asked by ABC's *Good Morning America* if he was scared, he replied, "No . . . well, maybe, a little scared." None of us will ever know how we will react in an emergency or if we have the right stuff. We can only whisper a prayer every morning that, if the occasion arises, so will the hero inside us. We might even take hope in something comedian Redd Foxx used to say:

Heroes aren't born. They're cornered.

Be strong and courageous! Do not be afraid and do not panic before them. For the LORD your God will personally go ahead of you. He will neither fail you nor abandon you.

DEUTERONOMY 31:6

The Miracle
of Thanksgiving

⌘

The Patuxet boy could not have imagined that he would create a nation. When white sailors came ashore, he welcomed them. They rewarded his friendliness by kidnapping him. He was hauled off to England, displayed to curiosity seekers, and then taught English. His captors used him as a scout and an interpreter on ships that explored the rugged coastline of the New World. After years of service, he was returned to his tribe.

Soon another English ship appeared on the horizon. When he led a party out to greet it, he and his Wampanoag friends were seized and transported to Spain, where they were sold as slaves. He was deathly ill when a monk purchased him. The brothers at the monastery nursed him back to health, and that nurturing love drew him to Jesus.

He found a boat and secured passage back to England. There he signed on to another ship. Six months later, he arrived in Massachusetts. There would be no happy reunion. Smallpox had ravaged his village, killing his family and wiping out his tribe. He was now alone, a stranger wandering forests with the ghosts of the departed. He was consumed by loneliness and despair.

Then he saw the familiar sails of another English ship. As it set anchor offshore, he hid among the trees and watched from a distance as settlers built crude huts. He saw them dying of starvation and disease during the harsh winter. He watched them bury half their number. Finally he marched up to their log stockade. At first they were frightened. Some cocked their muskets to shoot him. When he spoke to them in English, they were amazed. They could not imagine that this lonely survivor of a dead tribe was God's answer to the desperate prayers of the Plymouth Colony.

With this man's help, things turned around for the colonists in 1620. The Patuxet man led the Pilgrims to waters teeming with fish, taught them how to grow corn, showed them how to stalk game, and introduced them to friendly tribes. They thanked God for providing him for this moment in time. Without his aid, the English Puritans might not have gotten a toehold in Massachusetts. America as we know it would not exist. When the Pilgrims sat down for that first Thanksgiving feast, they praised God for this man history remembers as Squanto. In 1622, Governor William Bradford knelt at Squanto's deathbed. Squanto gasped, "Pray that I might go to the Englishman's God in heaven." Bradford later said, "Surely he now rests in heaven."

The Puritans who fled to America had a vision to build a city on a hill to light up the world. It seemed impossible that first winter, but God never gives vision without provision. They couldn't have known at the time how much help they'd receive from the lone survivor of a vanishing tribe. We are the blessed recipients of Squanto's amazing story. What's your vision today? The Bible says, "Where there is no vision, the people perish" (Proverbs 29:18, KJV). If yours is God's vision, you can take heart with this truth:

God will never give a vision without also supplying the provision.

This same God who takes care of me will supply
all your needs from his glorious riches, which
have been given to us in Christ Jesus.

PHILIPPIANS 4:19

664

The Scottish Nostradamus

eﾛⓇ⌒ɔ

He had what the Scots called the second sight—the ability to see into the future. The second sight was not considered witchcraft in Scotland, but a curse. It would become so for a seer in the 1600s, Coinneach Odhar, remembered as the Scottish Nostradamus. Odhar worked as a laborer in the highlands near Loch Ussie on the Brahan estate. What he saw in the distant future still astounds. As he walked across a field once, he cried, "Oh! Drumossie, thy bleak moor shall, ere many generations have passed away, be stained with the best blood of the Highlands. Glad am I that I will not see the day, for it will be a fearful period; heads will be lopped off by the score, and no mercy shall be shown or quarter given on either side."

On this same moor in 1746, a highlander army, fighting for Bonnie Prince Charlie against the British, suffered a crushing defeat at the Battle of Culloden. No mercy was shown or quarter given, just as Odhar had prophesied a hundred years before. He predicted that the Lochs in the Great Glen would be joined, something that happened when the Caledonian Canal was dug to connect them in the 1800s. He foresaw black iron horses blowing steam from their nostrils, pulling long lines of carriages through the glens two hundred years before railroads were built. Amazingly, he predicted "a black rain will bring riches to Aberdeen," which came true in the twentieth century with the discovery of North Sea oil. He said that Scotland would have its own parliament when men could walk on dry land from England to France. In 1991 Scotland's first session of Parliament was convened, just a few years prior to the opening of Channel Tunnel.

Odhar made startling predictions of gas pipes and water pipes in the

1600s. But his second sight became an affliction when Lady Isabella Seaforth asked the seer to tell her what her husband, the earl, was doing in France. When Odhar hesitated, she insisted that he give it to her straight. When he told her that the earl was having an affair with a Frenchwoman, adding that she was fairer than the countess, the enraged woman ordered him thrown into a barrel of boiling tar. Before he was killed, he gave a last prophecy: the end of the Seaforth line, with the final heir being unable to hear or speak. The countess's last descendant became deaf and dumb as a result of scarlet fever. He outlived his four children, thus becoming the final heir of the line.

The Scottish Nostradamus gave amazing prophecies. Some were true, and others require imagination to make them come true. But God has had a line of prophets who prophesied forty-four predictions about the coming Messiah, all of them fulfilled in the most exacting details. Hundreds of biblical prophecies have all come true. We might find Odhar, the Scottish Nostradamus, fascinating, but the ancient Jewish prophets, Jesus, and his apostles are absolutely trustworthy!

Biblical prophecies aren't given to scare us, but to prepare us.

No prophecy in Scripture ever came from the prophet's own understanding, or from human initiative. No, those prophets were moved by the Holy Spirit, and they spoke from God.

2 PETER 1:20-21

Making a Difference

⁂

Jimmy always wanted to be in law enforcement. From the time he was a little boy, he looked up to cops on the beat. Maybe it was because his dad died when he was only nine years old, leaving a huge hole in his heart. He missed those big arms that used to hold him tight, making him feel safe and secure. He thought that being a policeman would make others more secure in a world of danger. He often said that police work was the most noble profession in the world, and police officers must be the most important people of all. He went on to college, where he excelled, and then on to graduate school with a single purpose: to be the best police officer on the planet.

Jimmy was the proudest guy in New York when he got his badge and started working for the Port Authority Police Department. He rose through the ranks, impressing everyone with the fact that police work was his passion and never a job. In 1993 when a terrorist truck bomb hit the World Trade Center, he rushed into the thick black smoke to rescue people. Most people didn't know that Jimmy suffered from severe asthma. Afterward, he said to his worried brother, "You have to do what you have to do. There were people inside." Jimmy probably thought, *That's what my daddy would have done for me. That's what I would do for my two little girls.* Those he taught at the police academy reported that he often said: "You have to give your life for something that makes a difference."

On September 11, 2001, he was ready to teach classes in Jersey City when news of the terrorist attack broke. He rushed across the Hudson. Without regard for his asthma or his life, he rushed into one of the towers. He was last seen on the twenty-seventh floor, coughing in an asthmatic fit. Others told him that he had to get out while there was still time, but he stayed at his post, directing people down the stairs of a building minutes from disintegrating. The next day, his grief-stricken wife said of his heroic death, "He told me, 'When I go out of this world, I want to know that I made a difference.'"

The amazing story of Officer James Nelson challenges us all to ask, "What am I doing to make a difference?" Jimmy was only forty when he died. We can't know when there will be no more opportunities. A tragic postscript to Jimmy's story is that of his daughter, Caitlin. Fifteen years after her daddy died, this twenty-year-old college junior was participating in a pancake-eating contest with her sorority sisters when she choked to death. She had dreams of being a social worker and making a difference just like her father. We never know whether our final act will be one of heroism or choking on a pancake. We only know that the time we have is limited. As Jimmy's wife said of him, "He made the best of every day he lived."

Three things, once they've gone, never come back: words, opportunity, and time.

∽◌∾

Teach us to realize the brevity of life, so
that we may grow in wisdom.

PSALM 90:12

A Map to Nowhere

‿◦⊙◦‿

Losing your way can be fatal. George found that out the hard way. This dirt-poor farmer, with dreams of striking it rich, was in Springfield, Illinois, the day fast-talking James Reed held a crowd spellbound with tales of fabulous riches in California. Reed ended with a rousing challenge: "Come on, boys! You can have as much land as you want without it costing you anything."

Reed's promise of free land would cost everything for those who followed him, including George and his family. A lineup of wagons rolled out of Independence, Missouri, and by the time they arrived in Fort Laramie, they were already behind schedule. It was now July, and the wagons still had to cross a brutal stretch of mountains and badlands before winter set in. That's when Reed pulled out a book with a map that promised to cut some four hundred miles off the route to California, even though its author had never seen the trail. Neither had anyone else. Reed's map was based on rumor and legend. Frontiersmen warned that it was a fraud. But Reed convinced eighty-six people to join him. George was among those most enthusiastic. Maybe that's why the group elected him as their captain.

Their gamble proved disastrous. Heavy wagons had to be dragged over the rugged Wasatch Mountains and then across the Great Salt Lake Desert. By the time George's party found their way back to the California Trail, it was the end of September. Their "shortcut" had taken twenty-five days longer than the normal route. Weeks behind schedule and short on food, they reached California in late October.

The weary party might have made it up that last stretch of the Sierra Nevada had they not been hit by a freak blizzard. It was the first in a series of massive snowstorms leading to the worst winter in California history. The marooned party ate the last of their oxen, only to face five more months trapped. A desperate group, calling themselves the Forlorn Hope, set out for Fort Sutter on crudely fashioned snowshoes. Less than half of them made it.

Four search parties were turned back by blizzards before a handful of survivors were finally rescued in the spring of 1847. The rescuers were appalled to discover the grisly remains of half-eaten corpses. The survivors confessed that they had stayed alive by eating the frozen bodies of the dead. These reports of cannibalism became the fodder for sensational newspaper stories across a horrified nation.

George was not one of those eaten. But it would have only been a matter of time. This dreamer and schemer was found dead and half-frozen on his bed. Some 165 years later, history still recoils in horror at George's last name, Donner. His notorious name is indelibly etched in the history of the Old West. The bizarre story of the Donner Party is a sobering reminder of what can happen when people opt for the shortcut. The promise of a faster and easier way often leads to long delays. Bestselling author Orrin Woodward makes a lot of sense when he says this:

There are many shortcuts to failure, but no shortcuts to true success.

⎯⎯⎯ ⟨⟩ ⎯⎯⎯

There is a way which seems right to a man,
but in the end it leads to death.

PROVERBS 14:12, WEB

One Last Song
in a Tattered Coat

There was a time that he had written songs that made the whole world sing. Now he was just another drunken bum in the Bowery, ravaged with fever and starving to death. On a cold winter's morning, this shell of a man staggered out of his bed and stumbled to the public washbasin in a cheap flophouse. He fell and shattered the sink. They found him naked and incoherent, bleeding from a deep gash in his throat. A quack doctor was called to the scene. He used a string of black sewing thread to suture the wound. All the time the bum begged for a drink. A buddy shared the bottom of a bottle of cheap rum to dull his pain.

The bum was dumped into a police paddy wagon and dropped off at Bellevue Hospital, where he was left on a dirty gurney in the charity ward. He languished for three days without food or attention before he finally gasped his last breath. No one cared that a homeless drunk from the Bowery had died.

A friend came looking for him in the morgue. He found the body among rows of other nameless corpses with "John Doe" tags on their toes. When the friend gathered the man's meager belongings, he found a tattered coat with a few cents in one pocket and a scrap of paper in the other. Five words were scribbled on it: "Dear friends and gentle hearts." As the friend looked at these words, he wondered if they were the beginnings of a song.

Why would a Bowery bum carry around a line of lyrics? Could it be that he still believed he had the old magic? Was it possible that the heart of a genius still beat faintly in the emaciated body of a derelict? After all, there was a time long ago when he had written more than two hundred songs that are indelibly etched in our American heritage. Every schoolchild has sung his most famous songs: "Camptown Races," "Oh! Susanna," "My Old Kentucky Home," "Beautiful Dreamer," and "Jeanie with the Light Brown Hair." Who would have guessed that the Bowery bum was Stephen F. Foster, the most prolific songwriter in American history?

Is there anyone who is beyond redemption? At the dead end of his life, the father of American music still carried a scrap of hope in his tattered coat pocket. Every life, no matter how battered, still carries a scrap of hope and a melody waiting to be reborn. Some are in hospitals, others in nursing homes, and still others in prisons. Others are unwanted children in their mothers' wombs, but they still have a song to sing. Still others are people who slip into church each Sunday, but they are too discouraged to sing a song. Have the songs in your soul been silenced by the adversities of life? Don't lose heart. You still have songs locked in your soul, waiting to be written. Remember Stephen Foster's story in the light of this line from the blind hymn writer Fanny Crosby:

Chords that were broken will vibrate once more.

Let the ruins of Jerusalem break into joyful
song, for the LORD has comforted his
people. He has redeemed Jerusalem.

ISAIAH 52:9

An Elusive Seduction

❧

Paul fled the gray suffocation of an industrial revolution to find paradise in Tahiti. He lived in a state of euphoria, intoxicated by the sensual beauty of tropical colors, dizzying fragrances, mystical spirituality, and free love. When the artist returned to France, his tales of the South Pacific made him the darling of the Parisian café crowd. He set out to capture his paradise on canvas, shocking the art world with primitive forms on flat fields, one dimensional, out of proportion to reality, and in vibrant tropical colors. He called his works "the music of painting." But impressionist artists ridiculed his works as the crass attempt of a scheming money-grubber to cash in on the cravings of bourgeoisie Parisians for something exotic. Yet Paul Gauguin was sure he had found paradise and was using his canvas as a window to it. In the process, he became a bridge to modern artists like Matisse and Picasso. He is celebrated today as the quintessential romanticist, the 1800s hippie who found in Tahiti what we are all trying to find—paradise on earth!

Shocking new evidence paints a far uglier reality. Gauguin was a sadist and wife beater. His traumatized children wrote about watching their father repeatedly batter their mother. He abandoned his family for long periods of time and ultimately left them for good. He drank too much and was constantly in debt. His abuse and slander of Van Gogh helped drive that fragile artist to suicide. When the art world refused to recognize his genius, Gauguin fled back to Tahiti only to discover that his paradise was an illusion. He spent his last days in drunken disillusionment, infecting island girls with syphilis, and died a bitter and twisted man on May 8, 1903.

Like John Lennon's song "Imagine," Gauguin's paintings evoke within us that universal longing for paradise. But like most seductions, they sell something that doesn't exist. John Milton, in his *Paradise Lost*, speaks to Gauguin's delusion. He says that we live between the paradise that Adam lost and the one that Jesus will bring. In the "in-between" there is no paradise. The Garden of Eden has been turned into a tangle of thistles and thorns where the serpent still slithers about, seducing us with a lie that he holds the key to some faux paradise. Gauguin thought he found it in Tahiti. Marx and Lenin promised it in a worker's paradise. Philosophers, politicians, preachers, gurus, drug dealers, Madison Avenue hucksters, and even our own imaginations still promise utopia—if only we will buy the seductive sales pitch. But only Jesus can give an abundant life now and an eternal paradise later. The next time you gaze at a Paul Gauguin canvas, you might want to remember his tragic story in the light of something Karl Popper wrote:

Those who promise us paradise on earth never produced anything but a hell.

"You will not certainly die," the serpent said
to the woman. "For God knows that when
you eat from it your eyes will be opened, and
you will be like God, knowing good and evil."

GENESIS 3:4-5, NIV

The Funeral
That Killed Millions

୧ଠ୭ତ୬ଠ

The father of the Bolshevik Revolution was dying, and vultures were circling to seize his crown. In those last days of Vladimir Lenin's ebbing life, the proletariat masses held their collective breath while the politburo plotted. Russia was like a forest full of tense creatures that sense a wildfire is about to sweep through their timberlands.

Most thought that Lenin's heir apparent was Leon Trotsky, the leading intellectual among the party leadership. This Jewish Communist had paid his dues during the long years of revolution. He had been imprisoned, tortured, and exiled. He came home to lead the uprisings in Moscow that toppled Czar Nicholas. He served as the envoy that ended Russia's war with Germany and then led the Red armies to victory in a civil war. As Lenin deteriorated, the Machiavellian jockeying and plotting was bad enough. But after he suffered a massive stroke, the politics became deadly.

As Lenin slipped into a coma, only two contenders remained: Leon Trotsky, the passionate intellectual, and Joseph Stalin, the cunning backstabber. But history attests to the fact that the cunning invariably outfox the intellectual. While Trotsky formulated his policies, Stalin plotted his takeover. In late 1924 Trotsky was recuperating from an illness some distance from Moscow when Lenin died. Trotsky later wrote that Stalin sent this cable: "The funeral will take place on Saturday, you will not make it in time. The politburo considers that in your state of health you should continue to Sukhum. Stalin." Had he taken the time to check other communications, he would have discovered that the funeral had been moved to Sunday. The truth is: he could have made it in time, even if it had been held on Saturday. But Trotsky was a visionary who seldom paid attention to details.

Stalin gave a stirring eulogy and played the role of the father comforting a grieving nation. That funeral gave rise to Stalin's mystique and was the death knell to Trotsky's ambitions. Stalin quickly seized power and eliminated his rivals. Trotsky was accused of plotting against Stalin, was exiled to Kazakhstan, and eventually fled to Mexico where a KGB operative assassinated him.

The world can only wonder what might have been if Trotsky had showed up at Lenin's funeral. Had he become the party boss, Stalin's reign of terror wouldn't have happened. But history is shaped by mistakes and missed opportunities. "For the want of a nail the shoe was lost. For want of a shoe the horse was lost. For want of a horse the rider was lost. For want of a rider the message was lost. For want of a message the battle was lost. For want of a battle the kingdom was lost. All for want of a horseshoe nail." The amazing story of Trotsky's blunder is a warning to all of us who are lazy when it comes to the small details:

Seemingly unimportant acts or omissions can have grave and unforeseen consequences.

If you are faithful in little things, you
will be faithful in large ones.

LUKE 16:10

Ain't I a Woman?

ॐॐॐ

Isabella was one of twelve children born to an African slave couple. When the slave family's Dutch owner died in upstate New York, his greedy son broke up the family and sold them off. Isabella was peddled, along with a flock of sheep, for a hundred dollars to a master who abused her in unspeakable ways. She was sold twice more before she fell in love with Robert, a slave on a neighboring farm. Robert's owner forbade the marriage, lest any children born of the union should become the property of Isabella's owner. He forced her to marry an older slave named Thomas. It was a loveless union, but it produced a son and two daughters. Sadly her children became the property of her master.

New York's 1827 emancipation of slaves did not come soon enough for Isabella. After she escaped from her master, he sold her beloved son, Peter, to a plantation in Alabama. But she took him to court to have her son returned. Isabella became the first black woman in US history to sue a white man and win. The world should have taken notice of this fiery woman who would become a towering figure in the battle for civil rights and women's suffrage. It was during her stay with a Methodist family that she converted to Christianity. Later she worked as a housekeeper for an evangelist. It was there that she became a prophetess. Yet her unbroken string of family tragedies continued when Peter joined the crew of a whaling ship. When it returned to port in 1842, he was missing. She never heard from her son again.

Prophets are forged in the desert of affliction. So was this African American prophetess. In 1843 she changed her name to Sojourner Truth and teamed with Fredrick Douglass to tour the country preaching emancipation. Unable to read or write, she dictated a bestseller entitled *The*

Narrative of Sojourner Truth: A Northern Slave. She had no peer as a public speaker. Among her most ardent admirers was an Illinois lawyer by the name of Abraham Lincoln. She also spoke out for women's rights, electrifying an Ohio crowd with the soaring line "Ain't I a woman?" After the Civil War, she continued to agitate for social causes. In 1865 she boarded the whites-only section of a Washington, DC, streetcar, stood to her full six-foot height, and dared authorities to arrest her. Until the day she died in 1883, she spoke out against racial injustice, and she became the leading voice for women's rights. When people reminded her that she was in her nineties, she replied, "I'm not going to die. I'm going home like a shooting star."

This amazing story of a slave who became America's conscience in the 1800s reminds us that we are all sojourners on this earth. In the end, the only thing that will matter is what we have left behind when we move on. Her life was one of unspeakable personal tragedy, but ours are so much richer because she refused to be silent in the face of evil. We should take to heart something she said:

Truth is all powerful, and it will prevail.

———— ❧ ————

The very essence of your words is truth; all
your just regulations will stand forever.

PSALM 119:160

Taking Ten Rounds
for the Kids

❦

Jennifer Fulford-Salvano may be a petite blonde, but she is as tough as nails. This police officer from Orlando, Florida, is the kind of tough cookie you want patrolling your neighborhood. She was only out of the academy for three years when she was on patrol with police trainee Jason Gainor. Shortly before eight o'clock on the morning of May 5, 2004, an eight-year-old called 911 to say that strangers were in the house with his mom. It wasn't their zone, but the pair sped over to back up the primary responders, two other officers.

The neighborhood was in a section of Orlando that tourists headed for Disney World never see. The houses on these mean streets have windows covered with iron bars, and many are pockmarked with bullet holes. When Officer Fulford-Salvano pulled up, she saw a desperate woman standing on the front lawn. The woman immediately wanted to talk to the only female officer on the scene. All the time, she kept looking furtively at her house, while refusing to give details—even though her kids were inside. Something was suspicious. Later the officers discovered that she was in possession of over three hundred pounds of marijuana and $60,000 in cash stashed away from her husband's drug sales in Jamaica. The three robbers had invaded her home for an easy heist. Suddenly she saw the men shoving her three kids into a gold minivan in her garage. She began to scream hysterically, "My babies! My babies!"

As Jennifer ran toward the van, the robbers ambushed her. She took three shots to her armor, but seven more hit her in the arms, legs, and shooting hand before she could clear her holster. She went down, but knowing that there were three kids in the van, she managed to fire off a complete clip and reload in less than forty-seven seconds—using her nonshooting hand. One of the ambushers was instantly killed in the shoot-out. Another was shot in the head before the third surrendered. The firefight was like something out of an action movie. This courageous woman spent the next few days in the hospital, but earned the kudos of her fellow officers. It's no wonder that Jennifer Fulford-Salvano later received a dozen honors, including the International Association of Chiefs of Police Officer of the Year Award and the US Medal of Valor. But she is most proud that she saved three children.

Jennifer's story, like all of ours, is still being written. Thirty-eight days after her hospitalization, she returned to full duty. She also married her sweetheart, a firefighter. Today she is writing new chapters in her amazing story as a detective in the child abuse unit. Jennifer reminds us that a life given for children is the noblest one of all. Every parent, grandparent, teacher, coach, mentor, scout leader, or anyone else who invests in a kid's future, is as much a hero as Officer Jennifer Fulford-Salvano. Wess Stafford of Compassion International put it best:

Every child you encounter is a divine appointment.

⁂

Direct your children onto the right path, and
when they are older, they will not leave it.

PROVERBS 22:6

The FBI's Greatest Blunder

ᴄ⳾ᎬᎠᴖ

Since 1941, this amazing story has been hidden from the American public. It all began in Yugoslavia in 1939 when the Germans recruited Serbian playboy Dusko Popov to spy for them in England. But this recruit sold out to the British, becoming their most prized double agent. Popov was so good at his game that the Nazis never suspected he was a turncoat. After a couple of years, they sent him to the United States to set up a spy ring. When he informed the British, they alerted the FBI.

Upon his arrival in New York, Popov was grilled by FBI agents. He later wrote in his memoirs that he warned them to expect an attack on Pearl Harbor by year's end. He told them about a verbal communiqué from the German attaché in Tokyo that the Japanese were studying the tactics of a British air attack that had destroyed the Italian fleet in the Gulf of Taranto. More troubling was a telegram in his possession. Hidden on it was a microdot message with a series of questions from the Japanese to their German allies about US and Canadian defense installations, especially those at Pearl Harbor. The Germans were positive that Japan was planning to do to the Americans what the British air force had done to the Italian fleet. So the Nazi spymaster had instructed Popov to send sketches of Hickam, Wheeler, and Kaneohe airfields. Of highest priority were sketches of the installations at Pearl Harbor, together with information about depth of water, torpedo nets, and other details that clearly signaled a plan to attack the US fleet at anchor in Hawaii.

FBI agents quickly passed Popov on to J. Edgar Hoover. But the pint-size, prudish director disliked the suave and debonair playboy with the rakish good looks. His dossier on the spy was filled with stories of high-flying intrigue and sexual escapades that would later make Dusko Popov the inspiration for Ian Fleming's James Bond. Hoover spent most of their meeting rebuking the spy for his sexcapades. He never did pass Popov's warning on to the White House or naval intelligence. He did reveal some of the spy's microdot message to the Oval Office, but only to make the FBI look better than its rival US and British intelligence agencies. He never mentioned the part about Pearl Harbor.

The full text of Popov's report still remains buried in FBI files. The spy went to his grave wondering why his warning wasn't heeded. More than 2,400 military personnel and civilians killed on that December day might have wondered why America's top lawman didn't step in to save their lives. Nearly half a million US military casualties, together with their grieving families, might have been shocked to know that their FBI hero could have stopped an attack that led to war, if only he hadn't been so prudish, petty, and proud. Yet maybe we shouldn't be so quick to judge. Like J. Edgar Hoover, we often have plenty of evidence that there are dangers ahead. Yet we plow forward toward our own Pearl Harbor while forgetting this:

The world is not dangerous because of evil, but because of those who see it and do nothing.

⊰⊙⊱

Pride goes before destruction, and
haughtiness before a fall.

PROVERBS 16:18

They Died to
Make the Desert Bloom

⚬⚬⚬

Each year during the Christmas season, the Nevada City, California, woman lays flowers on the grave of her great-grandmother Marie Elizabeth Tierney Sherer. She spends the rest of the day thinking about the two men she never met. On December 20, 1922, Marie's husband, John, was part of a team doing survey work when they got caught in a flash flood. John was swept away by the raging Colorado River. Parties searched downriver for days, but they never found his body. John Gregory Tierney had the dubious distinction of being the first of ninety-six fatalities in the epic construction of the Hoover Dam.

It took two weeks for the news to reach Marie in Las Vegas. She was no stranger to heartbreak. Her three-year-old daughter had died of measles when John was mining in southeastern Arizona. But the death of her beloved John was more than she could handle. She took her twelve-year-old son, Patrick, back to Missouri. Years later, Patrick married Hazel, who gave birth to a boy. By now the nation was mired in the Great Depression, and the Hoover Dam project paid good wages. Patrick figured that the memories of his dad's death might get him hired. So he packed up his family and drove west. His mother was distraught. She had lost her husband to the Colorado River. She didn't want to lose her son, too.

Patrick wrote to his widowed mother, describing his work in Black Canyon—the grueling labor, hot weather, and steep terrain. Marie was on her way to spend the Christmas holidays with her son's family when, on December 20, 1935, Patrick slipped and fell more than three hundred feet from one of the intake towers of the dam. His body was recovered in twenty-five feet of the rising Lake Mead. In one of history's great ironies, John Tierney and his son Patrick were the first and last men to be killed on the Hoover Dam project, on exactly the same day thirteen years apart.

A memorial stands on the Nevada side of the Hoover Dam: a sculpture of a man in waist-deep water, with hands outstretched to the heavens. Its inscription reads, "They died to make the desert bloom." Indeed, their dam harnessed the volatile Colorado River, creating the modern Southwest by bringing water to thirty million people and netting $1.5 billion a year in agriculture.

So every year Sharon Tierney, a retired paramedic firefighter, makes a pilgrimage on December 20 to her great-grandmother's grave to place flowers in honor of a woman who sacrificed her great-grandfather, John, and her grandfather, Patrick. She says that the names of those two men are inscribed on that memorial at Lake Mead. But her great-grandmother, Marie, deserves to be remembered too. Christmas is a time when we remember our heavenly Father who gave his only begotten Son and a Galilean mother who sacrificed her boy to make a desert of sin bloom again.

The real miracle of Christmas is that God thought us worth the sacrifice of his Son.

❧

God showed his great love for us by sending
Christ to die for us while we were still sinners.

ROMANS 5:8

The African Napoleon

⤷◦⊙◦⤶

The African chief denied that the son she bore was his and called the baby boy the Parasite. The baby born out of wedlock and his mother were banished from the kraal, or fenced village. They spent the next several years as outcasts, traveling from kraal to kraal, begging for refuge. But the unwed mother and her little Parasite were invariably driven away with shouts of derision. They finally found refuge in the royal kraal of King Dingiswayo. For the first time in his life, the Parasite felt like he belonged. The proudest day of his life was when he was presented with his ox-hide shield and three long spears for throwing. But his first battle was disappointing. Battles among the tribes of Southern Africa were mostly for show. Combatants would stand a long way off from each other, shout obscenities, and throw spears harmlessly short of the mark. When one army finally had enough and headed for home, the other would declare victory.

But the Parasite had other ideas. He created a short-handled spear with a massive blade for hand-to-hand combat, and devised a deadly new tactic called the buffalo-horn formation, where the main body of men would charge en masse, with wings of warriors on either side to encircle the enemy in a pincer movement. The Parasite took his regiment of Zulu warriors on a twelve-year rampage that would change Africa. He marched against every kraal that had mistreated his mother and him during their outcast years, exacting revenge in the most unspeakable ways. Tribes either bowed their knee or were annihilated. His holocaust left a million dead. He is remembered as the military genius that created the Zulu Empire and ruled the southern half of Africa.

His childhood resentments also turned him into a psychopath who clubbed to death any Zulu warrior who showed fear in battle and who executed concubines who displeased him. When his beloved mother died, he lost all touch with reality. He ordered the murder of hundreds of loyal subjects, outlawed the planting of crops or drinking of milk for a year, and decreed death to any couple found pregnant. When mass starvation spread across Zululand, his half brothers had finally had enough. On September 22, 1828, they assassinated this African Napoleon and dumped him in an unmarked grave.

You may recall him by the Zulu word for parasite, *iShaka*. History remembers Shaka Zulu as a brutal conqueror. But isn't every conqueror brutal? A billion people have been killed in wars allegedly designed to bring world peace. Logic may question Jesus' beatitude "The meek will inherit the earth." Yet have strongmen or their armies ever inherited the world? Those who promise utopia invariably bring devastation. But there is a King who was born in a stable and died on a criminal's cross who alone conquers with love. Unlike Shaka, he does not take revenge on those who ridicule and betray him. Instead, he offers love and grace as a gift. No wonder wise men and women still bow before this King of kings.

Christ's greatest gift is forgiveness because that's what we need most.

———— ⁂ ————

I—yes, I alone—will blot out your sins for my
own sake and will never think of them again.

ISAIAH 43:25

'Tis the Season for . . .
Depression

෴

Her very name is synonymous with evil—*Jezebel*. When this princess of Lebanon married Israelite King Ahab, she brought along her Baal worship and established its altars throughout Israel. Baal was a horrific god that required infant sacrifice and unspeakable debaucheries. Jezebel converted her husband and then insisted that all Israel worship Baal. When people refused, this dragon lady unleashed a reign of terror.

But one desert prophet refused to buckle under. He declared that there would be no rain until Israel turned back to God. After three and a half years of drought, he challenged the Baal boys to a showdown on Mount Carmel. Whoever called down fire from heaven would win. It was like a heavyweight championship fight. "Ladies and gentlemen, in this corner we have Jezebel's boys, eight hundred fifty prophets of Baal and Asherah. And in the other corner, we have that desert scorpion, the prophet of doom, God's man— *Eliiijaaah!*" The Baal boys danced like whirling dervishes, mutilated themselves, and screamed at the skies until they fell down in a heap of exhaustion. Elijah drenched the altar in water and then calmly said, "Okay, God, do your thing." A fireball came out of heaven and consumed everything.

"The Champ" had the eight hundred fifty prophets slaughtered, pointed to a distant rain cloud, and said to Ahab, "Get home and tell Jezebel what happened today. Hurry up! There's a gullywasher coming!" Ahab took off in his chariot for Samaria, about twenty-five miles away. Elijah ran even faster, beating Ahab to the capital. He was sure that the Israelites would be tearing down the altars of Baal. Instead, he received a death threat from Jezebel.

You would think that the prophet who called down fire from heaven wouldn't fear threats from the Baal queen. But he hightailed it ninety miles out into the desert and whimpered, "The bad guys have won. I'm the only godly man left. But no one listens to me. So, God, kill me now!" Are you shocked that a great prophet would fall into suicidal depression? You shouldn't be. He was exhausted. His dreams were dashed. He felt all alone, without a friend in the world. God's greatest heroes have all gone through the dark night of the soul.

His story is perfect for Christmas. Depression is most prevalent in this season. Like Elijah, we wear out during this time of hyperactivity. God helped Elijah sleep, sent angels to feed him, and took him to a mountain getaway. It's critical to eat right and get rest during the holidays. Like Elijah, we feel alone. We aren't experiencing holiday cheer like everyone else. We think that we are the only one who knows the reason for the season. God told Elijah that seven thousand other people had not bowed their knee to Baal. God gave him a partner named Elisha and a new job to do. So grab your friends and do something for others. Above all else:

Don't believe what you tell yourself when you are sad and alone.

―――――✦―――――

Why am I discouraged? Why is my heart so
sad? I will put my hope in God! I will praise
him again—my Savior and my God!

PSALM 42:11

Christmas at
the South Pole

꿈꿈꿈

He was consumed with a single passion: to be the first man to reach the South Pole. Twice, he got tantalizingly close, only to come up short. When Roald Amundsen arrived there first, this intrepid explorer set a new goal: he and his team would be the first to cross the continent of Antarctica. Seamen at the South Georgia Island whaling station warned them that they were in danger of being trapped in ice floes at the Arctic Circle. But the explorer was not about to be stopped short of his dream for a third time. So his ship, the *Endurance*, plowed south, picking its way through the jigsaw maze of ice floes. In January of 1915 they were in sight of Antarctica when winds shifted and temperatures plummeted. Within hours the *Endurance* was trapped in solid ice.

By June men could hear the cracking of timbers as the ice slowly crushed the *Endurance*. When the thaws of October came, seawater rushed into the shattered vessel and the crew had to abandon ship. They would be spending Christmas in the ice. By April of 1916 they had been marooned on the ice for almost a year and a half, and their supplies were gone. That's when the twenty-eight-man team crowded into three small boats and headed out into the world's most dangerous waters. For seven days, they battled strong, icy winds and monster seas until they landed on Elephant Island off the southern tip of Cape Horn. It had been nearly five hundred days since they had last set foot on dry land.

Yet the team might as well have still been on those ice floes as on this uninhabited rock pile. So the intrepid explorer set out with five others in a lifeboat across the open seas to South Georgia Island. It was a miracle that they got there. But they were now on the opposite side of the island from the whaling station. So the explorer set off into the howling winds by himself and somehow trekked over mountains to get to the other side. Miraculously, on August 25, 1916, he returned to Elephant Island to rescue those left behind. Though Ernest Shackleton had ignored the warnings of seamen not to head to Antarctica, losing both his ship and dream to be the first to cross the continent, he had shepherded his men through almost two years of a frozen nightmare without losing a single one.

He later set off to circumnavigate Antarctica, but he suffered a heart attack and died aboard his ship. We might lament Ernest Shackleton's failure to realize a single dream, but we should celebrate that one entry he penned in his diary when the *Endurance* was trapped: "I pray God, I can manage to get the whole party to civilization." Shackleton's story is a challenge to every spouse, parent, pastor, or leader of people: we may not realize our personal goals, but if we help those under our care to get to the right place, we have done the far better thing.

Good shepherds get their flocks all the way home.

———— ⚬◯⚬ ————

This is the will of God, that I should not lose
even one of all those he has given me, but that
I should raise them up at the last day.

JOHN 6:39

A Seventeen-Year Prayer

❦

If it weren't for the city in California named after her, maybe no one would remember this woman at all. She was a quiet Christian teenager in North Africa when her father married her off to a much older man. He was an irascible character, given to violent outbursts of temper. But this gentle girl quietly went into her garden every day and prayed for him. Her godly spirit finally won her husband over, and he was converted to Christ on his deathbed.

But it was her son who really drove her to her knees. By the time he was sixteen, he was incorrigible. He spent nights carousing with prostitutes and drinking himself into a stupor. He later confessed, "I drank the cup of lust to its last bitter dregs." His mother prayed that he would find religion, but when he did, it was a heretical sect. He later wrote that his mother "wept on my behalf more than most mothers weep when their children die." At age seventeen, he sailed for Rome without so much as a good-bye. The more his mother prayed, the farther her prodigal son ran from God. The only good news was that her son had left the heretical sect. But he did so only to throw himself into more debauchery. He joked, "O Lord, make me chaste—but not yet."

When he took off for Milan, his mother boarded a ship in North Africa and caught up with him. By now he was living with a mistress and had fathered an illegitimate son. He was finally willing to go to church but only to study the preacher's rhetorical skills. By now she had prayed for her son for more than six thousand days straight. He was sitting in his garden when he heard children singing, "Take up and read! Take up and read!" He felt that God was speaking to him. So he began to read Paul's epistle to the Romans. That day, his mother's unceasing seventeen-year prayer was finally answered.

After her son and grandson were both baptized, they all headed home to North Africa. On the voyage, she became violently ill. As she lay on her deathbed, she whispered her final words, "I only wanted to live long enough to see you a Christian." Her son later confessed, "I wept for an hour, but it was so little in comparison to all the tears she had wept for me." We should be glad that Monica never stopped weeping for Aurelius Augustinus. The world remembers him as Saint Augustine, one of the towering figures in history. His book *The City of God* was the blueprint for the civilization that rose from the ashes of Rome, and his theological works paved the way for the Reformation one thousand years later. His mother's amazing story deserves more than the name of a California city: *Santa Monica*. She should encourage any of us who long to see loved ones come to their senses: we can quarrel, plead, nag, badger, and manipulate—or we can pray to God to intervene. Monica chose the way of a saint, and it paid off for us all. Arthur Ellis said it best:

The art of love is largely the art of persistence.

—∞—

You can pray for anything, and if you
have faith, you will receive it.

MATTHEW 21:22

Life in a Jar

~ↄⓄⓄↄ~

Little Irena watched her doctor daddy ignore the virulent anti-Semitism of his Polish town and tend to Jewish children during a typhoid epidemic. When neighbors asked her father why he would risk his life for Jews, he replied, "If you see someone drowning, you must jump in to save them, whether you can swim or not." It wasn't long before he contracted typhus and died. Irena never forgot her father's words. Saving the drowning would become her passion.

She was a twenty-nine-year-old social worker when the German blitz-krieg rolled over Poland. Within days, the SS was rounding up Jews, cramming more than four hundred thousand into the tiny Warsaw ghetto. Its inhabitants were forced to survive on daily rations of fewer than two hundred calories a person. Almost half died of disease, starvation, or random killings. The rest were shipped to Nazi death camps. Irena and her friends produced fake documents that helped three thousand Jewish families escape. She also used her Social Welfare Department permit to enter the Warsaw ghetto under the guise of checking children for typhus.

She asked Jewish parents to make a heartbreaking choice. She would get as many children out as possible, but they would be taken in by pre-dominantly Polish Catholic families and raised as Gentiles. Irena promised that she would keep a list of all the children and get them back to families that survived the Holocaust. Her ingenuity at getting those kids out was amazing. Once out, they had to attend churches and Catholic schools and learn how to recite Christian prayers—all to escape detection by the Gestapo. Yet Irena kept copious lists of all the Jewish children and their families, placed them in jars, and buried them under a tree in plain sight of the German army barracks.

From 1939 until 1945, Irena put her life on the line every time she jumped into shark-infested waters to rescue drowning children. Eventually the Gestapo arrested her. Irena was taken to Pawiak prison where interrogators broke her legs and feet. She was sentenced to die before a firing squad, but she miraculously escaped. She carried on her rescue efforts while a fugitive. Irena managed to save 2,500 children. After the Russians came, she dug up her jars and tried to reunite her rescued kids with their Jewish families. Tragically, almost all of their relatives had been killed at the Treblinka death camp.

Irena Sendler's heroism was hidden from the world for the next fifty years while Poland languished under Communism. But in 1999 a group of high school students in Kansas dug up her amazing story and brought it to light. By then she was an eighty-nine-year-old who still suffered nightmares from the Holocaust and worried that she hadn't done enough. At age ninety-seven, she was nominated for the 2007 Nobel Peace Prize. When she died the next year, you can bet that the angels in heaven were waiting to welcome her home. We should all remember what her father, Dr. Stanisław Krzyżanowski said:

If you see someone drowning, you must jump in to save them, whether you can swim or not.

If you try to hang on to your life, you will lose it. But
if you give up your life for my sake, you will save it.

LUKE 9:24

Stagecoach Mary

❧☙

Stagecoach Mary was one of those legendary figures who won the Old West. She was born in Tennessee but was no Southern belle. A big-boned woman of unusual height, she towered over most men. No one ever called Mary a lady, at least not out on the rugged frontier of Montana where she landed. She wore men's clothing, chewed tobacco, carried a shotgun, and could outcuss, outdrink, and outshoot any cowpoke that rode into the little town of Cascade.

Most folks would be surprised to know that Mary had worked for a convent in Toledo, Ohio. After the Mother Superior went out to Montana in 1884 to join the Jesuits at Saint Peter's Mission, she sent an urgent message for more staff to join her. Mary went out West with a party of nuns, most likely to provide protection from desperadoes who frequented the badlands. She stayed on at the mission, raising chickens, tending the gardens, and driving freight to the school from nearby Cascade. But this Amazon woman got a reputation as "having the temperament of a wild grizzly bear." Everyone also knew that they had better steer a wide path around those nuns and their students because Mary protected them with the ferocity of a mother grizzly. But her smoking, cussing, and fisticuffs got her in hot water with the bishop in Great Falls. When His Eminence banned her from the mission, it devastated Mary and broke the hearts of the nuns.

After two failed attempts as a restaurateur, she got a contract delivering the mail. The way she handled her team of horses—and any bandits foolish enough to try to hold up her stagecoach—became the stuff of legend. It didn't matter if renegades or desperadoes were on the prowl or if the roads seemed impassable because of blizzards or thunderstorms,

Stagecoach Mary got the mail to a frontier desperately in need of news and supplies. Mary was seventy years old when she finally retired. The locals said that she was "still as strong as bear's breath." She spent her last years finally wearing skirts, tending flowers, and babysitting children. A grateful community built a home for Mary in Cascade, where she died in 1914.

What most folks may not know is that Mary was born the daughter of a house slave and a field hand on a Southern plantation. When a grieving community laid her to rest, she was simply remembered as Stagecoach Mary, the first African American woman to carry mail for the US Postal Service. Maybe Montana-born, Hollywood cowboy star Gary Cooper summed up Stagecoach Mary best: she was born a slave, but "lived to become one of the freest souls to ever draw a breath or a .38." Mary Field's amazing story teaches us that we don't have to let others define us or society's conventions limit our freedom to be all we can be. Stagecoach Mary might say amen to something C. S. Lewis wrote:

We are what we believe we are.

———— ⦵ ————

You will know the truth, and the truth will set you free.

JOHN 8:32

The Greatest Gift of All

❧

Few people remember this Filipino kid from the slums. He wanted to get an education, but poverty forced him to work as a day laborer. Like all of us, he longed to do something significant with his life, but he would probably live out his days as a manual laborer on construction jobs. Then tropical storm Ketsana roared across the Philippines, bringing more rain than the islands had seen in forty years. Within hours, killer floods were rampaging across the nation, wiping out villages and sweeping whole families to their deaths. Almost a million people were left homeless in the wake of that monster storm.

When the floodwaters churned through his village, Muelmar tied a long rope around his waist. One by one, he got his mother and family to safety on higher ground. Then he went back to save others. He dove into the torrent and swam from rooftop to rooftop, rescuing mothers and their children. As he pulled them to safety, he was growing progressively weaker. No one knows how many times he dove into those deadly currents, but he managed to get thirty people to safety. The exhausted teen finally collapsed on dry ground, shivering with hypothermia. That's when he heard the frantic screams of Menchie. This young mother was being swept down the river as she clung desperately to a Styrofoam box with her six-month-old daughter in her arms. Muelmar ignored the warnings of his family and his dog-tired body to dive into the raging waters once again. No one knows how he managed to pull Menchie and her baby girl to safety. But even heroes finally give out. Those on the shores watched in horror as Muelmar was swept downriver. They found the teen's battered body a few days later.

As those he rescued gathered around his makeshift grave, his mother Maria wept uncontrollably. His father, Samuel, said to reporters from nearby Manila, "He always had a good heart. It was typical of him to have given his life for others." Menchie held on tight to her little one and said, "He gave his life for me and my baby, and I'll never forget his sacrifice." It's been a decade since Muelmar Magallanes gave his life to save those thirty people from certain death. In those September floods that came to the Philippines, he wrote the Christmas story all over again. God's Son dove into a raging flood of sin and misery, giving his life to rescue us. This is as good a time as any to remember the amazing story of a day laborer from the poor side of Manila. Say his name out loud: Muelmar Magallanes. Then go out and dive in somewhere to grab hold of someone who is being swept away. Grab on to them for dear life, just like Muelmar and Jesus.

In rescuing others from an unnecessary death, we rescue ourselves from a meaningless life.

———— ❧ ————

Rescue those being led away to death; hold
back those staggering toward slaughter. If you
say, "But we knew nothing about this," does
not he who weighs the heart perceive it?

PROVERBS 24:11-12, NIV

A Christmas Miracle?

∽⊙⊙⊙∾

The Reverend Howard Schade claimed that the story he wrote in a 1954 issue of *Reader's Digest* was true. Cynics argue that it was just too good to be true. Besides, fact-checkers can't verify it with the pastor, who died many years ago without naming the couple in his story. So you be the judge.

The story begins with water from a December storm creating an ugly hole in the plaster behind the Communion table. "Christmas is only two days away!" gasped the pastor's distraught wife. So the couple went to an auction where he placed the winning bid on a gold-and-ivory lace tablecloth. They hung the tablecloth over the hole in the wall as the centerpiece of their Christmas decorations. At noon on the blustery, cold, Christmas Eve day, the pastor noticed a woman standing at the bus stop near the church. When she told him that her bus wasn't due for forty minutes, he invited her to wait in his warm sanctuary.

She told him that she had taken the long bus ride out from New York City to apply for a job as a governess, but was turned down because of her broken English. Then she spied the tablecloth and excitedly pointed to the monogrammed initials in the folds. "That's my banquet cloth!" The woman told a tragic story about how her Viennese husband had the beautiful cloth made for her in Brussels. When the Nazis invaded Austria, he sent her out of the country. He was supposed to follow, but never came. She later heard that he died in a concentration camp and had grieved ever since. The pastor tried to make her take the banquet cloth, but she refused. He watched with an aching heart as she went out into the cold to catch her bus.

Everyone at the candlelight service admired the gold tablecloth. But a middle-aged jeweler was most intrigued. He said to the pastor in a heavy accent, "Many years ago, my wife—God rest her—and I owned such a cloth. In our home in Vienna, my wife put it on the table . . . only when the bishop came to dinner." When the stunned pastor told him about the visit of the woman that afternoon, the jeweler sobbed, "Can it be? Does she live?" Together the two men found the local family who had interviewed the woman for the governess job. With address in hand, they drove into New York City, where the couple had a miraculous Christmas reunion.

It's too bad that Christmas grinches can't fact-check this story. But does it really matter? We never learned the names of the magi, shepherds, or innkeeper in the Christmas story. Joseph and Mary are long gone. So are those who witnessed the birth, life, death, and resurrection of Jesus. Fact-checkers will never be satisfied with a story that is too good to be true. But since *Reader's Digest* labeled the story of the gold tablecloth "Drama in Real Life," those of us who believe that miracles still happen are willing to accept it as truth.

Just because you can't see something doesn't mean that you can't believe it.

———◈———

Faith shows the reality of what we hope for;
it is the evidence of things we cannot see.

HEBREWS 11:1

Hordos the Madman

〜◎〜

His subjects called him Hordos the Madman. Yet few kings have suffered the hatred that he endured for almost forty years. Society's elite dismissed him as a social climber. The political establishment resented him as an outsider. Patriots despised him as Rome's puppet king. Religious leaders condemned him as a heretic and a hedonist.

Hordos desperately tried to win the hearts of his subjects. He almost bankrupted his treasury building them a spectacular temple. He pulled off an unparalleled engineering feat when he constructed the world's greatest seaport. He did the impossible by erecting a city atop towering cliffs in the desert. Hordos wore himself out building highways, aqueducts, and sports arenas for his people.

His efforts earned him the coveted title *philokaisar*—"The One that Caesar Loves." His tiny country gained favored nation status and unprecedented prosperity. Yet all that mattered little to his ungrateful subjects. Almost daily the king uncovered assassination plots. A man can only try so long before his heart shrivels and dies. In the face of ingratitude, Hordos became resentful. Battered by political intrigue, he distrusted everyone. He married ten wives to shore up his political base. Yet his paranoia caused him to fear even his own family. He had his favorite wife executed on trumped-up charges, tortured his mother-in-law to testify against his daughter, and then killed her along with his brother-in-law. He even orchestrated the murder of three of his sons.

Surely Hordos had descended into madness. People who looked at him the wrong way disappeared in the night. Holy men who preached against him were burned alive. In his last days, his mind was eaten away by syphilis and his body infested with worms. He obsessed that his passing would cause rejoicing. So he had three hundred leading citizens rounded up and ordered their slaughter at his death so that there would be weeping in the land.

Hordos was his Hebrew name. But you know him as Herod the Great. Every Christmas he is remembered for a single act of savagery. To eliminate a potential rival, he ordered the butchery of every baby boy in the vicinity of Bethlehem. It is the one jarring note in a festive holiday season, the horror that mars the happiness of Christmas. But you would be mistaken to think that his attempt to kill the baby Jesus was the act of a madman. Herod understood that there can be only one king in a kingdom. Two people cannot occupy the same throne. It had to be either Jesus or him. One had to die if the other was to live. Isn't that exactly the message of King Jesus? "You have to die to self if I am going to live in you. You have to get off the throne if I am to reign in your life." Herod was sane enough to figure that out. Maybe we are the crazy ones when we divorce Christmas from the Cross. Herod grasped this much gospel truth:

You must either crucify or crown Jesus, but you can't compromise with him.

————— ✦ —————

He has performed mighty deeds with his arm; he
has scattered those who are proud in their inmost
thoughts. He has brought down rulers from
their thrones but has lifted up the humble.

LUKE 1:51-52, NIV

702

Black Magic at the Inn

They traveled more than twelve thousand miles, inching their way over towering mountains and across trackless wastelands. Bandits and beasts of prey dogged their every step. They were saddle sore, bone tired, and weather beaten. Yet these ancient stargazers relentlessly pushed westward. What drove them?

Matthew's Gospel alone mentions these high priests of Zoroastrianism called magi. But it doesn't tell you that they were likely sorcerers and astrologers who studied the stars, prepared daily horoscopes, read tarot cards, and told fortunes. The word *magi* comes from the same source as our word *magic*. They were also experts in the science of astronomy and the greatest scholars of their day. That's why they were called wise men. They were also mathematicians, philosophers, doctors, and legal authorities. Above all, they were famous as searchers of truth who plumbed the religions of the world and immersed themselves in the metaphysical. Their Zoroastrian religion had predicted a messiah to be born of a virgin, and they were on the lookout for that birth.

What was the star that they followed westward? Historians and scientists tell us that in 7 BC Jupiter, Saturn, and Earth came together in a conjunction so rare that it has only happened twice since then. This juxtaposition of planets lit up the night skies. To the ancients, Jupiter was the planet of kings, and Mars represented war. A warrior king was about to be born. Four years later, Jupiter came into conjunction with Regulus, the brightest star in the constellation Leo. The newborn ruler would be a Lion King. In 2 BC, Jupiter moved through Pisces, which was seen as the constellation of the Jews. The Lion King would be born in Israel. On top of that, the Hebrew word for Jupiter is *sedeq*, which means "righteousness." This newborn would grow up to be the King of Righteousness. Astronomers tell us that Jupiter would have been stationary above Palestine two years after Jesus' birth.

Beyond stars and planets, these mysterious magi found better answers in the Scriptures. Some five hundred years earlier, a Jewish captive became a magi in the court of Nebuchadnezzar of Babylon. His name was Daniel. He wrote a prophetic book about a great Israelite Warrior King who would rule the world in righteousness. The magi also possessed the prophecies of Isaiah, Jeremiah, and Ezekiel. All of these writings led these ancient truth searchers from Persia to Bethlehem.

The amazing story of stargazers who rode twelve thousand miles to worship a two-year-old toddler in Bethlehem should leave us all breathless. Perhaps you are discouraged today because you have come to Jesus, but those you love haven't. Keep praying for them. Remember, if God wants to get people to Jesus, he will move stars and planets to make it happen. So don't lose hope. In the meantime, live out your faith before them, knowing that, if God can use stars, ancient scrolls, and even Zoroastrian prophecies, he can use you, too. Like most Christmas sayings, this has been said before, but it always bears repeating:

Wise men [and women] still seek him.

They entered the house and saw the child with his
mother, Mary, and they bowed down and worshiped
him. Then they opened their treasure chests and
gave him gifts of gold, frankincense, and myrrh.

MATTHEW 2:11

The Story of
the Christmas Tree

∽◦⊚◦∾

I t has been vilified, banned, and outlawed. Kings have issued decrees, parliaments have passed laws, and preachers have railed against the Christmas tree. Although today it's considered a universal symbol of Christmas, its roots are in ancient paganism. King Tut never saw a Christmas tree, but the ancient Egyptians brought palm trees into their houses, decorated them with glittering objects, and fashioned wreaths of date palm leaves to hang on doors in honor of their gods. Canaanites decorated evergreen trees and danced around them in worship of their goddess Asherah. The Romans celebrated the winter solstice on December 25 by decorating trees, filling their houses with greens and candles, and exchanging gifts. In Northern Europe, Druid priests decorated their temples with evergreen boughs in December. They also hung mistletoe and burned Yule logs.

At first Christian missionaries forbade their converts to participate in these pagan celebrations. Then they stole solstice from the pagans—along with holly, mistletoe, wreaths, and decorated trees—and invested these symbols with Christian meaning. The ancient church changed winter solstice to Christ's Mass, or Christmas. After the Reformation, most Protestants rejected Christmas as pagan. The English Puritan Oliver Cromwell railed against "the heathen traditions" of Christmas carols and decorated trees. Governor William Bradford tried to stamp out "pagan mockery" in Plymouth Colony by penalizing Christmas frivolity. In 1659 Massachusetts enacted a law that made the observance of Christmas a penal offense. The hanging of any Christmas decorations was punishable by jail. In 1894 a Boston pastor was fired for putting a Christmas tree in his church. As late as 1900 public schools were open on Christmas Day. Only one in five American homes displayed a Christmas tree in 1900.

The first Christmas tree didn't appear in America until 1843. The German immigrant who set it up was almost run out of town by his irate Pennsylvania neighbors. But it's no wonder that it was a German Lutheran who introduced the Christmas tree to Americans. Some three hundred years earlier, as the story goes, Martin Luther was walking through a forest on a snowy evening. The stars shone brightly, causing the snow on the boughs to glisten like diamonds. Luther reflected on the beauty before him and suddenly realized that trees are at the heart of the gospel story. He cut one down, dragged it home, and his family decorated it for the Advent season, sparking a German love affair with Christmas trees. If you enjoy your Christmas tree, you can thank a German immigrant for bringing Luther's tradition to Pennsylvania during December of 1843. Martin Luther saw in the Christmas tree the true reason for the season: a Savior was born in a manger to be nailed to a tree outside Jerusalem thirty-three years later, carrying our sins and taking our punishment upon himself so that we might be forgiven by the grace of God. This year, as you decorate your tree and enjoy its beauty, think about this:

The best gift is not placed under a tree but was hung on one.

⸻

I resolved to know nothing while I was with you except Jesus Christ and him crucified.

1 CORINTHIANS 2:2, NIV

A Beauty in the Flaws

৵ৡ৩৶

Slats Grobnik scratched out a few bucks selling Christmas trees. Just before Christmas, when all the trees had been picked over, a ragged couple came onto the lot. As they turned the price tag over on each tree, it was obvious that they didn't have enough money to buy one. Then the woman spied a discarded Scotch pine consigned to the outer darkness of the lot. It didn't look so bad on one side, but it was terribly scrawny on the other. Not far away stood another pitiful tree with the needles on one side eaten away.

The woman whispered in her husband's ears, and he asked if three dollars would be enough to buy both trees. Slats figured that he couldn't sell them anyway, so he agreed. He watched as the couple dragged their two scraggly trees away, leaving a trail of pine needles in their wake.

A few evenings later, Slats was walking home when he spied a magnificent Christmas tree in the window of a dilapidated apartment building. The decorations weren't much, but it didn't matter because the tree was so thick and well formed. Then Slats saw the ragged couple sitting on the porch out front. "That's a beautiful tree up in the window," exclaimed Slats. "Yep," replied the man with pride. "That's our tree. Actually, it's the two trees we bought from you." "How can that be?" asked Slats. "I sold you the two worst trees on the lot." "I know," the man responded. Then he smiled at the mousy woman who clung to his arm. "But my missus is clever. She had me work the trees together where the branches are bare. We formed one tree out of the two and wired them together. The branches are so thick you can't even see the wire."

According to *Chicago Tribune* columnist Mike Royko, Slats Grobnik learned a secret that night. "You take two trees that aren't perfect, that have flaws, that might even be homely, that maybe nobody else would want. But if you put them together just right, you can come up with something really beautiful." Slats added, "Like two people, I guess. A skinny guy with a mousy wife and only three dollars between them can create a Christmas tree that brings joy to the whole neighborhood."

Christmas is the story of God taking the flawed and making it beautiful. The tree trunk became a cradle for the King of kings. A poor fisherman's wooden boat became his pulpit. A twisted tree became his cross to save the world. God can wire together an ordinary carpenter, an unwed teenage girl, a handful of shepherds, prostitutes, tax collectors, and flawed disciples to tell a Christmas story that brings joy to the whole world. Christmas is about God bringing beauty out of scrawny and scraggly things and saving us from the folly of a grandiose sense of greatness. When you feel like you are just a little person in a little place, take time to remember Slats Grobnik's amazing Christmas story.

God delights in using the ordinary to do the extraordinary.

⸻

God chose things despised by the world, things
counted as nothing at all, and used them to bring
to nothing what the world considers important.

1 CORINTHIANS 1:28

The Real Saint Nick

E very child thinks that you have to go to the North Pole to find Saint Nick. Actually, you have to go much farther—a circumnavigation of the globe from the Mediterranean to Northern Europe and across the ocean to the New World. The original Saint Nicholas was an ancient Greek bishop. When his bones were uncovered in 1951, forensic evidence showed that his nose had been broken, leaving it misshapen, probably during the persecution of the Roman emperor Diocletian.

Nicholas was quite the opposite of a rosy-cheeked, fat fellow whose belly quivers with laughter. He was a lean, mean, fiery bishop who went on the attack against heresy in the church and never backed down from Roman officials who tried to shut down his churches. Mostly, he was a fierce protector of children. When a desperate father was about to sell his three daughters into prostitution, Nicholas produced three bags of gold to pay off the man's debts. Tradition holds that when an innkeeper killed three boys, Nicholas raised them from the dead. By the Middle Ages, his legend had grown until he had become the patron saint of children. But his image fit with harsh medieval parenting: if children didn't behave, Saint Nicholas would come and take their presents away from them. As his image evolved in Northern Europe, Saint Nicholas was merged with old Germanic figures like Ru-klaus (Rough Nicholas), Aschenklas (Ashy Nicholas), and Pelznickel (Furry Nicholas): frightening ogres who kidnapped and whipped misbehaving children. One almost hears the lyrics from a Christmas song: "He's making a list, he's checking it twice, gonna find out who's naughty or nice."

But the Dutch children refused to give up Saint Nicholas as a cheerful gift bringer. They brought their *Sinterklaas* to America. And it is the habit of Americans to take the best of what immigrants bring and make it uniquely American. In 1809, New York writer Washington Irving turned the Dutch Sinterklaas into a pipe-smoking fat man flying in a wagon over rooftops, bringing presents to good boys and girls and switches to naughty children. But the greatest change to Saint Nick's image came in 1823 with the poem "The Night Before Christmas." To this day, he remains a fat, jolly Santa with a white beard in a flying sleigh pulled by eight familiar reindeer. All that was left was for country singer Gene Autry to add Rudolph the Red-Nosed Reindeer in his 1949 Christmas hit single.

Every child should be glad that gift-giving Sinterklaas, with an American makeover, won out over Ru-klaus, Aschenklas, and Pelznickel, the German kidnappers of naughty boys and girls. But we should never forget the original Saint Nicholas who passionately defended and protected children. It would make him angry to see the way children are neglected, abused, and abandoned today. But he would be happy to see the one season in the year when children are reminded on Christmas morning that others love them enough to give them gifts. May we love our children as lavishly the rest of the year too.

Your children know you love them by your presence, not your presents.

———— ⁕ ————

Beware that you don't look down on any of these
little ones. For I tell you that in heaven their angels
are always in the presence of my heavenly Father.

MATTHEW 18:10

The Day Christmas Stopped a War

಄ಀ

What happened that magical Christmas Eve has been told through a collection of eyewitness accounts, journal entries, and letters home. Historians disagree about the specifics, but everyone agrees that a miracle took place on the Western front. It was 1914, the first year of a horrific war that would leave fifteen million dead. Pope Benedict had called for a Christmas truce, but the generals agreed that a day of fraternization would dull the fighting edge of their soldiers. So the men on both sides hunkered down in muddy trenches, looking across no-man's-land at twisted barbed wire and the rotting corpses of men and horses.

But this Christmas Eve, snow—glistening like diamonds on a clear moonlit night—had covered the horror of war with a clean blanket. Maybe that's why the German soldiers began to sing: *Stille Nacht, heilige Nacht*. Across the way, French and Belgian troops joined in: *Douce Nuit, sainte Nuit*. Now the British were adding their voices to the song: *Silent night, holy night*. Maybe they were caught up in the magic of the moment, but German soldiers began to climb out of their trenches and walk across no-man's-land. At first, the Allied troops thought it was some kind of trick. But the Germans were unarmed. So the Brits began to climb out of their trenches. Within minutes, some two-thirds of the combatants were coming together to give Christmas greetings.

What took place between those one hundred thousand enemies during those few hours is the stuff of Christmas legend. It is beyond debate that mostly they sang familiar Christmas carols, celebrating their common belief in the birth of God's Son, in the middle of a war. Fires were started, and enemy soldiers shared their rations with each other. Some gave patches, helmets, and keepsakes from home as gifts. They spoke of home, family, and girlfriends. It has been said that there were even some friendly soccer matches, although historians hotly debate that part of the story. What isn't debated is that it was spontaneous on the part of both Germans and Allies, and for a brief moment in a horrifying and meaningless carnage, there was peace on earth.

When word of this outbreak of peace got back to the Allied and the German headquarters, the generals and field marshals on both sides ordered their men back into the trenches. In 1915 the War to End All Wars went into overdrive, full of horror beyond anything the world had ever witnessed. The Christmas truce of 1914 has never been repeated in the century since. The amazing story of what happened on that magical night should make us all wonder: What would take place if the nations of the world would bow their knee to the King of kings and Lord of lords? Surely there would be peace on earth as we forget our differences to focus on the only one who can bring us all together.

No Jesus, no peace. Know Jesus, know peace.

A child is born to us, a son is given to us.
The government will rest on his shoulders.
And he will be called: Wonderful Counselor,
Mighty God, Everlasting Father, Prince of Peace.

ISAIAH 9:6

The Blue-Collar Saint

❧

He was a bit player in the Nativity, appearing briefly and disappearing quietly. Who was Joseph? Only a few spare words sketch his character. He was a simple carpenter who labored with calloused hands in a little shop on the dusty road to nowhere. He lived in obscurity, labored long hours to keep a half step ahead of his creditors, barely kept his large family fed and clothed, got old before his time, and then disappeared without ever speaking a word.

Folks in the hills of Galilee knew him as Joe the Carpenter. When he finally scraped together enough money for a dowry, he entered into a marriage contract with the young woman in the village who had caught his eye. He may not have been rich, but her parents knew he would take good care of their girl. Joe left the engagement party feeling like the luckiest guy in the hill country. He was preparing his bachelor quarters for his new bride when his world fell apart. His little Mary was pregnant. At first, he couldn't believe it. She must have cheated on him. He could have dragged her before the synagogue court to be publicly humiliated and then demanded she be stoned to death for adultery. But he loved God and little Mary too much to do that. So brokenhearted Joe decided to get out of the marriage contract quietly.

Then the dreams started. Heaven whispered the truth to Joe: the child in Mary's womb was God's Son, and he had been chosen by God to protect and care for the mother and boy. The Bible says two things about this blue-collar carpenter: he obeyed God *immediately* and *silently*. He took Mary in and raised the heavenly Father's Son. Joe may have bought the story of a virgin birth, but other folks didn't. He was mocked as a fool, became the brunt of crude jokes, and lost customers. He would spend his life on the move—from Nazareth to Bethlehem to Egypt and back to the Galilean hills. Folks would always see him as a fool who got snookered by a pregnant girl to take in her illegitimate child. Yet he silently cared for God's Son until he silently disappeared.

Joe the Carpenter lived an amazing story. He is the patron saint of all blue-collar workers in the world who go about their daily business doing the ordinary things that make a big difference in the world. They seldom get noticed or are given the recognition we accord corporate bigwigs, hollow celebrities, or pontificating power brokers. But it's regular folks like Joe the Carpenter, who plod through everyday life quietly and faithfully doing the small things, that God entrusts with his only begotten Son and the best work of his Kingdom. When you begin to feel like you are a little person in a small place, remember that blue-collar saint, Joseph of Nazareth.

There are no little people, unimportant lives, or insignificant jobs.

❦

When Joseph woke up, he did as the angel of the
Lord commanded and took Mary as his wife.

MATTHEW 1:24

Simple Mary, Mother of God

❧⊙❧

A shadow moved across dusty hills and slipped into a hillbilly shack. The Spirit moved past snoring laborers to a sleeping girl. This teenage peasant girl would be flabbergasted to know that the Spirit hovering over her bed had traveled across galaxies to find her. Even now she felt nothing as he whispered a command and a miracle took place in her womb. She stirred ever so slightly, unaware that the fullness of God now dwelt in the microscopic cells that were the beginnings of a boy. In months to come, her belly would swell until she felt like she was going to explode. She would go through the crucible of a mother's labor until Jesus was born. Mary would wrap him in rags and present him as God's gift to the world.

After birthing Jesus, she would keep a home for her carpenter husband and give birth to several more children. Mary would manage her tribe of ragamuffin kids in primitive, impoverished conditions, working her fingers to the bone until she dropped off to sleep exhausted at each day's end. She would grow old before her time, worn and stooped over by the harsh conditions of a hardscrabble life. At the Cross, her poverty would be so pronounced that her crucified Son would tell a disciple to take her into his home. We last see her after the resurrection of Jesus, in the upper room. She is listed among the rest, no greater than anyone else in the room. After that, like her husband Joseph, she faded away into obscurity.

This is the *real* Mary, separated from myth. In a sense, she is no different from the rest of us. Like us, she had admirable qualities and glaring faults. Jesus saved some of his harshest rebukes for his mother. Though her conception of Jesus was miraculous, the Bible never presents *her* birth as immaculate. She is not a perpetual virgin, nor is she a Hallmark card saint. She was born a sinner like the rest of us. Surely, she was the most blessed of all women, given the privilege of carrying, birthing, and nurturing the only begotten Son of God. She also bore the excruciating sorrow of watching her beloved Son be rejected, despised, betrayed, tortured, and crucified. Hers was a mixed blessing.

Mary's amazing story teaches us that the Nativity scene is a collection of sinners, not stained glass saints with halos. Mary shows us that Christ is not conceived in those who *do* God favors, but in those *whom* God favors. Like Mary, we can have the very person of Christ conceived in us by the Holy Spirit. Like Mary, we can present him as a gift to the watching world. Like Mary, it will bring pain. But this much is true for Jesus, his heavenly Father and earthly mother, and you:

Love will cost you dearly and will break your heart, but in the end, it will save the world.

⟡

This is how God loved the world: He gave his
one and only Son, so that everyone who believes
in him will not perish but have eternal life.

JOHN 3:16

Wanda and Lucille's House

⸙

Mother and daughter looked more like twin sisters. Both were grossly overweight, and together they couldn't have possessed more than eight teeth. Their round faces were caked in heavy makeup beneath neon orange hair. Cheap perfume barely masked body odor that oozed through cast-off dresses and gaudy costume jewelry. Both had spent too many nights in jailhouses and skid row missions. As they lugged garbage bags full of their meager possessions past our church, Wanda and Lucille decided that it would be a good place to get religion again.

Their presence embarrassed me, especially when our paths crossed in public. They would waddle up, throw their pudgy arms around me, and loudly proclaim, "He's our pastor!" One night, I reluctantly went to their little house for dinner. They sat me on a wooden crate at a card table surrounded by stray cats and decor rescued from a junk heap. We ate fast-food fried chicken, fruit cocktail straight out of a can, and Wonder Bread served on worn plastic plates. Later that little shack became a house of evangelism. Almost weekly, they would phone me to come and share the gospel with bikers covered in tattoos, homeless drifters, or runaway teens—many high on drugs or reeking of booze. In five years, I led many people to Christ in their place on the poor side of Tulsa.

Whenever I announced from the pulpit that someone needed a place to stay, Wanda and Lucille always bulldozed over other parishioners to be the first to offer their home. I managed to find a tactful way to turn them down, embarrassed at the thought of anyone staying at their three-room shack. One day, my two friends set out on an odyssey to find their lost children. I can still see their round faces pressed against the rear window of a Greyhound bus. They mouthed a final good-bye through toothless grins.

They called me from Denver, and then I lost track of them. Almost thirty years later, I am ashamed that I didn't let Wanda and Lucille host any of our guests. I regret that I was mortified to be seen with them in public or embarrassed that they were part of our church.

Had Jesus come to Tulsa, Wanda and Lucille would have bullied their way past everyone to be first to host him. I would have found a polite way to steer Jesus toward a more impressive home. But he would have said, "No thanks, I want to stay at Wanda and Lucille's place. They'll wash my feet with tears of gratitude and wipe them dry with their hair. By the way, I've already been there a thousand times before. I slipped in with every down-and-outer they ever invited into their shack." The amazing story of Wanda and Lucille is a reminder that there was no room for Jesus in the inn. As a result, he was born among barnyard beasts to an unwed teenage mother so he could be crucified between two criminals. Surely, none of us can be so far gone that he won't come to our house.

Are you part of the Inn crowd, or the Stable few?

―――――∽◦∾―――――

God showed his great love for us by sending
Christ to die for us while we were still sinners.

ROMANS 5:8

Passing the
Point of No Return

⤳⟿⤶

Europe was climbing out of the Middle Ages in the early 1400s. There were oceans to cross, lands to explore, and treasures to be reaped by those willing to go where no European had gone before. But it would be another century before Galileo shocked the world with his assertion that the earth was round rather than flat.

Sailors at that time were sure that the ocean was like an infinity pool, with the distant horizon as its edge. Get too close, and your ship would fall off into an abyss. But the most frightening spot on the Atlantic Ocean was off the coast of Africa at the western end of the Sahara Desert. Cape Bojador was a place of strong currents and frequent storms, its shores littered with the skeletons of wrecked ships. Sailors called the waters south of Cape Bojador the Green Sea of Darkness. No ship had ever ventured into these uncharted waters and come back. Tall tales spoke of seas filled with monsters, witches, and demons.

But Portugal had a visionary prince. History remembers him as Henry the Navigator. He gathered the best mathematicians, astronomers, cartographers, and instrument makers to teach the art of sailing. His shipbuilders designed oceangoing vessels in an age when ships were built to hug the coastline. He was determined to see his ships go down the coast of Africa and around its southern tip to Asia. But someone had to possess the nerve to pass Cape Bojador. That man would be Gil Eannes.

Little is known about this mysterious man, except that he was a household servant in Henry's palace. Somehow he convinced Henry to give him a ship by promising that he would take it past Cape Bojador. But when his ship got close to the cape, his men mutinied, threatening to kill him if he went any farther. Henry was not pleased with Gil Eannes, but somehow the explorer convinced His Majesty to give him one more chance. He sailed again to the cape. His new crew was filled with dread, but this time they obeyed their captain and sailed past the point of no return. Ships would follow in his pioneering wake, but he would be the first to open the sea lanes that would eventually take European explorers around Africa to Asia.

Gil Eannes appeared out of nowhere and disappeared into obscurity. His one claim to fame was that voyage beyond the point of no return. But that one small step for humankind would open the world to Magellan, Columbus, and other intrepid explorers. Gil Eannes is the patron saint of those who dare to go beyond the point of no return. As you look forward to your new year, you might want to ask these questions: What is my Cape Bojador? What adventures am I missing because I'm afraid to venture out into the great unknown? Maybe like Gil Eannes you've tried to get beyond that cape before, but this year you have another chance. This much is sure: *The only trip that you will ever regret is the one you never took.*

_____

Farmers who wait for perfect weather never plant.
If they watch every cloud, they never harvest.
ECCLESIASTES 11:4

Jack's Redemption

❦

Jack was the golden boy of British politics. Born the son of a baron, he was educated at England's best schools: Harrow and Oxford. In 1940 he was elected as the youngest member of Parliament. As a second lieutenant in World War II, he distinguished himself in North Africa, Italy, and Normandy. The boy wonder rose to the rank of brigadier and was awarded the Order of the British Empire. He came home a war hero and was touted as a future political superstar.

He rose steadily up the ranks of government until he was appointed secretary of state for war in 1960. But power corrupts and so does the world of glamor. Jack and his wife became part of the swinging sixties lifestyle. When he wasn't at a cabinet meeting, he was in discos, dancing the night away with jet-set playboys and high-priced call girls. His closest friends whispered that he was in over his head, but Jack figured that he was bulletproof. Yet even Superman has to watch out for kryptonite. Jack's came in the form of Christine Keeler, a beautiful model turned prostitute. When he saw her swimming naked in the pool of a wealthy politician, it was lust at first sight. As the secretary of state for war carried on his torrid affair with Christine, his lover was also sleeping with a Soviet spy. Maybe no state secrets were passed during pillow talk, but when the news of Jack's affair hit the press, it was the biggest bombshell of the Cold War.

At first he lied about his affair. But the cover-up was exposed, and Jack had to resign in disgrace. The prime minister of England was forced to resign, and in the following parliamentary elections, Jack's Tory party was swept from power. This is where his story becomes amazing. The fallen political star took a dingy office at Toynbee Hall, doing charity work among London's poor. Cynics said that he was trying to rehabilitate his image. Friends worried that he was doing self-imposed penance. But Jack quietly continued his charity work for forty years, raising money for the least, last, and lost of society until old age and ill health confined him to a wheelchair.

When he died in 2006 at age ninety-one, the nation remembered him as a champion of the poor and oppressed. Former Tory leader Ian Duncan Smith said of Jack, "His enormous efforts will have changed the lives of many people and he will be sadly missed by them and many of us." His friends called him Jack, but the world also remembers him as John Profumo, the man whose affair with a prostitute nearly brought down the British government and endangered the West during the Cold War. His amazing story encourages us that grace is part of the word disgrace. Where sin abounds, grace abounds even more. Maybe you have messed up too. But like John Profumo, your story isn't over yet. A God of grace still has more chapters to write in your story. So grab hold of this hope:

Failure is not a disgrace, unless you allow it to become the last chapter of your book.

―――――― ❧ ――――――

As people sinned more and more,
God's wonderful grace became more abundant.

ROMANS 5:20

Falling through Ice

ᏋᏗᏇᏋᏇᎧᏉ

Carolyn was six years old when her mother ripped her out of the arms of her grandparents. She couldn't understand why her absentee mother wanted her back in her life. All she knew was that Rose was sadistic and vindictive, treating her more like an animal than a daughter. For the next few years, the girl endured a nightmare of unspeakable abuse. One morning she even woke up on hardwood floors, chained to a metal radiator.

Then one day Rose delivered her back to her grandparents. Perhaps the years of abuse had turned her from an adorable little girl into damaged goods. Carolyn sensed immediately that her grandmother, Betty, was now cold and distant. In the next few years, the teen was shuffled from one relative to another, always feeling unwelcome and unwanted. She was happy when her daddy took her in—until he began to sexually abuse her.

She got married young, thinking that her husband would give her all the love that she had missed as a child. Today she is quick to admit, "I married him for all the wrong reasons." When she wasn't able to create her dream family, Carolyn thought she could exorcise her childhood demons by rescuing abused kids. She started Texas Child Search, Inc. to track down and find missing children. With precious few funds and little police assistance, she rescued fifty-nine children. She was now a media darling, nominated by the *San Antonio Light* newspaper as their Woman of the Year. Then Carolyn fell through the ice.

She came home to discover her husband, Larry, engaging in inappropriate sexual behavior in her little girl's bed. Something inside Carolyn snapped. She arranged for a hit man to murder her husband. In her mind, she was getting rid of a sexual predator. Maybe she was also punishing those who had victimized her as a child or all the abusers of the kids she had rescued. When she drove with Larry to a New Orleans hotel, she expected the hit man to be waiting. Instead, the police were there to arrest her. Carolyn ended up in federal prison. Yet it was there that Carolyn finally found healing after she gave her life to Jesus Christ. She realized that if God could forgive her, she should forgive others. Somehow, she found the supernatural strength to forgive her sadistic mother, sexually abusive father, distant grandmother, and most of all, Larry.

Carolyn came out of prison to live the best chapters of her amazing story. She reunited with Larry and lived with him until his death in 1994. She has since married a man for all the right reasons. Perhaps you are struggling with bitterness toward those who abused you. Get hold of Carolyn Huebner Rankin's book *Falling through Ice*. She wants you to know, "No matter how deep the sewer . . . you can come out of it." Her amazing story of being able to forgive those who hurt her most reminds us of how to look at those who hurt us:

Forgiveness doesn't excuse their actions. It keeps them from destroying our heart.

Love is patient and kind. Love is not jealous or boastful or proud or rude. It does not demand its own way. It is not irritable, and it keeps no record of being wronged.

1 CORINTHIANS 13:4-5

Oceans of Mercy

ودوش

John still shakes his head in wonder. So do those who've had a front-row seat to his amazing story. It began when his invalid bedridden mother prayed for fifteen years that God would do great things through her boy. Then there was the person who challenged John to go on a mission trip to Haiti. He and his young bride had to make a difficult choice: use their savings to put a down payment on a house or to buy plane tickets. If John hadn't honored God by going to that impoverished island nation, he wouldn't have watched Haitians crowd into movie theaters to pay money they couldn't afford to see Hollywood movies they shouldn't watch. He left that country with a vision to bring redemptive movies to poor people of the world.

Later John felt led to go to India to make a movie about the life of Christ, using Indian actors and language. Though he was a pioneer of Christian television in America, he knew little about filmmaking, directing, or scriptwriting. Mostly, he had no financial backing. All he knew was that God had given him a vision. So he went to India by faith. There, he was stunned to see a billboard advertising a new movie on the life of Christ. Amazingly it had been directed and produced by a famous Bollywood director who was also a Hindu—as were most of the actors. As John sat in the theater watching this movie called *Dayasagar*, or "Oceans of Mercy," he was amazed to see Hindu and Muslim moviegoers falling in love with the Jesus who touched the untouchables, loved the unlovely, and stood up to the corrupt priests. He saw them weep when Jesus was crucified and cheer when he rose from the dead. John knew that he had found his film.

When he met Vijay, the film's director, he asked what motivated him to make *Dayasagar*. Vijay replied, "Jesus pushed me." John responded, "Jesus has pushed me to take this film to the villages of India." Through a miraculous deal, John got that film. In the first village, they stretched eight bedsheets tightly between bamboo poles as a screen and then called people to come. Though it was raining, two thousand people showed up. Later, teams went from village to village showing the film. They faced opposition, persecution, and death threats. But whole villages also came to see *Dayasagar*. The statistics are beyond belief. This film is the longest running in India. Since 1979, 335 million people have seen *Dayasagar*. Some 24 million viewers have made commitments to Jesus.

John Gilman's amazing story is one of impossible dreams coming true—not because of what John did, but because he stepped out in faith believing that he was acting on God's vision for India. As you look forward to a new year, remember *Dayasagar*. If your dreams and visions are from God, you can bank on his oceans of mercy. So go step out on faith, remembering this:

If God gives the vision, he will always give the provision.

――――― ⌒⊙⌒ ―――――

This same God who takes care of me will supply
all your needs from his glorious riches, which
have been given to us in Christ Jesus.

PHILIPPIANS 4:19

True Grit in
Those Pearly Whites

⌘

He was as smooth as butter. The impeccably dressed Syracuse grad with the pearly white teeth. The country clubber with a white tennis sweater casually draped across his shoulders to set off a perfect tan. He walked into the room with easy confidence, speaking in tones as rich as his privileged upbringing. Even his name reeked of privilege: Richard Augustus Wagstaff Clark Jr.

Hollywood and New York are dog-eat-dog worlds in which aspiring entertainers have to claw their way to the top. But Richard started at the peak. His rich uncle owned the radio station, and his dad managed it. Richard moved quickly from mail room to microphone. With the help of daddy's friends, he was soon standing in front of television cameras. His boyish good looks and easy manner were made for the new media. When the show's star was arrested for drunk driving, Richard got his big break. It seemed that success came easy for Richard.

Baby Boomers remember him by his stage name: Dick Clark. The host of *American Bandstand*. The guy with hip smoothness idolized by teenage girls and hated by gawky teen boys. The one suggesting clues on the mindlessly addictive *$100,000 Pyramid* right *after* the contestant loses. The ageless wonder on *New Year's Rockin' Eve*. New Year's Eves came and went, but Richard Augustus Wagstaff "Dick" Clark Jr. never got older, just richer. How could life be so doggone easy?

What his adoring public didn't know was that in 2004 America's oldest teenager suffered a debilitating stroke that marred his ageless youth and slurred his golden voice. He could hide out, announce his retirement, and give up. After all, he was in his seventies. But Dick Clark fought back. After two years of painful and exhausting therapy, he bravely appeared on the 2005 *New Year's Rockin' Eve* show before a shocked worldwide audience. His speech was slurred and his face partially paralyzed. America's teenager had grown painfully old overnight.

When he died in 2012, an obituary in the *New York Times* dismissed him in his own words: "I've always dealt with light, frivolous things that didn't really count; I'm not ashamed of that. . . . I've been a fluffmeister for a long time." But the ageless spinner of platters and the host of trivial game-show pyramids and TV bloopers cannot be dismissed as a fluffmeister.

There was true grit behind those pearly white teeth. For seven years he bravely battled to come back from a stroke resulting from diabetes. He had the courage to go public with it and to tell stroke victims everywhere that life can go on. Debilitation doesn't have to be debilitating. No matter what you are facing today, you can take heart from the story of a fluffmeister who became a champion. Surely Dick Clark would agree with this quote inspired by C. S. Lewis's work:

Hardships often prepare ordinary people for an extraordinary destiny.

———— ✺ ————

This is my command—be strong and courageous!
Do not be afraid or discouraged. For the LORD
your God is with you wherever you go.

JOSHUA 1:9

The Chosen Child

✧

She looked for love in all the wrong places. At age fifteen, she got pregnant. She had been with so many boys, she didn't know the identity of the father. She found her way to a home for unwed mothers, where she gave birth to her no-name boy. Later, she snagged a military man who was sent overseas. So she again went looking for love in all the wrong places.

She left her kids for days at a time while she was off on drunken binges. It was often worse when she came home with a boyfriend. One night she giggled as a drunk sodomized that now-six-year-old boy. The authorities intervened, and her children were put in the foster system. The boy was shuffled through several homes. In the first home, his foster father beat his wife to death with a hammer. In the second, the boy ate out of dog dishes. Even by the time he was twelve, he still wet the bed every night. Psychologists said that he had the sociability of a four-year-old. A sixth-grade teacher wrote on his report card, "This boy will never amount to anything." He still remembers the day that he shook his fist at the skies and said, "If there is a God, I hate you! I hate you!"

But God loved him. And he put that love in the heart of Mary Petterson. She desperately wanted children. So she went to the State Welfare Department, where she was shown a book with the photos of five hundred foster kids. She saw the no-name boy's picture and said, "That's the one I want." When she first saw him, she threw her arms around him and said, "Bobby, I love you!" It was the first time he had ever heard those words. Later, her husband, Arnold, asked, "Do you want to be our son?" A few days later, as he sat on his new Roy Rogers bunk bed, he whimpered, "Mom, tonight I am going to wet the bed, and you won't love me anymore." Mary wrapped her arms around the boy and said, "If you wet it tonight, we'll just change the sheets in the morning, and we won't love you any less." When kids at his new school teased, "You aren't a real kid; you're adopted," his new mother said, "Bobby, the rest of the parents had to take what they got in the hospital. But we went out and found you. You are special because you're a chosen child." Years later, when the wolves howl in his soul, he recalls those words, "You are a chosen child!"—chosen by Mary, Arnold, and God.

That no-name boy is the author of this book. This is my amazing story. Like your story, mine is amazing because it is *His* story—written by God. Like yours, my best chapters are yet to be written. I hope, like me, you will get up every day with excitement about the lines God will write today in your amazing story.

When God writes your story it has to have a happy ending.

———— ✎ ————

"I know the plans I have for you," says the LORD.
"They are plans for good and not for disaster,
to give you a future and a hope."

JEREMIAH 29:11

Sources

JANUARY 1 A DEVASTATING RESCUE
Hall, Allan. "Revealed: The Priest Who Changed the Course of History . . . by Rescuing a Drowning Four-Year-Old Hitler from Death in an Icy River." *Daily Mail*, January 5, 2012. http://www.dailymail.co.uk/news/article-2082640/How-year-old-Adolf-Hitler-saved-certain-death--drowning-icy-river-rescued.html.
Farrier, David. "New Evidence Suggests Priest Saved Young Hitler from Drowning." Newshub, June 1, 2012. http://www.newshub.co.nz/world/new-evidence-suggests-priest-saved-young-hitler-from-drowning-2012010617.
Willis, Amy. "Adolf Hitler 'Nearly Drowned as a Child.'" *Telegraph*, January 6, 2012. http://www.telegraph.co.uk/history/world-war-two/8996576/Adolf-Hitler-nearly-drowned-as-a-child.html.
Winston, George. "The Priest Who Saved a Four-Year-Old Hitler from Death in an Icy River." War History Online, February 9, 2014. https://www.warhistoryonline.com/war-articles/priest-saved-four-year-old-hitler-death-icy-river.html.

JANUARY 2 THE MOST COURAGEOUS MAN IN AMERICA
"Bob Wieland Walks across America on His Hands." YouTube video, 4:56. Posted by "TheSevenSunny," September 30, 2011. https://www.youtube.com/watch?v=TGPlBgFemx0.
Burns, James. "Double Amputee Bob Wieland Stands Tall on Veterans Day at NU." *NU News*, November 18, 2015. https://news.niagara.edu/news/show/double-amputee-bob-wieland-stands-tall-on-veterans-day-at-nu.
"President Ronald Reagan Names Veteran Bob Wieland Mr. Inspiration www.BobWieland.com." YouTube video, 9:01. Posted by Winning at the Race of Life, May 29, 2014. https://www.youtube.com/watch?v=quYtKUKBAlI.
Ungrady, Dave. "25 Years Later, a Marathon Finish Still Inspires." *New York Times*, November 5, 2011. https://mobile.nytimes.com/2011/11/06/sports/bob-wielands-athletic-accomplishments-continue-to-inspire.html.

JANUARY 3 THE IRRESISTIBLE POWER OF COURAGE
Early Church History. "Martyrs of Sebaste." Accessed January 9, 2018. https://earlychurchhistory.org/martyrs/forty-martyres-of-sebaste/.
Graves, Dan. "40 Martyrs of Sevaste." Christianity.com. Accessed January 9, 2018. https://www.christianity.com/church/church-history/timeline/301-600/40-martyrs-of-sevaste-11629648.html.
Tony Cooke Ministries. "The 40 Martyrs of Sebaste." Accessed January 9, 2018. Reprinted with permission by The Voice of the Martyrs. http://www.tonycooke.org/articles-by-others/voice_martyrs/.

JANUARY 4 WHO KILLED SUPERMAN?
McGasko, Joe. "The Superman Curse." Biography, June 18, 2013. https://www.biography.com/news/the-superman-curse-21259185.
Patterson, John. "Who Killed Superman?" *Guardian*, November 17, 2006. https://www.theguardian.com/film/2006/nov/18/features.weekend1.
Thill, Scott. "June 16, 1959: George Reeves, Superman, Felled by Speeding Bullet." *Wired*, June 16, 2009. https://www.wired.com/2009/06/dayintech-0616/.
Wood, Gaby. "Who Killed Superman? The Sinister True Story behind the Death of George Reeves." *Telegraph*, March 13, 2016. http://www.telegraph.co.uk/films/2016/04/14/who-killed-superman-the-sinister-true-story-behind-the-death-of/.

JANUARY 5 TAMERLANE'S CURSE
Advantour. "Tamerlane's Curse." Accessed January 24, 2018. https://www.advantour.com/uzbekistan/legends/tamerlane-curse.htm.

Jeffers, Jennifer. "Did the Curse of an Ancient Warlord Help the Nazis?" *The Raven Report* (blog), November 14, 2016. https://theravenreport.com/2016/11/14/the-curse-of-tamerlane-how-an-ancient -conquerer-may-have-helped-the-nazis-invade-russia/.

Lallanilla, Marc. "Real or Not? 6 Famous Historical Curses." Live Science, August 5, 2013. https://www.live science.com/38670-famous-historical-curses.html.

Mishkov, Aleksandar. "How the Curse of Timur's Tomb Changed the Course of World War II." Documentary Tube.com, April 19, 2016. http://www.documentarytube.com/articles/how-the-curse-of-timur-s-tomb -changed-the-course-of-world-war-ii.

JANUARY 6 THE BIGGEST NATION OF ALL

Boniface, Patrick. "Alexander the Great—The Greatest Leader of All Time?" Military History, October 10, 2010. https://www.military-history.org/intel/alexander-the-great.htm.

HistoryofMacedonia.org. "Alexander the Great." Accessed January 11, 2018. http://www.historyofmacedonia .org/AncientMacedonia/AlexandertheGreat.html.

Plutarch. *Plutarch Lives: Demosthenes and Cicero, Alexander and Caesar*, 7:665–78. Translated by Bernadotte Perrin. The Loeb Classical Library. Cambridge, MA: Harvard University Press, 1919.

Worthington, Ian. "How 'Great' Was Alexander?" The Circle of Ancient Iranian Studies. Accessed January 11, 2018. Previously published in *Ancient History Bulletin* 13.2 (1999). http://www.cais-soas.com/CAIS /History/Post-Achaemenid/alexander.htm#.

JANUARY 7 THE FORGOTTEN EXPLORER

Biography. "Matthew Henson." Updated March 31, 2016. https://www.biography.com/people/matthew -henson-9335648.

Chamberlain, Gaius. "Matthew Henson." Great Black Heroes, January 18, 2015. http://www.greatblack heroes.com/science/matthew-henson/.

Foulkes, Debbie. "Matthew Henson (1866–1955): First Person to Reach the North Pole." Forgotten Newsmakers, April 12, 2010. https://forgottennewsmakers.com/2010/04/12/matthew-henson-1866 -1955-first-person-to-reach-the-north-pole/.

Henderson, Bruce. "Who Discovered the North Pole?" *Smithsonian*, April 2009. https://www.smithsonianmag .com/history/who-discovered-the-north-pole-116633746/.

JANUARY 8 SAVED BY HIS UNBORN SON

Bible, Adam. "Inspiring Mountain Climber: Aron Ralston." *Men's Fitness*. Accessed February 11, 2018. https://www.mensfitness.com/training/endurance/inspiring-mountain-climber-aron-ralston.

Hannaford, Alex. "127 Hours: Aron Ralston's Story of Survival." *Telegraph*, January 6, 2011. http://www .telegraph.co.uk/culture/film/8223925/127-Hours-Aron-Ralstons-story-of-survival.html.

Today. "Hiker Who Cut Off Arm: My Future Son Saved Me." December 8, 2009. https://www.today.com /news/hiker-who-cut-arm-my-future-son-saved-me-wbna34325633.

Winters, Rebecca. "Survival of the Fittest." *Time*, May 4, 2003. http://content.time.com/time/magazine /article/0,9171,449493,00.html.

JANUARY 9 HISTORY'S STRANGEST SIEGE

Adams, Earnest W. Comment on "What Was Ancient Siege Warfare Like?" Quora, May 29, 2015. https:// www.quora.com/What-was-ancient-siege-warfare-like.

All Things Medieval. "The Story of the Sieging of a Medieval Castle: Chateau Gaillard." Accessed January 28, 2018. http://medieval.stormthecastle.com/essays/the-siege-of-chateau-gaillard.htm.

Archivist in Television. "Battle Castle: Chateau Gaillard, the Stronghold of Richard the Lionheart." *Medieval Archives* (podcast), March 1, 2012. Episode no longer available.

Janvier, Thomas A. "The Château Gaillard." *Harper's Magazine*, August 1904.

JANUARY 10 THE ULTIMATE COLD CASE

de Lisle, Leanda. "Did Richard III Kill the Princes in the Tower?" *Newsweek*, July 13, 2014. http://www .newsweek.com/did-richard-iii-kill-princes-tower-258395.

Gallagher, Paul. "The Princes in the Tower: Will the Ultimate Cold Case Finally Be Solved after More Than 500 Years?" *Independent*, August 21, 2015. http://www.independent.co.uk/news/uk/home-news/the -princes-in-the-tower-will-the-ultimate-cold-case-finally-be-solved-after-more-than-500-years-10466190 .html.

Johnson, Ben. "The Princes in the Tower." Historic UK. Accessed February 11, 2018. http://www.historic-uk .com/HistoryUK/HistoryofEngland/The-Princes-in-the-Tower/.

Lowery, Georgianna. "What Really Happened to the Princes in the Tower?" Owlcation, November 19, 2014. https://owlcation.com/humanities/The-Princes-In-The-Tower.

JANUARY 11 ANTONINA'S ARK

Linfield, Susie. "A Natural History of Terrible Things." Review of *The Zookeeper's Wife*, by Diane Ackerman. *Washington Post*, September 16, 2007. http://www.washingtonpost.com/wp-dyn/content/article/2007 /09/13/AR2007091301895.html.

Liphshiz, Cnaan. "When 300 Jews Escaped the Nazi Camps by Hiding in the Warsaw Zoo." JTA, March 23, 2015. https://www.jta.org/2015/03/23/news-opinion/world/when-jews-found-refuge-in -underground-warren-at-warsaw-zoo.

Oosterhoff, Inge. "The Zoo That Hid Jews from the German Army." Messy Nessy, December 3, 2015. http://www.messynessychic.com/2015/12/03/the-zoo-that-hid-jews-from-the-german-army/.

Vitone, Elaine. "True Story of Warsaw Zoo That Harbored Jewish Refugees during WWII." SFGATE, September 6, 2007. http://www.sfgate.com/books/article/True-story-of-Warsaw-zoo-that-harbored -Jewish-2504908.php.

JANUARY 12 THE EVOLUTIONARY MAN

Baig, Muneeb. "His Life Was a Series of Changes." Albalagh, February 9, 2003. https://www.albalagh.net /kids/history/malcolmx.shtml.

Blake, John. "Malcolm and Martin, Closer Than We Ever Thought." *In America* (blog). CNN, May 19, 2010. http://www.cnn.com/2010/LIVING/05/19/Malcolmx.king/index.html.

The Learning Network. "Feb. 21, 1965: Malcolm X Is Assassinated by Black Muslims." *New York Times*, February 21, 2012. https://learning.blogs.nytimes.com/2012/02/21/feb-21-1965-malcolm-x-is -assassinated-by-black-muslims/.

Worland, Justin. "On 50th Anniversary of Assassination, Malcom X's Legacy Continues to Evolve." *Time*, February 20, 2015. http://time.com/3715164/50-years-malcolm-x/.

JANUARY 13 THE SINGER WHO STOPPED WORLD WAR III

Chittenden, Maurice. "Rebel James Blunt Saved Us from War with Russia." *London Times*, November 14, 2010. https://www.thetimes.co.uk/article/rebel-james-blunt-saved-us-from-war-with-russia-qthpcdg0f6c.

Magrath, Andrea. "'I Stopped World War Three by Refusing US Orders to Destroy Russian Forces,' Claims James Blunt." *Daily Mail*, November 15, 2010. http://www.dailymail.co.uk/tvshowbiz/article-1329822 /James-Blunt-stopped-World-War-3-refusing-destroy-Russian-forces.html.

Peck, Tom. "How James Blunt Saved Us from World War 3." *Independent*, November 15, 2010. http://www .independent.co.uk/news/people/news/how-james-blunt-saved-us-from-world-war-3-2134203.html.

JANUARY 14 THE REAL LONE RANGER

Burton, Art T. "Bass Reeves." Fort Smith. National Park Service. Updated April 10, 2015. https://www.nps .gov/fosm/learn/historyculture/bass_reeves.htm.

Cellania, Miss. "The Life and Times of Deputy U.S. Marshal Bass Reeves." Mental Floss, January 17, 2013. http://mentalfloss.com/article/33537/life-and-times-deputy-us-marshal-bass-reeves.

Marcou, Dan. "Police History: Was U.S. Marshal Bass Reeves the Real Lone Ranger?" PoliceOne.com, August 26, 2013. https://www.policeone.com/police-heroes/articles/6408028-Police-History-Was -U-S-Marshal-Bass-Reeves-the-real-Lone-Ranger/.

McKay, Brett, and Kate McKay. "Lessons in Manliness from Bass Reeves." The Art of Manliness, April 24, 2011. https://www.artofmanliness.com/2011/04/24/lessons-in-manliness-from-bass-reeves/.

JANUARY 15 THE DEVIL'S DAUGHTER

Colley, Rupert. "Svetlana Alliluyeva (Lana Peters), Stalin's Daughter—A Brief Biography." *Rupert Colley .com* (blog), February 28, 2015. http://rupertcolley.com/2015/02/28/svetlana-alliluyeva-lana-peters -stalins-daughter-a-brief-biography/.

Grushin, Olga. Review. "*Stalin's Daughter*, by Rosemary Sullivan." *New York Times*, June 12, 2015. https:// www.nytimes.com/2015/06/14/books/review/stalins-daughter-by-rosemary-sullivan.html.

Nordlinger, Jay. "Stalin's Daughter, Her Own Woman." *National Review*, September 21, 2015. http://www .nationalreview.com/article/424288/stalins-daughter-her-own-woman-jay-nordlinger.

Trethewey, Rachel. "*Stalin's Daughter: The Extraordinary and Tumultuous Life of Svetlana Alliluyeva* by Rosemary Sullivan, Book Review." *Independent*, June 18, 2015. http://www.independent.co.uk/arts -entertainment/books/reviews/stalins-daughter-the-extraordinary-and-tumultuous-life-of-svetlana -alliluyeva-by-rosemary-sullivan-10328725.html.

JANUARY 16 THE SHAGGY HERO

Edelman, Adam. "Brave Teen Defends Central Michigan University Rape Victim from Crazed Attacker by Hiding Her in His Bathroom, Wielding Hunting Knife as Sex Fiend Tried to Break into His Home." *New York Daily News*, January 21, 2013. http://www.nydailynews.com/news/national/rape-suspect -posts-facebook-moments-shot-dead-article-1.1243611.

Ng, Christina. "Michigan 'Hero' Teen Hides Rape Victim from Alleged Attacker." ABC News, January 21, 2013. http://abcnews.go.com/US/michigan-hero-teen-hides-rape-victim-attacker/story?id=18272032.

Nye, James. "Hero Teenager Hid Terrified Rape Victim in His Home and Fended Off Her Crazed Attacker with a Knife as He Tried to Smash His Way into House." Daily Mail, January 20, 2013. http://www.dailymail.co.uk/news/article-2265678/Heroic-14-year-old-boy-lets-fleeing-rape-victim-house-fends-attacker-knife.html.

JANUARY 17 A DOG'S TALE

Daily Mail. "A Very Victorian Hoax! s Bobby Who Kept Vigil over His Master's Grave for 14 Years Was 'a Publicity Stunt.'" August 4, 2011. http://www.dailymail.co.uk/news/article-2021906/Greyfriars-Bobby-hoax-Dog-kept-vigil-masters-grave-publicity-stunt.html.

Johnson, Ben. "Greyfriars Bobby." Historic UK. Accessed February 11, 2018. http://www.historic-uk.com/HistoryUK/HistoryofScotland/Greyfriars-Bobby/.

Scotland Welcomes You. "Story of Greyfriars Bobby: A Truly Heartwarming and Inspiring Tale." Updated February 4, 2017. http://scotlandwelcomesyou.com/greyfriars-bobby/.

Strochlic, Nina. "Welcome to the Most Haunted Graveyard in the World. Safety not Guaranteed." Daily Beast, October 13, 2013. https://www.thedailybeast.com/welcome-to-the-most-haunted-graveyard-in-the-world-safety-not-guaranteed.

JANUARY 18 THE CHERNOBYL SUICIDE SQUAD

Higginbotham, Adam. "Chernobyl 20 Years On." Guardian, March 25, 2006. https://www.theguardian.com/world/2006/mar/26/nuclear.russia.

Kramer, Sarah. "The Amazing True Story behind the Chernobyl 'Suicide Squad' That Helped Save Europe." Business Insider, April 26, 2016. http://www.businessinsider.com/chernobyl-volunteers-divers-nuclear-mission-2016-4.

Molloy, Parker. "You Probably Don't Know Their Names, but 30 Years Ago, They Saved Europe." Upworthy, April 26, 2016. http://www.upworthy.com/you-probably-dont-know-their-names-but-30-years-ago-they-saved-europe.

JANUARY 19 YANKING ON SUPERMAN'S CAPE

Friebe, Daniel. "The Greatest Tour of All, by Greg LeMond." BikeRadar Blog. BikeRadar, July 16, 2009. https://www.bikeradar.com/us/blog/article/the-greatest-tour-of-all-by-greg-lemond-22419/.

Phelps, Don Don. "LeMond the Legend." Riding to Redemption (blog), October 30, 2012. http://ridingtoredemption.blogspot.com/2012/10/lemond-legend_30.html.

Swift, E. M. "Le Grand LeMond." Sports Illustrated, December 25, 1989. https://www.si.com/vault/1989/12/25/121301/le-grand-lemond-greg-lemond-1989-sportsman-of-the-year-rewrote-his-own-legend-with-a-heroic-comeback-and-a-magnificent-finish-in-the-tour-de-france.

Wallack, Roy. "Once Shunned, Greg LeMond Returns to Biking World and Road to Success." Los Angeles Times, February 20, 2015. http://www.latimes.com/health/la-he-greg-lemond-20150221-column.html.

JANUARY 20 THE ARYAN BROTHERHOOD OF AFRICA

Biswas, Soutik. "Was Mahatma Gandhi a Racist?" BBC News, September 17, 2015. http://www.bbc.com/news/world-asia-india-34265882.

India Today. "Bapu in Africa: 10 Things Mahatma Gandhi Did in South Africa." October 1, 2016. https://www.indiatoday.in/education-today/gk-current-affairs/story/bapu-in-africa-344314-2016-10-01.

NPR. "'Before India,' a Young Gandhi Found His Calling in South Africa." Morning Edition, April 16, 2014. https://www.npr.org/2014/04/16/303363995/before-india-a-young-gandhi-found-his-calling-in-south-africa.

Reddy, E. S. "Some of Gandhi's Early Views on Africans Were Racist. But That Was before He Became Mahatma." The Wire, October 18, 2016. https://thewire.in/73522/gandhi-and-africans/.

JANUARY 21 A LETTER FROM THE BIRMINGHAM JAIL

Abernathy, Ralph David. And the Walls Came Tumbling Down. New York: Harper & Row, 1989.

Garrow, David J. Bearing the Cross: Martin Luther King, Jr., and the Southern Christian Leadership Conference. New York: William Morrow, 1986.

King, Martin Luther, Jr. "Letter from Birmingham Jail." Christian Century 80 (June 12, 1963): 767–73.

JANUARY 22 THE PERFECT BOSS

Callan, Paul. "Hitler? Just a Big Softie." Sunday Express, November 19, 2009. https://www.express.co.uk/expressyourself/141442/Hitler-Just-a-big-softie.

Hall, Alan. "Hitler Was the Perfect Boss: Former Maid Breaks Her Silence on the 'Charming' Dictator." Daily Mail, December 4, 2008. http://www.dailymail.co.uk/news/article-1091768/Hitler-perfect-boss-Former-maid-breaks-silence-charming-dictator.html.

Herzog, Hal. "Was Hitler a Vegetarian? The Nazi Animal Protection Movement." *Psychology Today*, November 17, 2011. https://www.psychologytoday.com/blog/animals-and-us/201111/was-hitler-vegetarian-the-nazi-animal -protection-movement.

Oliphant, Vickiie. "Hitler as You've Never Seen Him—Unseen Photographs Attempt to Show SOFT Side." *Sunday Express*, March 31, 2017. https://www.express.co.uk/news/world/786214/Adolf-Hitler-dogs -animal-lover-photos-soft-side-Nazi-propaganda-Austria.

JANUARY 23 THE SCOTSMAN WHO FOUNDED AMERICA

Christianity Today. "John Knox." Previously published in *Christian History*, no. 46 (1995) and *131 Christians Everyone Should Know* (Nashville: Broadman & Holman, 2000). Accessed February 10, 2018. http:// www.christianitytoday.com/history/people/denominationalfounders/john-knox.html.

Fortson, Donald. "Scotland and the Birth of the United States." Ligonier Ministries. Accessed February 10, 2018. Previously published in *Tabletalk*, March 1, 2014. https://www.ligonier.org/learn/articles/scotland -and-birth-united-states/.

Graves, Dan, and John Knox. "John Knox and Scots Reform." Christian History Institute. Accessed February 10, 2018. https://christianhistoryinstitute.org/study/module/knox.

Parsons, Burk. "'Give Me Scotland or I Die.'" Ligonier Ministries. Accessed February 10, 2018. Previously published in *Tabletalk*, March 1, 2014. https://www.ligonier.org/learn/articles/give-me-scotland-or-i-die/.

JANUARY 24 THE REAL DR. JEKYLL AND MR. HYDE

Brocklehurst, Steven. "The Real Jekyll & Hyde? The Deacon Brodie Story." BBC News, January 29, 2015. http://www.bbc.com/news/uk-scotland-31018496.

Johnson, Ben. "Deacon Brodie." Historic UK. Accessed February 9, 2018. http://www.historic-uk.com /HistoryUK/HistoryofScotland/Deacon-William-Brodie/.

Scotsman. "Deacon Brodie: The Real Jekyll and Hyde?" Accessed February 9, 2018. https://www.scotsman .com/lifestyle/deacon-brodie-the-real-jekyll-and-hyde-1-465314.

JANUARY 25 RYAN'S SONG

Decker, Shawn. "The Importance of Remembering Ryan White." POZ, August 10, 2010. https://www.poz .com/article/Remembering-Ryan-White-18900-1961.

Johnson, Dirk. "Ryan White Dies of AIDS at 18; His Struggle Helped Pierce Myths." *New York Times*, April 9, 1990. http://www.nytimes.com/1990/04/09/obituaries/ryan-white-dies-of-aids-at-18-his -struggle-helped-pierce-myths.html.

Markel, Howard. "Remembering Ryan White, the Teen Who Fought against the Stigma of AIDS." *PBS NewsHour*, April 8, 2016. https://www.pbs.org/newshour/health/remembering-ryan-white-the-teen -who-fought-against-the-stigma-of-aids.

JANUARY 26 THE WAR STARTED BY A PIG

Coe, Alexis. "Inside the Pig War of 1859." Modern Farmer, March 14, 2014. https://modernfarmer.com /2014/03/inside-great-pig-war-1859/.

Johnson, Ben. "The Pig War." Historic UK. Accessed February 9, 2018. http://www.historic-uk.com /HistoryUK/HistoryofBritain/The-Pig-War/.

Thomas, Jeffrey A. "The Pig War." Military History Online. Accessed February 9, 2018. http://www.military historyonline.com/fiction/pigwar.aspx.

JANUARY 27 THE MAN BEHIND THE CURTAIN

Allen, Brooke. "The Man behind the Curtain." *New York Times*, November 17, 2002. http://www.nytimes .com/2002/11/17/books/the-man-behind-the-curtain.html.

Ferguson, Kelly K. "The Technicolor Life of L. Frank Baum, the Man Who Created Oz." Mental Floss.com. Accessed February 9, 2018. http://mentalfloss.com/article/25541/over-rainbow-technicolor-life-man-who -created-oz.

Fussell, James A. "Meet L. Frank Baum, the Man behind the Curtain." *Miami Herald*, August 31, 2014. http://www.miamiherald.com/news/business/banking/article1315566.html.

JANUARY 28 THE HIT MAN'S SON

Conradt, Stacy. "Woody Harrelson's Hitman Father." Mental Floss, July 28, 2015. http://mentalfloss.com /article/66602/woody-harrelsons-hitman-father.

Hattenstone, Simon. "Woody Harrelson: My Father, the Contract Killer." *Guardian*, February 17, 2012. https://www.theguardian.com/film/2012/feb/17/woody-harrelson-my-father-contract-killer-rampart.

History. "Woody Harrelson's Father Is Arrested for Murder." This Day in History: May 29, 1979. Accessed February 9, 2018. http://www.history.com/this-day-in-history/woody-harrelsons-father-is-arrested -for-murder.

Pow, Helen. "Woody Harrelson's 'Hit Man' Father 'Kidnapped and Murdered Salesman for $1,500' in 1968." *Daily Mail*, June 23, 2013. http://www.dailymail.co.uk/news/article-2346838/Woody-Harrelsons-hit-man -father-kidnapped-murdered-salesman-1-500-1968.html.

JANUARY 29 NEW YORK CITY'S FIRST IMMIGRANT

Feiden, Douglas. "Dominican Immigrant Was First Non-Indian Manhattan Settler." *New York Daily News*, October 5, 2012. http://www.nydailynews.com/new-york/manhattan/dominican-immigrant -non-indian-manhattan-settler-article-1.1175017.

Lewis, Jamie. "'Juan: Singular Sensation,' New York's First Immigrant." *New York Rediscovered* (blog), August 6, 2014. https://sites.newpaltz.edu/nyrediscovered/2014/08/06/juan-singular-sensation-new -yorks-first-immigrant/.

Niven, Steven J. "Jan Rodrigues: The 1st Black Man to Set Foot on the Island of Manhattan." The Root, February 1, 2016. https://www.theroot.com/jan-rodrigues-the-1st-black-man-to-set-foot-on-the-isl -1790854070.

Roberts, Sam. "Honoring a Very Early New Yorker." *City Room* (blog). *New York Times*, October 2, 2012. https://cityroom.blogs.nytimes.com/2012/10/02/honoring-a-very-early-new-yorker/.

JANUARY 30 FROM HOMELESS TO HARVARD

Adult Student.com. "From Homeless to Harvard—Liz Murray's Story." Accessed February 6, 2018. http:// adultstudent.com/students/tips/homeless-to-harvard-liz-murray/.

James, Susan Donaldson. "*Homeless to Harvard*: Child of Addicts Counsels Youth in Spirituality." ABC News, October 10, 2013. http://abcnews.go.com/Health/homeless-harvard-child-addicts-counsels-youth -spirituality/story?id=20523916.

O'Brien, Rebecca D. "After Harvard, a New Home." *Harvard Crimson*, April 14, 2003. http://www.the crimson.com/article/2003/4/14/after-harvard-a-new-home-the/.

Walters, Joanna. "Liz Murray: 'My Parents Were Desperate Drug Addicts. I'm a Harvard Graduate.'" *Guardian*, September 25, 2010. https://www.theguardian.com/world/2010/sep/26/liz-murray-bronx -harvard.

JANUARY 31 WHEN PATRIOTISM ISN'T ENOUGH

History. "British Nurse Edith Cavell Executed." This Day in History: October 12, 1915. Accessed February 6, 2018. http://www.history.com/this-day-in-history/british-nurse-edith-cavell-executed.

LaValley, Joy. "Edith Cavell, Fragile Martyr." With archival material assistance of Donna Cunningham. Worldwar1.com. Accessed February 6, 2018. http://www.worldwar1.com/heritage/e_cavell.htm.

Norton-Taylor, Richard. "Edith Cavell, Shot by Germans during WWI, Celebrated 100 Years On." *Guardian*, October 12, 2015. https://www.theguardian.com/world/2015/oct/12/edith-cavell-nurse -shot-by-germans-wwi-celebrated.

Rigby, Nic. "Nurse Edith Cavell and the British World War One Propaganda Campaign." BBC News, October 12, 2015. http://www.bbc.com/news/uk-england-norfolk-34401643.

FEBRUARY 1 THE SLAVE WHO CIVILIZED EUROPE

Blazeski, Goran. "Ziryab—The Slave Who Changed Society but Still Remains Anonymous in European History." The Vintage News, September 21, 2016. https://www.thevintagenews.com/2016/09/21/ziryab -slave-changed-society-still-remains-anonymous-european-history/.

Duane, Thomas. "Ziryab—The Leonardo da Vinci of Islam." Medium, June 3, 2016. https://medium.com /@thomasduane/ziryab-the-leonardo-da-vinci-of-islam-3ee176c00d11.

Lisapo ya Kama. "Ziryab, the Black Scholar Who Has Revolutionized Europe." African History, January 20, 2018. http://en.lisapoyakama.org/ziryab-the-black-scholar-who-has-revolutionized-europe/.

Worthington, Daryl. "Ziryab: A Forgotten Innovator of Music, Gastronomy and Style." New Historian, November 13, 2016. http://www.newhistorian.com/ziryab-forgotten-innovator-music-gastronome-style /7548/.

FEBRUARY 2 GENERALS AND SLAVES

Biography. "Ulysses S. Grant." Updated December 1, 2017. https://www.biography.com/people/ulysses-s -grant-9318285.

Blount, Roy, Jr. "The Civil War: Making Sense of Robert E. Lee." *Smithsonian*, July 2003. https://www .smithsonianmag.com/history/making-sense-of-robert-e-lee-85017563/.

Mikkelson, David. "The Truth about Confederate History: Part 2." Snopes, June 30, 2015. https://www .snopes.com/confederate-history-slave-ownership/.

WorldAtlas. "At the Start of the American Civil War, U.S. Grant Held Slaves, Robert E. Lee Did Not." Updated April 25, 2017. https://www.worldatlas.com/articles/at-the-start-of-the-american-civil-war-u-s -grant-held-slaves-robert-e-lee-did-not.html.

FEBRUARY 3 THE FOUR CHAPLAINS

American Veterans Center. "Greater Love: The Four Chaplains and the Sinking of the *Dorchester*." Accessed February 11, 2018. http://www.americanveteranscenter.org/avc-media/radio/documentaries/no-greater-love-the-four-chaplains-and-the-sinking-of-the-dorchester/.

Four Chaplains Memorial Foundation. "The Story." Accessed February 11, 2018. http://www.fourchaplains.org/the-saga-of-the-four-chaplains/.

Greene, Bob. "Real Heroes: Four Died So Others Might Live." CNN, February 3, 2013. https://www.cnn.com/2013/02/03/opinion/greene-four-chaplains/index.html.

McElhany, Gary. "The Four Chaplains: Forgotten Heroes." ThoughtHub, February 2, 2016. https://www.sagu.edu/thoughthub/four-chaplains-dorchester.

FEBRUARY 4 THE WOMAN WHO NEVER BACKED DOWN

Biography. "Rosa Parks." Updated August 7, 2017. https://www.biography.com/people/rosa-parks-9433715.

The Henry Ford. "What If I Don't Move to the Back of the Bus?" Accessed January 14, 2018. https://www.thehenryford.org/explore/stories-of-innovation/what-if/rosa-parks/.

RosaParksFacts.com. "Rosa Parks Early Life & Childhood." Accessed January 14, 2018. http://rosaparksfacts.com/rosa-parks-early-life-childhood/.

Theoharis, Jeanne. "How History Got the Rosa Parks Story Wrong." *Washington Post*, December 1, 2015. https://www.washingtonpost.com/posteverything/wp/2015/12/01/how-history-got-the-rosa-parks-story-wrong/?utm_term=.ddfa9f3dfa8f.

FEBRUARY 5 THE LONG TREK HOME

Flynn, Louise Jarvis. "Worst-Case Scenario." Review of *Miracle in the Andes: 72 Days on the Mountain and My Long Trek Home*, by Nando Parrado with Vince Rause. *New York Times*, July 30, 2006. http://www.nytimes.com/2006/07/30/books/review/worstcase-scenario.html.

Gibbs, Jeffrey. "Hero Story: Nando Parrado and Roberto Canessa." *Hero Stories* (blog), January 24, 2017. http://www.jeffreygibbs.org/inspirations/2017/1/24/hero-story-4-nando-parrado-and-roberto-canessa.

Parrado, Nando. "I Will Survive." *Guardian*, May 18, 2006. https://www.theguardian.com/books/2006/may/18/extract.features11.

Shelden, Michael. "'What Could We Eat but Our Dead Friends?'" *Telegraph*, May 25, 2006. http://www.telegraph.co.uk/culture/books/non_fictionreviews/3652636/What-could-we-eat-but-our-dead-friends.html.

FEBRUARY 6 THE TURKEY THAT SOARED

Eddie the Eagle. Directed by Dexter Fletcher. 20th Century Fox, 2016.

Lidz, Franz. "Whatever Happened to Eddie the Eagle, Britain's Most Lovable Ski Jumper?" *Smithsonian*, February 2014. https://www.smithsonianmag.com/history/whatever-happened-to-eddie-eagle-britains-most-lovable-ski-jumper-180949438/.

Oliver, Sarah. "Plight of the Eagle: Eddie's Wife Has Left Him, He's Working as a Plasterer and the New Film about His Life Won't Make Him a Penny Richer." *Daily Mail*, March 6, 2016. http://www.dailymail.co.uk/news/article-3478591/Plight-Eagle-Eddie-s-wife-left-s-working-plasterer-new-film-life-won-t-make-penny-richer.html.

FEBRUARY 7 THE RIVER OF DOUBT

Barcott, Bruce. "*The River of Doubt*: Cândido and Ted's Excellent Adventure." Review of *The River of Doubt: Theodore Roosevelt's Darkest Journey*, by Candice Millard. *New York Times*, October 16, 2005. http://www.nytimes.com/2005/10/16/books/review/the-river-of-doubt-candido-and-teds-excellent-adventure.html.

NPR. "Tracing Roosevelt's Path down the 'River of Doubt.'" *Morning Edition*, November 3, 2005. https://www.npr.org/templates/story/story.php?storyId=4986859.

Schwartz, Allan B. "Medical Mystery: Theodore Roosevelt and the River of Doubt." *Philadelphia Inquirer*, April 24, 2017. http://www.philly.com/philly/health/Medical-Mystery-Theodore-Roosevelt-and-the-River-of-Doubt.html.

Stockton, Richard. "5 Unbelievable Times Teddy Roosevelt Cheated Death." ATI. Updated January 17, 2018. http://allthatsinteresting.com/teddy-roosevelt-death.

FEBRUARY 8 JUST ANOTHER NIGHT ON THE JOB

Atwood, Liz. "Watergate Security Guard's Good Fortune Turns Sour." *Los Angeles Times*, October 24, 1993. http://articles.latimes.com/1993-10-24/news/mn-49168_1_security-guard.

Clymer, Adam. "Frank Wills, 52; Watchman Foiled Watergate Break-In." *New York Times*, September 29, 2000. http://www.nytimes.com/2000/09/29/us/frank-wills-52-watchman-foiled-watergate-break-in.html.

Winbush, Jeff. "Black History Month: The Forgotten Hero Who Toppled a President." *Zero Tolerance for Silence* (blog), February 1, 2012. https://jeffwinbush.com/2012/02/01/black-history-month-the-forgotten -hero-who-toppled-a-president/.

Woo, Elaine. "Frank Wills; Guard Discovered Watergate Break-In." *Los Angeles Times*, September 29, 2000. http://articles.latimes.com/2000/sep/29/local/me-28706.

FEBRUARY 9 THE INFINITE POSSIBILITIES OF HOPE

Kim, Eun Kyung. "'Hope Kept Me Going': Cancer Survivor with One Lung Climbs World's Tallest Peaks." Today, February 16, 2016. https://www.today.com/health/hope-kept-me-going-cancer-survivor-one -lung-climbs-world-t73781.

Mellino, Cole. "Cancer Survivor Climbs World's Tallest Peaks with Just One Lung." EcoWatch, February 18, 2016. https://www.ecowatch.com/cancer-survivor-climbs-worlds-tallest-peaks-helps-others-do-the-same -1882175533.html.

Minutaglio, Rose. "Two-Time Cancer Survivor with One Lung Prepares for North Pole Trek: 'I Want to Show People What's Possible.'" *People*, March 13, 2017. http://people.com/human-interest/two-time -cancer-survivor-one-lung-prepares-north-pole-trek/.

FEBRUARY 10 THE NIGHT WITCHES

Garber, Megan. "Night Witches: The Female Fighter Pilots of World War II." *Atlantic*, July 15, 2013. https://www.theatlantic.com/technology/archive/2013/07/night-witches-the-female-fighter-pilots-of -world-war-ii/277779/.

Grundhauser, Eric. "The Little-Known Story of the Night Witches, an All-Female Force in WWII." *Vanity Fair*, June 25, 2015. https://www.vanityfair.com/culture/2015/06/night-witches-wwii-female-pilots.

Holland, Brynn. "Meet the Night Witches, the Daring Female Pilots Who Bombed Nazis by Night." History, July 7, 2017. http://www.history.com/news/meet-the-night-witches-the-daring-female-pilots -who-bombed-nazis-by-night.

Monahan, Maureen. "The Lethal Soviet 'Night Witches' of the 588th Night Bomber Unit." Mental Floss, July 26, 2013. http://mentalfloss.com/article/51823/lethal-soviet-%E2%80%9Cnight-witches%E2%80 %9D-588th-night-bomber-unit.

FEBRUARY 11 THE OTHER LAFAYETTE

George Washington's Mount Vernon. "Lafayette's Testimonial to James Armistead Lafayette." Accessed February 3, 2018. http://www.mountvernon.org/george-washington/the-revolutionary-war/spying-and -espionage/american-spies-of-the-revolution/lafayettes-testimonial-to-james-armistead-lafayette/.

Oglesby, Lizzie. "Why We Need to Talk about James Armistead Lafayette." *Virginia Historical Society's Blog*, June 20, 2016. https://vahistorical.wordpress.com/2016/06/20/why-we-need-to-talk-about-james -armistead-lafayette/.

Quinn, Ruth. "James Armistead Lafayette (1760–1832)." U.S. Army, January 31, 2014. https://www.army .mil/article/119280/james_armistead_lafayette_1760_1832.

Salo, Jessica. "Lafayette, James Armistead (1760–1832)." BlackPast.org. Accessed February 3, 2018. http:// www.blackpast.org/aah/lafayette-james-armistead-1760-1832.

FEBRUARY 12 UNBROKEN BY FAILURE

Lincoln, Abraham. *Lincoln: Speeches and Writings 1832-1858*. Edited by Don E. Fehrenbacher. New York: Penguin, 1989.

FEBRUARY 13 DENIED IN LIFE, TOGETHER IN DEATH

Calhoun, David. "David Brainerd: 'A Constant Stream.'" C. S. Lewis Institute. Previously published in *Knowing and Doing*, Summer 2011. http://www.cslewisinstitute.org/David%20Brainerd_A_Constant _Stream_SinglePage.

Judy, Greg. "David Brainerd and Jerusha Edwards: A Colonial Love Story." *Salt of the Earth* (blog), February 16, 2013. http://salt-ofthe-earth.blogspot.com/2013/02/david-brainerd-and-jerusha-edwards.html.

Mahon, Brian. "A Model for Christian Women: Jerusha Edwards." *Grace, Glory, and Gospel Endeavor: Theology on Mission* (blog), June 19, 2010. https://brianrmahon.wordpress.com/2010/06/19/a-model -for-christian-women-jerusha-edwards/.

Marsden, George M. *Jonathan Edwards: A Life*. New Haven, CT: Yale University Press, 2003.

FEBRUARY 14 STRONG HEART

Catholic Online. "St. Valentine." Accessed March 12, 2017. http://www.catholic.org/saints/saint.php?saint _id=159.

Merrill, Mark. "The Real Story behind Valentine's Day." *Mark Merrill* (blog), February 14, 2011. http:// www.markmerrill.com/the-real-story-behind-valentines-day/.

Wikipedia, s.v. "Saint Valentine." Last modified March 7, 2017. https://en.wikipedia.org/wiki/Saint_Valentine.

FEBRUARY 15 UNLEASHING THE POWER OF MOM

History. "MADD Founder's Daughter Killed by Drunk Driver." This Day in History: May 3, 1980.
  Accessed February 3, 2018. http://www.history.com/this-day-in-history/madd-founders-daughter-killed
  -by-drunk-driver.
Koenenn, Connie. "The Company She Keeps: Drunk Driving: Candy Lightner Says She Still Wants Reforms.
  But Now That the MADD Founder Works for Restaurants, Some Wonder Whose Side She's Really On."
  Los Angeles Times, January 26, 1994. http://articles.latimes.com/1994-01-26/news/vw-15591_1_candy
  -lightner.
Lewin, Tamar. "Founder of Anti-Drunk-Driving Group Now Lobbies for Breweries." *New York Times*,
  January 15, 1994. http://www.nytimes.com/1994/01/15/us/founder-of-anti-drunk-driving-group-now
  -lobbies-for-breweries.html.
Smith, Lynn. "MADD at 20: Still a Force for Change." *Los Angeles Times*, April 2, 2000. http://articles
  .latimes.com/2000/apr/02/news/cl-15045.

FEBRUARY 16 THE HOUSE OF WISDOM

Bengoechea, Isabella. "Iraq's Golden Age: The Rise and Fall of the House of Wisdom." Culture Trip. Updated
  September 29, 2016. https://theculturetrip.com/middle-east/iraq/articles/iraq-s-golden-age-the-rise-and
  -fall-of-the-house-of-wisdom/.
Muzzafar, Zeynab. "Baghdad: Bayt al-Hikma (House of Wisdom) and the Destruction of Its Books." Facebook
  note, October 13, 2014. https://www.facebook.com/notes/zeynab-muzzafar/baghdad-bayt-al-hikma-house
  -of-wisdom-and-the-destruction-of-its-books/354693274692324/.
Sohma, Marina. "The House of Wisdom: One of the Greatest Libraries in History." Ancient Origins,
  January 1, 2017. http://www.ancient-origins.net/ancient-places-asia/house-wisdom-one-greatest-libraries
  -history-007292?nopaging=1.
Wilford, John Noble. "The Muslim Art of Science." Review of *The House of Wisdom*, by Jim al-Khalili. *New
  York Times*, May 20, 2011. http://www.nytimes.com/2011/05/22/books/review/book-review-the-house
  -of-wisdom-by-jim-al-khalili.html.

FEBRUARY 17 FROM LIBYA WITH LOVE

Branson-Potts, Hailey. "'I Know They Are Going to Die.' This Foster Father Takes in Only Terminally Ill
  Children." *Los Angeles Times*, February 8, 2017. http://www.latimes.com/local/lanow/la-me-ln-foster
  -father-sick-children-2017-story.html.
Bzeek, Mohamed. "A Foster Parent for Terminally Ill Children." Interview by Lulu Garcia-Navarro. *Weekend
  Edition Sunday*. NPR, February 19, 2017. https://www.npr.org/2017/02/19/516064735/a-foster-parent
  -for-terminally-ill-children.
Free, Cathy. "California Man Takes in Foster Kids Who Are Terminally Ill: 'Their Lives Have Value.'" *People*,
  June 16, 2017. http://people.com/human-interest/california-man-foster-kids-terminally-ill/.

FEBRUARY 18 LIVING FOR NINETY-NINE CENTS

Bloor West Villager. "From the Streets to Founding Second Cup." Toronto.com, September 17, 2010.
  https://www.toronto.com/community-story/55962-from-the-streets-to-founding-second-cup/. Post no
  longer available.
Clay, Chris. "Second Cup Founder Remembers Life on the Street." Mississauga.com, March 14, 2013. https://
  www.mississauga.com/community-story/3133251-second-cup-founder-remembers-life-on-the-street/.
Franklin, Jasmine. "Second Cup Co-Founder's Past." *Toronto Sun*, October 2, 2010.
Second Cup Coffee Co. "Our History." Accessed January 28, 2018. http://www.secondcup.com/our-story.

FEBRUARY 19 THE LAST SHOT OF THE CIVIL WAR

Dunham, Mike. "Civil War's Last Shots Were Fired in the Bering Sea." *Anchorage Daily News*. Updated
  September 29, 2016. https://www.adn.com/our-alaska/article/civil-wars-last-shots-were-fired-bering
  -sea/2011/04/17/.
FlameHorse. "9 Last Official Shots of Wars." Listverse, July 1, 2013. https://listverse.com/2013/07/01/9-last
  -official-shots-of-wars/.
History. "CSS Shenandoah Learns the War Is Over." This Day in History: August 2, 1865. Accessed
  January 28, 2018. http://www.history.com/this-day-in-history/css-shenandoah-learns-the-war-is-over.
Markowitz, Mike. "CSS Shenandoah and the Last Shot of the Civil War." Defense Media Network, April 9,
  2015. https://www.defensemedianetwork.com/stories/how-the-rebels-saved-the-whales/.

FEBRUARY 20 THE

Associated Press. "Mia Farrow's Son's Death Ruled a Suicide." Page Six, September 22, 2016. https://pagesix
  .com/2016/09/22/mia-farrows-sons-death-ruled-a-suicide/.
Biography. "Mia Farrow." Updated September 22, 2016. https://www.biography.com/people/mia-farrow
  -9292027.

Gotthelf, Michelle. "Mia & Son's Brave Battle to End Polio." *New York Post*, November 28, 2000. https://nypost.com/2000/11/28/mia-sons-brave-battle-to-end-polio/.

Rainey, Sarah. "Mia Farrow Drew Men to Her like a Magnet." *Telegraph*, October 3, 2013. http://www.telegraph.co.uk/news/celebritynews/10353209/Mia-Farrow-drew-men-to-her-like-a-magnet.html.

FEBRUARY 21 THE MAN WHO SAVED THE WORLD

Krulwich, Robert. "You (and Almost Everyone You Know) Owe Your Life to This Man." *Curiously Krulwich* (blog). *National Geographic*, March 25, 2016. https://news.nationalgeographic.com/2016/03/you-and-almost-everyone-you-know-owe-your-life-to-this-man/.

Watson, Leon, and Mark Duell. "The Man Who Saved the World: The Soviet Submariner Who Single-Handedly Averted WWIII at Height of the Cuban Missile Crisis." *Daily Mail*, September 25, 2012. http://www.dailymail.co.uk/news/article-2208342/Soviet-submariner-single-handedly-averted-WWIII-height-Cuban-Missile-Crisis.html.

Wilson, Edward. "Thank You Vasili Arkhipov, the Man Who Stopped Nuclear War." *Guardian*, October 27, 2012. https://www.theguardian.com/commentisfree/2012/oct/27/vasili-arkhipov-stopped-nuclear-war.

FEBRUARY 22 THE SILER CITY CAT HOUSE

Associated Press. "*Andy Griffith* Aunt Bee Recluse in Final Years." *Los Angeles Times*, January 17, 1990. http://articles.latimes.com/1990-01-17/entertainment/ca-368_1_aunt-bee.

Clarey, Brian. "Fresh Eyes: Aunt Bee's Siler City Cat House." *Fresh Eyes* (blog). Triad City Beat, May 28, 2014. Excerpted from Billy Ingram, *Reverend Buck Goes to College*. CreateSpace Independent Publishing Platform, 2014.

Lobosco, David. "What a Character: Frances Bavier." *Great Entertainers Archives* (blog), August 17, 2012. http://greatentertainersarchives.blogspot.com/2012/08/what-character-frances-bavier.html.

Washburn, Mark. "Secret Strife behind the Scenes in Mayberry." *Charlotte Observer*, November 3, 2015. http://www.charlotteobserver.com/entertainment/tv/media-scene-blog/article42732489.html.

FEBRUARY 23 TOBACCO WIVES

Cott, Nancy, ed. *No Small Courage: A History of Women in the United States*, 53. Oxford: Oxford University Press, 2000.

Erickson, Mark St. John. "Pioneering Female Colonists Changed Jamestown." *Daily Press*, March 19, 2016. http://www.dailypress.com/features/history/dp-fea-first-jamestown-women-20160319-story.html.

National Park Service. "The Indispensable Role of Women at Jamestown." Updated February 26, 2015. https://www.nps.gov/jame/learn/historyculture/the-indispensible-role-of-women-at-jamestown.htm.

Zug, Marcia. "The Mail-Order Brides of Jamestown, Virginia." *Atlantic*, August 31, 2016. https://www.theatlantic.com/business/archive/2016/08/the-mail-order-brides-of-jamestown-virginia/498083/.

FEBRUARY 24 CAN'T ACT. SLIGHTLY BALD. ALSO DANCES.

Biography. "Fred Astaire." Updated April 27, 2017. https://www.biography.com/people/fred-astaire-9190991.

Green, Anna. "14 Toe-Tapping Facts about Fred Astaire." Mental Floss, May 10, 2017. http://mentalfloss.com/article/76966/14-toe-tapping-facts-about-fred-astaire.

Jones, Jack. "Fred Astaire, Movies' Greatest Dancer, Dies." *Los Angeles Times*, June 23, 1987. http://www.latimes.com/local/obituaries/la-me-fred-astaire-19870623-story.html.

Shepard, Richard F. "Fred Astaire, the Ultimate Dancer, Dies." *New York Times*, June 23, 1987. http://www.nytimes.com/1987/06/23/obituaries/fred-astaire-the-ultimate-dancer-dies.html?pagewanted=all.

FEBRUARY 25 NEVER TOO OLD TO START

Biography. "Grandma Moses." Updated June 15, 2016. https://www.biography.com/people/grandma-moses-9416251.

New York Times. "Grandma Moses Is Dead at 101; Primitive Artist 'Just Wore Out.'" On This Day: December 14, 1961. Accessed January 28, 2018. http://www.nytimes.com/learning/general/onthisday/bday/0907.html.

Spencer, Amy. "Anna Mary Robertson 'Grandma' Moses (1860–1961)." Questroyal Fine Art. Accessed January 28, 2018. https://www.questroyalfineart.com/artist/anna-mary-grandma-robertson-moses/.

FEBRUARY 26 THE IMPERFECT STORY OF PERFECTION

Aronson, Brad. "Everything Counts—Third Grade Teacher's Small Act Still Inspires Baseball Legend Jim Abbott." *Brad Aronson's Blog*. Accessed January 28, 2018. http://www.bradaronson.com/jim-abbott/.

Rich, Charles. "Jim Abbott Has an 'Imperfect' Story to Tell." *Los Angeles Times*, June 5, 2012. http://www.latimes.com/tn-gnp-sp-abbott-20120605-story.html.

Salter, Susan. "Jim Abbott Biography—The Abbott Switch, into the Majors, Chronology, Down, but Not Out, Career Statistics." JRank, Famous Sports Stars. Accessed January 28, 2018. http://sports.jrank.org /pages/22/Abbott-Jim.html.

Schuler, Ryan. "Where Are They Now: Jim Abbott." USA Baseball, August 18, 2014. http://web.usabaseball .com/article_print.jsp?ymd=&content_id=90250838.

FEBRUARY 27 SECEDING FROM THE CONFEDERACY
Brody, Richard. "The Historical Imagination and *Free State of Jones*." *New Yorker*, June 23, 2016. https:// www.newyorker.com/culture/richard-brody/the-historical-imagination-and-free-state-of-jones.

CBS News. "The Story behind *Free State of Jones*." June 5, 2016. https://www.cbsnews.com/news/the-story -behind-free-state-of-jones/.

Grant, Richard. "The True Story of the *Free State of Jones*." *Smithsonian*, March 2016. https://www.smithsonian mag.com/history/true-story-free-state-jones-180958111/.

Karst, James. "The True Story of the *Free State of Jones*." Nola.com, June 24, 2016. http://www.nola.com /entertainment/index.ssf/2016/06/the_true_story_of_the_free_sta.html.

FEBRUARY 28 THE FOUNDING FATHERS OF DIRTY CAMPAIGNS
Benton, Michael. "Thomas Jefferson." John Adams. Updated November 6, 2013. http://johnadamsinfo.com /thomas-jefferson/70/.

History. "Thomas Jefferson and John Adams Die." This Day in History: July 4, 1826. Accessed January 27, 2018. http://www.history.com/this-day-in-history/thomas-jefferson-and-john-adams-die.

Pavellas, Ron. "John Adams & Thomas Jefferson: From Friendship to Antagonism to Reconciliation." *The Pavellas Perspective* (blog), February 3, 2010. https://pavellas.com/2010/02/03/john-adams-thomas -jefferson-from-friendship-to-antagonism-to-reconciliation/.

Swint, Kerwin. "Adams vs. Jefferson: The Birth of Negative Campaigning in the U.S." Mental Floss, September 9, 2012. http://mentalfloss.com/article/12487/adams-vs-jefferson-birth-negative-campaigning-us.

MARCH 1 THE PERSISTENT FISHERMAN
Markel, Howard. "The Infectious Disease That Sprung Al Capone from Alcatraz." *PBS NewsHour*, January 25, 2017. https://www.pbs.org/newshour/health/infectious-disease-sprung-al-capone-alcatraz.

Riedel, Michael. "Isolation, Madness and Syphilis: Inside Gangster Al Capone's Final Years, with the Man Once Named Public Enemy Number One Spending His Days Fishing and Doting on His Grandkids." *The Sun*, October 16, 2016. https://www.thesun.co.uk/news/1989213/inside-gangster-al-capones-final -years-with-the-man-once-named-public-enemy-number-one-spending-his-days-fishing-and-doting-on -his-grandkids/.

Taylor, Troy. "The Last Days of Al Capone." *American Hauntings* (blog), January 6, 2013. http://troytaylor books.blogspot.com/2013/01/the-last-days-of-al-capone.html.

MARCH 2 THE HEALER'S SONG
Biography. "Ronan Tynan." Updated April 1, 2014. https://www.biography.com/people/ronan-tynan-215201.

Leitch, Will. "The Misery Tenor." *New York*, January 3, 2010. http://nymag.com/daily/sports/2010/01/the _misery_tenor.html.

O'Dowd, Niall. "Irish Tenor Ronan Tynan Quits New York for Boston after Death Threats." Irish Central, March 6, 2010. https://www.irishcentral.com/opinion/niallodowd/irish-tenor-ronan-tynan-quits-new -york-for-boston-after-death-threats-86705637-238021391.

Paré, Gerri. "Ronan Tynan, M.D.: Inspirational Irish Tenor." Franciscan Media. Accessed January 27, 2018. https://www.franciscanmedia.org/ronan-tynan-m-d-inspirational-irish-tenor/.

MARCH 3 THE
Court, Simon. "10 Weird Stories about Famous People." Listverse, June 23, 2013. https://listverse.com/2013 /06/23/10-historical-figures-with-strange-and-awesome-stories-to-tell/.

Dickens London Tours. "Charles Dickens Biography." Accessed January 27, 2018. https://www.dickens londontours.co.uk/dickens-biography.htm.

Gorra, Michael. "Charles Dickens's Unhappy Children." Daily Beast, December 2, 2012. https://www.the dailybeast.com/charles-dickenss-unhappy-children.

Roberts, Mark D. "Christmas according to Dickens: What Made Scrooge Scrooge?" *Mark D. Roberts* (blog). Beliefnet. Accessed January 27, 2018. http://www.beliefnet.com/columnists/markdroberts/2010/12 /christmas-according-to-dickens-what-made-scrooge-scrooge.html.

MARCH 4 THE GREAT CANDY BAR DEBATE
Anderson, Jerry. "Was There Ever a Real 'Baby Ruth'?" History Spaces, December 12, 2015. http://www .historyspaces.com/u-s-history/was-there-ever-a-real-baby-ruth/.

Begley, Sarah. "The 13 Most Influential Candy Bars of All Time." *Time*, February 18, 2014. http://time.com/8195/13-most-influential-candy-bars-of-all-time/.

Klein, Christopher. "Babe Ruth v. Baby Ruth." History, September 25, 2014. http://www.history.com/news/hungry-history/babe-ruth-v-baby-ruth.

O'Hara, Patrick. "The Great Baby Ruth Debate—Resolved." *American Popular Culture*, October 2011. http://www.americanpopularculture.com/archive/sports/ruth.htm.

MARCH 5 THE MIRACLE THAT WON WORLD WAR II

EyeWitness to History. "The Evacuation at Dunkirk, 1940." 2008. http://www.eyewitnesstohistory.com/dunkirk.htm.

Gardner, David E. "The Miracle of Dunkirk: 70 Years On." Christians Together, May 28, 2010. https://www.christianstogether.net/Articles/200052/Christians_Together_in/Christian_Life/The_Miracle_of.aspx.

Knowles, David J. "The 'Miracle' of Dunkirk." BBC News, May 30, 2000. http://news.bbc.co.uk/2/hi/765004.stm.

Moore, James, and Reiss Smith. "The Miracle of Dunkirk: 40 Facts about the Famous Evacuation." *Daily Express*, May 23, 2017. https://www.express.co.uk/news/world/578885/Dunkirk-evacuation-World-War-Two-Germany-Britain.

MARCH 6 THE STAR OF DAVID GOES JAZZ

Armstrong, Louis. *Louis Armstrong, in His Own Words: Selected Writings*, chap. 1. New York: Oxford University Press, 1999.

Dalton, Anthony Jones. "Louis Armstrong's 'Karnofsky Document': The Reaffirmation of Social Death and the Afterlife of Emotional Labor." *Music & Politics* 9, no. 1 (Winter 2015). https://quod.lib.umich.edu/m/mp/9460447.0009.105/--louis-armstrongs-karnofsky-document-the-reaffirmation?rgn=main;view=fulltext.

Sher, Abby. "The Jews Who Adopted Louis Armstrong." Jewniverse, September 21, 2016. https://www.thejewniverse.com/2016/the-jews-who-adopted-louis-armstrong/.

Zax, Talya. "The Secret Jewish History of Louis Armstrong." *The Schmooze* (blog). *Forward*, August 24, 2016. https://forward.com/schmooze/346884/the-secret-jewish-history-of-louis-armstrong/.

MARCH 7 THE SWINDLE OF THE CENTURY

Economist. "The King of Con-Men." December 22, 2012. https://www.economist.com/news/christmas-specials/21568583-biggest-fraud-history-warning-professional-and-amateur-investors.

Hodson, Peter. "Kings of Con-Men: A Warning on Investing in a 'Sure Thing.'" *Financial Post*, January 10, 2013. http://business.financialpost.com/investing/kings-of-con-men-a-warning-on-investing-in-a-sure-thing.

Konnikova, Maria. "The Conman Who Pulled Off History's Most Audacious Scam." BBC, January 28, 2016. http://www.bbc.com/future/story/20160127-the-conman-who-pulled-off-historys-most-audacious-scam.

Taylor, Bryan. "The Fraud of the Prince of Poyais on the London Stock Exchange." Global Financial Data. Accessed January 24, 2018. https://www.globalfinancialdata.com/GFD/Article/the-fraud-of-the-prince-of-poyais-on-london-stock-exchange.

MARCH 8 THE ULTIMATE CLOSING ARGUMENT

Clay, Jeremy. "Victorian Strangeness: The Lawyer Who Shot Himself Proving His Case." *Magazine Monitor* (blog). BBC News, August 16, 2014. http://www.bbc.com/news/blogs-magazine-monitor-28805895.

Peters, Lucia. "The 6 Weirdest Deaths in History Remind Us of Our Own Fragile Mortality." Bustle, October 1, 2015. https://www.bustle.com/articles/114139-the-6-weirdest-deaths-in-history-remind-us-of-our-own-fragile-mortality.

Radeska, Tijana. "Clement Vallandigham—A Defence Lawyer Who Accidentally Shot Himself While Trying to Prove That Someone Shot Himself. He Died and the Defendant Was Set Free." The Vintage News, September 18, 2016. https://www.thevintagenews.com/2016/09/18/clement-vallandigham-defence-lawyer-accidentally-shot-trying-prove-someone-shot-died-defendant-set-free/.

MARCH 9 THE DAY JIM MET HIMSELF IN *THE TWILIGHT ZONE*

Matthews, Lindsay. "'Jim Twins,' Separated at Birth, Turned Out to Have the Same Life." IFLMYLIFE, December 1, 2016. http://www.iflmylife.com/health/jim-twins-separated-birth/.

Rawson, Rosemary. "Two Ohio Strangers Find They're Twins at 39—And a Dream to Psychologists." *People*, May 7, 1979. http://people.com/archive/two-ohio-strangers-find-theyre-twins-at-39-and-a-dream-to-psychologists-vol-11-no-18/.

Rindskopf, Jeffrey. "The Remarkable 'Jim Twins': Separated at Birth, They Shared the Same Life." First to Know, March 27, 2015. https://firsttoknow.com/jim-twins/.

MARCH 10 THE MARATHON WOMAN

Dempsey, James. "Half a Century after First Race, Kathrine Switzer Finishes Boston Marathon Again." Newstalk.com, April 18, 2017. http://www.newstalk.com/Half-a-century-after-first-race-Kathrine -Switzer-finishes-Boston-Marathon-again.

Grinberg, Emanuella. "1st Woman to Officially Run Boston Marathon Does It Again, 50 Years Later." CNN. Updated April 18, 2017. http://www.cnn.com/2017/04/17/us/boston-marathon-kathrine -switzer-trnd/index.html.

Mather, Victor. "First Woman to Enter Boston Marathon Runs It Again, 50 Years Later." *New York Times*, April 17, 2017. https://www.nytimes.com/2017/04/17/sports/boston-marathon-kathrine-switzer.html.

Switzer, Kathrine. "Episode 49: Kathrine Switzer." Interview by Christine Fennessy and Brian Dalek. *Runners World Show* (podcast), 1:19:29. April 13, 2017. https://www.runnersworld.com/the-runners-world-show /episode-49-kathrine-switzer.

MARCH 11 DYNAMITE IN A SMALL PACKAGE

Biography. "Dr. Ruth Westheimer." Updated July 6, 2016. https://www.biography.com/people/dr-ruth -westheimer-9542073.

Edwards, Jeff. "Dr. Ruth, the Famous Sex Therapist, Was Once a Sniper in the Israeli Army!" War History Online, November 25, 2015. https://www.warhistoryonline.com/featured/dr-ruth-americas-sex-therapist -israeli-trained-sniper.html.

Goldman, Laura. "Dr. Ruth's Advice: Put down the iPhone and No One Night Stands." HuffPost, December 6, 2017. https://www.huffingtonpost.com/laura-goldman/dr-ruths-advice-put-down-_b_8513878.html.

Hambleton, Laura. "Dr. Ruth Says Some Frank Things about Aging and Sex." *Washington Post*, June 24, 2013. https://www.washingtonpost.com/national/health-science/dr-ruth-says-some-frank-things-about-aging -and-sex/2013/06/24/f1aee184-bca8-11e2-89c9-3be8095fe767_story.html?utm_term=.b3afd1c0055b.

MARCH 12 THE FIFTY-WORD MASTERPIECE

Barajas, Joshua. "8 Things You Didn't Know about Dr. Seuss." *PBS NewsHour*, July 22, 2015. https://www .pbs.org/newshour/arts/8-things-didnt-know-dr-seuss.

Biography. "Dr. Seuss." Updated April 27, 2017. https://www.biography.com/people/dr-seuss-9479638.

Hiskey, Daven. "Dr. Seuss Wrote *Green Eggs and Ham* on a Bet That He Couldn't Write a Book with 50 or Fewer Words." *Today I Found Out* (blog), May 24, 2011. http://www.todayifoundout.com/index.php/2011 /05/dr-seuss-wrote-green-eggs-and-ham-on-a-bet-that-he-couldnt-write-a-book-with-50-or-fewer-words/.

Lewis, Dan. "Fifty Word Masterpiece." Now I Know, April 26, 2011. http://nowiknow.com/fifty-word -masterpiece/.

MARCH 13 THE CURSE OF CAMELOT

Collman, Ashley. "Rose Kennedy Talks about Daughter's Lobotomy, Banning Crying in the 'Cursed' Clan and How She Would Weigh Her Children Every Week in Recently Uncovered Interview." *Daily Mail*, November 24, 2015. http://www.dailymail.co.uk/news/article-3332512/Rose-Kennedy-talks -daughter-s-lobotomy-banning-crying-cursed-clan-weigh-children-week-recently-uncovered-interview .html.

Jones, Sam, and Mark Tran. "History of the Kennedy Curse." *Guardian*, August 26, 2009. https://www.the guardian.com/world/2009/aug/26/kennedy-curse-senator-ted-death.

Rothschild, Mike. "The Eerie Truth behind the Kennedy Curse." Ranker. Accessed January 21, 2018. https:// www.ranker.com/list/the-kennedy-curse-victims/mike-rothschild.

UncommonBusiness. "The Kennedy Curse." *True Conspiracy* (blog), August 28, 2006. http://trueconspiracy blog.blogspot.fr/2006/08/kennedy-curse.html.

MARCH 14 THE INCREDIBLE BRAIN

Alban, Deane. "72 Amazing Human Brain Facts (Based on the Latest Science)." *Be Brain Fit* (blog). Accessed January 21, 2018. https://bebrainfit.com/human-brain-facts/?fb_comment_id=862914153780501 _1221214211283825#fc43ebf677211c.

The CEU Group. "12 Surprising Human Memory Facts." Accessed January 21, 2018. http://www.theceugroup .com/12-surprising-human-memory-facts/.

Gupta, James. "10 Surprising Facts about Your Memory." *Synap* (blog). Accessed January 21, 2018. https:// blog.synap.ac/10-surprising-facts-about-your-memory/#.WmVUvainEdU.

Lu, Stacy. "Erasing Bad Memories." American Psychological Association. *Monitor on Psychology* 46, no. 2 (February 2015): 42. http://www.apa.org/monitor/2015/02/bad-memories.aspx.

MARCH 15 THE BIRDMAN OF NEW YORK

Jacobson, Rebecca. "8 Things You Didn't Know about Nikola Tesla." *PBS NewsHour*, July 10, 2013. https:// www.pbs.org/newshour/science/5-things-you-didnt-know-about-nikola-tesla.

King, Gilbert. "The Rise and Fall of Nikola Tesla and His Tower." *Smithsonian*, February 4, 2013. https://www.smithsonianmag.com/history/the-rise-and-fall-of-nikola-tesla-and-his-tower-11074324/.

Vujovic, Ljubo. "Tesla Biography: Nikola Tesla, the Genius Who Lit the World." Tesla Memorial Society of New York, July 10, 1998. http://www.teslasociety.com/biography.htm.

Whipps, Heather. "Nikola Tesla: Biography, Inventions & Quotes." Live Science, May 29, 2014. https://www.livescience.com/45950-nikola-tesla-biography.html.

MARCH 16 THE WORST SINGER IN THE WORLD

Nattrass, JJ. "'The Lady's a Lesson in Courage': Meryl Streep's Awful Singing Sets the Tone for the Funny yet Inspiring Tale of Florence Foster Jenkins in the Movie's First Full Trailer." *Daily Mail*, March 10, 2016. http://www.dailymail.co.uk/tvshowbiz/article-3485639/The-lady-s-lesson-courage-Meryl-Streep-s-awful-singing-sets-tone-funny-inspiring-tale-Florence-Foster-Jenkins-movie-s-trailer.html.

NPR. "Queen of the Night." *Snap Judgment*, August 1, 2014. http://ww.npr.org/2014/08/01/337096164/queen-of-the-night.

Thorpe, Vanessa. "How the World's Worst Opera Singer Finally Found Fame—and Redemption." *Guardian*, March 26, 2016. https://www.theguardian.com/film/2016/mar/27/florence-foster-jenkins-opera-films.

"Worst Singer Ever." YouTube video, 3:44. Posted by Jamie Frater, May 31, 2010. https://www.youtube.com/watch?v=DjURO9L5fdc.

MARCH 17 THE REAL HERO IN THOSE SWASHBUCKLERS

Damrosch, Leo. "The Third Musketeer." Review of *The Black Count*, by Tom Reiss. *New York Times*, September 14, 2012. http://www.nytimes.com/2012/09/16/books/review/the-black-count-by-tom-reiss.html.

Scutts, Joanna. "*The Black Count: Glory, Revolution, Betrayal, and the Real Count of Monte Cristo* by Tom Reiss." Review of *The Black Count*, by Tom Reiss. *Washington Post*, November 2, 2012. https://www.washingtonpost.com/opinion/the-black-count-glory-revolution-betrayal-and-the-real-count-of-monte-cristo-by-tom-reiss/2012/11/02/7552d290-1793-11e2-8792-cf5305eddf60_story.html?utm_term=.1907e7bfaa29.

Tonkin, Boyd. "The Role of Race in the Life and Literature of Alexandre Dumas: The Episode That Inspired the Man behind the Musketeers." *Independent*, January 16, 2014. http://www.independent.co.uk/arts-entertainment/tv/features/the-role-of-race-in-the-life-and-literature-of-alexandre-dumas-the-episode-that-inspired-the-man-9065506.html.

Wirth, Nikolaus. "Dumas, Thomas-Alexandre (1762–1806)." BlackPast.org. Accessed January 17, 2018. http://www.blackpast.org/gah/dumas-thomas-alexandre-1762-1806.

MARCH 18 CATS AND RATS

Abee, Holle. "Cats and the Black Plague." Owlcation. Updated February 4, 2010. https://owlcation.com/humanities/Cats-and-the-Black-Plague.

Andrews, Walter G. "Killing the Cats." Paper, December 2008. University of Washington. http://faculty.washington.edu/walter/Killing%20Cats3.html.

Damon. "That One Time the Pope Banned Cats and It Caused the Black Plague." History Things, November 14, 2016. http://historythings.com/one-time-pope-banned-cats-caused-black-plague/.

MARCH 19 SEEING THE EXTRAORDINARY IN THE ORDINARY

Bagley, Mary. "George Washington Carver: Biography, Inventions & Quotes." Live Science, December 6, 2013. https://www.livescience.com/41780-george-washington-carver.html.

Biography. "George Washington Carver." Updated January 16, 2018. https://www.biography.com/people/george-washington-carver-9240299.

Kettler, Sara. "7 Facts on George Washington Carver." Biography, March 1, 2015. https://www.biography.com/news/george-washington-carver-facts-national-peanut-month.

National Peanut Board. "Who Invented Peanut Butter?" Accessed January 17, 2018. http://nationalpeanutboard.org/peanut-info/who-invented-peanut-butter.htm.

MARCH 20 OVERCOMING PREJUDICE

Civil War Trust. "Robert Gould Shaw." Accessed January 14, 2018. https://www.civilwar.org/learn/biographies/robert-gould-shaw.

Hickman, Kennedy. "Civil War: Colonel Robert Gould Shaw." ThoughtCo. Updated January 3, 2018. https://www.thoughtco.com/civil-war-colonel-robert-gould-shaw-2360143.

Raimonto, Bob. "The Reluctant Abolitionist: Robert Gould Shaw." The Authentic Campaigner, March 10, 2007. http://www.authentic-campaigner.com/.

Teaching American History in South Carolina. "'Will I or Won't I?' Colonel Robert Gould Shaw, 54th Massachusetts Regiment." Accessed January 17, 2018. http://teachingushistory.org/lessons/pdfs_and_docs/documents/WillIorWontIColonelRobertGouldShaw54thMassachusettsRegiment.html.

MARCH 21 FOR SUCH A TIME AS THIS

This story is adapted from Esther 1–10.

Avraham, Rachel. "Incredible Parallels between the Purim Story and the Nazi Trials." United with Israel, March 10, 2014. https://unitedwithisrael.org/strange-parallels-between-the-purim-story-and-the-nuremberg-trials/.

Cohen, Yaacov. "The Tragic Life of Queen Esther." HuffPost, April 22, 2013. https://www.huffingtonpost.com/yaacov-cohen/the-tragic-life-of-queen-esther_b_2722130.html.

Crawford, Sidnie White. "Esther: Bible." Jewish Women's Archive. Encyclopedia. Accessed February 12, 2018. https://jwa.org/encyclopedia/article/esther-bible.

MARCH 22 FIFTEEN HUNDRED REJECTIONS

Biography. "Sylvester Stallone." Updated July 10, 2017. https://www.biography.com/people/sylvester-stallone-9491745.

Hainey, Michael. "Yo." GQ, September 7, 2010. https://www.gq.com/story/sylvester-stallone-yo-michael-hainey-cop-land-rocky-rambo.

New York Times. "'Rocky Isn't Based on Me,' Says Stallone, 'but We Both Went the Distance.'" November 1, 1976. http://www.nytimes.com/packages/html/movies/bestpictures/rocky-ar.html.

PlanetMotivation.com. "Never Quit—Ever!!" Accessed January 14, 2018. http://www.planetmotivation.com/never-quit.html.

MARCH 23 THE STRIKEOUT KING

Bumbar, Micky. "Babe Ruth, the Drunken Legend of American Baseball." Lords of the Drinks (blog), January 9, 2015. https://lordsofthedrinks.com/2015/01/09/babe-ruth-the-drunken-legend-of-american-baseball/comment-page-1/.

Corcoran, Cliff. "99 Cool Facts about Babe Ruth." Sports Illustrated, July 11, 2013. https://www.si.com/mlb/strike-zone/2013/07/12/99-cool-facts-about-babe-ruth.

James, Bill. "Life, Liberty, and Breaking the Rules." Slate, September 13, 2010. http://www.slate.com/articles/sports/sports_nut/2010/09/life_liberty_and_breaking_the_rules.html.

Sinek, Simon. "Are You Willing to Strike Out?" Simon Sinek Inc. Re:Focus (blog). Accessed January 14, 2018. http://sinekpartners.typepad.com/refocus/2010/03/are-you-willing-to-strike-out.html.

MARCH 24 THE CITY IN THE CLOUDS

Hearn, Kelly, and Jason Golomb. "Machu Picchu." National Geographic. Accessed January 14, 2018. https://www.nationalgeographic.com/archaeology-and-history/archaeology/machu-picchu-mystery/.

PBS. "A Marvel of Inca Engineering." Nova, January 1, 2010. http://www.pbs.org/wgbh/nova/ancient/wright-inca-engineering.html.

Peru for Less. "Machu Picchu History." Accessed January 14, 2018. https://www.machupicchu.org/machu_picchu_history.htm.

MARCH 25 THE BRAIN IS FASTER THAN THE TONGUE

Beattie, Andrew. "You Don't Know Jack Welch." Investopedia. Accessed January 14, 2018. https://www.investopedia.com/articles/financial-careers/09/jack-welch-ceo.asp.

The Famous People. "Jack Welch." Updated January 8, 2018. https://www.thefamouspeople.com/profiles/dr-john-francis-1713.php.

McKay, Reid. "How a Boy with a Stutter Became the Titan Who Transformed General Electric and Defined American Ingenuity—Jack Welch in Perspective." CEO.CA, May 3, 2013. http://blog.ceo.ca/2013/05/03/jack-welch/.

MARCH 26 THE DUMBHEAD

Bass, Matthew. "Albert Einstein Success Story." Success Groove, July 12, 2013. http://successgroove.com/success-stories/albert-einstein-success-story.html.

Chung, Arthur. "Albert Einstein. His Struggles. His Failures." Medium (blog), May 4, 2014. https://medium.com/@ArthurChung_/albert-einstein-his-struggles-his-failures-d7554f02b237.

Golden, Frederic. "Albert Einstein." Time, December 31, 1999. http://content.time.com/time/magazine/article/0,9171,993017,00.html.

Greeley (CO) Tribune. "Chautauqua: It Doesn't Take a Genius." August 6, 2009. https://www.greeleytribune.com/news/local/chautauqua-it-doesnt-take-a-genius/.

MARCH 27 THE PETER PAN SYNDROME

Daily Mail. "How Michael Jackson's Father Joe Whipped Him if He Missed a Note." June 26, 2009. http://www.dailymail.co.uk/news/article-1195847/How-Michael-Jacksons-father-Joe-whipped-missed-note.html.

Kimmel, Tim. "Michael Jackson: The Stolen Childhood of the King of Pop." *Family Matters Blog*, June 26, 2009. http://familymatters.net/blog/2009/06/26/michael-jackson-and-a-stolen-childhood/.

Orth, Maureen. "Nightmare in Neverland." *Vanity Fair*, January 1, 2007. https://www.vanityfair.com/magazine/1994/01/orth199401.

Weisberg, Jacob. "Arrested Development: The Tragedy of Michael Jackson." Slate, June 14, 2005. http://www.slate.com/articles/news_and_politics/the_big_idea/2005/06/arrested_development.html.

MARCH 28 THE MAN WHO FAILED TEN THOUSAND TIMES
Beals, Gerald. "The Biography of Thomas Edison." ThomasEdison.com. Accessed January 13, 2018. http://www.thomasedison.com/biography.html.

Feloni, Richard. "Thomas Edison's Reaction to His Factory Burning Down Shows Why He Was So Successful." Business Insider, May 9, 2014. http://www.businessinsider.com/thomas-edison-in-the-obstacle-is-the-way-2014-5.

Furr, Nathan. "How Failure Taught Edison to Repeatedly Innovate." *Forbes*, June 9, 2011. https://www.forbes.com/sites/nathanfurr/2011/06/09/how-failure-taught-edison-to-repeatedly-innovate/#63ac634865e9.

Hendry, Erica R. "7 Epic Fails Brought to You by the Genius Mind of Thomas Edison." *Smithsonian*, November 20, 2013. https://www.smithsonianmag.com/innovation/7-epic-fails-brought-to-you-by-the-genius-mind-of-thomas-edison-180947786/.

MARCH 29 THOSE MIRACLE FRUIT JARS
Herald of His Coming. "Circumstances Cannot Break God's Promises." November 2008. http://www.heraldofhiscoming.com/Past%20Issues/2008/November/circumstances_cannot_brake_god_s_promises.htm.

Milner, Melissa. "FRUIT JARS . . . A History Worth Remembering." *Bottles and Extras*, Winter 2004. https://www.fohbc.org/PDF_Files/Milner_FruitJars.pdf.

MARCH 30 BUTTERFLY MIRACLES
Petterson, Robert. *Desert Crossings*, 227–31. Naples, FL: Covenant Books, 2010.

MARCH 31 THE DESTRUCTIVE POWER OF BITTERNESS
Andrews, Evan. "10 Things You May Not Know about Genghis Khan." History, April 29, 2014. http://www.history.com/news/history-lists/10-things-you-may-not-know-about-genghis-khan.

Biography. "Genghis Khan." Updated April 27, 2017. https://www.biography.com/people/genghis-khan-9308634.

Szczepanski, Kallie. "The Mongol Empire." ThoughtCo. Updated October 18, 2017. https://www.thoughtco.com/the-mongol-empire-195041.

APRIL 1 A THAT SAVED AMERICA
Epstein, Daniel Mark. *The Lincolns: Portrait of a Marriage*. New York: Ballantine Books, 2008.

Goodwin, Doris Kearns. *Team of Rivals: The Political Genius of Abraham Lincoln*. New York: Simon & Schuster, 2005.

Gormley, Beatrice. *First Ladies Who Called the White House Home*. New York: Scholastic, 1997.

National First Ladies' Library. "First Lady Biography: Mary Lincoln." Accessed January 5, 2018. http://www.firstladies.org/biographies/firstladies.aspx?biography=17.

National Park Service. "Lincoln Home: Courtship and Marriage." Accessed January 5, 2018. https://www.nps.gov/liho/learn/historyculture/courtship.htm.

APRIL 2 THE BOWL OF SPAGHETTI
This true story is from the author's eyewitness account at age seventeen: as memorable an evening as there ever was.

APRIL 3 THE MAN WHO LOVED RACHEL
Andrew Jackson's Hermitage. "Orphan: Spark from the Start." Accessed March 14, 2017. http://thehermitage.com/learn/andrew-jackson/orphan/.

Burstein, Andrew. *The Passions of Andrew Jackson*. New York: Vintage Books, 2007. Kindle edition.

National First Ladies Library. "First Lady Biography: Rachel Jackson." Accessed March 14, 2017. http://www.firstladies.org/biographies/firstladies.aspx?biography=7.

Smolkin, Rachel, and Brenna Williams. "How Jackson Tried to Save His Wife's Honor." Presidential Places. CNN. Accessed March 14, 2017. http://www.cnn.com/interactive/2015/09/politics/andrew-jackson-hermitage-history/.

APRIL 4 THE SHANTUNG COMPOUND
Gilkey, Langdon. *Shantung Compound: The Story of Men and Women under Pressure*. New York: Harper & Row, 1966.

Price, Joseph L. "The Ultimate and the Ordinary: A Profile of Langdon Gilkey." Religion Online. Accessed January 5, 2018. Previously published in *Christian Century* (April 12, 1989), 380. https://www.religion -online.org/blog/article/the-ultimate-and-the-ordinary-a-profile-of-langdon-gilkey/.

APRIL 5 THE COVER-UP OF THE CENTURY
Hayman, Ronald. *Hitler and Geli*. New York: Bloomsbury USA, 1998.
Rosenbaum, Ron. "Hitler's Doomed Angel." *Vanity Fair*, September 3, 2013. https://www.vanityfair.com /news/1992/04/hitlers-doomed-angel.
Shirer, William L. *The Rise and Fall of the Third Reich: A History of Nazi Germany*. New York: Simon & Schuster, 1960.

APRIL 6 NEVER ENOUGH
Kennedy, John F. *Profiles in Courage*. New York: Harper, 1956.
Lamb, Brian. "Q & A with James Traub." C-SPAN, August 9, 2016. https://www.c-span.org/video/?413748-1 /qa-james-traub.
Traub, James. *John Quincy Adams: Militant Spirit*. New York: Basic Books, 2016.

APRIL 7 THE MAGNIFICENT SEVEN
Brown, Joshua. "The Nine Financiers, a Parable about Power." *Forbes*, July 25, 2012. https://www.forbes .com/sites/joshuabrown/2012/07/25/the-nine-financiers-a-parable-about-power/#7f9042e33126.
Goldsmith, Barbara. "What the Richest Men in the World Don't Know." Daily Beast, January 23, 2009. https://www.thedailybeast.com/what-the-richest-men-in-the-world-dont-know.

APRIL 8 BRINGING HOME THE GOLD
Bohnert, Craig. "Meet Douglas MacArthur: America's Olympic General." Team USA, July 4, 2016. https:// www.teamusa.org/News/2016/July/04/Meet-Douglas-MacArthur-Americas-Olympic-General.
Herman, Arthur. "Before Phelps, This American Brought Home 24 Gold Medals." Fox News, August 12, 2016. http://www.foxnews.com/opinion/2016/08/12/before-phelps-this-american-brought-home-24 -gold-medals.html.
Matthews, Lafayette. "Douglas MacArthur's Olympic Tradition." *Boundary Stones* (blog). WETA, August 5, 2016. https://blogs.weta.org/boundarystones/2016/08/05/douglas-macarthur%E2%80%99s-olympic -tradition.

APRIL 9 UNLUCKY IN LOVE
Briggs, John P., and John Briggs. "Unholy Desires, Inordinate Affections: A Psychodynamic Inquiry into John Wesley's Relationship with Women." Western Connecticut State University. Accessed January 5, 2018. Previously published in *Connecticut Review* 13 (Spring 1991): 1–18. http://people.wcsu.edu /briggsj/Wesley.html.
Busenitz, Nathan. "John Wesley's Failed Marriage." Cripplegate, March 28, 2013. http://thecripplegate.com /john-wesleys-failed-marriage/.
Christianity Today. "John Wesley and Women." Accessed January 5, 2018. http://www.christianitytoday.com /history/issues/issue-2/john-wesley-and-women.html.
Wesley, John. *The Journal of John Wesley*. Edited by Percy Livingstone Parker. Chicago: Moody, 1951.

APRIL 10 TOO BIG TO MISS
This story is adapted from 1 Samuel 17.

APRIL 11 STUTTERING TO STARDOM
Biography. "James Earl Jones." Updated December 7, 2017. https://www.biography.com/people/james-earl -jones-9357354.
Brown, Jeff. "From Stutterer to Star: How James Earl Jones Found His Voice." *PBS NewsHour*, October 12, 2014. https://www.pbs.org/newshour/amp/show/james-earl-jones-returns-broadway.
Hajek, Danny. "James Earl Jones: From Stutterer to Janitor to Broadway Star." *All Things Considered*. NPR, November 9, 2014. https://www.npr.org/2014/11/09/362328749/james-earl-jones-from-stutterer-to -janitor-to-broadway-star.
Hartley, Sarah. "James Earl Jones: My Stutter Was So Bad I Barely Spoke to Anyone for Eight Years." *Daily Mail*, March 6, 2010. http://www.dailymail.co.uk/health/article-1255955/James-Earl-Jones-My-stutter -bad-I-barely-spoke-years.html.

APRIL 12 DENIED A STAGE, GIVEN A NATION
Biography. "Marian Anderson." Updated February 15, 2015. https://www.biography.com/people/marian -anderson-9184422.

Hill, Alexis. "Marian Anderson and the Easter Sunday Concert, April 9, 1939." *Rediscovering Black History* (blog). National Archives, May 20, 2014. https://rediscovering-black-history.blogs.archives.gov/2014/05/20/marian-anderson-and-the-easter-sunday-concert-april-9-1939/.

Katz, Jamie. "Four Years after Marian Anderson Sang at the Lincoln Memorial, D.A.R. Finally Invited Her to Perform at Constitution Hall." *Smithsonian*, April 9, 2014. https://www.smithsonianmag.com/history/four-years-after-marian-anderson-sang-lincoln-memorial-dr-finally-allowed-her-perform-constitution-hall-180950468/.

Stamberg, Susan. "Denied a Stage, She Sang for a Nation." *Morning Edition*. NPR, April 9, 2014. https://www.npr.org/2014/04/09/298760473/denied-a-stage-she-sang-for-a-nation.

APRIL 13 SINGING TO JOHNNY

Haggai, John Edmund. *My Son Johnny*. Wheaton: Tyndale House, 1978.

APRIL 14 THE SECRET GARDEN OF LOVE

Christianity.com. "Odd Romance of John and Idelette Calvin." Accessed January 9, 2018. https://www.christianity.com/church/church-history/timeline/1501-1600/odd-romance-of-john-and-idelette-calvin-11629964.html.

Petersen, William J. "Idelette: John Calvin's Search for the Right Wife." Christian History Institute. Accessed January 9, 2018. Previously published in *Christian History*, no. 12 (1986). https://christianhistoryinstitute.org/magazine/article/idelette-john-calvins-search-for-the-right-wife.

Smyth, Thomas. *Calvin and His Enemies: A Memoir of the Life, Character, and Principles of Calvin.* Bellingham, WA: Logos Research Systems, 2009.

APRIL 15 THE STAYING POWER OF A MOMENTARY LAPSE

Beacom, Mike. "Why Woody Hayes Remains College Football's Most Complex yet Underappreciated Subject." ThePostGame, February 13, 2013. http://www.thepostgame.com/features/201302/woody-hayes-100-years-coach-ohio-state-buckeyes-college-football-columbus.

Bennett, Brian. "Woody Hayes' Last Game Coaching." ESPN, December 30, 2013. http://www.espn.com/college-football/bowls13/story/_/id/10215217/the-punch-ended-woody-hayes-career.

Bruce, David. *The Kindest People Who Do Good Deeds*. Vol. 2. Published by author. Copyright David Bruce, 2007.

BuckeyeFansOnly.com. "More Woody Hayes Stories & Quotes." Accessed January 9, 2018. http://buckeyefansonly.com/woody/woodyquotesandstories.html.

APRIL 16 THE LION WHO ROAMED GOOGLE EARTH

Kushner, David. "A Home at the End of Google Earth." *Vanity Fair*, October 8, 2012. https://www.vanityfair.com/culture/2012/11/india-orphan-google-earth-journey.

Loinaz, Alexis L. "The True Story behind *Lion*: How Lost Child Saroo Brierley Found His Birth Mother More Than 20 Years Later." *People*, December 8, 2016. http://people.com/movies/lion-movie-true-story-saroo-brierley/.

NPR. "With Memories and Online Maps, a Man Finds His 'Way Home.'" *All Things Considered*, June 22, 2014. https://www.npr.org/2014/06/22/323355643/with-memories-and-online-maps-a-man-finds-his-way-home.

Whitaker, Bill. "Man Returns to Childhood Home against the Odds." *Sixty Minutes*, CBS News, December 11, 2016. https://www.cbsnews.com/news/60-minutes-lion-movie-saroo-brierley-bill-whitaker/.

APRIL 17 THEO'S BIG BROTHER

Biography. "Vincent van Gogh." Last updated October 6, 2015. http://www.biography.com/people/vincent-van-gogh-9515695.

Kimmelman, Michael. "Van Gogh: The Courage & the Cunning." Review of *Van Gogh: A Power Seething*, by Julian Bell. *New York Review of Books*, February 5, 2015. http://www.nybooks.com/articles/2015/02/05/van-gogh-courage-and-cunning/.

Siegal, Nina. "Van Gogh's Pastoral Days." *New York Times*, March 12, 2015. https://www.nytimes.com/2015/03/13/arts/international/van-goghs-pastoral-days.html?_r=0.

APRIL 18 THE LEGEND OF THE LOST LEGION

Blundell, Nigel. "As a Hollywood Film Dramatises Ancient Tale, the 2,000 Year Riddle of Rome's Lost Ninth Legion Is Solved At Last." *Daily Mail*, February 22, 2011. http://www.dailymail.co.uk/sciencetech/article-1358700/Hollywood-film-The-Eagle-Romes-lost-Ninth-Legion-solves-riddle-last.html.

Hennessey, Andrew. "The Legend of the Lost 9th Legion." Whale. Accessed January 9, 2018. http://www.whale.to/b/hennessey5.html.

Lambert, Paddy. "In the Footsteps of the Missing Ninth Legion Hispana: Part One." HeritageDaily. Accessed January 9, 2018. https://www.heritagedaily.com/2013/03/in-the-footsteps-of-the-missing-ninth-legion -hispana-part-one/78078.

Russell, Miles. "The Roman Ninth Legion's Mysterious Loss." BBC News, March 16, 2011. http://www.bbc .com/news/magazine-12752497.

APRIL 19 THE PRINCE OF PREACHERS

Day, Richard Ellsworth. *The Shadow of the Broad Brim*, 171–79. Valley Forge, PA: Judson Press, 1934.

Drummond, Lewis. *Spurgeon: Prince of Preachers*, 237–61. Grand Rapids, MI: Kregel, 1992.

Spurgeon, C. H. *C. H. Spurgeon Autobiography: Volume 1: The Early Years*, 527–47. Reprint. London: Banner of Truth, 1973.

APRIL 20 NEVER THIN ENOUGH

Farr, John. "Where's That Rainbow? The True and Tragic Story of Judy Garland." Best Movies by Farr, June 24, 2015. https://www.bestmoviesbyfarr.com/articles/judy-garland-bio/2015/06.

Howe, Caroline. "'I Tried My Damnedest to Believe in the Rainbow That I Tried to Get over and I Couldn't. SO WHAT!' Judy Garland, in Her Own Words, on Drugs, Drink, Suicide Attempts and Her Loathing of Hollywood." *Daily Mail*, September 3, 2014. http://www.dailymail.co.uk/news/article-2740004/I -tried-damnedest-believe-rainbow-I-tried-I-couldn-t-SO-WHAT-Judy-Garland-words-drugs-drink -suicide-attempts-loathing-Hollywood.html.

Kettler, Sara. "'Stormy Weather': Judy Garland's Troubled Youth." Biography, June 21, 2017. https://www .biography.com/news/judy-garland-facts-bio.

APRIL 21 HISTORY'S STRANGEST FUNERAL

Chicago Tribune Editorial Board. "Editorial: Santa Anna's Leg? Come and Take It." *Chicago Tribune*, November 11, 2016. http://www.chicagotribune.com/news/opinion/editorials/ct-santa-anna-leg-dispute -illinois-texas-edit-20161111-story.html.

Conradt, Stacy. "The Pastries That Cost Santa Anna His Leg." Mental Floss, March 20, 2013. http://mental floss.com/article/49292/pastries-cost-santa-anna-his-leg.

Elizabeth. "That Time Santa Anna Held a Funeral for His Amputated Leg." History Things, January 6, 2017. http://historythings.com/time-santa-anna-held-funeral-amputated-leg/.

Galehouse, Maggie. "Texas Fighting for Santa Anna's Leg." *Houston Chronicle*, May 16, 2014. https://www .houstonchronicle.com/entertainment/article/Texas-fighting-for-Santa-Anna-s-leg-5483826.php.

APRIL 22 LATRODECTUS MACTANS

Forensic Outreach. "Black Widows: Four Chilling Differences between Female and Male Killers." Accessed March 14, 2017. http://forensicoutreach.com/library/black-widows-four-chilling-differences-between -female-and-male-killers/.

Strange Remains. "A Nightmare at Murder Farm: The Story of One of America's Most Prolific Serial Killers." May 18, 2014. https://strangeremains.com/2014/05/18/a-nightmare-at-murder-farm-the-story-of-one -of-americas-most-prolific-serial-killers/.

Szalay, Jessie. "Black Widow Spider Facts." Live Science, October 29, 2014. http://www.livescience.com /39919-black-widow-spiders.html.

APRIL 23 THE DEEPEST PIT OF ALL

Davis, Julie. "*The Hiding Place*: No Pit So Deep." Patheos, April 13, 2011. http://www.patheos.com/resources /additional-resources/2011/04/hiding-place-no-pit-so-deep-julie-davis-04-14-2011.

Ferreira, Patricia M. "Corrie ten Boom, a Dutch Savior." The International Raoul Wallenberg Foundation. Accessed January 11, 2018. http://www.raoulwallenberg.net/saviors/others/corrie-ten-boom-dutch-savior/.

PBS. "Corrie ten Boom." *The Question of God*. Accessed January 11, 2018. Reprinted with permission from *Guideposts*, 1972. http://www.pbs.org/wgbh/questionofgod/voices/boom.html.

APRIL 24 POSTCARDS FROM THE PRINCESS

Miller, Julie. "Inside Carrie Fisher's Difficult Upbringing with Famous Parents." *Vanity Fair*, December 27, 2016. https://www.vanityfair.com/style/2016/12/carrie-fisher-parents-debbie-reynolds-eddie-hollywood.

Molloy, Shannon. "The Story of Debbie Reynolds' Troubled Relationship with Daughter, Carrie Fisher." *Daily Telegraph*, December 29, 2016. https://www.dailytelegraph.com.au/entertainment/celebrity/the -story-of-debbie-reynolds-troubled-relationship-with-daughter-carrie-fisher/news-story/5d06926e68e0f7 ca65a24178818cbc91.

Phillips, Michael. "The Tragedy of Losing Debbie Reynolds and Carrie Fisher One Day Apart." *Chicago Tribune*, December 29, 2016. http://www.chicagotribune.com/entertainment/movies/ct-debbie-reynolds -carrie-fisher-appreciation-20161228-column.html.

Silva, Daniella. "Debbie Reynolds, Actress and Mother of Carrie Fisher, Dies at 84." NBC News, December 29, 2016. https://www.nbcnews.com/pop-culture/movies/debbie-reynolds-actress-mother-carrie-fisher-dies-84-n701026.

APRIL 25 THE FORGOTTEN GENIUS
Bartels, Meghan. "The Unbelievable Life of the Forgotten Genius Who Turned Americans' Space Dreams into Reality." Business Insider, August 22, 2016. http://www.businessinsider.com/katherine-johnson-hidden-figures-nasa-human-computers-2016-8.
Berman, Eliza. "This New Movie Tells the True Story of the Women Who Helped Put John Glenn into Space." Time, December 9, 2016. http://time.com/4594571/hidden-figures-john-glenn-space-race/.
Blair, Elizabeth. "'Hidden Figures' No More: Meet the Black Women Who Helped Send America to Space." Morning Edition. NPR, December 16, 2016. https://www.npr.org/2016/12/16/505569187/hidden-figures-no-more-meet-the-black-women-who-helped-send-america-to-space.
Bolden, Charles. "Katherine Johnson, the NASA Mathematician Who Advanced Human Rights with a Slide Rule and Pencil." Vanity Fair, August 23, 2016. https://www.vanityfair.com/culture/2016/08/katherine-johnson-the-nasa-mathematician-who-advanced-human-rights.

APRIL 26 DIVING INTO STARDOM
Ellis, Mark. "Charles Krauthammer Ruminates on God, Israel, and the Accident That Left Him Paralyzed." Godreports (blog), November 21, 2013. http://blog.godreports.com/2013/11/charles-krauthammer-ruminates-on-god-israel-and-the-accident-that-left-him-paralyzed/.
Hallowell, Billy. "Ever Wonder about the Story behind Charles Krauthammer's Tragic Accident? Conservative Star Opens Up." TheBlaze, October 28, 2013. https://www.theblaze.com/news/2013/10/28/krauthammer-opens-up-about-his-life-and-the-tragic-accident-that-forever-changed-it.
Tiffiny. "SCI Superstar: Charles Krauthammer." SPINALpedia.com (blog), June 18, 2015. https://spinalpedia.com/blog/2015/06/sci-superstar-charles-krauthammer/.
Vazquez, Maegan. "Fox News's Charles Krauthammer Describes the Injury That Left Him Paralyzed." Independent Journal Review, April 9, 2016. https://ijr.com/2016/04/580692-charles-krauthammer-paralysis/.

APRIL 27 THE NEWSPAPER CLIPPING
Asimakoupoulos, Greg. "Icons Every Pastor Needs: Six Ways to Remember Your Value." Christianity Today. Accessed January 13, 2018. http://www.christianitytoday.com/pastors/1993/winter/93l4108.html.
Flock, Elizabeth. "What They Found in Lincoln's Pockets the Night He Was Shot." U.S. News, May 24, 2013. https://www.usnews.com/news/blogs/washington-whispers/2013/05/24/what-they-found-in-lincolns-pockets-the-night-he-was-shot.
Goodwin, Doris Kearns. "The Night Abraham Lincoln Was Assassinated: What Happened on That Fateful Good Friday Evening." Smithsonian, April 8, 2015. https://www.smithsonianmag.com/history/abraham-lincoln-team-of-rivals-180954850/.
Marler, Don C. "The Deification of 'Honest Abe.'" Iconoclast (blog), March 25, 2012. https://donmarler.wordpress.com/2012/03/25/the-deification-of-honest-abe/.

APRIL 28 THE LONG PRAYER THAT CHANGED AMERICA
Hall, Peter Dobkin. "Doing Good in the World: Cotton Mather and the Origins of Modern Philanthropy." Documentary History of Philanthropy and Voluntarism in America project (work in progress), Harvard Kennedy School. Accessed January 13, 2018. https://sites.hks.harvard.edu/fs/phall/08.%20Mather.pdf.
Lambert, Frank. Inventing the "Great Awakening," 46–48. Princeton, NJ: Princeton University Press, 1999.
The Mather Project. "Biography: Cotton Mather (1662/3–1727/8)." Accessed January 13, 2018. http://matherproject.org/node/22.
Wendell, Barrett. Cotton Mather: The Puritan Priest, 297–307. New York: Dodd, Mead, and Company, 1891.

APRIL 29 THE RAIN OF FIRE
Catholic Online. "Martyrs of Japan." Accessed January 13, 2018. http://www.catholic.org/saints/saint.php?saint_id=4773#wiki.
Hoffman, Michael. "Christian Missionaries Find Japan a Tough Nut to Crack." Japan Times, December 20, 2014. https://www.japantimes.co.jp/news/2014/12/20/national/history/christian-missionaries-find-japan-tough-nut-crack/#.WlqfvqinEdU.
Josemaria, Anthony. "The Catholic Holocaust of Nagasaki—'Why, Lord?'" Homiletic & Pastoral Review, August 1, 2010. http://www.hprweb.com/2010/08/the-catholic-holocaust-of-nagasaki-why-lord/.
Magister, Sandro. "Nagasaki, the City of the Atomic Bomb—and of the Christian Martyrs." www.chiesa, October 30, 2007. http://chiesa.espresso.repubblica.it/articolo/173602bdc4.html?eng=y&refresh_ce.
Scorsese, Martin, and Jay Cocks. Silence. Directed by Martin Scorsese. Paramount Pictures, 2016.

APRIL 30 NOWHERE TO RUN, NOWHERE TO HIDE

Klein, Christopher. "How the Civil War Stalked Wilmer McLean." History, April 9, 2015. http://www.history
.com/news/how-the-civil-war-stalked-wilmer-mclean.

McTear, Rebecca. "The [American Civil] War Began in My Front Yard and Ended in My Parlor." *Today I
Found Out* (blog), March 18, 2013. http://www.todayifoundout.com/index.php/2013/03/the-american
-civil-war-began-in-my-front-yard-and-ended-in-my-parlor/.

MilitaryHistoryNow.com. "Meet Wilmer McLean—One of the Civil War's First and Last Victims." January 29,
2014. http://militaryhistorynow.com/2014/01/29/meet-wilmer-mclean-one-of-the-civil-wars-first-and
-last-victims/.

MAY 1 COMPOSERS AND THEIR CRITICS

Christianity.com. "Messiah and George Frideric Handel." Updated March, 2007. https://www.christianity
.com/church/church-history/timeline/1701-1800/messiah-and-george-frideric-handel-11630237
.html.

Davis, Mitch. "Ten Things Everyone Should Know about Handel's *Messiah*." OnFaith. Accessed January 13,
2018. https://www.onfaith.co/onfaith/2014/12/09/ten-things-everyone-should-know-about-handels
-messiah/35347.

Terry, Lindsay. *The Story of Handel's* Messiah. Wheaton, IL: Crossway, 2004. Accessed January 13, 2018.
https://www.crossway.org/tracts/the-story-of-handels-messiah-2559/.

Witherington, Ben. "Handel's *Messiah*—the Story behind the Classic." *Ben Witherington on the Bible and
Culture* (blog). Beliefnet. Accessed January 13, 2018. http://www.beliefnet.com/columnists/bibleand
culture/2009/12/handels-messiah-the-story-behind-the-classic.html.

MAY 2 THE DANCE OF FOOLS

This story is adapted from 1 Samuel 18–19; 25:44; and 2 Samuel 3; 6.

MAY 3 SINGING WITH DADDY

Biography. "Natalie Cole." Updated January 4, 2016. https://www.biography.com/people/natalie-cole
-37692.

Owen, Jonathan. "The Story of Nat King Cole and His Racist Neighbours." *Independent*, May 17, 2014.
http://www.independent.co.uk/arts-entertainment/music/news/the-story-of-nat-king-cole-and-his-racist
-neighbours-9391316.html.

Perrone, Pierre. "Natalie Cole: Singer Who Performed the First 'Virtual Duets' with Her Late Father
Nat 'King' Cole." *Independent*, January 3, 2016. http://www.independent.co.uk/news/obituaries
/natalie-cole-singer-who-performed-the-first-virtual-duets-with-her-late-father-nat-king-cole
-a6794906.html.

Rottenberg, Josh. "Natalie Cole Dies at 65; 'Unforgettable' Singer Was Daughter of Legendary Nat King
Cole." *Los Angeles Times*, January 1, 2016. http://www.latimes.com/local/lanow/la-me-ln-singer-natalie
-cole-dead-20160101-story.html.

Telegraph. "Natalie Cole, Singer–Obituary." January 3, 2016. http://www.telegraph.co.uk/news/obituaries
/12078977/Natalie-Cole-singer-obituary.html.

MAY 4 THE COUNTERFEIT ARTIST

Kaarre, Marty. "God Only Forgives People Who Are Wrong." *Story of the Day—ClimbingHigher* (blog),
November 25, 2013. https://kaarre.wordpress.com/2013/11/25/god-only-forgives-people-who-are
-wrong-2/.

Lewis, Dan. "The Unintentional Artist." *Now I Know* (blog), July 11, 2012. http://nowiknow.com/the
-unintentional-artist/.

Stevenson, Jed. "Pastimes; Coins." *New York Times*, April 8, 1990. http://www.nytimes.com/1990/04/08
/style/pastimes-coins.html.

MAY 5 THE PRICE WE PAY FOR GREATNESS

Biography. "Michelangelo." Updated August 28, 2017. https://www.biography.com/people/michelangelo
-9407628.

Bondeson, Lennart, and Anne-Greth Bondeson. "Michelangelo's Divine Goitre." *Journal of the Royal Society
of Medicine* 96, no. 12 (2003): 609–11. https://www.ncbi.nlm.nih.gov/pmc/articles/PMC539666/.

Il Mio Sogno (blog). "The Crucifix of Santo Spirito." September 28, 2010. http://whosedreamisit.blogspot
.com/2010/09/crucifix-of-santo-spirito.html.

Michelangelo: The Complete Works. "Biography of Michelangelo." Accessed January 13, 2018. https://www
.michelangelo-gallery.org/biography.html.

Sound Affairs. "Dissection." Accessed January 13, 2018. https://soundaffairs.wordpress.com/production
-themes/dissection/.

MAY 6 A MESSAGE IN A BOTTLE

Baldwin, Paul. "NASA's Voyager 2 Heads for Star Sirius . . . By Time It Arrives Humans Will Have Died Out." *Daily Express*, January 5, 2017. http://www.express.co.uk/news/world/567957/NASA-s-Voyager-2-sets -course-for-star-Sirius-by-time-it-arrives-human-race-will-be-dead.

NASA Jet Propulsion Laboratory. "What Is the Golden Record?" Voyager: the Interstellar Mission. Accessed March 13, 2017. http://voyager.jpl.nasa.gov/spacecraft/goldenrec.html.

Weber, Brandon. "A Spacecraft Launched 39 Years Ago Has Human Sounds Onboard—Now We Can Listen." Big Think, September 23, 2016. http://bigthink.com/brandon-weber/a-spacecraft-moving-at -35000-miles-per-hour-has-human-sounds-on-it-heres-how-to-listen.

MAY 7 THE POWER OF A STORY

Biography. "Arthur Miller." Updated March 22, 2017. https://www.biography.com/people/arthur-miller -9408335.

History. "Red Scare." Accessed January 14, 2018. http://www.history.com/topics/cold-war/red-scare.

Meyers, Kevin E. "Miller Tells of *Crucible* Origins." *Harvard Crimson*, May 12, 1999. http://www.thecrimson .com/article/1999/5/12/miller-tells-of-crucible-origins-parthur/.

Miller, Arthur. "Why I Wrote *The Crucible*." *New Yorker*, October 21, 1966. https://www.newyorker.com /magazine/1996/10/21/why-i-wrote-the-crucible.

MAY 8 THE RELUCTANT SPY

EyeWitness to History. "The Execution of Nathan Hale, 1776." Accessed March 13, 2017. http://www.eye witnesstohistory.com/hale.htm.

Phelps, M. William. *Nathan Hale: The Life and Death of America's First Spy*. Lebanon, NH: University Press of New England, 2014.

MAY 9 MUSSOLINI'S LAST BODYGUARD

Honey, Charley. "From Italian Fascist to Assembly of God Evangelist, Jenison Man Shares Lifetime of Stories, Travels." mLive, July 25, 2009. http://www.mlive.com/living/grand-rapids/index.ssf/2009/07 /from_italian_fascist_to_assemb.html.

Klein, Christopher. "How South America Became a Nazi Haven." History, November 12, 2015. http://www .history.com/news/how-south-america-became-a-nazi-haven.

Ward, C. M. *Frigoli: The Story of Bruno R. Frigoli: Former Fascist Now Serving Christ in Bolivia*. Springfield, MO: Assemblies of God, 1969.

Wieland, Carl. "Fighting for Mussolini: A Former Fascist Officer Makes a Remarkable Turnaround." Creation Ministries International. Accessed January 14, 2018. http://creation.mobi/fighting-for-mussolini.

MAY 10 FAILING ALL THE WAY TO GREATNESS

Biography. "Michael Jordan." Updated January 8, 2018. https://www.biography.com/people/michael-jordan -9358066.

Feeling Success. "Michael Jordan Failed Over and Over and That Is Why He Succeeded." August 20, 2015. https://www.feelingsuccess.com/michael-jordan-failure/.

Gordon, Jeff. "A Biography of Michael Jordan as a High School Basketball Player." LIVESTRONG.com, September 11, 2017. https://www.livestrong.com/article/450727-a-biography-of-michael-jordan-as-a -high-school-basketball-player/.

Poppel, Seth. "Michael Jordan Didn't Make Varsity—at First." *Newsweek*, October 17, 2015. http://www .newsweek.com/missing-cut-382954.

MAY 11 LET'S HEAR IT FOR THE BOLL WEEVIL

America's Story from America's Library. "The Boll Weevil Honored in Alabama: December 11, 1919." Accessed March 13, 2017. http://www.americaslibrary.gov/jb/jazz/jb_jazz_weevil_1.html.

Richardson, T. C., and Harwood P. Hinton. "Boll Weevil." In *The Portable Handbook of Texas*, edited by Roy R. Barkley and Mark F. Odintz, 696–99. Austin: Texas State Historical Association, 2000.

MAY 12 THE HAND THAT ROCKS THE CRADLE

Dallimore, Arnold A. *Susanna Wesley: The Mother of John and Charles Wesley*. Grand Rapids, MI: Baker Books, 1993.

MAY 13 THE MONKEY THAT ESCAPED THE NAZIS

Houghton Mifflin Books.com. "Curious George." Accessed January 14, 2018. http://www.houghtonmifflin books.com/features/cgsite/history.shtml#authors.

MacGregor, Jeff. "When Curious George Made a Daring Escape from the Nazis." *Smithsonian*, November 2016. https://www.smithsonianmag.com/arts-culture/curious-george-daring-escape-nazis-180960779/.

Smith, Dinitia. "How Curious George Escaped the Nazis." *New York Times*, September 13, 2005. http://www.nytimes.com/2005/09/13/books/how-curious-george-escaped-the-nazis.html.

MAY 14 CHARIOT WHEELS IN THE SEA
6000years.org. "Red Sea Crossing." Accessed January 14, 2018. http://www.6000years.org/frame.php?page=red_sea_crossing.

Kovacs, Joe. "Chariots in Red Sea: 'Irrefutable Evidence.'" WND, June 7, 2012. http://www.wnd.com/2012/06/chariots-in-red-sea-irrefutable-evidence/.

Nuwer, Rachel. "The Science of the Red Sea's Parting." *Smithsonian*, December 8, 2014. https://www.smithsonianmag.com/smart-news/science-red-seas-parting-180953553/.

Onion, Amanda. "Scientists Explain Red Sea Parting and Other Miracles." ABC News. Accessed January 14, 2018. http://abcnews.go.com/Technology/story?id=99580&page=1.

MAY 15 THE HEALING TOWN
Chen, Angus. "For Centuries, a Small Town Has Embraced Strangers with Mental Illness." NPR, July 1, 2016. https://www.npr.org/sections/health-shots/2016/07/01/484083305/for-centuries-a-small-town-has-embraced-strangers-with-mental-illness.

Jay, Mike. "The Geel Question." Aeon, January 9, 2014. https://aeon.co/essays/geel-where-the-mentally-ill-are-welcomed-home.

Wells, Karin. "Psychiatric Community Care: Belgian Town Sets Gold Standard." CBC News, March 9, 2014. http://www.cbc.ca/news/world/psychiatric-community-care-belgian-town-sets-gold-standard-1.2557698.

MAY 16 ONLY THE LONELY
Bullock, Philip Ross. *Pyotr Tchaikovsky*. London: Reaktion Books, 2016.

Greenberg, Robert. "5 (Pretty Dark) Facts about Composer Peter Tchaikovsky." Biography, May 7, 2015. http://www.biography.com/news/peter-tchaikovsky-facts-video.

Tommasini, Anthony. "The Patroness Who Made Tchaikovsky Tchaikovsky." Critic's Notebook. *New York Times*, September 2, 1998. http://www.nytimes.com/1998/09/02/arts/critic-s-notebook-the-patroness-who-made-tchaikovsky-tchaikovsky.html.

MAY 17 THE MAN WHO BROUGHT BAD LUCK
Biography. "Robert Todd Lincoln." Updated July 7, 2014. https://www.biography.com/people/robert-todd-lincoln-20989843.

KnowledgeNuts. "Robert Todd Lincoln Was Connected to Three Assassinations." December 7, 2013. http://knowledgenuts.com/2013/12/07/robert-todd-lincoln-was-connected-to-three-assassinations/.

Trex, Ethan. "5 Things You Should Know about Robert Todd Lincoln." Mental Floss, August 26, 2015. http://mentalfloss.com/article/22400/5-things-you-should-know-about-robert-todd-lincoln.

MAY 18 THE MAN WHO DIED THREE TIMES
Friedman, Jack. "Laszlo Tokes, the Pastor Who Helped to Free Romania, Is Home." *People*, February 5, 1990. http://people.com/archive/laszlo-tokes-the-pastor-who-helped-to-free-romania-is-home-vol-33-no-5/.

Louk, Lidia. "Laszlo Tokes: The Man Who Started the Romanian Revolution." *Epoch Times*, December 16, 2014. http://www.theepochtimes.com/n3/1146036-laszlo-tokes-the-man-who-started-the-romania-romanian/.

Wax, Trevin. "How a Reformed Church Overthrew Communism in Romania." *Kingdom People* (blog). The Gospel Coalition, December 22, 2009. https://blogs.thegospelcoalition.org/trevinwax/2009/12/22/how-a-reformed-church-overthrew-communism-in-romania/.

MAY 19 BOOED OFF THE STAGE
Biography. "Jerry Seinfeld." Updated April 28, 2015. https://www.biography.com/people/jerry-seinfeld-9542107.

Collis, Clark. "Jerry Seinfeld Talks Bombing Onstage in *Dying Laughing*." *Entertainment Weekly*, January 20, 2017. http://ew.com/movies/2017/01/20/jerry-seinfeld-dying-laughing-kevin-hart/.

Convery, Ann. "What Happened When Jerry Seinfeld Bombed Onstage—How to Turn Failure to Success." *Kill Jargon* (blog). Speak Your Business. Accessed January 14, 2018. http://speakyourbusiness.com/happened-jerry-seinfeld-bombed-onstage-turn-failure-success/.

Thompson, Kevin A. "What Jerry Seinfeld Knows about Success." *Kevin A. Thompson* (blog), July 7, 2014. http://www.kevinathompson.com/im-comedian/.

MAY 20 THE MIRACLE AT NASEBY
Fraser, Antonia. *Cromwell: Our Chief of Men*, 154–62. St. Albans, England: Panther Books, 1975.

Trueman, C. N. "The Battle of Naseby." History Learning Site. Updated August 16, 2016. http://www.historylearningsite.co.uk/stuart-england/the-battle-of-naseby/.

MAY 21 THE LONGEST-STANDING ARMY

Lubow, Arthur. "Terra Cotta Soldiers on the March." *Smithsonian*, July 2009. https://www.smithsonianmag
.com/history/terra-cotta-soldiers-on-the-march-30942673/.

Pruitt, Sarah. "5 Things You May Not Know about the Terra Cotta Army." History, March 28, 2014. http://
www.history.com/news/5-things-you-may-not-know-about-the-terra-cotta-army.

Roach, John. "Emperor Qin's Tomb." *National Geographic*. Accessed January 14, 2018. https://www.national
geographic.com/archaeology-and-history/archaeology/emperor-qin/.

MAY 22 SAVING MILLY

Groopman, Jerome. "Job's Doctors." Review of *Saving Milly*, by Morton Kondracke. *New Republic*, July 2,
2001. https://newrepublic.com/article/90613/jobs-doctors.

Kondracke, Morton. *Saving Milly: Love, Politics, and Parkinson's Disease*. New York: Ballantine, 2002.

MAY 23 THE EXORCISM OF A SAINT

Bindra, Satinder. "Archbishop: Mother Teresa Underwent Exorcism." CNN, September 7, 2001. http://
edition.cnn.com/2001/WORLD/asiapcf/south/09/04/mother.theresa.exorcism/.

Reaves, Jessica. "Did Mother Teresa Need an Exorcist?" *Time*, September 5, 2001. http://content.time.com
/time/world/article/0,8599,173791,00.html.

Van Biema, David. "Mother Teresa's Crisis of Faith." *Time*, August 23, 2007. http://time.com/4126238
/mother-teresas-crisis-of-faith/.

MAY 24 FREEDOM'S CRY

Loizides, Lex. "Moravians Sold into Slavery." *Church History Review* (blog), April 27, 2009. https://lexloiz
.wordpress.com/tag/moravians-sold-into-slavery/.

Zawacki, Tom. "John Leonard Dober and David Nitschman." *Emancipation of the Freed—Exploring the
Fullness of Freedom* (blog), January 21, 2007. http://emancipationofthefreed.blogspot.com/2007/01
/john-leonard-dober-and-david-nitschman.html.

MAY 25 THE RED PRIEST

Biography. "Joseph Stalin." Updated January 9, 2018. https://www.biography.com/people/joseph-stalin
-9491723.

Boer, Roland. "Stalin as a Theological Student." *Political Theology Today* (blog), November 12, 2014. http://
www.politicaltheology.com/blog/stalin-as-a-theological-student/.

Ghosh, Palash. "How Many People Did Joseph Stalin Kill?" International Business Times, March 5, 2013.
http://www.ibtimes.com/how-many-people-did-joseph-stalin-kill-1111789.

Kershaw, Tom. "The Religion and Political Views of Joseph Stalin." *The Hollowverse* (blog). Updated
September 17, 2012. https://hollowverse.com/joseph-stalin/.

MAY 26 DECISION AT TWENTY-NINE THOUSAND FEET

Fickling, David. "Climber Left for Dead Rescued from Everest." *Guardian*, May 29, 2006. https://www
.theguardian.com/world/2006/may/29/topstories3.mainsection.

Johnson, Richard, Bonnie Berkowitz, and Lazaro Gamio. "Scaling Everest." *Washington Post*. Updated May 12,
2016. https://www.washingtonpost.com/graphics/world/scaling-everest/.

Lauer, Matt. "Miracle on Mount Everest." Dateline NBC. Updated May 27, 2008. http://www.nbcnews.com
/id/13543799/ns/dateline_nbc/t/miracle-mount-everest/#.WMi2aDsrJQI.

NBC News and News Services. "Everest Climbers Recall Near-Death Experience." Updated June 12,
2006. http://www.nbcnews.com/id/13272568/ns/us_news-life/t/everest-climbers-recall-near-death-
experience/#.WMi5CTsrJQI.

Various Climbers. "The Route." Mount Everest. Accessed March 14, 2017. http://www.mounteverest.net
/expguide/route.htm.

MAY 27 LIEUTENANT BUTCH AND EASY EDDIE

Davis, John W., III. "The Murder of Al Capone's Lawyer Was Only Half the Story!" *Ruth Lilly Law Library*
(blog), September 30, 2015. https://rlllblog.com/2015/09/30/the-murder-of-al-capones-lawyer-was-only
-half-the-story/.

Ewing, Steve, and John B. Lundstrom. *Fateful Rendezvous: The Life of Butch O'Hare*. Annapolis: Naval
Institute Press, 1997.

St. Gabriel Parish. "Easy Eddie & Butch." Accessed March 13, 2017. Modified from "Easy Eddie and His
Son," Berean. http://www.stgabrielparish.com/Documents/Menu/9394.pdf.

MAY 28 THE WARRIOR SAINT

Castor, Helen. "The Real Joan of Arc." History Extra, October 23, 2014. Previously published in *BBC History
Magazine* (October 2014). http://www.historyextra.com/article/premium/real-joan-arc.

———. "Joan of Arc—Feminist Icon?" *Guardian*, October 17, 2014. https://www.theguardian.com/books/2014/oct/17/joan-arc-feminist-icon-uncomfortable-fit.

HistoryNet. "Joan of Arc." Accessed January 17, 2018. http://www.historynet.com/joan-of-arc.

O'Connor, William. "The Joan of Arc Nobody Knows." Daily Beast, June 8, 2015. https://www.thedaily beast.com/the-joan-of-arc-nobody-knows.

MAY 29 THE RECOVERING SKINHEAD

Lemons, Stephen. "Neo-Nazi Remorse? Ex-Skinhead Frank Meeink Says He Has It, and the Career Criminal Squad is Saved." *Phoenix New Times*, April 15, 2010. http://www.phoenixnewtimes.com/news/neo-nazi -remorse-ex-skinhead-frank-meeink-says-he-has-it-and-the-career-criminal-squad-is-saved-6432431.

Meeink, Frank. "Former Neo-Nazi Speaks Out on Charlottesville." Interview by Christi Paul. CNN video, 5:52. Posted August 20, 2017. http://www.cnn.com/videos/us/2017/08/20/american-history-x-neo-nazi -charlottesville-newday.cnn.

Nour, Särah. "10 Incredible Real-Life Stories of Redemption." Listverse, January 24, 2016. https://listverse .com/2016/01/24/10-incredible-real-life-stories-of-redemption/.

NPR. "A 'Recovering Skinhead' on Leaving Hatred Behind." *Fresh Air*, April 7, 2010. https://www.npr.org /templates/story/story.php?storyId=125514655.

MAY 30 THE QUADRIPLEGIC IRONMAN

"Dick & Rick Hoyt." YouTube video, 6:39. Posted by "Ironman Triathlon," February 5, 2007. https://www .youtube.com/watch?v=dDnrLv6z-mM.

Diorio, Gina L. "Inspirational Father-Son Team Dick and Rick Hoyt Race Their Last Boston Marathon." LifeNews.com, April 21, 2014. http://www.lifenews.com/2014/04/21/inspirational-father-son-team -dick-and-rick-hoyt-race-their-last-boston-marathon/.

Matson, Barbara. "Dick and Rick Hoyt Run 32nd and Last Marathon." *Boston Globe*, April 22, 2014. https://www.bostonglobe.com/sports/2014/04/22/dick-and-rick-hoyt-run-marathon-their-last-duo /0802xdlCGKe5Z84VmCgMpI/story.html.

MAY 31 FEEDING CANNIBALS

Fiji Sun. "How First Christian Missionaries Arrived in Fiji." August 14, 2008. http://fijisun.com.fj/2008/08 /14/how-first-christian-missionaries-arrived-in-fiji/.

Pacific Baptist Church. "James Calvert: The Printer-Missionary to Fiji." Accessed January 17, 2018. http:// www.pacificbaptist.com/missions/james_calvert_bio.pdf.

Squires, Nick. "Fijians Killed and Ate a Missionary in 1867. Yesterday Their Descendants Apologised." *Telegraph*, November 14, 2003. http://www.telegraph.co.uk/news/worldnews/australiaandthepacific/fiji /1446723/Fijians-killed-and-ate-a-missionary-in-1867.-Yesterday-their-descendants-apologised.html.

Vatunigere, Jonah. "A Brief History of Cannibalism in the Fiji Islands." *JonahVatunigere* (blog), April 18, 2011. https://jonahvatunigere.wordpress.com/2011/04/18/the-history-of-cannibalism-in-the-fiji-islands -4152011/.

JUNE 1 THE DAY AN ANGEL FED ANGELS

Lewis, Jaye. "Entertaining Angels." In *Chicken Soup for Every Mom's Soul: Stories of Love and Inspiration for Moms of All Ages*, edited by Jack Canfield, Mark Victor Hansen, Heather McNamara, and Marci Shimoff, 150–52. Cos Cob, CT: Backlist, 2012.

JUNE 2 WHEN FAITH WALKED ACROSS NIAGARA FALLS

Abbott, Karen. "The Daredevil of Niagara Falls." *Smithsonian*, October 18, 2011. http://www.smithsonian mag.com/history/the-daredevil-of-niagara-falls-110492884/.

CNN Wire Staff. "Daredevil Completes Walk across Niagara Falls." CNN, June 16, 2012. http://www.cnn .com/2012/06/15/us/niagara-falls-tightrope-nik-wallenda/index.html.

Hudson, Roger. "Niagara by Tightrope." *History Today* 62, no. 9 (September 2012). http://www.historytoday .com/roger-hudson/niagara-tightrope.

Thompson, Carolyn. "Nik Wallenda Faces Niagara Falls Tightrope Walk with Rich, but Tragic, Daredevil History." *National Post*, June 15, 2012. http://news.nationalpost.com/news/canada/nik-wallenda-faces -niagara-falls-tightrope-walk-with-rich-but-tragic-daredevil-history.

JUNE 3 WHEN THE SMALL STAND TALL

This story is adapted from Exodus 1.

JUNE 4 THE FACTORY WORKER'S DAUGHTER

Biography. "Melania Trump." Updated January 12, 2018. https://www.biography.com/people/melania-trump -812016.

Collins, Lauren. "The Model American." *New Yorker*, May 9, 2016. https://www.newyorker.com/magazine/2016/05/09/who-is-melania-trump.

Park, Andrea. "Inside the Small Slovenian Town Where Melania Trump Grew Up under the Communist Regime." *People*, February 25, 2016. http://people.com/politics/melania-trumps-childhood-in-communist-slovenia-in-poverty/.

Week. "Melania Trump: 20 Things You Might Not Know about the First Lady." December 11, 2017. http://www.theweek.co.uk/donald-trump/69907/melania-trump-17-things-you-might-not-know-about-the-first-lady.

JUNE 5 "VIVA CRISTO REY!"

Lopez, Kathryn Jean. "Armando Valladares, Witness to Truth." *National Review*, May 16, 2016. http://www.nationalreview.com/article/435409/castro-cuba-and-resistance.

Valladares, Armando. *Against All Hope: A Memoir of Life in Castro's Gulag.* Translated by Andrew Hurley. New York: Encounter Books, 2001.

JUNE 6 THE DEADLY REHEARSAL

Cumming, Jason. "The Disaster That May Have Saved D-Day." NBC News, June 5, 2009. http://www.nbcnews.com/id/30977039/ns/world_news-d_day_65_years_later/t/disaster-may-have-saved-d-day/#.WnY20qinEdU.

Gore-Langton, Robert. "The Tragedy of Slapton Sands: The Real Story of That Terrible Night." *Sunday Express*, May 12, 2014. https://www.express.co.uk/news/uk/475351/The-tragedy-of-Slapton-Sands-The-real-story-of-that-terrible-night.

Jones, Claire. "The D-Day Rehearsal That Cost 800 Lives." BBC News, May 30, 2014. http://www.bbc.com/news/uk-england-devon-27185893.

NPR. "Operation Tiger: D-Day's Disastrous Rehearsal." *All Things Considered*, April 28, 2012. https://www.npr.org/2012/04/28/151590212/operation-tiger-d-days-disastrous-rehearsal.

JUNE 7 THE AMAZING VISITATIONS

Alemayehu, Habtamu. "Ethiopia: Tamrat Layne and the Corruption Circus of the Mid-'90s." Nazret.com, April 19, 2015. http://nazret.com/blog/index.php/2015/04/19/ethiopia-tamrat-layne-and-the.

Baisley, Mark. "Tamrat Layne: Another Botched Marxist Rollout." Ethiopian News & Views, December 14, 2013. https://ecadforum.com/2013/12/14/tamrat-layne-another-botched-marxist-rollout/.

Berhane, Daniel. "Fmr. PM Tamrat Layne Claims 'Jesus Appeared before Him.'" Horn Affairs, May 6, 2013. https://hornaffairs.com/2013/05/06/ethiopia-tamrat-laye-encountered-jesus/.

Simply Jesus. "Meeting Jesus in Prison." Posted November 10, 2013. http://simplyjesusgathering.com/meeting-jesus-in-prison-tamrat-layne/.

JUNE 8 CANDY BOMBS

Ashley, O'rene Daille. "The Men Who Dropped the Bombs on Hiroshima and Nagasaki." *Today I Found Out* (blog), August 5, 2013. http://www.todayifoundout.com/index.php/2013/08/the-men-who-dropped-the-bombs-on-hiroshima-and-nagasaki/.

Biography. "Paul Tibbets." Updated September 14, 2015. https://www.biography.com/people/paul-tibbets-253510.

Goldstein, Richard. "Paul W. Tibbets Jr., Pilot of *Enola Gay*, Dies at 92." *New York Times*, November 2, 2007. http://www.nytimes.com/2007/11/02/obituaries/02tibbets.html.

Wells, Jeff. "The Day Baby Ruths Rained Down on Pittsburg." Mental Floss, October 19, 2015. http://mentalfloss.com/article/70002/day-baby-ruths-rained-down-pittsburgh.

JUNE 9 THE NIGHT OF THE LEPERS

This story is adapted from 2 Kings 6–7.

JUNE 10 A SHARECROPPER'S AUDACIOUS DREAM

Araton, Harvey. "Williams Sisters Leave an Impact That's Unmatched." *New York Times*, August 27, 2015. https://www.nytimes.com/2015/08/31/sports/tennis/venus-and-serena-williams-have-a-lasting-impact.html.

Broadbent, Rick. "Why Richard Williams Is No Longer Courtside." *Australian*, July 9, 2016.

Macguire, Eoghan, and Don Riddell. "Richard Williams: 'I Was Close to Being Killed So Many Times.'" CNN, December 16, 2015. http://www.cnn.com/2015/12/16/tennis/richard-williams-venus-serena-tennis/index.html.

St. John, Allen. "Is Richard Williams, Serena and Venus's Dad, the Greatest Coach of All Time?" *Forbes*, January 28, 2017. https://www.forbes.com/sites/allenstjohn/2017/01/28/is-richard-williams-serena-and-venuss-dad-the-greatest-coach-of-all-time/#ea0a15364317.

JUNE 11 NO FAIRY TALE
This story is adapted from Exodus 2–3.

JUNE 12 THE SAINT WHO TOOK DOWN THE MAFIA
Catholic Online. "Bl. Giuseppe 'Pino' Puglis." Accessed January 21, 2018. http://www.catholic.org/saints
/saint.php?saint_id=7733.
Gagliarducci, Andrea. "The First Martyr of the Mafia." *National Catholic Register*, May 27, 2013. http://
www.ncregister.com/daily-news/the-first-martyr-of-the-mafia.
Mazurczak, Filip. "The Priest Who Stood Up to Mafia." First Things, May 24, 2013. https://www.firstthings
.com/web-exclusives/2013/05/the-priest-who-stood-up-to-mafia.

JUNE 13 HISTORY ON THE CUTTING ROOM FLOOR
Fernandez de Castro, Rafa. "WATCH: That Time Fidel Castro Acted as an Extra in This Forgettable
Hollywood Flick." Splinter, September 17, 2015. https://splinternews.com/watch-that-time-fidel-castro
-acted-as-an-extra-in-this-1793850983.
Levenda, Peter. *Sinister Forces—The Manson Secret: A Grimoire of American Political Witchcraft*. Walterville,
OR: TrineDay, 2005.
Truthrambler. "Fidel Castro . . . Actor . . . Dead." *The Back Side of Fifty* (blog), November 26, 2016. https://
truthrambler.wordpress.com/2016/11/26/fidel-castro-actor-dead/.
WJY. "Fidel Castro, Movie Star." *Forgotten Hollywood History* (blog), July 5, 2009. http://forgottenhollywood
history.blogspot.com/2009/07/fidel-castro-movie-star.html.

JUNE 14 UNLOCKING THE GIFT OF POTENTIAL
CBN. "Patrick Henry Hughes: Pure Potential." Accessed February 4, 2018. http://www1.cbn.com/700club
/patrick-henry-hughes-pure-potential.
Hayes, Erin. "Blind, Wheelchair-Bound Student Doesn't Fail to Inspire." ABC News, November 10, 2006.
http://abcnews.go.com/WNT/story?id=2643340&page=1.
HuffPost. "Hero Dad Helps Disabled Son, Patrick Hughes, Fulfill His Dreams." March 14, 2012. https://
www.huffingtonpost.com/2012/03/14/hero-dad-helps-disabled-s_n_1344933.html.
Katzman, Christine Ngeo. Review of *I Am Potential*, by Zach Meiners, Bright Light Productions, 2015.
Halftime, December 13, 2015. http://www.halftimemag.com/noteworthy/i-am-potential-movie.html.

JUNE 15 STRAW DOGS
Goodman, David Zelag, Sam Peckinpah, and Gordon M. Williams. *Straw Dogs*. Directed by Sam Peckinpah.
ABC Pictures, 1971.
Wikipedia, s.v. "*Straw Dogs* (1971 film)." Last modified March 18, 2017. https://en.wikipedia.org/wiki
/Straw_Dogs_(1971_film).

JUNE 16 THE ONLY PLACE WITHOUT PREJUDICE
Al Jazeera. "Who Was Bessie Coleman and Why Does She Still Matter?" January 26, 2017. http://www
.aljazeera.com/indepth/features/2017/01/bessie-coleman-matter-170126114158228.html.
England, Charlotte. "Bessie Coleman: First African American Woman to Get International Pilot Licence."
Independent, January 26, 2016. http://www.independent.co.uk/news/world/americas/bessie-coleman-pilot
-first-african-american-woman-google-doodle-international-licence-queen-bess-150-a7547481.html.
Hill, Zahara. "Google Honors Bessie Coleman, America's First Black Female Pilot." HuffPost, January 26,
2017. https://www.huffingtonpost.com/entry/google-honors-bessie-coleman-americas-first-black-female
-pilot_us_588a1765e4b0737fd5cbdba8.
Zarrelli, Natalie. "Meet Bessie Coleman, the First Black Woman to Get a Pilot's License." *Atlas Obscura*,
March 1, 2017. https://www.atlasobscura.com/articles/bessie-coleman-aviator.

JUNE 17 THE BOY THEY CALLED SCARFACE
Chilton, Martin. "Frank Sinatra and His Violent Temper." *Telegraph*, May 14, 2016. http://www.telegraph
.co.uk/music/artists/frank-sinatra-and-his-violent-temper/.
Kaplan, James. *Sinatra: The Chairman*. New York: Doubleday, 2015.
Daily Mail. "'Obsessive Frank Sinatra Took 12 Showers a Day and Always Smelled of Lavender,' Reveals His
Widow." June 3, 2011. http://www.dailymail.co.uk/tvshowbiz/article-1392767/Obsessive-Frank-Sinatra
-took-12-showers-day-smelled-lavender-reveals-widow.html.

JUNE 18 WHEN DEATH BIRTHS A SONG
Bhebe, Enid, and Austin Bhebe. "Precious Lord—Take My Hand." *Enid & Austin Bhebe* (blog), August 10,
2012. https://austinbhebe.wordpress.com/2012/08/10/precious-lord-take-my-hand/.
Hawn, C. Michael. "History of Hymns: 'Precious Lord, Take My Hand.'" Discipleship Ministries. Accessed
January 23, 2018. https://www.umcdiscipleship.org/resources/history-of-hymns-precious-lord-take-my-hand.

Mikkelson, David. "Precious Lord and Tommy Dorsey." Snopes, January 12, 2010. https://www.snopes.com
/music/songs/precious.asp.

JUNE 19 THE SEAMSTRESS
Cope, Dorian. "14th November 1817—The Death of Policarpa Salavarrieta." *On This Diety* (blog). Accessed
January 23, 2018. http://www.onthisdeity.com/14th-november-1817-%E2%80%93-the-death-of
-policarpa-salaverreita/.
Phelan, Jessica. "7 of the Most Amazing Women You've Never Heard Of." Salon, January 20, 2014. Previously
posted in GlobalPost. https://www.salon.com/2014/01/20/7_of_the_most_amazing_women_youve
_never_heard_of_partner/.
Tudobeleza. "Policarpa Salavarrieta—Colombia's 1st Heroine." *Eyes on Columbia* (blog), September 3, 2010.
https://eyesoncolombia.wordpress.com/2010/09/03/policarpa-salavarrieta-colombias-1st-heroine/.

JUNE 20 SYMPHONIES AND PYRAMIDS
Johnson, Paul. *Mozart: A Life*. London: Penguin Books, 2013.
Krystek, Lee. "Khufu's Great Pyramid." Museum of Unnatural Mystery. Accessed March 13, 2017. http://
www.unmuseum.org/kpyramid.htm.
Moore, Charlotte. "The Mystery of Mozart's Burial Uncovered." *Limelight*, July 10, 2013. http://www.lime
lightmagazine.com.au/Article/349569%2Cthe-mystery-of-mozart-s-burial-uncovered.aspx.
Nelson, David. "Mozart's Unmarked Grave." In Mozart's Footsteps, August 16, 2010. http://inmozarts
footsteps.com/122/mozarts-unmarked-grave/.

JUNE 21 WHEN GREATEST ISN'T GOOD ENOUGH
Biography. "Michael Phelps." Updated January 22, 2018. https://www.biography.com/people/michael-phelps
-345192.
Crouse, Karen. "Seeking Answers, Michael Phelps Finds Himself." *New York Times*, June 24, 2016. https://
www.nytimes.com/2016/06/26/sports/olympics/michael-phelps-swimming-rehab.html.
GodUpdates. "Olympic Swimmer Michael Phelps Was on the Verge of Suicide until a Christian Friend
Stepped In." Accessed January 24, 2018. https://www.godupdates.com/olympic-swimmer-michael
-phelps-verge-suicide-christian-friend-saved/.
Neffinger, Veronica. "Did Olympic Swimmer Michael Phelps Give His Life to Christ?" Crosswalk.com,
August 8, 2016. https://www.crosswalk.com/blogs/religion-today-blog/did-olympic-swimmer-michael
-phelps-give-his-life-to-christ.html.
Zaimov, Stoyan. "Olympic Swimming Star Michael Phelps Says Rick Warren's *Purpose Driven Life* Saved
Him from Suicide." *Christian Post*, August 5, 2016. https://www.christianpost.com/news/olympic
-swimming-star-michael-phelps-says-rick-warrens-purpose-driven-life-saved-him-from-suicide-167539/.

JUNE 22 A LONG WALK FROM THE GRAVE
Boyle, Louise. "Woman Who 'Came Back from the Dead' in Car Crash Mistaken Identity Case Weds in the
Church Where Her Funeral Was Held." *Daily Mail*, May 21, 2012. http://www.dailymail.co.uk/news
/article-2147737/Whitney-Cerak-Mistaken-identity-teenager-family-believed-died-car-crash-weds-baby
.html.
Lauer, Matt. "A Twist of Fate." Originally aired on *Dateline NBC*, March 28, 2008. Updated December 26,
2008. http://www.nbcnews.com/id/23849928/ns/dateline_nbc-newsmakers/t/twist-fate/#.WmlD2KinEdU.
Stump, Scott. "Families Bonded over Emotional Mistaken Identity Case Find Strength in Faith." Today,
September 15, 2015. https://www.today.com/parents/families-bonded-over-emotional-mistaken-identity
-case-find-strength-faith-t44121.
Wagner, Meg. "Decade after Funeral, Woman Presumed Dead Talks about Mistaken ID." *New York Daily
News*, April 28, 2016. http://www.nydailynews.com/news/national/decade-funeral-woman-presumed
-dead-talks-mistaken-id-article-1.2617753.

JUNE 23 FAILING FORWARD
Astrum People. "Colonel Harland Sanders Biography: Inspiring History of KFC." Accessed March 13, 2017.
https://astrumpeople.com/colonel-harland-sanders-biography-inspiring-history-of-kfc/.
Whitworth, William. "Kentucky-Fried." *New Yorker*, February 14, 1970. http://www.newyorker.com/magazine
/1970/02/14/kentucky-fried.

JUNE 24 THE MAGNIFICENT FRAUD
Lucado, Max. *The Applause of Heaven*, chap. 13. Nashville: Thomas Nelson, 1999.
History. "The Taj Mahal." Accessed March 13, 2017. http://www.history.com/topics/taj-mahal#.
Daily News and Analysis. "Was Mumtaz Really Buried at Taj Mahal?" August 23, 2007. http://www.dnaindia
.com/india/report-was-mumtaz-really-buried-at-taj-mahal-1117182#.

JUNE 25 THE FORGOTTEN FALLEN

Allen, Thomas B. "Ask MHQ: British Revolutionary War Burials." HistoryNet, November 10, 2014. http://www.historynet.com/ask-mhq-british-revolutionary-war-burials.htm.

Six Foot Three. "Great Britain's War Dead Policy during American Revolutionary War?" City-Data.com, May 29, 2012. http://www.city-data.com/forum/history/1588419-great-britains-war-dead-policy-during.html.

Smith, G. S. "The Lost Troopers Beaufort, SC." Strange History, January 22, 2016. http://www.strange history.org/cms/.

JUNE 26 SERMONS FROM THE CRYPT

Bulfinch, Thomas. *Legends of Charlemagne*. Public domain.

Holloway, April. "1,200-Year-Old Bones Found in Aachen Cathedral in Germany Believed to Belong to Charlemagne, King of the Franks." Ancient Origins, February 1, 2014. http://www.ancient-origins .net/news-history-archaeology/carlemagne-bones-found-aachen-cathedral-germany-believed-10092938.

Lucado, Max. *The Applause of Heaven*, chap. 15. Nashville: Thomas Nelson, 1999.

JUNE 27 THE MOST EXPENSIVE BOOK IN THE WORLD

Bastian, Donald N. "How Much Does a Bible Really Cost?" *Just Call Me Pastor* (blog), November 30, 2015. https://justcallmepastor.wordpress.com/2015/11/30/how-much-does-a-bible-really-cost/.

BBC. "William Tyndale." Accessed January 24, 2018. http://www.bbc.co.uk/history/people/william_tyndale/.

Bos, Carole D. "William Tyndale—Burned for Translating the Bible into English." Awesome Stories. Updated October 6, 2017. https://www.awesomestories.com/asset/view/William-Tyndale-Burned-for-Translating -the-Bible-into-English.

Edwards, Brian H. "Tyndale's Betrayal and Death." Christian History Institute. Accessed January 24, 2018. Previously published in *Christian History*, no. 16 (1987). https://christianhistoryinstitute.org/magazine /article/tyndales-betrayal-and-death/.

JUNE 28 THE OTHER FIRE THAT NIGHT

Estep, Kim. "The Peshtigo Fire." National Weather Service. Accessed January 24, 2018. Reprinted with permission from the *Green Bay Press-Gazette*. https://www.weather.gov/grb/peshtigofire.

Havel, Gregory. "Remembering the Great Peshtigo Fire of 1871." *Fire Engineering*, October 8, 2007. http://www.fireengineering.com/articles/2007/10/remembering-the-great-peshtigo-fire-of-1871.html.

History. "Massive Fire Burns in Wisconsin." Accessed January 24, 2018. http://www.history.com/this-day-in -history/massive-fire-burns-in-wisconsin.

Rosenfeld, Everett. "Top 10 Devastating Wildfires: The Peshtigo Fire, 1871." *Time*, June 8, 2011. http://content.time.com/time/specials/packages/article/0,28804,2076476_2076484_2076503,00.html.

JUNE 29 A FROG WHO MARRIED A QUEEN

Mirror. "Elizabeth Taylor's Former Husband Larry Fortensky Opens Up for the First Time about Their Marriage." Updated February 3, 2012. http://www.mirror.co.uk/3am/celebrity-news/elizabeth-taylors -former-husband-larry-124663.

Graham, Caroline. "She Put on a Fur Coat over Her Nightdress and Fell Giggling in the Snow: Elizabeth Taylor's Builder Ex-Husband on Their Truly Bizarre Marriage." *Daily Mail*, April 23, 2011. http://www .dailymail.co.uk/femail/article-1380014/Elizabeth-Taylors-builder-ex-husband-Larry-Fortensky-bizarre -marriage.html.

JUNE 30 LIFE WITHOUT LIMBS

Attitude is Altitude. Accessed January 24, 2018. https://www.attitudeisaltitude.com/.

James, Susan Donaldson. "*Born without Limbs* Star Inspires with Courage and 'Trust in God.'" Today, June 17, 2015. https://www.today.com/health/born-without-limbs-star-nick-vujicic-lives-courage-t26796.

Life Without Limbs. YouTube channel. Accessed January 24, 2018. https://www.youtube.com/user/Nick VujicicTV.

Nandwani, Harshita. "No Arms, No Legs, No Worries." Achhikhabre, April 28, 2014. http://achhikhabre .com/arms-legs-worries-2/.

JULY 1 THE UNLIKELY LEADER

Hendricks, Howard, and William Hendricks. *As Iron Sharpens Iron*, chap. 4. Chicago: Moody Press, 1995.

Hyde, Douglas. *Dedication and Leadership*. South Bend, IN: University of Notre Dame Press, 1966.

Morgan, Kevin. "Obituary: Douglas Hyde." *Independent*, September 25, 1996. http://www.independent.co .uk/news/people/obituary-douglas-hyde-1365102.html.

JULY 2 THE BEAUTY AND THE BRAINS

Cowan, Lee. "Hedy Lamarr: Movie Star, Inventor of WiFi." CBS News, April 20, 2012. https://www.cbsnews .com/news/hedy-lamarr-movie-star-inventor-of-wifi/.

Greenfield, Rebecca. "Celebrity Invention: Hedy Lamarr's Secret Communications System." *Atlantic*, September 3, 2010. https://www.theatlantic.com/technology/archive/2010/09/celebrity-invention-hedy -lamarrs-secret-communications-system/62377/.

NPR. "'Most Beautiful Woman' by Day, Inventor by Night." *All Things Considered*, November 22, 2011. https://www.npr.org/2011/11/27/142664182/most-beautiful-woman-by-day-inventor-by-night.

Petersen, Anne Helen. "Scandals of Classic Hollywood: The Ecstasy of Hedy Lamarr." The Hairpin, August 8, 2013. https://www.thehairpin.com/2013/08/scandals-of-classic-hollywood-the-ecstasy -of-hedy-lamarr/.

JULY 3 FEATHERS IN THE WIND

This true story is from the author's personal experience. Names, places, and dates have been withheld to protect feelings still raw after several years.

JULY 4 TWO DAYS LATE AND A MONTH SHORT

Bingham, Amy. "Nine Things You Never Knew about the Fourth of July." ABC News, July 4, 2012. http:// abcnews.go.com/Politics/OTUS/things-fourth-july/story?id=16707033.

Handwerk, Brian. "4th of July: Nine Myths Debunked." *National Geographic*, July 4, 2012. https://news .nationalgeographic.com/news/2012/07/120704-4th-of-july-fourth-myths-google-doodle-nation -independence/.

Massachusetts Historical Society. "Letter from John Adams to Abigail Adams, 3 July 1776, 'Had a Declaration . . .'" Adams Family Papers: An Electronic Archive. Accessed January 25, 2018. https://www.masshist.org /digitaladams/archive/doc?id=L17760703jasecond.

Strauss, Valerie. "Why July 2 Is Really America's Independence Day." *Washington Post*, July 2, 2015. https://www.washingtonpost.com/news/answer-sheet/wp/2015/07/02/why-july-2-is-really-americas -independence-day/?utm_term=.850313687663.

JULY 5 THE SILENT HERO

James, Susan Donaldson. "Deciding to Marry a Quadriplegic: Couple Tells Love Story." ABC News, May 30, 2013. http://abcnews.go.com/Health/deciding-marry-quadriplegic-couple-tells-love-story /story?id=19282468.

Sells, Heather. "50 Years Later—Joni Eareckson Tada Talks of On-Going Struggles." CBN News, November 29, 2016. https://www1.cbn.com/cbnnews/us/2016/november/50-years-later-joni-eareckson-tada-talks-of-on -going-struggles.

Tada, Joni Eareckson. "Real Life with Joni and Ken." Focus on the Family. Accessed January 25, 2018. Previously published in *Thriving Family*, January/February 2014. https://www.focusonthefamily.com /marriage/facing-crisis/real-life-with-joni-and-ken.

Tada, Ken. "Caregiving: A Cause for Christ." Ligonier Ministries. Accessed January 25, 2018. Previously published in *Tabletalk* (October 1, 2011). https://www.ligonier.org/learn/articles/caregiving-a-cause -for-christ/.

JULY 6 A TALE OF TWO FAMILIES

Federer, Bill. "Jonathan Edwards v. Max Jukes." The Moral Liberal, October 4, 2011. http://www.themoral liberal.com/2011/10/04/jonathan-edwards-v-max-jukes/.

Fraser, Ryan. "What Legacy Are You Leaving for Your Family?" *Jackson Sun*. Updated October 11, 2014. http://www.jacksonsun.com/story/life/faith/2014/10/10/legacy-leaving-family/17054141/.

Winship, A. E. *Jukes-Edwards: A Study in Education and Heredity*. Reprint of the 1900 Harrisburg, PA, edition, Project Gutenberg, April 14, 2005. http://archive.org/stream/jukesedwards15623gut/15623.txt.

JULY 7 BE CAREFUL LITTLE EYES WHAT YOU SEE

Bundy, Ted. "Fatal Addiction: Ted Bundy's Final Interview." By James Dobson. Focus on the Family video, 32:51. January 23, 1989. http://www.focusonthefamily.com/media/social-issues/fatal-addiction-ted- bundys-final-interview.

Michaud, Stephen G., and Hugh Aynesworth. *Ted Bundy: Conversations with a Killer*. Irving, TX: Authorlink Press, 2000.

Truesdell, Jeff. "Who Was Ted Bundy? A Look at the Serial Killer's Trail of Terror." *People*, May 12, 2016. http://people.com/crime/who-was-ted-bundy-a-look-at-the-serial-killers-trail-of-terror/.

JULY 8 BOOMERANG JUSTICE

Biography. "Pontius Pilate." Updated November 11, 2014. https://www.biography.com/people/pontius -pilate-9440686.

Butcher, Kevin. "The Strange Afterlife of Pontius Pilate." *History Today*, March 25, 2016. http://www .historytoday.com/kevin-butcher/strange-afterlife-pontius-pilate.

Jackson, Wayne. "The Tragedy of Pontius Pilate." *Christian Courier*. Accessed January 26, 2018. https://www.christiancourier.com/articles/549-tragedy-of-pontius-pilate-the.

Knight, Kevin. "The Death of Pilate." New Advent. Accessed January 26, 2018. Based on *Ante-Nicene Fathers*, vol. 8. Translated by Alexander Walker. Buffalo, NY: Christian Literature Publishing, 1886. http://www.newadvent.org/fathers/0812.htm.

JULY 9 THE REAL WONDER WOMAN

Atoke. "BN Our Stories, Our Miracles: A Tragic Plane Crash, over 75 Surgeries Later, Kechi Okwuchi is the Beautiful Personification of Faith & Strength." Bella Naija, June 11, 2012. https://www.bellanaija.com/2012/11/bn-our-stories-our-miracles-a-tragic-plane-crash-over-75-surgeries-later-kechi-okwuchi-is-the-beautiful-personification-of-faith-strength/.

Guerra, Joey. "Plane Crash Survivor and Pearland Resident Kechi Okwuchi Wows *America's Got Talent* Judges." Chron, June 14, 2017. http://www.chron.com/entertainment/tv/article/Plane-crash-survivor-and-Houston-resident-Kechi-11217910.php.

Orubo, Daniel. "Kechi Okwuchi Is the Real Life Wonder Woman We Need Right Now." Konbini, June 14, 2017. http://www.konbini.com/ng/inspiration/kechi-okwuchi-is-the-real-life-wonder-woman-we-need-right-now/.

Weigle, Lauren. "Kechi Okwuchi—*America's Got Talent* Contestant Who Almost Died in a Plane Crash." Heavy, June 13, 2017. https://heavy.com/entertainment/2017/06/kechi-okwuchi-americas-got-talent-contestant-died-singer-plane-crash-before-and-after-flight-agt-deaths/.

JULY 10 CHRISTIANITY IN SHOE LEATHER

Dorsett, Lyle W. *A Passion for Souls: The Life of D. L. Moody*. Chicago: Moody Press, 1997.

Lutzer, Erwin. "D. L. Moody: An Unlikely Servant." *Moody Church Media*. Sermon preached January 19, 2014.

M'Millen, Thomas. "Abraham Lincoln Visits Moody's Sunday School." *Moody Church Herald*, December 1, 1908. Reproduced at The Moody Church. "Abraham Lincoln Visits Moody's Sunday School—Church History." Accessed March 12, 2017. http://www.moodychurch.org/150/teachings/abraham-lincoln-visits-moodys-sunday-school/.

Severance, Diane, and Dan Graves. "Dwight L. Moody Was Converted." Christianity.com. Last updated June 2007. http://www.christianity.com/timeline/1801-1900/dwight-l-moody-was-converted-11630499.html.

JULY 11 THE DANGLING TELEPHONE

Evans, Peter. "Marilyn Monroe's Last Weekend." *Daily Mail*. Updated August 2, 2010. http://www.dailymail.co.uk/femail/article-1299496/Marilyn-Monroes-weekend--told-time-eyewitnesss-account-row-Frank-Sinatra-friends-fear-signed-death-warrant.html.

John, Elton. "Candle in the Wind." *Goodbye Yellow Brick Road*. MCA Records, 1973.

Kashner, Sam. "Marilyn and Her Monsters." *Vanity Fair*, November 2010. http://www.vanityfair.com/culture/2010/11/marilyn-monroe-201011.

Luce, Clare Boothe. "What Really Killed Marilyn." *LIFE*, August 7, 1964.

JULY 12 OFF SCREEN

Chandler, Charlotte. "Daughter Dearest." *Vanity Fair*, February 8, 2008. https://www.vanityfair.com/news/2008/03/crawford200803.

Day, Elizabeth. "I'll Never Forgive Mommie." *Guardian*, May 24, 2008. https://www.theguardian.com/film/2008/may/25/biography.film.

Hartinger, Brent. "Review: A New Biography of Joan Crawford Claims *Mommie Dearest* Was Mostly a Lie." Logo, November 18, 2010. http://www.newnownext.com/review-a-new-biography-of-joan-crawford-claims-mommie-dearest-was-mostly-a-lie/11/2010/.

Schulman, Michael. "Surviving *Mommie Dearest*." *New Yorker*, May 10, 2013. https://www.newyorker.com/culture/culture-desk/surviving-mommie-dearest.

JULY 13 THE SECRET NO ONE KNEW

Gorman, Ashley. "The Tragedy of Robin Williams: Raising Awareness about Lewy Body Dementia." Morris Psychological Group, October 11, 2016. http://morrispsych.com/the-tragedy-of-robin-williams-raising-awareness-about-lewy-body-dementia-by-dr-ashley-gorman/.

Macatee, Rebecca. "Robin Williams: Look Back at His Life, Legacy and Career on the 1-Year Anniversary of His Tragic Death." E! News, August 11, 2015. http://www.eonline.com/news/684826/robin-williams-look-back-at-his-life-legacy-and-career-on-the-1-year-anniversary-of-his-tragic-death.

Smith, Nigel M. "Robin Williams' Widow: 'It Was Not Depression' That Killed Him." *Guardian*, November 3, 2015. https://www.theguardian.com/film/2015/nov/03/robin-williams-disintegrating-before-suicide-widow-says.

Youn, Soo. "Robin Williams: Autopsy Confirms Death by Suicide." *Hollywood Reporter*, November 7, 2014. https://www.hollywoodreporter.com/news/robin-williams-autopsy-confirms-death-746194.

JULY 14 THE FOLLY OF UNNECESSARY BATTLES
HistoryNet. "Battle of Gettysburg." Accessed March 12, 2017. http://www.historynet.com/battle-of -gettysburg.
Shaara, Michael. *The Killer Angels*. New York: David McKay Publications, 1974.
Tzu, Sun. *The Art of War*. Public domain.

JULY 15 THE SON FOR A SON
This story is adapted from Matthew 27:15-26; Mark 15:6-15; Luke 23:18-24; and John 18:40.
Johnson, S. Lewis. "Barabbas, the Man for Whom Christ Died." SLJ Institute. Accessed January 27, 2018. http://sljinstitute.net/featured/barabbas-the-man-for-whom-christ-died-matthew/.
Mathis, David. "Barabbas and Me." Desiring God, April 5, 2012. https://www.desiringgod.org/articles /barabbas-and-me.
Sumner, Paul. "Yeshua bar Abba." Hebrew Streams. Accessed January 27, 2018. http://www.hebrew-streams .org/works/ntstudies/yeshua-bar-abba.html.

JULY 16 THE LOST CITY OF EL DORADO
Berman, Eliza. "The True Story behind *The Lost City of Z*." *Time*, April 14, 2017. http://time.com/4735505 /the-lost-city-of-z-true-story/.
Grann, David. "*The Lost City of Z*: A Quest to Uncover the Secrets of the Amazon." *New Yorker*, September 19, 2005. https://www.newyorker.com/magazine/2005/09/19/the-lost-city-of-z.
———. *The Lost City of Z*, 1–36. New York: Vintage Books, 2010.
Rogers, S. A. "El Dorado? Lost City Found Using Google Earth." Mother Nature Network, January 19, 2010. https://www.mnn.com/green-tech/research-innovations/stories/el-dorado-lost-city-found-using -google-earth.

JULY 17 FROM AFRICA WITH LOVE
PBS. "The Queen of Sheba." *In Search of Myths and Heroes*. Accessed March 12, 2017. http://www.pbs.org /mythsandheroes/myths_four_sheba.html.
Women in the Bible. "The Queen of Sheba, Bible Woman." Accessed March 12, 2017. http://www.women inthebible.net/women-bible-old-new-testaments/queen-of-sheba/.

JULY 18 THE POWER OF A SINGLE SUPPER
Biography. "Jefferson Davis." Updated December 21, 2017. https://www.biography.com/people/jefferson -davis-9267899.
Davis, Varina. *Jefferson Davis: Ex-President of the Confederate States of America, a Memoir by His Wife*, vol. 2, chap. 71. Perseus Digital Library. Accessed January 27, 2018. http://www.perseus.tufts.edu/hopper/text? doc=Perseus%3Atext%3A2001.05.0038%3Achapter%3D71.
Flook, Daniel James. "Jefferson Davis's Imprisonment." Encyclopedia Virginia, March 9, 2010. https://www .encyclopediavirginia.org/jefferson_davis_s_imprisonment.
Methodist Review. "Religious Life of Jefferson Davis." Vol. 59 (1910): 334–42.

JULY 19 A VICTORY IN DEFEAT
Frye, David. "Greco-Persian Wars: Battle of Thermopylae." HistoryNet, June 12, 2006. http://www.history net.com/greco-persian-wars-battle-of-thermopylae.htm.
Herodotus. *The History of Herodotus*. Translated by George Rawlinson. Vol. 4, bk. 7. New York: D. Appleman, 1885. http://www.shsu.edu/~his_ncp/herother.html.

JULY 20 SKIING TO THE NORTH POLE
Collins, Lauren. "Top of the World." *New Yorker*, May 28, 2007. https://www.newyorker.com/magazine /2007/05/28/top-of-the-world.
Knapp, Sarah. "Barbara Hillary: Our Favorite Boundary Breaker." *Co-op Journal* (blog). REI Co-op. Accessed January 27, 2018. https://www.rei.com/blog/hike/barbara-hillary-favorite-boundary-breaker.
Pitts, Vanessa. "Hillary, Barbara (1931–)." BlackPast.org. Accessed January 27, 2018. http://www.blackpast .org/aah/hillary-barbara-1931.

JULY 21 THE LEPER WHO BECAME A SAINT
Catholic Online. "St. Damien of Molokai." Accessed March 12, 2017. http://www.catholic.org/saints/saint .php?saint_id=2817&+angels.
Senthilingam, Meera. "Taken from Their Families: The Dark History of Hawaii's Leprosy Colony." CNN, September 9, 2015. http://www.cnn.com/2015/09/09/health/leprosy-kalaupapa-hawaii/index.html.

JULY 22 TOO SMART TO BE PRESIDENT

History. "Albert Einstein: Fact or Fiction?" Accessed January 27, 2018. http://www.history.com/topics /einsteins-life-facts-and-fiction.

Lorenz, Jonna. "Albert Einstein, Israel President? Why Theoretical Physicist Turned Down Offer to Serve." Newsmax, December 14, 2014. https://www.newsmax.com/fastfeatures/albert-einstein-israel-president /2014/12/14/id/612969/.

Jewish Virtual Library. "Israel Modern History: Offering the Presidency of Israel to Albert Einstein." Accessed January 27, 2018. http://www.jewishvirtuallibrary.org/offering-the-presidency-of-israel-to -albert-einstein.

JULY 23 THE GODFATHER AND THE PRIEST

Curtis, Ken. "Savonarola's Preaching Got Him Burned—1498." Christianity.com. Accessed March 12, 2017. http://www.christianity.com/church/church-history/timeline/1201-1500/savonarolas-preaching-got-him -burned-1498-11632689.html.

Herbermann, Charles George, Edward A. Pace, Condé B. Pallen, Thomas J. Shahan, and John J. Wynne. *The Catholic Encyclopedia*, 13:190–92. New York: Encyclopedia Press, 1913.

Horsburgh, Edward Lee Stuart. *Lorenzo the Magnificent, and Florence in Her Golden Age*. London: Methuen, 1908.

Martines, Lauro. *Fire in the City: Savonarola and the Struggle for the Soul of Renaissance Florence*. Oxford: Oxford University Press, 2006.

JULY 24 THE WIDOW WHO LAUNDERED A FORTUNE

Bates, Daniel. "Exclusive: How McDonald's 'Founder' Cheated the Brothers Who REALLY Started Empire out of Hundreds of Millions, Wrote Them out of Company History—and Left One to Die of Heart Failure and the Other Barely a Millionaire." *Daily Mail*, May 5, 2015. http://www.dailymail.co.uk/news /article-3049644/How-McDonald-s-founder-cheated-brothers-REALLY-started-empire-300m-wrote -company-history-left-one-die-heart-failure-barely-millionaire.html.

Madhusoodanan, Sriram. "*The Founder* Reveals the Real Ray Kroc—but Not the Rest of the McDonald's Story." *Entrepreneur*, February 2, 2017. https://www.entrepreneur.com/article/288611.

Napoli, Lisa. "Meet the Woman Who Gave Away the McDonald's Founder's Fortune." *Time*, December 22, 2016. http://time.com/4616956/mcdonalds-founder-ray-kroc-joan-kroc/.

———. "*Ray and Joan* Chronicles Complex Life of Kroc's Philanthropic Wife." Interview by Scott Simon. *Weekend Edition Saturday*. NPR, November 19, 2016. https://www.npr.org/2016/11/19/502685423 /-ray-and-joan-chronicles-complicated-life-of-a-philanthropist-who-gave-away-mcdo.

JULY 25 THE UNWANTED BOY

Craddock, Fred B. *Craddock Stories*. Edited by Mike Graves and Richard F. Ward. St. Louis, MO: Chalice Press, 2001.

Hooper, Ben W. *Unwanted Boy: The Autobiography of Governor Ben W. Hooper*. Edited by Everett R. Boyce. Knoxville, TN: University of Tennessee Press, 1963.

Neely, Kirk H. "The Story of Ben Hooper." *Kirk H. Neely* (blog), June 8, 2009. https://kirkhneely.com/2009 /06/08/the-story-of-ben-hooper/.

JULY 26 PACO'S PAPA

Elder, Robert K., Aaron Vetch, and Mark Cirino. *Hidden Hemingway: Inside the Ernest Hemingway Archives of Oak Park*. Kent, OH: Kent State University Press, 2016.

Hemingway, Ernest. "The Capital of the World." In *The Fifth Column and the First Forty-Nine Stories*, chap. 2. New York: Scribner, 1938.

The Hemingway Resource Center. "Ernest Hemingway Biography." Accessed March 12, 2017. http://www .lostgeneration.com/.

Johnson, Paul. "Hemingway: Portrait of the Artist as an Intellectual." *Commentary*, February 1, 1989. https:// www.commentarymagazine.com/articles/hemingway-portrait-of-the-artist-as-an-intellectual/.

JULY 27 THE FILM NO ONE WANTED TO MAKE

Acuna, Kirsten. "George Lucas Recounts How Studios Turned Down *Star Wars* in Classic Interview." Business Insider, February 6, 2014. http://www.businessinsider.com/george-lucas-interview-recalls -studios-that-turned-down-movie-star-wars-2014-2.

Beggs, Scott. "How *Star Wars* Began: As an Indie Film No Studio Wanted to Make." *Vanity Fair*, December 18, 2015. https://www.vanityfair.com/hollywood/2015/12/star-wars-george-lucas-independent-film.

Myint, B. "George Lucas and the Origin Story behind *Star Wars*." Biography, December 16, 2015. https:// www.biography.com/news/george-lucas-star-wars-facts.

Smyth, Steve. Comment on "What Ever Happened to the Studio Executives That Turned Down the Original *Star Wars*?" Quora.com. Updated December 1, 2015. https://www.quora.com/What-ever -happened-to-the-studio-executives-that-turned-down-the-original-Star-Wars.

JULY 28 THE KING OF THE MOUNTAIN

Keith, Ted. "SI 60 Q&A: Gary Smith on Muhammad Ali, His Entourage and Memories of the Greatest." *Sports Illustrated*, October 14, 2014. http://www.si.com/boxing/2014/10/14/si-60-qa-gary-smith -muhammad-ali-entourage.

Lucado, Max. *The Applause of Heaven*, chap. 15. Nashville: Thomas Nelson, 1999.

JULY 29 WHEN WICKEDNESS PROSPERS

This story is adapted from Genesis 12–21.

Klein, Julia M. "Why Scholars Just Can't Stop Talking about Sarah and Hagar." *U.S. News*, January 25, 2008. https://www.usnews.com/news/religion/articles/2008/01/25/why-scholars-just-cant-stop-talking -about-sarah-and-hagar.

Siddiqui, Mona. "Ibrahim—The Muslim View of Abraham." BBC, September 4, 2009. http://www.bbc.co .uk/religion/religions/islam/history/ibrahim.shtml.

JULY 30 THE MAN WHO WAS BIGGER THAN GOD

Barlett, Donald L., and James B. Steele. *Howard Hughes: His Life and Madness*. New York: W. W. Norton, 2004.

Higham, Charles. *Howard Hughes: The Secret Life*. New York: St. Martin's Griffin, 2004.

Knight, Peter, ed. *Conspiracy Theories in America: An Encyclopedia*, 1:328–30. Santa Barbara, CA: ABC-CLIO, 2003.

JULY 31 UNIT 731

New York Times. "The Crimes of Unit 731." March 18, 1995. http://www.nytimes.com/1995/03/18/opinion /the-crimes-of-unit-731.html.

Rindskopf, Jeffrey. "Unit 731: The Horrors of the 'Asian Auschwitz' and Why You've Never Heard of It." First to Know, May 20, 2016. https://firsttoknow.com/unit-731-horrors-asian-auschwitz-youve-never -heard/.

Tatlow, Didi Kirsten. "A New Look at Japan's Wartime Atrocities and a U.S. Cover-up." *Sinosphere* (blog). *New York Times*, October 21, 2015. https://sinosphere.blogs.nytimes.com/2015/10/21/china-unit-731 -japan-war-crimes-biological/.

Winikoff, Janet. "Unit 731—A U.S. Cover-up of Cruelty." The Constantine Report, February 8, 2012. https://www.constantinereport.com/unit-731-a-u-s-cover-up-of-cruelty/.

AUGUST 1 THE CINDERELLA MAN

Huntington, Brennan. *Cinderella Man: Jim Braddock—The Real Story*. Directed by Brian Gillogly and John Preston. National Geographic Documentary, 2005. See "Cinderella Man—The Real Jim Braddock Story." YouTube video, 49:35. Posted by "ibhof2," March 7, 2012. https://www.youtube.com/watch?v =Bl6ER5pwOkU.

Schaap, Jeremy. *Cinderella Man: James J. Braddock, Max Baer, and the Greatest Upset in Boxing History*. New York: Houghton Mifflin Harcourt, 2005.

AUGUST 2 THE LAST LECTURE

Martin, Douglas. "Randy Pausch, 47, Dies; His 'Last Lecture' Inspired Many to Live with Wonder." *New York Times*, July 26, 2008. http://www.nytimes.com/2008/07/26/us/26pausch.html.

Martz, Geoff, Samantha Wender, and Chris Francescani. "Randy Pausch, 'Last Lecture' Professor Dies." ABC News, July 25, 2008. http://abcnews.go.com/GMA/randy-pausch-lecture-professor-dies/story?id =4614281.

"Randy Pausch Last Lecture: Achieving Your Childhood Dreams." YouTube video, 1:16:26. Posted by Carnegie Mellon University, December 20, 2007. https://www.youtube.com/watch?v=ji5_MqicxSo.

Walker, Tim. "Randy Pausch: The Dying Man Who Taught America How to Live." *Independent*, March 25, 2008. http://www.independent.co.uk/news/people/profiles/randy-pausch-the-dying-man-who-taught -america-how-to-live-800182.html.

AUGUST 3 LITTLE HERBIE STEALS A QUARTER

Krebs, Brock. *Leap into History: John Dillinger in Delaware County, Indiana*. BookBaby, 2015.

Matera, Dary. *John Dillinger: The Life and Death of America's First Celebrity Criminal*. New York: Carroll & Graf, 2004.

Peters, Robert. *What Dillinger Meant to Me*. New York: Sea Horse Press, 1983.

AUGUST 4 THE DISABILITY THAT SET A WORLD RECORD

Longman, Jeré. "Blurry Target Is No Trouble for Ace Archer." *New York Times*, July 28, 2012. http://www
.nytimes.com/2012/07/29/sports/olympics/with-impaired-vision-blurry-target-is-no-trouble-for-south
-korean-archer.html.

Pickup, Oliver. "London 2012 Olympics: Legally Blind South Korean Archer Im Dong-Hyun Eyes Gold
Medal at the Games." *Telegraph*, July 26, 2012. http://www.telegraph.co.uk/sport/olympics/archery
/9428260/London-2012-Olympics-legally-blind-South-Korean-archer-Im-Dong-Hyun-eyes-gold-medal
-at-the-Games.html.

The Week. "How Did a Blind Archer Set a World Record at the Olympics?" July 27, 2012. http://theweek
.com/articles/473520/how-did-blind-archer-set-world-record-olympics.

AUGUST 5 THE MONSTER IN THE MONK

Biography. "Ivan the Terrible." Updated April 27, 2017. https://www.biography.com/people/ivan-the-terrible
-9350679.

Bos, Carole D. "Ivan the Terrible and His Secret Police." Awesome Stories. Updated November 5, 2016.
https://www.awesomestories.com/asset/view/Ivan-the-Terrible-and-His-Secret-Police.

Orthodox Church in America. "Hieromartyr Philip the Metropolitan of Moscow and All Russia." Accessed
January 28, 2018. https://oca.org/saints/lives/2001/01/09/100135-hieromartyr-philip-the-metropolitan
-of-moscow-and-all-russia.

Seifi, Philip. "10 Things You Never Knew about Ivan the Terrible." *Lingualift* (blog). Accessed January 28,
2018. https://www.lingualift.com/blog/ivan-the-terrible/.

AUGUST 6 A LIFELINE FROM THE ASYLUM

Kauffman, Barry. "The Love of God." *Hymns with a Message* (blog), January 13, 2011. http://barryshymns
.blogspot.com/2011/01/love-of-god.html.

Ruffin, Mike. "Verse of Favorite Hymn Found on Wall in Insane Asylum." *Devotions* (blog), February 22,
2003. http://www.devotions.com/2003/02/verse-of-favorite-hymn-found-on-wall-in-insane-asylum.html
#respond.

AUGUST 7 THE MAN WHO KNEW INFINITY

Biography. "Srinivasa Ramanujan." Updated September 10, 2015. https://www.biography.com/people
/srinivasa-ramanujan-082515.

Ellis, Ian. "The Mystery of Srinivasa Ramanujan's Illness." Today in Science History. Accessed January 28,
2018. https://todayinsci.com/R/Ramanujan_Srinivasa/RamanujanSrinivasa-IllnessMystery.htm.

Rao, K. Srinivasa. "Srinivasa Ramanujan—From Kumbakonam to Cambridge." *Asia Pacific Mathematics
Newsletter* 7, no. 1 (2017). http://www.asiapacific-mathnews.com/01/0102/0001_0007.html.

Valiant Woman in Training. "Ramanujan's Wife." *The Valiant Woman Project* (blog), September 8, 2016.
http://valiantwomanproject.blogspot.com/2016/09/ramanujans-wife_8.html.

AUGUST 8 KISSING THE BEGGAR'S LIPS

Acocella, Joan. "Rich Man, Poor Man: The Radical Visions of St. Francis." *New Yorker*, January 14, 2013.

Englebert, Omer. *St. Francis of Assisi: A Biography*. Cincinnati, OH: Franciscan Media, 2013.

Sweeney, Jon M. "The Real Francis: How One Saint's Ancient Insights Are Transforming Today's Church."
America Magazine, September 22, 2014. http://www.americamagazine.org/issue/real-francis.

AUGUST 9 WRIGHT-MARE IN WISCONSIN

Conradt, Stacy. "The Terrible Crime at Frank Lloyd Wright's Taliesin." Mental Floss, December 5, 2017.
http://us2.mentalfloss.com/article/28519/taliesin-tragedy.

Klein, Christopher. "The Massacre at Frank Lloyd Wright's 'Love Cottage.'" History, June 8, 2017. http://
www.history.com/news/the-massacre-at-frank-lloyd-wrights-love-cottage.

New York Times. "Frank Lloyd Wright Dies; Famed Architect Was 89." On This Day: April 10, 1959. Accessed
January 28, 2018. http://www.nytimes.com/learning/general/onthisday/bday/0608.html.

Stamberg, Susan. "Novel Sheds Light on Frank Lloyd Wright's Mistress." *Morning Edition*. NPR, August 7,
2007. https://www.npr.org/templates/story/story.php?storyId=12536605.

AUGUST 10 THE PRICE WE PAY FOR LOVE

Lewis, C. S. *A Grief Observed*. San Francisco: Harper & Row, 1961.

Sibley, Brian. *Through the Shadowlands: The Love Story of C. S. Lewis and Joy Davidman*. Grand Rapids, MI:
Revell, 2005.

AUGUST 11 VICTORIA'S SECRET

Greene, Mary. "Victoria's Secret Crush: How Queen Fell Under the Spell of Indian Servant after Death of
Ghillie Companion John Brown." *Daily Mail*, April 20, 2012. http://www.dailymail.co.uk/news/article
-2132054/Queen-Victoria-Abdul-Karim-After-John-Browns-death-Queen-fell-Indian-servant.html.

Lawson, Alastair. "Queen Victoria and Abdul: Diaries Reveal Secrets." BBC News, March 14, 2011. http://
www.bbc.com/news/world-south-asia-12670110.

Leach, Ben. "The Lost Diary of Queen Victoria's Final Companion." *Telegraph*, February 26, 2011. http://
www.telegraph.co.uk/news/uknews/theroyalfamily/8349760/The-lost-diary-of-Queen-Victorias-final
-companion.html.

Sanghani, Radhika. "How I Uncovered the Hidden Friendship between Queen Victoria and Her Indian
Servant Abdul." *Telegraph*, July 22, 2017. http://www.telegraph.co.uk/women/life/uncovered-hidden
-friendship-queen-victoria-indian-servant-abdul/.

AUGUST 12 WANDERING TO GLORY

AD2000. "John Bradburne: Zimbabwe Martyr and Lepers' Friend." Vol. 13, no. 6 (July 2000). http://www
.ad2000.com.au/john_bradburne_zimbabwe_martyr_and_lepers_friend_july_2000.

Dove, John. *Strange Vagabond of God: The Story of John Bradburne*. Dublin: Ward River Press, 1983.

Howse, Christopher. "Sacred Mysteries: How John Bradburne's Life of Failure Made Him a Saint." *Telegraph*,
July 23, 2017. http://www.telegraph.co.uk/opinion/2017/07/23/sacred-mysterieshow-john-bradburnes
-life-failure-made-saint/.

Moore, Charles. "John Bradburne: A Martyr Who Turned Love into the Divine." *Telegraph*, September 14,
2009. http://www.telegraph.co.uk/comment/columnists/charlesmoore/6189629/John-Bradburne-a
-martyr-who-turned-love-into-the-divine.html.

AUGUST 13 THE BROKEN HARPSICHORD

Lucado, Max. *When God Whispers Your Name*. Dallas: Word, 1994.

Morris, Edmund. *Beethoven: The Universal Composer*. New York: HarperCollins, 2005.

AUGUST 14 HISTORY'S FORGOTTEN HALF

Dvorak, Petula. "This Woman's Name Appears on the Declaration of Independence. So Why Don't We
Know Her Story?" *Washington Post*, July 3, 2017. https://www.washingtonpost.com/local/this-womans
-name-appears-on-the-declaration-of-independence-so-why-dont-we-know-her-story/2017/07/03
/ce86bf2e-5ff1-11e7-84a1-a26b75ad39fe_story.html?utm_term=.ed38f8ffbcbe.

———. "History's 'Unknown Woman.' Few Cared Who She Was or What She Accomplished." *Washington
Post*, July 20, 2017. https://www.washingtonpost.com/local/historys-unknown-woman-few-cared-who
-she-was-or-what-she-accomplished/2017/07/20/3868c52c-6d62-11e7-96ab-5f38140b38cc_story.html
?utm_term=.31f8137d5a30.

George, Christopher T. "Mary Katherine Goddard and Freedom of the Press." BaltimoreMD.com. Accessed
January 28, 2018. http://www.baltimoremd.com/monuments/goddard.html.

History. "Patriot Printer, Publisher and Postmistress, Mary Katharine Goddard Born." This Day in History:
June 16, 1738. Accessed January 28, 2018. http://www.history.com/this-day-in-history/patriot-printer
-publisher-and-postmistress-mary-katharine-goddard-born.

AUGUST 15 THE MONSTER FROM MILWAUKEE

Ratcliff, Roy, with Lindy Adams. *Dark Journey Deep Grace: Jeffrey Dahmer's Story of Faith*. Siloam Springs,
AR: Leafwood Publishers, 2006.

Ross, Bobby, Jr. "Inside Story: Did 'Jailhouse Religion' Save Jeffrey Dahmer?" *Christian Chronicle* (August
2010). http://www.christianchronicle.org/article/did-jailhouse-religion-save-jeffrey-dahmer.

Terry, Don. "Jeffrey Dahmer, Multiple Killer, Is Bludgeoned to Death in Prison." *New York Times*, November 29,
1994. http://www.nytimes.com/1994/11/29/us/jeffrey-dahmer-multiple-killer-is-bludgeoned-to-death-in
-prison.html.

AUGUST 16 TRUTH AND ITS CONSEQUENCES

Associated Press. "Guatemala Frees Colonel Accused of Killing Bishop Juan Jose Gerardi." *Washington Times*,
July 15, 2012. https://www.washingtontimes.com/news/2012/jul/15/guatemala-frees-colonel-accused
-of-slaying-bishop/.

Curiel, Carolyn. "Murder in Guatemala." Review of *The Art of Political Murder*, by Francisco Goldman. *New
York Times*, September 30, 2007. http://www.nytimes.com/2007/09/30/books/review/Curiel-t.html.

Guatemala Human Rights Commission. "Assassination of Bishop Gerardi." Accessed February 3, 2018.
http://www.ghrc-usa.org/our-work/important-cases/assassination-of-bishop-gerardi/.

Rohter, Larry. "Bishop's Death Shakes Hopes for Guatemala Peace." *New York Times*, May 9, 1998. http://
www.nytimes.com/1998/05/09/world/bishop-s-death-shakes-hopes-for-guatemala-peace.html.

AUGUST 17 THE MIDNIGHT RIDE

DeBenedette, Valerie. "The 16-Year-Old Revolutionary Who Outrode Paul Revere." Mental Floss, April 18,
2016. http://mentalfloss.com/article/78686/16-year-old-revolutionary-who-outrode-paul-revere.

Michals, Debra, ed. "Sybil Ludington." National Women's History Museum, 2017. https://www.nwhm.org
/education-resources/biographies/sybil-ludington.

Pavao, Paul, Janelle Whitelocke, and Esther Pavao. "Sybil Ludington." Revolutionary-War.net. Accessed
February 3, 2018. https://www.revolutionary-war.net/sybil-ludington.html.

AUGUST 18 GEORGE WASHINGTON'S LIAR

Creighton, Linda L. "Benedict Arnold: A Traitor, but Once a Patriot." *U.S. News*, June 27, 2008. https://
www.usnews.com/news/national/articles/2008/06/27/benedict-arnold-a-traitor-but-once-a-patriot.

Palmer, Dave Richard. *George Washington and Benedict Arnold: A Tale of Two Patriots*. Washington, DC:
Regnery, 2006.

Philbrick, Nathaniel. "Why Benedict Arnold Turned Traitor against the American Revolution." *Smithsonian*,
May 2016. http://www.smithsonianmag.com/history/benedict-arnold-turned-traitor-american
-revolution-180958786/.

AUGUST 19 FLYING WITHOUT WINGS

Dei, Nicole. "Born without Arms, Record-Setting Pilot Jessica Cox Inspires: 'I Don't Give Up.'" Today,
July 2, 2015. https://www.today.com/money/born-without-arms-jessica-cox-sets-guinness-pilot-record
-t29936.

Dioquino, Rose-An Jessica. "Armless Fil-Am Woman Pilot Jessica Cox Afraid of Flying?" GMA News
Online, November 4, 2011. http://www.gmanetwork.com/news/news/pinoyabroad/237511/armless-fil
-am-woman-pilot-jessica-cox-afraid-of-flying/story/.

Dunn, James. "Woman Born without Arms Became a Martial Arts Expert, Learned to Fly, Drive, and Even
Play PIANO with Her Feet." *Daily Mail*, June 29, 2015. http://www.dailymail.co.uk/news/article
-3143119/Arizona-Woman-Jessica-Cox-born-without-arms-learnt-fly-feet.html.

Gandhi, Lakshmi. "Disability Activist, Pilot Jessica Cox Shares Story in *Right Footed* Documentary." NBC
News, May 18, 2017. https://www.nbcnews.com/news/asian-america/disability-activist-pilot-jessica-cox
-shares-her-story-right-footed-n761186.

AUGUST 20 THE SHIP THAT GOD COULDN'T SINK

History. "Titanic." Accessed March 11, 2017. http://www.history.com/topics/titanic.

Jeffress, Robert. *Not All Roads Lead to Heaven*, chap. 6. Grand Rapids, MI: Baker, 2016.

Mendelsohn, Daniel. "Unsinkable: Why We Can't Let Go of the Titanic." *New Yorker*, April 16, 2012.
http://www.newyorker.com/magazine/2012/04/16/unsinkable-3.

AUGUST 21 LETTERS FROM LIZZIE

Baylor University. "The Browning Letters." Digital Collections. Accessed March 11, 2017. http://digital
collections.baylor.edu/cdm/landingpage/collection/ab-letters.

King, Steve. "The Brownings: 'Dared and Done.'" Today in Literature. Accessed March 11, 2017. http://
www.todayinliterature.com/stories.asp?Event_Date=9/12/1846.

Markus, Julia. *Dared and Done: The Marriage of Elizabeth Barrett and Robert Browning*. New York: Knopf,
1995.

AUGUST 22 THE KINGDOM BUILT ON FAILURE

Byrd, Ian A. "The Surprising Financial Failures of Walt Disney." Byrdseed. Accessed February 3, 2018.
http://www.byrdseed.com/the-surprising-financial-failures-of-walt-disney/.

Kober, Jeff. "Of Failure and Success: The Journey of Walt Disney." MousePlanet, August 26, 2010. https://
www.mouseplanet.com/9365/Of_Failure_and_Success_The_Journey_of_Walt_Disney.

Reed, Lawrence W. "Failure Made Disney Great." Foundation for Economic Education, April 15, 2016.
https://fee.org/articles/failure-made-disney-great/.

Schochet, Stephen. "Walt Disney's Failures Could Inspire Entrepreneurs." Hollywood Stories. Accessed
February 3, 2018. http://www.hollywoodstories.com/pages/disney/d3.html.

AUGUST 23 THE GOOSE FROM GOOSE TOWN

Christianity Today. "John Huss." Accessed March 11, 2017. http://www.christianitytoday.com/history/people
/martyrs/john-huss.html.

Poggius the Papist. *Hus the Heretic*. Ithaca, MI: AB Publishing, 1997.

Schaff, David S. *John Huss: His Life, Teachings and Death after 500 Years*. Eugene, OR: Wipf and Stock, 2001.

AUGUST 24 THE PARTING SHOT

FlameHorse. "9 Last Official Shots of Wars." Listverse, July 1, 2013. https://listverse.com/2013/07/01/9-last
-official-shots-of-wars/.

Hattem, Michael D. "The Story of 'Evacuation Day.'" *The Junto* (blog), November 25, 2014. https://early
americanists.com/2014/11/25/the-story-of-evacuation-day/.

Roberts, Sam. "Celebrating 225 Years Since the British Left Town." *New York Times*, November 25, 2008. https://cityroom.blogs.nytimes.com/2008/11/25/celebrating-225-years-since-the-british-left-town/.

AUGUST 25 SEEING WITH EARS

Capretto, Lisa. "A Touching Update on the Blind Boy Who Could 'See' with Sound." HuffPost, April 13, 2016. https://www.huffingtonpost.com/entry/blind-ben-underwood-update_us_570d729fe4b0ffa5937d6926.

Cruz, Stefanie. "Elk Grove Blind Teen Who Used Sound to See: 5 Years Later." FOX40. Updated May 3, 2014. http://fox40.com/2014/05/02/elk-grove-blind-teen-who-saw-without-eyes-5-years-later/.

Jewell, Hannah. "Even after His Death, This Incredible Blind Teenager Continues to Inspire People." BuzzFeed, September 5, 2014. https://www.buzzfeed.com/hannahjewell/this-blind-teenager-could-see-using-sound?utm_term=.acXZQYJ7Ek#.ruY1Y7Pl5v.

People. "The Boy Who Sees with Sound." July 14, 2006. http://people.com/premium/the-boy-who-sees-with-sound/.

AUGUST 26 THE MAN WHO CHANGED WASHINGTON

Footnotes Since the Wilderness (blog). "George Washington Mobilized the Monks of Ephrata for the American Revolution." Posted by "deor12," August 3, 2010. https://footnotessincethewilderness.wordpress.com/2010/08/03/george-washington-mobilized-the-monks-of-ephrata-for-the-american-revolution/.

———. "George Washington Pardons Traitor Michael Widman." Posted by "deor12," June 29, 2010. https://footnotessincethewilderness.wordpress.com/2010/07/29/george-washington-pardons-traitor-michael-widman/.

AUGUST 27 CARPENTER TO THE STARS

Biography. "Harrison Ford." Updated December 7, 2017. https://www.biography.com/people/harrison-ford-9298701.

Jones, Ross, and Rebecca Hawkes. "Harrison Ford: 12 Things You Didn't Know." *Telegraph*, March 6, 2015. http://www.telegraph.co.uk/films/2016/04/19/harrison-ford-12-things-you-didnt-know/.

Newsweek. "Carpenter to Han Solo—Star Wars' Impact on Harrison Ford's Career." December 4, 2016. http://www.newsweek.com/how-star-wars-advanced-harrison-ford-acting-career-527310.

Pallotta, Frank. "Harrison Ford Explains How He Went from Full-Time Carpenter to Han Solo in *Star Wars*." Business Insider, April 14, 2014. http://www.businessinsider.com/harrison-ford-reddit-ama-from-carpenter-to-han-solo-in-star-wars-2014-4.

AUGUST 28 THE MIRACLE ON FLIGHT 255

Biolchini, Amy. "U-M Staff Recalls Unforgettable 'Miracle Child' on Anniversary of Deadly Flight 255 Crash." *Ann Arbor News*, August 16, 2012. http://www.annarbor.com/news/unforgettable-miracle-child-breaks-silence-for-anniversary-of-deadly-flight-255-crash/.

Flight 255 Memorial. "The Crash." Accessed March 10, 2017. http://www.flight255memorial.com/thecrash.html.

Ryan, Scott. "Sole Survivor of Metro Airport Crash Breaks Her Silence." CBS Detroit, June 11, 2012. http://detroit.cbslocal.com/2012/06/11/sole-survivor-of-metro-airport-crash-breaks-her-silence/.

AUGUST 29 WHEN WHALES FIGHT BACK

CNN. "Sunken Ship of *Moby-Dick* Captain Found." February 12, 2011. http://www.cnn.com/2011/US/02/12/hawaii.shipwreck/index.html.

Cockayne, Angela. "*In the Heart of the Sea*: The Horrific True Story behind *Moby-Dick*." The Conversation, December 28, 2015. https://theconversation.com/in-the-heart-of-the-sea-the-horrific-true-story-behind-moby-dick-51685.

Hoare, Philip. "When Whales Attack: The Horrific Truth about *Moby-Dick*." *Telegraph*, December 26, 2015. http://www.telegraph.co.uk/films/2016/04/14/when-whales-attack-the-horrific-truth-about-moby-dick/.

King, Gilbert. "The True-Life Horror That Inspired *Moby-Dick*." *Smithsonian*, March 1, 2013. https://www.smithsonianmag.com/history/the-true-life-horror-that-inspired-moby-dick-17576/.

AUGUST 30 SEARCHING FOR HEAVEN

Biography. "Jackie Gleason." Accessed March 10, 2017. http://www.biography.com/people/jackie-gleason-9542440?page=4#!.

Pace, Eric. "Jackie Gleason Dies of Cancer; Comedian and Actor was 71." *New York Times*, June 25, 1987. http://www.nytimes.com/1987/06/25/obituaries/jackie-gleason-dies-of-cancer-comedian-and-actor-was-71.html.

Rich, Frank Kelly. "The Great Drunk: Lushing Large with Jackie Gleason, Part 1: The Thirsty Years." *Modern Drunkard*, February 5, 2005. www.drunkard.com/02-05-jackie-1/.

The University of Miami Library. "Spectral Collections: The Jackie Gleason Collection." Special Collections, The Mosaic, October 22, 2014. https://library.miami.edu/specialcollections/2014/10/22/spectral-collections-the-jackie-gleason-collection/.

AUGUST 31 THE SWEET POTATO THAT DESTROYED CHINA
Mann, Charles. *1493: Uncovering the New World Columbus Created*, chap. 5. New York: Knopf, 2011.

SEPTEMBER 1 THE HERO OF NANKING
Melvin, Sheila. "Nanjing: Death Dances with Remembrance." *New York Times*, September 14, 2005. http://www.nytimes.com/2005/09/14/arts/nanjing-death-dances-with-remembrance.html.

Perlmutter, Tammy. "Minnie Vautrin: Staring Down Death." *The Mudroom* (blog), March 13, 2015. http://mudroomblog.com/minnie-vautrin-staring-down-death/.

Van Maren, Jonathon. "Minnie Vautrin: The Woman Who Would Not Leave Nanking." *End the Killing* (blog). Canadian Centre for Bio-Ethical Reform, April 20, 2012. https://www.endthekilling.ca/blog. Post no longer available.

Working, Russell. "China Salutes Illinois Hero of Massacre by Japanese." *Chicago Tribune*, September 25, 2005. http://articles.chicagotribune.com/2005-09-25/news/0509250254_1_iris-chang-massacre-nanjing.

SEPTEMBER 2 HUGS FOR THE PRESIDENT
Lavin, Cheryl. "Family Outcast: A Reagan Son Sadly Remembers Years of Neglect." *Chicago Tribune*, April 17, 1988. http://articles.chicagotribune.com/1988-04-17/features/8803090826_1_michael-reagan-four-reagan-children-maureen.

Reagan, Michael, with Jim Denney. *Lessons My Father Taught Me*. West Palm Beach, FL: Humanix Books, 2016.

Reagan, Michael, Patti Davis, and Ron Reagan Jr. "Transcript: Reagan's Children Deliver Remarks at Service." *The Washington Post*, June 11, 2004. http://www.washingtonpost.com/wp-dyn/articles/A36014-2004Jun11.html.

SEPTEMBER 3 SHOT FOR GOING TO SCHOOL
Brenner, Marie. "The Target." *Vanity Fair*, March 15, 2013. https://www.vanityfair.com/news/politics/2013/04/malala-yousafzai-pakistan-profile.

Gidda, Mirren. "Malala Yousafzai's New Mission: Can She Still Inspire as an Adult?" *Newsweek*, January 11, 2017. http://www.newsweek.com/2017/01/20/exclusive-malala-yousafzai-interview-davos-540978.html.

Husain, Mishal. "Malala: The Girl Who Was Shot for Going to School." BBC News, October 7, 2013. http://www.bbc.com/news/magazine-24379018.

The Nobel Prize Foundation. "Malala Yousafzai—Biographical." Nobelprize.org, 2014. Accessed May 12, 2018. https://www.nobelprize.org/nobel_prizes/peace/laureates/2014/yousafzai-bio.html.

SEPTEMBER 4 THE POSSIBILITIES AND LIMITS OF FORGIVENESS
Associated Press. "Nazi Hunter Simon Wiesenthal Dies at 96." NBC News. Updated September 20, 2005. http://www.nbcnews.com/id/9404749/ns/world_news/t/nazi-hunter-simon-wiesenthal-dies/#.WMLD_jvysdU.

Facing History and Ourselves. "The Sunflower Synopsis." Accessed March 10, 2017. https://www.facinghistory.org/sunflower-synopsis.

Simon Wiesenthal Center. "Simon Wiesenthal Biography." Accessed March 10, 2017. http://www.wiesenthal.com/site/pp.asp?c=lsKWLbPJLnF&b=4441351.

Wiesenthal, Simon. *The Sunflower*. Translated by H. A. Piehler. London: W. H. Allen, 1970.

SEPTEMBER 5 A RESURRECTION IN THE VALLEY OF DEATH
Richardson, Don. *Lords of the Earth*. Bloomington, MN: Bethany, 1977.

Schenk, Ruth. "Missionaries Risk All to Witness to Cannibals." Emmanuel Baptist Church. Accessed March 9, 2017. http://ib-emmanuel.org/clientimages/55879/mission_to_cannibals.pdf.

World Team. *The Yali Story*. Directed by Dianne Becker. Rolling Shoals, 2004. See "The Yali Story (Bruno de Leeuw)." YouTube video, 27:09. Posted by "Yopi Dopi," March 9, 2015. https://www.youtube.com/watch?v=nlI9B1uGOHo.

SEPTEMBER 6 THE FLOOD THAT CHANGED AMERICA
Barry, John. "The Mississippi Flood of 1927." Interview by Linda Wertheimer. *Weekend Edition Saturday*. NPR, September 3, 2005. https://www.npr.org/templates/story/story.php?storyId=4831423.

Hambling, David. "The Mississippi Flood That Changed Destinies." *Guardian*, May 9, 2017. https://www.theguardian.com/news/2017/may/09/the-mississippi-flood-that-changed-destinies.

Risk Management Solutions. *The 1927 Great Mississippi Flood: 80-Year Retrospective*. Accessed February 5, 2018. http://forms2.rms.com/rs/729-DJX-565/images/fl_1927_great_mississippi_flood.pdf.

Watkins, T. H. "Boiling Over." Review of *Rising Tide: The Great Mississippi Flood of 1927 and How It Changed America*, by John M. Barry. *New York Times*, April 13, 1997. http://www.nytimes.com/books /97/04/13/reviews/970413.13watkint.html.

SEPTEMBER 7 OLD WOOM'S WINNIE

Discovery. "Winston Churchill Biography." May 8, 2015. http://veday.discoveryuk.com/winston-churchill -biography/.

Johnson, Boris. "The Woman Who Made Winston Churchill." *Boris Johnson* (blog). *Telegraph*, October 12, 2014. http://www.telegraph.co.uk/news/politics/conservative/11155850/Boris-Johnson-the-woman-who -made-Winston-Churchill.html.

Kent, Richard L. "A Woman of No Importance: Elizabeth Everest." *The Tattered Remnant* (blog), December 31, 2009. http://tatteredremnants.blogspot.com/2009/09/tattered-remnants-002-elizabeth-everest.html.

Labrecque, Ellen. *Who Was Winston Churchill?* New York: Grosset & Dunlap, 2015.

SEPTEMBER 8 PREMATURE BURIALS

Angelone, Caitlin. "'To Be Buried Alive Is, beyond Question, the Most Terrible of These Extremes Which Has Ever Fallen to the Lot of Mere Mortality.'" *Fugitive Leaves* (blog). College of Physicians of Philadelphia Historical Medical Library, March 30, 2016. http://histmed.collegeofphysicians.org/to-be-buried-alive -is-beyond-question/.

Bondeson, Jan. "Lifting the Lid on the Macabre History of Those Buried Alive." *Daily Mail*, March 12, 2010. http://www.dailymail.co.uk/news/article-1257330/Lifting-lid-macabre-history-buried-alive.html.

Finn, Alan. "7 Weird Graveyard Inventions." Mental Floss, October 22, 2014. http://mentalfloss.com/article /59584/7-weird-graveyard-inventions.

Morton, Ella. "Scratch Marks on Her Coffin: Tales of Premature Burial." *Atlas Obscura* (blog). Slate, October 7, 2014. http://www.slate.com/blogs/atlas_obscura/2014/10/07/buried_alive_victorian_vivisepulture_safety _coffins_and_rufina_cambaceres.html.

SEPTEMBER 9 THE COMPASSIONATE PURITAN

Christianity Today. "Jonathan Edwards." Accessed March 9, 2017. http://www.christianitytoday.com/history /people/theologians/jonathan-edwards.html.

Marsden, George M. *A Short Life of Jonathan Edwards*. Grand Rapids, MI: Eerdmans, 2008.

Piper, John. "The Pastor as Theologian: Life and Ministry of Jonathan Edwards." Desiring God, April 15, 1988. https://www.desiringgod.org/messages/the-pastor-as-theologian.

SEPTEMBER 10 LOVING DADDY'S KILLER

Beliefnet. "Learning to Forgive." Accessed February 6, 2018. http://www.beliefnet.com/entertainment/movies /2006/01/learning-to-forgive.aspx.

Fickas, Tamara D. "Jim Elliot Biography." Inspirational Christians. Accessed February 6, 2018. http://www .inspirationalchristians.org/biography/jim-elliot/.

Overstreet, Jeffrey. "*End of the Spear.*" Review by Lisa Ann Cockrel of *End of the Spear*, by Bill Ewing, Bart Gavigan, and Jim Hanon. Directed by Jim Hanon. Every Tribe Entertainment, 2005. *Christianity Today*, January 20, 2006. http://www.christianitytoday.com/ct/2006/januaryweb-only/endofthespear.html.

Von Buseck, Craig. "*End of the Spear*: The True Story." CBN, accessed February 6, 2018. http://www1.cbn .com/end-spear-true-story.

SEPTEMBER 11 LET'S ROLL

History. "Flight 93." Accessed February 15, 2018. http://www.history.com/topics/flight-93.

NBC News. "Heroes of Flight 93." December 8, 2003. http://www.nbcnews.com/id/3080117/ns/dateline _nbc-newsmakers/t/heroes-flight/#.WoZCXqinEdU.

Pynchon, Victoria. "September 11 and the Heroes of Flight 93." *She Negotiates* (blog). *Forbes*, September 10, 2011. https://www.forbes.com/sites/shenegotiates/2011/09/10/september-11-and-the-heroes-of-flight -93/#6c1bf1e36260.

Vulliamy, Ed. "'Let's Roll . . .'" *Guardian*, December 1, 2001. https://www.theguardian.com/world/2001 /dec/02/september11.terrorism1.

SEPTEMBER 12 THE ARMY THAT ATTACKED ITSELF

ER. "The Battle of Karansebes." Naked History, January 20, 2017. http://www.historynaked.com/the-battle -of-karansebes/.

Knight, David. "The 5 Most Idiotic Wars Ever Fought." Cracked, March 6, 2009. http://www.cracked.com /article_17123_the-5-most-retarded-wars-ever-fought.html.

Upton, Emily. "Did the Austrian Army Really End Up Fighting Itself in a Major Battle?" *Today I Found Out* (blog), April 21, 2014. http://www.todayifoundout.com/index.php/2014/04/battle-karansebes/.

WorldAtlas. "Did You Know the Austrian Army Defeated Itself in the 1788 Battle of Karansebes?" Updated April 25, 2017. https://www.worldatlas.com/articles/did-you-know-the-austrian-army-defeated-itself-in -the-1788-battle-of-karansebes.html.

SEPTEMBER 13 THE CURSE OF THE CONTROL FREAK
Schickel, Erika. "At Zorthian Ranch, a Return to Bohemia." *LA Weekly*, July 8, 2014. http://www.laweekly .com/music/at-zorthian-ranch-a-return-to-bohemia-4832037.
Statesville Daily Record. "Tragedy Marks Efforts for Safety." February 12, 1948. https://www.newspapers.com /newspage/3285983/.
Swindoll, Charles R. *Man to Man.* Grand Rapids, MI: Zondervan, 1996.

SEPTEMBER 14 THE SCANDALOUS MISSIONARY
Christianity Today. "Hudson Taylor: Faith Missionary to China." Previously published in *131 Christians Everyone Should Know* (Nashville: Broadman & Holman, 2000). Accessed February 7, 2018. http://www .christianitytoday.com/history/people/missionaries/hudson-taylor.html.
Covell, Ralph R. "Taylor, James Hudson (1832–1905)." Boston University School of Theology. Reprinted with permission from *Biographical Dictionary of Christian Missions* (New York: Macmillan Reference USA, 1998). Copyright 1998 Gerald H. Anderson. http://www.bu.edu/missiology/missionary-biography /t-u-v/taylor-j-hudson-1832-1905/.
OMF. "James Hudson Taylor." Accessed February 7, 2018. https://omf.org/us/about/our-story/james-hudson -taylor/.
Piper, John. "The Ministry of Hudson Taylor as Life in Christ." Desiring God, February 5, 2014. https://www .desiringgod.org/messages/the-ministry-of-hudson-taylor-as-life-in-christ.

SEPTEMBER 15 WHEN DOGS ROUTED A TANK DIVISION
Pile, Stephen. *The (Incomplete) Book of Failures: The Official Handbook of the Not-Terribly-Good Club of Great Britain.* Boston: E.P. Dutton, 1979.
Upton, Emily. "The Exploding Anti-Tank Dogs of World War II." *Today I Found Out* (blog), December 2, 2013. http://www.todayifoundout.com/index.php/2013/12/anti-tank-dogs-world-war-ii/#disqus_thread.

SEPTEMBER 16 FROM RAGS TO RICHES
Gillett, Rachel. "From Welfare to One of the World's Wealthiest Women—The Incredible Rags-to-Riches Story of J. K. Rowling." Business Insider, May 18, 2015. http://www.businessinsider.com/the-rags-to -riches-story-of-jk-rowling-2015-5.
Greig, Geordie. "'I Was as Poor as It's Possible to Be . . . Now I Am Able to Give': In This Rare and Intimate Interview, JK Rowling Reveals Her Most Ambitious Plot Yet." *Daily Mail*, October 26, 2013. http:// www.dailymail.co.uk/home/event/article-2474863/JK-Rowling-I-poor-possible-be.html.
Hastings, Chris. "Tears as JK Rowling Returns to Where It Began." *Telegraph*, December 23, 2007. http:// www.telegraph.co.uk/news/uknews/1573476/Tears-as-JK-Rowling-returns-to-where-it-began.html.
Ray, Sanjana. "The Remarkable Story of J. K. Rowling—From Rags to Some Serious Riches." YourStory, June 10, 2016. https://yourstory.com/2016/06/jk-rowling-story/.

SEPTEMBER 17 CONCEIVED IN SHAME, BORN FOR GREATNESS
The basis of this story is found in greater detail for those willing to plow into the Yalkut HaMachiri and Sefer HaTodaah (section on Sivan and Shavuot) or Torah commentaries of Radak and Abarbanel to 1 Samuel 16:3.
Weisberg, Chana. "Nitzevet, Mother of David." *Chabad.* Accessed March 9, 2017. http://www.chabad.org /theJewishWoman/article_cdo/aid/280331/jewish/Nitzevet-Mother-of-David.htm.

SEPTEMBER 18 THE NIGHT MARS INVADED NEW JERSEY
CBS. "The War of the Worlds" (radio drama). *The Mercury Theatre on the Air*, originally aired October 30, 1938. See "War of the Worlds—Original 1938 Radio Broadcasts (2011 Remastered Version)." YouTube video, 59:17. Posted by "Orchard Enterprises," February 24, 2015. https://www.youtube.com/watch?v =9q7tN7MhQ4I.
Dixon, George. "'War of the Worlds' Broadcast Causes Chaos in 1938." *Daily News*, October 29, 2015. http://www.nydailynews.com/news/national/war-worlds-broadcast-caos-1938-article-1.2406951.
New York Times. "Radio Listeners in Panic, Taking War Drama as Fact," headline story October 31, 1938. http://www.war-of-the-worlds.org/Radio/Newspapers/Oct31/NYT.html.
Schwartz, A. Brad. "Orson Welles and History's First Viral-Media Event." *Vanity Fair*, April 27, 2015. http:// www.vanityfair.com/culture/2015/04/broadcast-hysteria-orson-welles-war-of-the-worlds.
Welles, Orson. "The War of the Worlds." Sacred Texts. Accessed March 7, 2017. Radio broadcast transcript of Orson Welles and *The Mercury Theatre on the Air* in *The War of the Worlds* by H. G. Wells, October 30, 1938. http://www.sacred-texts.com/ufo/mars/wow.htm.

SEPTEMBER 19 MEN AGAINST THE SEA

Alexander, Caroline. "Mutiny on the *Bounty*: The True Story of Captain Bligh's Mutineers." *Telegraph*, March 12, 2017. http://www.telegraph.co.uk/men/the-filter/mutiny-bounty-true-story-captain-blighs -mutineers/.

Klein, Christopher. "Mutiny on the *Bounty*, 225 Years Ago." History, April 28, 2014. http://www.history .com/news/mutiny-on-the-bounty-225-years-ago.

Murche, Guy, Jr., "Mutiny Victims Battle Sea's Terror in Open Boat." *Chicago Tribune*, May 10, 1936.

Rose, Alexander. "Captain Bligh: A Man Misunderstood and the Epic High Seas Drama on HMS *Bounty*." gCaptain, October 24, 2011. http://gcaptain.com/captain-bligh-misunderstood-epic/.

SEPTEMBER 20 THE FIFTEEN-MINUTE SUPERSTAR

Danger, Nick. "Superstar USA—The Meanest Show Ever." Blogcritics, May 18, 2004. http://blogcritics.org /superstar-usa-the-meanest-show-ever/.

Katner, Ben. "Superstar Jamie Squeals!" *TV Guide*, June 15, 2004. http://www.tvguide.com/news/jamie -spears-superstar-37489/.

The WB Television Network. *Superstar USA*. Episode 7, originally aired June 14, 2004. See "WB Superstar USA—Jamie—'My Heart Will Go On.'" YouTube video, 3:27. Posted by "grobisher's channel," July 31, 2009. https://www.youtube.com/watch?v=5q5u5bFatic.

SEPTEMBER 21 AMERICA'S FAIRY GODMOTHER

Berger, Danielle. "Website Shows Foster Kids Their Wishes Are Worthwhile." CNN, October 28, 2013. https://www.cnn.com/2013/03/07/us/cnnheroes-gletow-foster-wishes/index.html.

Gletow, Danielle. "The Power to Change a Child's Life." HuffPost, March 2, 2017. https://www.huffington post.com/entry/the-power-to-change-a-childs-life_us_58b84d72e4b051155b4f8c86.

Gomez, Alanna. "Danielle Gletow: Fairy Godmother to America's Foster Children." *End the Killing* (blog). Canadian Centre for Bio-Ethical Reform, July 19, 2013. https://www.endthekilling.ca/blog. Post no longer available.

Ippolito, Amanda. "Founder of Trenton-Based One Simple Wish in the Running for CNN Hero of the Year." *Times of Trenton*, November 22, 2013. http://www.nj.com/mercer/index.ssf/2013/11/founder_of_trenton -based_one_simple_wish_in_the_running_for_cnn_hero_of_the_year.html.

SEPTEMBER 22 THE CHAMBERMAID'S CHOICE

Alvarez, Alonso, Ricardo Colorado, Alejandro Monteverde, and Leo Severino. *Crescendo I*. Directed by Alonso Alvarez. Wama Films, 2011. See "Crescendo," YouTube video, 15:03. Posted by "MovietoMovement," October 20, 2014. https://www.youtube.com/watch?v=CafJJNETvqM.

Morris, Edmund. *Beethoven: The Universal Composer*. New York: Harper Perennial, 2010.

SEPTEMBER 23 A MAGNIFICENT CASE OF MALPRACTICE

Adams, Anne. "Fanny Crosby, Hymnwriter." *History's Women* (blog). Accessed February 9, 2018. http://historys women.com/blog/fanny-crosby/.

Christianity.com. "Fanny Crosby: America's Hymn Queen." April 28, 2010. https://www.christianity.com /church/church-history/timeline/1801-1900/fanny-crosby-americas-hymn-queen-11630385.html.

Christianity Today. "Fanny Crosby." Accessed February 9, 2018. Previously published in *131 Christians Everyone Should Know* (Nashville: Broadman & Holman, 2000). http://www.christianitytoday.com /history/people/poets/fanny-crosby.html.

Miller, Basil. "Fanny Crosby, Famous Blind Hymn Writer." Truthful Words. Accessed February 9, 2018. https://www.truthfulwords.org/biography/crosbytw.html.

SEPTEMBER 24 THE SONG OF A HUMAN TRAFFICKER

Dallas, Kelsey. "Don't Mess with the Music: Why Changing Hymn Lyrics Can Be Dramatic." *Deseret News*, March 12, 2016. http://www.deseretnews.com/article/865649845/Dont-mess-with-the-music-Why -changing-hymn-lyrics-can-be-dramatic.html.

Metaxas, Eric. *Amazing Grace: William Wilberforce and the Heroic Campaign to End Slavery*. New York: HarperCollins, 2007.

Phipps, William E. *Amazing Grace in John Newton: Slave-ship Captain, Hymnwriter, and Abolitionist*. Atlanta: Mercer University Press, 2004.

Sheward, David. "The Real Story behind 'Amazing Grace.'" Biography, August 11, 2015. http://www .biography.com/news/amazing-grace-story-john-newton#!.

SEPTEMBER 25 MORAL PAP FOR THE YOUNG

NPR. "Alcott: 'Not the Little Woman You Thought She Was.'" *Morning Edition*, December 28, 2009. https://www.npr.org/templates/story/story.php?storyId=121831612.

O'Connor, Roisin. "Louisa May Alcott: Five Things You Might Not Know about the Author of *Little Women.*" *Independent*, November 29, 2016. http://www.independent.co.uk/arts-entertainment/books/features/louisa-may-alcott-little-women-google-doodle-writer-author-5-things-you-didnt-know-a7445106.html.

Raga, Suzanne. "10 Little Facts about Louisa May Alcott." Mental Floss, November 29, 2017. http://mentalfloss.com/article/89228/10-little-facts-about-louisa-may-alcott.

Scribbling Women. "Louisa May Alcott." *A Whisper in the Dark.* https://scribblingwomen.chass.ncsu.edu. Site no longer available.

Stossel, Sage. "Louisa May Alcott in *The Atlantic.*" *Atlantic*, July 1995. https://www.theatlantic.com/magazine/archive/1995/07/louisa-may-alcott-in-the-atlantic/308868/.

SEPTEMBER 26 THE ASTERISK IN AN OBITUARY
Martin, Douglas. "Annette Funicello, 70, Dies; Beloved as Mouseketeer and a Star of Beach Movies." *New York Times*, April 8, 2013. http://www.nytimes.com/2013/04/09/movies/annette-funicello-mouseketeer-dies-at-70.html.

Moore, Frazier, and Bob Thomas. "Annette Funicello Obituary." Legacy, April 8, 2013. http://www.legacy.com/ns/annette-funicello-obituary/164132356.

Shapiro, Marc. *Annette Funicello: America's Sweetheart.* Riverdale, NY: Riverdale Avenue Books, 2013.

SEPTEMBER 27 TOUCHING ALL BASES
Brady, Erik. "A Father's Day Story That Touches All the Bases." *USA Today.* Accessed February 9, 2018. https://www.usatoday.com/story/sports/2017/06/15/fathers-day-story-touches-all-bases/395402001/.

Tarapacki, Thomas. "St. Francis Welcomes New Hall of Fame Members." *Am-Pol Eagle*, July 21, 2017. http://ampoleagle.com/st-francis-welcomes-new-hall-of-fame-members-p11126-208.htm.

WGRZ. "A Father's Day Story for the Ages." June 16, 2017. http://www.wgrz.com/article/news/a-fathers-day-story-for-the-ages/449758393.

SEPTEMBER 28 THE TREASURE OF THE SALINAS DE SAN ANDREAS
Cool, Paul. *Salt Warriors: Insurgency on the Rio Grande.* College Station, TX: Texas A&M University Press, 2008.

SaltWorks. "History of Salt." Accessed March 7, 2017. https://www.seasalt.com/salt-101/history-of-salt.

Ward, Charles Francis. "The Salt War of San Elizario (1877)." Master's thesis, University of Texas, 1932.

SEPTEMBER 29 THE MAN OF A THOUSAND FACES
Corliss, Richard. "That Old Feeling: Who Was Peter Sellers?" *Time*, February 10, 2003. http://content.time.com/time/arts/article/0,8599,421269,00.html.

Jones, Jerene. "Peter Sellers' Mask of Comedy Hid a Flawed, Spiteful Man, His Sorrowful Children Claim." *People*, February 1, 1982. http://people.com/archive/peter-sellers-mask-of-comedy-hid-a-flawed-spiteful-man-his-sorrowful-children-claim-vol-17-no-4/.

North, Dan. "'There Used to Be a Me': Peter Sellers on the Muppet Show." *Spectacular Attractions* (blog), September 26, 2008. https://drnorth.wordpress.com/2008/09/26/there-used-to-be-a-me-peter-sellers-on-the-muppet-show/.

Time. "Who Is This Man? The Many Faces of Peter Sellers." Cover story, March 3, 1980.

SEPTEMBER 30 THE FLYING PARSON
Find a Grave. "Rev. Gilbert Lothair 'Gil' Dodds." August 14, 2012. https://www.findagrave.com/memorial/95344887/gilbert-lothair-dodds#.

Larson, Mel. *Gil Dodds: The Flying Parson.* Special edition for National Youth for Christ. Chicago: Evangelical Beacon, 1945. Posted at the Evangelical Christian Library. http://www.ccel.us/gildodds.toc.html.

New York Times. "Gil Dodds, Former Mile Record-Holder, Dead at 58." February 5, 1977. http://www.nytimes.com/1977/02/05/archives/gil-dodds-former-mile-recordholder-dead-at-58.html.

OCTOBER 1 THOMAS CLARKSON'S BOX
The Abolition Project. "Thomas Clarkson—Key Events." Accessed February 10, 2018. http://abolition.e2bn.org/box_59.html.

BBC. "Thomas Clarkson (1760–1846)." Accessed February 10, 2018. http://www.bbc.co.uk/history/historic_figures/clarkson_thomas.shtml.

The Clarksons Society. "Thomas Clarkson." Frequently Asked Questions. Accessed February 10, 2018. http://www.thomasclarkson.org/tcfaq.htm.

OCTOBER 2 THE PREACHER AND THE GUNSLINGER
FrontierTimes.com. "John Wesley Hardin." Accessed February 10, 2018. http://www.frontiertimes.com/outlaws/hardin.html.

History. "John Wesley Hardin Killed in Texas." This Day in History: August 19, 1895. Accessed February 10, 2018. http://www.history.com/this-day-in-history/john-wesley-hardin-killed-in-texas.

Montgomery, Murray. "The Killing of John Wesley Hardin." TexasEscapes.com, May 2001. http://www.texas escapes.com/DEPARTMENTS/Guest_Columnists/Times_past/KillingOfJohnWesleyHardin1.htm.

Spangenberger, Phil. "Hardin's Deadly Tools." *True West*, March 12, 2012. https://truewestmagazine.com /hardins-deadly-tools/.

OCTOBER 3 THE MAN IN THE IRON LUNG

Bamigboye, Baz. "Claire and Andrew Bring to Life a Remarkable Love Story: Actress Tells Baz Bamigboye about Her Role in New Film *Breathe*." *Daily Mail*, March 16, 2017. http://www.dailymail.co.uk /tvshowbiz/article-4322262/Claire-Foy-Andrew-Garfield-star-new-film-Breathe.html.

Bradshaw, Peter. "*Breathe* Review—Andrew Garfield Fronts Poignant Biopic of Wheelchair Pioneer." Review of *Breathe*, by William Nicholson, directed by Andy Serkis (Imaginarium Productions, 2017). *Guardian*, September 15, 2017. https://www.theguardian.com/film/2017/sep/15/breathe-review-andrew-garfield -andy-serkis-robin-cavendish-toronto-film-festival-tiff.

Renton, Alice, and Tim Renton. "Obituary: Robin Cavendish." *Independent*, August 10, 1994. http://www .independent.co.uk/news/people/obituary-robin-cavendish-1382697.html.

OCTOBER 4 THE WORLD'S MOST-ADMIRED WOMAN

Battle, Michael. *Practicing Reconciliation in a Violent World*. New York: Morehouse, 2005.

Harm, Frederick R., Paul E. Robinson, Glen W. McDonald, and Harold C. Warlick. *Sermons on the Second Readings*. Lima, OH: CSS Publishing, 2002.

Maasburg, Fr. Leo. *Mother Teresa of Calcutta: A Personal Portrait*. San Francisco: Ignatius Press, 2011.

OCTOBER 5 THE RACE OF THE CENTURY

Hale, Ron. "Seabiscuit vs. War Admiral the Greatest Match Race of the Century." ThoughtCo. Updated June 23, 2017. https://thoughtco.com/seabiscuit-vs-war-admiral-3862278.

Loverro, Thom. "Seabiscuit vs War Admiral: The Horse Race That Stopped the Nation." *Guardian*, November 1, 2013. https://www.theguardian.com/sport/2013/nov/01/seabiscuit-war-admiral-horse -race-1938-pimlico.

Mezger, Raelyn. "Biography." Seabiscuit: An American Legend. Accessed February 10, 2018. http://tbgreats .com/seabiscuit/bio.html.

Pedulla, Tom. "Seabiscuit: A True Rags-to-Riches Story." America's Best Racing, April 21, 2016. https://www .americasbestracing.net/the-sport/2016-seabiscuit-true-rags-riches-story.

OCTOBER 6 SCRUBBING THE TOMBSTONE

Associated Press. "25 Years Later, Chucky Mullins Remains Remembered by Ole Miss, Brad Gaines." *Gulflive.com* (blog). *Mississippi Press*, September 5, 2014. http://blog.gulflive.com/mississippi-press -sports/2014/09/25_years_later_chucky_mullins.html.

ESPN. "*SEC Storied*: It's Time—Chucky Mullins." ESPN video, 0:59. From *SEC Storied*, September 4, 2014. http://www.espn.com/video/clip?id=11426259.

Organ, Mike. "'Brad Gaines/Chucky Mullins Story' Has Emotion, Healing." *Tennessean*, September 3, 2014. https://www.tennessean.com/story/sports/college/vanderbilt/2014/09/03/brad-gaineschucky -mullins-story-emotion-healing/15039463/.

OCTOBER 7 THE FORGOTTEN FATHER

The American View. "Dr. Joseph Warren—Humble Patriot." June 12, 2014. https://www.theamericanview .com/dr-joseph-warren-americas-first-hero/.

Beck, Derek W. "The Circumstances of the Death of Dr. Joseph Warren." Derek W. Beck, April 4, 2011. http://www.derekbeck.com/1775/info/circumstances-of-warrens-death/.

Klein, Christopher. "10 Things You Should Know about Joseph Warren." History, January 22, 2015. http:// www.history.com/news/10-things-you-should-know-about-joseph-warren.

National Park Service. "Doctor Joseph Warren." Boston National Historical Park. Updated March 24, 2017. https://www.nps.gov/bost/learn/historyculture/warren.htm.

OCTOBER 8 THE OTHER ROSA PARKS

Biography. "Elizabeth Jennings Graham." Updated October 20, 2015. https://www.biography.com/people /elizabeth-jennings-graham-091415.

Greider, Katharine. "The Schoolteacher on the Streetcar." *New York Times*, November 13, 2005. http://www .nytimes.com/2005/11/13/nyregion/thecity/the-schoolteacher-on-the-streetcar.html.

Irwin, Demetria. "[Unsung Sheroes] Elizabeth Jennings Graham: A 19th Century Rosa Parks." *Ebony*, March 3, 2016. http://www.ebony.com/black-history/elizabeth-jennings-graham-new-york-womenshistory.

OCTOBER 9 THE DAY THE MUSIC DIED

Egan, Timothy. "Kurt Cobain, Hesitant Poet of 'Grunge Rock,' Dead at 27." *New York Times*, April 9, 1994.

Fricke, David. "100 Greatest Guitarists: David Fricke's Picks." *Rolling Stone*, December 2, 2010. http://www.rollingstone.com/music/lists/100-greatest-guitarists-of-all-time-19691231.

Marcus, Stephanie. "Courtney Love Admits to Using Heroin While Pregnant with Frances Bean Cobain." *Huffington Post*, January 28, 2015. http://www.huffingtonpost.com/2015/01/28/courtney-love-heroin-pregnant_n_6565528.html.

Rolling Stone. "100 Greatest Singers of All Time." December 2, 2010. http://www.rollingstone.com/music/lists/100-greatest-singers-of-all-time-19691231.

OCTOBER 10 THE IMAGINARY HOME

Gitner, Jess. "At 40, 'Take Me Home, Country Roads' Still Belongs." *Morning Edition.* NPR, April 6, 2011. https://www.npr.org/2011/04/06/135150085/at-40-take-me-home-country-roads-still-belongs.

Harlan, Will. "Country Roads: West or Western Virginia?" Blue Ridge Outdoors, April 10, 2009. http://www.blueridgeoutdoors.com/go-outside/country-roads-west-or-western-virginia/.

Songfacts. "Take Me Home Country Roads by John Denver." Accessed February 10, 2018. http://www.songfacts.com/detail.php?id=2409.

OCTOBER 11 THE SHORTEST WAR IN HISTORY

Higgins, Malcolm. "The Shortest Wars in Military History." War History Online, March 9, 2017. https://www.warhistoryonline.com/history/five-shortest-wars-military-history.html.

Johnson, Ben. "The Shortest War in History." Historic UK. Accessed February 10, 2018. http://www.historic-uk.com/HistoryUK/HistoryofBritain/The-Shortest-War-in-History/.

Smithfield, Brad. "The Shortest War in History Was between England and Zanzibar and It Lasted for a Full 38 Minutes!" The Vintage News, March 22, 2016. https://www.thevintagenews.com/2016/03/22/the-shortest-war-in-history-is-between-england-and-zanzibar-and-it-lasted-for-a-full-38-minutes-copy/.

OCTOBER 12 A SHOEMAKER WHO CHANGED THE WORLD

Beck, James R. *Dorothy Carey: The Tragic and Untold Story of Mrs. William Carey.* Grand Rapids, MI: Baker, 1992.

Christianity Today. "William Carey." Christian History. Accessed March 6, 2017. http://www.christianitytoday.com/history/people/missionaries/william-carey.html.

Walker, F. Deaville. *William Carey: Missionary Pioneer and Statesman.* Chicago: Moody, 1951.

OCTOBER 13 THE MYSTERIOUS MONK

Ripley, Robert LeRoy. *Ripley's Giant Book of Believe It or Not!* New York: Grand Central, 1983.

Unremitting Failure (blog). "Art Expert Unremitting Failure Squints at the Works of: Joseph Matthäus Aigner and Ashley Snow Macomber!" May 5, 2011. http://futility.typepad.com/futility/2011/05/art-expert-unremitting-failure-squints-at-the-works-of-joseph-matth%C3%A4us-aigner-and-ashley-snow-macomb.html.

Wagner, Stephen. "True Stories of Amazing Coincidences." ThoughtCo, August 10, 2017. https://www.thoughtco.com/stories-of-amazing-coincidences-2594414.

OCTOBER 14 VENGEANCE AND SURVIVAL

Barcott, Bruce. "A True Story of Vengeance and Survival." *Outside*, August 13, 2010. https://www.outsideonline.com/1825626/true-story-vengeance-and-survival.

Montgomery, Sy. "Review of John Vaillant's *The Tiger: A True Story of Vengeance and Survival.*" *Washington Post*, August 29, 2010. http://www.washingtonpost.com/wp-dyn/content/article/2010/08/27/AR2010082702288.html.

NPR. "The True Story of a Man-Eating Tiger's 'Vengeance.'" *Morning Edition*, September 14, 2010. https://www.npr.org/templates/story/story.php?storyId=129551459.

Tigers-World. "Siberian Tiger." January 16, 2014. http://www.tigers-world.com/siberian-tiger/.

OCTOBER 15 THE MAN WHO VOLUNTEERED FOR AUSCHWITZ

Lucjan, Damian. "Witold Pilecki—The Incredible Story of the Man Who Volunteered for Auschwitz." War History Online, September 15, 2016. https://www.warhistoryonline.com/world-war-ii/story-of-the-man-who-volunteered-for-auschwitz.html.

NPR. "Meet the Man Who Sneaked into Auschwitz." September 18, 2010. https://www.npr.org/templates/story/story.php?storyId=129956107.

Reed, Lawrence W. "Witold Pilecki: Bravery beyond Measure." Foundation for Economic Education, October 23, 2015. https://fee.org/articles/he-volunteered-to-go-to-auschwitz/.

Sola, David de. "The Man Who Volunteered for Auschwitz." *Atlantic*, October 5, 2012. https://www.theatlantic.com/international/archive/2012/10/the-man-who-volunteered-for-auschwitz/263083/.

OCTOBER 16 THE MAN OF A MILLION LIES

Burgan, Michael. *Marco Polo: Marco Polo and the Silk Road to China*. Minneapolis: Compass Point Books, 2002.

Edwards, Mike. "Wonders and Whoppers." *Smithsonian*, July 2008. http://www.smithsonianmag.com /people-places/wonders-and-whoppers-27166/.

Polo, Marco. *The Travels*. Translated by Ronald Latham. London: Penguin Classics, 1958.

OCTOBER 17 THE TRIUMPH OF BUBBLES

Sills, Beverly. *Bubbles: A Self-Portrait*. New York: Bobbs-Merrill, 1976.

———. "Peter and Beverly Sills Greenough." Interview by Mike Wallace. Televised July 6, 1975, on *60 Minutes* by CBS. YouTube video, 6:21. Posted by "Beverly Sills," September 8, 2006. https://www .youtube.com/watch?v=3kRpzn5lf0k.

Tommasini, Anthony. "Beverly Sills, All-American Diva, Is Dead at 78." *New York Times*, July 3, 2007. http://www.nytimes.com/2007/07/03/arts/music/03sills.html.

OCTOBER 18 LOOKING FOR THAT HOME

Biography. "Janis Joplin." Updated April 27, 2017. https://www.biography.com/people/janis-joplin-9357941.

Brown, Mick. "How Never-Seen-Before Letters Reveal the Inner World of Janis Joplin." *Telegraph*, January 28, 2016. http://www.telegraph.co.uk/music/artists/how-never-seen-before-letters-reveal-the -inner-world-of-janis-jo/.

Lloyd, Robert. "Beyond the Tragedy, *Janis: Little Girl Blue* Reveals Joplin as a Smart, Funny, Vulnerable Feminist Conundrum." Review of *Janis: Little Girl Blue*, by Amy Berg. Directed by Amy Berg. Disarming Films and Jigsaw Productions, 2015. *Los Angeles Times*, May 2, 2016. http://www.latimes .com/entertainment/tv/la-et-st-janis-little-girl-blue-review-20160501-snap-story.html.

Schulman, Michael. "My Big Sister, Janis Joplin." *New Yorker*, October 29, 2013. https://www.newyorker .com/culture/culture-desk/my-big-sister-janis-joplin.

OCTOBER 19 THE RELUCTANT HERO

Adams, Noah. "Remembering Sgt. York, a War Hero Who Built a School." *All Things Considered*. NPR, November 11, 2015. https://www.npr.org/sections/ed/2015/11/11/455368998/remembering-sgt-york -a-war-hero-who-built-a-school.

Cellania, Miss. "Sergeant Alvin York." Mental Floss, September 15, 2009. http://mentalfloss.com/article /22768/sergeant-alvin-york.

Crocker, Brittany. "Walk in the Footsteps of WWI Hero Alvin York." *USA Today*, April 6, 2017. https:// www.usatoday.com/story/travel/nation-now/2017/04/06/world-war-i-hero-alvin-york/100145516/.

Timbs, Larry. "A Sergeant's Story: Tennessee Preserves Memory of Humble Hero Alvin York." *Charlotte Observer*, August 28, 2015. http://www.charlotteobserver.com/living/travel/article32560584 .html.

OCTOBER 20 A TEACHER'S FINAL LESSON

Bacon, John. "Report: Teacher Tried to Divert Shooter." *USA Today*, December 16, 2012. https://www .usatoday.com/story/news/nation/2012/12/16/newtown-shootings-gunman-soto-details/1772791/.

Berger, Joseph. "Remembering the Passion of a Teacher Who Died Protecting Students." *New York Times*, December 19, 2012. http://www.nytimes.com/2012/12/20/nyregion/remembering-the-passion-of -victoria-soto-a-sandy-hook-teacher.html.

Pelley, Scott. "60 Minutes Returns to Newtown, 4 Years Later." CBS News, April 16, 2017. https://www .cbsnews.com/news/return-to-newton-ct-sandy-hook-school-shooting-4-years-later/.

Williams, Matt. "Victoria Soto: Sandy Hook Teacher Who Wanted to Mould Young Minds." *Guardian*, December 15, 2012. https://www.theguardian.com/world/2012/dec/15/sandy-hook-teacher-victoria -soto.

OCTOBER 21 THE MAN WHO FELL TO EARTH

Broad, William J. "Russian Space Mementos Show Gagarin's Ride Was a Rough One." *New York Times*, March 5, 1996. http://www.nytimes.com/1996/03/05/science/russian-space-mementos-show-gagarin-s -ride-was-a-rough-one.html.

Krulwich, Robert. "Cosmonaut Crashed into Earth 'Crying in Rage.'" *Krulwich Wonders* (blog). NPR, March 18, 2011. https://www.npr.org/sections/krulwich/2011/05/02/134597833/cosmonaut-crashed -into-earth-crying-in-rage.

Rodgers, Paul. "Yuri Gagarin: The Man Who Fell to Earth." *Independent*, April 2, 2011. http://www .independent.co.uk/news/science/yuri-gagarin-the-man-who-fell-to-earth-2257505.html.

Schupak, Amanda. "6 Surprising Facts about the First Manned Space Mission." Live Science, April 6, 2011. https://www.livescience.com/33185-yuri-gagarin-vostok-1-faq-facts.html.

OCTOBER 22 A MOUSE THAT ROARED

Hamilton, Duncan. *For the Glory: Eric Liddell's Journey from Olympic Champion to Modern Martyr.* New York: Penguin Press, 2016.

Magnusson, Sally. *The Flying Scotsman: A Biography.* New York: Quartet Books, 1981.

McCasland, David. *Eric Liddell: Pure Gold.* Grand Rapids, MI: Discovery House, 2010.

Pettinger, Tejvan. "Eric Liddell Biography." Biography Online. Last updated August 7, 2014. http://www.biographyonline.net/sport/athletics/eric-liddell.html.

OCTOBER 23 THE WOMAN WHO TORE DOWN THE WALL

Angelo, Bonnie. *First Mothers: The Women Who Shaped the Presidents.* New York: Harper Perennial, 2001.

D'Souza, Dinesh. *Ronald Reagan: How an Ordinary Man Became an Extraordinary Leader.* New York: Free Press, 1997.

OCTOBER 24 COLLAPSING TO VICTORY

Crouse, Lindsay. "For Runner with M.S., No Pain while Racing, No Feeling at the Finish." *New York Times,* March 3, 2014. https://www.nytimes.com/2014/03/04/sports/for-runner-with-ms-no-pain-while-racing-no-feeling-at-the-finish.html.

Kissane, John A. "For Teen Runner with MS, a Season of Change." *Runner's World,* December 10, 2014. https://www.runnersworld.com/web-exclusive/for-teen-runner-with-ms-a-season-of-change.

Morley, Gary, and Lisa Cohen. "Kayla Montgomery: Young Runner's Brave Battle with MS." CNN, May 10, 2015. https://www.cnn.com/2015/05/20/sport/kayla-montgomery-multiple-sclerosis-athletics-feat/index.html.

Polachek, Emily. "Kayla Montgomery, Runner with Multiple Sclerosis, to Receive Award." Competitor Running, June 30, 2016. http://running.competitor.com/2016/06/news/runner-multiple-sclerosis-kayla-montgomery-receive-award-independence-day_152654.

OCTOBER 25 SIXTY-SIX SHINING LIGHTS

Brogadir, Josh. "Family 'Glad' Britney Gengel's Body Recovered." NECN, March 25, 2014. https://www.necn.com/news/new-england/_NECN__Family__glad__Britney_Gengel_s_Body_Recovered_NECN-252141821.html.

Friedman, Emily. "Parents Devastated after Daughter Declared Still Missing in Haiti." ABC News, January 15, 2010. http://abcnews.go.com/WN/HaitiEarthquake/missing-haiti-len-gengel-searches-daughter-britney-florida-student/story?id=9574373.

Salomon, Sanjay. "Remembering Britney Gengel." WGBH. Accessed February 16, 2018. http://www.wgbh.org/articles/Remembering-Britney-Gengel-1623.

Twomey, Karen. "Britney Gengel's Parents Visit Haiti Orphanage 5 Years after Deadly Quake." CBS Boston, January 12, 2015. http://boston.cbslocal.com/2015/01/12/britney-gengels-parents-visit-haiti-orphanage-5-years-after-deadly-quake/.

OCTOBER 26 THE TEENAGE CARDINAL

PBS. "The Characters: Pope Leo X." Accessed February 11, 2018. http://www.pbs.org/empires/martinluther/char_leo.html.

ReligionFacts. "Giovanni de' Medici." Updated November 22, 2016. http://www.religionfacts.com/pope-leo-x.

Webley, Kayla. "Top Ten Controversial Popes." *Time,* April 14, 2010. http://content.time.com/time/specials/packages/article/0,28804,1981842_1981844_1981624,00.html.

OCTOBER 27 THE ANGEL IN THE RED BANDANA

Baker, KC. "9/11 Hero Welles Crowther, 'the Man in the Red Bandana,' Still Inspires Others to Do Good." *People,* April 27, 2017. http://people.com/human-interest/911-hero-welles-crowther-the-man-in-the-red-bandana-still-inspires-others-to-do-good/.

Kilgannon, Corey. "Saved on 9/11, by the Man in the Red Bandanna." *New York Times,* September 8, 2017. https://www.nytimes.com/2017/09/08/nyregion/welles-crowther-man-in-red-bandanna-911.html.

Kramer, Peter D. "9/11: Tom Rinaldi Shares Story of Man in the Red Bandanna, Who Died Saving Others." *USA Today,* September 7, 2016. https://www.usatoday.com/story/news/nation-now/2016/09/07/911-tom-rinaldi-shares-story-man-red-bandanna-who-died-saving-others/89952504/.

OCTOBER 28 THE FIXER

Biography. "Martin Luther." Updated August 8, 2017. https://www.biography.com/people/martin-luther-9389283.

Jacobsen, Herbert K. "Martin Luther's Early Years: Did You Know?" *Christianity Today.* Accessed February 18, 2018. Previously published in *Christian History,* no. 34 (1992). http://www.christianitytoday.com/history/issues/issue-34/martin-luthers-early-years-did-you-know.html.

Lawson, Steven. "Fortress for Truth: Martin Luther." Ligonier Ministries, September 11, 2017. Excerpted from Steven J. Lawson, *Pillars of Grace*. Reformation Trust, 2016. https://www.ligonier.org/blog /fortress-truth-martin-luther/.

OCTOBER 29 THE CURSE OF MACBETH

Kemp, Stuart. "Macbeth: The Curse of the Scottish Play." *Telegraph*, September 18, 2015. http://www.telegraph .co.uk/film/macbeth/scottish_play_curse/.

MacGowan, Doug. "The Macbeth Curse." Historic Mysteries, May 19, 2012. https://www.historicmysteries .com/the-macbeth-curse/.

Palmer, Mary. "7 Sinister Examples of the Curse of Macbeth ahead of the Blockbuster Cinema Release." Scotland Now, September 10, 2015. http://www.scotlandnow.dailyrecord.co.uk/news/7-sinister-examples -curse-macbeth-6419261.

Schumm, Laura. "Why Do Actors Avoid the Word 'Macbeth'?" History, April 9, 2014. http://www.history .com/news/ask-history/why-do-actors-avoid-the-word-macbeth.

OCTOBER 30 HELPER OF THE HELPLESS

Bradfield, Haley. "Amy Carmichael Biography." Inspirational Christians. Accessed February 11, 2018. http:// www.inspirationalchristians.org/biography/amy-carmichael-biography/.

Christianity.com. "Amy Carmichael Helped the Helpless." July 16, 2010. https://www.christianity.com /church/church-history/church-history-for-kids/amy-carmichael-helped-the-helpless-11634859.html.

MacKenzie, Catherine. "Amy Carmichael." Review of *Amy Carmichael: Beauty for Ashes*, by Iain Murray. The Gospel Coalition, April 1, 2015. https://resources.thegospelcoalition.org/library/amy-carmichael.

OCTOBER 31 OF SPIRITS

Harlan, Susan. "Guilt House." Curbed San Francisco, June 23, 2016. https://sf.curbed.com/2016/6/23 /11994078/winchester-mystery-house-architecture-history.

Leah. "We Welcome You to the Winchester Mystery House." Ripley's Believe It or Not! May 1, 2017. http:// www.ripleys.com/weird-news/winchester-mystery-house/.

Marck, John T. "Sarah Winchester and Her Mystery House." About Famous People. Accessed February 7, 2018. http://www.aboutfamouspeople.com/article1231.html.

Stollznow, Karen. "The Winchester Mystery House." CSI, December 29, 2011. https://www.csicop.org /specialarticles/show/the_winchester_mystery_house.

NOVEMBER 1 THE CHIEF INSPIRATOR

Berrios, Valerie. "So What Do You Do, Toan Lam, 'Chief Inspirator' for Social Activism Site GoInspireGo .com?" Mediabistro, February 5, 2014. https://www.mediabistro.com/interviews/so-what-do-you-do -toan-lam-chief-inspirator-for-social-activism-site-goinspirego-com/.

Fernando, Aneya. "How Former TV Reporter Toan Lam Became a Social Activist." TVSpy, February 6, 2014. http://www.adweek.com/tvspy/how-former-tv-reporter-toan-lam-became-a-social-activist/115792.

Fox, MeiMei. "This Immigrant Found His 'American Dream' in Inspiring Others to Give Back." *Forbes*, May 8, 2017. https://www.forbes.com/sites/meimeifox/2017/05/08/this-immigrants-american-dream-is -to-inspire-others-to-live-a-life-of-service/#10108714224a.

HuffPost. "Toan Lam." Accessed February 18, 2018. https://www.huffingtonpost.com/author/toan-lam.

NOVEMBER 2 BARBARIANS AT THE GATES

History. "Punic Wars." Accessed February 12, 2018. http://www.history.com/topics/ancient-history/punic-wars.

Kiernan, Ben. "The First Genocide: Carthage, 146 BC." Yale University Genocide Studies Program. Previously published in *Diogenes* 51, no. 3 (2004). https://gsp.yale.edu/sites/default/files/first_genocide.pdf.

Scullard, Howard Hayes. "Scipio Africanus the Younger." *Encyclopedia Britannica Online*. Updated November 15, 2017. https://www.britannica.com/biography/Scipio-Africanus-the-Younger.

Whitworth, Lou. "Living in the New Dark Ages." Probe Ministries. Accessed February 12, 2018. Material quoted and paraphrased from Charles Colson, *Against the Night: Living in the New Dark Ages*. With Ellen Santilli Vaughn. Ann Arbor, MI: Servant, 1989. http://www.leaderu.com/orgs/probe/docs /darkages.html.

NOVEMBER 3 HISTORY'S GREATEST ATHLETE

Biography. "Jim Thorpe." Updated February 5, 2016. https://www.biography.com/people/jim-thorpe -9507017.

Greene, Bob. "Tortured Life of World's Greatest Athlete." CNN, August 1, 2010. http://www.cnn.com /2010/OPINION/08/01/greene.jim.thorpe/index.html.

Jenkins, Sally. "Why Are Jim Thorpe's Olympic Records Still Not Recognized?" *Smithsonian*, July 2012. https://www.smithsonianmag.com/history/why-are-jim-thorpes-olympic-records-still-not-recognized -130986336/.

New York Times. "Jim Thorpe Is Dead on West Coast at 64." On This Day: March 29, 1953. Accessed February 12, 2018. http://www.nytimes.com/learning/general/onthisday/bday/0528.html?mcubz=1.

NOVEMBER 4 THE COP WHO COULDN'T BE BOUGHT

Alm, David. "Frank Serpico Speaks, in a New Documentary about the Legendary Ex-Cop." *Forbes*, April 25, 2017. https://www.forbes.com/sites/davidalm/2017/04/25/frank-serpico-speaks-in-a-new-documentary -about-the-legendary-ex-cop/#180fe71013a1.

Garcia, Maria. "'Frank Serpico': A Portrait of the Legendary Whistleblowing Cop." Biography, April 26, 2017. https://www.biography.com/news/frank-serpico-documentary-review.

Kilgannon, Corey. "Serpico on Serpico." *New York Times*, January 22, 2010. http://www.nytimes.com/2010 /01/24/nyregion/24serpico.html?pagewanted=all.

Perry, Douglas. "Why Frank Serpico Still Gets Hate Mail: 5 Things Everyone Should Know about the Iconic Cop." *Oregonian*, October 30, 2014. http://www.oregonlive.com/today/index.ssf/2014/10/why_frank _serpico_still_gets_h.html.

NOVEMBER 5 THREE MINUTES AND SEVENTEEN SECONDS THAT CHANGED FOOTBALL

Hale, Jon. "Amid Protests, Kentucky Football Statue Takes On More Meaning in Lexington." *Louisville Courier-Journal*, August 27, 2017. https://www.courier-journal.com/story/sports/college/kentucky /2017/08/27/confederate-statues-kentucky-football-wilbur-hackett-nate-northington-greg-page-houston -hogg/589665001/.

Kindred, Dave. "The Forgotten Trailblazer." Sports on Earth, November 5, 2013. http://www.sportsonearth .com/article/63673094/nate-northington-sec-segregation-university-of-kentucky-ole-miss.

Story, Mark. "UK's Nate Northington: Integrating SEC Football Was 'More Difficult Than I Anticipated.'" *Lexington Herald-Leader*, September 29, 2017. http://www.kentucky.com/sports/spt-columns-blogs /mark-story/article176106916.html.

White, Bob. "SEC Pioneer Northington Subject of Documentary." *Louisville Courier-Journal*, February 14, 2015. https://www.courier-journal.com/story/sports/college/kentucky/2015/02/14/kentuckys-sec -pioneer-louisville-native-nate-northington-subject-cbs-documentary/23431657/.

NOVEMBER 6 THE JEWEL THIEF WHO BECAME A COP

HuffPost. "Larry Lawton, Former Jewel Thief, Is First Ex-Con to Become Honorary Police Officer." August 18, 2013. https://www.huffingtonpost.com/2013/08/18/larry-lawton-ex-con-honorary-police_n_3768977 .html.

Mitchell, Anita. "Larry Lawton: The Reality Check Program Is My Legacy." Broward People, March 26, 2016. www.browardpeople.com/larry-lawton-the-reality-check-program-is-my-legacy/. Article no longer available.

Nissen, Dory. "Larry Lawton Finds His Purpose in Prison." CBN. Accessed February 12, 2018. http://www1 .cbn.com/larry-lawton-finds-his-purpose-prison.

NOVEMBER 7 THE SECRET MISSION THAT CHANGED AMERICA

Axelrod, Alan. "Joe Kennedy Jr.: Fallen Hero of Operation Aphrodite." The History Reader, May 26, 2015. http://www.thehistoryreader.com/military-history/joe-kennedy-jr-fallen-hero-operation-aphrodite/.

Historic Wings. "Operation Aphrodite." August 12, 2012. http://fly.historicwings.com/2012/08/operation -aphrodite/.

History. "Joseph Kennedy Jr." Accessed February 12, 2018. http://www.history.com/topics/joseph-kennedy-jr.

World War II Today. "Joseph P. Kennedy Jr. Dies in Secret Drone Mission." Accessed February 12, 2018. http://ww2today.com/12-august-1944-joseph-p-kennedy-jr-dies-in-secret-drone-mission.

NOVEMBER 8 WHEN SAINTS DOUBT

This story is adapted from Matthew 3; 11; and Mark 6.

Akin, Jimmy. "Who Was John the Baptist? (11 Things to Know and Share)." *National Catholic Register*, August 28, 2013. http://www.ncregister.com/blog/jimmy-akin/who-was-the-baptist-11-things -to-know-and-share.

Amazing Bible Timeline. "John the Baptist in the Bible, Biography." February 16, 2013. https://amazing bibletimeline.com/blog/john-the-baptist-in-the-bible-biography/.

Goldberg, G. J., ed. "John the Baptist and Josephus." Josephus.org. Accessed February 12, 2018. http://www .josephus.org/JohnTBaptist.htm.

NOVEMBER 9 THE COMEBACK KING

Biography. "George Foreman." Updated November 3, 2017. https://www.biography.com/people/george -foreman-9298881.

May, Michael. "Total Failure: How George Foreman's Losses Showed Him the Light." *All Things Considered.* NPR, May 24, 2017. https://www.npr.org/2017/05/24/528995768/total-failure-how-george-foremans-losses-showed-him-the-light.

Sugar, Bert Randolph. "Boxing's Greatest Fighters: George Foreman." ESPN, October 18, 2006. Excerpted from Bert Randolph Sugar, *Boxing's Greatest Fighters.* Guilford, CT: Lyons, 2006. http://www.espn.com/sports/boxing/news/story?id=2631852.

Walsh, S. M. "George Foreman's 12 Kids: 5 Fast Facts You Need to Know." Heavy, August 30, 2016. https://heavy.com/entertainment/2016/08/george-foreman-kids-children-family-sons-daughters-wife-married-better-late-than-never-nbc/.

NOVEMBER 10 THE DECISION

Jerome, Richard. "Cold Mountain." *People,* February 9, 2004. http://people.com/archive/cold-mountain-vol-61-no-5/.

Reed, Susan, and Laura Sanderson Healy. "Left for Dead on a Peruvian Peak, Joe Simpson Survives to Write Movingly about the Climbers' Code." *People,* May 1, 1989. http://people.com/archive/left-for-dead-on-a-peruvian-peak-joe-simpson-survives-to-write-movingly-about-the-climbers-code-vol-31-no-17/.

Simpson, Joe. "Joe Simpson: My Journey Back into the Void." Interview by Peter Stanford. *Telegraph,* October 22, 2007. http://www.telegraph.co.uk/news/features/3634463/Joe-Simpson-My-journey-back-into-the-void.html.

Traditional Mountaineering. "Notable Mountain Climbing Accidents Analyzed by Experts." Accessed February 14, 2018. http://www.traditionalmountaineering.org/FAQ_NoteableAccidents.htm.

NOVEMBER 11 THE UNEXPECTED HERO

Faraci, Devin. "The Time Daniel Inouye Pried a Grenade from His Severed Arm." BirthMoviesDeath, December 17, 2012. http://birthmoviesdeath.com/2012/12/17/the-time-daniel-inouye-pried-a-grenade-from-his-severed-arm.

Hersh, Seymour M. "Daniel Inouye's Conscience." *New Yorker,* December 18, 2012. https://www.newyorker.com/news/news-desk/daniel-inouyes-conscience.

National Park Service. "Daniel Inouye: A Japanese American Soldier's Valor in World War II." Accessed January 11, 2018. https://www.nps.gov/articles/inouyeww2.htm.

PBS. "As 'Nisei' Soldier, Sen. Daniel Inouye Fought to Prove His Loyalty to America." *NewsHour,* December 18, 2012. https://www.pbs.org/newshour/politics/as-nisei-soldier-sen-daniel-inouye-fought-to-prove-his-loyalty-to-america.

NOVEMBER 12 FROM TRAILER PARK TO TINSELTOWN

Biography. "Hilary Swank." Updated April 27, 2017. https://www.biography.com/people/hilary-swank-9542281.

Hiscock, John. "Hilary Swank: I Like to Take On Roles That Scare Me." The National, November 12, 2010. https://www.thenational.ae/arts-culture/hilary-swank-i-like-to-take-on-roles-that-scare-me-1.511000?videoId=5594734385001.

Palmer, Martyn. "'I Know What It's Like to Be the Outsider': Hilary Swank on Her Journey from Trailer Park to Tinseltown." *Daily Mail,* January 7, 2011. http://www.dailymail.co.uk/home/you/article-1341187/Hilary-Swank-journey-trailer-park-Tinseltown-I-know-like-outsider.html.

Witteman, Kate M. "Stars Who Were Once Homeless: Hilary Swank." *Time,* July 11, 2013. http://newsfeed.time.com/2013/07/11/stars-who-were-once-homeless/slide/hilary-swank/.

NOVEMBER 13 BLINKING A BESTSELLER

Davis, Charles Patrick. "Locked-in Syndrome." MedicineNet.com. Reviewed March 18, 2016. https://www.medicinenet.com/locked-in_syndrome/article.htm#locked-in_syndrome_facts.

Di Giovanni, Janine. "The Real Love Story behind *The Diving Bell and the Butterfly.*" *Guardian,* November 29, 2008. https://www.theguardian.com/lifeandstyle/2008/nov/30/diving-bell-butterfly-florence-bensadoun.

Mallon, Thomas. "In the Blink of an Eye." Review of *The Diving Bell and the Butterfly,* by Jean-Dominique Bauby. *New York Times,* June 15, 1997. http://www.nytimes.com/books/97/06/15/reviews/970615.mallon.html.

Schneider, Karen S. "Blink of an Eye." *People,* June 2, 1997. http://people.com/archive/blink-of-an-eye-vol-47-no-21/.

NOVEMBER 14 LEFT BEHIND IN AFRICA

Biography. "David Livingstone." Updated April 2, 2014. https://www.biography.com/people/david-livingstone-9383955.

Nuwer, Rachel. "Decoding the Lost Diary of David Livingstone." *Smithsonian,* November 24, 2014. https://www.smithsonianmag.com/history/decoding-lost-diary-david-livingstone-180953385/.

Schrope, Mark. "Dr. Livingstone's Diary on 19th-Century Africa, Now Uncensored." *Washington Post*, November 1, 2011. https://www.washingtonpost.com/lifestyle/style/dr-livingstones-diary-on-19th -century-africa-now-uncensored/2011/10/31/gIQAUsB2aM_story.html?utm_term=.2399e6b8d7b0.

Wholesome Words. "David Livingstone." Accessed February 15, 2018. Copied from *Christian Heroism in Heathen Lands*, by Galen B. Royer. Public domain. https://www.wholesomewords.org/missions/bliving2 .html.

NOVEMBER 15 CRAWLING A PICKET FENCE TO THE OLYMPICS

Dubin, Burt. "Story of Determination: Glenn Cunningham." WantToKnow.info. Accessed February 15, 2018. https://www.wanttoknow.info/050702powerofdetermination.

Rogers, Thomas. "Glenn Cunningham, 78, Premier Miler of 1930's." *New York Times*, March 11, 1988. http://www.nytimes.com/1988/03/11/obituaries/glenn-cunningham-78-premier-miler-of-1930-s.html.

Watson, Leroy, Jr. "Forgotten Stories of Courage and Inspiration: Glenn Cunningham." B/R, June 12, 2009. http://bleacherreport.com/articles/198249-forgotten-stories-of-courage-and-inspiration-glenn -cunningham.

NOVEMBER 16 THE DELI SANDWICH

Butcher, Tim. "The Lie That Started the First World War." *Telegraph*, June 28, 2014. http://www.telegraph .co.uk/history/world-war-one/10930829/The-lie-that-started-the-First-World-War.html.

Espino, Fernando. "6 Random Coincidences That Created the Modern World." Cracked, April 27, 2009. http://www.cracked.com/article_17298_6-random-coincidences-that-created-modern-world.html.

Hornshaw, Phil. "*Fargo* Fact Check: Did a Sandwich Really Help Start World War I?" TheWrap. Updated May 24, 2017. https://www.thewrap.com/fargo-fact-check-sandwich-world-war/.

Raub, Olivia. "Princip's Sandwich Starts a War." *History as You Were Never Taught* (blog). Sites at Penn State, October 24, 2013. http://sites.psu.edu/interestinghistory/2013/10/24/princips-sandwich-starts-a-war/.

NOVEMBER 17 THE PARALYZED ACTION STAR

Brian, Sascha. "What If I Told You Sylvester Stallone Has Been Paralyzed Since Birth?" Like a Boss, September 29, 2014. http://www.likeaboss.com/news/what-if-i-told-you-sylvester-stallone-has-been -paralyzed-since-birth/.

Gilbey, Ryan. "Sylvester Stallone: The Wacky People's Champ Who Battled His Own Ego." *Guardian*, February 24, 2016. https://www.theguardian.com/film/2016/feb/24/sylvester-stallone-profile-creed -rocky.

Hawker, Tom. "25 Things You (Probably) Didn't Know about Sylvester Stallone." IGN, January 30, 2013. http://www.ign.com/articles/2013/01/30/25-things-you-probably-didnt-know-about-sylvester-stallone.

Stanley, Tim. "Rocky, the Raging Optimist Who Floored America." *Telegraph*, January 14, 2016. http://www .telegraph.co.uk/film/creed/rocky-sylvester-stallone-making-of-trivia/.

NOVEMBER 18 STARVING FOR A STRANGER

Binder, David. "Franciszek Gajowniczek Dead; Priest Died for Him at Auschwitz." *New York Times*, March 15, 1995. http://www.nytimes.com/1995/03/15/obituaries/franciszek-gajowniczek-dead-priest-died-for -him-at-auschwitz.html.

Biniaz, Benjamin. "Religious Resistance in Auschwitz: The Sacrifice of Saint Kolbe." *Through Testimony* (blog). University of Southern California Shoah Foundation, August 12, 2016. https://sfi.usc.edu/blog /benjamin-biniaz/religious-resistance-auschwitz-sacrifice-saint-kolbe.

Hitler's Children. "Father Maximilian Kolbe and His Sacrifice." Accessed February 15, 2018. http://www .hitlerschildren.com/article/1465-father-maximilian-kolbe-and-his-sacrifice.

Pettinger, Tejvan. "Maximilian Kolbe Biography." Biography Online. Updated June 26, 2017. https://www .biographyonline.net/spiritual/maximilian-kolbe.html.

NOVEMBER 19 TWO MINUTES THAT CHANGED HISTORY

Conant, Sean, ed. *The Gettysburg Address: Perspectives on Lincoln's Greatest Speech*. New York: Oxford University Press, 2015.

Georgia Info. "This Day in Georgia Civil War History: December 5, 1863, *Harper's Weekly* Commented on Gettysburg Address." Accessed March 11, 2017. http://georgiainfo.galileo.usg.edu/thisday/cwhistory /12/05/harpers-weekly-commented-on-gettysburg-address.

Los Angeles Times. "Abraham Lincoln Gettysburg Address: They Get Longer, but Not Better." Top of the Ticket: Political Commentary from the *LA Times*, November 19, 2010. http://latimesblogs.latimes.com /washington/2010/11/gettysburg-address-abraham-lincoln.html.

NOVEMBER 20 A RIGHTEOUS EVIL

Bordewich, Fergus M. "John Brown's Day of Reckoning." *Smithsonian*, October 2009. https://www .smithsonianmag.com/history/john-browns-day-of-reckoning-139165084/.

De Togni, Elisa. "The Abolitionist's John Brown." Civil War Trust. Accessed February 15, 2018. https://www.civilwar.org/learn/articles/abolitionists-john-brown.

HistoryNet. "John Brown." Accessed February 15, 2018. http://www.historynet.com/john-brown.

Timmons, Greg. "Terrorist or Freedom Fighter? John Brown's Raid on Harpers Ferry." *Biography*, October 15, 2015. https://www.biography.com/news/john-brown-biography-harpers-ferry-raid.

NOVEMBER 21 THE CANDY MAN CAN

Biography. "Milton Hershey." Updated April 27, 2017. https://www.biography.com/people/milton-hershey-9337133.

Entrepreneur. "Milton S. Hershey." October 8, 2008. https://www.entrepreneur.com/article/197530.

Masters, Marsha. "Spotlighting Entrepreneurs: The Sweet Success of Milton Hershey." EconEdLink. Updated May 19, 2015. https://www.econedlink.org/teacher-lesson/1069/Spotlighting-Entrepreneurs-Sweet-Success-Milton-Hershey.

Shapiro, Phil. "The Story of Milton Hershey." Phil Shapiro's website. Accessed February 21, 2018. http://www.his.com/~pshapiro/milton.hershey.html.

NOVEMBER 22 ONLY ONE CAME FORWARD

The Billy Graham Library. "This Date in History: Nov. 1, 1934—Billy Graham Accepts Christ." November 1, 2012. https://billygrahamlibrary.org/this-date-in-history-nov-1-1934-billy-graham-accepts-christ/.

Coppenger, Mark. "What I Learned from Mordecai Ham." *Christianity Today*. Accessed February 15, 2018. Previously published in *Leadership Journal* (Fall 1988). http://www.christianitytoday.com/pastors/1988/fall/8814032.html.

Laurie, Greg. "The Impact of One." Daily Devotion. Harvest, January 15, 2013. https://www.harvest.org/devotions-and-blogs/daily-devotions/2013-01-15.

Sanders, Fred. "Mordecai Ham Tried to Baptize a Cat." The Scriptorium Daily, April 2, 2009. http://scriptoriumdaily.com/mordecai-ham-tried-to-baptize-a-cat/.

NOVEMBER 23 LESSONS FROM THE CONCENTRATION CAMP

Barnes, Henry. "Viktor Frankl's Book on the Psychology of the Holocaust to Be Made into a Film." *Guardian*, June 9, 2015. https://www.theguardian.com/film/2015/jun/09/viktor-frankls-book-on-the-psychology-of-the-holocaust-to-be-made-into-a-film.

PBS. "Viktor Frankl." *The Question of God.* Other Voices. Reprinted with permission from *Man's Search for Meaning* (Boston: Beacon, 1959). Accessed February 16, 2018. http://www.pbs.org/wgbh/questionofgod/voices/frankl.html.

Smith, Emily Esfahani. "There's More to Life Than Being Happy." *Atlantic*, January 9, 2013. https://www.theatlantic.com/health/archive/2013/01/theres-more-to-life-than-being-happy/266805/.

NOVEMBER 24 THE MAN TIME FORGOT

Berman, Mark. "The Guy Missouri Forgot to Imprison for 13 Years Has Been Cleared of New, Different Charges." *Washington Post*, February 6, 2015. https://www.washingtonpost.com/news/post-nation/wp/2015/02/06/the-guy-missouri-forgot-to-imprison-for-13-years-has-been-cleared-of-new-different-charges/?utm_term=.f8f2ae8a7fc9.

Crimesider Staff. "Man Who Went to Prison 13 Years Late Ordered Released." CBS News, May 5, 2014. https://www.cbsnews.com/news/man-who-went-to-prison-13-years-late-ordered-released/.

Pearce, Matt. "Missouri Ex-Convict Freed after Another Bizarre Brush with the Law." *Los Angeles Times*, February 5, 2015. http://www.latimes.com/nation/la-na-missouri-charges-dropped-20150205-story.html.

Williams, Aja J. "Judge Frees Man That Clerical Error Kept from Prison." *USA Today*, May 5, 2014. https://www.usatoday.com/story/news/nation/2014/05/05/judge-frees-robber-who-skipped-prison/8722645/.

NOVEMBER 25 PITCHING YOUR TENT TOWARD SODOM

This story is adapted from Genesis 13–19.

Ark Discovery International. "Sodom and Gomorrah." Accessed February 16, 2018. http://www.arkdiscovery.com/ sodom_&_gomorrah.htm.

Lovett, Richard A. "Bible Accounts Supported by Dead Sea Disaster Record?" *National Geographic*, December 8, 2011. https://news.nationalgeographic.com/news/2011/12/111208-dead-sea-bible-biblical-salt-dry-science/.

NOVEMBER 26 SURRENDERING TO LORD NELSON

BBC. "Admiral Horatio Lord Nelson (1758–1805)." Accessed February 16, 2018. http://www.bbc.co.uk/history/historic_figures/nelson_admiral_horatio_lord.shtml.

Crockett, Kent. "The Sword First, Then the Hand." *Kent Crockett's Devotionals* (blog), April 19, 2010. http://kentcrockett.blogspot.com/2010/04/sword-first-then-hand.html.

Ryan, Michael. "Lord Nelson: Hero and . . . Cad!" *Smithsonian*, February 2004. https://www.smithsonian
mag.com/history/lord-nelson-hero-andcad-105811218/.

Sanders, J. Oswald. "Spiritual Discipleship—page 3." C. S. Lewis Institute. Accessed February 16, 2018.
Excerpted from *Spiritual Discipleship*, by J. Oswald Sanders. Previously published in *Knowing & Doing*
(Summer 2011). http://www.cslewisinstitute.org/Spiritual_Discipleship_page_3.

NOVEMBER 27 BAREFOOT IN THE SNOW

ABC News. "Boy, 7, Saves Mom after Car Wreck." December 18, 2002. http://abcnews.go.com/GMA/story?id
=12551&page=1.

Harlow, Kristance. "10 Amazing Child Heroes." Listverse, December 9, 2013. https://listverse.com/2013
/12/09/10-amazing-child-heroes/.

Singleton, Don. "Barefoot Boy Braves Snow to Save Mom." *New York Daily News*, December 1, 2002.
http://www.nydailynews.com/archives/news/barefoot-boy-braves-snow-save-mom-article-1.498636.

NOVEMBER 28 THE MIRACLE OF THANKSGIVING

Biography. "Squanto." Updated November 22, 2017. https://www.biography.com/people/squanto-9491327.

Colson, Charles. "The Story of Squanto." Bible.org, February 2, 2009. Previously published in BreakPoint
Commentary, November 25, 1998. https://bible.org/illustration/story-squanto.

Metaxas, Eric. "Thanksgiving and the True Story of Squanto." Interview by Terry Meeuwsen. CBN. Accessed
January 26, 2018. http://www1.cbn.com/churchandministry/thanksgiving-and-the-true-story-of-squanto.

Wilson, Ralph F. "Squanto—God's Special Indian, a Thanksgiving Story." Joyful Heart. Accessed January 26,
2018. http://www.joyfulheart.com/thanksgiving/squanto.htm.

NOVEMBER 29 THE SCOTTISH NOSTRADAMUS

Jeffers, Regina. "Scotland's Nostradamus: The Brahan Seer." *English Historical Fiction Authors* (blog),
December 1, 2011. https://englishhistoryauthors.blogspot.com/2011/12/scotlands-nostradamus-brahan
-seer.html.

Johnson, Ben. "The Brahan Seer—The Scottish Nostradamus." Historic UK. Accessed February 16, 2018.
http://www.historic-uk.com/HistoryUK/HistoryofScotland/The-Brahan-Seer-the-Scottish-Nostradamus/.

Munro, Bruce. "Brahan Seer: The Scot Who Could See the Future." BBC, July 7, 2011. http://www.bbc.co
.uk/scotland/history/brahan_seer.shtml.

Undiscovered Scotland. "The Brahan Seer." Accessed February 16, 2018. https://www.undiscoveredscotland
.co.uk/usbiography/b/brahanseer.html.

NOVEMBER 30 MAKING A DIFFERENCE

Blackhurst, Kathryn. "6 Astonishingly Heroic Acts of Police Officers." *Newsmax*, June 11, 2015. https://
www.newsmax.com/fastfeatures/police-officer-heroic-acts/2015/06/15/id/650007/.

Chambers, Steve. "James Nelson." *New Jersey Star-Ledger*, August 23, 2011. http://blog.nj.com/lives
_remembered/2011/08/james_nelson_40_he_made_a_diff.html.

Collins, Dave. "Caitlin Nelson, Daughter of Fallen 9/11 Cop, Dies after Pancake-Eating Contest." HuffPost,
April 3, 2017. http://www.huffingtonpost.ca/2017/04/03/woman-dies-pancake-eating-contest_n
_15786168.html.

Remo, Jessica. "Clark Remembers 9/11, Honors Victim James Nelson." Clark Patch, September 12, 2013.
https://patch.com/new-jersey/clark/clark-remembers-911-honors-victim-james-nelson.

DECEMBER 1 A MAP TO NOWHERE

PBS. "American Experience: *The Donner Party*." Film Resources: The Diary of Patrick Breen. Accessed
March 7, 2017. http://www.pbs.org/wgbh/americanexperience/features/primary-resources/donner
-diary-patrick-breen/.

Rarick, Ethan. *Desperate Passage: The Donner Party's Perilous Journey West*. Oxford: Oxford University Press,
2008.

Weiser, Kathy. "The Donner Party Tragedy." Legends of America. Updated April 2015. http://www.legends
ofamerica.com/ca-donnerparty.html.

DECEMBER 2 ONE LAST SONG IN A TATTERED COAT

Songwriters Hall of Fame. "Stephen Foster Biography." Accessed March 12, 2017. http://www.songwriters
halloffame.org/exhibits/bio/C10.

Swindoll, Charles R. "Insight for Today: Who Cares?" Insight for Living Ministries, July 26, 2015. http://
www.insight.org/resources/daily-devotional/individual/who-cares.

DECEMBER 3 AN ELUSIVE SEDUCTION

The Art Story. "Paul Gauguin." Accessed February 18, 2018. http://www.theartstory.org/artist-gauguin-paul
.htm.

Artble. "Paul Gauguin." Accessed February 18, 2018. https://www.artble.com/artists/paul_gauguin.

Hill, Amelia. "Gauguin's Erotic Tahiti Idyll Exposed as a Sham." *Guardian*, October 7, 2001. https://www.theguardian.com/world/2001/oct/07/arts.highereducation.

Smart, Alastair. "Is It Wrong to Admire Paul Gauguin's Art?" *Telegraph*, September 19, 2010. http://www.telegraph.co.uk/culture/art/8011066/Is-it-wrong-to-admire-Paul-Gauguins-art.html.

DECEMBER 4 THE FUNERAL THAT KILLED MILLIONS

Jones, Nigel. Review of *Stalin's Nemesis: The Exile and Murder of Leon Trotsky*, by Bertrand M. Patenaude. History Today. Accessed February 18, 2018. http://www.historytoday.com/nigel-jones/stalin%E2%80%99s-nemesis-exile-and-murder-leon-trotsky.

SparkNotes. "Joseph Stalin." Accessed February 18, 2018. http://www.sparknotes.com/biography/stalin/.

Thatcher, Ian D. "Trotskii and Lenin's Funeral, 27 January 1924: A Brief Note." *History* 94, no. 2 (April 2009): 194–202.

Trotsky, Leon. *My Life*, chap. 41. New York: Charles Scribner's Sons, 1930. PDF e-book. Marxists Internet Archive. Accessed February 18, 2018. https://www.marxists.org/archive/trotsky/1930/mylife/ch41.htm.

DECEMBER 5 AIN'T I A WOMAN?

Biography. "Sojourner Truth." Updated February 8, 2018. https://www.biography.com/people/sojourner-truth-9511284.

History. "Sojourner Truth." Accessed February 18, 2018. http://www.history.com/topics/black-history/sojourner-truth.

PBS. "Sojourner Truth." This Far by Faith. Accessed February 18, 2018. http://www.pbs.org/thisfarbyfaith/people/sojourner_truth.html.

Pope-Levison, Priscilla. "Truth, Sojourner, Isabella Baumfree (ca. 1791–1883)." BlackPast.org. Accessed February 18, 2018. http://www.blackpast.org/aah/truth-sojourner-isabella-baumfree-ca-1791-1883.

DECEMBER 6 TAKING TEN ROUNDS FOR THE KIDS

Chaplain 81. "47 Seconds." *Free from the Fire* (blog), January 7, 2016. https://freefromthefire.com/2016/01/07/47-seconds-2/.

Gebhart, Lindsay. "Fla. Officer Takes 10 Rounds to Save Children, Her Own Life." PoliceOne.com, November 2, 2005. https://www.policeone.com/police-heroes/articles/120351-Fla-officer-takes-10-rounds-to-save-children-her-own-life/.

Gutierrez, Pedro Ruz, Henry Pierson Curtis, and Rich Mckay. "7 Bullets Couldn't Stop Orange Deputy." *Orlando Sentinel*, May 6, 2004. http://articles.orlandosentinel.com/2004-05-06/news/0405060307_1_fulford-north-charleston-home-invaders.

Prickett, Greg. "Driving to the Sound of Gunfire." Mimesis Law, December 11, 2015. http://mimesislaw.com/fault-lines/driving-to-the-sound-of-gunfire/5379.

DECEMBER 7 THE FBI'S GREATEST BLUNDER

Macintyre, Ben. "Why the FBI's J. Edgar Hoover Snubbed James Bond." *Australian*, December 12, 2014.

O'Toole, Thomas. "Did Hoover Know of Pearl Harbor?" *Washington Post*, December 2, 1982. https://www.washingtonpost.com/archive/lifestyle/1982/12/02/did-hoover-know-of-pearl-harbor/7510d069-2ac9-4512-a543-d2ce1aceca7c/?utm_term=.b0d2f786cb0d.

War History Online. "Scandal of the Century—New Book Claims USA Knew of Pearl Harbor Plans for Months." June 8, 2016. https://www.warhistoryonline.com/history/scandal-of-the-century.html.

Zimmerman, Dwight Jon. "Dusko Popov, Real Life James Bond, Ran Afoul of the FBI." Defense Media Network, September 1, 2011. https://www.defensemedianetwork.com/stories/dusko-popov-real-life-james-bond-ran-afoul-of-the-fbi/.

DECEMBER 8 THEY DIED TO MAKE THE DESERT BLOOM

Brean, Henry. "Father and Son Died on the Same Day, 14 Years Apart While Working on Hoover Dam." *Las Vegas Review-Journal*, December 18, 2016. https://www.reviewjournal.com/local/local-las-vegas/father-and-son-died-on-the-same-day-14-years-apart-while-working-on-hoover-dam/.

Gamble, Kelly Stone. "Hoover Dam Stories: Two Deaths." *Staring Out the Window* (blog), November 12, 2011. http://kellystonegamble.blogspot.com/2011/11/hoover-dam-stories-two-deaths.html.

Robison, Mark. "Fact Checker: A Look at Nevada Myths: Hoover Dam Deaths, Union Gold, 501 Jeans Origin." *Reno Gazette-Journal*, June 1, 2015. http://www.rgj.com/story/news/2015/06/02/fact-checker-a-look-at-nevada-myths-hoover-dam-deaths-union-gold-501-jeans-origin/28325399/.

Weinstein, Arthur. "5 Strange Ironies and Coincidences in U.S. History." Listosaur.com, November 7, 2011. https://listosaur.com/history/5-strange-ironies-and-coincidences-in-us-history/.

DECEMBER 9 THE AFRICAN NAPOLEON

Austin, Julia. "16 Things That Made Shaka Zulu a Military Genius." AFKInsider, August 25, 2014. https://afkinsider.com/57305/16-things-made-shaka-zulu-a-military-genius/.

Dhwty. "Shaka Zulu: The Story of a Ruthless Ruler." Ancient Origins, October 15, 2015. http://www.ancient-origins.net/history-famous-people/shaka-zulu-story-ruthless-ruler-004191.

South African History Online. "Shaka Zulu." Updated February 7, 2018. http://www.sahistory.org.za/people/shaka-zulu.

Wilkinson, Stephan. "Shaka Zulu: Africa's Napoleon?" HistoryNet, March 14, 2017. http://www.historynet.com/shaka-zulu-africas-napoleon.htm.

DECEMBER 10 'TIS THE SEASON FOR . . . DEPRESSION

This story is adapted from 1 Kings 16–19.

Boucher, Chris. "Finding Hope for Depression: Lessons from Elijah." *RPM Ministries* (blog). RPM Ministries, July 21, 2010. http://www.rpmministries.org/2010/07/finding-hope-for-depression-lessons-from-elijah/.

Heitzig, Skip. "Journey through Spiritual Depression." *Christianity Today*. Accessed February 18, 2018. http://www.christianitytoday.com/pastors/2001/february-online-only/cln10214.html.

Moen, Chris. "Elijah the Prophet." Life, Hope & Truth. Accessed February 18, 2018. https://lifehopeandtruth.com/prophecy/prophets/prophets-of-the-bible/elijah-the-prophet/.

DECEMBER 11 CHRISTMAS AT THE SOUTH POLE

Arbuckle, Alex Q. "1914–1916: The *Endurance*." Mashable. Accessed February 18, 2018. https://mashable.com/2015/10/10/the-endurance/#otAe2VB92iq8.

Biography. "Ernest Shackleton." Updated February 3, 2016. https://www.biography.com/people/ernest-shackleton-9480091.

Koehn, Nancy F. "Leadership Lessons from the Shackleton Expedition." *New York Times*, December 24, 2011. http://www.nytimes.com/2011/12/25/business/leadership-lessons-from-the-shackleton-expedition.html.

Tharoor, Ishaan. "Captain Scott and Captain Shackleton: A 100 Year Old Expedition." *Time*, December 15, 2011. http://time.com/3783925/captain-scott-and-captain-shackleton-a-100-year-old-expedition/.

DECEMBER 12 A SEVENTEEN-YEAR PRAYER

Christianity Today. "386 Augustine Converts to Christianity." Accessed February 18, 2018. Previously published in *Christian History*, no. 28 (1990). http://www.christianitytoday.com/history/issues/issue-28/386-augustine-converts-to-christianity.html.

Hawkins, Susie. "Monica, the Mother of St. Augustine—A Portrait of a Praying Mother." Passionate Faith on Display: Portraits of Significant Women in Church History, part 2. Transcript. Edited by Marilyn Fine. Bible.org, September 17, 2008. https://bible.org/seriespage/2-monica-mother-st-augustine-portrait-praying-mother.

Nichols, Stephen. "Monica: A Mother's Prayer." 5 Minutes in Church History, March 5, 2014. Podcast and transcript. https://www.5minutesinchurchhistory.com/monica-a-mothers-prayer/.

Severance, Diane. "Augustine Couldn't Outrun Mother's Prayers." Christianity.com, April 28, 2010. https://www.christianity.com/church/church-history/timeline/301-600/augustine-couldnt-outrun-mothers-prayers-11629656.html.

DECEMBER 13 LIFE IN A JAR

Bellafante, Ginia. "A Female Oskar Schindler of the Warsaw Ghetto." *New York Times*, April 17, 2009. http://www.nytimes.com/2009/04/18/arts/television/18hear.html.

Hevesi, Dennis. "Irena Sendler, Lifeline to Young Jews, Is Dead at 98." *New York Times*, May 13, 2008. http://www.nytimes.com/2008/05/13/world/europe/13sendler.html.

Kroll, Chana. "Irena Sendler: Rescuer of the Children of Warsaw." Chabad.org. Accessed February 18, 2018. http://www.chabad.org/theJewishWoman/article_cdo/aid/939081/jewish/Irena-Sendler.htm.

Lowell Milken Center for Unsung Heroes. "Life in a Jar." Accessed February 18, 2018. https://lowellmilkencenter.org/irena-sendler/.

DECEMBER 14 STAGECOACH MARY

Enss, Chris. "Stagecoach Mary." *True West*, January 22, 2016. https://truewestmagazine.com/stagecoach-mary/.

Everett, George. "Mary Fields: Female Pioneer in Montana." HistoryNet, June 12, 2006. Previously published in *Wild West* (February 1996). http://www.historynet.com/mary-fields-female-pioneer-in-montana.htm.

PJB5. "10 African-American Cowboys Who Shaped the Old West." Listverse, April 4, 2016. https://listverse.com/2016/04/04/10-african-american-cowboys-who-shaped-the-old-west/.

WHM. "The Life and Legend of Mary Fields." Women's History Matters, April 8, 2014. http://montana
womenshistory.org/the-life-and-legend-of-mary-fields/.

DECEMBER 15 THE GREATEST GIFT OF ALL
Mahr, Krista. "The Top 10 Everything of 2009: Top 10 Heroes." *Time*, December 8, 2009. http://content
.time.com/time/specials/packages/article/0,28804,1945379_1944701_1944711,00.html.
Marks, Kathy. "'He Saved Us, and Then He Was Gone.'" *Independent*, September 28, 2009. http://www
.independent.co.uk/news/world/asia/he-saved-us-and-then-he-was-gone-1794710.html.
Shears, Richard. "Philippines Floods: Hero Teenager Saves More Than 30 Lives before He Is Swept Away."
Daily Mail, September 29, 2009. http://www.dailymail.co.uk/news/article-1216643/Philippines-floods
-Hero-teenager-saves-30-lives-swept-away.html.
Villegas, Dennis. "The Short and Heroic Life of Muelmar Magallanes." *Dennis Villegas* (blog), October 7,
2009. http://dennisvillegas.blogspot.com/2009/10/short-and-heroic-life-of-muelmar.html.

DECEMBER 16 A CHRISTMAS MIRACLE?
Fader, Carole. "Fact Check: Could Inspirational Story Be True?" *Florida Times-Union*, December 24, 2016.
http://www.jacksonville.com/reason/2016-12-24/fact-check-could-inspirational-story-be-true.
Snopes. "The Gold and Ivory Tablecloth." Updated January 7, 2011. https://www.snopes.com/glurge
/tablecloth.asp.
Wetzstein, Cheryl. "Wetzstein: 'Tablecloth' Is a Love Story." *Washington Times*, December 22, 2009. https://
www.washingtontimes.com/news/2009/dec/22/tablecloth-is-a-love-story/.
WFP. "The Gold and Ivory Tablecloth—by Howard C. Schade." CNN iReport, December 3, 2010. http://
ireport.cnn.com/docs/DOC-524834.

DECEMBER 17 HORDOS THE MADMAN
This story is adapted from Matthew 2.
Encyclopedia of World Biography. "Herod the Great Biography." Accessed February 19, 2018. http://www
.notablebiographies.com/He-Ho/Herod-the-Great.html.
Onion, Amanda. "Researchers Diagnose Herod the Great." ABC News, January 25, 2002. https://abcnews
.go.com/Technology/story?id=98107&page=1.
Trivedi, Bijal P. "What Disease Killed King Herod?" *National Geographic*, January 28, 2002. https://news
.nationalgeographic.com/news/2002/01/0128_020128_KingHerod.html.
Vander Laan, Ray. "Herod the Builder." That the World May Know. Accessed February 19, 2018. https://
www.thattheworldmayknow.com/herod-the-builder.

DECEMBER 18 BLACK MAGIC AT THE INN
This story is adapted from Matthew 2.
Ashby, Chad. "Magi, Wise Men, or Kings? It's Complicated." *Christianity Today*, December 16, 2016.
http://www.christianitytoday.com/history/holidays/christmas/magi-wise-men-or-kings-its
-complicated.html.
Morris, Henry M. "When They Saw the Star." Institute for Creation Research. Accessed February 20, 2018.
http://www.icr.org/home/resources/resources_tracts_whentheysawthestar/.
Weintraub, David A. "Can Astronomy Explain the Biblical Star of Bethlehem?" The Conversation, December 23,
2014. http://theconversation.com/can-astronomy-explain-the-biblical-star-of-bethlehem-35126.

DECEMBER 19 THE STORY OF THE CHRISTMAS TREE
Barnes, Alison. "The First Christmas Tree." *History Today*, December 12, 2006. http://www.historytoday
.com/alison-barnes/first-christmas-tree.
History. "History of Christmas Trees." Accessed February 20, 2018. http://www.history.com/topics/christmas
/history-of-christmas-trees.
Puiu, Tibi. "The Origin and History of the Christmas Tree: From Paganism to Modern Ubiquity." ZME
Science. Updated December 8, 2017. https://www.zmescience.com/science/history-science/origin
-christmas-tree-pagan/.
Tait, Edwin Woodruff, and Jennifer Woodruff Tait. "Why Do We Have Christmas Trees?" *Christianity
Today*, December 11, 2008. https://www.christianitytoday.com/history/2008/december/why-do-we
-have-christmas-trees.html.

DECEMBER 20 A BEAUTY IN THE FLAWS
Ciccone, F. Richard. "Introducing Slats Grobnik, Mike Royko's Alter Ego." *Chicago Tribune*, June 13,
2001. http://articles.chicagotribune.com/2001-06-13/features/0106130008_1_mike-royko-slats
-grobnik-gun-club.
Men of Integrity. "Christmas Tree-Parable." *Christianity Today*. www.christianitytoday.com/moi/2009/003
/may/christmas-tree-parable.html. Article no longer available.

Royko, Mike. "A Lovely Couple, Bound with Love." *Chicago Tribune*, December 24, 1985. http://articles
.chicagotribune.com/1985-12-24/news/8503290225_1_christmas-trees-secret-christmas-eve.

DECEMBER 21 THE REAL SAINT NICK
Biography. "St. Nicholas." Updated December 7, 2017. https://www.biography.com/people/st-nicholas
-204635.
Handwerk, Brian. "Saint Nicholas to Santa: The Surprising Origins of Mr. Claus." *National Geographic*,
December 20, 2013. https://news.nationalgeographic.com/news/2013/12/131219-santa-claus-origin
-history-christmas-facts-st-nicholas/.
Olsen, Ted. "The Real Saint Nicholas." *Christianity Today*, August 8, 2008. http://www.christianitytoday
.com/history/2008/august/real-saint-nicholas.html.
Whychristmas?com. "St. Nicholas, Santa Claus & Father Christmas." Accessed February 20, 2018. https://
www.whychristmas.com/customs/fatherchristmas.shtml.

DECEMBER 22 THE DAY CHRISTMAS STOPPED A WAR
Bajekal, Naina. "Silent Night: The Story of the World War I Christmas Truce of 1914." *Time*, December 24,
2014. http://time.com/3643889/christmas-truce-1914/.
Dash, Mike. "The Story of the WWI Christmas Truce." *Smithsonian*, December 23, 2011. https://www
.smithsonianmag.com/history/the-story-of-the-wwi-christmas-truce-11972213/.
DeGroot, Gerard. "The Truth about the Christmas Day Football Match." *Telegraph*, December 24, 2014.
http://www.telegraph.co.uk/history/world-war-one/11310353/The-truth-about-the-Christmas-Day
-football-match.html.
History. "Christmas Truce of 1914." Accessed February 21, 2018. http://www.history.com/topics/world-war
-i/christmas-truce-of-1914.

DECEMBER 23 THE BLUE-COLLAR SAINT
This story is adapted from Matthew 1 and Luke 2.
Biography. "St. Joseph." Updated April 2, 2014. https://www.biography.com/people/st-joseph-9358199.
Martin, Harold S. *Joseph—The Husband of Mary and Foster Father of Jesus.* Hanover, PA: Bible Helps,
2008. http://biblehelpsinc.org/publication/josephthe-husband-of-mary-and-foster-father-of-jesus/.
Stewart, Don. "What Do We Know about Jesus' Earthly Parents: Joseph and Mary?" Blue Letter Bible.
Accessed February 21, 2018. https://www.blueletterbible.org/faq/don_stewart/don_stewart_198.cfm.

DECEMBER 24 SIMPLE MARY, MOTHER OF GOD
This story is adapted from Matthew 1–2; 12:46; Luke 1–2; John 2:1-11; 19:25-27; and Acts 1:14.
Brown, Kristine. "3 Things You Didn't Know about Mary (Mother of Jesus) in the Bible." Crosswalk.com,
June 3, 2016. https://www.crosswalk.com/faith/women/3-things-you-didn-t-know-about-mary-mother
-of-jesus-in-the-bible.html.
Chadwick, Patricia. "Mary: Mother of Jesus." History's Women. Accessed February 21, 2018. http://www
.historyswomen.com/womenoffaith/mary.htm.
White, Lesli. "6 Fascinating Facts about Mary, Mother of Jesus." Beliefnet. Accessed February 21, 2018. http://
www.beliefnet.com/faiths/christianity/galleries/6-fascinating-facts-about-mary-mother-of-jesus.aspx.

DECEMBER 25 WANDA AND LUCILLE'S HOUSE
This true story is from the author's personal experience. It can be attested to by the author, his family, and
the hundreds of people who personally witnessed the amazing story of these two ladies.

DECEMBER 26 PASSING THE POINT OF NO RETURN
Enchanted Learning. "Gil Eannes: Explorer of Coastal Africa." Accessed February 21, 2018. http://www
.enchantedlearning.com/explorers/page/e/eannes.shtml.
Frater, Jamie. "10 Unforgettable Stories History Forgot." Listverse, December 28, 2010. https://listverse.com
/2010/12/28/10-unforgettable-stories-history-forgot/.
Hernández, Diego. "The Life and Adventures of Gil Eanes." Prezi presentation, May 12, 2014. https://prezi
.com/ehoyenykwcci/the-life-and-adventures-of-gil-eanes/.
The Mariners' Museum and Park. "Prince Henry the Navigator." http://exploration.marinersmuseum.org
/index.php?type=explorer&id=33. Article no longer available.

DECEMBER 27 JACK'S REDEMPTION
Cowell, Alan. "John Profumo, British Minister Ruined by Sex Scandal, Dies." *New York Times*, March 10,
2006. http://www.nytimes.com/2006/03/10/international/europe/john-profumo-british-minister-ruined
-by-sex-scandal.html.
Gold, Tanya. "The Profumo Affair: Where Is the Redemption of Christine Keeler?" *Guardian*, December 4,
2013. https://www.theguardian.com/commentisfree/2013/dec/04/profumo-affair-christine-keeler
-stephen-ward.

Noonan, Peggy. "How to Find Grace after Disgrace." *Wall Street Journal*, July 12, 2013. https://www.wsj.com /articles/SB10001424127887324425204578600230806506440.

Tweedie, Neil. "John Profumo: Scandal Minister Who Found Redemption." *Telegraph*, March 11, 2006. http:// www.telegraph.co.uk/news/uknews/1512691/John-Profumo-scandal-minister-who-found-redemption.html.

DECEMBER 28 FALLING THROUGH ICE

Hallowell, Billy. "One Woman's Life Story That's Filled with So Much Tragedy—and Inspiration—That You Just Have to Read It." TheBlaze, November 1, 2013. https://www.theblaze.com/news/2013/11/01 /one-womans-incredibly-wild-journey-of-finding-god-and-redemption-after-hiring-a-hitman-to-kill-her -husband.

New Orleans Times-Picayune. "Family Violence Adviser Is Held in Plot to Have Husband Killed." Front page headline, May 27, 1987.

Rankin, Carolyn Huebner. *Falling through Ice*. With Rosetta D. Hoessli. Houston, TX: Crossover, 2011.

DECEMBER 29 OCEANS OF MERCY

Gilman, John. "*Dayasagar* and the Life of Christ in India." *Lausanne World Pulse*, no. 9 (2006). https://www .lausanneworldpulse.com/perspectives-php/470/09-2006.

"John Gilman Journeys to India after Receiving a Vision from God." YouTube video, 10:30. Posted by *The 700 Club*, October 1, 2014. https://www.youtube.com/watch?v=UgdNp4Quuc4.

Shibley, David. "The Dalit Revolution." *Ministry Today*, April 30, 2006. https://ministrytodaymag.com /197-archives/world4/12963-the-dalit-revolution.

Virginia Beach Daily Press. "Carolyn Ross Wood Gilman." August 13, 2005. http://www.legacy.com/obituaries /dailypress/obituary.aspx?n=caroline-ross-wood-gilman&pid=14807877.

DECEMBER 30 TRUE GRIT IN THOSE PEARLY WHITES

Drevitch, Gary. "Dick Clark Was Much Tougher Than We Thought." Next Avenue, April 20, 2012. http:// www.nextavenue.org/dick-clark-was-much-tougher-we-thought/.

Lynch, Rene. "Dick Clark Dies: Entertainment Icon Became Hero to Stroke Victims." *Los Angeles Times*, April 19, 2012. http://articles.latimes.com/2012/apr/19/nation/la-na-nn-dick-clark-dies-hero-to-stroke -victims-20120419.

Stogel, Stewart. "Dick Clark's Triumph over Adversity." WND, April 19, 2012. http://www.wnd.com/2012 /04/dick-clarks-inspirational-story-of-courage/.

Taylor, Elise. "Dick Clark Will Always Be Part of *New Year's Rockin' Eve*—and That's a Great Thing." *Vanity Fair*, December 31, 2015. https://www.vanityfair.com/hollywood/2015/12/remembering-dick-clark -new-years-rockin-eve-barry-adelman.

DECEMBER 31 THE CHOSEN CHILD

The author takes the liberty and joy of sharing his own amazing story.

Topical Index

September 18
September 26
September 29
November 12
November 17
December 30

CHRISTMAS
October 28
December 8
December 10
December 11
December 15
December 16
December 18
December 19
December 20
December 21
December 22
December 23
December 24
December 25

CIVIL WAR
February 2
February 12
February 19
February 27
March 20
April 1
April 27
April 30
May 17
July 14
November 19
November 20
December 5

COMMITMENT
January 28
February 17
March 22
April 1
May 5
May 22
July 5
July 10
August 10
August 28
September 26
October 12
October 24
November 30
December 23
December 24

COMMUNION
July 18

COMPASSION
January 11
February 17

May 26
June 1
July 21
August 8
August 12
September 1
September 9
October 4
October 30
November 13
November 14
November 18
December 29

COMPOSERS
March 6
May 1
May 16
June 18
June 20
August 13
September 22
September 23
December 2

CONSEQUENCES
January 1
January 9
March 13
April 5
April 15
April 29
June 3
June 26
July 8
July 29
August 3
August 9
August 16
August 20
September 6
September 13
September 22
October 17
October 22
November 7
November 25
December 1
December 7
December 23
December 27

CONTENTMENT
January 6
February 5
February 24
April 4
April 6
June 21
June 26
August 13

August 30
September 29
October 17

COURAGE
January 2
January 3
January 16
January 18
January 31
February 3
February 4
February 6
February 7
February 9
February 10
February 21
March 16
March 21
April 3
April 10
May 7
May 8
May 18
May 27
May 31
June 2
June 3
June 12
June 15
August 23
September 1
September 5
September 9
September 19
September 22
September 26
October 5
October 12
October 22
November 4
November 11
November 18
December 6
December 15
December 24

COVER-UPS
January 10
January 22
February 22
April 5
June 6
August 11
August 16
November 4
December 7

CROSS OF JESUS
January 18
January 25

April 2
April 19
April 22
May 6
May 18
May 26
May 31
June 4
July 11
July 15
August 28
August 30
October 1
October 6
October 15
November 8
November 18
December 9
December 15
December 19

DECISIONS
January 8
January 9
January 12
January 16
January 18
February 3
February 5
February 7
February 17
February 21
February 27
March 13
March 21
April 1
May 13
May 19
May 26
June 3
July 5
July 8
July 22
July 29
August 3
August 10
August 20
September 1
September 2
September 4
September 11
September 13
September 19
September 22
September 26
October 15
October 17
October 22
November 7
November 10